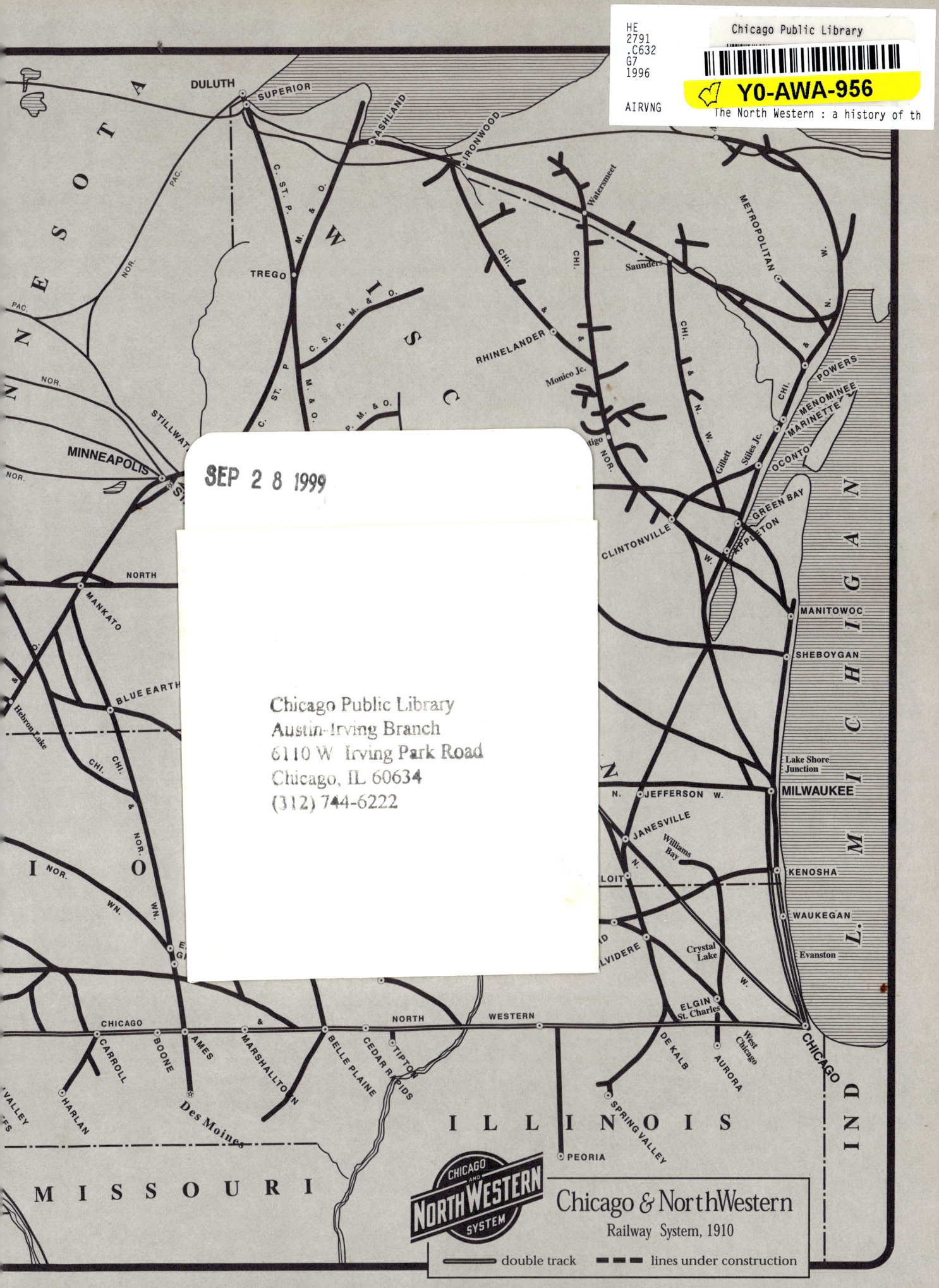

Chicago Public Library
Austin-Irving Branch
6110 W Irving Park Road
Chicago, IL 60634
(312) 744-6222

THE NORTH WESTERN

THE NORTH WESTERN

A HISTORY OF THE
CHICAGO & NORTH WESTERN
RAILWAY SYSTEM

H. Roger Grant

NORTHERN ILLINOIS UNIVERSITY PRESS
DeKalb 1996

© 1996 by Northern Illinois University Press

Published by the Northern Illinois University Press,

DeKalb, Illinois 60115

Manufactured in the United States

using acid-free paper

All Rights Reserved

Design by Julia Fauci

Library of Congress
Cataloging-in-Publication Data
Grant, H. Roger, 1943–
The North Western : a history of the Chicago &
North Western Railway system / H. Roger Grant.
    p.   cm.
Includes bibliographical refrences and index.
ISBN 0-87580-214-1 (alk. paper)
1. Chicago and North Western Transportation
Company—History. 2. Railroads—Illinois—History
I. Title.
HE2791.C632G7   1996
385'.06'5773—dc20
96-12686   CIP

Frontispiece and logo courtesy of
North Western/Union Pacific.

Dedicated to
Jessie Powell Prizer (1871–1955)
A family friend who nutured my excitement for the past

Contents

Preface ix

1 The Galena 3
2 The North Western Emerges 25
3 Years of Expansion, 1877–1892 43
4 The Omaha Road 69
5 The Hughitt Era 83
6 "The Best of Everything" 101
7 The Great War and the Roaring Twenties 127
8 The Great Depression and Bankruptcy 153
9 The Second World War and Postwar Railroading 171
10 The Heineman Era 189
11 Employee Ownership and After: The Provo and Wolfe Administrations 219
12 The Final Years 247

Notes 255
Additional Works on the North Western 281
Index 283

Preface

The Chicago & North Western Railway has been part of my professional life for more than a decade. After completing *The Corn Belt Route: A History of the Chicago Great Western Railroad Company*, which Northern Illinois University Press published in 1984, I decided to study the North Western. From my work on the "Great Weedy," which included research at North Western headquarters in Chicago, I knew that the historically significant North Western lacked a modern, scholarly treatment and that abundant materials existed. Since several of the Midwest's premier carriers, including the Milwaukee Road and Rock Island, remained understudied, an examination of the North Western would contribute to an understanding of this once mighty "granger" group of roads.

This general history covers the North Western from its earliest years until its recent sale to the Union Pacific. Within this narrative spanning more than a century, I develop several themes. Foremost is the greatness of the company. The North Western grew into a robust carrier that truly could boast the "Best of Everything" credo. Enormously profitable from the mid-nineteenth century until the early twentieth century, it fashioned a major rail network in the Midwest and Great Plains during these years, creating an excellent physical plant and providing quality service. At times the North Western was an innovator, and often it set standards for the industry.

A second theme is the role that the North Western and its affiliated companies played in shaping the "Great West." Under William Ogden and Marvin Hughitt, two of the most gifted railroad leaders of the nineteenth century, the company bolstered the growing strength of Chicago by funneling freight and passenger traffic to and from the metropolis and also advanced western settlement and town making, particularly during the "Great Dakota Boom" of the early 1880s.

The matter of challenge and response constitutes an important theme as well. The narrative focuses on the impact of state and national regulation, modal competition, financial depressions, labor problems, corporate mergers, and partial federal deregulation since 1980. The quality of company leadership has been an important factor. The railroad suffered from a certain ossification after the Hughitt years but enjoyed a rebirth in the mid-1950s under the guidance of Ben W. Heineman. Finally, what happened to the North Western during its nearly 150 years of corporate life was typically part of railroading in the region and nation.

The structuring of material for a comprehensive history of the North Western takes into account several audiences. While some readers may find the construction portions tedious, the building of an extensive network of trackage was a remarkable accomplishment and a triumph worthy of attention. Moreover, anyone intensely interested in the North Western will want to know when and why a particular line appeared. Since this history represents a thorough study of the North Western, the building activities, especially during the 1880s, cannot be dismissed with a meaningless phrase like "the company added numerous appendages." Later, when the North Western suffered from an overbuilt network, management eventually "rationalized" mileage and corrected the problems caused by earlier achievements. Although I do not build every line tie by tie, some readers may want to skip ahead. Others may conclude that the latter part of the book smacks of trade journalism, yet the general history approach means describing and explaining recent events in detail. I hope the two constituencies, scholars and railroad enthusiasts, find information to their liking.

As with all academic projects, a variety of institutions helped to make this book possible; so, I wish to recognize their support: California State Railroad Museum, Sacramento; British Museum, London, England; The Center for Western Studies, Sioux Falls, South Dakota; Chicago & North Western Transportation Company, Chicago; Chicago Historical Society, Chicago; Illinois State Historical Society, Springfield; Interstate Commerce Commission Library, Washington, D.C.; James Jerome Hill Reference Library, St. Paul, Minnesota; John W. Barriger III National Railroad Library of the Mercantile Library, St. Louis; Lake Forest College Library, Lake Forest, Illinois;

Library of Congress, Washington, D.C.; Milwaukee Public Library, Milwaukee; Minnesota Historical Society, St. Paul; The National Archives, Washington, D.C.; Nebraska State Historical Society, Lincoln; Newberry Library, Chicago; Northern Illinois University Regional Archives, DeKalb; Northwestern University Library, Evanston, Illinois; Princeton University, Firestone Library, Princeton, New Jersey; Railroad Museum of Pennsylvania, Strasburg, Pennsylvania; Railway & Locomotive Historical Society Archives, Sacramento, California; Smithsonian Institution, Washington, D.C.; South Dakota State Historical Society, Pierre; State Historical Society of Iowa, Iowa City; State Historical Society of Wisconsin, Madison; Union Pacific Museum, Omaha; University of Akron Archives, Akron, Ohio; University of Iowa Libraries, Iowa City; University of South Dakota Library, Vermillion; West Chicago Historical Society, West Chicago, Illinois; and the Wyoming State Archives, Museums and Historical Department, Cheyenne.

Portions of my research were underwritten by several institutions. A Faculty Research Committee grant from the University of Akron, a stipend from the James Jerome Hill Reference Library, a summer fellowship from the Newberry Library, and financial and other support from the Chicago & North Western expedited this work. I am grateful for this assistance.

While scores of individuals to whom I owe debts of gratitude have contributed to this book, I especially thank Charles Shannon, Arlington Heights, Illinois, and James A. Zito, St. Charles, Illinois, for providing valuable insights into the history of the North Western during the last half century. As usual the staff of Bierce Library at the University of Akron, most of all Sarah Akers and John Ball, assisted in locating materials. And I appreciate the suggestions made by Boris Blick, Keith L. Bryant Jr., Robert W. Downing, Don L. Hofsommer, John C. Kenefick, and Thomas J. Lamphier, whose efforts considerably improved the manuscript. I remain responsible for errors of fact and interpretation, however.

Finally, my wife, Martha Farrington Grant, has consistently been my best critic. She is always willing to help, even though busy with her own career as a social worker. She made this book possible, far beyond the normal sense of the phrase, and so it is truly hers too.

THE NORTH WESTERN

Early American railroads universally revealed a primitive nature, including their motive power. The locomotive *Whirling Thunder* of the Galena, new in 1853, rebuilt in 1862 and again in 1884, pauses in 1867 on the Aske Arch Culvert near Rockford, Ill. By this time the engine, renamed *Thunder,* was part of the North Western fleet. The fenders over the driving wheels prevent mud from splashing onto the highly decorated boiler. (North Western/Union Pacific)

CHAPTER One

THE GALENA

The railway age in America officially dawned during the early 1830s. Although a few companies had earlier secured corporate charters, commenced construction, and, in the case of the Baltimore & Ohio Railroad, opened with horses pulling "rail wagons," it was not until Christmas 1830 that scheduled steam-powered railroad service began. On that auspicious day *The Best Friend of Charleston*, the first steam locomotive made in America for commercial use and weighing four and one-half tons, pulled a train of "carriages" over the initial segment of the South Carolina Canal & Rail Road Company between Line Street in Charleston and a point six miles distant. The *Charleston Courier* considered it as an exhilarating trip for the 141 passengers: "We flew on the wings of the wind at the varied speed of fifteen to twenty five miles an hour, annihilating 'time and space.'" Since the fastest horse could not have moved nearly as fast over this stretch of land, such press comment was hardly exaggerated.[1]

This highly publicized event and others that followed excited the public, and "railroad fever" spread rapidly. The growth of successful railroad projects was truly amazing. The year the tiny *Best Friend of Charleston*, the mechanical herald of a new era, chugged out of Charleston, only 23 route miles of spindly track were in operation. But by 1840 the rail total reached 2,808 miles, surpassing even Great Britain, the birthplace of the steam car. By midcentury ribbons of iron totaled 9,021 miles, an immense increase of 300-plus percent in a decade. Most of these pioneer pikes were shortlines rather than through routes. "Iron bands" commonly connected established communities with bodies of water or merely wandered into the hinterlands to tap agricultural or mineral traffic.[2]

The modern railway evolved steadily during its formative or demonstration period. Steam locomotives, specialized rolling stock, solid-metal rails, and wooden crossties became widely recognized hallmarks of this promising mode of transport. Still, railroading retained a raw flavor, and promoters lacked universal standards. The width between the rails prompted considerable debate. A gauge of four feet eight and one-half inches was enthusiastically used in England and eventually became standard in America, though it took nearly half a century to achieve dominance. Railroad builders in the South generally preferred a five-foot width, while their counterparts in the North employed a wider range. Gauges there ran the gamut from "broad" or "Erie Gauge" (six feet) to "English Gauge" and ultimately to "narrow gauge" (three feet), with several intermediate variations. This profusion of gauge hampered the interchange of rolling stock and lessened the impact of the steam car civilization.[3]

Another obstacle involved debate over something as basic as the roadbed. What later smacked of lunacy found dedicated champions in the 1830s and early 1840s, the concept of "railroads-on-stilts." This meant placement of rails and ties upon a wooden platform supported by massive stakes driven deeply into the ground. The advantages were thought to be obvious. "[A pile roadway] . . . is not liable to derangement by frosts," argued an adviser to the New-York & Erie Rail Road (Erie) in January 1840; "it is not liable to be obstructed by snow; it is free from dangers of a graded road in consequence of the washing of the banks by flood and rains, and settling when set up in soft bottom, thereby requiring constant expense to adjust the road and replace the earth materials." Proponents argued that "the interest on the money saved by building a pile road instead of a graded road will renew the piles, if necessary, every five years."[4]

Several firms embraced railroads-on-stilts. In the case of the Erie, the company installed more than 100 miles of wooden pilings in southern New York. The strategy, however, proved unsatisfactory when construction difficulties increased costs. Officials finally conceded that a graded roadbed was the practical solution. When the line eventually opened between the New York communities of Piermont and Dunkirk in 1851, the price tag was several times the original estimate; miles of rotting oak posts contributed to this overrun.[5]

Despite conflicting notions of gauge and roadbed, railroad pioneers believed their form of transport would end isolation for virtually any area and create what they called the "oxygen of trade," in much the same way that turnpike and canal advocates earlier had promoted their grand projects. Railroaders strongly emphasized their form's superior qualities, especially speed and continuous operation. Even with all the limitations of the first up-start railroads, road and canal builders must have had premonitions of approaching ruin.[6]

While railroads possessed distinct advantages over competitors, not all of the early projects succeeded. The century of construction launched in the 1830s contained many examples of "paper" or "hot-air" schemes that failed to materialize. Furthermore, years might pass before a proposed railroad turned a wheel. Financial troubles regularly stopped construction, and problems associated with legal disputes, routing difficulties, and inept leadership had their crippling effects.[7]

Railroad promoters surely recognized early on that there were no guarantees for completion of their plans, yet builders often remained undeterred. Despite setbacks and failures these indefatigable promoters saw their efforts increasing prosperity and fostering a united republic.[8]

A largely isolated Territory of Illinois entered the Union on December 3, 1818, and it took years before the twenty-first state would shed its frontier character. The population of Illinois stood at only 55,211 in 1820, and while it reached 157,445 a decade later, vast areas experienced little or no development. The majority of the Euroamerican residents lived in the southern part, having arrived there largely from states south of the Mason-Dixon line. Soon, however, the defeat of the Sauk and Fox tribes, the remaining Native Americans within the Prairie State, in the brief but locally significant Black Hawk War of 1832, opened for settlement a rich region from the southern half of Lake Michigan westward to the Mississippi River. An influx of immigrants, mostly from places other than Dixie, selected land in the northern sections and elsewhere in the state. By the 1830s Illinois was a logical place to settle: vast tracks of rich prairie soil could be purchased cheaply. The population data revealed an impressive surge by 1840: enumerators counted 476,183 inhabitants in the sixth federal census.[9]

Fortunately for those individuals who wished to move to Illinois, improvements in internal transport made their journeys easier and cheaper. Waterways were the most convenient; steamboats plied the Ohio and Mississippi rivers and their principal tributaries; steam-powered packets served Great Lakes ports, and canal boats operated on a sprawling network of recently dug "ditches" in New York, Pennsylvania, Ohio, and Indiana. Wagon roads, too, were somewhat better built and more convenient than they had been in the past. Still, the federally financed National Road, "the grand portage between the Ocean and the Western Rivers," stretched only from Maryland to Ohio and would not enter Illinois until the 1840s. Railroads, although rare in the Old Northwest, provided the fastest and most dependable service.[10]

One Illinois community that benefited from improved water transport was Chicago. Strategically situated at the mouth of the Chicago River on the southwestern shore of Lake Michigan and thus part of the vital Great Lakes–Erie Canal–Hudson River route to New York City, the village quickly developed. The shacklike settlement around Fort Dearborn, a small military post, contained only 350 inhabitants in 1833, but by 1837, the year Chicago was incorporated as a municipality, its population reached 4,170. In the 1840s the community burgeoned; the Census of 1850 listed nearly 30,000 inhabitants.[11]

Chicagoans expected great things of their fledgling hometown and showed a fierce determination for their community to grow. Residents correctly perceived that transportation was both a cause and result of urban development, and they strove to enhance their facilities. Fortunately, they were blessed with good location, strong leadership, and considerable luck.

Initially, better transportation meant better waterways. Chicagoans strongly supported river and lakefront improvements, most notably removal of a troublesome sandbar where the Chicago River emptied into Lake Michigan. But soon many were caught up in the canal craze that swept parts of New England, the Mid-Atlantic states, and the Old Northwest following the opening of the stunningly profitable Erie Canal in 1825. Residents believed that if an artificial channel connected Lake Michigan with the Illinois River, they might capture the trade of the adjoining areas and possibly much of the developing upper Mississippi Valley as well. Asked a citizen in 1835, the year the legislature authorized the Illinois & Michigan project, "What would be the value of even the fertile Prairies of Illinois, remote from her large rivers, without a canal?"[12]

Dreams of a 96-mile-long Illinois & Michigan Canal between Chicago and La Salle, Illinois, below the rapids of the Illinois River, started to materialize in 1836. Dignitaries ceremonially turned the first shovels of earth on the Fourth of July, always considered to be an auspicious day. These hopeful enthusiasts planned a "deep-cut" or "steamboat" (60-feet wide and 6-feet deep) canal, something more versatile and more costly than the typical ditch. Aided by a handsome federal land grant of nearly one-half million acres and by generous state support, prospects for rapidly completing the more than $8 million undertaking seemed promising. But the negative impact of the Panic of 1837 and the following depression, coupled with financial mismanagement, halted construction in 1843.[13]

The Illinois & Michigan Canal, nevertheless, did not remain unfinished and useless. Refinancing two years later and a less-expensive "shallow-cut" (40-feet wide and 4-feet deep) plan allowed workers to complete their assignments; the longed-for water artery, with its 15 locks and 4 aqueducts, opened for commercial traffic on April 23, 1848, at a cost of $6.4 million. "The Canal is said to be in excellent navigable order, both for packet [passenger] and transportation [freight] lines," reported the *Weekly Chicago Democrat*, the city's first newspaper, soon thereafter. "Two daily lines of packets leave Chicago and Peru [near La Salle] morning and evening. The fare through, including meals, is four dollars." By the end of the first 180-day navigation season, 162 boats had paid nearly $90,000 in tolls, and the canal was on its way to bolstering the economic base of Chicago and northern and central Illinois. Yet a decade after the waterway's opening, Chicagoans considered it "an old fogy institution—one of the things that were to be superseded by new inventions." Competing railroads had rendered it obsolete.[14]

Long before boats moved through the region's best canal corridor, railroad promotion in Illinois had become a popular topic of conversation and the subject of some action. One early scheme involved building a rail line from the junction of the proposed Illinois & Michigan Canal and the Illinois River south to the confluence of the Ohio and Mississippi rivers. "It will make the southern and interior counties," argued Circuit Judge Sidney Breese in October 1835, "cause them to settle, raise the value of their lands (which are intrinsically as good as any), and furnish the means of transportation for their products either to a Northern or Southern market, of which they are now destitute." Concluded the judge, "I hope some gentlemen may feel sufficient interest in this matter to consider it maturely. . . . It is a great, magnificent, and feasible project. It can—it will, be accomplished."[15]

Judge Breese soon realized part of his wish. When legislators gathered for their winter session of 1836–1837 in Vandalia, the capital, they overwhelmingly approved "An Act to establish and maintain a general system of Internal Improvements." The price tag exceeded $20 million, a staggering commitment since Illinois contained only 400,000 mostly impecunious inhabitants. With this ambitious program the Prairie State kept pace with Indiana and Michigan, which dedicated large sums of public monies for improved transport. While lawmakers designated some funds for river improvements, they earmarked more than 90 percent for approximately 1,300 miles of railroads. Politicians, whether in Illinois or elsewhere, wanted to invest heavily in nascent rail projects for the public's (and their own) benefit, and disregarded the issue as to whether these enterprises would likely prove profitable in the near term. Specifically, they allotted about $3.5 million, which exceeded a third of the railroad budget, for the Central Railroad. This was to be a north-south intrastate line that would link Galena, a booming lead-mining camp of about a thousand residents in the northwestern hill country, with Cairo, a village of several hundred on the Ohio River near its mouth.[16]

The Central Railroad, however, failed to stable the first iron horse in Illinois. For largely political reasons work progressed more rapidly on another state-sponsored project, the Northern Cross Rail Road. This route was designed to connect Quincy, on the Mississippi River, with Danville, near the Indiana border, thus bisecting the state's midsection. But builders completed a substantially shorter line, a poorly constructed 24-mile road from Meredosia, a settlement on the Illinois River, eastward to Jacksonville. Service started in November 1838. Then in March 1842, the Northern Cross reached Springfield, the new capital, 55 miles east of Meredosia. But the road, which cost $250,000, languished, and the state sold it at auction on April 26, 1847, for a paltry $21,000. This distressing event convinced residents that private enterprise should assume the risks, and for the next generation they advocated laissez-faire as strenuously as they earlier had embraced public sponsorship. A similar consequence occurred elsewhere: various governments had boldly entered the field of state enterprise in the 1830s and 1840s, and most suffered severe financial difficulties.[17]

The Central Railroad undertaking profited greatly from the Internal Improvement Act of 1837. Yet, as with the Northern Cross, the state's largess did not ensure success. While surveyors staked out the 350-mile path and graders shaped sections of the roadbed, workers did not install track. Just as the Panic of 1837 delayed completion of the Illinois & Michigan Canal, so it crippled this north-south rail artery. The state abandoned its efforts shortly thereafter; private investors sought unsuccessfully to revitalize the project in the early 1840s. Only after the federal government, cajoled by masterful Senator Stephen A. Douglas, granted 2.5 million acres of the public domain to the road did it move forward as an investor-owned project. When the 705-mile carrier, renamed the Illinois Central Railroad, finally opened in September 1856, it accounted for nearly a third of the state's railroad mileage and claimed to be the world's longest railroad. Specifically, the company operated a Y-shaped system: its main stem extended from Dunleith, on the Mississippi River near Galena, to Cairo, and a 252-mile "branch" connected Centralia, approximately 100 miles north of Cairo, to Chicago. Illinois Central officials correctly recognized the promise of the Lake City.[18]

Agitation for better transportation during the 1830s involved efforts by residents of Chicago and sections of northern Illinois to get their own railroad, which seemed a sensible way to improve connections with the commercial world and to make money. Ambitious merchants in Chicago eagerly sought to bolster trade; they saw the funneling of lumber, manufactured goods, wheat, livestock, and other agricultural products through their community as a sure means to riches. It was generally agreed that railroads would raise land values, and tax revenues would increase as property values mounted. Some Chicagoans expressed keen interest in a railroad between their wharves and the Illinois River, and others pressed for a southerly rail route into the Wabash River valley. While the former scheme became the Illinois & Michigan Canal, the latter failed to progress beyond the paper Chicago & Vincennes Railroad, which the state chartered in January 1835. Another plan involved a railroad through the fertile, albeit transportation-starved, areas northwest of Chicago, ultimately reaching the Galena lead district. Farmers and townspeople outside of Chicago, who considered the Illinois & Michigan Canal project to be inconvenient or impractical, embraced the iron horse. Such sentiment does much to explain why lawmakers on January 16, 1836, passed "An Act to Incorporate the Galena & Chicago Union Railroad Company."[19]

The Illinois General Assembly granted the Galena & Chicago Union, the "Galena," a charter that contained several attractive provisions. Although it called for a railroad (promoters could substitute a turnpike) from "the town of Galena, in the county of Jo Daviess, to such point at the town of Chicago as shall be determined," the company might have "such appendages as may be deemed necessary." The firm also could "unite with any other Railroad Company already incorporated" and control its future "rates of toll." And the state allowed the incorporators three years in which to begin work.[20]

What was remarkable about the Galena's charter was not that backers won it—state governments, of course, strongly encouraged transportation betterments at this time—but that it gave them largely carte blanche authority to shape their venture. The explanation likely involved more than the plan's basic soundness: two members of the powerful internal improvements committees, Representative John Hamlin of Galena and Senator James Stroude of Chicago, played a critical role in the legislative victory. There was merit, too, in the observation made by a student of the Galena in 1879: "The charter was made very liberal to induce capitalists to take hold of it."[21]

The principal instigators of the Galena & Chicago Union, a combination of business and professional men from Chicago, moved quickly to breathe life into their charter. At the organizational meeting held in the Chicago law office of Ebenezer Peck on May 23, 1836, local investors subscribed to the one thousand shares (par value of $100 each) authorized by the lawmakers. Yet little money entered the treasury. The newly named seven directors, headed by Theophilus Smith, a state supreme court justice, Chicago attorney, and insurance company executive, met periodically to discuss financial strategies. While the company failed to win a federal land grant, it received positive charter revisions, which on March 17, 1837, gave the road "the right of way through such portions of public land belonging to this State as remain unsold" and increased the limit on capital stock.[22]

Even before the Galena achieved a semblance of financial order, directors sent a party of surveyors into the countryside. They hired James Seymour, "then just from the [New-York &] Erie road," and he finished his work by April 1837. Seymour and his assistants did not fix the line and determine construction costs for the entire distance between Chicago and Galena, but rather they examined the approximately 10 miles from Chicago "due west" to the Des Plaines River. The company hoped to make a positive start and to tap nearby traffic and still planned to push to Galena "in a reasonable period of time." Yet this modest objective made a lasting impression on the Seymour group. "We began our survey at the foot of Dearborn Street," recalled John Wentworth, a participant, decades later, "and ran three lines nearly due west to the Des Plaines River. Much of the time we waded in water, waist deep. . . . The high grass, where the fire had not swept over it, required four-foot stakes, which we *backed* [*sic*] for miles."[23]

The Galena's directors readily accepted Seymour's work. It offered a direct route between the city and the river at an affordable cost. The price tag for building a double-tracked roadbed with a single line amounted to $73,952, or about $7,500 per mile. This included the expense of extensive piling and stringer work through portions of the undrained prairie. Obviously, here the concept of the pile roadway did not seem too foolish.[24]

The Seymour report was not followed by substantial action. A steadily worsening economic climate hurt the fledgling enterprise, and laborers drove only a few piles along Madison Street in Chicago. Coupled with hard times was a dramatic shake-up in the ownership of the company in late 1837, following which the youthful Elijah Kent Hubbard, banker, freight forwarder, and real estate speculator, gained 79 percent of the stock. Then Hubbard suddenly died on May 26, 1839. The bulk of the securities of this moribund and leaderless railroad entered his estate.[25]

As the 1840s began, supporters of a railroad between Chicago and Galena expected little. The Galena & Chicago Union had seemingly fizzled; the state of Illinois verged on insolvency; and financial conservatism reigned supreme. Still, depression and disappointments failed to destroy a deep-seated faith in progress. The only consolation for the region's populace, which urgently required better transportation, came with the opening of four and one-half miles of poorly constructed turnpike west from Lake Street in Chicago over the marshlands and soggy prairie to a sandy glacial moraine known as Berry's Point.[26]

Improved roadways, in fact, appeared for some to be the likely way of upgrading intercity commerce in the foreseeable future. The fad of plank roads swept sections of Canada and the East beginning in the mid-1830s, and these wooden arteries laid in a network strongly appealed to Chicago-area residents. They applauded the placement of wide, heavy hemlock or oak planks across wooden stringers to create a solid surface over the wettest and hence muddiest stretches of road. "No section of the Union is better adapted for the building of plank roads than northern Illinois," concluded the *Joliet*

Signal. "[A]nd no other region would be more benefitted by them. The people are becoming awakened on the subject, and are beginning to view the matter in its proper light."[27]

The chief advantage of plank roads involved cost. The cheapest railroad, which employed "strap" or "flat" iron rail, ran about $6,000 to $8,000 per mile to build, while a plank road usually could be installed for much less, commonly $500 to $1,500 per mile. Wherever stands of trees grew, builders could erect small sawmills to convert the native wood into planks and then place them over existing public roads, thus saving the expense of grading, draining, and perhaps bridging.[28]

Antimonopoly sentiment, widespread during the Age of Jackson, entered the rhetoric of plank road promoters and hinted at future conflict between the public and railroads. One Chicagoan envisioned these pikes being "brought into every street and alley; to every ware house and manufactory in our city:—in the country; to the villages, settlements, and farm houses; all sections *are alike benefitted by them*." He added, "They do not enhance one man's property, and depress that of others; the farmer can take his produce to market, when his time is of little or no value. When a sudden advance in the staples of the country takes place, there are no railroad directors, or officers to reap the benefits of it." This champion of plank roads assumed that they would be free to users, paid for from tax collections. Yet while publicly chartered, most of these improvements were privately controlled, and tolls were charged.[29]

Since plank roads frequently offered a cost-effective means of keeping vehicles out of the mud, they became somewhat commonplace in Illinois and other sections of the Midwest. Between 1848 and 1854, for example, seven such thoroughfares radiated out of the Chicago area alone: three to the north of the city, one to the west, and three to the south. Soon, however, railroads brought ruin to turnpikes. But even when a transportation monopoly, plank road companies often experienced difficulties. Most of all they faced the continual expense of upkeep: surfaces, weakened by use and decay, menaced patrons if not repaired. Few of these wooden routes generated profits for their owners.[30]

Even before plank roads appeared, Chicago-area railroad supporters rebounded. One event energized them: the Rockford railroad convention of 1846. In vogue during the early years of railroading, this type of meeting could spark successful railroad-building projects. The individuals who assembled in Rockford were upbeat; they played on their generation's notions that railroads created wealth, benefited everybody, and signified progress for the state and nation.[31]

Convened in Rockford, a county-seat community 92 miles northwest of Chicago, the meeting's overall purpose was clear: "[To take] measures for the construction of the road [Galena & Chicago Union] at the earliest possible time." After preliminary work, 319 delegates, who represented the service territory of the projected line, gathered on January 7, 1846. Their discussions revealed strong sentiments and the likelihood of considerable financial support for the project. The body unanimously approved a resolution presented by Chicago businessman Walter Newberry: "RESOLVED, If a satisfactory arrangement can be made with the present holders of the stock of the Galena and Chicago Union Railroad Company, that the members of this convention will use all honorable measures to obtain subscriptions to the stock of said company." Newberry's role was hardly accidental. While Galena backers hailed from nearly a dozen counties, those from Chicago and Cook County dominated the convention, and they formulated the agenda.[32]

The Rockford assembly yielded more than good intentions. The Chicago representatives and their associates, encouraged by this tangible showing of public support, mindful of the need for the railroad, and buoyed by a healthier economic climate, moved with dispatch. They acquired the securities held by the Hubbard estate and vigorously pushed subscriptions of the company's stock.[33]

This "new" Galena & Chicago Union attracted talented live wires. Foremost among them was an uprooted New Yorker, William Butler Ogden (1805–1877), whose powerful presence left a deep impression on the project. Ogden's hustle and vision did much to convert notions of a Chicago-based railroad into a profitable reality.[34]

Ogden lived the American dream. Born on

June 15, 1805, in Walton, New York, a village in heavily forested Delaware County in the Southern Tier, he entered the business world in his early teens. Because of his father's poor health he assumed many responsibilities of the family's small sawmill. These pressing demands limited Ogden's opportunities for a formal education; yet his early career convinced him that hard work made personal prosperity possible and likely. He proclaimed later in his life that "I was born close by a saw-mill . . . , christened in a millpond, graduated at a log-school-house, and, at fourteen, fancied I could do any thing I turned my hand to, and that nothing was impossible, and ever since . . . I have been trying to prove it, with some success." Ogden illustrated the type of person about whom French traveler Alexis de Tocqueville in the 1830s concluded: "Every American is eaten up with longing to rise."[35]

This ambitious young man moved beyond lumber to other activities. Ogden became postmaster at Walton and, in 1834, won election on the Democratic ticket to the New York Senate. But a year later he decided to leave the Empire State when his prosperous brother-in-law Charles Butler urged him to move to Chicago. Butler had become heavily involved in the city's intense real estate speculation. He had spent $100,000 to buy a thousand lots north of the river and persuaded Ogden to join his American Land Company. Butler made an excellent choice; Ogden excelled in this work. Later Ogden acquired his own property and gained a personal fortune from the land boom that came with the return of prosperity in the 1840s.[36]

A "natural leader," a "natural orator," and "a man of noble ambitions and high resolves," Ogden emerged as a popular figure in Chicago. When the community became incorporated, he won election as its first mayor. Throughout his tenure Ogden used his public powers to boost his adopted hometown, whose image of "miserable little hamlet . . . set down in the mud about the forks of the Chicago River" gradually disappeared. And Ogden did not stop his promotion of the town when he left politics. Ogden's first concern became the languishing Illinois & Michigan Canal project, and through his political and financial contacts he did much to bring about its completion.[37]

Ogden grasped the potential of the railway. During his brief senatorial career in New York he urged public support for construction of the New-York & Erie Railroad, a line projected from the Hudson River to Lake Erie. In remarks to fellow lawmakers Ogden seemingly possessed clairvoyant powers; he foresaw "continuous railways from New York to Lake Erie, and south of Lake Erie, through Ohio, Indiana, and Illinois, to the waters of the Mississippi, and connecting with railroads running to Cincinnati, and Louisville in Kentucky, and Nashville in Tennessee, and to New Orleans." And he added, "[They] will present the most splendid system of internal communication ever yet devised by man." Ironically, Ogden ended up shaping the railroad map himself, at least to the north and west of Chicago, and assisted in developing a link to the "Father of Waters" slightly more than a decade after his optimistic oration.[38]

William Butler Ogden did not create the Galena single-handedly. Other influential Chicagoans contributed their homespun talent and initiative, including Walter Newberry, a merchant, banker, and real estate promoter; Thomas Dyer, partner in the beef-packing house of Wadsworth, Dyer & Chopin and first president of the Chicago Board of Trade; and Charles Walter, a prosperous agricultural commodities broker and farm implements dealer. These "prudent businessmen," collectively known as the "Chicago Group," left a positive legacy.[39]

Before construction of the Galena & Chicago Union could commence, the Chicago Group needed capital and thus aggressively sought financing. They won state approval in February 1847 of an increase in capital stock to $3 million. During the summer and fall of 1847 company president William Ogden spearheaded a drive in Chicago to solicit support. Two railroad representatives canvased each of the city's nine wards and "disposed [of stock] . . . principally to mechanics." Similar efforts were mounted along the projected route and in all did remarkably well. "The success in obtaining subscriptions along the line of the route," observed the *Rockford Forum*, "has been greater than was at first anticipated, from $250,000 to $300,000 having been subscribed. Winnebago [County] . . . [has] subscribed between $23,000 and $25,000 for stock." County governments also helped; they imposed special "railroad taxes" for the purchase of company securities.[40]

The Chicago Group initially avoided national and foreign money centers. "The directors of the company are prudent business men," concluded the *American Railroad Journal*, "and will not jeopard[ize] the interests of stockholders or give to eastern capitalists the control of the road." Moreover, eastern financiers continued to distrust Illinois-based transportation projects as memories of the state's acute financial problems following the Panic of 1837 lingered.[41]

Another major step toward developing the Galena required obtaining a detailed study of the proposed line. The board wisely hired an experienced civil engineer, Richard Price Morgan, who examined the terrain between Chicago and Galena with his associates in 1847. His findings soon became available. Morgan estimated the cost of constructing the 182 miles of standard gauge single track, with bridges designed for double track, at $2,648,000 or $14,550 per mile.[42]

The board members warmly received Morgan's 18-page report. Expected construction expenses were neither unreasonable nor excessively high. If the company acquired mostly second-hand materials, including locomotives, rolling stock, and strap rail, the cost per mile could be cut further. They undoubtedly appreciated Morgan's view that "if the country between the Mississippi and Lake Michigan were a perfect desert, there would be enough business in a few years concentrated at Galena, from the western shores of that great stream, to give ample support to a railroad connecting that city with Chicago." Morgan estimated receipts from freight and passenger revenues at $393,000 and operating costs of $176,500. "[I]n the very first year that the Galena Railroad shall be in operation, over 8 per cent. will be gained on the capital expended." The confident predictions of the Morgan study were later confirmed.[43]

Although backers of the Galena ultimately intended to reach the lead-mining district, they initially concentrated on opening the 41 miles between Chicago and Elgin. This section not only could generate traffic immediately but could be built easily. "[T]he grades on that portion of the road between Chicago and Elgin are scarcely equalled by any other road in the country," commented Ogden in April 1848, "the maximum grade going east, being but six feet, and going west, but twenty feet to the mile." Furthermore, the road could be fashioned "in straight lines, and the few curves there are, all

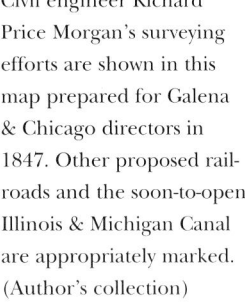

Civil engineer Richard Price Morgan's surveying efforts are shown in this map prepared for Galena & Chicago directors in 1847. Other proposed railroads and the soon-to-open Illinois & Michigan Canal are appropriately marked. (Author's collection)

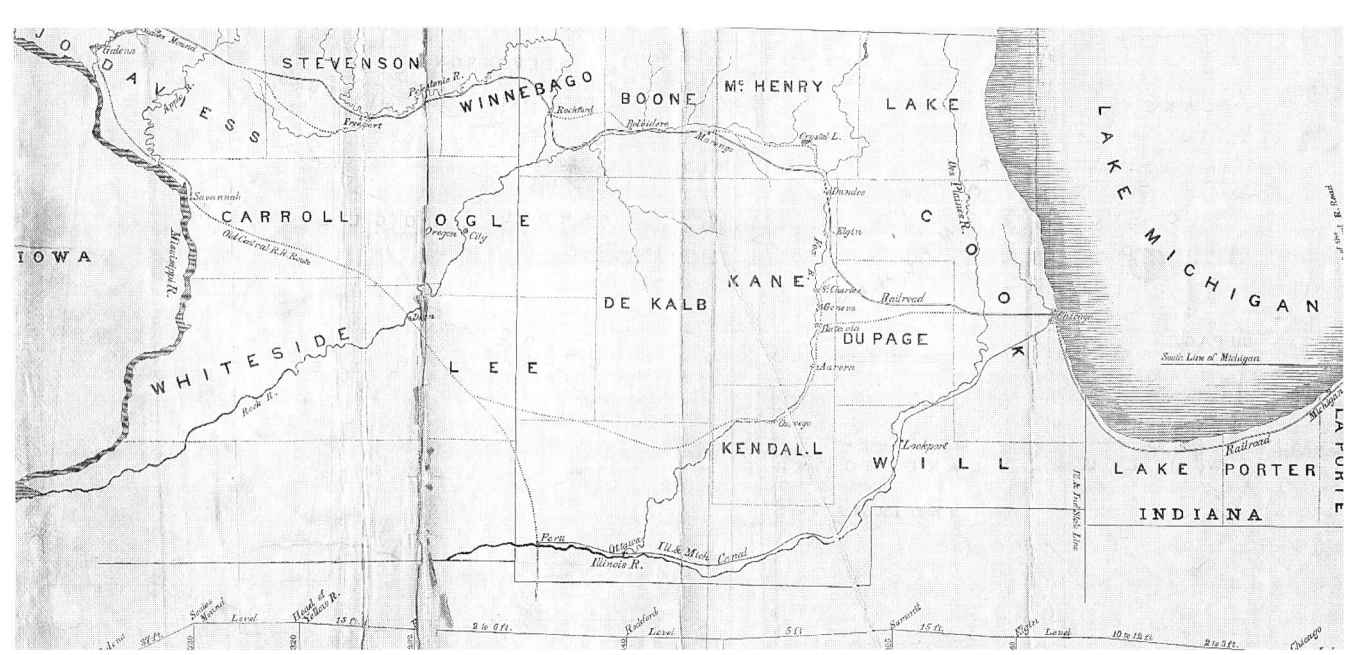

having large radii, requiring but trifling increase of power as compared with a straight line." Finally, bridge work would not be costly either. The road would encounter no major streams, and the once swampy prairies had become drier to some extent. "Owing to the champion character of the country over which the road passes, the consequent absence of any considerable floods in the streams it crosses, the cost of grading and bridging from Chicago to Elgin, and of the entire construction of the road," noted the account, "will be greatly less than of most other roads, probably much less than that of any other substantial, well constructed road, of equal length ever built." A railroad, at least between Chicago and Elgin, seemed assured.[44]

Construction of the Galena finally began in June 1848 when workers drove the first grade peg near the corner of Kinzie and Halsted streets on the outskirts of Chicago. By August 21 the Weekly Chicago Democrat could report that "the work upon the grading of this road as far West as the Du Page River, is progressing rapidly to completion." And by late fall laborers had completed 10 miles from Chicago toward Elgin. The road, however, did not reach its intermediate destination until January 1850.[45]

Like most other western railroads of the 1840s, the Galena avoided the blunders some eastern and southern roads made with gauge and grade during the demonstration period of American railroading. And like neighboring carriers, the project was not designed to be state-of-the-art. Company officials envisioned a practical and inexpensive road; they wanted to reduce costs by acquiring used materials and equipment. "It is anticipated that Iron and Engines, of good quality may be obtained on advantageous terms," commented chief engineer John Van Nortwick in April 1848, "from some of the many eastern companies, who are substituting the T for flat [strap] rail, and who are desirous of disposing of the light engines, (which are best suited to the wants of this road,) and substituting those of greater weight and power."[46]

The "able and indefatigable" Van Nortwick correctly anticipated the nature of the emerging Galena. The roadway at first used discarded, obsolescent flat or strap-iron rail. At that time several eastern states, New York in 1847 for example, had outlawed this rail for safety reasons. The 20- to 25-foot strips of iron, bolted to wooden beams, occasionally worked loose and curled up under the weight of passing trains. These "snakeheads" might then break through a coach floor and injure or even kill its occupants and halt the train, much the way sawyers and snaps could impale and sink a riverboat. The Galena was willing to risk strap-rail accidents and apparently encountered no major difficulties.[47]

Just as tons of strap iron became available, so too did the light steam locomotives that manufacturers had designed to run over these primitive tracks. The Galena's first piece of motive power, the 10-ton *Pioneer*, was built by prominent locomotive manufacturer Matthias W. Baldwin in his firm's Philadelphia shops in the early 1840s and featured the popular six-wheel arrangement (4-2-0). While the *Pioneer*'s background is not fully known, the Galena may have purchased it from the Tonawanda Railroad, a later component of the New York Central. Apparently the Galena also acquired a few cars and 42 miles of strap rail from this western New York carrier. Soon after laborers unloaded the wood-burning *Pioneer* from a lake schooner on the west bank of the Chicago River on October 10, 1848, the locomotive began to pull cars laden with supplies and workers for the advancing line. According to the *Gem of the Prairie* of October 28, "the untiring iron horse maintained a steady speed of sixteen miles per hour over the shaky metal-capped, wooden track." Within a month the Galena reached the Des Plaines River, near present-day Maywood.[48]

Quickly the Galena attracted traffic. The road's first business, however, added nothing to company coffers. Millican Hunt, an Ogle County farmer, remembered nearly 50 years later that the Galena's initial cargo consisted solely of dressed hogs. "I traded some wheat with my neighbor . . . for live hogs, which according to our agreement, he was to slaughter and dress and I was to come after them," Hunt recalled. "During the first part of December [1848] I went for the hogs, loaded them on a sled, and, with John Worthington, who also had a load, started for Chicago." Yet their journey into the city did not go as expected. "There was about fifteen inches of snow on the ground. After more than two days' travel—a distance of eighty odd miles—we arrived at the Oak Ridge house, where Oak Park is now located, and found that little snow had fallen there and in Chicago. We could scarcely get along with our sleds on the bare ground. At this time the track of the . . . Galena railroad had been laid from Chicago as far as the Oak Ridge house, and when we arrived there a construction train was standing on the track. There was a small engine, since called the Pioneer, and other small flat cars with several hands operating the train." Hunt then described the arrangement for transporting the meat to market by rail. "Mr. Worthington asked the conductor if he would take our hogs on the cars into Chicago, so we could go in there with empty sleds. The conductor said he would do so if we would transfer the hogs within 15 minutes. I then said, 'Captain, we will pay you well for this when we get into Chicago.' The conductor said, 'Boys, do you know you are going to be the first shippers by railroad into Chicago?' I said, 'No, sir,' and he replied: 'Well you are, and you shall have it free. You will find your hogs on the cars about a quarter of a mile this side of the river. If we are not there, you just unload them and take them away."[49]

This impromptu shipment of meat at the beginning of December 1848 demonstrated the potential market for freight business. Even a Lilliputian road could serve customers, and the railroad rapidly met their needs with a profit. "Yesterday the covered cars for the transportation of produce were placed upon the track," reported the *Weekly Chicago Democrat* of December 5, 1848. "Over thirty loads of wheat were at the Des Plaines river waiting transportation into the city." Westbound movements began thereafter when a Chicago merchant "forwarded a number of boxes of goods for Dupage County." These events thrilled most residents of the area; rail transport significantly cut shipping costs and transit time and augured well for the economic health of the region.[50]

Passenger service probably followed on a "mixed" train for several months, with both freight cars and likely a makeshift coach attached to the *Pioneer*. In the spring of 1849 the *Weekly Chicago Democrat* revealed that "one thousand two-hundred and twenty-one passengers have been carried on the railroad during the month of April. The road is now finished twelve miles, or one mile beyond the Des Plaines River. The cars, however, only run to the river." The Galena did not operate a bona-fide passenger car until July 4, 1849, when it opened to Cottage Hill (Elmhurst), 18 miles west of Chicago. The equipment pleased the *Chicago Journal:* "The first passenger car . . . will be in running order tomorrow [July 4]. It is an elegant vehicle, built by Messrs. Welch & Launder, of this city, at an expense of over $2,000. All aboard, gentlemen, for Cottage Hill!"[51]

The emerging Galena owned pieces of rolling stock that, like the *Pioneer*, were smaller versions of later nineteenth-century equipment. Freight cars during the demonstration period resembled simple wooden boxes and seldom held cargoes greater than 10 tons. Passenger coaches were not much larger and were nearly as spartan, especially before the Civil War, except possibly for ornamental paint on their exteriors. Lighting and heating equipment were minimal, and seats were closely spaced.[52]

The opening of the first segment of the Galena demonstrated that the railroad was a dramatically superior form of transport, regardless of the equipment. Since the climate of the region followed a cold-hot and wet-dry cycle, commerce fluctuated widely from season to season. Whether it was ice on Lake Michigan or quagmires on county roads, shippers and travelers needed to adjust their schedules to conform with those of nature. But the iron highway largely solved the problems associated with life in a temperate climate; it set off a true transportation revolution. If patrons gained convenient access to the rails, seasonal inconveniences might be forgotten. "The 'Open Sesame' . . . has been spoken through the railroad-whistle," observed Michigan writer Caroline Kirkland a decade after the *Pioneer* first got up a head of steam. "Railroads cannot make mines and quarries, and fat soil and bounteous rivers; yet railroads have been the making of Illinois. Nobody who has ever seen her spring roads, where there are no rails, can ever question it. From the very fatness of her soil, the greater part of the State must have been one Slough of Despond for three quarters of the year, and her inhabitants strangers to each other, if these iron arms had not drawn the people together and bridged the gulfs for them."[53]

Throughout 1849 the construction of the Galena & Chicago Union continued, more rolling stock became available, and freight and passenger traffic increased. By the time the Galena reached Cottage Hill, receipts averaged about $60 daily, and the company's securities finally gained respectability. "Stock, which had gone down to 75 or 80 cents on the dollar, was no longer considered a dead loss, and hopes were entertained that the predictions of the Engineer . . . might be verified." In late November the Galena extended 30 miles, and its tiny trains became even busier. "It is estimated that it might require some thirty or forty cars to do the business in Elgin—it will take at least a hundred. There are now more than fifty freight cars, and they cannot do the business." When the company reached Elgin on January 22, 1850, business boomed. The firm's third annual report, issued in May 1850, indicated that its four locomotives, which included three new 15-ton 4-4-0 or "American Standard" types built by Norris & Company in New Jersey, 67 freight cars, and eight passenger coaches could barely handle the volume of goods and people. "The business of the Road," commented the *Chicago Daily Tribune* at year's end, "has thus far exceeded the expectation of the most sanguine of its friends." The company earned $22,529.89 from freight between June 1849 and May 1850 and $22,802.07 from passengers. Operating expenses totaled $18,519.82, which produced net earnings of $26,812.14. In an August 1850 editorial the *American Railroad Journal* stated: "The portion opened is doing so well, the company will, we presume, find no difficulty in obtaining sufficient means for the vigorous prosecution of the remainder of the line." The trade journal added: "The success of that part opened must inspire confidence in the ability of the company to meet all liabilities incurred on account of construction."[54]

Running even a shortline necessitated many improvements, and the Galena responded as best it could. The state of this thriving property is revealed in the chief engineer Van Nortwick's description of facilities as of May 1, 1850:

> The depot and station buildings constructed, are a substantial freight house at Chicago, 50 by 150 feet, including the necessary offices for the accommodation of all business of the Company at this place. One engine house and smith's shop, 30 by 60 feet, with an addition 18 by 60 feet, and a temporary building, 26 by 90 feet, used for a car shop. At the junction of the Aurora Branch Rail Road [Turner Junction], a permanent freight house 28 by 60 feet, has been constructed, also a wood shed and water station building, 30 by 40 feet, and a temporary engine house. At Elgin, a permanent building 30 by 40 feet, has been erected for an engine house and water station. At Desplaines [sic] and Babcock's Grove [Lombard], water stations have been provided, and temporary freight houses have been built at Cottage Hill, Babcock's Grove and Wheaton's.[55]

The Van Nortwick commentary reveals a common practice of pioneering railroads, namely, not erecting special passenger facilities except perhaps at their terminals. With finite financial resources companies decided to spend their money where it was needed most—on track, equipment, and freight facilities. This last one was particularly important because cargoes required protection from weather and theft.[56] Passengers, however, could fend for themselves; there had been no tradition of providing shelter for passengers anyway. Stagecoach travelers usually waited in roadside inns, taverns, or stores, much like intercity bus riders a century later. Many early railroads, including the Galena, continued this money-saving practice for some years after completion of their initial lines.[57]

Finally the "First Division" of the Galena, this 42.44 miles of main line from the Chicago River northwestward to Elgin, was complete. The cost averaged about $9,000 per mile for a total of slightly more than $405,000. Directors took pride in their achievement and immediately focused on the next segment.[58]

The "Second Division" involved construction of the 50 miles of line between Elgin and Rockford. Work moved haltingly: the first 12 miles northwest of Elgin opened on September 15, 1851, the next dozen miles on October 18, and the 12 miles to Belvidere on December 3. Severe winter weather delayed laying track to Cherry Valley, in eastern Winnebago County, until March 10, 1852. The iron horse finally arrived in Rockford, seven miles west of Cherry Valley and 92 miles from Chicago, on August 2, 1852.[59]

The Second Division cost considerably more than the First. The bill exceeded $800,000, or about $16,000 per mile. By this time the Galena wisely opted for standard T rail; the iron came from Welsh mills and weighed 56 pounds to the linear yard. The quality, of course, greatly surpassed strap rail, and by now the company could afford this desirable improvement. It replaced the strap iron on the First Division with the all-metal variety by summer 1853. In contemporary railroad tradition the Galena sold the second-hand rail to two struggling railroads in Wisconsin.[60]

Reaching Rockford, a good source of traffic, did not end the second wave of expansion. The Galena continued with its "Third Division," designed to extend from the Winnebago County seat, on the east side of the Rock River, westward to Freeport, 29 miles, and a connection with the projected Illinois Central Railroad. Unlike much of the Chicago-Rockford route, this extension crossed some rough terrain and necessitated bridging the troublesome Rock River at two points. On September 1, 1853, the Galena arrived at Freeport, 121 miles from Chicago, and at a cost of nearly $20,000 per mile for the third leg.[61]

At the same time as the construction of the Freeport division, the Galena embarked upon two new line additions, the "Beloit Branch" and the "Dixon Air Line." The former diverged from the main stem at Belvidere and ran for 21 miles to the Illinois-Wisconsin border at Beloit. There the extension connected with the Beloit & Madison Railroad, a firm that tried mightily to link its namesake communities and also planned to push from Madison to Portage City (Portage) on the Wisconsin River "and to the pineries north." While the Galena opened this appendage on November 14, 1853, the Beloit & Madison did not reach the Wisconsin capital for another decade and then under the Galena's control. The second project, the Dixon Air Line, however, shortly thereafter changed the character of Chicago's pioneer carrier.[62]

It soon became apparent that the Galena & Chicago Union Railroad had been misnamed. When residents of Galena and Jo Daviess County welcomed steam cars in the fall of 1854, they belonged to the Illinois Central Railroad. That carrier, not the Galena road, installed the 51 miles of track between Freeport and Galena. Even though the Galena never reached its namesake western terminus, it still captured traffic from the lead district, and it alone offered a direct route to Chicago and the East. The company could hardly be accused of running from "nowhere to nowhere in particular"; it was much more than a local tap line.[63]

Directors of the Galena decided that they needed their own route to the Mississippi River rather than trackage to Galena. "The company wanted a new main line," concluded an early observer. These individuals had their eyes on the "West," perhaps envisioning an extension to the Pacific Ocean. Such thoughts, while premature, were not entirely in the realm of fantasy. As early as the mid-1840s a plan to construct a rail line from Lake Michigan to Oregon provoked widespread discussion. In a less visionary fashion leaders of the Galena fretted about other railroads building directly west from Chicago. Reports about the plans of the Chicago, St. Charles & Mississippi Air Line Railroad, which expected to parallel the Galena from Chicago to the Fox River and then extend directly to the Mississippi River at Savanna, were troublesome. Worrisome, too, were the intentions of the Chicago & Rock Island and the Michigan Southern & Northern Indiana railroads, of which the latter was about to reach Chicago.[64]

Galena officials responded shrewdly. The core of their projected line would be apart from the sphere of influence of the developing Chicago & Rock Island Railroad. That carrier, launched in 1851 with authority to build between the cities in its corporate title, would parallel the Illinois & Michigan Canal southwest of Chicago and then extend westerly to the Mississippi River at Rock Island, Illinois, approximately 75 miles south of Galena. Indeed, the Rock Island company boldly executed its plans: the road opened the initial segment between Chicago and Joliet in October 1852, reached Peru the following spring, and arrived in Rock Island on Washington's birthday in 1854. With the routing strategy of the Rock Island known, the Galena in April 1853 announced its determination to build an "Air Line" or direct route to the Mississippi River at Savanna, approximately 40 miles south of Galena. It would also largely usurp the projected route of what was becoming the moribund "St. Charles Air Line." Any remaining threat from that firm ended in 1854 when the Galena acquired its assets.[65]

Leaders of the Galena moved with dispatch on the Dixon Air Line extension. They could do so because the company's success and promise gave it access to pools of capital, both local and national. Lawmakers also promptly agreed to increase the road's capital stock "to a sum not exceeding five millions of dollars."[66]

Surveyors promptly went to work. They located the line westward from Junction (shortly Turner and later West Chicago), 30 miles west of Chicago where the 12-mile Aurora Branch Railroad, the core component of the Chicago, Burlington & Quincy Railroad, had met the Galena in September 1850. The route passed through Dixon, where the railroad would cross the Galena-Cairo line of the Illinois Central, and terminated at Fulton City (soon shortened to Fulton), about 25 miles south of Savanna, the original destination. The Dixon Air Line would be 135 miles long, "being the shortest practicable line between Chicago and any point on the Mississippi River."[67]

Progress was steady. Graders and tracklayers completed 45 miles west of Junction in January 1854, "but [the track] was not in a condition to be fully opened for business until about the 1st of May [1854]." The line reached Dixon, 68 miles from Junction, on December 4, 1854; Sterling on July 22, Morrison on September 23, and Fulton on December 16, 1855. Construction labors benefited from the partially completed earthen work between Dixon and Fulton instigated by the failed Mississippi & Rock River Junction Railroad a year or so earlier. In February 1855 the Galena absorbed the assets of that firm, which had sought to become a feeder of the Illinois Central.[68]

Shortly after trains reached Fulton, Galena crews installed an electric telegraph line from Turner to the end of track, just as they had done a year earlier along the original line. Noted the *Tenth Annual Report* for 1857, "[The General Office] . . . is also connected with the telegraph lines of the Chicago, Burlington & Quincy, and of that portion of the Illinois Central upon which the joint business is done." The latter involved trackage between Freeport and Galena.[69]

A formal gala to welcome the iron horse had become a tradition along newly completed rail lines. One such celebration took place at Sterling; elated residents decided to make the welkin ring. "Simeon Coe furnished a three-year old ox, which was roasted on a primitive arrangement of forked sticks, and then borne in triumph, bedecked with flags and oranges, to an immense arbor of branches near the present Central school," recounted a local historian in 1908. "After the banquet, B. F. Taylor, the poet, made a flowery address. The lion of the day was Stephen A. Douglas, who talked to the masses in his own earnest style. . . . Estimates of the multitude ran as high as five thousand."[70]

The enthusiasm generated by completion of the Dixon project extended to more than individuals who gained direct access to the line. With this strategic artery in place and with prospects growing for reaching the developing Iowa frontier, the larger business community recognized the Galena's considerable progress. The feeling grew among investors, including those from principal money centers, that the company's securities, unlike those of some pioneer pikes, particularly in the South, represented a highly attractive investment. The *Ninth Annual Report,* presented to stockholders on June 4, 1856, showed that the carrier generated gross earnings of nearly $2.5 million and had operating expenses of approximately $1.2 million. The Galena retained a surplus of almost $400,000 "after paying 22 per cent. in Dividends and all expenses and interests properly chargeable to income account." Its soundness was evident in the policy of paying cash for construction and equipment and "never resort[ing] to the modern practice of paying stocks and bonds to contractors."[71]

The sterling qualities of the Galena stemmed from more than good luck. The road tapped traffic from expanding agricultural, commercial, and manufacturing operations in a region with enormous potential for growth. From the first the company profited from its mostly unchallenged local monopolies. "In its early days the Galena R. R. was the only way for people and their goods to reach the marketplace," observed a journalist in 1884. "[The railroad] did not have to worry about either competitors or hostile lawmakers."[72]

Strong leadership also contributed to making the Galena a vibrant enterprise. Some observers thought that the company would suffer when William Ogden, the stellar force behind the firm's gestation, resigned from both the presidency and the directorship in June 1851. The reason for his departure was not loss of faith in the company or in railroading, but rather a controversial business transaction. Several fellow directors charged Ogden with impropriety; namely, they objected to the firm's buying construction materials from McCagg, Reed & Company, a concern in which Ogden served as a "special partner." Ogden was not involved directly, although he used his contacts to assist the struggling road. Supplies were contracted *below* market price and were furnished on credit to the then cash-hungry carrier. In a subsequent trial a court vindicated Ogden's conduct, and his reputation remained untarnished. "[Ogden] had given his time, his money, and his credit to push on the Road," related Isaac Arnold, a Chicago lawyer. "[A]nd [he] had risked in it his private fortune, and I regarded the defense of this case, and the attack made upon his integrity, as most unjust and ungrateful." Added Arnold, "I remember few, if any, cases in my professional life, in which I felt a deeper personal interest." Trouble at the Galena did not sour Ogden on either the property or rail transport, and he re-entered the company's affairs near the close of the Civil War.[73]

Following the departure of William Ogden, a capable and prudent executive took charge, John Bice Turner (1799–1871). A native of New York's Southern Tier, he joined the fledgling railroad industry as a construction contractor in the mid-1830s and worked on several rail and canal building projects in New York before he moved to the Chicago area in 1843. After briefly raising sheep, Turner returned to railroading. By the late 1840s he worked closely with Ogden in soliciting funds for the Galena and later helped to supervise its construction.[74]

John Turner embraced a judicious strategy as the Galena's chief officer. He wanted his company to upgrade its physical plant and to focus on main rather than branch line expansion. As for the latter, Turner agreed that a successful carrier required feeders, but he thought it better that local boosters take the financial risks for them. The Galena would still gain from these appendages as it would receive freight and passenger traffic from these interchange partners. If any of these shortlines failed, the Galena could likely acquire them at the foreclosure sale for a bargain-basement price.[75]

An illustration of Turner's commitment to a stronger railroad was the double-tracking of the original core line between the Wells Street terminal in Chicago and Junction (renamed Turner in 1857 "by the people of that place"). This construction, which began in 1855, was hardly an extravagance: the company dispatched increasing numbers of trains over its Freeport and Fulton lines as did the Chicago, Burlington & Quincy, which rented rights to this 30-mile funnel route. The double-tracking became the first major project of its kind in Illinois and the harbinger of large-scale improvements to manage rising traffic.[76]

This betterment of the Turner era also created one of the hallmarks of the Galena and later of the Chicago & North Western system: left-handed train operations. The Galena had placed its stations north-of-track, and this became a concern when double-tracking occurred. If inbound passenger trains to Chicago ran on the right, patrons would need to cross the outbound line, a potentially dangerous situation. If inbound trains operated to the left, the hazard would be avoided. Officials also realized that travelers to Chicago commonly arrived at the station in the morning shortly before train time and required a waiting room and likely the services of the ticket seller. In the evening they got off the train and usually went directly home. Left-handed running would not interfere with this practice, and the company consequently could avoid the expense of relocating depots. Indeed, the Galena already had established itself as a company that watched its pennies.[77]

Development of the former St. Charles Air Line was another notable improvement during the Turner years. Its 10 miles of unfinished right-of-way from the South Branch of the Chicago River to a connection with the Galena at Harlem (Oak Park) finally opened on January 1, 1856, as the St. Charles Air Line Branch, and gave access to the Air Line's strategic real estate near Chicago's commercial core. The acquisition of the potential rival also provided convenient connections with railroads to the East and facilitated movement of interline freight traffic.[78]

Hardly as strategic as the St. Charles Air Line properties, but contributing further to the Galena's well-being, was its association with a feeder road from East Elgin northward to Richmond, Illinois, near the Wisconsin border. This

33-mile shortline, chartered in 1852 as the Fox River Valley Railroad and reorganized seven years later as the Elgin & State Line Railroad, served a flourishing farming area in eastern McHenry County. The Galena took control of the company's operations in 1858 and leased the line in 1863.[79]

The Turner regime, nevertheless, remained committed to a trunk-line strategy and did so in a conservative fashion. In the mid-1850s two ambitious railroad projects developed across the Mississippi River from the Galena's western terminus at Fulton. One was the Iowa Central Air Line Railroad, projected from Lyons City (later Lyons) northwesterly through Maquoketa and "thence . . . as near as practicable to the 42nd parallel across the state of Iowa to the Missouri River." This company planned a 335-mile trans-Iowa route and considered itself "destined to be the most important link in the great chain which is to connect the Atlantic and Pacific Oceans." The other was the Chicago, Iowa & Nebraska Railroad (CI&N), proposed from Clinton, several miles south of Lyons and nearly opposite Fulton, westward to Cedar Rapids and then northwesterly toward Minnesota and a connection with the yet unbuilt Minneapolis and Cedar Valley railroad to St. Paul. After a portion of this Hawkeye State trackage opened, the Galena leased it in perpetuity, even though the Galena had not been involved directly in either its promotion or construction.[80]

Although the Iowa Central Air Line possessed a generous land grant that Congress had allotted to Iowa in 1856, it never evolved beyond sections of naked grade between Lyons and Anamosa, a distance of about 65 miles. Inept, even dishonest management limited progress, and then the Panic of 1857 dealt the knockout punch. "Efforts were made to bolster it [Iowa Central Air Line] up and retain the grant," observed a local historian in 1878, "but the main purpose was carefully avoided by the manipulators of the funds, and the public became disgusted with the policy of the corporation."[81]

The CI&N, on the other hand, evolved steadily. With ample financing, principally from New England and New York investors, construction began shortly after the company's official organization on January 26, 1856. The project witnessed the first tracklaying in October 1856, and the line opened to Cedar Rapids, 82 miles west of Clinton, in June 1859, having been delayed by the hard times following the panic.[82]

Resembling the Dixon Air Line, the Hawkeye State road served a rich territory with a promising future. "The entire scope of the country penetrated by the CHICAGO, IOWA & NEBRASKA RAILROAD is unsurpassed in the West for beauty, healthfulness and fertility," bragged a company prospectus published in early 1857. "Much of it is thickly settled; as much so as any portion of Iowa; and now yields annually an amount of agricultural products far beyond the capacity of any present mode of transportation to market possessed by the people." This was not an exaggeration. The CI&N became a busy artery once the economy rebounded from the national depression: cattle and grain moved eastbound, and lumber and merchandise went westward.[83]

After the CI&N reached the Cedar River at Cedar Rapids, its owners discarded their initial routing strategy. The railroad never veered toward Minnesota; instead backers decided to turn west. While they did not go so far as to suggest that the Pacific Ocean was their ultimate destination, their eyes were on the Missouri River. These promoters contemplated a line across the wilds of Iowa as a logical portion of a future Chicago-to-Pacific rail link and as a means of boosting the value of their original property.[84]

The thrust toward the Missouri River did not take place under the aegis of the CI&N, however. Promoters of the extension, which included directors of the CI&N and several prominent Cedar Rapids residents, launched another firm on June 14, 1859, the Cedar Rapids & Missouri River Rail Road (CR&MR), to realize their objective. They did so to secure from state lawmakers the land grant earlier bestowed on the moribund Iowa Central Air Line. Backers of the CR&MR knew that they needed public assistance if they were to cross a sparsely settled region, particularly the projected route through western Iowa.[85]

The transfer of the land grant by the state government did not follow automatically. Although officers of the Iowa Central Air Line lacked credibility, lobbyists representing two competing roads that sought to reach the Missouri River caused some difficulty. "The measure was vigorously opposed by a strong combination of the city of Dubuque, and by the Dubuque & Pacific Railroad interest, on the north, and the Mississippi & Missouri and Rock Island interests, on the south," reported CR&MR president Lucius B. Crocker. These groups wanted the land grant awarded to another company, which they would control. The CR&MR overcame its opponents, however, in March 1860.[86]

The real estate meant much to the project. Specifically, the CR&MR gained access to "the unsold alternate sections or parts of sections of land situated within fifteen miles of the line of road that should be constructed on or near the 42nd parallel, and authorized the State [of Iowa] to sue the same for such purpose." If the railroad reached its destination, it would receive title to approximately 900,000 acres of some of the most fertile lands in North America. President Crocker expected land sales to generate from $2.50 to $5.00 per acre, or about $2.25 million to $4.5 million for the company's treasury. This substantial public largess was not the only incentive; the terrain itself was "remarkably adapted to the construction of a railroad of easy grade and small cost."[87]

The building started promptly. Even though the outbreak of the Civil War caused difficulties, including shortages of labor and materials, trains reached Otter Creek Station (Chelsea), 41 miles west of Cedar Rapids, by the end of 1861, and Marshalltown, 69 miles west of Cedar Rapids, in January 1862. Residents in the latter community showed "intense excitement over the event, and proper observance of it was made." Steam cars arrived in State Center, 15 miles west of Marshalltown in December 1863, and Nevada, 29 miles from Marshalltown, on July 4, 1864, and then Boone, 23 miles farther west, in December 1865.[88]

The steady progress of the CR&MR during a time of national crisis can be explained partly by the involvement of a remarkable individual, John Insley Blair. This wealthy, hard-driving New Jersey industrialist and railroad executive sensed the potential for railroads in the West when he visited eastern Iowa in the summer of 1860. "Blair seems to have no sooner touched Iowa soil," observed a biographer, "whereupon he perceived the boundless opportunities for opening up the West and the great possibilities of a trans-continental railroad with all its advantages to the Union." Blair soon acquired a major position in the CR&MR, about 15 percent of its common stock, and participated in a survey expedition during the summer of 1863 to determine the best route westward. In charge of the road's building arm, the Iowa Railroad Construction Company, Blair effectively solicited aid from local communities, and later oversaw extension of the line between Marshalltown and the Missouri River. Blair also headed the Iowa Railroad Land Company, which profitably sold the land grant real estate.[89]

No one considered the Iowa roads to be insignificant shortlines wandering aimlessly over the prairies. By the close of the Civil War the CR&MR emerged as a strong contender to best affiliates of the Burlington and the Rock Island railroads to the Missouri River at Council Bluffs, the projected milepost 1 of the future transcontinental railroad. Already the CR&MR had created a continuous line of 317 miles between Chicago and central Iowa, except for the gap caused by the Mississippi River.[90]

While laborers hammered spikes and surfaced track west of Cedar Rapids, the CI&N worked to span the Mississippi River. When the railroad began service, it used a steam-powered ferryboat to interchange cars with the Galena at Fulton. Then in January 1860 the CI&N linked the east channel from the Illinois side below Fulton to Little Rock Island with a seven-span wooden truss bridge; the company continued to cross the navigation channel by ferry. "This arrangement has proven very satisfactory, and no change of cars is now necessary in transferring freight and passengers from one road to the other, and an uninterrupted line is thus formed between Chicago and Cedar Rapids, a distance of 218 miles," reported the Galena in its *Fourteenth Annual Report,* published in 1861. "A contract has been entered into for a close running connection between the two companies." Still, the CI&N planned to install a drawbridge over the west or main channel. This engineering feat, however, did not happen until 1865. By then the CI&N had entered the orbit of the expanding Chicago & North Western Railway.[91]

While the great explosion of system building in the railroad industry occurred during the 1880s, the Galena disclosed its intention to expand much earlier. It leased both the CI&N and the CR&MR roads on July 3, 1863. As these Iowa lines evolved into going concerns, leaders of the Galena watched them closely and reported their development to stockholders. Yet they did little to finance these properties; rather, they only "form[ed] close business relations with them." This meant coordinated freight and passenger schedules and tariffs, extended terms on freight charges for construction materials hauled from Chicago, and construction of a short extension from Fulton to the CI&N bridge. Galena officials remained attached to their economical ways. As the *Chicago Tribune* accurately reported, "[The] Galena Company has thus far received the business of the Iowa roads without bearing any of the burdens of obtaining it." Admittedly, Galena managers worried that any investments in the Iowa roads could be lost if they failed to establish legally binding arrangements with them. "[A]s matters stand now," wrote Galena general superintendent Edward Talcott to John Blair, "our Co. have [*sic*] no assurance that whatever aid we may give will not hereafter be diverted from us."[92]

The Galena's lack of major financial ties to the Iowa roads stood in sharp contrast to what was becoming a general practice. Larger firms often strengthened their relationships with connecting feeders by buying their securities. The aggressive Pennsylvania Railroad reflected this trend. After 1852 the company invested heavily in several roads that were emerging west of Pittsburgh.[93]

The relationship between the Galena and the combined CI&N and the CR&MR was hardly an equal partnership. "The Iowa roads have never assumed to 'dictate' [to the Galena]," observed a journalist in 1862. "Their attitude . . . has been that of constant supplication, which was again and again renewed, in spite of repulses rendered most humiliating by the haughtiness on the part of the Galena. . . ." As the Galena considered itself the "Alpha and Omega of all railroads," the directors of the Iowa roads contemplated finding another eastern connection. Most likely it would have been at Dubuque, approximately 60 miles north of Clinton, and access to the Illinois Central via ferries to its rail head at Dunleith, Illinois. But when the Galena offered an acceptable lease arrangement, the Iowa roads cast their lot with a prosperous and potentially powerful concern. It was a sensible union. The properties fit together perfectly and foreshadowed the combined roads becoming a link in the "Overland" transcontinental route.[94]

The Galena may not have been the Alpha and Omega of all railroads by the early 1860s, but it had few equals in the Midwest. The company had enjoyed profitability almost from the start. Even when the Panic of 1857 devastated the national economy, especially that of the frontier, the Galena maintained its financial health. When the road's freight and passenger business declined precipitously, a cautious management responded prudently by cutting the company's workforce from 1,904 employees in August 1857 to only 722 in January 1858, and its monthly payroll correspondingly dropped from $68,318 to $27,864. The Galena's ratio of expenses to earnings remained at comfortable levels from 1856, when the Dixon Air Line opened, to 1864, when the Galena lost its corporate identity. The best year was 1856, when the rate stood at an astonishing 45 percent; it climbed to 63 percent during the second half of 1857; dropped to 52 percent in 1861, and increased to 58 percent in 1863. Just as the Panic of 1857 adversely affected the company, so too did the Civil War years, which created "the higher value of fuel, material and labor."[95]

The robust Galena Railroad consistently sought to upgrade its equipment and physical plant, a rehearsal for the "Best of Everything" credo of the latter-day Chicago & North Western. Modern motive power was among the Galena's most notable betterments. With adequate financial resources by the early 1850s, the company started to assemble a fleet of heavier (mostly 28 ton) "American Standard" 4-4-0 type locomotives from the country's premier builders: Baldwin; Rogers, Ketchum & Grosvenor; and Schenectady. Although a North Western publicist in 1902 would write that these general-purpose iron horses "possessed small hauling capacity, wheezed and leaked, [and] spread the earth with cinders," they were at the time of purchase wonderful machines. These

American Standard locomotives with such distinctive names as *Cloud, Hercules,* and *Whirling Thunder* pulled passenger trains of several cars at 20 to 25 miles per hour and freight trains of 10–15 cars at about half those speeds, far surpassing the power of the *Pioneer* and other early lightweight engines.[96]

The Galena furthermore expanded and improved its rolling stock. In 1863 the company possessed not only 74 locomotives, mostly wood-burning, but also 1,540 "cars of all description." Its passenger equipment, in particular, ranked with the best in operation. For example, the Galena, along with the Camden & Ambroy and the Troy & Boston, used the first gas units for illuminating coaches, a vast improvement over candles. More memorable, perhaps, was the Galena's employment in 1858 of some of the earliest sleeping cars in the Midwest. The road offered passengers who traveled overnight "Woodruff-style sleepers" between Chicago, Galena, and Fulton. Although this service was short-lived, the company reintroduced sleeping equipment in the early 1860s.[97]

Trackside facilities also underwent a metamorphosis. The stations in Chicago illustrate these steady improvements. A modest single-story frame structure, located near the intersection of Canal and Kinzie streets, served patrons at the initiation of service in 1848–1849. Remodeling followed; the depot gained a partial second story for offices and a large cupola. The latter added more than a decorative touch. "Mr. Turner often watched for the incoming of his trains, with the aid of a long, old fashioned 'marine' telescope that he possessed," noted William Stennett, a student of the North Western, "and thus could announce the coming of a train while it was yet as far away as Austin, six miles." In the early 1850s the Galena relocated its principal passenger terminal to a nearby site at Water and Wells streets on the east side of the North Branch of the Chicago River. This building, which the company designed for both passenger and office purposes, was a 45 x 45 foot brick and stone edifice and featured an attached train shed. But growth of business subsequently left this depot wanting. The Galena, spurred to make modifications when the city raised the level of Wells Street to eliminate its "muddiness," enlarged this second passenger depot and office facility in 1862–1863. At a cost of $20,000 it lengthened the structure by 30 feet and added a third story. This substantial facility remained a beehive of activity until it was consumed in the Great Fire of 1871.[98]

Just as Chicago received improved depots so too did lesser communities. The Galena realized that it must provide more than inexpensive freight shelters at these stations. In what evolved into a common practice in the industry, especially in the Midwest and West, the company erected "combination" depots. Usually built of wood these buildings provided under one roof space for storage of baggage, express and less-than-carload freight; an office for the agent; and a waiting area for patrons. Management reported in 1861 that "station buildings are now being framed to replace the . . . sheds [on the Dixon Air Line] at Lodi, Bement, Ogle, Nachusa, Como and Round Grove."[99]

Passenger service on the Galena rivaled the best of the era. Its trains served more than 40 communities along the principal Freeport and Fulton routes with runs twice daily. This "OLDEST AND MOST RELIABLE ROUTE TO THE NORTH WEST" resembled most trunk roads by not dispatching expresses, instead ordering each train to stop at every station. Still, by the eve of the Civil War Galena passenger trains averaged speeds of about 25 miles per hour, an impressive rate for the time. Travelers also enjoyed such services as "A MAGNIFICENT SLEEPING CAR Attached to every Night Train" and "BAGGAGE CHECKED THROUGH TO ANY POINT, and carefully handled, free of charge."[100]

For the nearly 15 years that the Chicago & Galena Union operated independently, it profoundly affected the inhabitants along its expanding network of iron rails. Even before the company extended much beyond Chicago, it made its presence felt. Not only did area farmers and merchants gain ready access to markets, but also new patterns of social intercourse emerged. "The railroad is a great convenience to the inhabitants of the towns of the Fox River," concluded the *Weekly Chicago Democrat* as early as December 1849. "Persons . . . often ride into the city by the evening train, visit their friends, transact business, go to the theatre or some other place of public amusement, and return in the

During the fall of 1848 the Galena erected the first railroad depot in Chicago. The historic one-story building stood west of Canal Street and south of Kinzie Street. In 1849 the company added a second floor for office space. By the 1870s the depot principally served North Western employees as the Railway Men's Reading Room. (Author's collection)

morning train to their homes." The newspaper wryly observed, "Some of the young gentlemen's mothers never suspect they've been out, before they are at home and at business as usual."[101]

The scope of rail service grew increasingly complex. In early 1850, for instance, the Post Office Department awarded the Galena a contract to move "pouched" mail. No longer would letters travel on much slower and irregular stagecoaches. Galena trains also began to carry small packages. Though the shipment of parcels by railways was just beginning at midcentury, Galena customers, as others did elsewhere, turned their items over to reliable crew members. "Mr. Germain is the gentlemanly conductor," observed a Chicago reporter in October 1850. "[T]he public may be assured of his strict attention to packages and whatever else may be entrusted to his charge."[102]

Though the Galena never hired an army of workers, its steady growth increased local employment opportunities by offering a variety of positions, whether office work, train service, or equipment and roadway maintenance. Scattered biographical sketches of Galena employees, which appeared mostly in the *North-Western Magazine* during the early part of the twentieth century, suggest that the workforce consisted of mostly young males, who left agriculture for railroading in what was surely their first wage-earning experience. The Galena also recruited elsewhere, hiring personnel from the ranks of local clerks and stagecoach employees as well as skilled eastern artisans and mechanics. Once the workforce became established, the company commonly tolerated and even encouraged nepotism. This practice, particularly promoted by foremen, continued on the North Western and most other railroads for generations.[103]

The corporate culture of the Galena involved more than growing numbers of kith and kin; it included a spirit of paternalism that was widespread at the time. Industrialists frequently expressed compassion toward workers even though they generally preached a laissez-faire ideology. Officials often knew their employees on a first-name basis and felt personal ties to them; after all, their companies were relatively small and closely knit. They also recognized that a large portion of their personnel had become dependent upon the wage system. If the breadwinner died or was seriously injured, the future of a family was threatened, especially if there were young dependents. During the Galena's lifetime, little in the way of a safety net existed for the unfortunate. Public bodies, mostly units of county government, provided limited assistance, and private charities, the mainstay for the troubled, offered only slightly greater assistance. Moreover, railroad brotherhoods, which sought to shelter members and their families from economic distress, were only evolving. The first permanent trade union organization of railway workers, the Brotherhood of Locomotive Engineers, did not appear until the Civil War.[104]

The leadership of the Galena then filled the welfare void as it thought appropriate. An illustration of one of its acts of compassion is a resolution of November 2, 1852, passed by the Board of Directors:

> Charles Gary, an engineer . . . was accidentally killed on the 31st [of] October, while conducting his train westward. . . . [T]he company have lost an honest, upright and intelligent officer, whose place it will be difficult to fill; and inasmuch as Mr. Gary has left a Widow and three small children who were wholly dependent upon his labor for their support, and with a view to relieve the wants of those who are thus deprived of their natural protector and father, it is further revolved that the Sum of five hundred and forty dollars be paid to his Widow, it being the sum which would have been due him for his year's services if his life had been spared.[105]

As with other roads that took a paternalistic attitude toward their employees, the Galena never realized the ideal atmosphere of a totally happy family. While information about workers' attitudes toward management is scarce, likely the severe cuts in the workforce prior to the Civil War caused hard feelings. Discontent erupted near the end of Galena's corporate life when engineers struck over wages and work rules. While management agreed to their request for an increase of 75 cents per day in 1864, it demanded some unpopular concessions. Engineers and firemen would be expected either to work on their locomotives or to perform other shop work as directed by the master mechanic for four hours per working day or forfeit one-sixth of a day's pay. And if runs were doubled, that is, if two days' work in the same working period was required, the pay would not be doubled, but increased only one-half of a standard day's pay. A strike ensued, but the disgruntled members of Division Number 6 of the Brotherhood of Locomotive Engineers chose the wrong course of action. The Galena broke the protest with the assistance of other Chicago-based carriers that supplied strikebreakers to run the many wartime trains. The failure of this work stoppage had a far-reaching impact upon the newly launched engineers' union. "The defeat of the engineers during the strike," concludes labor historian Walter Licht, "was largely responsible for the adoption by the Brotherhood of Locomotive Engineers of a more conservative stance." The engineers then concentrated on mutual insurance and temperance work.[106]

Although the Galena & Chicago Union merged with the Chicago & North Western on a troubled note, the company had been a "splendid affair, prosperous in the extreme, finely equipped, and a huge factor in promoting Chicago's growth." *The Annual Review of the Trade, Business and Growth of Chicago* concluded in 1865 that the "value of that trade to our city [via the Galena] we should not dare to estimate, as any figures drawn from its amount last year [1864], and its prospective growth, would appear wild and chimerical." The period from 1836 to 1848 admittedly represented years of struggle, but once the firm opened its First Division between Chicago and Elgin, it thrived. Sensible expansion followed, and the company prospered even during the vicissitudes of depression and war. The strength of the Galena encouraged other railroad promoters in the Midwest, although they customarily met with less success. William Stennett, the chronicler of the company, expressed this point well. "The Galena and Chicago Union served as the model for all other railroads in the West, and if and when others failed it was not the fault of the model, but rather the fault of those whose efforts could not match the works of the men who built Chicago's first Rail Road."[107]

The North Western, a profitable and technological advanced carrier, had the wherewithal and desire to acquire the finest equipment. Customers made few complaints about the physical conditions of the carrier; indeed, the arrival of the North Western was a triumph for any community. Built by Baldwin in 1867, the *Crawford* represented the best motive power that was available during the early Gilded Age. (Railway & Locomotive Historical Society)

CHAPTER

TWO

THE NORTH WESTERN EMERGES

Railroads during the antebellum years rarely grew into long-distance routes organized under a single corporate structure. Yet scores of projects sought that lofty objective. An early exception was the 447-mile New-York & Erie Railroad (Erie), which completed the "Grand Iron Highway from the Ocean and the Lakes" in 1851. Erie trains linked the New York communities of Piermont on the Hudson River and Dunkirk on Lake Erie. While the Illinois Central Railroad soon became the Erie of the Midwest, the neighboring Galena & Chicago Union Railroad evolved in a more customary fashion. Just as Chicago's first carrier emerged as a gradual assemblage of little companies, its merger partner in 1864, the Chicago & North Western Railway (North Western), shared a similar corporate genealogy.[1]

The immediate forerunner of the North Western—the Chicago, St. Paul & Fond du Lac Railroad (Fond du Lac), launched in March 1855—consisted of two small, associated predecessor roads, the Rock River Valley Union Railroad and the Illinois & Wisconsin Railroad. The former received authorization from Wisconsin authorities in February 1850 to tie the Rock River at Janesville with Lake Superior via Fond du Lac, a settlement on the southern shores of Lake Winnebago. The company's promoters, a combination of local and eastern investors, subsequently received permission to expand northwestward from southern Wisconsin to La Crosse on the Mississippi River and St. Croix Falls on the St. Croix River. As was common in such ambitious schemes, little happened. Although surveyors fixed a much longer route, the Rock River Valley Union completed only a 29-mile line southwesterly from Fond du Lac. "We ran the preliminary line that winter [1852–1853] from Fond du Lac through Waupun, thence skirting Winnebago Marsh on the east, through Avoca and Mayville to Hosicon and Watertown," related a member of the locating party. "[We] disband[ed] at the latter place when spring opened and the call of the plow and the hoe was heard in the land."[2]

The Illinois & Wisconsin evolved into a more substantial enterprise, however. In fall 1853, nearly two years after its incorporation in Illinois, some of the same surveyors who had earlier trudged through the swamps and forests of Wisconsin established a line from Chicago to Janesville, the anticipated interchange point with the Rock River Valley Union. These part-time locators worked for mostly eastern investors who sensed potential for Wisconsin rail traffic and the continued growth of Chicago. Soon a graded right-of-way and then track replaced the survey stakes. Service started on the 38 miles between Chicago and Carey, Illinois, by fall 1854, and reached Janesville, 91 miles from Chicago, two years later.[3]

Construction of the Illinois & Wisconsin went less smoothly than had the Galena, the region's premier carrier. Inadequate resources, which had completely stalled the Rock River Valley Union, delayed completion of the Illinois & Wisconsin. This company also was a victim of financial misconduct. As a conversant builder explained: "I was assigned to a division overseeing the construction from Fox river to Woodstock . . . . The contractors for the work were Bradly, Page and Co. who sub-let to other parties one of whom on our division, a Mr. Church, decamped with the pay roll funds for his gang." And there was a problem with the money itself. "Our pay was in the notes of a recently established wild-cat Connecticut bank which in the course of time duly suspended leaving a trail of doleful farmers and merchants to agitate for more stringent banking laws."[4]

The troubles of the Illinois & Wisconsin could have been further exacerbated had it selected the wrong track gauge. "The road . . . came very near involving the management in what would have proved to be a most disastrous investment," voiced a participant. "Our consulting engineer Mr. Broadhead who had supervised the construction of the Erie road was a strenuous advocate for the adoption of the six feet system gauge but was fortunately overruled and the standard gauge decided on, thereby saving to the stockholders an outlay similar to that which the Erie was compelled subsequently to face by its necessary abandonment of the broad gauge with the consequent alterations of road bed and equipment."[5]

To improve the chances of completing the Chicago-to-Wisconsin rail route, state authorities and shareholders approved consolidation of the Rock River Valley Union and the Illinois & Wisconsin. The troubled properties officially merged on March 31, 1855, and the reorganized company became the Chicago, St. Paul & Fond du Lac Railroad, a name expressing the expected symbiotic relationship between these communities.[6]

Once the Fond du Lac's rails connected Chicago with Janesville, its backers were encouraged. Grain, white pine lumber, and general merchandise filled the freight trains, and passengers crowded the coaches; earnings figures looked promising. In October 1856, for example, receipts exceeded $50,000 for the month and surpassed the company's estimates. The road's entry into Chicago likewise augured well for the future. "That the city of Chicago is to become the commercial metropolis of the northwest, we have no doubt," editorialized the *Janesville Gazette*. "It is no longer a matter of prediction—it is now a *fact*." The Fond du Lac, moreover, forged a valuable connection at Janesville with the Milwaukee and Mississippi Rail Road, which had reached Prairie du Chien, Wisconsin, in spring 1857. The Fond du Lac consequently became "part of a *through* route of 227 miles from Chicago to the Mississippi River, at that point." And the company already served a flourishing territory of farms and villages. "The great value of this trade and travel can be appreciated only by those who have visited the region . . . ," opined the *Gazette*. "It is now settling more rapidly than any other portion of the United States by a Yankee population."[7]

While the Fond du Lac's future was expected to shine as brightly as the Galena's, the new corporation soon could be compared to a falling star. It not only failed to achieve its major short-term goal of linking Janesville with the southern terminus of the former Rock River Valley Union, a distance of 57 miles, but the company slipped into bankruptcy. The hard times that followed the Panic of 1857 finished it off. Additional line construction or any other major betterment was inconceivable.[8]

Failure of the Fond du Lac caused considerable hardships. While its freight and passenger service continued, the company fell into arrears in payroll and other obligations. Employees who had become wholly dependent upon the wage system and others whose livelihood was tied to their income were especially affected. "Nobody wanted [Fond du Lac workers] as borders because they could not pay their board for five months," remembered a former jobholder. "Mr. [Robert] Tarrant [the master mechanic] persuaded a Mrs. Near, who lived not far from the shops [in Chicago], to take quite a lot of Fond du Lac boarders. Perhaps she forgave him later, but it was a tough proposition." The recorder recalled: "On one occasion, [Mrs. Near] came into the dining room with tears in her eyes and said, 'Boys, I do not know how I can set another table. The grocers will not trust me any more, the butchers will not, and I cannot buy another thing, and what shall I do? I cannot turn you away; many of you owe me at lot of money, but I know you cannot get it, and what shall I do?'" Her boarders, fortunately, took action. "One man . . . said, 'Well, I am going to lay off for a quarter of a day and go and see the paymaster, Geo. P. Lee, and try and get something.' Others said they would try it also; so ten or twelve went down to the general office on the corner of Lake and Clark streets, and practically got down on their knees to Mr. Lee, and he . . . gave to each one $10.00, and Mrs. Near got it all. Mr. Lee then stated that the road very soon expected to pay up all arrears in full; and sure enough, not long after this it did pay everybody all that was coming, and Mrs. Near was made the happiest woman in Chicago." Though employees received their back pay, the Fond du Lac again encountered financial difficulties, and likely the Mrs. Nears along the road extended credit and hoped for a better day.[9]

That better day came on June 2, 1859. The court-appointed receivers sold the Fond du Lac at auction in Janesville to a group of affiliated investors. The successor firm, the Chicago & North Western Railway, chartered by the state of Illinois five days later, acquired the assets of the troubled company, and the North Western's first president, William B. Ogden, immediately took charge. No stranger to regional transport affairs, he had already been deeply involved with the property as a major Fond du Lac bondholder, director, and officer.[10]

The railroad regrouped nicely. With a scaled-down debt, management placed its financial house in good order. This meant a settlement with employees over unpaid wages. Those who were entitled to compensation received common stock in the new company equal to their claims, and "that stock was a good investment [for them]." Optimism in the carrier's future returned, and the recovery of the economy also inspired confidence. Soon construction workers joined the two isolated units of the property. Remarked a chronicler of the road several decades later, "It truly became the Chicago and North-Western."[11]

Still, William Ogden and his associates wanted more than a through line between Chicago and Fond du Lac. These men had two primary destinations in mind: the resource-rich Upper Peninsula of Michigan and St. Paul, Minnesota, the head of navigation on the Mississippi River. Such extensions would improve the North Western's long-term financial health and stimulate the growth of Chicago, a city where Ogden and others linked to the company had major business interests.[12]

The desire to boost Chicago compelled North Western leaders to protect their headquarters city. During the 1850s Milwaukee, Wisconsin, the Lake Michigan port community 85 miles north of Chicago, showed signs of becoming a major metropolis. The nucleus of the future Chicago, Milwaukee & St. Paul, the later fierce rival of the North Western system, emerged in 1850 when the Milwaukee & Mississippi Rail Road opened a 10-mile line between Milwaukee and Elm Grove, Wisconsin. By the time the Panic of 1857 struck, quickly throwing all Wisconsin-based railroads into receivership and temporarily ending new construction, the road had reached the Mississippi River at Prairie du Chien. When the North Western emerged, Milwaukee seemed to be strengthening its railroad position at the expense of Chicago. But North Western strategists believed that their building policy could divert trade from Milwaukee's hinterlands directly to their city by the lake.[13]

Although the North Western waited until the 1870s before gaining access to the St. Paul gateway, it moved ahead with attempts to tap the Great Lakes frontier. In 1859, the year it forged the Fond du Lac-to-Chicago connection, the company pushed 17 miles northward along the western shores of Lake Winnebago to Oshkosh. Then between 1861 and 1862 the North Western added 48 miles of iron rails when it reached Green Bay, Wisconsin (then Fort Howard), and the vital Great Lakes shipping corridor. Moreover, the company became the first important lumber-carrying railway in Wisconsin. With this extension it tapped extensive pineries, thus providing timber firms an alternative to the dangers and uncertainties of water transport.[14]

Government largess speeded completion of the northern extension. The North Western effectively utilized a federal land grant given to Wisconsin in 1856. State lawmakers initially had awarded it to the Wisconsin & Superior Rail Road, but that company failed to construct the line. Nevertheless, these public lands, amounting to approximately 4,000 acres per track mile, went for their intended purpose of promoting a railroad through the northeastern section of the state. When the Fond du Lac acquired the Wisconsin & Superior in 1857, it received this heavily forested real estate thick with prized white pines.[15]

The project won even more external support. The federal government gave the North Western a special grant of 80 acres from its Fort Howard military reservation for station facilities in Green Bay. William Ogden described this strategic acreage as being "large water-front and ample dimension, [and] is of great value and convenience to the Company."[16]

While Green Bay remained the northern terminus of the North Western in Wisconsin until 1871, the company entered the Upper Peninsula of Michigan during the Civil War. Soon after the conflict began, William Ogden and "capitalists in the main unconnected with the Chicago and North Western" acquired rights for a rail line from Little Bay de Noquet on the shores of Lake Michigan northward into the wilds of Delta and Marquette counties. They sought to serve their copper and iron ore holdings and to transship minerals directly from Lake Superior ports to the lower lakes. Under the banner of the Peninsula Rail-Road of Michigan, a North Western subsidiary, rails tied Escanaba with Negaunee (Jackson Mines) by 1864. This 62-mile shortline, subsequently the Peninsula Division, provided additional business for its parent company; lumber, merchandise, and passenger traffic also became important. In order to link the Michigan unit with the North Western, three vessels, operated by the satellite Green Bay Transit Company, plied Lake Michigan during the navigation season. When ice blocked commerce, goods (except for bulk commodities) and people traveled on stages owned by another firm controlled by the railroad, Lake Forwarding Company.[17]

Further trackage appeared during the formative years of the North Western. The principal addition was a 72-mile line, which opened on that most glorious of national holidays, the Fourth of July, in 1861, between Kenosha, Wisconsin, a village on Lake Michigan 50 miles north of Chicago, and Rockford, Illinois. This largely east-to-west artery served a thriving farming area that clamored for more rail service. Its completion gave patrons some useful routing options: the line interchanged with the North Western at Harvard, Illinois, and met the Galena at Caledonia on the Madison branch and Rockford on the original main line. Like the Peninsula Rail-Road, the Kenosha-to-Rockford property flew its own corporate flag, Kenosha, Rockford & Rock Island Rail-Road, and again William Ogden was involved. The company remained independent until 1864, but to prevent it from "falling into the then unfriendly hands of the Galena & Chicago Union Company," the North Western acquired it through an exchange of common stock. The Ogden road then operated the property as its Kenosha Division.[18]

The year 1864 marked more than the addition of the Kenosha, Rockford & Rock Island to the developing network of North Western trackage in Illinois, Michigan, and Wisconsin. Under the leadership of the visionary Ogden, management consummated one of the first large mergers of the railway age: fusion of the Galena & Chicago Union with the Chicago & North Western. Because of its scope, this corporate arrangement attracted considerable attention. "[The merger] was talked about from the Atlantic to the slopes of the Missouri River, and opinions were as varied about it as were the people that gave them." News of the consolidation surely must have been a pleasant diversion from reports of bloody Civil War battles.[19]

The Great Consolidation, as it was called, happened quickly. Stockholders of both railroads readily consented to the plan, and on June 2, 1864, "it was virtually effected and carried out." Then on February 15, 1865, state legislative enactments completed the process. Owners of the Galena, the larger and more profitable road, received appropriate compensation; a share of Galena common yielded one share of North Western preferred, one share of North Western common, and a cash payment of $3.[20]

A group of dissident Galena shareholders, however, led by New York lawyer Julius Wadsworth, sued in federal court in Chicago to prevent the merger from being implemented. Fortunately for proponents of union, these efforts failed. The legal action, according to a financial observer, "was prompted partly by malice but more by a desire to make money by depressing the Stock [of the North Western]." The dissidents later wanted to capitalize on what they expected to be a run-up in the value of North Western shares. Some Galena shareholders also resented Ogden's earlier departure from the company and his subsequent push for its securities.[21]

Investors and noninvestors alike sensed that merger presaged bright prospects for the enlarged Chicago & North Western and as well as Chicago and the Midwest. In a *Circular to the Stockholders of the Chicago & North-Western R'y Company,* dated June 20, 1864, management explained why consolidation represented a wise course of action. "The union of both gives greater strength and power, favoring more advantageous and extended connections, and better relations with other railroads built and to be built, and will aid to prevent the construction of such roads as would only serve to create injuri-

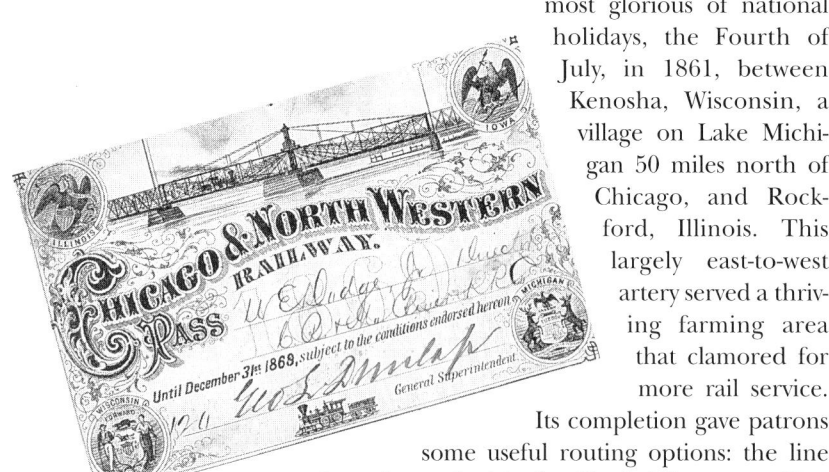

During the formative years the North Western regularly commissioned fancy artwork for its annual passes. These cards were issued to employees, "foreign" railroaders, and friends of the company. The 1868 pass includes the official seals of the four states that the railroad served, Illinois, Iowa, Michigan, and Wisconsin, and displays the new draw span across the Mississippi River at Clinton, Iowa. (Author's collection)

ous competition, without any adequate increase of the aggregate earnings of the roads competing." Further advantages were stressed: "Decided economy, material reduction of expenses, and increased and more profitable service of engines and cars, will also be the result of co-operation in the place of competition, and of one management of both Roads." Surely a combined Galena and North Western would strengthen the Chicago economy and enhance its claim as "Nature's Metropolis." Common wisdom accepted the notion that the North Western was good for Chicago and its hinterland and vice versa.[22]

The "new" North Western, directed by William Ogden and backed by directors who mostly came from Chicago and New York, discarded the Galena & Chicago Union name. The Galena had never reached the lead-mining center on its own rails, and there was no reason to that name. Rather, officials called their expanded property the Chicago & North Western Railway. "[This] involved no change of books or blanks, and is sufficiently comprehensive to include the large territory now penetrated by the united roads."[23]

The banner of the Chicago & North Western flew over a large railroad. To the core North Western, with its 315 route miles, was added the 545 route miles, including leased trackage, of the Galena, creating an 860-mile property. For the moment it could claim to be the longest carrier in America. Only the Illinois Central with its 706 miles of track was nearly as large, although the 359-mile Pennsylvania would shortly take control of the 467-mile Pittsburgh, Fort Wayne & Chicago.[24]

The leaders of the North Western eagerly anticipated a greater property. Only the crippling panics of 1873 and 1893 interrupted ongoing expansion during the remainder of the century. The 1880s, a decade of intense railroad construction, witnessed the spectacular growth of the North Western. Officials wanted a larger carrier for various reasons; longer hauls meant more income per train mile, access to new markets, and control over their operations. Railroaders then as later wished to avoid sharing trackage with a competitor, fearing the owning road could trouble the tenant. As a result additional construction and "system building" swept the industry during these halcyon times.[25]

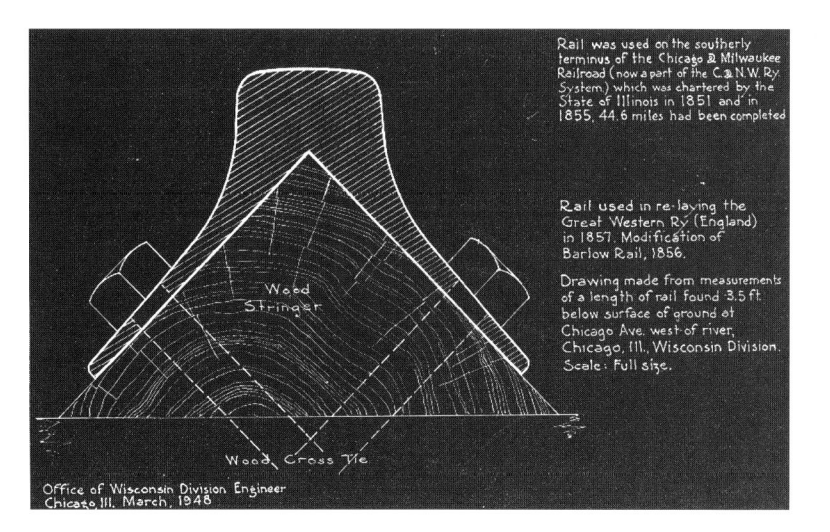

From 1865 until the economic dislocations of the mid-1870s, the North Western considerably increased its territory. This meant filling gaps within its perimeter of lines as well as expanding outward. The first important enlargement of the merged company involved acquisition of the profitable and strategic Chicago & Milwaukee Railway (C&M). Built by area promoters in the early 1850s as two separate entities, namely the Illinois Parallel Railroad from Chicago to the Wisconsin state line and the Green Bay, Milwaukee & Chicago Railroad from Milwaukee to a connection with the Illinois Parallel, these properties had formally consolidated in June 1863. But at first "everything was transferred" at State Line, Illinois, according to a former C&M employee in 1910, "then passengers and baggage were run through without transfer and later freight also was seen through."[26]

The shortline status of the Chicago & Milwaukee ended when the North Western acquired it through a perpetual lease in May 1866. The North Western acted prudently; the acquisition generated immediate income and offered much promise. "The gross earnings of the Chicago and Milwaukee Railway Company for the past year [1865] . . . were $1,063,164.21 [and interest on debt totaled $127,832]," reported William Ogden, "showing that on the basis of earnings as well as for the purpose of securing more perfect combinations and preventing undue competition, the purchase of this road was a desirable transaction to this Company." With

Even in the 1850s railroads in the Midwest selected unusual varieties of rail. The Milwaukee & Chicago acquired England-manufactured "Barlow" rail, which was not standard or widely used, rather than more common "T-rail." (North Western/Union Pacific)

this 85-mile route the North Western won access to a superb corridor between two vibrant metropolises and subsequently witnessed the building of "Beautiful Suburban Towns" along the line north of Chicago. And the company protected its home turf.[27]

Like the Chicago & Milwaukee, a rented property until merged with the parent system in 1881, the Iowa roads, acquired with the Galena, were leased until about the same time. While the C&M never expanded, the Cedar Rapids & Missouri River pushed westward during the 1860s. The destination was Council Bluffs and a connection with the gestating Union Pacific. Tracklayers worked steadily and hammered down their last spikes on January 17, 1867, fashioning the first trans-Iowa rail artery.[28]

As with most construction achievements, a gala took place at an auspicious moment. On February 8, 1867, passenger service was inaugurated between Chicago and Council Bluffs, a distance of 488 miles. "The arrival of the first regular passenger train was marked by a joyous celebration," reported the Council Bluffs *Nonpareil*. "Cannon[s] were fired and a long procession of wagons, artillery and citizens marched to the station to greet the train. Mayor Frank Street and other prominent citizens addressed the assembly between selections by the band and the salutes of the cannon. Telegrams were sent to the mayors of Chicago and other eastern cities and many telegrams of congratulation were received."[29]

With track to the Missouri River the North Western positioned itself for future long-distance freight and passenger traffic. The "wedding of the rails" at Promontory Summit, Utah Territory, on May 10, 1869, meant that the Chicago to Council Bluffs line became the eastern segment of the "Overland Route" to the Pacific. The Union Pacific connected the "Bluffs" with the Central Pacific at Ogden, Utah, giving access to the Central's milepost 1 at Sacramento, California, and from there water passage to San Francisco. But the North Western soon encountered rivals: the Rock Island reached Council Bluffs on June 5, 1869, and the Burlington arrived on January 18, 1870. Although these competitors operated slightly longer routes, each totaling 499 miles, they served somewhat less fertile sections of Iowa. The North Western remained optimistic. "Situated as one of the earliest, most direct and favorable connections of the Pacific Railways, and enjoying amicable relations for the interchange of business, we may confidently rely upon receiving a due share of the through traffic passing over those lines; and we shall hereafter participate in the benefits of the new business in direct proportion to the success of those great national routes in influencing the course of business across the continent."[30]

By the early 1870s the North Western controlled more than the strategic Omaha line into the trans-Mississippi West. It also dominated rails that crossed the wooded hills and tall-grass prairies of southern Minnesota. Just as the Cedar Rapids & Missouri River built the final segment of the Chicago to Council Bluffs line, the Winona & St. Peter Railroad (W&StP) promoted trackage in Minnesota. A liberal charter from territorial lawmakers in 1855 spurred efforts to construct a railroad westward from the Mississippi River at Winona. But the Transit Railroad Company and its successor, the Winona, St. Peter & Missouri River Railroad, never turned a wheel. The difficult economic times of the pre–Civil War years discouraged efforts to attract capital for these frontier enterprises. The third attempt was successful, beginning in 1862 with incorporation of the W&StP. What saved this undertaking from becoming another stillborn venture was a land subsidy.[31]

Unquestionably, land grants stimulated scores of western railroad projects. Although a line across southern Minnesota was inevitable, a generous subsidy made possible an iron artery that mostly preceded settlement. The measure, approved by Congress on July 13, 1866, and subsequently awarded by Minnesota, gave the company odd sections of 640 acres within 20 miles of the completed right-of-way. When the W&StP reached Watertown, Dakota Territory, 323 miles west of the Mississippi River in 1874, it had obtained nearly 1.7 million acres of the public domain, including some of the most fertile wheat lands on the continent. The company made its selections of land with care, but this policy angered some residents of the area. "[The] land grant . . . was an inducement to make the road as long as possible and to run it where it would take the best lands," complained an early chronicler of Lyon County, Minnesota, and a booster of the village of Lynd. "Instead of running anywhere near in a straight line west it therefore ran northwest from one corner of the county to the other leaving Lynd ten miles or so south of the road. This broke up the metropolitan prospects of Lynd, at least until some other railroad shall reach that locality."[32]

Yet the Winona & St. Peter could not immediately realize large amounts of cash from its prudent use of the law. After prosperity returned in the late 1870s, the company's land department sold much of this real estate at prices ranging from $2 to $8 per acre. Purchasers found the W&StP lands attractive because of their general fertility and the "title is absolute and indisputable." The latter was not the case with some of the acreages peddled by other railroads from their public allotments.[33]

The complexion of the W&StP rapidly changed. The property fell into the hands of eastern investors, guided by Danford Barney, William Fargo, and Angus Smith. Between 1864 and 1867 these individuals had provided funds for construction of 105 miles from Winona to Waseca, Minnesota. The Barney group sold its controlling position in October 1867 to an eager and pleased North Western. "The earnings of the Winona Road which will be greatly augmented by its proposed extension to the Minnesota River [at St. Peter], led to the confident belief that it will not only be self-sustaining, but profitable," explained the company to shareholders, "and prove to be a valuable and important auxiliary to the business of our Western and North-Western lines." The W&StP shortly reached the rich valley of the Minnesota River and also penetrated the fertile prairies of eastern Dakota.[34]

The Barney group did more than prepare the way for the North Western to serve Minnesota and Dakota; it made available a "keystone" component, the La Crosse, Trempealeau & Prescott Railroad (LT&P). This company, incorporated in 1857, planned an approximately 100-mile route between the Wisconsin communities of La Crosse and Prescott on the east bank of the Mississippi River via Trempealeau and Fountain City. But the venture never evolved beyond the planning stage until the Barney interests took charge and sold it to the North Western as part of the W&StP transaction. Using the LT&P charter, the North Western opened 28 miles in 1870; this trackage extended from a point opposite Winona, Minnesota, to Winona Junction, Wisconsin, about 3 miles east of La Crosse. (The Mississippi River was not bridged at Winona until 1872.) The North Western eventually connected the LT&P with its own Madison line; the first revenue train rolled over that 129-mile link in 1873. In the interim traffic from the West reached North Western rails at Madison via the Milwaukee & St. Paul Railroad.[35]

The decision by the North Western to unite the Minnesota and Wisconsin lines involved more than the obvious desire to own contiguous trackage. The company's Madison Division, the former Beloit & Madison Rail Road, which came with the Great Consolidation, had not done well. "The business on this Madison line," noted the North Western in 1871, "has ever been comparatively light." But an extension between Madison and Winona Junction would make this early appendage part of a through route and would serve the rail-starved Baraboo Valley, described as a "productive and well-settled country." Generating both additional long- and short-haul traffic held a persuasive logic. Then there was also the matter of protecting what the company felt to be its "rightful" territory. "Unless the Chicago and North Western Company stepped in and occupied the field," the railroad stated, "other parties, independent of them, would construct the line, and the opportunity which such a project afforded of connecting the unprofitable Madison Division with the detached La Crosse, Trempealeau and Prescott, and Winona and St. Peter Rail-Roads, would be lost."[36]

Before the Panic of 1873 dried up investment money, the North Western steadily added to its network of rail lines. Mileage, standing at 1,156 on May 31, 1869, by five years later had increased to 1,499. With inclusion of the "Proprietary Roads," the total reached 1,990 as of May 31, 1874. These satellite companies included the Winona & St. Peter, with its 330 miles (four of which belonged to its Winona, Mankato & New Ulm Railroad subsidiary); La Crosse, Trempealeau & Prescott with 29 miles; Iowa Midland Railway with 69 miles, and the North Western Union Railway with 63 miles of line.[37]

The last two roads, the Iowa Midland and North Western Union, entered the sphere of the North Western in the early 1870s. The Iowa Midland, successor of the ill-fated Iowa Central Air Line of the 1850s, opened in 1871 along part of

Engine No. 4 of the Winona & St. Peter Railroad, built in 1883 by the Schenectady Locomotive Works, waits with its crew in Green Bay, Wisc., in 1899. The locomotive subsequently became North Western No. 892. (Railway & Locomotive Historical Society)

the original survey from Lyons, near Clinton, "through the beautiful and well settled country of the Maquoketa Valley" to Anamosa, seat of Jones County. "The Iowa Midland Company reaped the benefit of this work [extensive grading by the Air Line] at very small cost, and encouraged by some local aid, undertook the construction of the line, which [was] transferred by lease and control of stock, to the Chicago & North Western Company." As with the Baraboo Valley extension, North Western officials worried about encroachments by other carriers. The railroad also wanted to create a network of branch or feeder lines to its main stems, in this case an appendage to the Omaha or "Fulton Line" at Clinton. "The control of this project, aside from any local merits it might possess," the company disclosed in 1871, "was regarded as a measure of protection to the interests of the Chicago & North Western Company; and as the business which might reasonably be expected to originate on this road would be valuable, if made tributary to the Fulton line."[38]

The absorption of the Iowa Midland was followed by that of the North Western Union. This captive corporation, a creature of North Western management, began service in 1873 between Milwaukee and Fond du Lac, Wisconsin. It, too, joined the expanding North Western system because of strategic and traffic considerations. "The necessity for this line to protect our business north of Fond du Lac, from the effect of the competition of new roads on shorter lines to Milwaukee and Chicago, was none too soon seen and provided for," observed the North Western's *Fourteenth Annual Report*. "With this connection, a new route for all that region is opened to Milwaukee, a fine local business insured, and by the use of this line, and of our Chicago and Milwaukee road, a shorter route by at least 29 miles is made for all the Chicago business."[39]

While the North Western Union contributed traffic to its parent, it turned out to be more expensive than anticipated. Construction costs exceeded $2.2 million. North Western leaders had expected substantial financial aid from the Milwaukee business community. Such funds never materialized, however, and the satellite incurred steep payments for parcels of urban real estate. This financial outlay led to the shelving of plans to build between Milwaukee and Lodi, Wisconsin, near Madison, thus forging a direct linkage with the Winona & St. Peter.[40]

North Western officials might complain about the costliness of portions of the North Western Union, but they could crow about the overall financial picture since the Great Consolidation. Admittedly a national depression that settled over the country by 1874 damaged corporate earnings and dampened optimism, but the period from 1864 to 1873 proved to be generally positive for investors. The company usually paid dividends of 7 or 10 percent to holders of preferred shares and as much as 10 percent to owners of common stock during five of the ten years. The North Western generated revenues of $6,820,749 in fiscal year 1864–1865, of which freight produced $4,448,598 and passengers $2,167,901. The comparable figures for fiscal year 1872–1873 were $12,736,606, $8,614,260, and $3,509,702 respectively.[41]

Those who guided the North Western constantly sought not only to gratify investors, but also to upgrade the road's physical state. These two objectives were hardly unrelated. "The general condition of the entire property has been improved by the addition of facilities afforded by new construction and equipment, and by the renewals and repairs put upon the road," observed the *Fourteenth Annual Report* for 1872–1873. Management, of course, understood that utopia had not been realized; no railroad could ever reach that exalted level of perfection. Technological improvements were ongoing, and most possessed practical applications.[42]

One notable advancement was steel rail. Its durability far exceeded that of iron. Used in a significant quantities on the Pennsylvania Railroad during the Civil War, steel rails quickly demonstrated their superiority. "The general introduction of steel rails is now wholly a commercial question in which the cost of increased capital required for their purchase become the chief impediment to their general adoption," commented Pennsylvania President J. Edgar Thomson in 1866. Fortunately for Thomson's road and other carriers, the high cost would gradually be reduced through the genius of steel czar Andrew Carnegie. The North Western observed in 1873 that it was embarking upon a program to replace its obsolete iron rails. "The greatest economy of operations is . . . attainable only by the substitution of steel rails on all our main lines, where the traffic is heavy, and there the destruction of iron reaches its maximum at great cost to the Company." Even though the hard times of the mid-1870s severely limited this undertaking, the company indicated that the "first important step has been taken [1873], and ten thousand tons of steel rails have been ordered, which will be laid down as fast as they can be delivered. . . . This, with sufficient equipment, will constitute the chief want of the Company hereafter for the movement of the large traffic which will press upon the road."[43]

Although the management of the North Western ran a profitable and technologically proficient enterprise, the hierarchy itself experienced difficulties during the immediate post–Civil War period. William Ogden, the driving force behind both the Galena and the North Western and in charge from the start, resigned on June 4, 1868. He also left the Board of Directors. Ogden was 63 and wanted to curtail his business obligations in preparation for retirement. The Board appropriately honored his involvement with the North Western and its predecessor firms:

Baraboo, Wisc., located between Madison and Elroy, received an engine facility in the 1870s. This early view shows a wood-burning 4-4-0 locomotive, a water tank with an unusually placed clock, and a massive pile of cordwood in the right foreground. (North Western/Union Pacific)

A commercial portrait photographer in New York City captured a mature William B. Ogden, the first president of the North Western. Ogden did yeoman service in creating railroads, in building Chicago, and in promoting the "Great Northwest." (Chicago Historical Society)

Resolved: That . . . [William Ogden's] connection with this Company, dating back for a period of twenty-one years, his disinterested labors in its behalf without fee or reward during the whole time, the benefit he has conferred upon it and the country, demand our grateful acknowledgements.[44]

No one of Ogden's caliber and dedication was at the president's desk until Marvin Hughitt assumed the post in 1887. Yet during those 19 years the four chief executives at least possessed better than average talent. The difficulty with their leadership mostly involved personal commitment to an independent North Western.

Financier Henry Keep replaced William Ogden, but his tenure as president lasted only 13 months; he died on July 30, 1869. Born in upstate New York, on June 11, 1818, Keep lived the Horatio Alger rags-to-riches story. When Keep's father died in 1835, the family sought refuge in the Jefferson County poorhouse. Having experienced great poverty and without much formal education, Keep, who was bright and diligent, pulled himself up the ladder of success a rung at a time. He worked as a teamster and hackman before he transformed his small savings into a considerable sum. Keep displayed his business acumen by cleverly exploiting changes in the value of local and Canadian bank notes. Success in speculation led him to banking in Watertown, New York, and ultimately to his own stock brokerage firm in New York City. Keep became particularly adept in the field of railroad securities. After the Panic of 1857, for example, he developed a sizable position in a choice midwestern carrier, the Michigan Southern and Northern Indiana Railroad, a property that subsequently became part of the massive Vanderbilt family holdings. On his way to becoming a multimillionaire, Keep, with the assistance of Chicago businessman Rufus Hatch, secured financial control of the North Western.[45]

The death of Henry Keep created a major void, but the Board of Directors filled the vacancy on September 1, 1869, with another wealthy businessman and enthusiastic railroader, Alexander Mitchell. This third president of the North Western was born on October 18, 1817, into a large middle-class family in Aberdeenshire, Scotland. He immigrated to Milwaukee, Wisconsin, in 1839. A shrewd and energetic individual with a reputation for ruthless dealings, Mitchell became secretary of the Wisconsin Marine and Fire Insurance Company, which he cofounded during his first year in America. In reality the insurance operation dealt only secondarily with marine and fire underwriting; rather it provided general banking services.[46]

Like many financiers who controlled investment capital, Alexander Mitchell became interested in railroads. He appears to have entered the field largely out of loyalty to Milwaukee. Mitchell knew that his home community needed railroad connections if it were to thrive. By the Civil War Mitchell and other Milwaukee business leaders could see how the aggressive North Western had constantly strengthened Chicago. An exceptional opportunity to serve Milwaukee came in 1865 when Mitchell became director and then president of the troubled Milwaukee & St. Paul. He activated the property and extended control over several other roads, including the debt-ridden yet well-located Milwaukee & Prairie du Chien acquired in December 1867.[47]

As part of Mitchell's plan to strengthen both

Milwaukee and the Milwaukee & St. Paul (the company became the Chicago, Milwaukee & St. Paul in 1874), he saw archrival North Western as a "natural" merger partner. Using his considerable financial connections and aided by the death of Henry Keep, Mitchell soon stood at the helm of two leading midwestern railroads. His elevation to the North Western presidency attracted much attention. "History repeats itself," commented the *Chicago Post*. "The tears of Alexander the Great, because he had no more worlds to conquer, are familiar to every schoolboy, and there we have another Alexander, surnamed Mitchell, who starting out with the Milwaukee & St. Paul railroad, first gobbled the Old Milwaukee and La Crosse, then the Prairie du Chien, then half a dozen small railroads in Wisconsin, Iowa, and Minnesota, . . . and now *eheu iam satis!* [That's enough!] the Northwestern, with all its branches, spurs, divisions, and ramifications!" Concluded the *Post*, "As there are still other lines to gobble, however, we suppose the weeping will not commence until such little sidetracks as the Union Pacific, New York Central, etc. are added to the inventory."[48]

While "Alexander the Great" of Milwaukee sought what would have been a megamerger in the Gilded Age, he failed in that objective. This dour Scot was hardly a likable sort, but it was not his personality that wrecked the grand plan. Those who opposed him, including members of the North Western board, had no desire to see the Chicago carrier lose its corporate identity in some type of "Chicago, Milwaukee, St. Paul & North Western" arrangement. Adding to Mitchell's distress was the acquisition of a sizable block of North Western securities by a group of speculators in the spring of 1870. Mitchell, therefore, resigned his North Western executive and board positions on June 30, 1870, but he continued to lead the "St. Paul" until his death in 1887.[49]

Attempts to create a community of interest between the St. Paul and North Western had come to naught. Nevertheless, the North Western formed close links to another expanding midwestern road, the Chicago, Rock Island & Pacific. The fourth president of the North Western, John F. Tracy, who served from June 3, 1870, until June 19, 1873, had labored hard to create a flourishing Rock Island.[50]

Little is known about the background of John Tracy until he joined the Rock Island as superintendent in the mid-1850s. Originally from Buffalo, he had worked for the New-York & Erie before seeking his fortune on the transportation frontier. "[Tracy] was a first-rate operating officer and a hard driver of men," notes a historian of the Rock Island Lines. "He asked no questions but took hold of a job and personally saw to it that the job was successfully accomplished." Tracy did well on the Rock Island and won its presidency in 1865.[51]

Unlike either Henry Keep or Alexander Mitchell, Tracy exhibited a pronounced speculative bent. Throughout his executive career he made heavy, personal commitments in securities and traded them on both the long and short side. His frequently risky investments later caused his financial ruin and his departure from the Rock Island shortly before his death in 1878.[52]

The plunger and expansionist characteristics of John Tracy made possible his presidency at the North Western. But he did not operate alone. Financial backing from a group linked with the Pennsylvania Railroad gave him control of this formidable foe of the Rock Island. The Tracy crowd acquired a substantial number of North Western shares with borrowed money, and this leveraged stock served as collateral.[53]

As head of the North Western, John Tracy had two primary objectives: to increase his personal wealth and that of his investor friends through the coordinated operations of the Rock Island and North Western and to protect these properties from any aggressive acts on the part of the Burlington and its combative president, James F. Joy. Tracy especially wished to keep the Burlington at bay in the lucrative Illinois and Iowa marketplace. "It is impossible to remain stationary," argued Joy in his characteristic fashion. "If the Company's owning and managing roads there do not meet the wants of the adjoining country and aid in its development, other alliances are sure to be found which end in rival roads and damage to existing interests." The Burlington executive, of course, had no intention of allowing the Tracy roads to dominate traffic west of Chicago.[54]

The competitive atmosphere intensified following the golden spike ceremony at Promontory in May 1869. By January 1870 the Burlington had joined the North Western and Rock

Island in providing connecting service between the transcontinental Central Pacific–Union Pacific route at Council Bluffs and the Chicago gateway. This meant an increase in traffic for the three Chicago carriers, but the resulting cutthroat rates meant that their revenues failed to keep pace with business.[55]

Fortunately for the companies' balance sheets, the competitive problem was largely resolved. Tracy suggested a workable approach, which the three roads soon implemented. The solution, dubbed the "Iowa Pool," became the prototype of the nonlegally binding "gentlemen's agreements" that swept the business community during the Gilded Age. This pooling arrangement permitted each carrier to retain 50 percent of its freight revenues and 45 percent of its passenger income for movements between the two terminals. These monies supposedly would pay for these freight and passenger operations. The balance of the income would be divided equally among the three railroads. While Tracy, Joy, and their colleagues considered the Iowa Pool to be an experiment, it functioned relatively well until mostly outside forces caused its collapse in the early 1880s. If unabated rate cutting had continued during the depression of the mid-1870s, the three companies might have failed or would have become so weakened that they could not have expanded readily during the boom years of the 1880s.[56]

The handiwork of John Tracy in rate pooling benefited the North Western. But his taste for speculation could have damaged a property long identified with financial soundness. Even though the North Western never faced bankruptcy during Tracy's tenure, its floating debt rose to troubling levels. Remittances from bond subscriptions, mostly purchased by Dutch investors, prevented a cash crisis. Tracy lessened his grip, however, when he stepped down from the presidency in 1873, so that he could "participate more actively in the field of corporate expansion." Still, Tracy remained on the Board of Directors and the influential Executive Committee until shortly before his death five years later.[57]

The North Western charted to a more conservative course after Tracy's resignation. The Board of Directors named another uprooted New Yorker, Albert Keep (apparently unrelated to Henry Keep), as the company's fifth president. Without his predecessor's speculative mania, he cultivated his managerial skills.[58]

The background of Albert Keep resembles that of many captains of industry; he rose from poverty to wealth largely through his own initiative and good fortune. Born in Homer, in central New York, on April 30, 1826, Keep came from a family of modest means. Following his formal education at an undistinguished local academy, he migrated to the southern Wisconsin community of Whitewater, where he established the dry-goods firm of Peck, Keep & Co. In 1851 Keep relocated to Chicago and operated a similar business. Within a few years he also entered the field of real estate. Railroads, too, attracted Keep, and he won a seat on the board of the Lake Shore & Michigan Southern, a unit of the future New York Central system.[59]

Albert Keep performed well in his new capacities at the North Western: president, board member, and head of the Executive Committee. The Board of Directors represented several shareholding groups, including those associated with the two previous regimes, and some took a speculative viewpoint. Greater stability, however, came in 1879 when the Vanderbilts gained considerable influence. William H. Vanderbilt, who assumed control of the transportation empire created by his father "Commodore" Cornelius Vanderbilt following his death in 1877, represented family and associated interests. Keep prospered; he had enjoyed the trust of the Vanderbilts earlier while serving on the Lake Shore & Michigan Southern board; in fact, he kept that seat until 1883.[60]

Keep's generally conservative approach to railroading won endorsement of the sizable number of Dutch security holders. Since 1872 J. L. ten Have, a banker from Amsterdam, had represented these foreign investors on the North Western board. "They were . . . drawn to the more solid American railroad bonds of companies like the Illinois Central or the Chicago & North Western," concludes historian Augustus J. Veenendaal Jr. "Securities of this type generally yielded between 5 and 6 percent, but they were respectable and safe." A spokesman for the Dutch investors expressed support of Keep and his non-speculative tendencies. "We are convinced here that the present President (Mr. Keep) is an honest man," he told the *Railroad Gazette,* a trade publication, in 1875. "This, in our opinion, is the chief question for American investments. We do not like such things as the payment of dividends without taking care for the future and without providing for the payment of enormous sums due within a few year." Money from Dutch rather than British parties remained a principal European source of funding for American railroads for several decades. Understandably, the company published a Dutch-language edition of its annual report.[61]

Even the presence of Jay Gould, "one of the most sinister figures that have ever flitted bat-like across the vision of the American people," failed to disrupt Albert Keep and his administration. Gould bought enough stock in the North Western to gain a board seat in 1877; he already served on the board of the Rock Island. Gould controlled the Union Pacific and wished to protect that road's traffic with its eastern interchange partners. Yet as his latest biographer concludes, "His toehold in Northwestern and Rock Island had brought meager results," and he would leave the two Iowa Pool partners in 1884. On balance, Jay Gould caused little, if any mischief during his tenure at the North Western.[62]

If there were demons that plagued the Chicago & North Western during the 1870s, they were the "Grangers." In the early part of the decade the granger movement swept into political power in the upper Mississippi River valley. Members of the recently formed farmers' organization—the Patrons of Husbandry—joined by a coalition of merchants and commercial groups and working through the dominant Republican party, sought to bring area railways under the public's thumb. These carriers heretofore had been essentially free of government regulation. The Grangers pressed hard for the creation of state railroad commissions with powers to supervise companies and thus to protect their perceived rights. Most of all, they spearheaded efforts to reduce freight and passenger rates and to end long- and short-haul discrimination. The latter practice could arise when a railroad enjoyed a local transportation monopoly and allegedly charged "what the traffic would bear." Reformers considered carriers obligated to provide their services inexpensively, conveniently, and predictably. They did not understand that market forces dramatically affected rates.[63]

The granger victories were impressive. Stringent railroad regulatory acts passed in Illinois, Iowa, Minnesota, and Wisconsin. The most drastic was Wisconsin's Potter Railroad Law, which took effect on May 1, 1874. This controversial act arranged freight and passenger traffic into classifications and established maximum rates for items within each category. Generally the measure ended the popular practice of carriers setting a higher rate per ton mile and per passenger mile for the shorter haul. The Potter Law also created a three-member Board of Railroad Commissioners to enforce the statute. This enactment established a precedent of dangerous inflexibility in rates, especially for freight, and it accepted the mistaken assumption that "reasonable" charges were based *solely* upon distance.[64]

No wonder Charles Francis Adams Jr., architect of railroad regulation in Massachusetts and soon-to-be president of the Union Pacific Railroad, drew national attention to the misguided Potter Law. He called it the "most ignorant, arbitrary, and wholly unjustifiable law to be found in the history of railroad legislation." By slashing rates as much as "twenty to fifty percent," Adams charged, the act "seemed designed as practical confiscation of the many millions of foreign capital invested in the public improvements of that state. . . . If ever a problem called for wise legislation, founded upon careful and patient study, this one certainly did. The Granger legislatures, however, went at it like so many bulls at red rags."[65]

In the same year Wisconsin regulated its railroads, so did Iowa. The state's popular Republican governor Cyrus Clay Carpenter proclaimed, "In my judgment the time has arrived when a limit to freight charges on our Iowa railroads should be fixed by law." The governor's initiative prompted legislators to consider the demands of the nearly 40,000 local members of the Patrons of Husbandry for railroad control. The final measure lacked strong farmer backing, however. It failed to create a board of railroad commissioners as Iowa agrarians had proposed and instead imposed a maximum rate or "cast-iron tariff" on freight charges. This pleased eastern Iowa merchants who ardently campaigned for the lowest rates possible. The railroads, needless to say, keenly felt the bitter sting of consumer rage.[66]

The rate policies of the North Western during this time do not appear to be unfair. In Iowa, for example, the Patrons of Husbandry disclosed that the company's short-haul charges were next to the lowest locally and that its long-haul rates to Chicago were the cheapest. Furthermore, Hawkeye State Grangers praised the quality of service and the condition of the property.[67]

Understandably the North Western could not ignore this first great outburst of state regulation. The Potter Law and similar legislation elsewhere gravely affected its financial condition. In 1873 the road's interest payments on its 565 miles of line in Wisconsin were $1,350,135, but the net income for the best year during the act's operation stood at only slightly more than $1 million.[68]

Initially, North Western officials, directed by Albert Keep, tried to educate lawmakers and the public concerning the serious defects of mileage-based rate controls. In one "Memorial" or white paper Keep joined Alexander Mitchell, president of the St. Paul, to argue the railroads' case. Their "equal mileage rates are inexpedient" position embraced the following logic about the opposition's policy:

> a) It would prevent railway companies from lowering their fares and rates so as to compete with traffic by sea, by canal, or by a shorter or otherwise cheaper railway, and would thus deprive the public of the benefit of competition and the company of a legitimate source of profit.
>
> b) It would prevent railway companies from making perfectly fair arrangements for carrying at a lower rate than usually goods brought in large and constant quantities, or for carrying for long distances at a lower rate than for short distances.
>
> c) It would compel a company to carry the same rate over a line which has been very expensive in construction, or which, from gradients or otherwise, is very expensive in working at the same rate as which it carries over other lines.[69]

The position of the North Western was somewhat naive. A Keep associate predicted in 1873: "Through the process of informing the citizens about the true nature of railroad affairs, we can prevent cruel laws from happening." The shock of the Potter Law and the Iowa "cast-iron tariff" prompted the company and other roads to become more realistic and forceful. Their principal response ultimately entailed direct legislative lobbying. The degree to which the North Western lobbied in Madison, Des Moines, and elsewhere is not clear, but "the C&NW made its case heard before the proper authorities." There is no evidence that the company took exceptional measures or did anything that smacked of blatant corporate arrogance. The St. Paul, on the other hand, was more aggressive. Mitchell refused to build much-needed grain-storage facilities in Milwaukee until reformers halted their attacks.[70]

The most restrictive acts of the Granger phenomena soon became only unpleasant memories. Wisconsin repealed the Potter Law in 1876, and two years later in Iowa the General Assembly replaced the 1874 statute with a more reasonable Board of Railroad Commissions, the basic objective of the Iowa Grange. Nevertheless the era of laissez-faire had practically ended with establishment of regulatory commissions. Carriers could no longer rely upon the law of supply and demand and pooling agreements to determine their rate structure. The era of public scrutiny had arrived.[71]

By the end of the 1870s Grangerism had mostly run its course. A stronger economy and more transportation options largely explain the decline in regulatory agitation. But the railroads had learned an important lesson: they needed to monitor state legislatures and employ lobbyists. Once the North Western took this course of action, it coped with the impending excesses of the populist and progressive reform crusades more effectively.[72]

The Grangers displayed a capacity for critical judgment. These Gilded Age reformers avoided attacking the North Western on its quality of service and its physical plant. The company continually sought to accommodate patrons even though the 1870s were difficult years. After all, the road endured the ravages of the Chicago fire of October 1871. This massive conflagration caused nearly $180,000 in damages to company property (insurance coverage came to only $68,400), temporarily forced diversion of traffic from Chicago, and for months disrupted the commercial life of the city. Moreover, the company coped with a national depression after 1873, which sent 30 percent of all railroad mileage into court-ordered receivership. The North Western also faced stressful managerial problems.[73]

The leadership of the North Western understood clearly that a commitment to serving the commonweal could in the long run raise income, and it endeavored to do so in various ways. One response, the railway post office (RPO) car, significantly affected the company, the industry, and indeed the nation. Railroads liked to claim "firsts," and the North Western, no exception to this generalization, proudly touted the employment of the first RPO car in which mail was gathered, sorted, and dropped off along a regular route.[74]

Mail has always been a precious lading. Attempts to dispatch it more quickly and efficiently have been continuous since the rise of the Republic. As early as 1837 letters began to move by train, but this "pouched mail," secured in locked canvas bags, was handled the same way as it traveled on stagecoaches and steamboats. A breakthrough came with the inaugural of the Pony Express on April 3, 1860. The first sack of oilskin-wrapped envelopes reached St. Joseph, Missouri, from the East by a special train operated by the Hannibal & St. Joseph Railroad. Sometime later a regular mail car was assigned for letters bound for California destinations; this high-priority mail was organized en route in a former baggage car. The equipment remained in service only briefly because the telegraph supplanted the Pony Express in 1862.[75]

The use of a mail car on the Hannibal & St. Joseph was a warm-up for what was about to happen on the North Western. The principal force behind the introduction of the RPOs was George Armstrong, an assistant postmaster in Chicago. Troubled by the chaos of mail handling caused by the unprecedented volume generated by the Civil War, Armstrong conceived of "a post office on wheels." As he commented in a letter to Postmaster General Montgomery Blair in the summer of 1864: "Passengers travelling over railroad routes generally reach a given point in advance of letters, when to that given point letters must pass, under the present system, through a distributing office, and when letters are subject to a distributing process in more than one distributing office as is largely the case now, the tardiness of a letter's progress toward its place of destination is proportionately increased." And Armstrong concluded, "But a general system of railway distribution obviates this difficulty. The work being done while the cars are in motion and transfers of mails from route to route and for local delivery on the way, as they are reached, letters attain the same celerity in transit as persons making direct connections."[76]

Postmaster General Blair readily granted Armstrong authority to test his idea for "simplifying the mail service." On August 28, 1864, the country's first railway post office, housed in a remodeled baggage car and furnished with letter and newspaper cases, rolled between Chicago and Clinton, Iowa. This trip was fairly rough, according to James Medill, editor of the *Chicago Tribune*, who seemed bothered by the experiment. "Why, Mr. Armstrong, your plan is the craziest idea I ever heard of in regard to mail distribution. If it were to be generally accepted by the Post Office Department, the government would have to employ a regiment of soldiers to follow the cars and pick up the letters that would blow out of the train." Medill later recanted and enthusiastically endorsed the new service.[77]

More activity followed with the Railway Post Office scheme. During 1864 and 1865 the North Western built five "mail cars" in its shops at Fond du Lac, Wisconsin, and they operated between

Management of the North Western enthusiastically promoted its passenger service. This advertisement appeared in the *Chicago City Directory* of 1873. (Author's collection)

Public timetables of the North Western included more than the arrival and departure times of trains; schedules typically publicized travel and equipment. The company proudly informed readers in the May 28, 1874, issue that its rolling stock featured "Miller Platforms." In the mid-1860s Ezra Miller developed an improved passenger car that contained couplers that eliminated the link and pin and a combination trussed-end platform, lessening the likelihood of the car telescoping in a wreck. (Author's collection)

Chicago and Green Bay. Then in 1867 similar equipment entered service between the Iowa communities of Boone and Council Bluffs, and shortly thereafter on additional parts of the system. Other railroads acquired this specialized rolling stock as well. Rather than handling sealed sacks of mail, postal workers instead opened them, "worked" their contents, and re-pouched the mail for on-line destinations and for connections. The federal government rewarded Armstrong with an appointment to head the Railway Mail Service, which began in 1869. For nearly a century Armstrong's innovation was the backbone of the nation's intercity postal distribution system.[78]

The rolling stock that caught the public's eye was surely not the RPO equipment but rather the Pullman sleeping car. Although the North Western operated its share of "accommodations," namely local trains with their one or two spartan day coaches, the company provided select patrons luxurious sleeping cars that incorporated the latest features of the builders' art. The most popular sleepers by the 1870s belonged to the Chicago-based Pullman Palace Car Company. By 1875 the Pullman fleet of approximately 800 cars operated on about 30,000 miles of line, including the Overland Route.[79]

Florence Leslie, wife of the owner of *Frank Leslie's Illustrated Newspaper* of New York, gave a glowing account of her trip westward from Chicago on the North Western in 1877. She found the quality of the newly introduced "Pullman Hotel Car" to be unequaled:

> First, we are impressed with the smooth and delightful motion, and are told it is owing to a new invention, in the shape of paper wheels applied to this car [introduced by Richard Allen in 1869 and extensively used between 1880 and 1900], and incredible though the information sounds, meekly accept it, and proceeded to explore the internal resources of our kingdom. We find everything closely resembling our late home, except that one end of the car is partitioned off and fitted up as a kitchen, storeroom, scullery—reminding one, in their compactness and variety, of the little Parisian *cuisines,* where every inch of space is utilized, and where such a modicum of wood and charcoal produces such marvelous results.[80]

The Leslie commentary concurred with a contemporary advertising broadside issued by the North Western's Passenger Department:

> The Chicago and North Western Railway is the PIONEER LINE And the only one that can offer you Pullman Hotel Cars West of Chicago. By this Route you can have these celebrated Hotel Cars to Council Bluffs, And from Council Bluffs to Denver you can take Through PULLMAN SLEEPERS. No other Route can truthfully offer you these advantages.[81]

Florence Leslie discovered other pleasures beyond comfortable sleeping arrangements. She appreciated the opportunity to select such unusual game dishes as prairie chicken, pheasant, quail, plover, snipe, blue teal, woodcock, mallard, canvas back duck, pigeon, widgeon, and venison steak. Her more colloquial remark rang true: "We ate high on the hog!"[82]

Others observers commented on more than the state-of-the-art Pullman service provided on the North Western's section of the Overland

Route. Henry T. Williams, for one, in his widely consulted travel handbook, *Williams' Pacific Tourist and Guide across the Continent,* published a year before Florence Leslie made her grand "land voyage," noted that "the Chicago and North-Western Railroad . . . is the shortest line [between Chicago and Council Bluffs]. . . . The eating-stations on this route are all very fine. . . . [T]hey are the best of the Iowa railroads."[83]

The riders who chose to sleep and eat their way across Illinois and Iowa in the lap of luxury numbered far fewer than those who used another new service of the period, the commuter train. After the Civil War the North Western developed an extensive commuter business in the Chicago area, which the railroad expanded as the city and its "steamcar suburbs" blossomed.[84]

The descriptive narrative *Chicago and Its Suburbs,* written by publicist Everett Chamberlin and published in 1874, described the scope of the North Western's early commuter business. Communities along the railroad's three main stems, which radiated from Chicago, enjoyed access to convenient local runs. In the commentary on Winnetka, situated on the Milwaukee Division, Chamberlin noted: "The train service is excellent, and the commutation yearly ticket only $76." As for Palatine: "Its location is twenty-two miles from the city, on the Wisconsin Division . . . and sixteen passenger trains call at its depot each day." In the entry for River Forest, a stop on the Galena Division, he wrote: "The station has a service of 12 trains each day." Chamberlin concluded that the company provided commuter trains that were "adopted to the wants of city workers."[85]

Travelers could select destinations other than Chicago during those years. Whether they rode fancy Pullmans or simple coaches, they could take advantage of pleasure outings or business opportunities. Like most large carriers the North Western became heavily involved in promoting vacation sites for the affluent few and new land and communities for everyone. While the greatest developmental efforts occurred later, the company early on resorted to broadsides, newspaper advertisements, pamphlets, and other publications to promote its services.

An example of an ever eager North Western was its joint efforts with the Burlington & Missouri River Railroad in Nebraska to stimulate interest in the trans-Missouri West. A Chicago press agent wrote these observations for a broadside distributed in August 1875:

The chance to go and see for yourselves that the Grasshopper stories are false. That this is one of the best countries the sun ever shone upon, and a larger harvest per acre is already harvested and in the field, then you have in Wisconsin or Illinois—both small grains and corn—and for a Hog, Cattle and Sheep country it can best you all hollow![86]

In a more general approach were these typical statements that appeared on the back cover of a North Western public timetable for October 1874:

RUNNING THROUGH FIVE STATES,
THIS GREAT RAILWAY LINE,
Made up of over TWO THOUSAND MILES of
the best Railroad there is in the NORTHWEST,
Offers inducements to the
traveling public second to none in the
country, and SUPERIOR to any offered
by its competitors. Steel Rail,
Shortest and Quickest Routes,
Westinghouse Safety Air Brakes,
Miller's Safety Platforms, Pullman
Place Cars.
SPEED, COMFORT & SAFETY ARE COMBINED
And render this the Great Route for the PEOPLE[87]

While the North Western might be guilty of hyperbole, it hardly violated conventional standards of truth in advertising. Any possible public doubts or criticisms about the road would be mostly laid to rest during the forthcoming regime of Marvin Hughitt, the "second William Ogden" and the force that shaped the property for nearly a half century.

North Western locomotive No. 75, a popular 4-4-0 American Standard, rests on a gallows turntable in an unidentified location, perhaps in eastern Dakota Territory. The Hinkley Locomotive Works built No. 75 in 1855 as the *Woodstock* for the Chicago, St. Paul & Fond du Lac Railroad. Following additional refurbishings, this Class H-3 locomotive was scrapped in 1905. (George Krambles collection)

CHAPTER Three

YEARS OF EXPANSION, 1877–1892

While volatility characterized the leadership of the Chicago & North Western Railway following the resignation of William Ogden in 1868, it vanished once Albert Keep assumed power. The company's fifth president, a persevering, systematic man, provided an important steadiness during his 14-year tenure that began in 1873. Keep's skills won him universal respect, including that of the Vanderbilt family, an emerging force on the Board of Directors.[1]

The North Western also reaped the insights of Keep's principal subordinate, Marvin Hughitt, who served as general manager. As Hughitt gained major responsibilities, he shaped important matters of policy, and his work did much to make the company one of the nation's premier roads. After Keep's departure in 1887, Hughitt guided the railroad for more than a generation. During this long tenure he symbolized the stability and profitability of the property. The venerable Hughitt remained in the executive suite until 1910 and exercised influence as a board member until his death in 1928. "Tall, straight of figure, broad of shoulder, firm of face and alert of step, Mr. Hughitt is the very personification of success and power," observed a Chicago journalist. "He is the North-Western Railway." Hughitt's sobriquet, "King Marvin," was not off the mark.[2]

The background of Marvin Hughitt resembles that of many rising businessmen of the era. His roots were in rural America, he received only a modicum of formal education, and he worked elsewhere before he "went railroading." An editorial in the *Chicago Railway Review* of March 1872 described his personal traits: "He has comprehension, energy and enterprise . . . [and] has perfect integrity and straightforwardness." Hughitt's strict personal code, considerable intelligence, and eagerness to please his superiors hardly made him exceptional. Thomas C. Cochran in his monumental study *Railroad Leaders, 1845–1890: The Business Mind in Action* contends that these executives possessed high moral standards, preferred honesty in their business transactions, and felt content if their properties produced reasonable profits.[3]

Hughitt hailed from upstate New York. He was born on a farm in Cayuga County in the Finger Lakes district on August 9, 1837. At 15 he joined the New York, Albany & Buffalo Telegraph Company in its office in Albany, where he quickly mastered the complexities of the cryptic Morse code. Two years later Hughitt moved to Chicago where he honed his telegraphic skills with his new employer, the Illinois & Missouri Telegraph Company. In 1857 he entered railroad service as a trainmaster and superintendent of telegraph for the St. Louis, Alton & Chicago Railway (later the Chicago & Alton) in Bloomington, Illinois.[4]

During the early months of the Civil War Hughitt changed employers. He left the Alton to become the superintendent of the Southern Division of the Illinois Central and called Centralia

The North Western frequently used this formal portrait of Marvin Hughitt, which dates from about 1900. Hughitt richly deserved the sobriquet "King Marvin," for he, more than any other company official, shaped the modern North Western System. (North Western/Union Pacific)

his hometown. Through much of the conflict, Hughitt sustained an unpredictable and at times overwhelming workload. On at least two occasions he toiled without rest for more than 36 hours to expedite troop and supply trains.[5]

Hughitt avoided becoming a "lifer" with the Illinois Central. Although promoted to the general superintendency of the road in 1864, he left in 1870 to become assistant general manager of the Chicago, Milwaukee & St. Paul Railroad in Chicago. The next year Hughitt assumed the general managership of the Pullman company but resigned on March 1, 1872, to accept a similar job with the North Western. He won promotion in 1880, becoming vice president and general manager, the position he held until taking the presidency seven years later.[6]

Marvin Hughitt displayed the qualities generally ascribed to other self-made railway executives of the post–Civil War era. He wanted to "know the facts" about his company's operations and the region it served or planned to reach. Hughitt had a good command of finances as well, and he consistently showed a sense of commitment to the public. While optimistic about the future of the North Western and its territory, Hughitt resisted needless expansion, although he considered a possible extension to the Pacific coast. Similarly, he revealed an antispeculative bent, something that set him apart from more colorful contemporary railroad leaders. "Hughitt liked to stick to his knitting," remarked an associate. He did, and the North Western prospered.[7]

Hughitt managed the daily affairs of the railroad in a reasonable manner. He expected subordinates to be loyal and to do their best. If they performed well, rewards followed, namely job security and promotions. The few employees of color, who confronted nearly universal discrimination, prospered under Hughitt's reign. John Johnson was one such person. Born a slave at Culpapel Court House, Virginia, in 1840, Johnson escaped from bondage in 1863 and eventually made his way to Chicago. After a stint as a Pullman porter, he joined the North Western in 1881 as a waiter on the company's first dining car. Because of his skills and dedication he won assignment to Hughitt's business car two years later. Johnson's outstanding work as an attendant allowed him to remain with Hughitt for decades. Even after he left his longtime assignment, Johnson continued to draw a monthly paycheck until his death in 1922. Hughitt insisted that management employ him in odd jobs at corporate headquarters.[8]

The management of the Chicago & North Western had broad ambitions. While it wanted a productive and dedicated workforce, the principal objective was to strengthen the property. This meant more than short-term profitability, but betterments and expansion to ensure lasting financial health.

The North Western resembled other businesses when it experienced a severe financial downswing after the Panic of 1873, which set off the first full-scale depression since the late 1850s. The collapse of several railroads, most notably the Northern Pacific, shattered a somewhat jerry-built national economy. Happily hard times did not throw the North Western into the hands of a court-appointed receiver. Other carriers were not so fortunate; more than a quarter of the American railway network, or about 20,000 miles, fell into receivership between 1874 and 1877. By the time the depression was only a year old, 108 companies had defaulted on their bonds, some $497 million in securities.[9]

The Keep-Hughitt administration monitored carefully the financial situation. The Panic sharply reduced the value of North Western common stock from a high of 64 $3/4$ to a low of 40 in 1873. Even so the carrier fared better than most of its competitors. Security prices remained depressed for the next four years, and the malaise inevitably had an adverse effect on income. For the fiscal year from June 1, 1873, to May 31, 1874, the company's gross earnings stood at $14,351,523, the highest ever. But they dropped to $12,707,726 in the next reporting period, and subsequently fell to $11,877,500 for the 1876–1877 fiscal year. The predepression level of gross earnings would not be equaled until 1878–1879. Net earnings paralleled this decline; they dropped from $2,183,913 for fiscal year 1872–1873 to a low of $1,078,226 in 1876–1877. Net earnings rebounded the following year to $2,464,487.[10]

Prosperity returned during the 1880s for the nation and the railroad industry. The annual gross income for the North Western between 1880 and 1893, when hard times returned with a vengeance, averaged more than $25.3 million, and net earnings commonly ran at slightly more than $10 million annually. These impressive figures would have been much greater had stiff freight-rate competition in the Midwest not burgeoned during part of this period.[11]

A barometer of the financial strength of the company was its record of dividend payments. Although the Board of Directors voted to skip dividends on both preferred and common stock during the worst years of the depression, it granted a 2 1/4 percent dividend to owners of preferred shares in 1877. Between 1878 and 1881 these security holders received 7 percent, were paid 7 1/4 percent in 1882, and 8 percent in 1883, 1884, and 1885. The 7 percent rate was reestablished in 1886 and lasted for the remainder of the century. Holders of common stock received 3 percent in 1878, 4 percent in 1879, 6 percent in 1880 and 1881, 6 1/2 percent in 1882, 7 percent in 1883, 1884, and 1885, and 6 percent from 1886 through 1894. "The Northwestern is a prince of a railroad," concluded Stephen C. Millett, a New York investment specialist, in 1889. "At times the Northwestern could have paid 10% on both classes of its stock and still have had a tidy surplus."[12]

With policies based on a long-standing tradition of sensible responses to economic conditions, North Western management acted prudently during the troublesome 1870s and then adopted an expansive outlook throughout the halcyon 1880s. The most visible manifestation of the new dynamism, aside from payment of ample dividends, was renewed construction. Such building occurred in two waves during the 1870s, specifically before and after the financial stringency brought on by the depression. Trackage increased from 1,382 miles in 1870 to 2,512 miles 10 years later. The predepression activities involved mainly the building of the Menominee Extension, 115 miles laid down between Fort Howard (Green Bay), Wisconsin, and Escanaba, Michigan, in 1871 and 1872; the Madison Extension, 129 miles that linked Madison, Wisconsin, with Winona Junction, Wisconsin, and a connection with the proprietary Winona & St. Peter Railroad (W&StP); and the expanding St. Peter road itself, which stretched more than 300 miles across southern Minnesota and into eastern Dakota Territory by 1874. Construction, too, entailed the opening of the 69-mile Iowa Midland and the 63-mile North Western Union, both controlled properties like the St. Peter.[13]

A combination of renewed confidence and better earnings brought construction workers back to the North Western system. As the demand for iron ore increased, the company sought to gain more of this traffic through expansion of trackage to additional mine sites in the Upper Peninsula. A 25-mile branch line known as the Menominee River Railroad opened between the Michigan communities of Powers and Quinnesec in 1877. The appendage left Powers, 41 miles north of Menominee on the Green Bay to Escanaba line, and extended in a northwesterly direction. "The most sanguine views are held out by the owners of the new mines of their extent and value," reported Albert Keep in May 1877, "and the assurance is given that their products will largely increase the revenues of the Company, not only from the working of the branch, and the employment of the present equipment of ore cars and docks, but also from the utilization of 22 miles of our present main line to Escanaba, upon which this traffic will be clear gain."[14]

The North Western initiated construction of another profitable branch line, which also opened in 1877 and was designed to handle mainly agricultural traffic in western Iowa. Built under the corporate banner of the Maple River Rail-Road and controlled by the North Western-leased Cedar Rapids & Missouri River Railroad, the 60-mile extension left the Omaha line at Maple River Junction, four miles west of Carroll, and extended northwesterly to Mapleton, in the valley of the Maple River, a tributary of the Missouri River. "The road will open up some of the best and most fertile portions of Western Iowa," noted Keep, "and become a feeder to 400 miles of the present main line to Chicago." He was correct; the building strategy was wholly sound. A year later workers installed a 13-mile "twig" from Wall Lake, Iowa, 17 miles from Maple River Junction, northward to Sac City.[15]

Still more branches appeared by the end of the decade. The North Western backed construction of four additional feeder lines, all of which connected with the W&StP at various points along its Minnesota main stem and were built by separate companies. These included the

Minnesota Valley Railway, which laid a 24-mile line northwest of Sleepy Eye to Redwood Falls; the Rochester & Northern Minnesota Railway, which built a 25-mile pike from Rochester north to Zumbrota; the 15-mile Plainview Rail-Road that linked Eyota north to Plainview; and the 12-mile Chatfield Rail-Road that extended south from Eyota to Chatfield. Although these four satellite companies were legally independent, the North Western guaranteed their first-mortgage bonds. In 1881 the W&StP absorbed these firms.[16]

The practice of creating subsidiaries continued during this time of expansion. The North Western was hardly unusual in employing this tactic. Most large railroads pursued a similar course, and advantages were numerous. Charters for these roads were easily extracted from state governments as they were popular with local residents. Future patrons not only wanted rail service, but also they liked having their hometown, county, or geographic locality part of the official name, reinforcing their booster spirit in a tangible way. Another benefit was that at times the real intentions of the financial backers could be disguised; a localized shortline might actually become a springboard for a more ambitious project. By the Gilded Age carriers became increasingly sensitive to incursions by competitors into what they considered to be their territories. Such incursions needed to be concealed as retaliations might follow. Furthermore, when using a subsidiary, if the project failed, it would not adversely affect the financial health of the controlling company. Since the North Western commonly held the first mortgage, its investment was reasonably secure. The principal drawback was the additional paperwork generated by these separate entities. The desire to streamline the corporate structure often led to their demise except when financial or political considerations necessitated their preservation.[17]

Beyond the direct promotion of new rail lines, the North Western absorbed several shortlines toward the end of the decade. The three that came under the company's control were narrow-gauge (3' 0") roads in Iowa and Wisconsin. Shortly after the Civil War a cadre of railroad promoters considered standard-gauge (4' 8½") lines to be impractical for certain transportation needs. Instead, they argued, the slimmer pikes held several crucial advantages, namely, that they were easier and cheaper to build, maintain, and operate. A surprising number of their dreams became reality: a building boom between 1871 and 1883 created approximately 12,000 miles of narrow-gauge lines. Most of this trackage, however, was not connected with other slim-width properties, although attempts were made to create regional and even interregional networks. In time many of the surviving narrow-gauge roads were converted to standard gauge because of the impracticality of a multiple-gauge interchange. The builders of the narrow-gauge lines erred when they reasoned that the smaller gauge was cheaper and better. Transportation economist George W. Hilton concludes that, "the experience of the narrow gauge movement demonstrated definitively that gauges under 4'-8 ½" are less than optimal for general transport purposes."[18]

The first of the narrow-gauge railroads that the North Western acquired was the Des Moines & Minnesota Railroad (DM&M). Although backers of the DM&M planned a 250-mile line from the Iowa capital to Minneapolis, they did little for several years following the firm's chartering in 1870. In 1874 the company opened 37 miles between Des Moines and Ames, a college town located on the Omaha line. Following a financial reorganization in 1877 as the Des Moines & Minneapolis Railroad, the company again pushed northward. This time workers spiked down about 20 miles of track between Ames and the new settlement of Callanan. Although described by the *Railway World* as the "only first-class narrow-gauge railroad in Iowa," the company again experienced difficulties, defaulting on its bonds in July 1879. Soon, however, the North Western leased the 57-mile road and widened the more important segment between Ames and Des Moines in 1880. It converted the remaining portion two years later.[19]

The former DM&M fit well into the North Western system. It not only served some rich agricultural lands and thriving communities but also provided the company access to Iowa's greatest metropolis. The DM&M furthermore tied together the east-west main line with the newly opened Toledo & North Western, a proprietary firm, which met the old DM&M near Callanan, relocated and renamed Jewell Junction.[20]

Two additional narrow-gauge railroads, the

A narrow-gauge passenger train of the North Western pauses between Fennimore and Woodman in Grant County, Wisc., in 1896. Locomotive No. 278, a 4-4-0 built as No. 5 for the Des Moines & Minneapolis Railroad in 1879, soon became a North Western possession. When the North Western converted the DM&M to standard gauge in 1880, the engine entered service on the former Chicago & Tomah Railroad, a narrow-gauge shortline that the North Western had recently acquired. (Railway & Locomotive Historical Society)

Galena & Southern Wisconsin (G&SW) and the Chicago & Tomah Railroad (C&T), entered the North Western's fold in 1880. These neighboring properties, totaling 92 miles, developed independently of one another though they both sought to improve transportation in a rugged section of southwestern Wisconsin. The G&SW began its corporate existence in 1872 and two years later completed a nine-mile line north of Galena, Illinois. The company reached Platteville, 30 miles from Galena, in 1875. Although the G&SW entertained some expansion plans, including an extension to Madison, it never advanced any farther than a few miles northeast of Platteville. The company failed in 1879, and reorganization later that year as the Galena & Wisconsin Railroad kept the trains running.[21]

A sister carrier of sorts was the somewhat less woebegone Chicago & Tomah Railroad, launched in 1872. Its promoters expected to build from Freeport, Illinois, through the lead belt of southwestern Wisconsin, to Tomah in the western part of the Badger State. In addition to minerals the completed road would also carry agricultural and lumber products. Better economic conditions allowed the C&T to connect the Wisconsin communities of Woodman, Fennimore, and Lancaster, a distance of about 30 miles in 1878. A year later a 14-mile extension tied Lancaster to Montfort, a village east of Fennimore. While this shortline graded additional right-of-way north of Woodman, it never finished any trackage.[22]

With these narrow-gauge roads failing to complete their intended objectives and suffering from poor earnings, the North Western stepped in and acquired them cheaply. The explanation of these acquisitions involved more than cost. The trackage allowed the company to enter a region that had remained largely isolated and could generate considerable mixed traffic. Galena, however, was no longer considered to be the big prize as lead mining in the immediate vicinity had either declined or was controlled by the Illinois Central.[23]

The Galena & Southern Wisconsin and the Chicago & Tomah then became part of the Milwaukee & Madison Railway, a subsidiary of the North Western, and were soon joined south of Montfort. The combined roads remained isolated from the parent firm, but this trackage did not stay unconnected for long. The Milwaukee & Wisconsin built a 61-mile standard-gauge line west from Madison through Dodgeville to Montfort in 1881 and subsequently widened the narrow-gauge network, except for the 16 miles between Woodman and Fennimore. The latter retained its slim width until it was abandoned in 1926; construction costs and traffic considerations did not warrant conversion.[24]

The 1880s found both the North Western and the American railroad enterprise poised for massive development. In 1880 slightly more than 93,000 miles of railway were in operation; a decade later the figure exceeded 166,000 miles.

Never before or since have so many new rails been spiked to ties in 10 years. With access to ample funds, the North Western embarked on an expansion program in the Midwest and Great Plains. By 1890 the company's mileage stood at 4,250, a 59.1 percent increase from 1880; it had become a major interterritorial system.[25]

Iowa became a primary focus of the North Western's expansion plan. The attractiveness of the state steadily grew. Its population increased significantly: 674,913 in 1860, 1,194,020 in 1870, and 1,624,615 in 1880. Then during the 1880s the population rose 17.7 percent; census enumerators counted 1,912,297 residents in 1890. Iowa's economic base was maturing as the raw frontier stage had largely disappeared by 1880. Although claiming other industries, the state was becoming the heart of the nation's breadbasket. Hawkeye State farmers, abandoning their reliance upon a cash grain economy, were switching to livestock raising. Indeed, the introduction and propagation of distinctive beef-cattle breeds reached boom proportions in the 1880s.[26]

Although the North Western certainly did not monopolize the Iowa market, it became a dominant carrier. The company built through the richest agricultural lands of the state; it generally avoided the rugged terrain of the northeast and the "pot and kettle" topography of the southern and south-central sections. The strategy was to build new lines mostly north of the Omaha stem, although short extensions radiated both north and south from this artery. The company already controlled the Iowa Midland Railway and in 1872 had the Stanwood & Tipton Railway, a subsidiary, cross the nine miles between the main line at Stanwood in eastern Iowa and Tipton, seat of Cedar County. A similar feeder line opened in western Iowa in 1882, when the Iowa South-Western Railway built 35 miles from Carroll, a thriving county seat on the Omaha line, to the village of Kirkman, and from Manning, situated on the Kirkman branch, to Audubon, the Audubon County capital, a distance of 17 miles.[27]

The exception to the general philosophy of avoiding southern Iowa was the Ottumwa, Cedar Falls & St. Paul Railway. This satellite, which never reached any of the places in its corporate name, extended southward from Belle Plaine, 116 miles west of Clinton, through several villages to the coal camp of Muchakinock in Mahaska County. This 60-mile branch, opened in 1884, was designed chiefly to haul coal, partially for use as locomotive fuel, from the rich and developing bituminous fields of the Des Moines River valley. Because the North Western no longer relied on wood-burning locomotives, access to a dependable and cheap supply of "black diamonds" was essential. Early in the twentieth century the Muchakinock line was extended into neighboring Monroe County, and some observers believed that it might eventually reach St. Joseph or Kansas City, Missouri.[28]

The principal construction project in Iowa involved the 385-mile Toledo & North Western Railway (T&NW), a wholly controlled subsidiary. Although the road was shaped between 1880 and 1885, most of the grading and tracklaying was done in 1881 and 1882. The T&NW left the Omaha line at Tama, 132 miles west of Clinton, and angled to the northwest. The three miles between Tama and Toledo were quickly installed in 1880, and later that year the line reached Webster City, a prosperous county seat, 80 miles from Toledo. During 1881 track gangs completed 15 miles of line north of Webster City to Eagle Grove, 30 miles northwest from Eagle Grove to Willow Glen (Bradgate), and 15 miles west from Jewell Junction, south of Webster City, to Stratford. Even more T&NW mileage materialized in 1882. North of Eagle Grove 66 miles of track were put in to the Minnesota state line at Elmore, Minnesota, and a connection with the Chicago, St. Paul, Minneapolis & Omaha ("Omaha Road") for the Twin Cities. Two miles were built between Jewell Junction and the end of track of the newly acquired DM&M narrow-gauge road; 115 miles of line extended from Willow Glen to Hawarden near the boundary of Dakota Territory; and 42 miles stretched west from Stratford to Lake City. Then four years later a line spanned the 15 miles between Lake City and Wall Lake Junction, and an interchange with the Maple River Railroad. A projected line between Gladbrook, 18 miles northwest of Tama, and Anamosa, the end of the Iowa Midland, never materialized, even though the T&NW conducted the survey work. An unrelated, yet North Western–controlled venture, the 26-mile Chicago, Iowa & Dakota Railway, opened from the T&NW near Gifford (Eldora

Junction), 40 miles from Tama, northward through Iowa Falls to Alden in 1884.[29]

The web of trackage that the Toledo & North Western created fully justified the expenditure of nearly $5.8 million that was financed conservatively through long-term debt. Built to quality standards, furnished with good equipment, and free from watered stock, the T&NW offered much to its parent. Concerned about the possibility of incursions into this territory by other carriers, especially the Chicago, Milwaukee & St. Paul, President Keep sanctioned the project because "[it] will prevent the diversion to other roads of traffic which we now enjoy, and will secure a large accession of new [on-line] business."[30]

Other benefits included the connection with the Omaha Road at Elmore, Minnesota, which completed a network of company and company-controlled lines, and a useful route to Dakota. In 1883 the North Western, through its Dakota Central Railway subsidiary, installed a 125-mile line between the T&NW at Hawarden, Iowa, and Iroquois, Dakota Territory, which formed "the shorter outlet of the Dakota lines as an alternate with the Winona & St. Peter." Furthermore, the T&NW trackage from Tama to Lake View Junction and then a 20-mile extension of the Maple River Railroad from Mapleton to Onawa, which opened in 1886, linked with the Sioux City & Pacific Railroad (by then part of the North Western) for Council Bluffs. This forged 210 miles of line paralleling the Chicago and Omaha artery and relieved congestion on the busy Omaha stem without necessitating a second mainline track. Had the 75-mile Gladbrook-Anamosa project become a reality, the North Western would have owned a second trans-Iowa artery.[31]

The Toledo & North Western disappeared without fanfare on June 6, 1890, when the North Western merged it into the corporate structure. Like other carriers the company frequently absorbed its subsidiaries. On October 24, 1884, the North Western had eliminated several branch-line subsidiaries, including the Iowa Midland, Iowa South-Western, and Stanwood & Tipton, "in pursuance of the policy of the Company to reduce the number of its minor corporations." A much more significant transaction had taken place a few months before when the North Western purchased the "Iowa Leased Lines" or Blair Roads. Specifically, the company acquired the Chicago, Iowa & Nebraska (83 miles), Cedar Rapids & Missouri River (274 miles), and Maple River (131 miles) railroads and their "tributary and natural extensions, to-wit, the Sioux City & Pacific Railroad from Sioux City to Missouri River Junction, thence across the Missouri River to a connection with the Union Pacific Railway at Fremont, Neb., 107.42 miles; the Missouri Valley and Blair Railway & Bridge Company, owning the bridge and its approaches over the Missouri River at Blair, and the Fremont, Elkhorn & Missouri Valley Railroad, from Fremont to Valentine, . . . Neb., with the Creighton Branch, 3ll miles." The cost was $27,875,100, a fair price.[32]

The reasons for the acquisition of the Blair Roads were several. The North Western wanted to guarantee control of these essential lines; it sought to provide additional access to the trans-Missouri West; and it wanted to save money. As President Keep explained to shareholders: "The annual charge to the Chicago & North-Western Railway Company, by assuming the bonds and obligations of the purchased properties, and by paying 7 per cent on the new stock to be issued therefor, will be less than the amount of rental now accruing under the leases, after deducting the new income derived from the business of the tributary roads." A Nebraska newspaper reported that the savings would amount to about $150,000 annually.[33]

The North Western leadership had no misgivings about this addition. "It is a natural step in the developing the North Western," observed Marvin Hughitt. "The Company can afford this commitment and . . . it will offer opportunities for logical growth in our region of business." Keep and Hughitt were well aware that competitors were in an expansive mood. The Burlington, for one, had leaped from central Nebraska westward to Denver, Colorado, in 1881–1882. The railroad map of the nation's midsection had hardly jelled, and neither had the route structure of the North Western.[34]

When the North Western brought the Iowa Leased Lines fully into its corporate fold, two affiliated properties remained legally separate, the Sioux City & Pacific (SC&P) and the Fremont, Elkhorn & Missouri Valley Railroad (FE&MV).

The former officially joined the North Western on August 28, 1901, and the latter on February 28, 1903. Yet the North Western operated them as its "Trans-Missouri Lines" for more than three decades as part of its expanding system. Both the SC&P and FE&MV were associated with the Blair Roads, handiwork of John Insley Blair, the archetypical nineteenth-century entrepreneur who made much of his estimated $70 million fortune from the development of railroads and land promotion in the West.[35]

The SC&P took shape soon after the Civil War and was designed as its corporate name implied to share in the nation's rapidly progressing transcontinental railroad network. The first segment of the SC&P linked Missouri Valley, Iowa, 21 miles east of the new western terminus of the CR&MR at Council Bluffs, with an impressive-sounding settlement, California Junction, Iowa, a distance of only six and one-half miles. The construction, officially undertaken by the Cedar Rapids road, occurred in autumn 1867. By February 1868 track laborers finished the SC&P northward for 70 miles along the eastern bank of the Missouri River from California Junction to Sioux City, a growing regional trading center with a population of 3,401 in 1870. A year later crews completed their work between California Junction and Fremont, Nebraska, 32 miles to the west. As the *Fremont Tribune* described the work in Nebraska, "only the best equipment was used—oak ties, the best American iron for rails, level grade, fills and ditching in the best of manner." Railroad cars moved by "a large and powerful" ferryboat across the meandering "Big Muddy" until it froze and then on a temporary wooden structure. In 1883 a high-level, heavy-duty steel, stone, and timber bridge opened under the auspices of the Missouri Valley & Blair Railway & Bridge Company. The Nebraska segment, which briefly flew the banner of the Northern Nebraska Air Line Rail Road, created a direct route between Sioux City and the Union Pacific transcontinental line.[36]

The SC&P was more than a well-positioned property. It swiftly captured traffic from the slow-moving steamboats that served landings along the Missouri River south of Sioux City, and it tapped potentially productive agricultural territory. Yet the area traversed by the new railroad could not immediately generate substantial freight and passenger business, a drawback mitigated somewhat by a land grant awarded upon the project. When Congress passed the Pacific Railway bill in 1862, it expected the Union Pacific Railroad to build a branch to or from Sioux City. But two years later it decided not to burden the struggling transcontinental road with an extension into northwestern Iowa. Lawmakers offered to provide public lands to any railroad that undertook the project just as they had promised the Union Pacific; thus the SC&P received 42,500 acres of land in Iowa. The federal government also repeated its commitment in the Act of 1862 by making a loan of 6 percent, 30-year bonds to the extent of $16,000 per mile of line constructed between Fremont and Sioux City. These securities comprised a first mortgage on the property.[37]

Backers of the SC&P wisely took control of the mostly "paper" Northern Nebraska Air Line that had planned to link the Missouri River near De Soto with Fremont. The most attractive feature of this local line was 75 sections of land (48,000 acres) given it by the state of Nebraska. This largess rewarded legislators from along the projected line who had backed the successful effort to move the capital from Omaha to Lincoln. Washington County (De Soto) also issued bonds in the amount of $75,000.[38]

Even with a good location, a promising region, and substantial public assistance, the SC&P failed to make money. The railroad was hurt by the hard times of the 1870s, which greatly depressed the real estate market and commerce generally, and it could not generate enough through and local traffic. The SC&P lost its monopoly in the Sioux City market when the Iowa Falls & Sioux City Railroad, initially attached to the Dubuque & Pacific Railroad and ultimately absorbed by the Illinois Central, opened a trans-Iowa line between Dubuque and Sioux City in mid-1870. John Blair, the ubiquitous investor, incidentally held a substantial interest in the Iowa Falls & Sioux City project. The financial pressures on the SC&P forced the Iowa Leased Lines to assist it in paying interest on its bonds. This shortage of cash explains why an independent bridge company, a cooperative venture of the Iowa Leased Lines, North Western, and SC&P, spanned the Missouri River. When the North Western acquired the Blair roads, it obtained the equity the Iowa Leased Lines had in the SC&P, namely, more than 90 percent of its common stock.[39]

The Fremont, Elkhorn & Missouri Valley, the other Blair Road affiliate, had developed into a much larger property. It was approximately three times the length of the Sioux City & Pacific at the time of the sale in 1884. The Elkhorn Road was not designed to be a feeder, rather the initial backers of the FE&MV fantasized about building across the northern part of the newly admitted state of Nebraska, and then westward to a possible junction with the Central Pacific at Ogden in Utah Territory, thus roughly paralleling the Union Pacific. If they failed in reaching that objective, the road's advocates hoped to extend the line approximately 200 miles northwest to the confluence of the Missouri and Niobrara rivers. With that water connection it "will carry trade of Montana and Idaho away from Sioux City and give it to her southern neighbors." One supporter even thought about a line "reaching from the Niobrara [River] and prairies of the north, to the Gulf of Mexico in the south." But in 1874 the electrifying news came that gold had been discovered in the Black Hills of Dakota Territory, and that region became part of the scheme. During the first decade of its existence, however, the FE&MV did not become much more than a shortline wandering across the prairies northwest of its interchange with the SC&P at Fremont. Between 1869 and 1878 the company constructed only a 52-two mile line from Fremont to Wisner, Nebraska.[40]

The genesis of the "Elkhorn Route" came from among civic boosters in Fremont, Nebraska. The project was spearheaded by Robert Kettle and several fellow businessmen. Their community, which claimed only 1,195 residents in 1870 (the population grew to 3,013 by 1880), enjoyed access to both the SC&P and Union Pacific railroads, but like most every "burg" in the country, it was not content with the status quo. More railroads, it was believed, meant a bright future, and progress meant growth, growth in population and real estate values.[41]

The plan for the new Fremont-based carrier took a major step forward on January 20, 1869, with formal organization of the company. Promoters intended to move quickly into the largely empty lands north and west of Fremont, which entailed building through the broad valley of the Elkhorn River, described as "one of the loveliest [and] richest . . . regions of the State." The task was not considered to be either too difficult or excessively expensive.[42]

Backers of the Elkhorn Route had good reason to be sanguine about their undertaking. Not only was the economy healthy and the population steadily increasing, but government was likely to assist their cause. Nebraska lawmakers energized the evolving railroad when they passed the Land Grant Act of 1869. Under this statute the state would award 20,000 acres of land for every 10-mile segment of new construction. No company could receive more than 100,000 acres, however, and a special board would be required to inspect the construction before state officials would transfer land titles.[43]

When railroads built through lightly populated areas, promoters often demanded, or at least expected, direct local financial assistance. Such minor subdivisions as towns and townships, and especially counties, would vote special bond subsidies to help finance construction within their jurisdictions. Communities and individuals also might donate real estate for the right-of-way, station sites, and related support facilities. A major commitment came from potential patrons on November 4, 1869, when voters of Dodge County (Fremont) overwhelmingly endorsed a bond issue of $120,000. When the results of the balloting became known, an impromptu celebration ensued. Fremont residents fervently believed that their hometown would become "the railroad center of Nebraska." If it did not develop into a second Chicago, it would surely be the "Indianapolis of the West."[44]

The favorable outcome in Dodge County was a harbinger of further bond victories. By the time the FE&MV officially joined the North Western system in 1903, it had received $660,000 in bonds from local taxing authorities. This direct funding invigorated the road and gave communities their essential rail connections.[45]

Proponents of the Elkhorn Route concluded that the railroad required much more money than local governments in a frontier region could possibly provide. The stock subscription drives also seemed destined to fall short of financial needs. In the autumn of 1869, Robert Kettle, who represented the incorporators, asked John Blair for assistance. Because of Blair's ties to the SC&P, he was known and respected. Given assurances that voters of Dodge County would provide start-up capital and aware of the excellent prospects for state lands, Blair and his associates, who included the wealthy Oakes Ames and William Glidden, agreed to participate. The SC&P would soon lease the developing road. The presence of Blair contributed enormously to the emergence of the FE&MV.[46]

Buoyed by the Dodge County bond vote, construction began the day after the election. John Blair encouraged this work as he wanted at least 10 miles completed so the company could receive its first state land. If these pieces of real estate were acquired by spring, the FE&MV could expect to earn better retail prices before the growing season, bolstering the corporate treasury. While the frozen ground made grading difficult, it was done with dispatch, and tracklayers hurriedly finished their work. On New Year's Day 1870 a modest ceremony took place at the end-of-track site called Maple Creek. Robert Kettle spoke to the gathering and helped to drive in the final spikes. The high point of the celebration came when officials invited a Native American from the crowd to join the spike pounding. "The Indian tried to do so [with a maul] but missed the spike entirely, but then he took out his tomahawk and gave it a few taps."[47]

"A few taps" symbolized the immediate future of the Elkhorn Route. The company finished another 25 miles between Maple Creek (later Nickerson) and West Point in 1870, financed in part by a $100,000 bond issue from Cuming County. During the following year, the road reached Wisner, 17 miles to the northwest and 52 miles from Fremont. This community, developed by FE&MV affiliate Elkhorn Land and Town Lot Company, honored S. P. Wisner, the road's attorney and lobbyist, a common naming practice when railroads created trackside settlements.[48]

The railroad stalled at Wisner until the national economy and local agricultural conditions improved. Not only did the Panic of 1873 stymie railroad building, but a drought on the Central Plains in 1873 dried up most of the field crops. Then a biblical-like invasion of grasshoppers stripped the greenery bare during the late summer of 1874. As a resident from West Point described an aspect of that calamity: "Much to my surprise, I found what stopped the [FE&MV] train was a cloud of grasshoppers. They covered the rails and the engine. As their wings and bodies were crushed, the slippery mass solidified and it could only be removed with chisels and hard labor." Unfortunately, drought and grasshoppers continued to menace plains agriculturalists through 1876. These adversities hardly put Nebraskans in an expansive mood. When people scrawled "Eaten out by grasshoppers, Going back East to live with the wife's folks" on the ragged covers of their wagons, the FE&MV understandably waited for better times to resume construction. The company's having received its allotment of state lands, some 97,546 acres, did not mean economic salvation. The road found it nearly impossible to sell the real estate at satisfactory prices.[49]

Another factor that adversely affected expansion was the negative image some residents held of railroad projects. A backlash of sorts occurred in northern Nebraska when the Covington, Columbus & Black Hills Railroad (CC&BH) failed to become much more than a "hot air" proposition. The company's promoters were excessively optimistic; they planned to create a narrow-gauge (3' 6") road from Covington, Nebraska, located on the west bank of the Missouri River opposite Sioux City, Iowa, to the Black Hills. They also projected a branch southward to Columbus, Nebraska, and a connection with the main line of the Union Pacific. Although the CC&BH finished 26 miles of track between Covington and Ponca, seat of Dixon County, in 1876, it never added another mile. Voters of Knox County, on the route surveyed west of Sioux City, approved a handsome bond subsidy, but for a time the empty promises of the CC&BH poisoned receptivity area residents might have had toward more financial aid for other railroads.[50]

Even though the CC&BH fiasco damaged the mid-1870s efforts by the Elkhorn Route to obtain additional public funds, the road profited from the inability of the narrow-gauge company to compete in northern Nebraska and western Dakota. As economic conditions improved, railroad-starved settlers renewed their interest in the projected course of the FE&MV, and they backed more subsidies. Both Stanton County and Stanton, the county seat, for example, endorsed bonds for the railroad in 1878. Residents grasped the argument advanced by a company official: "We cannot afford to extend much in advance of population and production but if the people think they can promote their interests by aiding us to build sooner than we otherwise could, let them say so and we will give them a railroad and a depot." Fortunately for those who wanted railroad service, this was not an iron-clad rule.[51]

Construction resumed in 1879 when the Elkhorn Route completed its longest addition ever, 59 miles between Wisner and Oakdale. The line, however, avoided Norfolk, the major metropolis of the region. This seemingly odd decision reflected the company's intent to punish residents for failing to contribute bond money and for the unwillingness of Norfolk officials to donate a parcel of land, 250 by 2,000 feet, for a rail yard. Instead the FE&MV passed within a mile of this Madison County community and placed its depot "one and one-half mile south of town with the intention of building up a point of stock and produce shipment that would ruin the town." Presumably the plan was to profit from the creation of this rival settlement, appropriately named South Norfolk.[52]

The scheme failed to develop as intended. When the Omaha, Niobrara & Black Hills Railroad (ON&BH), an affiliate of the Union Pacific, reached Norfolk from the south in 1880, its impending arrival forced the Elkhorn Route to rethink the issue of service to the Madison County community. The FE&MV did not want to lose any more business to the ON&BH, so it pushed an extension, the Niobrara branch, northward through Norfolk toward the Missouri River. The first segment of this feeder, 32 miles northwest of Norfolk Junction (Norfolk), opened in 1880. The lines of the FE&MV, advancing in two directions from Madison County, did discourage further building by the ON&BH, and the Blair road realized a virtual rail monopoly in northern Nebraska. The only competitor of note appeared in 1890, when the Nebraska & Western Railroad, the self-proclaimed "Pacific Short Line," built 130 miles directly west of Covington (Sioux City) to O'Neill, Nebraska. While originally a local company, the property soon passed into the hands of the Great Northern and later the Burlington.[53]

The Elkhorn Route kept advancing northwestward. Most of this construction was financed by the company through long-term first mortgage bonds and common stock. After all, the route was often being built ahead of major settlements, and important local subsidies were impossible to obtain. Although efforts in 1880 were focused on the Niobrara branch, the main line reached Neligh, seat of Antelope County, five miles northwest of Oakdale. More hurried building took place in 1881. The Niobrara branch moved forward 10 miles from Plainview, in Pierce County, to Creighton, seat of Knox County, and the main line reached Long Pine, Brown County, 98 miles from Neligh. Construction slowed the following year, but the company extended the main line from Long Pine to Thatcher, near Fort Niobrara and Valentine, in Cherry County, 49 miles. Tracklayers connected Thatcher with Valentine, a six-mile link, in 1883.[54]

By the time the Elkhorn Road entered the orbit of the North Western, the property was more than an insignificant shortline. Its 311 miles of track served a thriving livestock trade and ever more acres of hard spring wheat ("Turkey Red") and prairie hay. Ranchers in Knox and Pierce counties, located on the Niobrara branch, for example, produced an estimated three-quarters of a million head of cattle in 1880. In the early 1880s abundant rainfall, good crops, and strong commodity prices sent settlers streaming into the region. Traffic increased as the new residents required a vast range of processed and manufactured goods, and their demand for lumber seemed almost limitless.[55]

Nevertheless the balance sheet of the Elkhorn Route was disappointing. The more the railroad grew, the more revenues it generated, but because of high operating expenses, profits remained small. On the eve of the North Western takeover, gross earnings totaled $294,377, and the net, after deductions for interest payments, stood at only $45,786. While land sales and local subsidies were important, they hardly compensated for what officials considered to be "disappointing" earnings from freight and passenger traffic. The company had pushed through a thinly populated country, a dramatically different situation from what the

Galena & Chicago Union had done a quarter of a century before in Illinois.[56]

Several factors explain the North Western's involvement with the Elkhorn Route. The weak earnings of the SC&P and the FE&MV partially account for their sale. Moreover, John Blair had largely completed his agenda: he liked to develop a frontier pike, promote townsites, and dispose of land, and then sell or lease the railroad to another company. By the mid-1880s Blair had achieved the status of senior citizen, and it was time to consider retirement or at least a less-strenuous business life. He also had developed a close relationship with North Western management, particularly Marvin Hughitt. And Hughitt, who wished to increase the North Western's presence on the Great Plains, recognized the potential value of the Blair holdings. At the same time Hughitt fully understood their less-than-stellar financial performance and that "the Blair system is hardly up to the standard condition of the North Western."[57]

The decision by the North Western to acquire the Elkhorn Route was directly related to problems within the Iowa Pool as well. This "gentlemen's agreement," declining for some time, fell apart in 1884. Its principals, the Burlington, North Western, and Rock Island, had become less willing to refrain from invading the territory of the others. Even had the pool continued, the North Western would hardly have wanted to share its trans-Missouri traffic. "We cannot in the justice of our shareholders," wrote Hughitt, "admit the claim of any company to share in the advantages to be derived from the construction of those systems simply because they are west of the River."[58]

The collapse of the Iowa Pool meant that the jostling railroads could expand whenever and wherever they pleased. While Hughitt deplored "the needless paralleling of existing systems," he logically concluded that self-defense of his company was the practical policy. Hughitt and his fellow executives fumed when they learned in late 1883 that the Burlington planned to create the Chicago, Burlington & Northern Railroad, which would establish a rival line between Chicago and the Twin Cities. This could potentially sap the North Western of its lucrative interchange traffic, including cars from the newly completed Northern Pacific, the nation's first northern transcontinental artery. Unhappiness with the Burlington and its aggressive leader, Charles Perkins, explains why the North Western would soon spin a web of rails in Nebraska under the aegis of the FE&MV. The North Western not only pushed the FE&MV into the Black Hills and Wyoming but sent appendages south of the Platte River, a clear intrusion into Burlington domain.[59]

The desire to expand in the trans-Missouri West and ample financial resources permitted the main line of the Elkhorn Route to move forward rapidly toward its new destinations. Track reached the Dawes County seat of Chadron, near the Wyoming and Dakota border in 1885, a distance of 137 miles from Valentine, the previous terminus. That same year witnessed the opening of a line into the southern portion of the Black Hills. Completion of 56 miles between Chadron and Buffalo Gap, Dakota Territory, made the FE&MV the first trunk railway in that region. During the construction season of 1886, what was called the "main stem" advanced from Dakota Junction, Nebraska, five miles northwest of Chadron, to the Wyoming border, a distance of 58 miles. An affiliated company, the Wyoming Central Railway, with a charter from the Territory of Wyoming, built 77 miles to Douglas in 1886; 29 miles to Glen Rock a year later; and then 25 miles to the east-central commercial center of Casper in 1888. Rumors spread that the Wyoming Central was headed toward either Ogden or the Yellowstone Park country, but officials in Chicago had not decided on a route, if any, west of Casper.[60]

In 1886 tracks entered the heart of the Black Hills. Workers installed the 48 miles from Buffalo Gap to Rapid City, Dakota Territory, the major city of the region. The arrival of the first train of the Elkhorn Route into Rapid City prompted the local newspaper editor to publish a front page story that recounted this momentous occasion: "On Sunday [July 4] large numbers of people came in, and all Sunday night and early Monday they kept coming. It seemed as if the population of our neighboring towns had locked their doors and came en masse to rejoice with us in our prosperity." The article added: "The prosperity of Rapid City is the prosperity of the Hills, and in all the huge crowd assembled here on Monday was not one mind so narrow, one heart so selfish as to begrudge to our people the eminent satisfaction shown on every hand." The future of this "Hills" community seemed bright, indeed.[61]

The presence of Elkhorn Route trains in the Black Hills preceded by about four years the first of two competitors, the Burlington and the Milwaukee Road. While the latter did not reach Rapid City until 1907, the former arrived in the area at the end of 1889. The Burlington line from Alliance in northwestern Nebraska, somewhat parallel to the FE&MV but more to the south, sliced through the southwestern corner of South Dakota (a state after November 2, 1889) and proceeded northwestward into Wyoming.[62]

The North Western and the Burlington eagerly sought to exploit the freight and passenger business of the Black Hills. By the late 1880s the area produced minerals, primarily gold and coal, and lumber from extensive stands of spruce and pine forests. Prospects for shipments of livestock and hay also looked encouraging. There was a potential for tourism, particularly at Hot Springs in the southern hills. Both roads reacted similarly; they either built or cobbled together a network of lines and appendages.[63]

The North Western, through the Elkhorn Route, led the way with improved transportation to the region. Tracks of the FE&MV extended northward from Rapid City to Whitewood, 37 miles, in 1887, and three years later they reached Belle Fourche, another 21 miles to the north. The road opened two important feeders in 1890, one 14 miles between Buffalo Gap and Hot Springs and another nine miles from Whitewood to Deadwood, in the heart of the mining district. The parent North Western, namely Hughitt, soon decided to stop building standard-gauge trackage to serve those mines and to use 3' 0" gauge instead. During the summer of 1891 the FE&MV finished about 18 miles of narrow-gauge track from Deadwood south and west into the Ruby Basin. Later, in 1902, a three-mile dual-gauge spur connected Blacktail Junction, near Deadwood, to Lead, location of the Homestake Mine, the richest gold operation on the continent. These narrow-gauge extensions were assumed to be cheaper to build and operate than conventional ones in this rough terrain, a dubious conclusion. Similar "tap" lines, however, had already been in service in the Hills for some time. The strategy of the rival Burlington had been to snap up two previously independent slim-width roads—the Black Hills & Fort Pierre Railroad, which had operated its first train between Lead and Woodville in 1881, and the Deadwood Central Railroad, which opened from Deadwood to Lead in 1889.[64]

Entry into the Black Hills and the monotonous high plains of Wyoming largely satisfied the North Western management's strategy of creating a network of feeder and secondary lines to "strengthen our primary routes." The company had not finished its network of branches in Nebraska, however. An important addition to the subsidiary Elkhorn Route came in 1886 when a line was installed west of Scribner to Lindsay, 61 miles, and the following year westward from Lindsay to Albion and north to Oakdale, 53 miles. This cutoff, which connected with the main artery at Scribner and Oakdale, largely a southern parallel route, served an expanding agricultural area. Even though the FE&MV failed to receive bond money from the several counties it traversed, the investment was sound. The territory was "one of the most fertile regions of Nebraska in which many settlers had already made their homes." Furthermore, the North Western characteristically wanted to discourage competitors from this part of Nebraska. Except for a branch the Union Pacific built south from Albion to a main-line connection at Columbus, the plan succeeded.[65]

The company did not ignore the 42-mile Niobrara branch. It added another 12 miles in Knox County between Creighton and Verdigre in 1888. Because construction was much more expensive than nearly anywhere in the state, due to the roughly broken country in the vicinity, and the broad and shifting Niobrara River had to be spanned, further work was halted until 1902. The FE&MV then built northwesterly 69 miles beyond Verdigre to Bonesteel, South Dakota.[66]

While leaders of the Burlington presumably cared little about the cutoff between Scribner and Oakdale or the Niobrara appendage, they felt differently about another project in 1886, construction of the 52-mile Lincoln line. The Elkhorn Route, aided by bond money from Lancaster County (Lincoln), rapidly staked, graded,

To tap traffic from the Homestake Mine at Lead, S.Dak., the Fremont, Elkhorn & Missouri Valley Railroad constructed a three-mile mixed-gauge spur in 1902 between Gayville and Lead. Hourly trains began running through Deadwood Gulch (pictured at right), which is between Deadwood and Lead, in the fall of that year. (North Western/Union Pacific)

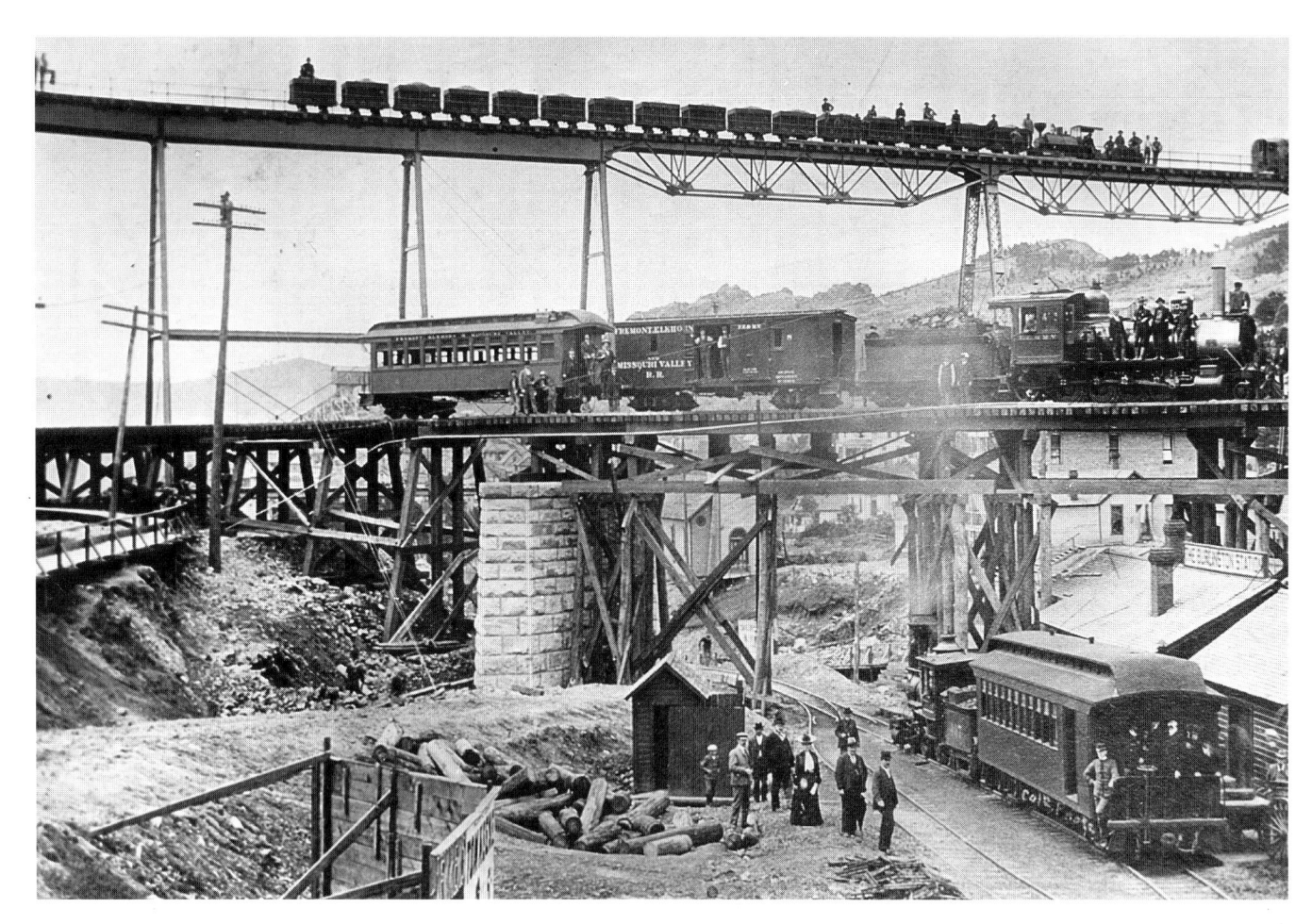

Mining activities in the Black Hills necessitated a maze of railroad facilities. This circa 1900 photograph at Lead shows the industrial trackage of the Homestake Mine at the top, the Fremont, Elkhorn & Missouri Valley Railroad in the middle, and the Chicago, Burlington & Quincy Railroad at the bottom. The two common carriers used narrow-gauge track. (North Western/Union Pacific)

and installed a branch south from Fremont through Wahoo to the Nebraska capital, a focal point of Burlington operations in the state. The principal challenges for the FE&MV were erecting a bridge over the shallow but treacherous Platte River near Fremont and redesigning a nearby freight yard. Fortunately the company could share facilities in Lincoln with another new arrival, Jay Gould's Missouri Pacific.[67]

Lincoln was not the only main-line community on the Burlington where the Elkhorn Route competed. The company pushed a 28-mile extension in 1887 from Arlington, eight miles east of Fremont on the SC&P, southward to Omaha. It also built a 10-mile arm from near Irvington, in the Omaha area, to connect with the stockyards and meat-packing plants of South Omaha.[68]

The Omaha and South Omaha lines were well-conceived additions. The FE&MV secured a second connection with the North Western to Chicago; it linked up with another affiliate, the Omaha Road (see chapter 4), in the rapidly growing city of Omaha (140,452 residents in 1890). And the new construction forged a convenient route for the marketing of livestock from the range lands of Nebraska, South Dakota, and Wyoming. The immense stock-gathering facilities and the packing district at South Omaha offered great economic promise. This municipality, begun in 1884 under the auspices of the South Omaha Land Company, had truly become the "Magic City" of its promoters' claims; South Omaha claimed more than 10,000 inhabitants by 1890. The town's yards could handle thousands of cattle daily, and Cudahay Packing Company, Geo. H. Hammond & Company, Omaha Packing Company, and Swift & Company, the local "Big Four," emerged as leading employers.[69]

Expansion south of the Platte River did not stop with extensions to Lincoln and Omaha. The Elkhorn Route used the Platte River bridge when it built an 120-mile branch from near Fremont (Platte River Junction) southwest to Hastings, seat of Adams County. This line, which was finished in October 1887, took advantage of local subsidies and became the second railroad in several thriving farming communities, including David City, Harvard, and York. Some observers thought that this addition might be a springboard for a line to Denver, Colorado, or some other Rocky Mountain or western terminus. But management denied this, publicly commenting that such an extension would face head-on competition from the recently opened Burlington route to Denver.[70]

The final foray into the heartland of the Burlington in Nebraska was a 115-mile branch from Linwood, 17 miles west of Fremont, generally in a southerly direction to Superior, Nebraska, located on the border with Kansas. The first 78 miles of track between Linwood and Geneva opened in 1887, and the remaining 47 miles from Geneva to Superior were completed the next year. Superior was turning into a minor railroad center; in addition to the FE&MV, the Burlington, Missouri Pacific, and Santa Fe served this Nuckolls County community. The North Western eventually forged a brisk traffic interchange with the friendly Santa Fe.[71]

As with the Hastings branch the trackage to Superior was thought by some to be merely the first part of a longer line, in this case perhaps one that would eventually reach Garden City or Wichita, Kansas, or even Oklahoma and Texas. Resembling the extension to Hastings, the Superior line funneled agricultural goods, particularly grain and livestock, to regional markets.[72]

The presence of the Elkhorn Route in so many Nebraska communities was widely welcomed. Residents felt that they needed these ribbons of steel to ensure their involvement in commercial agriculture. When the FE&MV extended into the South Platte Country, the public believed that it would gain more than greater convenience in transportation: another railroad would undoubtedly foster competitive rates. Similarly by the 1880s a perception prevailed that the state's two principal carriers, the Burlington and Union Pacific, were too powerful and that they had become a political "ring." Their officers, many thought, wielded much influence in the election of the two United States senators; there was allegedly a "Burlington man" and a "Union Pacific man." Some newspaper editors, imbued with a reform spirit, named the FE&MV the "people's railroad," and others concurred.[73]

Public aid came to the Elkhorn Route as a result. The total reached $660,000 by the late 1880s. When the Hastings and Superior lines were built, various towns and townships voted bond money. The citizens of Hastings, for example, contributed $60,000 to attract the North Western affiliate. The only difference in this support was that it flowed largely from localized units instead of from counties as had earlier been common. Individuals who lived in sections of a county missed by a projected rail line grumbled about *their* tax dollars supporting betterments that they could not fully enjoy. In an age of horse transport and poor public roads a rural resident often could not reach a railroad a dozen or so miles away, while residents of a town or township through which a rail line passed had no such problem.[74]

By the 1870s the Dakota Territory, like the state of Nebraska, attracted widespread public interest. While the Black Hills gold rush initially captured newspaper headlines, the territory's agricultural potential attracted the attention of many. Farmers started to arrive in large numbers, mostly repeating the pattern of populating sections of Nebraska. Settlers earlier had been discouraged by the presence of roaming Native Americans, thought by most whites to be "bloodthirsty savages" and "red devils." Settlement too was hindered by the lack of adequate long-distance transportation except on those few streams that could accommodate shallow-draft steamboats. Moreover, good land opportunities existed elsewhere, and reports of drought and grasshoppers dampened enthusiasm. Agricultural settlement until 1878 had been generally confined to the region along the border with Iowa and Minnesota, scene of a minor land rush between 1868 and 1873.[75]

Much of the eastern half of present-day South Dakota experienced the "Great Dakota Boom" that lasted from 1878 until 1887. One of the monumental land-development events in American history, it was the result of a combination of factors: deceptively abundant rainfall, good soil, a decline of the "Indian problem," disappearance of free or inexpensive lands elsewhere, increasing demands for wheat, better farm implements, and even improved milling techniques. The iron horse, of course, facilitated this development and was warmly welcomed. Locomotive whistles were "the sweetest music a resident of the broad prairies . . . could hear," remarked a territorial official. Or as the editor of the *Britton Daylight* put it: "About noon the construction train came thundering in while the old locomotive whistled out the signal and glad tidings of its approach, casting joy and delight into the very receptacles of our hearts." No wonder a Dakotan exclaimed: "Crops, ideas, people, fortunes, and everything else grow so vast that it makes a down-easter's head swim like a fishing cork in a maelstrom." For roughly a decade thousands of pioneers found this vast expanse of prairie country to their liking. The population of southeastern South Dakota soared from approximately 80,000 in 1880 to about 250,000 five years later. Farmers' shacks and what novelist Hamlin Garland called those "flimsy little wooden towns" became ubiquitous.[76]

The North Western entered Dakota (South Dakota) in 1873. In September of that year the affiliate Winona & St. Peter completed a 154-mile extension from New Ulm, Minnesota, to Lake Kampeska, Codington County, Dakota. This trackage opened only a few months after the state's first pike, the locally sponsored Dakota Southern Railroad, completed a 61-mile link between Sioux City, Iowa, and Yankton, the territorial capital. Although the Lake Kampeska line allowed the W&StP to qualify for a land grant, the company's western section, which "ran only through buffalo country," soon became streaks of rust. The Panic of 1873 and the ensuing depression made it uneconomical to operate in Dakota. With the return of better times after 1877, however, the W&StP reconstructed the track from Gary, on the Dakota-Minnesota border, to Watertown (Lake Kampeska).[77]

The reopening of the 35 miles between Gary and Watertown was a prelude to what became a 724-mile building spree in Dakota. This developmental mileage proliferated like milkweed. Construction coincided almost exactly with the Great Dakota Boom, and it was closely supervised by Marvin Hughitt. After visiting the territory in the late 1870s, he concluded that "it was good business to extend railroads across [open land] . . . as an inducement to settlement." Although branch lines were always something of a speculation, Hughitt was right. The opening of the main core of the Dakota Central Railway, a newly formed subsidiary that the W&StP eventually absorbed, created a leading route into the region. Almost immediately thousands of settlers surged onto the prairies. Unlike the W&StP

the Dakota Central did not receive public lands to help offset the cost of construction. The North Western financed the new mileage through bond and stock issues. Its Western Town Lot Company developed scores of communities, often profitably.[78]

Even without land grants the federal government aided the ventures of the North Western in Dakota, just as it had done elsewhere in the trans-Mississippi West. The new residents who farmed often did so on free public acres, ones that Washington officials had acquired from Native Americans in a series of land cessions between 1858 and 1873. Settlers usually qualified for quarter sections (160 acres) under provisions of the Homestead Act of 1862. The Timber Culture Act of 1873 gave farmers an additional quarter section if they planted 40 acres of trees and tended them for 10 years. Specifically, the act was designed to alter the climate of the "Great American Desert"; proponents optimistically argued that groves of trees would reduce winds, attract more rainfall, and provide fuel and building materials.[79]

Surveyors, graders, and tracklayers energetically immersed themselves in their specialized assignments in 1879. That year the Chicago & Dakota Railway, an affiliate of the W&StP, built some 46 miles from Tracy, Minnesota, on the New Ulm to Watertown line, to the Dakota border. Tracy became the starting point for the Dakota extension: a route could be pushed directly westward across the territory to Deadwood, a path to the Black Hills that would bisect the best lands east of the Missouri River.[80]

The commercial and trade press was filled with reports during the early 1880s of building activities in eastern Dakota. The 25-mile line from the Minnesota border to Volga, in Brookings County, opened in 1879, and in 1880 this trackage reached Pierre, the future state capital, a distance of 185 miles. But the line stalled at this terminus on the east bank of the Missouri for 25 years. Although the *Railroad Gazette* reported in early 1881 that the "company is putting in a winter bridge over the Missouri at Pierre, Dak., for the purpose of carrying across material for the extension to the Black Hills, on which work will be resumed in the spring," nothing happened except for a survey. The problem involved the Great Sioux Reservation between the Missouri River and the Black Hills. While persistent efforts made by the North Western and its principal rival in South Dakota, the Milwaukee Road, resulted in the opening of the Indian lands between the Cheyenne and White rivers in 1890, this was a hollow victory; the Great Dakota Boom had largely ended. The North Western could have surely won an easement for its nearly 170 miles of track through Sioux country just as the Elkhorn Route had done in scattered areas of northwestern

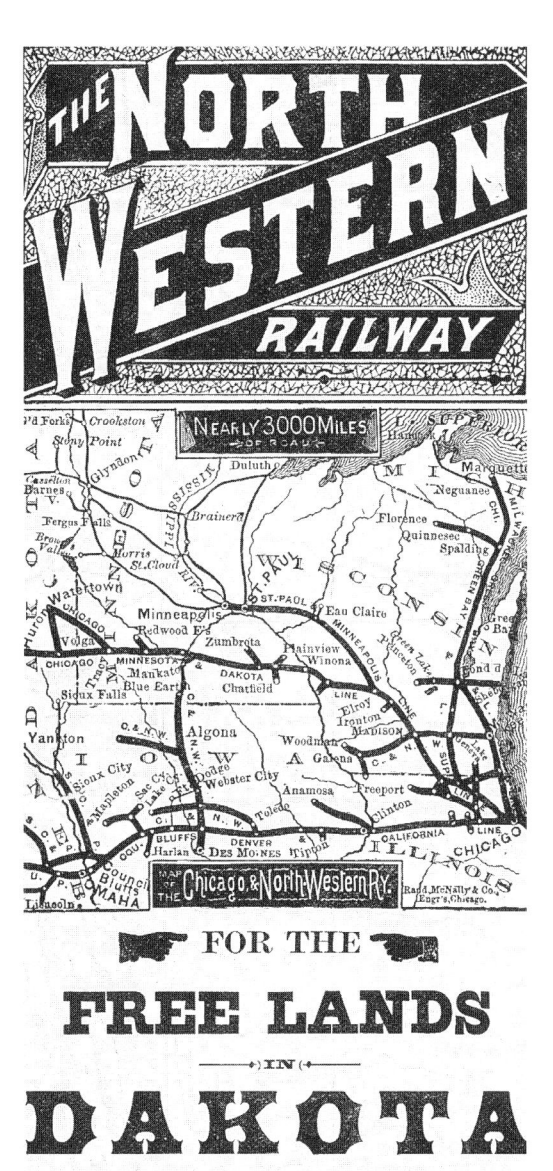

The North Western actively promoted Dakota during the great land boom of the early 1880s. The company public timetable for April 20, 1882, told readers of real estate opportunities in the territory. (Author's collection)

Nebraska about the same time, but Hughitt concluded that traffic to and from the Hills would not justify the cost. The FE&MV's heading toward the region from Nebraska also influenced the decision not to built west of the Missouri River. Furthermore, the railroad could make direct connections with the Northwestern Express and Transportation Company, a stage line, for the Hills. With through cars between Chicago and Pierre, a traveler encountered only one change between Chicago and Deadwood for this 950-mile journey.[81]

While the Dakota Central never penetrated the West River country, it added connectors and branches in the eastern part of the territory. In 1881 the company built 88 miles northward through the James (Dakota) River valley from west of Huron on the main stem to Ordway in Brown County. The Dakota Central added five miles a year later when it reached Columbia, 15 miles north of Aberdeen. In 1886 the line was extended to Oakes in Dickey County (North Dakota) and an interchange with a branch of the Northern Pacific. This 39-mile segment formed a through route to Jamestown and Bismarck, the territorial capital from 1883 to 1889. Speculation followed that the Dakota Central would push beyond Oakes to Bismarck, thus providing another but potentially better connection with the Northern Pacific and tapping additional wheat lands.[82]

Another connector line nearly as long opened in 1883. The Dakota Central installed 125 miles of track between Hawarden, Iowa, on the Big Sioux River and an end point of the Toledo & North Western, and Iroquois, Dakota, 18 miles east of Huron. This southeast-to-northwest diagonal provided the North Western with a convenient route from Chicago to the Northern Plains and to the Pacific Northwest via a connection with the Northern Pacific at Oakes.[83]

The secondary branches put down by the Dakota Central resembled others along the system; they either paralleled a more important route or cut through the hinterland in a perpendicular fashion. During the 1882 building season the company added a line 71 miles west of Watertown to Redfield, seat of Spink County and a community already served by the Ordway branch. The next year a 44-mile line linked Watertown with the Tracy-Pierre main stem at Castlewood Junction, a few miles west of Brookings. It served fertile lands along the valley of the Big Sioux River. In 1885 a 28-mile spur left the Hawarden-Iroqouis line at Centerville, Turner County, for Yankton. Contemporary reports suggested that this appendage would be "extended from Yankton westward up the Missouri [River]." Construction gangs in 1886 and 1887 built west of Redfield 33 miles to Faulkton, seat of Faulk County, and 43 miles to Gettysburg, seat of Potter County, near the Missouri River. The Watertown to Gettysburg line paralleled the main stem about 40 miles to the north. The final work done by the Dakota Central involved a 38-mile appendage that ran due north of Doland, a Spink County village 21 miles east of Redfield, through Verdon, end of track in 1886, to Groton, Brown County, which was reached the following year.[84]

The North Western through the Dakota Central was not alone in contributing to the Great Dakota Boom. The Milwaukee Road became even more involved in the territory; its network of lines exceeded 1,200 miles by 1887, including the pioneer Dakota Southern. The trackage tended to lie north and south of the Dakota Central. The major Milwaukee Road arteries in Dakota extended from Iowa through Canton and Mitchell to Chamberlain on the Missouri River; across southern Minnesota through Madison and Woonsocket; and from the Twin Cities through Aberdeen to near the Missouri River. The company's line from Sioux City through Mitchell to north of Aberdeen closely followed the Oakes branch of the Dakota Central.[85]

While the North Western and Milwaukee Road never came to physical blows over routings in Dakota, they caused each other to build for protection and equally to fight for every possible advantage. "Our lines in . . . South Dakota reflect our concern about the St. Paul [Milwaukee Road] during the construction period," reflected a North Western official in 1901. "With an exception or two, we did not over-build for the anticipated and real needs of the public." The Yankton branch of the Dakota Central, which clearly challenged the Milwaukee Road's domination of the southern part of the Territory, is probably the best illustration of unnecessary and even spiteful trackage.[86]

There were hard feelings when the Milwaukee Road outmaneuvered the North Western in the James River valley. Initially the Dakota Central expected to build what became the Oakes branch almost directly north from Huron. But the secretary of the interior set aside three townships of public land in Spink County on the projected route for a reservation for Sioux Chief Drifting Goose and his band. The company then altered its route about 10 miles west of the original survey. The plan for the proposed reservation was not carried out, but by then the line was under construction. An alert Milwaukee Road seized the opportunity to outflank its competitor. It constructed an "air line" south from Aberdeen to Redfield, and by being between the North Western and the river took "almost complete control of the district which the C&NW managers had intended to occupy." A compromise might have been possible in later years, preventing these closely spaced tracks. But the idea of two railroads sharing a common line was an anathema to industry leaders during this era. The North Western, nonetheless, mostly held its own against the Milwaukee Road. The fact that Pierre rather than Mitchell, on the Milwaukee, became the state capital in 1889 attests to the power and skills of the Hughitt road.[87]

The North Western not only encountered the rivalry of the Milwaukee Road, it also faced incursions by the "Manitoba." Officially the St. Paul, Minneapolis & Manitoba Railway, renamed the Great Northern Railway in February 1890, and led by James Jerome Hill, this company and this man caused Marvin Hughitt and the North Western considerable grief in Dakota during the late 1880s. Although the two executives easily squelched the independent Duluth, Huron & Denver Railway, which seemed on the verge of building from Sauk Center, Minnesota, southwestward into east-central South Dakota, the territories of both the Manitoba and North Western, Hill approved construction into the North Western's service area of three heavy-duty lines: from Breckenridge, Minnesota, to Aberdeen; from Benson, Minnesota, to Watertown and Huron; from Willmar, Minnesota, to Sioux Falls. When Hughitt learned in July 1886 that the Manitoba planned to survey a route to Watertown, he told Hill: "Whatever the future may develope [sic] I shall have the personal and official satisfaction of having done all I could to urge upon you not to extend your system of roads . . . [and] to antagonize good neighbors and friends. You have all of Minnesota, north of the parallel of Minneapolis into which to expand your system. It is a large and valuable field, and should, I think content your people." And he added, "The extension of your lines north-ward and west-ward of that parallel is natural and makes your system homogeneous and united, and you will pardon my opinion, but I believe you will have a better property if you confine your operations to that field, then to build south-westerly thereof, into territory already quite well supplied with railway facilities." Hughitt's argument failed to impress Hill, and the Manitoba drained business that the North Western had counted on from its Dakota lines.[88]

The timing of the construction of the rail network in Dakota Territory was excellent. The North Western took considerable risk with this ambitious expansion; it constructed track mostly ahead of substantial population. Yet the company was responding sensibly. "Where new territory is to be opened for settlement by new railroads, the roads should be built so as to bring in the settlers while they are coming," argued an industry expert in 1882. "They may be built too early, and lie in the wilderness, with rails rusting, till growth recommences; and they may be built too late, when the ground is preoccupied." Although the Winona & St. Peter extension to Lake Kempeska was certainly premature, the North Western made a commitment to expansion once the boom commenced. Moreover, it halted building when the economy soured at the end of the decade. A combination of events hardly made Dakota a place for profitable rail building: a severe winter during 1886–1887, which devastated the cattle industry on the northern range; steadily falling prices of wheat; and a widespread drought that began in 1887 and continued into the mid-1890s. By the end of the 1880s local agriculturalists found it difficult to cope with the heavy financial obligations that many had assumed so gladly during the years of prosperity. Still a reporter for the *New York Tribune*, who visited the region in 1889, concluded that "Dakota has been made by the railroads." No one really challenged the notion that the magic touch of a new railway promised a bright future for residents in the surrounding territory.[89]

On the eve of the worst economic depression in the American experience, the North Western made its last major acquisition of the waning century. The company purchased the 757-mile Milwaukee, Lake Shore & Western Railway (MLS&W), a well-positioned hauler of iron ore, lumber, and agricultural products in Wisconsin and the Upper Peninsula of Michigan. As did other medium-size carriers of the era, the MLS&W had evolved from a combination of predecessor roads and acquisitions.[90]

The core of the MLS&W, called the "Lake Shore Road," tangibly took shape in the early 1870s when several communities along Lake Michigan north of Milwaukee sought to improve transportation in the region. They bitterly resented plans of a Chicago, Milwaukee & St. Paul affiliate, the Milwaukee & Northern, to build on a north-south axis about 10 to 20 miles west of Lake Michigan between Milwaukee and Green Bay. Formation of the Milwaukee, Manitowoc & Green Bay Railroad in March 1870 became the response of the lakeshore towns of Manitowoc, Port Washington, and Sheboygan. This firm sought to join the places of its corporate title, and it did so with some success. During 1872 and 1873 the company completed a 74-mile line from Lake Shore Junction, a few miles north of Milwaukee and an interchange with the North Western, through Sheboygan and into Manitowoc. By the time of this construction the company renamed itself the Milwaukee, Lake Shore & Western Railroad.[91]

The Lake Shore was initially local in character. The physical plant resembled a branch rather than a main line. It was cheaply built and modestly equipped. Its leaders were mostly on-line businessmen and included Manitowoc lumber manufacturer Joseph Vilas, described as a "master organizer" who "displayed managerial abilities of a high order." The company relied heavily on financial assistance from grass-roots sources including $480,000 in public subsidies.[92]

A related and somewhat earlier property was the nearby Appleton & New London Railroad. Chartered in 1866, this firm proposed connecting Appleton, near the northern edge of Lake Winnebago, with the nearby village of New London. This venture remained a paper proposition until Vilas took charge about 1870. Aided by his considerable business acumen and tax support, the Appleton road decided to build not to New London but rather eastward to Manitowoc, 43 miles, in 1871 and 1872. It thus connected with Vilas's other interest, the Lake Shore Road.[93]

The Appleton & New London and the Lake Shore Road became largely one road by 1873. Yet the combination failed to energize growth, except for the opening in 1874 of a six-mile branch from Manitowoc to Two Rivers, another Manitowoc County lake port. Neither Green Bay nor any other long-distance destination materialized, even though the approximately 120-mile network connected Milwaukee with several important Badger State communities. The hard times that gripped the country adversely affected the Vilas lines, and their ledgers hemorrhaged red ink. Poor earnings led to a foreclosure sale on December 10, 1875, and reorganization as the Milwaukee, Lake Shore & Western Rail*way*, a company that formally fused together the assets of the Appleton and Lake Shore properties. While Vilas joined the board of the rehabilitated corporation, local control ended. The new Lake Shore Road was dominated by eastern financiers, headed by Frederick William Rhinelander, the Harvard-educated scion of a socially prominent New York family.[94]

Even with a restructured debt and stronger financial support the Lake Shore Road saw only modest betterments until the economy recovered. Just the earlier projected 20-mile connection between Appleton and New London, which handled its first train in 1876, came into existence. With better times President Rhinelander and his associates decided to build toward Lake Superior and to gain access to immense stands of white and Norway pine trees in the North Woods counties. While lumber production in the Great Lakes region declined precipitously after a peak during the early 1890s, there was plenty of wood to transport for a decade or so. Yields were often as much as 40,000 board feet an acre. Furthermore, leaders of the MLS&W firmly believed that the plow would follow the ax. As timber shipments declined, surely agricultural products would fill that void. The company misjudged the prospects for successful farming, however, as the soil was generally too thin and infertile.⁹⁵

The business projections did point to two sources of dependable earnings. The Rhinelander group recognized the enormous traffic potential of iron ore. If the railroad reached the rich mineral deposits of the Upper Peninsula, the mix of commodities hauled would be further strengthened. The road also found a way of filling its passenger coaches. "The company is giving especial attention this season to the excursion and picnic business from Milwaukee," noted a trade publication in 1879, "and is meeting with much success as the road reaches many pleasant places along the lake shore." The firm expanded this business after it reached attractive inland lakes and streams, and it erected a large hotel at Lake Gogebic, Michigan, which "proved very successful." The company perceived that scenery was also a natural resource.⁹⁶

The Lake Shore Road advanced slowly but steadily toward the projected terminus of Ashland. Construction parties installed track between New London and Clintonville, 16 miles, in 1878; Clintonville and Tigerton, 19 miles, in 1879; and Tigerton and Aniwa, 32 miles, in 1880. Also in 1880, a 24-mile branch was pushed westward from Eland Junction, between Tigerton and Aniwa, to Wausau, the Marathon County capital. Twelve years later the MLS&W extended this line southwestward 40 miles to Marshfield. Another appendage was installed about the time of the Wausau construction, a 23-mile branch from Hortonville, near New London, and was finished in 1880 to Oshkosh, a manufacturing center on the west shore of Lake Winnebago. Work continued in 1881 on the main stem toward Ashland. Between Aniwa and Summit Lake 26 miles were added; workers in 1882 and 1883 laid 86 miles from Summit Lake into Gogebic

In the early 1890s a construction gang installs a culvert along the emerging line of the Milwaukee, Lake Shore & Western Railroad in Marathon County, Wisc. Workers completed the 40-mile Marshfield-Wausau branch in 1892. (State Historical Society of Wisconsin)

The crew of a Milwaukee, Lake Shore & Western 4-4-0 locomotive pauses in 1884 with a pay train on a trestle over the Fox River at Appleton, Wisc. (State Historical Society of Wisconsin)

County, Michigan, site of vast quantities of iron ore. Then the final 81 miles were built in a mostly westerly direction to Ashland during the next two years. A developing seat of Ashland County with an 1880 population of only 951, Ashland was both a port on Lake Superior and an evolving railroad center. Once in Ashland, the company constructed giant timber and steel ore docks to serve the Michigan mines.[97]

The route structure of the MLS&W did not end with reaching Ashland, the pineries of the North Woods, and the Gogebic Range. By 1889 the company had developed a shorter line to Ashland and one that also served more timberlands. This 89-mile cutoff started in 1882 with a 16-mile line from Monico to Pelican Rapids (renamed Rhinelander in November 1882 to honor the MLS&W president) in Oneida County and later extended through Lac du Flambeau to Hurley, 39 miles east of Ashland on the original trackage.[98]

The MLS&W also acquired or built several minor appendages, mostly during the late 1880s, to reach additional stands of pines. The Wisconsin River Branch, for one, leased in 1888 and purchased a year later, ran from Pratt Junction, located between Summit Lake and Monico, westward through Langlade and Lincoln counties. Much of this trackage was laid in 1885 and 1886 by the Wolfe & Wisconsin Rivers Railroad, a company controlled by Oshkosh lumberman George Pratt; the project promoted the settlements of Harrison and Parrish.[99]

The Lake Shore Road did more than absorb the Appleton & New London; it took possession of an adjoining shortline with a pretentious name, the St. Paul Eastern Grand Trunk Railway (StPEGT). This 56-mile road connected Oconto, seat of Oconto County near the western shore of Green Bay, with Clintonville to the southwest and a tie-in with the MLS&W. While the StPEGT proposed to become a trans-Wisconsin line with an extension to Marinette, Michigan, it completed only 10 miles from Oconto to an interchange with the Milwaukee & Northern Railroad at Stiles Junction in 1882, several years after its incorporation. In 1884 tracks reached Clintonville when the MLS&W gained control. A subsidy of 200,000 acres of mostly timber land in Oconto and Shawano counties partially explains the modest success of the StPEGT. The road, which remained a leased property, became a viable branch for the MLS&W and later the North Western.[100]

The construction and acquisition strategies of the Lake Shore Road, coupled with steady physical improvements and better rolling stock, produced a favorable balance sheet. Gross earnings rose steadily: $315,943 in 1879, $2,317,802 in 1886, and $3,534,104 in 1891. The company consistently made a sizable annual profit, an amount that stood at $555,589 in 1891. Its debt structure was also reasonable.[101]

The North Western moved toward control of the Milwaukee, Lake Shore & Western in early 1891. The agreement between the two companies resulted in an exchange of 10 shares of North Western common for nine shares of

MLS&W preferred and four shares of North Western common for five of MLS&W common. This transaction began in December 1891, leading to the formal merger of the railroads. On September 1, 1893, the MLS&W ceased to exist. The former Lake Shore Road trackage became the Ashland Division of the North Western.[102]

The official explanation for the step taken by the North Western was not surprising. Marvin Hughitt told shareholders in the spring of 1892 that a "growing business, common to both roads, has been developed and built up at various points on the main lines in Eastern and North Wisconsin, by co-operation of service and interchange of connecting traffic, which it is in the interest of both companies to foster and preserve." He noted that the North Western found the Lake Shore Road attractive because of "the transportation of iron ore . . . [and] forest products."[103]

The years of expansion added even more route miles to the North Western system. As on previous occasions most of this trackage entered the company through subsidiaries. The North Western preferred this approach until it resumed expansion after the depression of the 1890s. By then it generally constructed new trackage under its own name for the sake of corporate simplicity.

Most of the remaining growth before 1893 took place in the Upper Peninsula of Michigan. Like earlier construction in the region it was designed to reach mineral deposits, mostly iron ore in the Menominee Range. The company's Menominee River Railroad, which had built between Powers and Quinnesec in 1877, added more than 60 miles within a few years, extending northwestward to Crystal Falls and Stambaugh in Iron County. Similarly, the Escanaba & Lake Superior Railroad (unrelated to a later shortline by the same name) connected in 1882 North Western trackage at Narenta, southwest of Escanaba, with Metropolitan, 55 miles, and expanded to local iron mines. The Iron Range Railway constructed about 35 miles northwest of Escanaba in 1889; it linked Ishpeming with Republic and Clowry with Michigamme. A year earlier the Iron Range Railway had extended the Menominee River line to Watersmeet and linked up with the Lake Shore Road.[104]

The search for minerals, in this case coal, explains why the North Western built a 76-mile feeder in north-central Illinois in 1885. Under the flag of the Northern Illinois Railway, tracks extended south from Belvidere, a Boone County village on the former Galena Road, through Sycamore, where they met the five-mile Sycamore and Cortland branch, built by North Western predecessor Sycamore & Cortland Railroad in 1859, to DeKalb and a crossing of the Omaha stem. The rails proceeded southwestward to the Bureau County mining camp of Spring Valley. This area along the Illinois River in Bureau and neighboring La Salle counties was emerging as an important soft coal district.[105]

The North Western also added miscellaneous lines during the boom years that followed the depression of the 1870s. The two most important were the Sheboygan & Fond du Lac Railroad (S&F) and the Milwaukee & Madison Railway, and together they increased the system by nearly 180 miles. The S&F, acquired in October 1879, totaled 79 miles. It extended west from Sheboygan through Fond du Lac to Princeton, in Green Lake County, Wisconsin. Local interests had built the property in four segments: 14 miles between Sheboygan and Plymouth in 1859 by the predecessor Sheboygan & Mississippi River Railroad; six miles from Plymouth to Glenbeulah by that same company a year later; 23 miles from Glenbeulah to Fond du Lac in 1868 by the S&F; and last, 35 miles from Fond du Lac to Princeton in 1871. When the North Western later pushed this modestly profitable line to Marshfield, 86 miles beyond Princeton, the former S&F gained greater value. The slightly longer Milwaukee & Madison ran in an "air-line" fashion west of Milwaukee to Madison, 80 miles. Built in 1882 under the auspices of this subsidiary, the trackage served mostly rural village, but it offered a better route from Milwaukee to the Twin Cities and points to the west and south.[106]

Several additions were less significant. One was the Rock River Railway, which was constructed between the southern Wisconsin towns of Janesville and Afton, six miles, in 1880. This spur shortened the line from Beloit to Fond du Lac and Green Bay. Another addition that also saved mileage was the 16-mile Janesville & Evansville Railway, a road that tied the two places of its corporate title and created a more direct route between Chicago and Madison. Also included were the Galesville & Mississippi River Railroad, which in 1883 linked the western Wisconsin towns of Trempealeau and Galesville on the Madison-to-Winona (Minnesota) line, and the Lake Geneva & State Line Railway, which added six miles to the "Crystal Lake Short Line" from Lake Geneva to Williams Bay in southeastern Wisconsin during 1888. The earlier segments of this branch, Elgin, Illinois, to Genoa, Wisconsin, had been built by the Fox River Valley Railroad in 1854, and from Genoa to Lake Geneva, by the State Line & Union Railroad in 1871. In 1880 the later company joined the Elgin & State Line Railroad, successor to the Fox River Valley, and in 1883 the North Western absorbed the combined properties.[107]

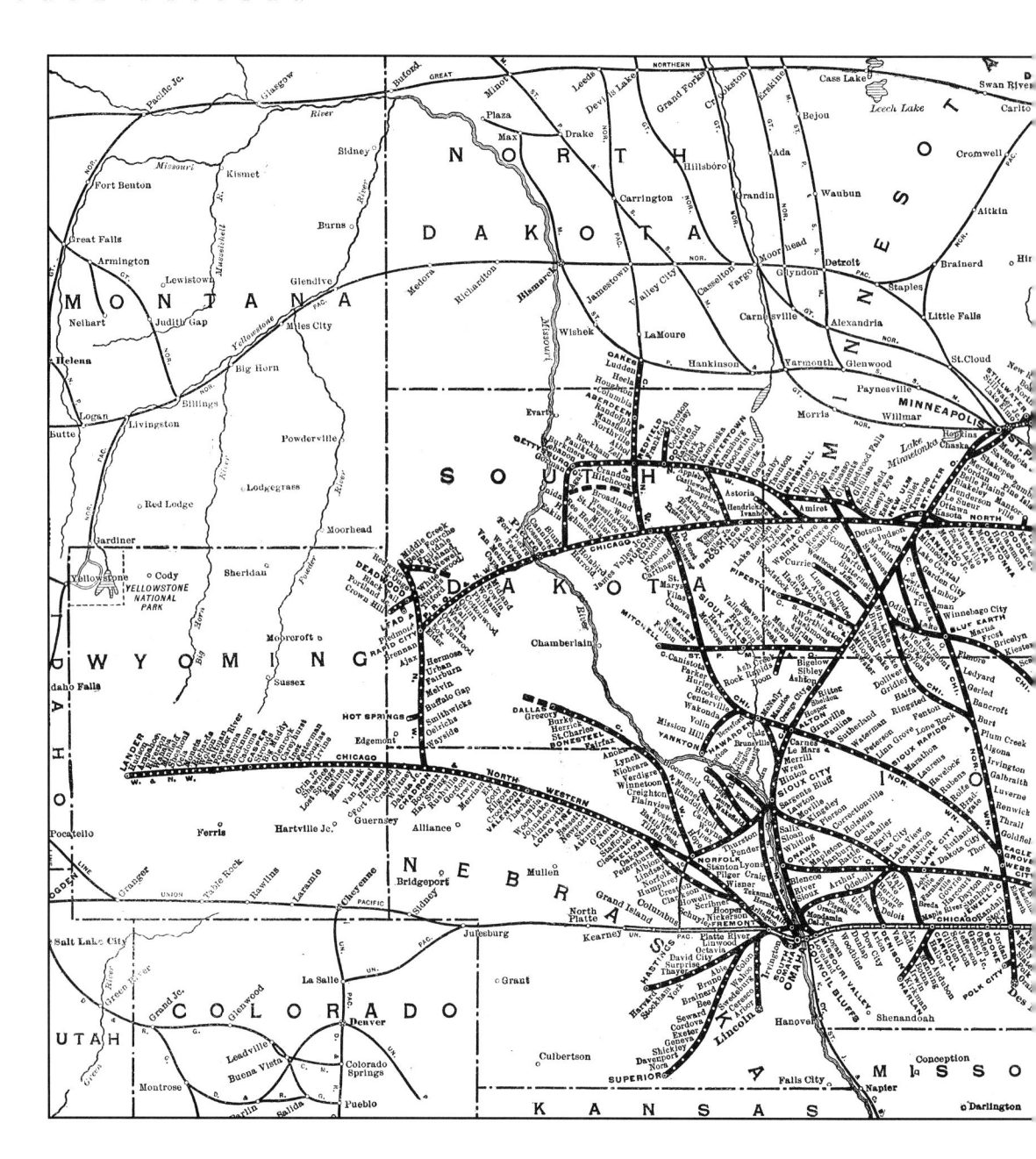

Finally, the North Western constructed modest mileage in the greater Chicago area. In 1883 it opened six miles from Batavia south to Aurora, a continuation of a three-mile appendage constructed 11 years earlier from the Omaha stem at Geneva to Batavia. This trackage simply extended a branch built by the St. Charles Railroad in 1871, two miles north of the main line from Geneva to St. Charles. (The St. Charles Railroad later joined the Elgin & State Line and then was dissolved as a separate entity.) And the North Western's Junction Railway Company completed an eight-mile freight transfer route in 1889 between Montrose and North Evanston.[108]

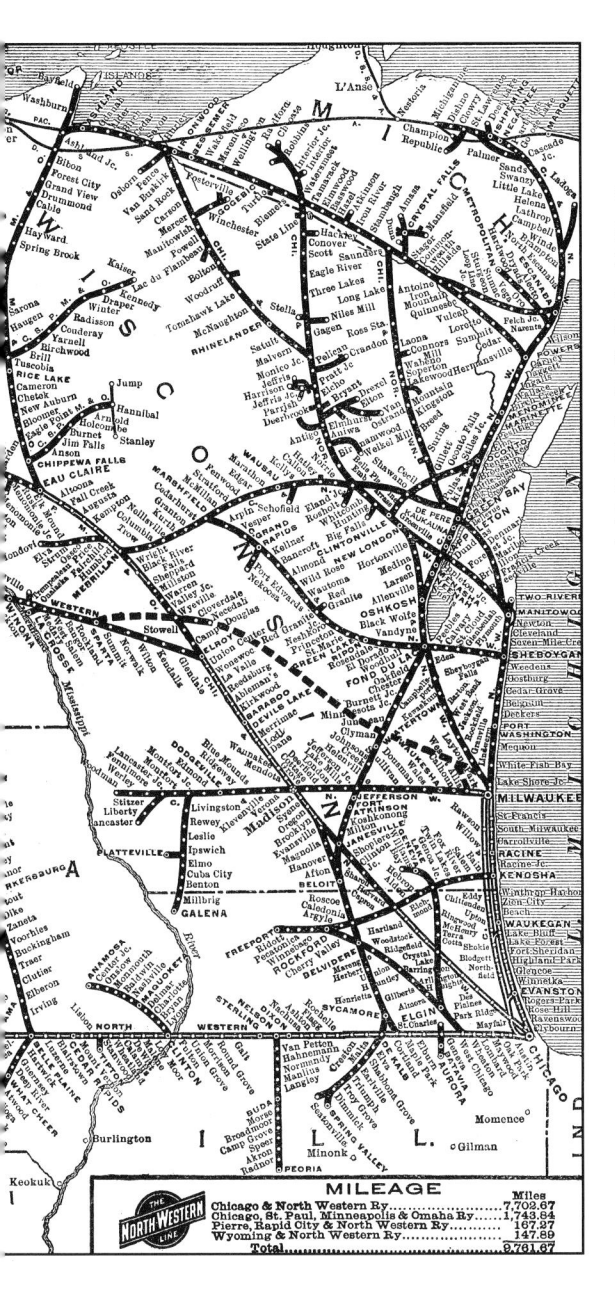

When the North Western published its system map in November 1910 the network of main, secondary, and branch lines revealed an American railroad behemoth. "The North Western system covers its territory like a morning dew," opined a Huron, South Dakota, newspaper editor in 1907. (Author's collection)

The troubled years that followed the panic on Wall Street in May 1893 had a sobering effect on the North Western, the entire railroad enterprise, and the nation generally. The company weathered the economic storm, but it wisely followed a conservative policy regarding expansion, doing virtually nothing until signs of economic recovery became apparent. "I believe that the Chicago & North-Western has not yet grown to the extent that it some day will," observed Marvin Hughitt in early 1896. Perhaps he contemplated an extension to the Pacific Ocean; the possibility of purchasing the bankrupt Union Pacific, which would later be sold at a sheriff's sale in Omaha; or construction of additional branches and acquisition of more short-lines to tap traffic and to discourage invasions from other roads.[109]

While there were uncertainties, the North Western by the mid-1890s had established itself as one of America's foremost railroads. It controlled a profitable and impressive network of trackage. Specifically, the firm as of May 31, 1894, owned 5,031 miles of line, divided into nine operating divisions. Not counted in this total, however, was the 1,439-mile Chicago, St. Paul, Minneapolis & Omaha Railway, a company that the North Western had controlled through majority stock ownership since 1882. Although it functioned separately, the Omaha Road nevertheless was and would continue to be a vital part of the North Western system.[110]

This crew of Omaha Road No. 252, a high-stepping 4-4-0, helped the Chicago, St. Paul, Minneapolis & Omaha Railway keep its five states linked to the nation. (Author's collection)

CHAPTER

Four

THE OMAHA ROAD

A distinguishing feature of the Chicago & North Western Railway for decades was its control of the Chicago, St. Paul, Minneapolis & Omaha Railway. This approximately 1,700-mile railroad, popularly called the "Omaha Road" or simply the "Omaha," developed three principal lines that radiated from the St. Paul: one to Omaha, Nebraska, via Sioux City, Iowa; one to Elroy, Wisconsin, which made a direct connection with the North Western to Chicago; and one to Ashland-Bayfield, Wisconsin, and Duluth, Minnesota. Although the North Western purchased a controlling interest in the Omaha's stock in 1882, it did not lease the carrier until 1957. The North Western finally acquired the Omaha in 1972. The company owned only a bare majority of the common and preferred shares until the mid-1920s when it substantially increased its holdings. Thus the relationship between the North Western and the Omaha differed markedly from the Elkhorn and Lake Shore roads. "[The] Northwestern [has] avowed a policy of concentration and has since taken in a very considerable mileage in accordance with it, [but the] Omaha has never yet been absorbed," observed a financial writer in 1902. "Whether this is due to a policy of exception to prove the rule, or to legal obstacles, only those in the confidence of the Northwestern's management know."[1]

The development of the Omaha Road itself was hardly unusual. Like many railroads during the Gilded Age the Omaha began not as a single carrier that constructed most of its own mileage, but rather as an outgrowth of several smaller, at times related, properties. The corporate genealogy consisted of four distinct parts: St. Paul & Sioux City Railroad, West Wisconsin Railway, North Wisconsin Railway, and expansion as the Omaha after its formal organization on May 26, 1880.[2]

The earliest component of the Omaha Road appeared in Minnesota. Building the Minnesota Valley Railroad, later the St. Paul & Sioux City, must have seemed extremely arduous to its backers. Beginning in 1855 with incorporation of the Root River Valley & Southern Minnesota Rail Road Company, shortened to the Southern Minnesota Rail Road two years later, local promoters sought to tie St. Paul, the territorial capital (state capital after 1858), to the "mouth of the Big Sioux River," at Sioux City, Iowa. As planned, the Southern Minnesota would have linked two major Upper Midwest rivers, the Mississippi and Missouri, and followed a portion of the Minnesota River. These streams being navigable would have provided connections with seasonal steamboat service. Even with a generous land grant, the project failed because of the terrible times after the Panic of 1857. It became virtually impossible to sell any of the nearly 1.2 million acres of land that the state of Minnesota had awarded the fledgling firm.[3]

In 1864, however, the Minnesota Valley Railroad rose phoenixlike from the remains of the original undercapitalized corporation. Supported by the land grant and by greater investments, the road's trains began to roll in 1865 over the 22 miles of iron rails from Mendota, a village opposite St. Paul, southwestward to Shakopee, a community in Scott County. Workers installed track through the valley of the Minnesota River to Belle Plaine, 19 miles, in 1866. That same year they also completed a key six-

This distinctive combination-type locomotive and coach, built by the Columbus Car Works in 1865 for the Minnesota Valley Railroad, plied the rails of this future component of the Omaha Road in the late 1860s. (Railway & Locomotive Historical Society)

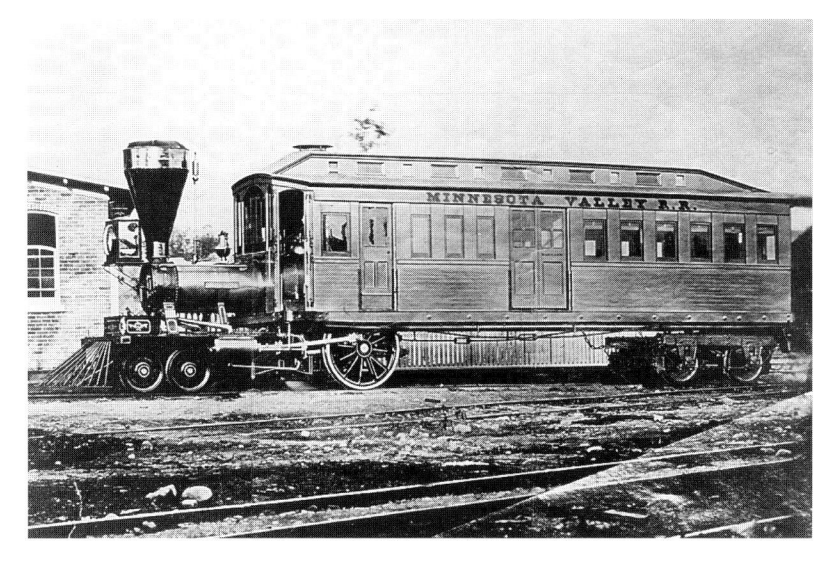

mile extension between Mendota and West St. Paul. The Minnesota Valley and a neighboring shortline, the Minnesota Central Railroad, joined forces to bridge the Mississippi River at West St. Paul. The impressive span of iron and timber opened to the capital city in 1869.[4]

The original objective of Sioux City remained in the minds of the backers of the Minnesota Valley Railroad. Better economic conditions and public largess, including a land grant of nearly 400,000 acres from the state of Iowa to a subsidiary firm, the Sioux City & St. Paul Railroad Company (SC&StP), stimulated the project. Agricultural expansion along the projected route also encouraged the mostly Twin Cities promoters. More farmers were raising spring wheat, a popular crop that was easily grown, conveniently shipped, and always marketable. The output of wheat in Minnesota by 1880 was twice the combined production of barley, corn, flaxseed, and oats. The promise of the prairies seemed well on the way to fulfillment. "Building between St. Paul and Sioux City after the Civil War was not a risky gamble," concluded a company officer several decades later. "The wholly uninhabited prairies were starting to fill up and we knew that once a rail line was put through, there would be plenty of wheat to haul and goods to bring the residents." During this period railroads repeatedly opened the plains to plows and profits.[5]

Construction progressed at a steady, modest pace. Tracks reached Le Sueur in 1867, Mankato in 1868, Lake Crystal in 1869, and St. James in 1870. When crews pushed beyond Lake Crystal, they left the river valley for the expansive grasslands. Here, except for some meandering streams, the fledgling road encountered no major physical obstacles. Once in St. James, the company operated a 120-mile line that connected the Twin Cities with southwestern Minnesota.[6]

The Minnesota Valley, officially the St. Paul & Sioux City (StP&SC) after January 9, 1869, fortunately reached its destination of Sioux City before the hard times of the mid-1870s stymied most construction. With the affiliated Sioux City & St. Paul Railroad and trackage rights, through freight and passenger traffic became possible between St. Paul and Sioux City in October 1872. Specifically, the SC&StP, bolstered by a large gift of land, built from Le Mars, seat of Plymouth County, Iowa, to St. James, 123 miles, and rented the 25 miles between Le Mars and Sioux City from the Iowa Falls & Sioux City Railroad, part of the Illinois Central system.[7]

Officials of the St. Paul & Sioux City now wanted more than a line between their original building destinations. By the time the North Western took control, the StP&SC had added several feeder and connector lines in Minnesota, Iowa, and Dakota. As was common elsewhere, subsidiaries carried out much of this construction. The longest addition, 98 miles, was spiked down between 1876 and 1880 and ran westward from Sioux Falls Junction, Minnesota, near Worthington, through Sioux Falls to Salem, seat of McCook County, Dakota Territory. After 1883 Salem became an interchange point with the Iroquois to Hawarden line of the Dakota Central. The company also opened a 28-mile appendage from the Dakota extension at Luverne, Minnesota, southward to the village of Doon, in Rock County, Iowa, in 1879. Another feeder had begun business a year earlier between Heron Lake, Jackson County, Minnesota, and Woodstock, a hamlet in Pipestone County, 44 miles to the northwest. This branch would be extended 11 miles to Pipestone, the county seat, in 1884. A more important route was readied in 1881: a 43-mile line that ran from Lake Crystal to Elmore, Minnesota, on the Iowa border. This trackage gave the StP&SC access to the soon-to-

Railroading has always been capital and labor intensive. Omaha Road employees work with a pile driver on a bridge near Sibley, Iowa, in the 1880s. Locomotive No. 41, a Schenectady product of 1855, was used in work-train service before being scrapped in 1888. (Railway & Locomotive Historical Society)

be completed Toledo & North Western Railway and better connections to the south and east.[8]

In 1880, the year before the St. Paul & Sioux City reached Elmore, Minnesota, the carrier took possession of the Sioux City & Nebraska Railroad. This company controlled approximately 140 miles of railroad in Nebraska, including a route between Sioux City and Omaha. The purchase represented quintessential mini-system building.[9]

As with most modest-size carriers of the period, the Sioux City & Nebraska tied together predecessor firms. What subsequently became the Omaha Road in Nebraska began with the Omaha & North Western Railroad (O&NW). This carrier, incorporated in 1869, sought to build from Omaha, the rapidly developing railroad hub and true "Gate City to the West," northwestward to the mouth of the Niobrara River. Unlike the rival Fremont, Elkhorn & Missouri Valley, the O&NW never approached its announced destination. Instead the company completed a 25-mile segment from Omaha to Blair in 1870 and a connection with the Sioux City & Pacific. Between 1871 and 1876 the O&NW struggled to expand but installed only 17 miles of track from Blair to Tekamah, seat of Burt County, by the nation's centennial year. This construction failed to save the company financially, and it entered bankruptcy in 1877. The O&NW handled insufficient traffic, something that bedeviled many developmental roads, but nevertheless the line remained in operation. A new corporation, the Omaha & Northern Nebraska Railway (O&NN), created by the eastern bondholders of the defunct O&NW, assumed control. Not long after the O&NN made its debut, workers added 16 miles of line. By 1880, the road stretched 58 miles from Omaha on the south to Oakland on the northwest.[10]

By the time the Omaha & Northern Nebraska headed northward, Elias F. Drake, president of the StP&SC and a "financially successful" St. Paul businessman, became actively involved as he and his colleagues wanted to reach Omaha. The Drake interests seized the chance to acquire the financially distressed Covington, Columbus & Black Hills Railroad (CC&BH), a narrow-gauge pike that had earlier worried backers of the Elkhorn Route. The CC&BH was not much of a property, but it ran in the right direction. The road, built in 1877, stretched from Covington (South Sioux City) to the southwest and then northwest to Ponca in an adjoining county, a distance of 26 miles. It was conveyed in December 1879 to the newly formed Sioux City & Nebraska Railroad (SC&N). Soon thereafter the SC&N not only widened and improved the former CC&BH but pushed it southward from Coburn Junction, 10 miles below Covington on the former narrow gauge, to Oakland, 54 miles, and to linkage with the O&NN. This astonished no one; the SC&N had previously agreed to acquire the Omaha to Oakland trackage. Then on March 2, 1880, the enlarged SC&N "conveyed all its railroad, both acquired and under construction, in the State of Nebraska, to the Saint Paul and Sioux City Railroad Company." This included an affiliate of the Sioux City & Nebraska, the Missouri River Transfer Company, which in 1880 laid connecting track to the riverbank and operated a car ferry for the interchange of freight and passenger equipment between Covington and Sioux City. A bridge replaced this traffic bottleneck in 1886.[11]

Acquisition of the Nebraska trackage served the StP&SC well. Even though this was not the best line to Omaha (it was 24 miles longer than the joint Sioux City & Pacific–North Western route via California Junction and Council Bluffs), the trackage still provided single-corporation access to a bustling gateway. Furthermore, the Nebraska artery tapped a growing farm country between Sioux City and Omaha, which it largely monopolized. Only a branch of the Burlington Route eventually competed, but then not directly. This 103-mile Burlington appendage opened in 1916 between the Nebraska towns of Laketon, near Sioux City, and Ashland.[12]

Before the StP&SC disappeared as a legal entity, it had spawned a nearly 700-mile network in southern Minnesota and adjoining sections of Dakota, Iowa, and Nebraska that served promising agricultural localities and several expanding commercial centers. With multiple rail connections the road developed strategic importance. An array of local subsidies, including grants of the public domain, and successful sales of securities made possible this component of the Omaha Road.

With the StP&SC successfully penetrating territory to the southwest of the Twin Cities, the

Locomotive No. 21, the *T. C. Pound*, of the West Wisconsin Railway, gleams as the shop and maintenance-of-way workers gather for this 1870s photograph. (State Historical Society of Wisconsin)

West Wisconsin Railway emerged as a valuable road to the southeast. The company traced its origins to the incorporation of the Tomah & Lake St. Croix Railroad in 1863, a project that sought to tie Tomah, located on the cross-state Milwaukee & St. Paul Railroad, with the St. Croix River valley, part of the boundary between Minnesota and Wisconsin.[13]

The prospects looked encouraging. "The country through which the Road passes has been most liberal in its support of the Company," commented the New York investment house of White, Morris & Co. in 1871. "By authority of the Wisconsin legislature, each of the eleven counties through which the Road runs, donated 50,000 dollars of their bonds, with the Right of Way." In addition the railroad received 6,400 acres of public land for every mile of line completed, which ultimately yielded nearly a million acres.[14]

After several false starts the Tomah road gave way to the West Wisconsin in 1867. The successor firm, which had reaped the same financial incentives, took advantage of the postwar boom. It quickly installed 10 miles of track from Tomah northward to another Monroe County community, Warren's Mills (Warren). Five years later the line reached the St. Croix River town of Hudson, in St. Croix County. This nearly 175-mile road, which followed an old stage route, passed through the growing communities of Black River Falls, Merrillan, and Eau Claire. Service, however, did not end at Hudson. Arrangements with the St. Paul, Stillwater and Taylors Falls Rail Road (StPS&TF), a company controlled by business interests from the Twin Cities including individuals linked to the StP&SC, made possible direct access to St. Paul. Indeed, the 20-mile StPS&TF had been launched in late 1869 in anticipation of West Wisconsin rails reaching the St. Croix River. Subsequently, in October 1871, the West Wisconsin leased the recently finished StPS&TF, including rights to the firm's drawbridge over the St. Croix River. Nearly a decade later, the StP&SC absorbed the StPS&TF, a prelude to the fusion of the core parts of the Omaha Road.[15]

With access into the Twin Cities, the West Wisconsin soon dramatically improved its other principal outlet. While Tomah made a logical starting place, a better southern terminus was soon located at the Juneau County village of Elroy, 32 miles southeast of Warren. Here in 1872 the company formed a friendly connection with the North Western, which was building from Madison to Winona Junction, Wisconsin, on the east bank of the Mississippi River opposite Winona, Minnesota. The connection at Elroy created a convenient and competitive through route between Chicago and St. Paul, something neither road independently had.[16]

The process of restructuring proceeded rapidly. In one of the first abandonments in the Midwest the West Wisconsin scrapped the

Tomah to Warren appendage in 1872, the year it reached Elroy. It used track materials from the former line to construct the latter. The Tomah section had generated scant local business, and the company could continue to connect with the Milwaukee & St. Paul by creating an interchange at Camp Douglas, a station between Warren and Elroy. Nevertheless some individuals affected by the Tomah retirement howled and took the matter to court. Although winning several favorable decisions, they never regained service.[17]

Formation of "The Elroy Route" or "The Chicago, Madison and St. Paul Line" was important. "The Great Route Between Chicago, Madison and St. Paul Without Change of Cars" proclaimed a joint public timetable published in January 1876, three months before the official signing of the Abstract of Agreement. It informed readers that "The Distance from Chicago to St. Paul by this Route is Only 409 Miles. SPEED, COMFORT AND SAFETY ARE COMBINED, And render this the Great Route of the People." The competing Milwaukee Road undoubtedly considered this hyperbole, but while its rails from Chicago to St. Paul measured the same distance, its equipment and travel times were hardly better.[18]

Since the West Wisconsin opened a largely transportation-starved region, its presence delighted residents. The arrival of the iron horse was greeted with expectations of further progress and by at least one grand celebration or "blow out." Although far from unusual during the construction era, the citizenry of Eau Claire demonstrated great enthusiasm for the coming of the steam car civilization. With committees on invitations, reception, entertainment, refreshments, toasts, music, and finance and $1,500 in contributions, all was readied for the momentous day in August 1870 when the train of celebrants arrived. Cannon fire, food, drink, and speeches greeted residents, and "people from up and down the Chippewa Valley poured into town to swell the throng." In the festive parade were brightly decorated banners with such proclamations as "Chippewa Falls to Eau Claire, Greeting: We Rejoice in Your Prosperity" and "West Wisconsin Railroad, Now by St. Paul, the Work Goes Bravely on." Participants long remembered the dinner in the eating pavilion. "A large 'wigwam,' open at the sides and roofed with evergreens, held ten tables, each seating seventy persons and presided over by the representative ladies of the city," recounted a local historian in 1914. "[The tables] . . . were spread with linen, silver and dainty food from their homes, decorated with flowers from their gardens and the feast was enjoyed to the fullest extent by the guests, who voiced their appreciation enthusiastically."[19]

Notwithstanding traffic arrangements with the North Western, which generated more than half of its annual revenues, and public approval of the "Elroy Route," the West Wisconsin found it necessary to default on its debt obligations in 1877; foreclosure came a year later. The hard times of the mid-1870s created the financial crisis. The railroad, which had been supported by investors from Wisconsin and the East, principally D. A. Baldwin of Hudson and Jacob Humbird of Baltimore, the former a small-town miller and real estate promoter and the latter a railroad contractor, could not stave off creditors. The West Wisconsin apparently made a gallant attempt, though, and offered itself to the North Western, but President Albert Keep concluded that his company already owned "too much railroad." This was a sane conclusion considering the uncertainties caused by a deepening depression. Furthermore, the carrier registered a flat traffic pattern during most of the decade.[20]

A new day, however, was about to dawn for

The seven-stall enginehouse of the West Wisconsin Railway, probably at Hudson, Wisc., is a beehive of activity in the late 1870s. (State Historical Society of Wisconsin)

The North Western and West Wisconsin railroads actively promoted the "Elroy Route." The timetable of June 1, 1873, spotlights the newly forged "Chicago and St. Paul Through Line." (Author's collection)

the West Wisconsin. A committee of the holders of the road's three bond issues received court approval to reorganize the property, a typical response to a railroad failure. Led by Chicago railroader and company president Henry H. Porter, these interests, largely from Chicago and New York, transformed the defunct firm into the Chicago, St. Paul & Minneapolis Railway, which started up on April 30, 1878.[21]

Not long after the Porter group took charge, the new company made arrangements to serve Minneapolis and to do so joined forces with the Milwaukee Road to create a terminal and industrial switching road, the Minneapolis Eastern Railway. Both carriers wanted economical access to the lucrative milling district. Their shortline opened on June 1, 1879.[22]

The Porter-led road spent heavily in Minneapolis. Surely the savings that resulted from the cooperative Minneapolis Eastern project allowed major capital improvements in the city. One betterment was a massive freight house. "The depot . . . is of brick and fire-proof, 45x330 ft.," reported the *St. Paul Pioneer Press* in October 1880. "It extends from Fourth to Fifth Avenue, without crossing a railroad track. Underneath the whole building is a cellar 10 ft. deep blasted out of the solid [rock] ledge, making one of the best storage rooms in the city." Neither the North Western nor any other railroad had a monopoly on quality facilities.[23]

While never as busy as the mileage of the former West Wisconsin, the North Wisconsin Railway developed into an active unit of the future Omaha Road. By the time the Omaha appeared in 1880, the track of the North Wisconsin headed northward toward Lake Superior from an interchange with the West Wisconsin, appropriately named North Wisconsin Junction, three miles east of Hudson. This project, backed by those involved with the StP&SC and the West Wisconsin, received permission from Wisconsin lawmakers in November 1871 "to construct, maintain and operate a line of railroad from . . . St. Croix [River] . . . to or near Bayfield [Wisconsin]."[24]

Tracklaying progressed haltingly. The North Wisconsin extended only from North Wisconsin Junction to New Richmond, 13 miles, by 1872, and then to Clayton, 25 miles to the north, in 1874. The depression delayed further building until 1878, when the road added 18 miles from Clayton to Cumberland and another 26 miles from Cumberland to beyond Chandler, Washburn County, the following year.[25]

Although the line begun by the North Wisconsin did not reach Lake Superior until later, the initial segment between North Wisconsin Junction and Chandler developed into an important artery for forest products. Trainloads of logs moved to nearby sawmills, and cars of finished lumber traveled south. Passenger business was modest, however; lumberjacks mostly occupied seats in the road's few coaches. Unlike the West Wisconsin, which annually transported thousands of through travelers in state-of-the-art equipment, the North Wisconsin was a parochial, even primitive carrier.[26]

The North Wisconsin managed to weather the economic dislocations of the mid-1870s. When the depression struck, the company suspended its expansion plans. While its revenues were much smaller than those for the West Wisconsin, its daily operating costs were substantially lower. To reduce these expenses further the North Wisconsin attached a passenger car to a scheduled freight train for patrons along its 38-mile route. A "mixed" train was much cheaper to operate than conventional passenger service. This response probably did not upset many riders; no one expected luxury accommodations.[27]

This lumber-carrying road remained subsidy poor but land rich during its less than 10 years of corporate life. The company generated only modest public support, receiving aid from just three communities totaling a mere $35,000. Building through the North Woods tapped only minor population centers, and local governments possessed meager financial resources. But following a pattern of railroad building in parts of the Upper Midwest and Great Plains, the North Wisconsin received public lands as the beneficiary of a grant made by the state of Wisconsin in 1864 to the ill-fated St. Croix & Lake Superior Railroad. These several hundred thousand acres were nearly all heavily forested and worth far less than those fertile prairie parcels granted the StP&SC. There was little likelihood that tree stumps would give way to cornstalks and wheat fields.[28]

Before its corporate demise the North Wisconsin expanded somewhat. The return of better times toward the end of the 1870s prompted local businessmen in River Falls, an inland community 12 miles southwest of Hudson, to join forces with the backers of the North Wisconsin and the StPS&TF to launch the Hudson & River Falls Railway. They worked swiftly, and the line opened in 1878. Two years later the shortline was conveyed to the North Wisconsin. Then in 1885 the Omaha Road extended the appendage to Ellsworth, 14 miles southeast of River Falls.[29]

The fashionable process of system building continued. The formation of the Chicago, St. Paul, Minneapolis & Omaha in the spring of 1880 exemplified the trend of smaller roads either joining other smaller railroads or uniting with much larger companies. Initially the carrier consisted of only the Chicago, St. Paul & Minneapolis and the North Wisconsin roads. Even this modest consolidation brought a loss of power for local businessmen, a widespread phenomenon. A group of New York investors took over and shrewdly placed a prominent Wisconsinite, Philetus Sawyer, who owned one-fourth of the stock in the North Wisconsin, on the Board of Directors. This self-made lumberman and millionaire from Oshkosh was also a powerful Republican politician. He effectively aided the company, especially with matters that related to land grants and timber claims.[30]

Within a year after the Omaha Road was formed, it absorbed the StP&SC minisystem. The now greatly enlarged Omaha was nicely positioned to reward investors, serve patrons, and expand into what it considered its domain. In the first annual report President Porter correctly suggested that the Omaha was evolving into an even greater property. "[I]t will be seen that the roads which the Company now have [sic] under construction are not 'branches' in the ordinary sense of the term, but are lines either connecting its system of railway with Lake Superior at important points, where the lake transportation steamers owned by and running in connection with the eastern trunk lines of railroad receive and deliver cargoes, as well as where a heavy lumber traffic originates." Added Porter: "[The Omaha will] join . . . its present system of railroads with important railways running west, two of them through to the Pacific Coast."[31]

Before the 1890s depression interrupted construction, the Omaha Road not only added some short branches along its multistate system but also built several important lines. First, the company completed the former North Wisconsin. It reached Lake Superior at Bayfield, 180 miles north of Hudson, in 1883, as well as Ashland, a more important port community, doing so with a four-mile stub that left the main line at Ashland Junction, 21 miles south of Bayfield.[32]

The Omaha further extended its mileage in northwest Wisconsin by pushing northward 160 miles from Eau Claire through Chippewa Falls and Spooner to Superior-Duluth. This expansion, facilitated by subsidiaries Chippewa Falls & Northern Railway and the Eau Claire & Chippewa Falls Railway, came about rather slowly, the work occurring between 1881 and 1884. Duluth was located at the head of navigation on the Great Lakes and was served by the Northern Pacific, the new northern transcontinental road. Henry Villard, who led the Northern Pacific, originally had intended for his company to build through western Wisconsin. Financial problems and the willingness of the Omaha Road to provide a convenient route to Milwaukee and Chicago prompted "the Villard management and the Omaha directors . . . [to] come to an amicable understanding." The Superior-Duluth extension operated over the Bayfield line for about five miles between Spooner and Superior Junction (later Trego), and this reduced construction and maintenance costs.[33]

The Omaha Road also expanded in Nebraska and South Dakota. The company installed 47 miles of track during 1881 and 1882 from Emerson Junction, near Covington, through Wayne to Norfolk, connecting with the main line of the Elkhorn Road and a branch of the Union Pacific. From this extension it added 43 miles northwestward from Wayne through Randolph to Bloomfield in Knox County; work was completed in

1890. Three years later the company extended the Ponca spur 11 miles northwestward to Newcastle. Finally, it entered the backyard of the Milwaukee Road in 1887, when it lengthened the Salem line 33 miles to Mitchell, the thriving seat of Davison County and a growing center of Milwaukee Road operations in the territory. The mileage for the Omaha amounted to an impressive 1,482 as of December 31, 1892; it was a noteworthy regional carrier.[34]

The connection at Elroy alone made the Omaha Road of interest to the North Western. If the joint trackage could not be operated for through service, especially passenger traffic, between Chicago and the Twin Cities, then the North Western would need to build, buy, or lease an alternative route. The two roads also interchanged with each other at several strategic points and ultimately that number increased to seventeen junctions.[35]

Thus the North Western carefully watched the growth of the Omaha. It may have planned early on to acquire at least a portion of the properties that became the unified company. Certainly the West Wisconsin was vital to the North Western. Direct financial involvement came in November 1882. The decision to invest more than $10.5 million, financed through $10 million of 5 percent, 50-year debenture bonds, was made because the North Western feared that the Omaha would fall into the hands of the Chicago, Rock Island & Pacific. The North Western no longer felt that it had "too much railroad"; times had changed dramatically from the mid-1870s.[36]

The Rock Island, like the North Western, was another Chicago-based granger road. By 1880 it linked Chicago with Omaha and eastern Iowa with northeastern Kansas. The firm controlled additional rail lines in Illinois, Iowa, and Kansas. A reorganization in 1880 created an invigorated company that was eager to expand. The driving force behind the Rock Island was Ransom Reed Cable, who displayed "belligerent" tendencies toward competitors and sought to have his road dominate as much territory as possible. He had his eyes on varied destinations: the Rocky Mountain West, Texas, and the Upper Midwest. Cable was rising quickly in the ranks: director in 1877, second vice president in 1880, and vice president and general manager in 1881. This ambitious railroader became president and general manager in 1883. "The title of president wasn't enough for Cable," observes a chronicler of the Rock Island. "He tacked onto it words 'general manager.' He wanted the world to know that he was the whole Rock Island road—the supreme boss."[37]

Ransom Cable worried the North Western. President Albert Keep observed in 1880 that "R. R. Cable is capable of causing great harm to our Company." The likely reason for Keep's concern stemmed from the Rock Island's joint purchase with the Burlington of the Burlington, Cedar Rapids & Northern Railway (BCR&N) in the summer of 1879. The main line of this interstate carrier extended 253 miles from the Mississippi River community of Burlington, Iowa, northward through Cedar Rapids to the southern Minnesota town of Albert Lea.[38]

The relationship between the Rock Island and the BCR&N was not the only troubling matter for North Western officials. On its Board of Directors the new Omaha Road had "Rock Island men," including Cable, David Dows, and Henry Porter. Dows was a New Yorker, who represented investors with major holdings in the Rock Island, and Porter, the first president of the Omaha, was a former Rock Island director. While the BCR&N did not connect with the Omaha, new or leased trackage could easily bind them together in southern Minnesota. And, too, the 98-mile "Milwaukee Division" of the BCR&N, running from Cedar Rapids northeastward to Postville, Iowa, was only approximately 75 miles away from Elroy, Wisconsin.[39]

Since the Rock Island threatened "to upset the Northwestern's apple cart," the Keep administration decided to gain control of the Omaha Road. A financial expert observed years later, "The first object sought was the protection of Northwestern's territory, which was attained and . . . more than paid for the investment." The multimillion dollar commitment was hardly imprudent as the Omaha was not a struggling concern. It remained profitable, at times exceedingly so, until the 1930s. During the 1880s and prior to the Panic of 1893, gross earnings averaged $6.27 million and net earnings $1.94 million. Shortly after the turn of the century, an informed commentator emphasized that the

North Western had followed a judicious course. "[The Omaha] had paid its proprietors handsomely in the long run, as any reasonably conceived and wisely managed railroad property in the country seems bound to do." The bond structure of the Omaha was simple and revealed a financially sound corporation. "Down to 1912 the Company had never issued debentures," reported Wood, Struthers & Co. in 1920. "Its funded debt prior to 1912 had consisted solely of several issues of divisional first mortgage bonds, the latter have been sold, from time to time, to refund maturing first mortgage bonds and to pay for extensions, other additions to the property and improvements."[40]

The Omaha Road remained an independent railroad. "[It is] a distinct property," noted the *Railroad Gazette,* "and presents a separate annual report." Its four operating divisions—Eastern, Northern, St. Paul & Pacific, and Nebraska—retained the interests of its predecessor components, and this organizational structure largely remained intact for decades. The headquarters was not located in Chicago but rather in an imposing brick and masonry general office building at the corner of Fourth and Rosabel streets in St. Paul. The North Western, the dominant stockholder, placed its representatives on the Omaha board, however. They included several from the board of the North Western, as well as Minneapolis flour magnate William Drew Washburn, who had extensive railroad experience. Marvin Hughitt succeeded Henry Porter as the Omaha president.[41]

The North Western treated the two roads as if they were one physically. "It coordinated the property with its own building and expansion plans," observed a business journalist in 1887. When, for example, in the mid-1880s the North Western acquired the 16-mile Princeton & Western Railway, a shortline that united the western Wisconsin communities of Wyeville and Necedah, it possessed trackage that connected only with the Omaha at Wyeville. This line remained isolated from the North Western until the 135-mile "Adams Cutoff" opened between Necedah and Lindwerm, Wisconsin, near Milwaukee, in 1911. In another example the Omaha, which already linked Merrillan and Neillville, Wisconsin, in Trempealeau and Clark counties, lengthened this 15-mile branch northeastward to Marshfield in Wood County, 23 miles, in 1891. The company sought, in part, to "open up a large section of hardwood country and . . . reach some standing pine timber." A year later the North Western backed construction to Marshfield of a 40-mile extension of the

The year is 1892, the place the Robert Street freight station in St. Paul, Minn., and the occasion the appearance of an Omaha Road pay train. Railroads, America's first "big business," pumped large amounts of money into local economies and altered national life with more than its trains. (State Historical Society of Wisconsin)

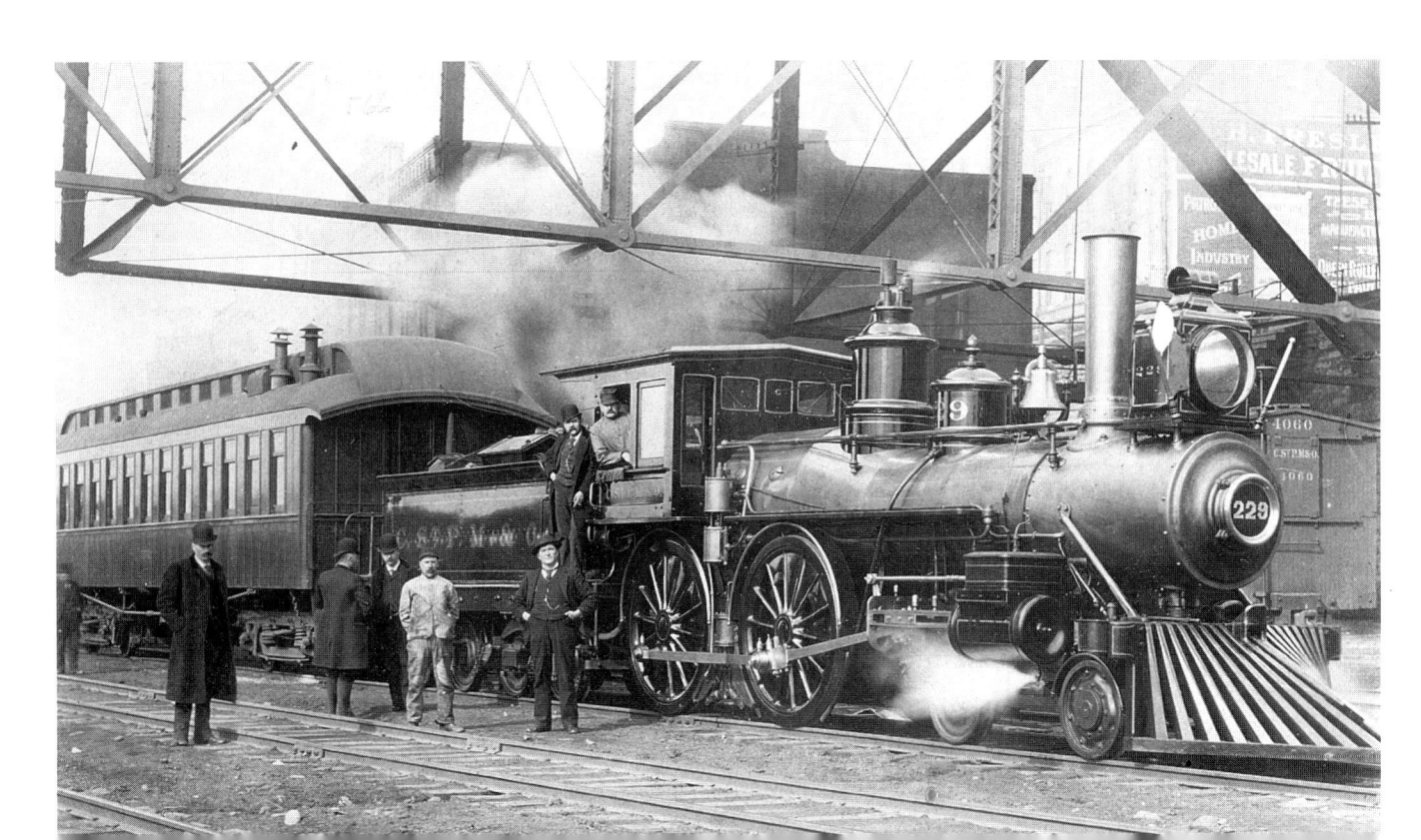

An Omaha Road "fast freight" races along a main line early in the twentieth century. (Author's collection)

Milwaukee, Lake Shore and Western's Wausau branch. This created an important transstate route much as the Adams Cutoff would nearly two decades later.[42]

The North Western did more than increase physical contacts with the Omaha Road. It included the smaller company's schedules in its public timetables, various promotional folders, and advertisements. Separate Omaha timetables appeared, but they nearly always featured the North Western logo, along with the "C.St.P.M.& O. Ry." identification. The Omaha name was emblazoned on pieces of rolling stock, but as with printed matter, the North Western herald was usually displayed. More important, the two traffic departments, while separate in organization, solicited business jointly. The companies fit together well, for "once the Omaha came under the control of the North-Western, a perfectly matched system in so many ways was forged."[43]

The flow of freight demonstrated this "perfectly matched system." Even before the Omaha fully evolved, its individual components generated traffic that was sent to or received from sites along the North Western. When the Omaha came together, a triangular trade emerged. Boxcars of wheat from Nebraska farms moved over the Omaha to milling facilities in Minneapolis; the finished flour traveled by the Elroy Route to Chicago warehouses; and these cars carried a variety of goods from Chicago and eastern businesses to stores in Nebraska. The Omaha, too, "gave to the Winona and St. Peter and Dakota Central Roads easy access by short hauls to the unrivalled milling facilities of Minneapolis," reported a North Western official. "It was all like the veins in your hand, interconnected and practical."[44]

Lumber was another commodity that moved in a predictable way. Saw-milling centers in western Wisconsin relied heavily on the Omaha and North Western by the 1880s. Prairie dwellers needed large quantities of wood products, and their requirements were readily handled by this developing rail network. As early as 1879 the Chicago, St. Paul & Minneapolis, St. Paul & Sioux City, and Sioux City & Pacific signed a pooling compact for rates on shipments of forest products. This "Wisconsin Lumber Line" agreement, later extended to additional roads, generated a brisk and profitable business.[45]

Other types of interchange business flourished. Coal, for example, passed conveniently between the roads. Thousands of gondola cars from Illinois and Iowa mines traveled annually via such connections as Alton, Iowa, and Elmore, Minnesota, to points on the Omaha. Similarly large numbers of animals were shipped from North Western system stations on the Great Plains to stock yards on the Omaha near the Twin Cities and Sioux City. "There were a lot of stock extras by the latter part of the [nineteenth] century," wrote an officer of the Omaha in 1907. "That traffic continues to move from the west and . . . is important to us."[46]

The North Western knew it had a valuable partner. "Some of [the Omaha's] lines have become indispensable," Albert Keep affirmed in 1883, "and others greatly necessary to the integrity and completeness of the Chicago and North Western Railway system in the Northwest." Few questioned this assessment.[47]

As with the North Western, the Omaha Road provided "high grade" service. While it operated poky way freights and passenger locals, it also had better trains, including time freights and "limiteds," to serve the public. The firm's premier trains raced along the Elroy Route, its showcase line. Reports from state regulatory bodies reveal few substantial or sustained complaints. Grumpy employees, it seems, tarnished the road's image more than anything else.[48]

New equipment and improved trackside facilities helped to satisfy patrons. Betterments continued uninterrupted, except during those five troubled years in the 1890s. The road's annual reports, the trade press, and on-line newspapers regularly chronicled this material progress. "The company is making considerable improvements to its roadbed," noted the *Railroad Gazette* in 1892. "The road is replacing a number of small wooden bridges with steel structures, and the use of wooden culverts is rapidly being done away with, stone taking the place of wood in the larger ones and iron pipe being substituted for the lesser ones." The *Gazette* added, "Several of the grades on the Eastern division have been reduced, and wherever it was possible the track has been straightened." The public, too, commented on the physical condition. "The Omaha Company is a fine appearing railroad," opined a stockman from near Mankato, Minnesota, in 1889. "[It] keeps everything in tip-top condition." Ample income, low debt, and capable managers doubtless were contributing factors in this unsolicited testimonial.[49]

No American corporation, particularly a railroad with its quasi-public functions, could ever fully satisfy everyone. Even the Omaha Road had its critics. Sometimes tensions that erupted between the railroad and the public looked trivial to outsiders, but they could become highly charged locally.

A dispute about the location of the depot in Butterfield, Minnesota, during the late 1890s is illustrative. The inhabitants of this Watonwan County village, situated on the Twin Cities to Sioux City line, appeared content with the overall services of the Omaha Road. That changed in 1899 when the Minnesota & Iowa Railway, a North Western subsidiary, built a 92-mile feeder from Burt, Iowa, to Sanborn, Minnesota, which crossed the Omaha at Butterfield. While the completion of another rail line should have elated residents, townsfolks instead castigated the Omaha's decision to move its depot to the crossing site, which was not within easy walking distance of the commercial heart of Butterfield. A complaint was lodged with the Minnesota Railway and Warehouse Commission, and an investigation ensued. The regulatory body, however, backed the railroad's right to relocate the depot "to a logical place," and praised it for grading and graveling a half-mile public roadway between the village and station. Later the company annoyed merchants further when it permitted a restaurant in the depot.

Crew members of an Omaha Road 0-6-0 switch engine pause from their assignments in the Sioux City, Iowa, yards about 1890. Fireman Nels Canfield is seated on the handrail, standing in the cab is engineer James Harrington. (State Historical Society of Wisconsin)

Early in the twentieth century, residents of the hamlet of Bennett, Wisc., received only a car body for their depot, perhaps temporarily. According to the caption on this 1908 picture postcard, Halloween pranksters placed portions of a carriage on the shelter's roof. (Author's collection)

It's train time early in the twentieth century in Mankato, Minn. The passenger train in the foreground stands on Omaha Road rails and the train behind awaits a highball on the North Western's Winona-Pierre line. The mail is being "worked" at the Omaha's Railway Post Office car. (Cornelius W. Hauck collection)

"[This has] caused our restaurants and hotels a great loss of revenue," complained the *Butterfield Times* in 1901. The newspaper demanded "that the whole question as to the rights of removal of the Omaha passenger depot outside of the village limits be reopened, and a vigorous action instituted to have it moved back to its former location." When the side of the status quo prevailed, hard feelings remained.[50]

A more intense, widespread, and prolonged confrontation between the Omaha Road and the public took place somewhat earlier. When wheat farmers suffered severe financial reversals during the late 1880s and early 1890s because of plummeting commodity prices and a prolonged drought, they swelled the ranks of antibusiness forces. Their shrill cries for reform could be heard throughout large parts of the company's territory. They were not so much troubled with any specific acts of corporate arrogance but rather tarred the Omaha for being part of the sordid world of "big biz." "No railroads in our state or anywhere else for that matter should be making profits for the already pampered rich," concluded a Populist from Wayne, Nebraska, a town on the Omaha, in 1891. "Railroads should be run like the postal operations with the people and not the plutocrats being the owners." The Omaha was merely guilty of being a public utility.[51]

Neither Marvin Hughitt nor lesser officials of the Omaha were targets of the Populists and their sympathizers. Instead, trouble came from the presence of members and associates of the prominent Vanderbilt family on the Board of Directors and the Executive Committee. Cornelius Vanderbilt II, the titular head of the clan after 1885, and his younger brother, William K., were vigorously involved in the affairs of the company. Knowledgeable individuals within the industry sensed potential public-relations difficulties. Commented a business associate of James J. Hill in late 1882, "I quite agree with you that control of the Omaha Road passing into the hands of the Vanderbilt party will be apt to stimulate the [reform] movement." This observation was made not long after William Henry Vanderbilt, the son of flamboyant "Commodore" Cornelius Vanderbilt, creator of the mighty New York Central system and father of Cornelius II and William K., allegedly told a reporter in Chicago: "The public be damned!" This widely publicized yet "entirely fictitious 'interview'" made William H. Vanderbilt an instant target of public wrath. It did not matter that the average person knew next to nothing about him. Most Americans for years considered every Vanderbilt to be part of an insensitive and money-hungry railroad family. The Omaha and the North Western suffered because of the presence of these "villains."[52]

Branding railroads as poor corporate citizens was a generally unfair criticism. Ironically transportation costs actually *dropped* during the late nineteenth century when carriers were being blasted for gouging consumers. Cheap, dependable haulage of goods and people had become an industry norm, and unmistakably an Omaha Road standard. This ongoing trend resulted from better equipment and physical plant; more skilled managers; intervention into the rate-making process by state railroad commissions in the 1870s; creation of the Interstate Commerce Commission, the product of the Interstate Commerce Act of 1887, which required rates to be "reasonable and just"; and massive new construction, hence greater competition, during the 1880s.[53]

While these public relations problems affected the Omaha negatively, the opening of competing long-distance lines proved especially troubling. In his report to shareholders in 1889, Marvin Hughitt noted that "the situation regarding nearly all competitive freight traffic presented new complications, some of which were very difficult to deal with." As he explained, the "business which formerly yielded fair returns to this Company as one of the older roads between Minneapolis and St. Paul and Chicago, has not increased in sufficient volume to fill the channels which are now opened by the existence of six competing lines and, in addition to these, another through route still further dividing and diverting the traffic was opened during the past year [1888] in the North, from St. Paul and Minneapolis to Sault Ste. Marie [Soo Line], in connection with the Canadian Pacific Railway, thus creating a seventh line for the through Eastern traffic, which is Inter-national and operated for the most part independently of the restrictions imposed by the Inter-State Commerce Law upon American railroads." Customers thus did well at the expense of the company.[54]

The Omaha Road found itself increasingly in a straitjacket. Public intervention was becoming a pronounced trend within the railroad industry. "I must think that there are becoming so fewer options to create revenues," lamented an officer of the troubled Erie Railroad in 1896, and colleagues from even the richest roads agreed. Leaders of the Omaha hoped that better economic conditions would stimulate both local and through traffic and that their continued commitment to excellence would generate and keep business.[55]

It was hoped that specific self-help activities might provide both short- and long-term financial benefits. The Omaha remained active in promoting sales of its land grant and in stimulating community development. A more heavily populated and thriving environment meant more revenues. James E. Moore, who headed the road's small but vigorous town lot company, for example, labored in the early 1890s to develop Avoca, Minnesota, a village located in Murray County on the Pipestone branch. "I am very much in earnest in trying to procure for Avoca a bank, a good hotel and a drug-store," he told a resident in November 1892, "and I do not propose to rest content with the situation, until your town is supplied with all three."[56]

The relationship between the North Western and the Omaha Road worked well. Even though the former delayed the absorption of the latter for a long time, there was really no compelling reason to alter the arrangement. The Omaha was large and prosperous enough to stand alone, and it functioned effectively as a mostly separate corporation. "The Omaha was about the right size to get your hands on," remarked a onetime official of the North Western. "It could be operated efficiently." Actually, the company was somewhat more substantial than its independent neighbors the Chicago Great Western and the Minneapolis & St. Louis, carriers that were generally well run, although less profitable. With control of the Omaha Road, the North Western hardly worried about losing this prized property. The onetime suitor of the Omaha, the Rock Island, had turned elsewhere to satisfy its ambition to serve the region. It chose the Burlington, Cedar Rapids & Northern as the vehicle, buying it outright from the Burlington in 1902. By World War I the Rock Island owned considerable mileage in southern Minnesota and a line that served eastern South Dakota.[57]

Although the entry and expansion of the Rock Island into the backyard of the Omaha Road annoyed the North Western, the Omaha possessed the superior railroad. In a reflective moment Marvin Hughitt called the affiliate "a bright and precious jewel." Not surprisingly the Omaha referred to itself officially as the "Royal Route," and it was.[58]

Employees at the shops in Boone, Iowa, take a break from their routine for their photograph, about 1895. Railroading, on the North Western and elsewhere, was often a male world, filled with dirty, dangerous work assignments. (Author's collection)

CHAPTER

Five

THE HUGHITT ERA

By the dawn of the twentieth century Marvin Hughitt reigned over an imposing railroad. The Chicago & North Western owned 5,767 route miles of line, and it controlled even more trackage. The system included the additional 1,591 miles of the Omaha Road and 1,300 miles of the Elkhorn Route. The editor of a daily newspaper in Huron, South Dakota, was so impressed with the size of the combined property that he told readers, "[I]f [its rails were] laid from east to west [they] would reach one-third way around the globe, or if extended through it would stick out at both ends, or reach from pole to pole."[1]

The company's annual income reflected the size of this sprawling nine-state carrier. For the fiscal year that ended on May 31, 1901, the core company generated gross earnings in excess of $43 million and net earnings that stood at nearly $16 million. Few railroads in the United States were larger or more prosperous. Not unexpectedly a financial writer for the *New York Times* termed the North Western the "Greatest of All the Grangers."[2]

Hughitt and the North Western established a reputation at home and abroad for a conservative approach to railroading. The regular and handsome dividends the company paid on its securities (usually 7 percent on preferred and 6 percent on common) commanded the respect of the investment community. The North Western contributed mightily to the nation's railway enterprise, whose stock dominated trading on Wall Street. The financial world carefully watched the road. "Chicago & Northwestern is such an important property, and the results of its operation so typical of the conditions in the settled Northwest," concluded a financial writer in 1903, "that its statements are received with as much interest as are those of [the] Pennsylvania in their relation to business conditions in the East." The Pennsylvania Railroad at the time immodestly called itself the "Standard Railroad of the World," a claim that was fully defensible. The North Western might have adopted a "Standard Railroad of the Midwest" slogan, for it was a stellar enterprise, and its future seemed particularly bright. No one then could have imagined that the railroads, including Hughitt's well-managed and thriving company, would in the not so distant future confront a serious competitive threat from motorized vehicles.[3]

Although no decade again equaled the new-line construction of the 1880s, considerable expansion occurred between the end of the depression of the 1890s and the outbreak of World War I. The national railroad map contained 193,346 miles in 1900 and 240,293 a decade later; it peaked at 254,251 miles in 1916. During this time the North Western contributed approximately 2,000 miles, and the Omaha Road added about 250 miles to the nation's most dynamic and visible industry.[4]

Feeder trackage dominated this expansion. Marvin Hughitt and his associates endorsed the concept of a "dense network of lines." While one official later jokingly described the system map as "resembling a plate of wet spaghetti," the building that occurred early in the century was not ill conceived. Most additions were designed to haul out grain or forest products and bring in coal, merchandise, and industrial goods. The company referred to these appendages as "gathering branches," an apt description. Business on them might boom for a few months during the "grain rush" or the seasonal tree harvesting and become somewhat somnolent during the remainder of the year. Not only did these branch lines tap traffic, they also discouraged invasions from other roads.[5]

Although many of these feeders would eventually be abandoned, they functioned for decades as commercial lifelines. Not until after World War I did the automobile, bus, and truck become alternative forms of transport. Even if internal combustion vehicles were reliable, and most were not, the terrible condition of roads in the North Western's domain made travel virtually impossible at times. The Upper Midwest had a large number of the "mud road states," and few residents were sanguine about solving the problem of "viscous and vicious" mud. The old

By 1892 the sprawling North Western system extended from Chicago to Duluth-Superior and on to Pierre, S.Dak., and Casper, Wyoming. When the hard times of the 1890s ended, the company constructed even more lines. (Author's collection)

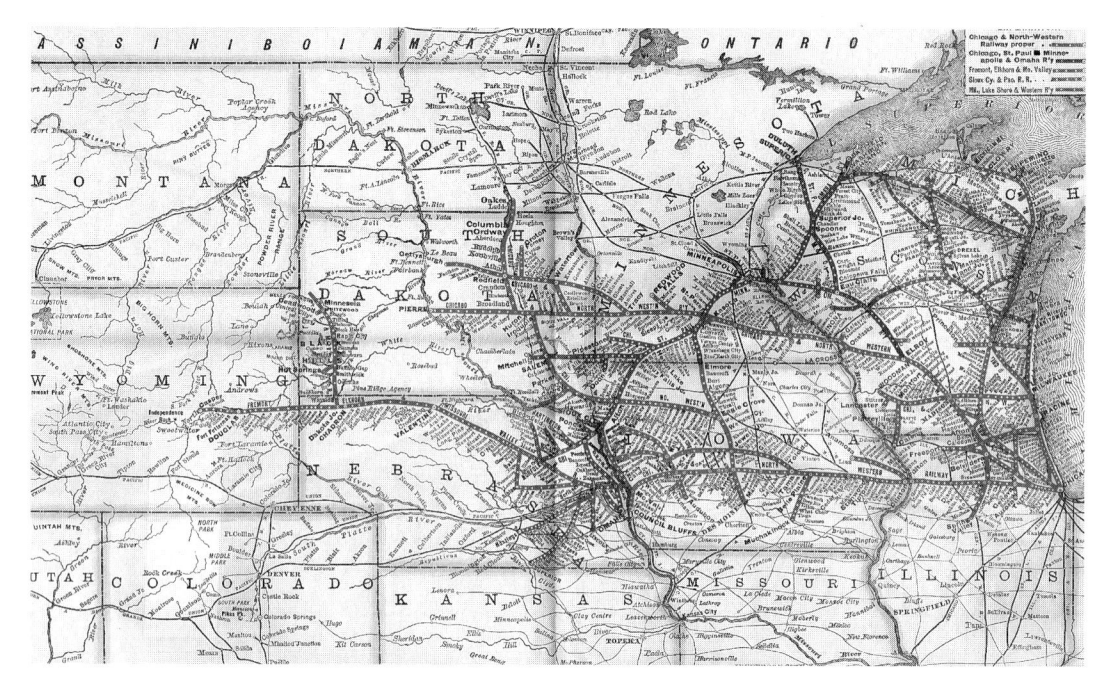

"Trade cards" were the rage in Gilded Age America, and the North Western used them to promote itself. (Author's collection)

adage rang true that "the better the soil, the poorer the roads."[6]

Iowa was an example. The state in 1904 possessed more than 100,000 miles of roadways; only Texas and Missouri claimed a more extensive network. These public roads were nearly all unimproved, that is, consisting of dirt, dust, or mud depending upon the season. All-weather highways in the Hawkeye State were rare: 1,408 miles of gravel, 241 miles of macadam or stone surface, and 20 miles of "other," probably brick. An observer, about 1905, commented: "It seems absurd that in a state so wealthy and prosperous, so advanced in education and intelligence the entire agricultural economy and the basis for practically all business activity should be left to the mercy of bad weather on account of roads which would be a disgrace even to a barbarian."[7]

The process of adding branches to feed the main lines of the North Western began anew toward the end of the 1890s. Once again the Hughitt road used subsidiaries to carry out much of the work. In 1899 the company, wishing "to reach and accommodate new business" in western Iowa and "for protection of its traffic," launched the Boyer Valley Railway. Soon this affiliate completed a 25-mile branch from Denison, a county seat on the Omaha stem, northeastward to Wall Lake, a hub of branch-line operations, and a 65-mile line from Boyer, near Wall Lake, southwestward to Mondamin, a station on the Sioux City & Pacific, 10 miles north of California Junction. These two lines crossed fertile farm lands and roughly paralleled the newly opened 131-mile "Omaha Extension" of the Illinois Central. Likely the North Western realized its objectives with this trackage.[8]

Even as the Boyer Valley Railway took shape, the North Western lengthened another branch in western Iowa, seven miles from Kirkman to Harlan, seat of Shelby County. This work was done under the auspicious of the Harlan & Kirkman Railway. In 1881 the North Western's Iowa South-Western Railway had installed 35 miles of track from Carroll, on the main line, to the hamlet of Kirkman. Construction stopped there, probably because Harlan, while close by, was considered to be in "Rock Island Country." Three years earlier the Avoca, Harlan & Northern Rail Road, a Rock Island affiliate, had reached Harlan from Avoca, located on its cross-state artery. The energetic actions of Ransom Cable surely ended any hesitations about serving Harlan. While the Rock Island did not strike back locally, the aggressive Chicago Great Western Railway later caused considerable consternation. Its dynamic president, A. B. Stickney, pushed an extension from Fort Dodge to Omaha alongside the Carroll to Harlan branch early in the twentieth century and captured much of the traffic.[9]

The North Western did not have to worry about competitors when in July 1900 it opened a 32-mile branch from Tyler, Minnesota, on the Winona & St. Peter, to Astoria, an "inland" village in Deuel County, South Dakota. This line, built by the Minnesota & South Dakota Railway, was the ideal appendage. Its rails stretched through transportation-starved sections of wheat country that annually generated hundreds of carloads of grain.[10]

Two years later a more ambitious branch was constructed nearby under the guidance of the Minnesota Western Railway. It created a 40-mile mostly grain-gathering line between the communities of Evan and Marshall. While this trackage never hummed with traffic, it provided a useful parallel route to portions of the main line west of Sleepy Eye. The Minnesota Western began at Evan on the Redwood Falls branch near Sleepy Eye, and proceeded westward through Redwood and Lyon counties to Marshall, a regional emporium. The Marshall terminus allowed trains to continue directly to Watertown, Redfield, and Gettysburg and later Pierre, South Dakota.[11]

Understandably the North Western invested heavily in branch lines throughout sections of the wheat belt, particularly South Dakota. The Great Plains, in the minds of many Americans, was the "Last Best West," and here remained opportunities to acquire free or inexpensive land and to participate in town building. Both were theoretically lucrative activities. The federal government stimulated development early in the century when it opened large tracts of former Indian reservations in the "West River Country" for settlement. Railroad service beyond the Missouri River, except in the Black Hills, was minimal, and the North Western sought to increase it. The company, however, encountered vigorous competition from its old nemesis, the Milwaukee Road.[12]

Hughitt and the Board of Directors endorsed several feeder projects in South Dakota. Extensions to the Verdigre branch were the most significant. The initial segment, built by the Elkhorn Route, had reached Verdigre, Nebraska, from South Norfolk, 54 miles, in 1888. Shortly before the company officially entered the North Western fold in 1903, it pushed the line northward 69 miles across the Missouri River to Bonesteel, in Gregory County, where

Well-dressed travelers assemble at the Boyer, Iowa, North Western station, around 1900. (Author's collection)

the terminus remained for several years. Once the economy and weather improved, settlers rushed in to acquire farm and village real estate made available by the earlier closing of the Fort Randall Reservation. When the government threw open the eastern part of the Rosebud Indian Reservation in 1904, additional public acres became accessible, and more were offered in 1908. Since much of this land was in neighboring Tripp County, northwest of Bonesteel, the thousands of expectant pioneers needed a railroad, and the North Western obliged. Crews put into place 26 miles of track between Bonesteel and Gregory in 1907, five more miles to Dallas the following year, 11 additional miles to Colome in 1910, and another 11 miles to Winner, the seat of Tripp County, a year later. The 175-mile Winner branch served a vast territory from the West River Country to northeastern Nebraska and gave patrons a direct route to Omaha and convenient connections to other midwestern destinations.[13]

A part of South Dakota, long open to settlement but developed fully only after the turn of the century, was the grassland section north and east of Pierre. The North Western claimed this general territory when its rails reached Gettysburg, seat of Potter County, from Faulkton and the east in 1887. That same year the Milwaukee Road had made a modest foray into the vicinity of Faulkton with a north-south branch from Eureka to Orient. But the collapse of the Great Dakota Boom further delayed expansion.[14]

A new building phase began in 1910. The North Western organized the James River Valley & North Western Railway to construct two sizable branches, though only one became a reality, a 40-mile line that stretched southward from Gettysburg through Oneida, seat of Sully County, to Blunt in Hughes County on the main line from Tracy to Pierre. The other project would have paralleled the main line for approximately 80 miles from Oneida eastward to Hitchcock on the Oakes, North Dakota, branch. Why the company shelved the latter construction is not clear; it conducted the survey work and briefly noted this trackage (in a broken line) on its official maps. Perhaps North Western officials assumed that the Milwaukee Road was unlikely to meddle in the area because its recent leap to the Pacific Northwest dramatically increased its debt.[15]

The North Western finished the better part of the James River Valley & North Western project. With the line from Gettysburg to Blunt, the company created a loop, which employees dubbed the "hump," from Tracy to Pierre, permitting more efficient use of equipment and more convenient scheduling of passenger trains. While the Oneida-to-Hitchcock line would have served more acres of grain and would have spawned several towns, the railroad already enjoyed a virtual monopoly on the business in this area. The problem was that farmers had to make longer, time-consuming trips to reach a station.[16]

In 1910, the year the Gettysburg-to-Blunt extension opened, the North Western turned to an undertaking north of the Black Hills. Its Belle Fourche Valley Railway constructed 23 miles of line between Belle Fourche, end of track of the former Elkhorn Route, eastward along the Belle Fourche River to Newell. This developing agricultural area needed a railroad. The Federal Bureau of Reclamation, created by the Newlands Act of 1902, selected the locality for one of its earliest ventures, and by 1912 the Belle Fourche Irrigation Project provided ample water to farmers. This was made possible by the Orman Dam, two major supply canals, and a companion maze of irrigation ditches.[17]

The Belle Fourche Valley could possibly have become more of a cutoff than a stub-end piece of trackage. Officials considered extending the branch from Newell southeastward to join the Winner line, but this plan never evolved much beyond the discussion stage. The *Railroad Age Gazette* speculated that the appendage would be pushed eastward from Newell to Gettysburg, consequently forging a second trans-Dakota route. This might involve construction of a bridge over the Missouri River with the Minneapolis & St. Louis Railroad near Le Beau, western terminus of that Minneapolis-based granger road, which apparently had its eyes on the vast cattle county of northern South Dakota, where it would compete with the Milwaukee Road. Apparently some survey work and negotiations occurred.[18]

While agricultural branches predominated new construction during the early part of the century, the North Western built appendages to reach exploitable natural resources, usually stands of timber. Unless streams were adequate, lumbermen needed railroad cars to haul logs to mills and take the finished products to markets.

Even before the depression loosened its grip on the Upper Midwest, the North Western authorized construction of an important lumber feeder. In 1895 it incorporated the Wisconsin Northern Railway "to construct a railroad from a point of connection with the Chicago & North Western Railway at or near the station of Big Suamico in Brown County . . . , and running in a northwesterly and northerly direction through parts of Brown, Oconto, Shawano, Forest, and Florence counties to the boundary line between the States of Wisconsin and Michigan, an approximate distance of 115 miles." Because of hard times, the North Western wanted to increase sales of its timber lands, but poor transportation made them "of low practical value and unavailable for profitable development." The company thought that once the trees were harvested a "considerable tract of good agricultural land will ultimately be redeemed from the forest and brought under cultivation." Such a branch seemed to be a sound long-term investment as well as an immediate source of income from land sales and freight charges.[19]

Construction of the Wisconsin Northern began slowly. Rails were not laid on the southern portion of the projected route until 1897. The starting point, however, was Gillett (Northern Junction) on the leased St. Paul Eastern Grand Trunk Railway rather than Big Suamico near Green Bay. Trains ran initially over the 46 miles between Gillett and Wabeno, in Nicolet County. The North Western subsequently discarded the Wisconsin Northern corporation and extended the branch under its own authority 15 miles northward to Lacona. This Nicolet County lumber camp remained the end of track from 1899 until 1906. Then the North Western added another 30 miles, making connection at Saunders, Michigan, with its east-west Powers–Iron Mountain–Ashland line.[20]

As the new century began, the North Western installed a 17-mile branch to the west of the Wisconsin Northern. This appendage extended northeasterly through remote sections of Oneida and Nicolet counties from Pelican, on the former Lake Shore Road, to Crandon. But unlike the Wisconsin Northern, this line never reached another North Western artery.[21]

Railroad construction continued, however, in the area after the North Western arrived at Crandon. The Wisconsin & Northern Railroad, an independent road that the Soo Line later acquired (and not to be confused with the Wisconsin Northern), built through Crandon on a north-south axis. The North Western was forced to share some of the lumber traffic with its new rival.[22]

As workers toiled in the North Woods of Wisconsin, others laid 24 miles of "spur track" from Perkins (later called Winde), Michigan, on the Escanaba-to-Isheming line, in a northerly direction through land grant acres of Alger and Delta counties to a terminus called Ladosa. Service on this cheaply built Upper Peninsula branch began in 1901, but traffic must have been minimal. Public timetables did not list scheduled passenger trains, although riders may have traveled in the caboose of a logging run.[23]

It was coal and not lumber that induced the North Western to form the Southern Iowa Railway in 1901. The company had served the softcoal fields in Mahaska County, Iowa, since the 1880s, and a maze of track tied together the diggings. When more coal sites developed southwest of the Des Moines River in Monroe County at the turn of the century, the North Western built 22 miles of line from Stark, a station near the end of the Belle Plaine–Muchakinock branch, to Buxton in northern Monroe County. This terminus, which became the headquarters of the railroad's Consolidated Coal Company, boomed. Most of Buxton's estimated 6,000 residents were African Americans, unique for an

The North Western published a foreign-language folder at the turn of the century to promote German settlement in Michigan and Wisconsin. The company touted the availability of thousands of acres of "Forest and Cleared Land." (Charles H. Stats collection)

Iowa community, and a huge company store served their needs. The branch reached the western part of Monroe County about the time of World War I; its official end of track was Consol, another Consolidated Coal town, which flourished until the Great Depression.[24]

Before World War I American railroad owners invested heavily in what became the second building of their vast enterprise. They did so because of an unprecedented demand for freight and passenger services. A variety of betterments followed: the laying of thousands of miles of heavier steel rails; installation of modern signaling devices; and a plethora of rebridging, regrading, and line-straightening projects. This last included pieces of "cutoff" trackage that were designed to facilitate a more efficient flow of traffic.[25]

Outside the Chicago area, where construction of cutoffs, track elevations, and a massive passenger terminal cost millions of dollars (see chapter 6), the North Western also spent heavily on streamlining its expansive network. Some of this work created line additions that generated considerable business, having the same impact on the system as did contemporary agricultural, lumber, and coal appendages.

Formation of the Mankato & New Ulm Railway in 1899 was a quintessential cutoff project. This satellite firm constructed a 26-mile line relocation between the two Minnesota communities of its corporate name. Completion of this alternative route to the original Winona & St. Peter main line in mid-1900 provided several improvements: trackage across the state was reduced by slightly more than eight miles; residents of Mankato, a thriving market and college town, received superior service; and interchange with the Omaha Road's Twin Cities-to-Sioux City line was improved. The earlier route, via St. Peter, remained but slipped to branch-line status.[26]

A much larger undertaking that affected southern Minnesota was the simultaneous work conducted by another affiliate, the Minnesota & Iowa Railway. This company built a 119-mile line that consisted of both branch and cutoff components. The feeder portion connected the Redwood County, Minnesota, villages of Vesta on the northwest and Sanborn on the southwest, a distance of 26 miles. The latter community was also a station on the cross-state main line. The cutoff section, which extended for 93 miles from Sanborn southeasterly to the northern Iowa town of Burt, Kossuth County, met the old Toledo & North Western. The new trackage gave the North Western a much improved route between points in western Minnesota and eastern South Dakota and those to the east and south. It roughly paralleled and served the same purpose as the much more westerly trackage between Iroquois, South Dakota, and Hawarden, Iowa, which similarly connected with a former Toledo & North Western line.[27]

Another lengthy cutoff that "filled out the system well" was the 195-mile Iowa, Minnesota & North Western Railway. Its first 55-mile portion was spiked down in 1899 from Blue Earth City (Blue Earth), Minnesota, southeast to Mason City, Iowa. The former community was located on the Omaha Road's busy Elmore line, and the latter, the prosperous seat of Cerro Gordo County, gave the company entry into a traffic-rich area.[28]

The Iowa, Minnesota & North Western completed its work in 1900 with two projects. One involved the installation of 29 miles of track west from Blue Earth to Fox Lake, Minnesota, and a junction with the Minnesota & Iowa. This extension also offered an interchange with the recently opened 30-mile north-south Medalia-Fairmont branch of the Omaha Road at Fairmont, situated about midway between Blue Earth and Fox Lake.[29]

The second project, the last and longest span of the Iowa, Minnesota & North Western, was the 107-mile extension southeast of Mason City to the Omaha stem at Belle Plaine. While this construction missed every county seat and important community along its path, including the Waterloo–Cedar Falls population center, it traversed some of the nation's best corn and hog country. Where the company developed a monopoly, it generated a brisk local business. The Belle Plaine-to-Fox Lake line, moreover, made a practical cutoff for traffic in and out of eastern South Dakota and southern Minnesota. It also provided an economical way to transport coal from southern Iowa to the prairie regions of the northwest. "I can still see in my mind's eye those long trains of coal, grain and merchandise rumbling behind those little ten-wheelers down the line," recalled a resident of Mason City. "There was a lot of business there in the 1920s," and that observation held true for the previous twenty years as well.[30]

Not long after the Iowa, Minnesota & North Western opened, the North Western focused on southern Wisconsin, fashioning a combination cutoff and branch network between Princeton and Marshfield. Using the corporate entity of the Princeton & North Western Railway, the Hughitt road built an additional 105 miles of trackage during 1901 and 1902. Specifically, the Princeton & North Western extended the Fond du Lac–Princeton branch, which the Sheboygan & Fond du Lac Railroad had built in 1871, northwestward through the counties of Green Lake, Marquette, Waushara, Portage, and Wood to Marshfield and the Omaha Road's Merrillan-Marshfield line. This construction created another trans-Wisconsin route; it provided a direct path connecting Sheboygan, Fond du Lac, Marshfield, Merrillan, Eau Claire, and the Twin Cities. The Princeton & North Western installed two small appendages: eight miles from Bannerman to Red Granite (Waushara County) in 1901, and seven miles from Grand Rapids to Nekoosa (Wood County) the following year. The main stem served an important manufacturing center, Grand Rapids, later renamed Wisconsin Rapids, and a growing number of summer lake resorts.[31]

Two major cutoffs that appeared during this period were also located in Wisconsin and arguably held greater strategic value than most others. The North Western had debated whether the first of these should be built at all because of political factors. In 1900 famous "progressive boss" Robert M. La Follette Sr. and his fellow Republican insurgents came to power in the state. These reformers seemed determined to "crucify" the large railroads, burdening them with high property taxes and other restrictive regulations. Although the Badger State would not be "redeemed" until the election of Republican stalwart Emanuel L. Philipp to the governorship in 1914, the company decided to proceed with its needed building program. "The La Follette crowd and its anti-railroad intentions were ignored," noted a Wisconsin journalist. But this was not the full explanation. The North Western and other principal carriers developed a more comfortable relationship with the energized Wisconsin Railroad Commission. A painstaking study of that body during this period concluded that the commission ultimately aided the railroads "by a greater insulation from the threat that the politics of reform would disrupt their operations." Thus the regulated essentially captured the regulators.[32]

The project Marvin Hughitt and his associates debated was whether to construct the Manitowoc, Green Bay & North Western Railway. When the green light came in 1905, workers laid 36 miles of track northward from Manitowoc to near Green Bay. From there they built in two directions: northwestward 30 from Duck Creek (Green Bay) to an intersection with the Ashland Division (the former Wisconsin Northern Railroad) north of Gillett, in Oconto County, and largely westward 48 miles from Pulaska, a station on the Duck Creek-to-Gillett line, to Eland Junction, in Shawano County. The intent was to link the Ashland and Peninsula divisions more effectively. "[It] will affect important savings in distance between points on those divisions in North Wisconsin and Michigan and points south of Manitowoc, as compared with the distances which obtain via the existing lines through Green Bay and Fond du Lac, over which a large volume of traffic now passes," explained Marvin Hughitt. "The maximum grades and curvatures on the new railway will also be much less than on the old lines."[33]

While the Manitowoc, Green Bay & North Western trackage primarily facilitated freight traffic between the Upper Peninsula and northern Wisconsin and Milwaukee and Chicago, the Milwaukee, Sparta & North Western Railway contributed markedly to future movements of both freight and passengers. Better known as the Adams Cutoff (named for a station near Necedah, Wisconsin), this "direct route with low grades" took shape during 1910 and 1911 and linked Lindwerm, eight miles north of Milwaukee, with Sparta, a town in the western Wisconsin county of Monroe. The 135-mile line, which used the existing but wholly rebuilt 13-mile Necedah-Wyeville branch, forged connections with the Omaha Road to the Twin Cities at Wyeville, 23 miles east of Sparta, and with the old Winona & St. Peter to South Dakota at Sparta.[34]

Tracklayers install the Nelson-Peoria line near Buda, Ill., in 1901. (Railway & Locomotive Historical Society)

The Milwaukee, Sparta & North Western also created a belt line around Milwaukee. This involved an eight-mile cutoff between the new construction at Butler, six miles west of Lindwerm, and West Allis, on the Madison line near the Wisconsin metropolis. "[It] will afford great relief from congestion at the terminal within that city," noted Hughitt in 1910. "All through traffic may be diverted to the best line and a considerable portion of the local traffic distributed at its terminal yards." The Butler to West Allis and the Lindwerm to Clayman Junction (44 miles) portions of the Milwaukee, Sparta & North Western were double-tracked, and "they handled all trains with dispatch."[35]

The final cutoff construction involved trackage installed by the Sioux City, Dakota & North Western. This Iowa endeavor reached fruition in 1910, the year work began on the Adams Cutoff. The Hawkeye State affiliate completed approximately 28 route miles from a point near Hinton, Iowa (Wren), 12 miles north of Sioux City, northwest to Hawarden, the Sioux County town where the Iroquois line of the former Dakota Central met the Eagle Grove line of the former Toledo & North Western. When the Sioux City, Dakota & North Western opened, the North Western possessed a shorter and better engineered route between Sioux City, the ranking city in the region, and stations in South Dakota. The Hughitt road, moreover, signed an agreement with the Illinois Central "providing for perpetual trackage rights over the main line of the Illinois Central Railroad Company between Sioux City and Hinton." Omaha Road trains, however, continued to use the full 26-mile segment of the Illinois Central between Sioux City and Le Mars, Iowa.[36]

While not every piece of postdepression trackage fits neatly into one of the three basic categories, several additions could best be described as extensions. They were usually longer lines that reached into new territory or at least had the potential for doing so. Officials likely did not consider them as either appendages or improvements to existing parts of the system.

Although the North Western already had reached several bituminous coal fields in Illinois and Iowa, it wished to tap even more acres of black diamonds. Moreover it eyed the central Illinois city of Peoria, a burgeoning manufacturing metropolis of 57,578 residents in 1900. The company further contemplated expansion to St. Louis, the country's second greatest railroad center. These objectives led to still more subsidiaries, the Peoria & North Western Railway in 1901, and the St. Louis, Peoria & North Western Railway a decade later.[37]

The first part of the expansion agenda in Illinois involved the Peoria & North Western. Construction of this affiliate began in March 1901, from the Omaha stem at Nelson, near Dixon, southward 85 miles to Peoria. Workers finished the line 10 months later. The company arranged with the Peoria & Pekin Union Railway, a terminal property, to provide access to the greater Peoria freight business. The North Western also became a tenant in Peoria's union passenger station.[38]

The second segment began to take shape in 1913 when the St. Louis, Peoria & North Western commenced construction of a line 90 miles southward to Girard in Macoupin County. It laid 14 miles of rail between Peoria and Pekin in 1913, and 78 miles between Pekin and Girard the following year. At its southern extremity the subsidiary connected with the Macoupin County Railway, another North Western satellite. This coal carrier had completed 24 miles of track between Girard and Benld in 1904, following an earlier report made by a consulting engineer that mineral lands should be acquired and developed because the "coal is of a superior quality, easily mined [and] free from dirt and waste." The thrust from Peoria southward prompted William A. Gardner, Hughitt's successor, to observe: "[It] will give the Company direct access to its extensive coal fields in Southern Illinois and insure to it an economical, adequate and reliable supply of fuel." That was largely the explanation an official of the North Western gave the Interstate Commerce Commission in 1927: "[T]he extension from Peoria to Girard was built for the purpose of hauling our own coal from our own mines on our own line, so that we would not have to ship it over foreign railroads any longer." It was the same strategy employed by the Burlington when it pushed into the region at approximately the same time.[39]

The additional mileage did more than reach fuel, however; the North Western gained access to St. Louis rail connections. An interchange with the Litchfield & Madison Railway, the self-proclaimed "St. Louis Gateway Route," a 45-mile shortline that linked its namesake towns, and trackage rights gave entrance into the teeming freight yards of East St. Louis, Illinois. In 1958 the North Western acquired this well-positioned road.[40]

The other line extensions took place in the trans-Missouri West between 1906 and 1907. Specifically, they involved the construction activities of the Pierre, Rapid City & North Western Railway, which installed 165 miles of track through the West River Country from Fort Pierre (opposite Pierre on the Missouri River) to Rapid City, and the Wyoming & North Western Railway, which built from Casper to the western Wyoming settlements of Shoshoni, "a new town located near the eastern boundary line of the Shoshoni Indian Reservation," 102 miles, and Lander, 45 miles southwest of Shoshoni.[41]

The Pierre, Rapid City & North Western provided everything that the North Western wanted: a means to reach a developing agricultural country; a cutoff from the northern part of the system to the Black Hills; and a potential springboard to the West, perhaps ultimately to the Pacific Ocean. "This line was really one of the last key lines that needed to be built," concluded a company official in 1918. "[It] . . . potentially gave us a further way to the West." As early as 1903 John E. Blunt, the company's chief engineer, had seen value in the route solely on the merits of local traffic: "The astonishing influx of settlers in that country has changed the situation so materially as to invite the building of railroads to the Hills."[42]

Construction went swiftly. The sections from Fort Pierre to Philip and Rapid City to Wasta were finished in 1906; the remaining 44-mile gap

A crowd gathers in 1906 to welcome the first North Western passenger train to arrive in Lander, Wyo. The construction train stands on a siding in the background. (North Western/Union Pacific)

Early in the twentieth century the North Western considered at least two routes to the Pacific Ocean from Lander, Wyo. (Author's collection)

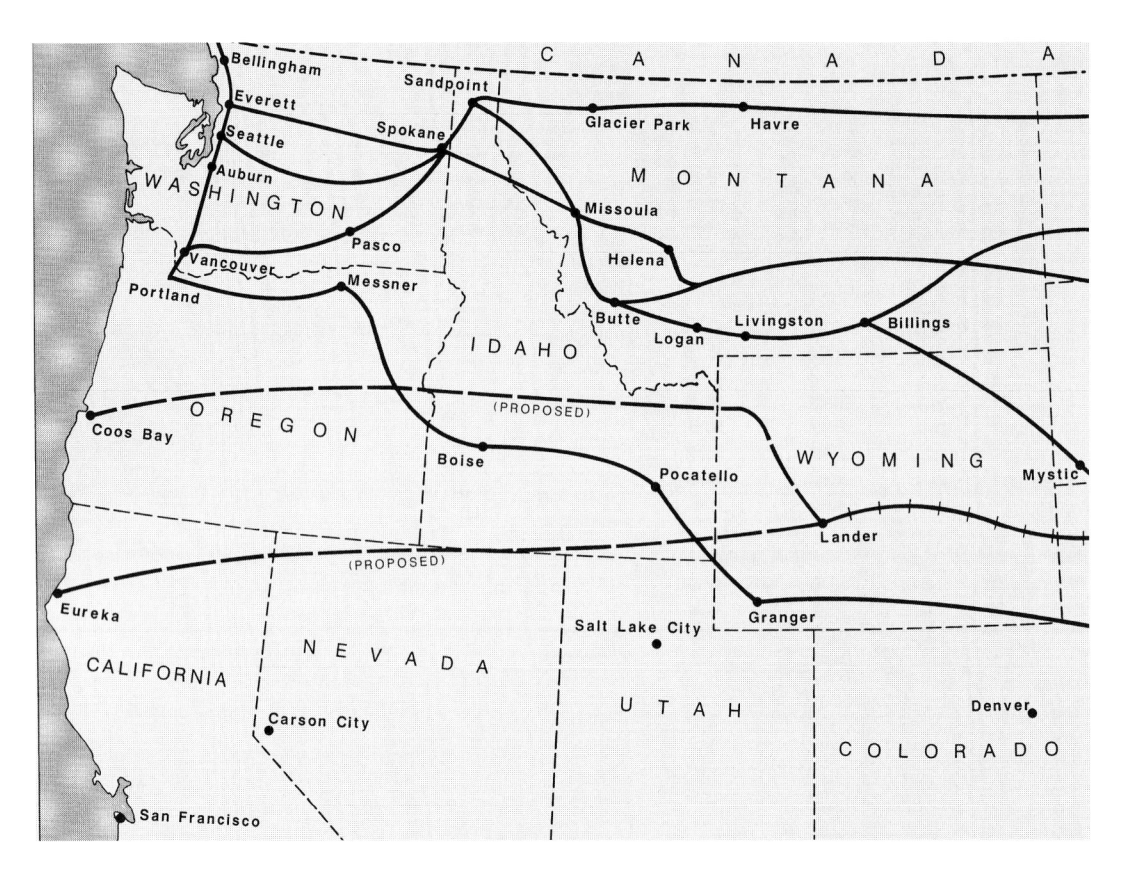

was closed the following year. Yet the project was a challenge. A shortage of white laborers prompted the employment of Native Americans "on the rougher work"; Indians were hired seemingly out of desperation. Since the line crossed little level terrain, crews encountered major grading problems, particularly near Wall in the Badlands. And there was the need to span scores of streams, especially the meandering and occasionally dry Bad River and its tributaries. A clever wag called the company "*P*retty *R*ough *C*ountry & *No Water*," and the nickname stuck.[43]

Observers of the North Western expected that when the company launched the Wyoming & North Western and headed westward from Casper, it was contemplating more than agricultural development of the over 1.4 million acres of former Shoshoni Indian lands that the federal government opened for settlement in 1906. Yet that was the announced purpose when the first regularly scheduled train steamed into Lander, 1,246 miles from Chicago, on October 17, 1906. While the Lander extension "sewed up parts of [Wyoming] for Mr. Hughitt," it seemed destined to become part of an even more ambitious project.[44]

Such speculation seemed warranted. The North Western at this time considered at least two routes from Wyoming to the Pacific Ocean. One would run from Lander westward along the Idaho, Utah, and Nevada state lines into northern California, with Eureka, a costal community of some 7,300 residents, the probable destination. The other line would extend northward from Shoshoni and then bend to the west from the southern boundary of Yellowstone National Park through central Idaho and Oregon to Coos Bay, a port that "could rival Portland and San Francisco." Conceivably Hughitt discussed these schemes and perhaps others with E. H. Harriman, who had taken control of the Union Pacific in the late 1890s and was converting it into a "first-class" property. They likely talked about some type of cooperative venture. Harriman, a tough negotiator, surely told Hughitt to keep his end of track in South Dakota or Wyoming. Harriman already faced conflict with James J. Hill in the Pacific Northwest; the two men soon battled over control of Deschutes Canyon and a route through central Oregon. Entry by the North Western, even under a joint arrangement with the Union Pacific, would only complicate matters. Harriman no doubt encouraged the North Western to remain primarily a granger operation.[45]

In conjunction with its expansion in Wyoming and its evaluation of California and Oregon termini, the North Western considered forming a partnership with the Milwaukee Road, its longtime rival, for a line to the Pacific Northwest. This well-managed firm, like the North Western, found a Pacific extension an interesting possibility. Hughitt did not personally enter negotiations with his counterpart, Albert J. Earling. Rather, William K. Vanderbilt of the North Western's Executive Committee discussed the matter with William Rockefeller, the Standard Oil Company executive who served in a similar capacity with the Milwaukee. From these conversations a joint routing strategy emerged. Construction would extend westward from South Dakota, likely from Rapid City, which both companies had reached from the east by 1907, through Montana and Idaho to the Washington cities of Seattle and Tacoma.[46]

Nothing of significance followed the Vanderbilt-Rockefeller parley. Although details of the negotiations are sketchy, it seems that various forces undermined a joint agreement. The matter of cost probably caused the North Western to back off. The price tag likely came to between $50 and $75 million. Furthermore, there was that "tradition of mutual distrust" between the two roads, and surely neither Harriman nor Hill would have approved. An undismayed Hughitt urged associates to "stick to our knitting, develop this railroad in its present territory and let the Milwaukee build to the coast if it wants to," which is what happened. Hughitt seemed content, in the words of a published report, for his company to "remain the great local line which it now is."[47]

Anytime there were hints of North Western expansion to the Pacific, individuals and groups along anticipated routes expressed enthusiasm. Often proponents promised to assist the project through a local tax or by donating land for the right-of-way and station sites. Rumors of a joint North Western and Milwaukee Road move toward Puget Sound brought this comment from a Kittitas County, Washington, resident: "If the Northwestern and St. Paul [Milwaukee Road] build through Ellensburg, there will be rejoicing in the streets." Yet the North Western, with its cautious management, never allowed public opinion to stampede it into what might have been a bad business decision. Recalled a company official in 1928, "Mr. Hughitt refused to get caught up in that hysteria to add 'Pacific' to his road's corporate name."[48]

The Hughitt "stick-to-our-knitting" philosophy turned out well. The Panic of 1907 dashed most plans for westward expansion as hard times crippled a large portion of the railroad industry. All was quiet at North Western headquarters. The company weathered this business crisis and remained a darling with investors. On the other hand the Milwaukee Road, which installed the final rails of its Pacific coast extension west of Garrison, Montana, on May 14, 1909, experienced immediate and long-term economic problems and soon lost its blue chip standing.[49]

After 1910 the railroad world lacked the ambitious drive of the previous decade. Companies still laid more track, and most of it appeared west of the Missouri River, but no one built to the Pacific, with the exception of the Western Pacific Railroad in 1910. This western leg of the George Gould system proved to be financially disappointing.[50]

Marvin Hughitt's prudence involved more than rejecting a Pacific extension once its costs and risks were fully understood. He would not become "Mr. Construction" solely for company or personal aggrandizement, preferring a positive image based on his reflective, cautious actions. Throughout his tenure Hughitt sought to enrich the long-term economic base of the railroad. He fervently believed that what was best for the North Western's territory was best for the property.

Hughitt's efforts focused on bolstering farm income. He backed creation of one of the industry's first agricultural development departments, complete with several full-time experts. In this he was hardly unique among railroad executives. Prominent railroad leader James J. Hill also fostered trackside agriculture; he advocated "dual-purpose" cows (for meat and milk), swine, and potatoes. Hughitt championed much the same, but alfalfa especially fascinated him. Realizing that wheat growers on the Great Plains had suffered terribly in the early 1890s because of drought and low prices, he concluded that a self-help solution lay with diversification, a move to cattle raising or perhaps dairying. Alfalfa could play a critical role, for this easily produced legume made an excellent and economical livestock feed and contributed to soil improvement.[51]

A man of direct action, Hughitt promoted alfalfa at every opportunity. The North Western printed an array of special educational pamphlets, of which *Alfalfa: The Money Crop of the West and Northwest* was among the most widely distributed. The company also operated alfalfa demonstration trains that were aimed at monocrop farmers, and it financed alfalfa-related research at several agricultural colleges. Early in the century Hughitt personally asked Nebraska farmers to try the crop. Those who agreed were accorded cheap leases on portions of the railroad's right-of-way and other lands.[52]

Hughitt and the North Western deservedly won praise for their aggressive and continuing alfalfa campaign. "President Hughitt has revolutionized agriculture in Antelope County," commented a Neligh, Nebraska, newspaperman. "The successful culture of alfalfa means good income for farmers and townspeople . . . and for the North Western as well."[53]

The journalist was right. Hughitt knew that if agrarians prospered so would his company. That is why he endorsed more than alfalfa. Experts from the North Western and the University of Wisconsin Extension Service, for example, worked with members of the local Potato Growers' Association to promote the "spud." The railroad's "Potato Exhibit Car" toured that state just as did its "land-clearing" trains. The company wished to show Wisconsinites how stump-pulling machines and dynamite could clear the land and make possible production of potatoes and other crops.[54]

The Hughitt road did much more than promote specific agricultural products. It pioneered a crop-reporting service in the mid-1880s. This useful information was generally collected by station agents and then sent by the company to the local and regional press. The sophistication of this data gathering later improved, much to Hughitt's satisfaction.[55]

When crops failed, the North Western responded with equal concern. It was hardly a "soulless corporation." After troubles struck the wheat belt during the early 1890s, the company slashed freight rates for seed grains to one-quarter of the normal charges and hauled cattle feed and coal at half price.[56]

While the railroad suffered during times of farm distress—everyone understood the adage that "when there's no rain on the plains, there's no grain in the trains"—the commitment to agricultural development paid off handsomely. In 1900 raw agricultural goods amounted to nearly 20 percent of the company's gross-ton miles of freight, and Hughitt accurately predicted that this "could be raised significantly . . . and profitably."[57]

Concern by Marvin Hughitt for the well-being of agrarians, while admittedly self-serving, paralleled his view of the company's employees. Throughout his tenure the North Western enjoyed a commendable record of labor-management relations. Although no railroad ever created a worker's paradise, the company was a good place for a lifetime career. It adopted a generous pay policy and offered various supportive programs. Consequently the North Western experienced only minor disruptions during the bitter general strikes of 1877 and 1894; it was blessed with labor peace for decades.[58]

Even though Hughitt was not the only one responsible for a reasonably contented workforce, he played a positive, nurturing role. He favored liberal rates of pay, and the company regularly granted employees wages that equaled or surpassed those of its competitors. "I have always believed that our people should be rewarded with a decent living wage," Hughitt told the press during a brief wildcat strike by telegraph operators on the Peninsula Division in 1893. "I do not feel that we should cut wages during hard times. It is foolish in the long run to obtain labor at the cheapest price."[59]

This conviction sharply contrasted with views held by Charles Perkins, president of the Burlington Railroad and a classic laissez-faire advocate. He thought that workers should be paid entirely on the basis of supply and demand or what he called the "natural law." Not unexpectedly, in 1888 the Burlington suffered a bitter strike by its locomotive engineers, mainly because their pay was so much less than that of their colleagues on neighboring roads. "Hoggers" who handled the Burlington's "fast mails," for example, received $87.50 for 26 days of work; those on the North Western earned $120 for approximately the same assignment.[60]

Marvin Hughitt was not an aggressive Charles Perkins. The North Western head was a more caring individual, and the policies of the railroad toward its employees reflected his personal outlook. Managements of a number of other carriers took a similar stance. But opinions and sentiments were diverse, and some roads strongly opposed assuming any paternalistic functions.

Historical records offer an abundance of examples of North Western benevolence during the Hughitt era. The company, for instance, had long followed a compassionate policy toward injured workers. When Peter Johnson, a student brakeman, made his first trip in July 1908, he suffered a critical accident near Lake Benton, Minnesota. "[Johnson] fell directly under the [freight car] wheels and one pair of wheels passed over his legs below the knees severing both limbs from the body." The train crew summoned a local physician and then took Johnson to Tracy, Minnesota, the nearest division point and his hometown, for additional medical attention. The company surgeon decided that Johnson required the care of specialists at the Mayo Brothers' Clinic, and "a special train was made up which took him to Rochester." Although the young man's career as a railroader ended abruptly, his life was saved.[61]

While the tragedy that befell brakeman Johnson and the response made by the North Western received limited press attention, the actions of heroine Kate Shelley generated considerable and sustained interest and again revealed a compassionate corporation. A series of cloudbursts struck central Iowa on July 8, 1881, severing the Omaha line, and the 15-year-old daughter of the widow of a section foreman and farmer near Moingona, six miles west of Boone, responded in an extraordinary fashion when a locomotive and its crew plunged into the raging waters of Honey Creek near her home in the late evening. Shelley sought to alert the eastbound *Atlantic Express*, scheduled to pass through Moingona shortly after midnight. This meant crawling across the 600-foot railway bridge over the Des Moines River amid driving rain and dangerous lightning. Her task was made all the more difficult by spikes placed in the bridge ties to deter trespassers. Shelley finally reached her destination, the depot at Moingona, and there she reported the wreck at Honey Creek. Unknown to her the company had already ordered trains halted at the edge of

Kate Shelley, the widely acclaimed heroine who helped to save the lives of two North Western crewmen, stands on the platform at Moingona, Iowa, about 1904, shortly after her appointment as station agent. After the original two-story depot burned in 1901, the modest wooden structure served the public on this North Western appendage. (North Western/Union Pacific)

the storm. Shelley then guided a rescue party that saved two stranded crew members; two others had already drowned.[62]

The actions subsequently taken by the North Western were magnanimous. It gave $5,000 to two families of the flood victims, $2,500 to a third family, and $100 to a fund sponsored by the community to reward Kate Shelley and assist her impoverished family. Later the company sent the Shelleys "a car of hard coal, two barrels of flour, a sack of coffee, chest of tea, potatoes, soap and a quantity of wearing apparel." Subsequently in October 1903 the railroad hired Shelley as its station agent at Moingona; previously she had worked intermittently as a rural school teacher. Since the company had recently relocated the main line over the Des Moines River, the village received only limited service, and so Shelley's duties were modest, appropriately so since her health was fragile. She mostly sold passenger tickets and billed freight shipments, remaining at the depot until her death in 1912.[63]

Although Peter Johnson labored for only a single day and Kate Shelley died while still on the job, thousands of workers served many years before leaving the North Western. Retired workers commonly did not expect a pension. Although such government-administrated schemes had developed in a limited fashion in Europe before World War I, most Americans persisted in thinking that security for illness and old age was strictly a private matter. It took the ravages of the Great Depression of the 1930s to persuade federal lawmakers to break with tradition and pass the Social Security Act in August 1935. Incredible in retrospect, some railroad companies anticipated this momentous social change decades earlier. Most notably, the Baltimore & Ohio had launched the country's first railroad pension plan in 1884 as part of its general relief program. Employees, who were 35 years old and who had worked for the company 10 years or longer, could retire and receive benefits.[64]

Even before the railroads created their own pension schemes, employees had gained a measure of security as a result of particular hiring practices. The earliest workers frequently came from farm backgrounds—railroads served as the first wage-earning experiences for many lads— but gradually this situation changed. By the end of the nineteenth century nepotism in hiring widely prevailed. Most carriers, including the North Western, tolerated or even encouraged the practice. Hughitt himself took part and never tried to change it. "I see the employment of good men from good North-Western Ry. families a benefit," he wrote Frederick D. Underwood, who headed the Erie Railroad, a carrier noted for favoritism. "This means that these men will act in a dependable way. They will not want to injure their own family members and friends." He added, "We can never expect to be a big family on this railroad because of our many thousands of employees, but that can happen on the individual divisions and in the shops."[65] And Hughitt's own family benefited. His son, Marvin Jr., joined the freight department in 1881, when he was 20, and steadily advanced through the ranks. By 1906 the younger Hughitt was serving as the road's freight traffic manager.[66]

Another bond that fostered job security and contributed to family connections on the North Western was membership in the Freemasons. While the company employed hundreds of non-Masons, including Roman Catholics, a tradition developed among workers, particularly those in train service, to join Masonic lodges. This secret, Christian-based society was popular throughout the system, and it made the North Western a "Protestant" road of sorts. Those men who gained positions of responsibility and authority frequently belonged to this fraternal group.[67]

In addition to the unwritten code of family and fraternal connections, employees of the North Western gained a degree of financial protection through the evolving seniority system. Managers frequently gave experienced workers choice assignments and protected them during times of retrenchment. Before the company adopted a pension plan in December 1900, veteran employees constituted an important part of the workforce. For example, there were locomotive engineers past the age of 70, and a few even in their 80s, who operated some of the first-class passenger trains. If senior employees still needed regular paychecks but were unable to hold demanding assignments, they might take a menial task such as road-crossing flagman, station attendant, and office messenger.[68]

The complexion of the workforce began to change after 1900. Longtime North Western employees could expect to supplement their savings with modest monthly pension checks, and they could afford to retire and enjoy their twilight years. The company's stated policy was to reward personnel "who have rendered it long and faithful service," by granting "monthly allowances" based on longevity of employment. Individuals 70 years of age or older and with 30 years or more on the job "shall be retired and pensioned." Others, too, received coverage. "All employees sixty-five to sixty-nine years of age, inclusive of both years, who have been thirty or more years in the service, and who have become incapacitated, may be retired and pensioned." Payment was determined in this fashion: "For each year of service one per cent. of the average regular monthly pay for the ten years next preceding retirement; provided, however, that the annual pension disbursement of the company shall not exceed two hundred thousands dollars." If that amount was reached and the Board of Directors refused to commit additional funds, "a new rate shall be established proportionately reducing all allowances."[69]

When it came to a pension program, the North Western was not an innovator but an imitator, turning to the Pennsylvania Railroad for its model. That mammoth Philadelphia-based carrier had launched its retirement plan on January 1, 1900, and claimed to be "the first railroad in the United States to institute a formal pension plan covering all its employes." The details were largely the same as those incorporated into the North Western program a year later. Both railroads were profitable and well managed, and the Pennsylvania influence on the North Western is understandable. Alexander J. Cassat, the Pennsylvania president from 1899 to 1906, had been heavily involved in preparing the pension scheme, and he and Hughitt knew each other well.[70]

The pension program of the North Western functioned smoothly. The owners of the *Chicago Tribune* were so impressed that they adopted much of it for their employees in 1911. The North Western in that same year reported that after a decade of operation, hundreds of workers had received checks totaling more than $1 million. The number of retirees on the pension rolls averaged 600 monthly. While individual benefits varied, the person with the largest amount, a former locomotive engineer, had taken in the princely sum of $9,000. He had been a pensioner for nearly 10 years after having compiled 45 ½ years of continuous company service. Arthur Finnegan, a retired trainman from Boone, Iowa, characterized the thoughts of many: "By doing the right thing for the Company in your best years you will reap the harvest of a liberal pension when you reach the age when you are to be retired." This point of view helped both railroad and employee.[71]

The North Western already provided "relief" services before it embarked upon its popular pension plan. A good illustration is the Surgical Department, created in the early 1870s and continually enlarged and improved. Because of the concentration of employees in Chicago, the department provided its own facilities at the downtown Wells Street passenger station to handle all but the most difficult medical cases. Hospitals there and elsewhere by arrangement gave this care. Like other trunk lines, the North Western retained private medical doctors in its divisions to examine and treat workers. These practitioners were divided into two categories: local surgeons and district surgeons. The former were found in every important on-line community and the latter traveled as needed. The chief surgeon, a salaried employee based in Chicago, supervised these physicians. The company customarily paid these doctors for mandated physical examination of employees and for treatment of their job-related injuries and gave them annual passes for passenger travel.[72]

In addition to programs developed by the leadership of the North Western for its more than 40,000 employees, a wide range of self-help activities, mostly outside the corporation, contributed to improving the employee's situation. Many began during the formative years of the company and continued beyond the tenure of Marvin Hughitt.

Foremost among endeavors by railroad personnel to improve the work environment and quality of life were the various union brotherhoods. Though none of these groups traced their origins to the North Western system, they soon appeared. The Brotherhood of Locomotive Engineers, for example, the first permanent trade union of American railroad workers and launched in 1863, rapidly established a membership among engineers on the Galena & Chicago Union and the North Western. The same held true for other unions, whether conductors, telegraphers, or trackmen. Their respective brotherhoods became part of the labor mosaic at the company.[73]

Although brotherhoods evolved into modern trade organizations, with the emphasis on "bread and butter" issues, that is, the quest for higher wages, shorter hours, and improved working conditions, they generally began as mutual aid societies. Brotherhoods provided members with various programs of accident, death, and burial insurance; they were truly "coffin clubs." A worker might pay a dollar or less each month for this security.[74]

The pioneer brotherhoods offered more. In an era when fraternal societies and lodges attracted tens of thousands of members, these incipient railroad unions sponsored various activities, including ritualistic initiations, regular meetings, and ever popular suppers and dances. Newspapers in communities with sizable concentrations of railroad workers chronicled these events; the balls inevitably became the social events of the year.[75]

A typical railroad social evening occurred in Huron, Dakota, on the evening of February 3, 1887. Sponsored by the local trainmen's brotherhood, the festivities seemed in trouble at first when the band of the 11th U.S. Infantry, stationed at Fort Sully near Pierre, canceled because of bad weather. The snow and cold also disrupted the travel plans of other out-of-town guests. But the trainmen were determined to hold their "Second Annual Ball," and they did. It was apparently a delightful affair. "The hall was beautifully decorated," reported the *Daily Huronite*. "Two switch stands flanked either side of the entrance door with their white and red lights; two locomotive headlights were placed at either end of the hall and shed their flashing rays upon the throng. Hundreds of lighted railway lanterns adorned the gallery circle; mottoes were, 'Industry,' 'Charity,' and 'Sobriety.' Over the stage in large letters was the word 'Welcome.' Many banners also . . . [hung] from the arch over the stage, such as 'Welcome, B.L.E.'; 'Welcome, B.L.F.'; 'Welcome, O.R.C.' From the ventilating dome in the center of the hall was suspended a large brake wheel, encircled with different colored lights. Bunting was everywhere." The enthusiastic description continued. "And the music, well, it was a surprise to many. The new orchestra has only been organized a short time, and they have but five members, but it was wonderful how well they filled the hall with music. Many well merited compliments were bestowed upon them. And it was remarked that if we cannot get the Ft. Sully orchestra we can do pretty well at home. Caterer Eberhart served an elegant supper at 12 o'clock . . . . Dancing was kept up till four o'clock. The boys did well."[76]

Marvin Hughitt and fellow officials accepted the brotherhoods, except when they called strikes, which was an infrequent occurrence on the North Western. Management warmly applauded the objectives of charity, industry, and sobriety. "Our Labor organizations bring stability to the railroad," opined an executive in 1899. "They [are of] . . . good intent." To this Hughitt added, "The laboring men's organizations contribute much to the smooth workings of our railroad . . . , and I respect their many noble objectives."[77]

When employees displayed their public commitment to temperance, officials seemed especially pleased. Hughitt himself was a "dry" and strongly supported efforts to find acceptable substitutes for saloons and other "Sodoms." He warmly applauded the work of the Railroad Division of the Young Men's Christian Association. Various North Western centers featured these specialized "Y"s. And the Hughitt regime strictly enforced the industry's "Rule G," actually "Rule No. 12" on the North Western. As railroad bureaucracies developed, they adopted a "book of rules" for their operating employees. The one that involved drink was simple and blunt: "Intoxication, or even the occasional use of intoxicating liquors, on the part of employees, will be sufficient reason for dismissal."[78]

Not a brotherhood, but resembling the established activities of unions, was the Employe Mutual Aid Association. This group of approximately 1,000 shop personnel from the Chicago area was formed on January 10, 1897, with the backing of the company. The purpose was largely twofold. First, it was a traditional coffin club: "The object of the Association is the raising of a fund by monthly contribution of the members, for the purpose of rendering assistance to its members in case of sickness or phys-

North Western employees decorated locomotive No. 608, a Class C-2 4-4-0, for the 1889 Fourth of July celebration in Kenosha, Wisc. One of the portraits on the pilot is of President Benjamin Harrison. (Author's collection)

ical disability, caused by accident, or to their families in case of death." Second, it provided members with social opportunities. The most popular event was the annual summer picnic. On Saturday, August 21, 1909, the association held its "twelfth annual outing and excursion" at Dellwood Park, west of Chicago, and the railroad provided shuttle service between the downtown station and the park for the happy celebrants. The Employe Mutual Aid Association was not a substitute for a bona fide union, however. Most shop workers belonged to the Brotherhood of Railway Carmen, the International Association of Machinists, the International Brotherhood of Blacksmiths, or the National Brotherhood of Boilermakers.[79]

Not all self-help and social functions centered on male-dominated organizations. The North Western had a variety of female groups, usually auxiliaries of the several brotherhoods. Their memberships were large and their activities varied. In Huron, for example, the Prairie Rose #5 Chapter, Ladies of the Locomotive Firemen & Enginemen, flourished early in the century. A popular local event was its "Thimble Bee or Kensington" where "railroad ladies are invited to come and bring their own needlework."[80]

Marvin Hughitt shaped the North Western. In no way did this durable railway executive fit the "robber baron" stereotype; he was a builder and a benevolent leader. When Hughitt resigned from the presidency in 1910, he was still a vigorous 73; he remained active on the Board of Directors and continued to work for the company's betterment until his death in 1928.[81]

The importance of Hughitt as a driving force behind the development of a giant railroad corporation was widely recognized. Comments of an official of the Delaware, Lackawanna & Western, a prosperous anthracite road, made when Hughitt left the president's office, were typical: "Mr. Hughitt has built up a wonderful railroad. . . . While our company is the envy of many here in the East, the North-Western is our equal or better in that vast region north and west of Chicago." These remarks recognized the North Western's impressive profitability, large size, and committed workforce. They were also likely influenced by the company's adherence to a corporate motto that truly characterized the property: "The Best of Everything."[82]

During the passenger-train era, the North Western spent heavily on selling itself as a premier carrier. The company consistently tapped the best designers and printers for its widely distributed promotional literature. This 1897 brochure reflects the ornate style typical of the time. (Author's collection)

CHAPTER Six

"THE BEST OF EVERYTHING"

The Chicago & North Western Railway gained extraordinary stature through its development by Marvin Hughitt and others. Service, equipment, structures, and a consumer-sensitive attitude combined to make the company a respected property. "The C.& N.-W. Ry. is in a category with only a few railways in America," concluded an English railway official who visited the United States in 1911. "I comprehend why the C.& N.-W. Ry. has selected the Best of Everything words to represent itself."[1]

Following the Civil War the North Western diligently worked to lay the foundation for "The Best of Everything," and this involved polishing its public image. Although it would be decades before American corporations, including railroads, employed advertising professionals, businesses realized the value of trademarks and slogans for their products or services. Officials sensed that a consumer revolution was in the making and wished their companies to be recognized positively. Railroads, which felt the wrath of Grangers and other "anti-monopolists," were eager to demonstrate that they subscribed to a "public be served" rather than a "public be damned" philosophy. Good promotion also had its practical considerations. Carriers needed emblems for easy recognition, symbols they could place on calendars, stationery, timetables, buildings, and rolling stock. A freight car with an imaginative logo or slogan emblazoned on its sides became an eye-catching traveling billboard.

The North Western experimented with insignias during the 1870s. For several years starting around 1873 the company used a shield that served as the prototype for the widely recognized "ball and bar" logo, which was adopted nearly 20 years later. That initial creation employed a tilted parallelogram with the words "North Western." A subsequent trademark, devised in the late 1870s, suggested the ball and bar design as well, but the words had no pronounced slant. In the late 1870s and early 1880s the railroad also used a bland logo that faintly resembled the head-end view of a passenger coach. And here "Northwestern," one word, was again on a 30-degree angle.[2]

During much of the 1880s a colorful trademark that differed sharply from earlier images was used. Since the North Western was expanding steadily, management claimed that "there was no better railroad under the sun than the North Western." To make this point, Old Sol appeared in the upper left corner of the design, beaming down on "Chicago and North Western Railway." A few years later, the sunburst format vied with the corporate name, placed at that earlier 30-degree angle, inside a rectangle.[3]

Then in the early 1890s the ball and bar replaced both monograms. The name on this ultimate logo evolved over time, however: from "The North-Western Line" to "Chicago and North Western Line" to "Chicago and North Western System." This basic design remained for good reasons: it had distinctive qualities, and the bar suggested motion, ideal for a transportation company. "[T]he 30-degree angle [gave] the effect of a Civil War cannon capable of motion yet solid and stable with one end dragging the ground," argues historian James A. Ward. "The inherent tension between motion and rest is a pleasant one, especially since the parallelogram [bar] points upward towards the circle's otherworldliness."[4]

About the time the ball and bar emblem became fixed, the North Western chose a slogan for its advertising: "The Best of Everything." It was likely a refinement of "The Best Is Good Enough," which had been used occasionally in the 1880s. The company regularly employed the Best of Everything phrase until the 1930s; the slogan was direct and aptly described the property. "The Best of Everything . . . captures the spirit of our railway," remarked David Hoops, the company's general agent in Denver in 1906, and few would quibble with him. The phase was a change from "The Pioneer Line," which appeared in the 1870s, or "The Great Route for the PEOPLE," coined somewhat later.[5]

Other premier carriers advanced slogans that made similar extraordinary claims. The New York Central Railroad in the late 1890s proclaimed that it was the "Greatest Railroad in the

The North Western used its famous logo in varied ways. Early in the twentieth century the company distributed lapel buttons to show support for a scientific agriculture that would help farmers and their communities. (Author's collection)

World," although it quickly turned to less hyperbole with "The Great Four Track Trunk Line of the United States" and later "The Water Level Route—You Can Sleep." The fierce competitor of the Central, the Pennsylvania Railroad, selected an equally self-serving motto, "The Standard Railroad of the World," which it long refused to alter. Even lesser roads made grand assertions: "America's Most Popular Railway" (Chicago & Alton) and "The Scenic Line of the World" (Denver & Rio Grande).[6]

If there had been truth-in-advertising laws when the North Western promised "The Best of Everything," no judge would have ever issued a cease and desist order. As did the New York Central and the Pennsylvania, the company operated an excellent railway. It provided fine service, possessed a modern physical plant that the Chicago passenger terminal symbolized, and displayed a deep commitment to patrons and concern for the well-being of employees.

The traveling public by the 1880s had become familiar with luxury travel on the North Western's two great lines, the Chicago and Council Bluffs (Omaha) route and the Elroy Route (via Elroy, Wisconsin, and connection with the Omaha Road) between Chicago and St. Paul–Minneapolis. The following decades saw equipment and service repeatedly upgraded. These changes nearly always attracted attention; they were welcome news to the public.

Service on the Omaha line was impressive even before Marvin Hughitt assumed the presidency. A tradition of excellence had been firmly established; the North Western had earlier basked in the spotlight of positive notoriety when it introduced opulent Pullman hotel cars between Chicago and Council Bluffs in the late 1870s. "[T]hey differ from the ordinary dining-car," explained the *Railroad Gazette*, "being a Pullman sleeping or salon car, with the addition of a well-furnished kitchen and larder, from which meals can be furnished to the passengers as they may desire and from a liberal bill of fare."[7]

While hotel cars subsequently disappeared from the standard consist, other equipment remained first-rate. The April 1, 1884, timetable for the two limited trains each way between Chicago and Council Bluffs, the *Denver Express* and the *Pacific Express* (*Atlantic Express* eastbound), listed "Palace Sleeping Cars" and "North Western Dining Car." According to company claims, these "are the most modern, complete and magnificent productions of human skill and ingenuity in existence, and are managed entirely in the interest of the patrons of this road." And, this glowing commentary continued, the "meals provided include all the delicacies of the season, and equal those furnished by any first class hotel."[8]

In the fall of 1887 a major change occurred, continuing the tradition of excellence. The North Western joined the Union Pacific and the Southern Pacific to introduce the *Overland Flyer*, offering daily service with through cars between Chicago and San Francisco. "The make-up and movement of this train," observed the *Chicago Journal*, "has been arranged with studious care to afford the greatest convenience and best service to the patrons of the North Western." Two years later the *Flyer* became the "crack train" of the route and offered such amenities as cars with reclining chairs, sleepers, and a diner. This train, known as the *Overland Limited* after November 1896, retained its preferred status and was upgraded periodically. "To 'The Overland Limited,' which leaves San Francisco daily at 6:00 p.m., is attached a new and elegant Gas-Lighted Pullman Buffet Sleeping Car, containing, in addition to the usual number of double upper and lower berths, two spacious drawing-rooms, and carr[ies] passengers through to Chicago without change in ONLY 3 BUSINESS DAYS," affirmed a company folder issued in November 1897. "The advantages of this arrangement will be readily apparent to those who have experienced the annoyances incident to changes of cars at unreasonable hours, and it should be remembered that NO EXTRA CHARGE is made for the THROUGH CAR SERVICE offered to patrons of the Chicago, Union Pacific & North-Western Line, the rates at all times being as favorable as by inferior routes."[9]

The *Overland Limited* was completely refurbished in 1902. "Pullman delivered 2 million dollars worth of new wooden cars," notes Arthur D. Dubin in *Some Classic Trains*. "Each was built on a steel frame covered with 'a new material known as monolith.' The term was an early name for concrete, and this method of construction prevailed to the end of the heavy-

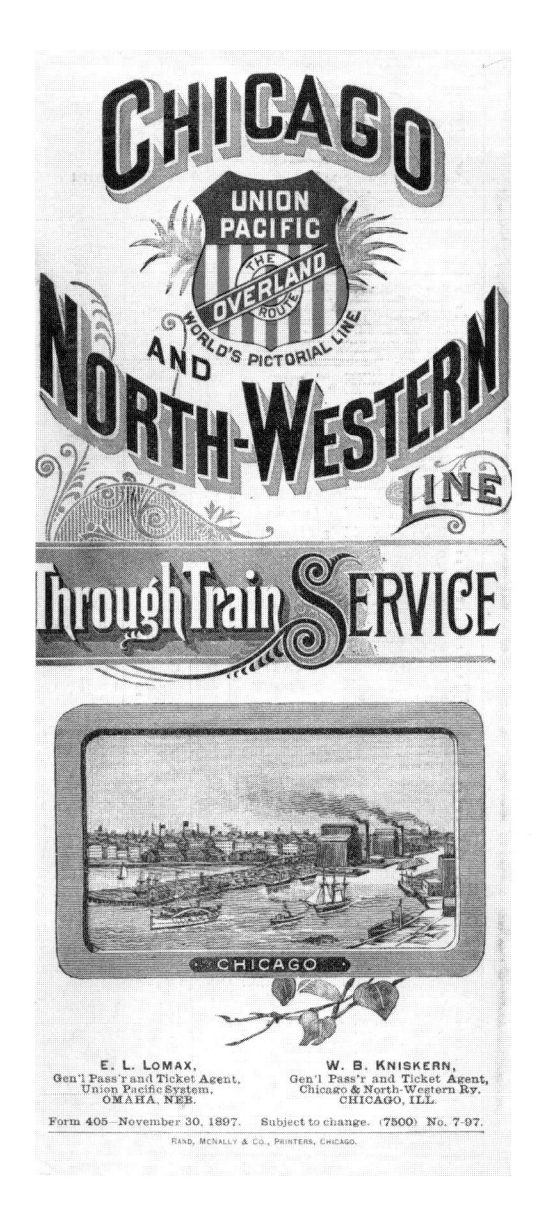

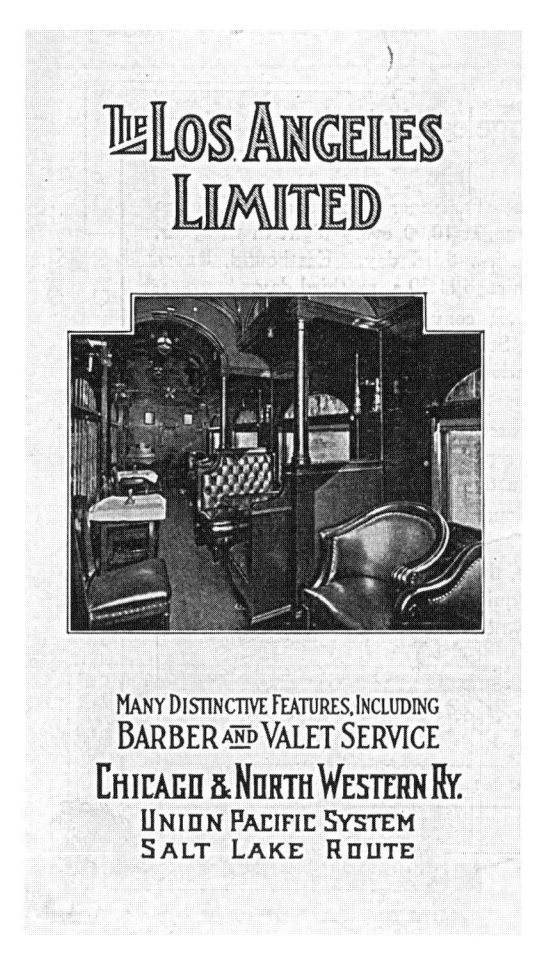

The North Western and Union Pacific jointly promoted passenger service on the transcontinental "Overland Route." This November 30, 1897, folder describes the trains and includes a condensed timetable. (Author's collection)

The *Los Angeles Limited* was a popular name train that traveled the Overland Route. The on-board staff provided passengers with barber and valet services. (Author's collection)

weight [car] era." The Best of Everything theme was strikingly apparent in a novel piece of equipment: a telephone. A special uniformed attendant supervised this communication device in the observation lounge.[10]

Another premier passenger train that raced across the prairies of Illinois and Iowa was the *Los Angeles Limited*. This "palatial train for particular people," which made its debut on December 15, 1905, operated over the Union Pacific to Salt Lake City, and to the City of the Angels over the San Pedro, Los Angeles & Salt Lake Railroad, later part of the Union Pacific system. As the North Western described the *Overland Limited* and the *Los Angeles Limited* in November 1909: "The trains are electric lighted throughout. The dining car service is of the highest standard of excellence. The equipment includes buffet, library and observation cars, private compartment, drawing-room and standard section sleeping cars on both trains. Pullman tourist sleeping cars are also included on the Los Angeles Limited."[11]

The North Western was able to please its patrons because of the excellent relations it enjoyed with its interchange partners. This element was critical if the popular post–Civil War strategy of creating a through passenger "Line" or "Route" were to be effective. The North Western and the Union Pacific formalized their already close ties on October 18, 1889. The two companies signed a 10-year agreement for creation of a "Chicago, Union Pacific and North-Western Line," which provided established through passenger service between Chicago and points on the Union Pacific system, a basic arrangement that lasted for more than 60 years.[12]

Similarly, the relationship strengthened passenger service ties between the North Western and Southern Pacific. E. H. Harriman played a major role. After taking charge of the Union Pacific in the late 1890s, this Merlin of railroading

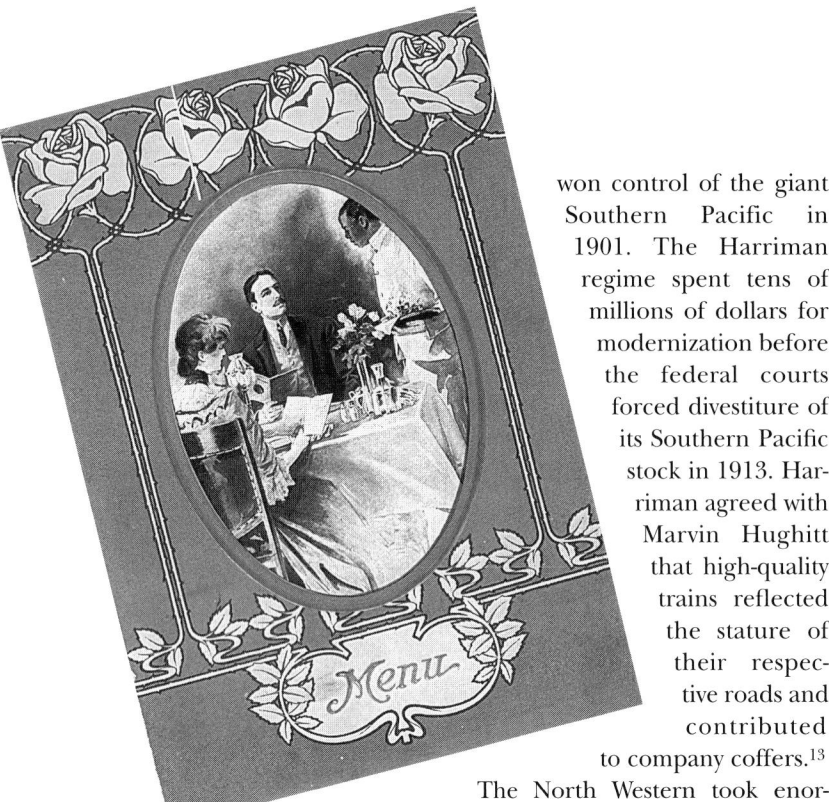

Because of the thrill of eating in the dining car, patrons often kept their menus as souvenirs of their rail adventures. The North Western turned to Poole Brothers, a prominent Chicago printer, to furnish attractive breakfast menus for the *North Western Limited*. (Author's collection)

won control of the giant Southern Pacific in 1901. The Harriman regime spent tens of millions of dollars for modernization before the federal courts forced divestiture of its Southern Pacific stock in 1913. Harriman agreed with Marvin Hughitt that high-quality trains reflected the stature of their respective roads and contributed to company coffers.[13]

The North Western took enormous pride in its service on what the Union Pacific called the Overland Route, especially with the upgraded *Overland Limited*. The company distributed a reprint of a richly illustrated article, "From Prairie Schooner to the Overland Route," from the July 1902 issue of the respected national magazine, *The Monthly Review of Reviews*. The message was progress and was backed with abundant evidence that the "New Overland Limited" was a remarkable train. "The traveler of the seventies woke weary and worn out after a night in a stuffy little low-roofed car. The traveler of to-day goes from his bed to the bath, from the bath to the barber shop, from the shop to the cafe, strolls into the smoking room, or smokes in his private compartment, reads the latest papers in the library car, and steps from the train at his destination rested and refreshed." The piece closed with the frequently repeated claim: "Then, as now, the service of the North-Western Line gave to the traveler 'the best of everything.'"[14]

It is small wonder that the *Overland Limited* became an American icon. "In the fullness of time," concluded railroad aficionado Lucius Beebe, "the name of the *Overland Limited* was to become, with the single exception of its eastern counterpart, *The 20th Century Limited*, the most radiant and celebrated train name in America." Many passengers agreed that the *Overland Limited* was a delightful way to cross the western half of the continent. The train made such a positive impact on S. S. Pierce, the prominent Boston grocer, that he distributed the popular "Overland" cigar whose colorful label sported a view of the speeding limited. And boys—perhaps their fathers, too—wanted a metal toy train called the "Overland." The name also graced such commercial establishments as hotels, eateries, and saloons. Even Hollywood made a feature-length film in 1926 called *The Overland Limited*, starring Alice Lake and Malcolm McGregor.[15]

Nearly all of the crack trains that traveled the Omaha line were linked with the Union Pacific. By the early years of the twentieth century the *Overland Limited*, *California Limited* (*Atlantic Express* eastbound), *Oregon Express* (*Eastern Express* eastbound), and the *Colorado Special* (*Chicago Special* eastbound) gave patrons in the principal stations along the North Western superb service. Moreover the company provided additional passenger trains, although most were locals. While the Burlington, Milwaukee Road, and Rock Island offered strong competition between Chicago and Omaha, no carrier overshadowed the North Western.[16]

While the Overland Route required cooperation with the Pacific roads, the North Western controlled the Elroy Route or "Twin Cities Route" between Chicago and St. Paul-Minneapolis once the Omaha Road entered the North Western's orbit. Even before that control was established in 1882, the company strove to make the principal trains—the *St. Paul and Minneapolis Express* and its successors, the *Vestibuled Limited* and the *North Western Limited* most of all—exceptional. "DO NOT FORGET!" the Passenger Department told readers of its June 9, 1879, public timetable, "The CHICAGO, ST. PAUL & MINNEAPOLIS LINE IS THE ONLY LINE THAT RUNS PULLMAN SLEEPERS north from Chicago, and that runs to and from the SAME DEPOT AT ST. PAUL with the St. Paul & Pacific, St. Paul & Duluth and Northern Pacific Railroads without omnibus transfer. IT IS THE BEST AND DIRECT SHORT LINE."[17]

The North Western consistently improved the quality of passenger service on this major traffic way. While the *St. Paul and Minneapolis Express* took 19 hours to complete its 407-mile run from Chicago to St. Paul in 1885, a decade later the *North Western Limited* cut the run to less than 13 hours. When the company renovated the

Limited with electric lights in 1898, the *St. Paul Pioneer Press* expressed wonder and delight: "The Aladdin of the North Western Line has rubbed his lamp again and set to work the 19th century genie of mechanics, electricity, and art. Their work far surpasses even the wonders of the Arabian Nights, for they have produced the new *North Western Limited* by which one may dream himself to and from Chicago while in a bed that has all the comforts of home."[18]

With keen competition from the Chicago, Milwaukee & St. Paul Railway for through passengers between Chicago and the Twin Cities, the North Western "never seemed to let up" on making its flagship trains on the Elroy Route the "acme of travel comfort, convenience, safety, and service." In 1912 the company introduced the "new" *North Western Limited.* "Standing in the trainshed, the yellow and green cars and the glistening black Pacific [locomotive] were a sight to behold," opines Arthur Dubin. "The shaded silver lettering on the steel cars and the new illuminated C&NW trademark on the brass railing of the observation car were details that set the *Limited* apart from other trains in the depot." And the interior was equally impressive. According to a contemporary folder, "compartments may be opened en suite, and each is provided with its own toilet facilities." It noted too that "provision is also made in each compartment and drawing room for control of the electric fans and vapor heat to suit the comfort of the occupants" and that the "lounging car with its spacious club rooms is a distinctive feature. Each is equipped with lounging chairs and sofas, richly upholstered in Spanish leather." Even coach passengers enjoyed a pampered ride: "The Reclining Chair Car is equipped with seats of the most improved pattern, which are readily adjustable for reclining and resting as may be desired. It is also vapor heated and brilliantly lighted by electricity."[19]

Patrons on other North Western routes likewise encountered fine North Western "varnish." At the beginning of the twentieth century, the road operated a fleet of trains providing parlor, dining, and Pullman accommodations. These included the *Ashland Limited, Peninsula Express* (for the "Copper Country" of northern Wisconsin and Michigan), *Iron Range Express,* and the *Eastern Express* (Sioux City and the Black Hills);

these names became household words, standing for pleasant and dependable travel.[20] To its numerous quality name trains, the North Western added the *Duluth-Superior Limited* (called *Chicago Limited* when going southbound) in 1906. This overnight train covered the 479 miles from Chicago, via Madison and Eau Claire, Wisconsin, to the "Head-of-the-Lakes." Representative of other runs over "secondary" main lines, the *Limited* was set up to satisfy its clientele. "The train is composed of buffet-smoking car, Pullman standard drawing-room sleeping cars, dining cars, free reclining chair cars (with porter) and standard coaches, making a solid vestibuled train through without change."[21]

Although branch-line and local passenger trains were seldom glamorous, the North Western generally offered ample service and good accommodations. From most places along the sprawling system a person could travel to principal trading centers, conduct business or visit, and return the same day. In the early twentieth century residents who lived north of Belle Plaine, Iowa, on the Fox Lake branch, for example, could catch a morning train for a midday arrival in Mason City, a busy market town. After sufficient time for their affairs, which might include supper in a downtown restaurant, they could board an 8:30 P.M. train for a late-evening return to their hometown station.[22]

Such a trip in all probability did not involve riding in a rickety, antique coach. The company might assign rolling stock that recently had served main-line patrons or by 1910, self-propelled,

The promotional budget for the *North Western Limited* was considerable. The railroad distributed this advertising card about 1920. (Author's collection)

A North Western passenger train passes through Sheboygan, Wisc., in 1909. The "varnish" is traveling on the Milwaukee-Manitowoc–Green Bay line. (George Krambles collection)

The North Western operated a variety of passenger trains, including "mixed" runs. About 1890 a small American Standard locomotive rumbles into the station at Plainview, Minn., with several freight cars and a coach. (Author's collection)

internal combustion equipment. Riders who used the 137-mile branch between Huron, South Dakota, and Oakes, North Dakota, for one, were not disappointed. "Oakes service of the North Western line is superb," editorialized *The Daily Huronite* in 1898. "Modern, gas lighted and steamheated coaches with double windows are run on these trains, insuring every comfort to the traveler." This same newspaper a decade later reported that "The Chicago & North Western Railway is using a gasoline motor car . . . with what are understood to be very flattering results. The car at present is in operation between Norfolk, Neb., and Bonesteel, S.D., making the trip of 152 miles daily in each direction. The car is said to be popular with the traveling public."[23]

The management of the North Western hardly reserved the Best of Everything for just its passengers. The company consistently tried to please shippers. They deserved attention; the bulk of the company's gross earnings originated from freight traffic. In 1900 this income totaled $32 million, while passenger revenues generated $9 million, and express, mail, and miscellaneous services brought in $1.9 million. Top officers undoubtedly saw their crack limiteds as having considerable "marquee" advertising value, and so resembled industry leaders whom *London Times* reporter Edwin Pratt interviewed at the turn of the century. "Railway officials in America have an axiom that a man 'ships' his merchandise by the route he travels, so that, if they can only secure his patronage as a traveler, which in itself may not be much, they will count on carrying his merchandise or agricultural products, which may amount to a great deal."[24]

The North Western commitment to improving freight service was genuine. Merchants in South Dakota, for example, expressed delight when the railroad inaugurated a fast freight from Chicago to "Dakota points" in 1888. This meant that the Huron Furniture Company in Huron received excellent service: "goods were shipped [from Chicago] on November 9th and arrived here on the 13th."[25]

Just as the North Western issued lavish folders for the *Overland Limited, North Western Limited,* and other fine trains, it produced somewhat more formal publications for freight patrons. In November 1899 the General Freight Department, based in Chicago, distributed a 10-page brochure, "Special Fast Freight Service from Chicago, Milwaukee, and Manitowoc to the Principal Points in the West and Northwest." In it the company boasted that it "reaches with its own rails the famous WATER POWERS, COAL FIELDS, IRON ORE RANGES, [AND] HARD AND SOFT LUMBER DISTRICTS [and] . . . has on its line more manufactories than has any other western railroad." Most of this brochure provided "Time Freight" schedules between Chicago, Milwaukee, and Manitowoc and points on the system as well as "foreign" (off-line) destinations. For instance, a time freight left Chicago bound for Huron at 6:20 P.M. and arrived there at 1:25 P.M. on the second day; another left the Windy City at 7:05 P.M. for Ogden, Utah, and reached that strategic western point at 2:30 A.M. on the fourth day.[26]

By the early part of the century the North Western deservedly gained recognition for its freight operations. The road's handling of fragile and perishable commodities attracted the attention of traffic experts Grover Huebner and Emory Johnson. "The C&NW Railway's time freight arrangements cover about 161 articles of a perishable, high-class, or otherwise urgent nature," they explained in a 1911 publication. "It is not called a redball system, but in its main essentials is similar. Time freight is shipped on special freight trains, and is billed only from certain designated 'time freight billing stations.'" About the same time a journalist from Ashland, Wisconsin, observed that "The Northwestern moves some of its cargoes better than some lines move passengers." In a sense he was right.[27]

The North Western transported freight, whether expedited or not, in modern rolling

Not all individuals who traveled on the North Western purchased tickets. These "boes," migratory workers heading for the wheat harvest in North Dakota, are photographed on August 13, 1914, near Hecla, S.Dak., about 20 miles south of Oakes, N.Dak., the end of this branch. (Don L. Hofsommer collection)

A longtime source of freight traffic for the North Western came from the iron mines in the Lake Superior region. In August 1881, for example, the company deposited 270,000 tons of the reddish mineral at the Escanaba, Mich., docks for transfer to Great Lakes vessels. The "Norris Group No. 3" at Ironwood, Mich., annually filled thousands of ore cars. (North Western/Union Pacific)

stock. It routinely retired old cars and acquired replacements. The fleet too had grown impressively: from 5,982 units in 1870 to 40,846 in 1900. Also, the size and quality of these cars had increased as well. Fewer units of a specific type at times meant a greater carrying capacity. "A reduction in the total number of iron ore cars," observed Marvin Hughitt in 1892, "[was] caused by substitution of large, double hopper, standard cars for the old style small car, but the capacity of the equipment has been enlarged in the decreased count, in which is included an addition of 500 new cars." These and other pieces of freight equipment came with air brakes and automatic "Janney"-type couplers rather than the primitive and dangerous "link-and-pin" devices.[28]

The company took pride in the talents of its mechanical department personnel who managed this rolling stock. One creative employee, Hugh Gray, is credited with introducing the grain door. With this contrivance boxcars could be used as bulk carriers; the door eliminated the need to bag corn, oats, and wheat for shipment by rail.[29]

The theme of quality in freight transport can be observed in the movement of livestock. The North Western contributed greatly to making Chicago the "butcher of the world." Trains loaded with cattle, hogs, and sheep traveled from farms and ranches of the Midwest and Great Plains to "Packingtown." "The Chicago & North-Western has the largest live stock traffic of any road into Chicago," reported the *Railroad Gazette* in 1905. "During the calendar year of 1904 it carried into the city over 3,600,000 head—62,000 cars—of live stock." Some of these "moves" operated in a unit-train fashion; a locomotive pulled several dozen stock cars with an

The North Western handled thousands of cars of apples from various on-line locations in Michigan and Wisconsin. The firm of Wilcox and Glenn readies an apple shipment from Saranac, Mich., on November 2, 1909. (Author's collection)

attached "drovers" caboose. This equipment, while hardly regal, was at least comfortable for cattlemen who accompanied their animals to market. The North Western and other granger roads gave stock shippers a complementary "trip" or "drovers" pass for their personal transportation. Occasionally, the company even attached a sleeping car to a stock extra.[30]

When valuable horses were to be shipped, the North Western provided an unusual conveyance, a baggage car specially fitted for equine passengers. In 1898 the company unveiled the horse car *Northwest*, which offered stable room for a dozen animals. "Canvas collapsing sleeping berths for two men are provided," noted a trade journal, "and a tool and a hay box are carried underneath the car floor." The *Northwest* also contained steam heating and a water system. These accouterments ensured that a high-spirited animal would arrive at its destination in good condition.[31]

The high quality of a North Western time freight and its equipment are described by "boomer" Union Pacific brakeman Charles P. Brown, who traveled between Council Bluffs and Chicago in 1902. The slogan Best of Everything can be applied appropriately to the hauling of both "hogs and humans":

> Well when I got to Omaha, I went over to the Chicago and North Western railroad yards, in Council Bluffs, and found out from the yardmen that there was a regular fast freight due out at seven P.M. for Chicago, and I made up my mind to tie into the conductor on this highball run to see if he would carry me over his division, as I was now a railroad man and in good standing in the order of the Brotherhood of Railroad Trainmen. . . . [S]o about six thirty pm, I went over to the yards again, and the train was already made up, with the engine and caboose coupled on, and the air brakes were being tested, so I tied into the conductor for a ride, and he sent me to his hind man [rear brakeman], and he said if the hind man would vouch for me, that I could ride, so I went back to the caboose where the hind man was, and told him what the conductor had said, then I showed him my Brotherhood traveling car, and receipts, and told him that I was a trainman off the U.P. in Wyoming, and was headed for Chicago, then he put me through the works and saw that I was right up-to-date, and when the conductor came to the caboose, the rear brakeman told him that I was jake. . . . So at seven pm they pulled out of there right on the cathop [on time], and believe me they sure did wheel them too, and about nine pm the hind man says to me, listen brother, don't you want to take a flop in the hay, and get some shuteye, for we run right through on this run two divisions to Marshalltown [Iowa], and I told him that I would be glad to. Now this caboose had upper berths something like a pullman (of course not so fine), for the North Western handled lots of stock trains, and these berths were for the accommodation of the travelling stockmen, so he pulled down one of them and fixed the bed, and I piled in and had a good sleep, and when we arrived in Marshalltown the next morning, the conductor squared me out on the same train with the next crew, and I rode with them to Clinton, Iowa, . . . and the next crew that got the train at Clinton took me right into Chicago, so I rode the same fast freight across two states . . . with three different train crews, and . . . I could not keep from thinking how different it was to be a railroad man and belong to one of the big brotherhoods, and get to ride in a caboose, than to be a poor hobo, and have to ride in a boxcar.[32]

When trainman Brown mentioned "wheeling," he indicated that the North Western had not ignored motive power in its quest for quality. Like most major roads, the company adopted bigger and better steam locomotives for its freight, passenger, and switching operations. "[A]dding to the efficiency and strength of the motive power," Marvin Hughitt told shareholders in 1896 "[are] large engines of the highest type and most approved construction." The railroad spent heavily on advanced power. In May 1900, for example, the company reported that "82 Locomotives have been purchased during the year in replacement of a like number of Locomotives retired, or to be retired, from service, and their cost [is] $1,015,040.33." The North Western preferred 10-wheel (4-6-0 Class R) locomotives for freight service and both 8-wheel (4-4-0 Class A and Class C) "American Standards" and 10-wheel (4-4-2 Class D) "Atlantics" to power passenger assignments. The company either sold or scrapped much of its old and vast fleet of 4-4-0s, the traditional heart of its motive power for half a century.[33]

The North Western tended to avoid impetuous experimentation with its motive power; it was neither a Baltimore & Ohio nor an Erie in this field. When the company acquired a fleet of high-stepping 4-4-0s from the Schenectady Locomotive Works in 1899 for its "fast mails," *The American Engineering and Railroad Journal* commented that "these engines have no novel features. They represent the best of present practice and the chief interest in the details lies . . . in the elimination of unnecessary weight in order to favor the boilers to the utmost." These were hardly daring products of the locomotive builder's art.[34]

The motive power selected by the Hughitt regime made sense for its freight operations. Hughitt firmly and wisely believed in "running shorter trains and running them faster as productive of the best service for patrons." Not only did short, fast trains please customers, but, as a Southern Pacific civil engineer revealed in the 1920s through a sophisticated costing procedure, they were much more economical to operate than long, heavy drags. The North Western thus avoided pioneering in the adoption of monster motive power, a policy that did not change markedly until the late 1920s when it acquired a fleet of enormous 4-8-4 (Class H) locomotives.[35]

The North Western did consider cutting-edge technology. In 1895 it opened a locomotive testing plant at the West Fortieth Street shop in Chicago. During this time the company gave thought to cross-compound engines; it wanted to determine if a compound engine with both high and low pressure cylinders would be superior to a simple engine. The compound approach was not promising, however, although superheaters, which the road later adopted for its newest locomotives, ultimately bolstered engine efficiency. The North Western did much better in its experiments with new energy sources, namely lignite and oil. These alternatives to bituminous coal worked reasonably well; scores of locomotives assigned to western Nebraska and Wyoming after 1910 were fired with these locally plentiful and inexpensive fuels.[36]

More efficient train operations entailed improving the physical plant. With passenger and freight traffic increasing, management faced the enviable problem of finding ways to accommodate growth. During the late nineteenth and early twentieth centuries the North Western in-

The North Western, like every railroad, experienced deadly wrecks. This scene, captured by a commercial photographer from Logan, Iowa, may have been the tragedy that took place on July 11, 1896, near this western Iowa community. Telescoped cars, especially of wooden construction, were often the cause of crew and passenger injuries and deaths. (Author's collection)

Part of the relocation and double-tracking of the central Iowa main line involved construction of a "high bridge" over the Des Moines River. Later, this massive structure, which the North Western claimed to be the longest double-track span in the world, was named the Kate Shelley Bridge. (Author's collection)

At the turn of the century the North Western spent heavily to relocate its main line west of Boone, Iowa. A huge fill near the Des Moines River required vast quantities of dirt and rock. (North Western/Union Pacific)

vested heavily in a profusion of betterments: heavier steel rail, hardwood crossties and crushed rock ballast, automatic and block signals, new bridges, longer passing sidings, a high-density freight line in greater Chicago, elevated tracks away from public streets in Chicago, Evanston, and Milwaukee, and double-tracking of the busiest routes.[37]

The construction of double main-line tracks showed improvements that demonstrated the Best of Everything thinking. The concept, hardly novel, had occupied the attention of management from nearly the inception of the road. But the crush of longer and more frequent freight, commuter, and long-distance passenger trains on the three principal routes that radiated from Chicago necessitated additional lines. From the 1880s to the early 1890s the company spent millions of dollars on these essential betterments. Not only did workers install a second and occasionally a third or fourth main track, they also reduced grades, improved alignments, and upgraded bridges along these congested arteries.[38]

The largest of the double-tracking projects involved the Omaha line. This task, which had begun before the Civil War immediately west of Chicago, was completed to the Mississippi River by 1891. That year 40 miles of second track opened west of Clinton and 14 miles near Cedar Rapids. But the depression of the mid-1890s postponed further work. Then a terrible wreck, in which a fast freight rammed a crowded excursion train and killed 31 passengers on the single track in western Iowa, dramatically demonstrated the need for this project to be swiftly completed. This much publicized tragedy of July 11, 1896, near Logan, Iowa, might have

For nearly 30 years patrons of the North Western in Chicago used the Wells Street Station. In the foreground are several omnibuses marked "North Western Ry. Depot." (North Western/Union Pacific)

been avoided had a double track spanned the Hawkeye State.[39]

A healthier business climate after 1897 allowed resumption of the double-track work. "The Company's main line between Chicago and the Missouri River at Council Bluffs, a distance of 490 miles," reported Hughitt in May 1901, "is now a Double Track Railway with the exception of one section of 67 miles, between Maple River Junction [west of Carroll] and Missouri Valley, Iowa." And he correctly expected the remaining work to move ahead rapidly.[40]

Approximately seven miles of the improved Omaha line consisted of new construction in central Iowa built by the Boone County Railway, a subsidiary. Much of the original route between Boone and Ogden, about 11 miles, was a traffic bottleneck caused by extensive curves and the Moingona Hill, "on which there is a grade of 79 feet per mile, requiring expensive pusher [locomotive] service." Moreover, the old single-track span across the Des Moines River needed to be replaced. This $1.1 million project, finished by late 1900, created a shorter and less-rugged double-track line and included an impressive 2,685 foot double-track steel viaduct and bridge.[41]

By early 1902 trains finally could cross Illinois and Iowa on a dual-track speedway. The company took such pride in the renovation of the Omaha stem that it issued a richly illustrated pamphlet, *Over Half a Century of Progress, 1848–1902: The Only Double Track Railway between Chicago and the Missouri River*. Produced and distributed by the Traffic Department in 1902, the publication described the road's continued improvements and stressed the Best of Everything theme: "Double steel tracks, perfect ballast, steel bridges . . . [and] magnificent engines, greyhounds of steel."[42]

The North Western did not believe that its other double-tracking projects needed similar publicity. Still, the company noted in various advertisements that it possessed an extensive network of dual main stems. The actual total was almost 800 miles by 1902. In addition to the Omaha line, the "North Line" from Chicago to Lake Shore Junction, Wisconsin, several miles north of Milwaukee, was double-tracked, and the "Northwest Line" from Chicago to the Omaha Road connection at Elroy, Wisconsin, was similarly equipped, except between Harvard, Illinois, and Evansville, Wisconsin. A second route existed between these two communities, however: Harvard to Evansville via Beloit, Wisconsin. Thus the entire length of route between Chicago and Elroy offered dual tracking.[43]

Although the double-track speedways attracted public attention, the foremost symbol of the North Western providing the Best of Everything was its Chicago passenger terminal. This "great portal to the west," which officially opened on June 4, 1911, was a magnificent facility. "The new passenger station of the Chicago & North Western in Chicago is a splendid example of much that is best in passenger terminal design not only as regards beauty and convenience but also as regards the number and completeness of its facilities," concluded John A. Droege, a New Haven Railroad official and an authority on urban terminals. The only criticism was that the North Western should have built this grand monument to the Railway Age a decade or so earlier.[44]

Officials of the North Western had the best interests of Chicago travelers in mind. When the Great Fire of 1871 consumed the Wells Street depot, located at the corner of North Wells and East Kinzie streets, the company was forced to erect a "temporary wooden shed." That utilitarian affair gave way in 1881 to an elegant, $250,000 red-pressed brick and grey sandstone station with Gothic and Neo-Greco elements designed by Chicago architect William W. Boyington. Unlike its predecessor, the "New" Wells Street terminal served every train on the three trunk lines radiating from the city. Understandably the railroad ballyhooed the opening of its convenient, consolidated facility. "ARISE AND SING!" proclaimed an advertising broadside. "ON AND AFTER Monday, May 23rd, 1881, ALL PASSENGER TRAINS OF THE CHICAGO & NORTH-WESTERN RAILWAY (RUNNING INTO CHICAGO,) Will arrive at and depart from the NEW DEPOT. LET EVERY ONE REMEMBER IT!" Patrons clearly liked what they saw: the handsome structure contained a functional and attractive 144 x 60 foot main waiting room, which "is, without doubt, one of the most complete and commodious passenger rooms yet erected." The building briefly reigned as "the largest and finest passenger station in Chicago."[45]

The Wells Street Station made a positive first impression, but it soon became too small. Remodeling barely kept up with the ever growing volume of trains and passengers. By the turn of the century the North Western concluded that further expansion was out of the question. Most of all the station, hemmed in by the Chicago River on the south and west, Kinzie Street on the north, and Wells Street on the east, had no space to grow. Furthermore, the throat of the terminal yard crossed the north branch of the Chicago River over which a movable bridge had to be maintained because of commercial navigation. A less restricted, yet central location became the sensible alternative.[46]

The North Western pushed ahead with the passenger terminal project in late 1905. A general plan, supervised by civil engineer John Wallace, came out within a year and with an ordinance passed by Chicago City Council on December 17, 1906, the company received special legal rights for the construction. Land acquisition and extensive preparatory work followed. "The terminal territory was all improved city property and covered with buildings of various types," noted a professional engineering journal. "The buildings were sold to wrecking contractors, who wrecked them, retained the salvage and cleaned up the debris, or moved them bodily to other sites. In all there were 455 buildings wrecked or removed, 66 of which were four stories or more in height."[47]

The ongoing project received considerable press attention in the summer of 1908, when the company made its plans for the station public. The Board of Directors had selected the Chicago architectural firm of Frost & Granger, and for good reasons. This company had designed other North Western facilities, including the massive Victorian Gothic depot in Milwaukee, which had opened in 1889, and the recently completed La Salle Street Station in the Windy City. And Charles S. Frost, partner with Alfred Hoyt Granger, was Marvin Hughitt's son-in-law. "These drawings indicated that the new terminal will be one of the finest architectural features of the city—a splendid structure of classic design,"

Those travelers who passed through the Wells Street depot could partake of free attendant service. A folder published in 1899 also told patrons that the station provided a "Bureau of Information" for their assistance. (Author's collection)

The North Western for years provided an array of services to the public from a downtown Chicago office in the Sherman House located at 62 South Clark Street. Similar offices of aggressive competitors could be found in nearby locations. The photograph dates from 1886. (Author's collection)

commented the editor of the *Daily Huronite*. "[T]he essential feature of which is a great colonnaded entrance or portico of lofty proportions, monumental in type, that towers to a height of one hundred and twenty feet above Madison street."[48]

Professional journals seemed more intrigued with the proposed train shed. "One of the most important features, from an architect's point of view, is the treatment of the train shed," observed the *Railroad Age Gazette*. "This structure will be 840 ft. long, extending over three city squares, but it will not have the usual long black expanse of sooty roof that offends the eye. On the contrary, the facade running north and south along Canal street and Clinton street will be a finished and artistic curtain wall of brick and granite, 48 ft. high, and including in its length the fine portal of the Washington street subway."[49]

The favorable commentary about the emerging Chicago passenger terminal must have pleased Marvin Hughitt and his associates. After all, the North Western was spending heavily on this Italian Renaissance structure and its many accouterments. The final cost exceeded $23 million, a princely sum for the time.[50]

Neither the railroad nor the public was disappointed when the station opened to its first trains. The facility had especially impressive practical dimensions and contained state-of-the-art features. Marvin Hughitt had made it clear that he wanted the "best, most efficient, most complete, and most comfortable station for passengers that is possible," one that "will be a credit to Chicago, our home." The station, for example, had numerous electrical devices, including 23 elevators, as well as several pneumatic tubes for communications and belt conveyors for the unloading and transferring of mail. The track layout was carefully conceived; trains bound for Milwaukee, Minneapolis, or Omaha could easily reach their main-line speedways.[51]

The station offered a myriad of creature comforts. The structure sported an elegant dining room "with service equal to the best metropolitan cafes." There were women's rooms equipped with writing desks and supplies, manicuring and hairdressing services, and a "maid in waiting." The special needs of male patrons were fully accommodated, including a smoking room and a capacious barber shop. Available to all were the many telephone booths "so arranged that the opening of the door starts an electric fan and turns on the light," a garage for private cars, and a drugstore.[52]

Travelers could also get specialized assistance in the terminal. As in other great monuments to railway transport, the station had a conveniently located information bureau, where personal help on travel matters could be obtained. This kiosklike facility, which opened as soon as the station complex did, provided a popular and efficient public service.[53]

Immigrants too could receive attention. Thousands of them patronized the railroad annually until World War I dramatically lessened their numbers. These "strangers in our gates" usually traveled in family or even larger groups, often with children and infants, and were laden with personal possessions. Those who came from non-English-speaking countries frequently found their new homeland bewildering. The North Western wished to help. Many of these immigrants planned to settle along the system, usually in the trans-Missouri West, and, if ignored, they could burden station and train personnel. And there was a sense of justice. "But is the immigrant, once admitted," asked a company pamphlet, "to drift at the mercy of every wind of change when transplanted to American soil where language and conditions are entirely foreign to his experience?" The railroad concluded that "the first need of the immigrant, at the very moment of his arrival in the large cities, which are centers of distribution, is to have safeguards thrown around him until he can get in communication with his relatives or friends or reach his ultimate destination."[54]

Immigrants had been assisted in the former Wells Street Station, but in the new terminal they found a more welcoming environment. No American railroad cared for them better than did the North Western. Not long after the station opened, the company issued a pamphlet, *The Care and Protection Afforded the Immigrant in the New Passenger Terminal*, which explained the way these travelers were aided. The folder described the large "Immigrant Waiting Room," with its paid attendants, the modern and sanitary restrooms, a bathroom for women and children, a laundry room, and a lunch counter. The company rightfully won widespread praise for these wide-ranging and free services. "There is one station in Chicago where immigrants are well protected," concluded Alexander McCormick, president of the Immigrants' Protective League,

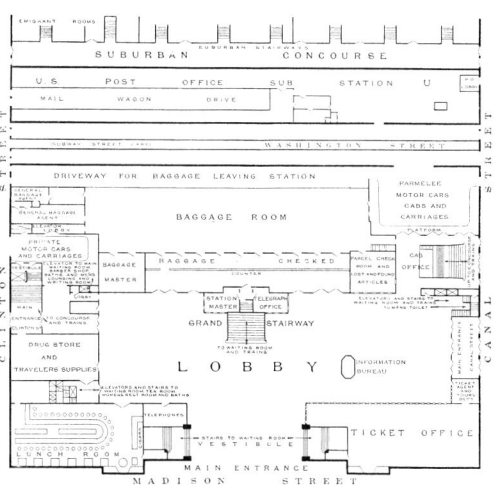

The North Western began advertising the Chicago passenger terminal soon after its completion. Picture postcards offered views of the imposing structure, and brochures provided readers with detailed floor plans of the massive facility. (Author's collection)

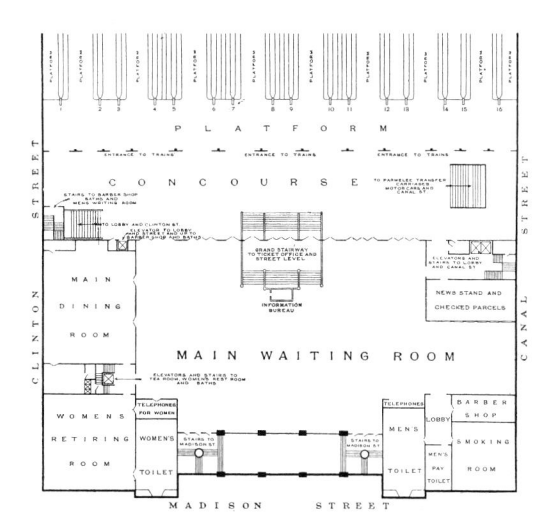

CHICAGO PASSENGER TERMINAL

The North Western took enormous pride and effort to create a beautiful passenger station that would become the envy of its competitors. Everyone agreed it represented the road's commitment to the "Best of Everything." (Author's collection)

Women's Retiring Room

Tea Room

Main Waiting Room

Train Concourse

Grand Staircase

The North Western and its predecessor and affiliated companies selected various architectural styles for their small-town depots. The structure at Carpentersville, Ill., located on the Williams Bay, Wisc., branch, reflects popular building tastes of the Victorian era. A northbound train glides into the station in 1908. Passenger service ended at Carpentersville 24 years later. (North Western/Union Pacific)

The North Western picked an architecturally plain and inexpensive frame depot for the village of Elburn, Ill., a station between Geneva and DeKalb on the Omaha line. (Author's collection)

"and that is at the new Chicago and North Western Railway Passenger Terminal." The *Chicago Evening Post* noted that the "protection of the immigrant passing through Chicago 'from every wolf that roams the streets,' as well as the ministering to the physical comforts of the foreigners who are temporarily in the city, has been provided for by the Chicago and North Western Railway."[55]

If anyone became ill at the new station, medical assistance was readily available. The sick received attention in one of two hospital rooms, one for men, one for women. "Furnished with comfortable white beds, these rooms are well lighted, providing cheerful surroundings and are so situated that the prevalent quiet throughout the station is there intensified," reported a feature story in the company magazine. "A trained nurse is in attendance at all times and the wants and needs of the sick are taken care of promptly and in an expert manner. If the case demands the attention of a physician, one is called immediately."[56]

The terminal was more than a utilitarian place; it possessed considerable beauty and exuded opulence. Visitors delighted in the six immense granite columns of the portico at the main entrance on Madison Street, "the sort of entrance first designed and built for holy temples now invites the traveling public." And back of the colonnade was the high-vaulted vestibule with granite stairways, brass-railed and with treadlights, leading to the great three-story waiting room. And this public space, which measured 202 x 117 feet, was truly spectacular. "[It is] a Roman atrium with barrel-vault roof," observed John Droege. "The pilasters and the entire order up to the spring of the vaulted ceiling are of dull-finished Tennessee marble, the columns being of Greek Appolino marble, of a delicate green

During the summer of 1909 the station agent at Auburn, a farming village on a branch line in northwestern Iowa, faces the camera of a commercial postcard maker from St. Paul. The agent wears his required cap, mandated by the book of rules. The depot represents a popular, standard plan. (Author's collection)

The North Western erected a standard depot at its station in Lodi, Wisc., near Madison. In this circa 1915 scene, a passenger train is approaching and, on the right, shipments of less-than-carload freight and express are about to be loaded. (Author's collection)

hue." The public, too, admired the attractiveness of the specialized rooms, their furnishings, lighting, and decorations. Another compelling feature was a "high power" searchlight whose beam could been seen over a great distance.[57]

The railroad and the city had every right to laud the terminal. "It will be exhibited with pride even when our long-looked-for neighbors, the Martians, arrive on this terrestrial sphere," wrote essayist John Anson Ford. Construction of this splendid facility led to negative comments about the nearby Union Station. "It is ugly, dirty, dark, smelly, too small by far for the business that passes through it, cold in winter, hot in summer—in brief, almost everything that a modern passenger station in a city such as Chicago ought not to be," pronounced the *Railroad Age Gazette*. "The station being such as it is, and the Pennsylvania system, the Burlington, St. Paul [Milwaukee Road] and the Alton being such roads as they are, we confidently anticipate that the time will not be long before these roads will do their patrons and themselves the justice of building a station that will take its proper rank among the great passenger terminals of the country." They eventually did, but not before the mid-1920s, nearly two decades after the North Western started work on its "Temple of Progress."[58]

Although public attention during the early twentieth century centered on the Chicago passenger terminal, the North Western regularly upgraded its station facilities elsewhere. Typically the locations that received new depots were larger, growing communities, often county seats. They likely had a wooden structure from the time of the earliest service, and usually were of

The North Western selected a typical brick depot for DeKalb, Ill., a lively trading center and, after 1895, college town. (George Krambles collection)

the popular combination design, with separate parts for a waiting room, office, and freight-baggage section. But when business grew, the railroad preferred a detached freight and express building and a roomy brick passenger depot. The latter might contain an individual waiting room for women and children; the desire persisted to isolate the "vile and coarse" males from the "fairer" sex. In 1900 the road opened "conveniently arranged" brick and stone passenger depots at Clybourn Junction (Chicago) and Highland Park, Illinois; Denison and Jefferson, Iowa; and Oconto, Wisconsin. While the Chicago terminal was the foremost symbol in brick and mortar of company commitment to the Best of Everything, the wave of replacement "county-seat" depots, which appeared systemwide about the same time, made a similar, albeit less grandiose, statement.[59]

One did not need to visit a modern North Western depot to sense a mighty, consumer-oriented railroad. An individual had only to stand at trackside and watch the passage of an "on-time" crack train. After the turn of the century, the "Age of Speed" or "ballast scorching" had arrived on America's premier railways. "The people demand it," contended *The World's Work* in 1907. "The railroads must obey."[60]

The North Western obliged. It could dispatch its limiteds and fast mails at a breath-taking clip since it possessed a superior physical plant, which, of course, included several "raceways." Speed had long been part of the company's operational history. Newspapers, magazines, and trade journals after the 1870s continually reported impressive times for both scheduled and "special" trains.[61]

Two accounts of "fast times" made on North Western rails attest to the outstanding quality of the road, reinforcing the public's positive perception of it. While the report appearing in the *Chicago Herald* of April 22, 1891, smacks of yellow journalism, the wire service account of August 17, 1909, is straightforward.

> For long distance running, . . . the [Jay] Gould special has earned the palm. Yesterday Superintendent Miller of the Galena Division of the Chicago and North-western, submitted a report of the wonderful run to the general manager's office. The time given on this report was taken by watches on the train. It shows that the train left the Broadway Depot in Council Bluffs promptly at 6 a.m. and made the run over the Iowa Division to Clinton in seven hours and five minutes. This was for a distance of exactly 350 miles. The amount of time lost in taking water and changing engines is not yet reported, but can be safely estimated at twenty-five minutes, leaving 400 minutes for a 350 miles run on a single track which carries the heaviest traffic of any road crossing the State of Iowa. . . .
>
> From Clinton eastward is where coal was burned, steam made and miles were covered in the most rapid manner ever known on any railroad in the world. Four minutes were lost in changing engines, and at 1:09 p.m. the three-car special pulled slowly across the great bridge over two wide channels of the Mississippi. Fulton, on the east bank of the Mississippi, 2.6 miles, was reached in 4 minutes, or at 33 miles an hour, which is fast time under ordinary circumstances. The next 7.9 miles, Union Grove, was reached in 8 minutes. From Round Grove to Rock Island Junction a speed of 76 miles an hour was attained. All the way to De Kalb a speed varying from forty-five to seventy-six miles an hour was maintained. . . . The report of the superintendent who was on the train taking time by his watch shows that the special left De Kalb at 2:47 and made the run to Elburn, fourteen and three-tenth miles, including the time lost in getting under headway, in sixteen minutes. The superintendent's report shows that the distance from Elburn to La Fox, three and four-tenth miles, was run in three minutes, or at sixty-eight miles an hour, while the five and one-tenth miles from La Fox to Geneva occupied four minutes, the hurricane rate of seventy-six and one-half miles an hour being attained.

The "deepo" often became the focal point of important community events. On April 30, 1898, hundreds of residents from Boone, Iowa, and surrounding areas flocked to the North Western station to bid farewell to soldiers bound for service during the Spanish-American War. (Author's collection)

Here is where 102 miles an hour was really made, if the sending operators at Elburn, La Fox and Geneva and the receiving operator at the Turner [West Chicago] registry station are correct. When the train stopped at Turner to change engines, a reporter for THE HERALD was informed by the operator that the La Fox operator had sounded the special passing two minutes after Elburn reported and that just three minutes later Geneva had sounded. There is everything in favor of the correctness of the operator's figures in the minds of many railroad officials.[62]

A better-documented report summarized a "fast run":

One of the fastest runs ever made by any railway between St. Paul and Chicago was recorded today by The North Western Line.

A special train, bearing the Chicago American's Round-the-World Race, left the Union Station, St. Paul, at 8.12 a.m., arriving at the Wells St. Station, Chicago, 3.35 p.m., a total of seven hours and twenty-three minutes for 407 miles, including the necessary stops and delays incident to the run. . . .

Some very fast time was made at different stages of the journey, the run from St. Paul to Elroy, a distance of 194 miles, was made in 198 minutes elapsed time, 189 minutes actual running time, and between Elroy and Madison, 74 miles, in 78 minutes. All records between the two cities were broken.[63]

With increasing speeds came a heightened concern for safety. The North Western wisely extended its Best of Everything credo to include protection of patrons, employees, and everyone who physically came into contact with the property. By the 1910s the company had established itself as a leader in the drive for "safety first," doing so with both good equipment and education. "The Chicago & North Western stands out conspicuous among American railroads for efficiency in all those things which relate to public safety," editorialized the *Sioux City Journal* in 1914. "It has been in fact a pioneer therein. On its part there has been no halting or grudging compliance with all legal requirements in safety appliances. On the contrary it has on its own motion gone far beyond the requirements of the law." Added the *Journal*, "In addition it has for many years had in force a system of special training, in hearty cooperation with its employees, for safe-guarding travelers . . . , a system which is a model to other progressive carriers."[64]

Even before Congress passed the Safety Appliance Act of 1893, which required automatic couplers and air brakes on freight trains (most passenger trains had Westinghouse-type brakes by 1890), the North Western had already installed these devices on its freight cars. The company was unusual as numerous carriers were either apathetic or openly hostile to mandatory legislation. The North Western management grasped the salutary impact safety appliances would have on public and employee welfare and sensed the positive financial implications. The company could only benefit from reduced accident claims and wear and tear on its rolling stock.[65]

But no amount of modern equipment could make the North Western or any railroad accident proof. Mishaps occurred, and the local press duly chronicled the more arresting ones. The reports graphically revealed the dangers that were found along the railroad corridor and conveyed the human suffering involved. A representative account appeared in a South Dakota newspaper during the mid-nineties, about "a family man with a child." According to this front-page story, "One of the saddest accidents which has occurred on the Dakota Central Division . . . for a long time occurred Saturday morning at Canova, resulting in the loss of his right arm of William Pigney, a brakesman [*sic*] who has been in the employ of the company for the past seven years. At the time of the accident . . . Pigney was braking [*sic*] on the south freight under Conductor Harry Shirk, and was making either his first or second trip on that run." Explained the reporter: "While switching at Canova, Mr. Pigney was hanging to the side ladder of the car when the slide cattle chute, which had been left unclosed, threw him to the ground in such a manner that his right arm was across the rail and was run over between the elbow and shoulder. He was carried to Salem where medical attention was secured." A surgeon amputated the mangled arm, and Pigney's career with the North Western probably came to an end.[66]

The railroad continued to pose dangers, not so much to patrons, but to workers such as brakeman Pigney. In 1910 Ralph C. Richards, longtime general claim agent, made these apt remarks in a speech to employees:

Think of it! Every third day some employe is killed on the North Western . . . , and every fifty minutes one of you men are injured, not passengers, not outsiders, but you employes. Now isn't it high time that you men who are paying this awful toll, remember it isn't the company, it isn't the officers, it isn't the passengers or the people who are crossing our tracks that are paying this toll, it is your people, you employes of the road. It is not a question of dollars and cents, it is just a question of saving human life. . . . It is trying to save men from losing their legs or their arms that can never be put back, trying to save making widows and orphans, trying to save destitution and misery. The officers can't do this, the laws can not do it, there is no one to do it but just you. . . .[67]

Ralph Richards did a remarkable job for safety on the North Western, and it involved more than thoughtful rhetoric. Beginning about 1910, he started formulating what he called the "safety-first" program. Backed by management and formally launched on January 1, 1911, Richards's effort focused local, national, and even international attention on railroad safety issues. He quickly became known as the "father of the railroad safety movement," with widespread recognition due partly to his gifts as a proselytizer.[68]

When asked in 1913 to describe the origins of the safety-first program, Richards replied with these words:

The year that we commenced this work on our road, our records showed that our accidents, deaths as well as injuries to our men, increased 37 per cent over what they were the year before. Because, perhaps, of my long experience in the investigation and settlement of accident claims and the settlement of them, as well as my acquaintance on the road, having spent all my life on the North-Western, I was assigned to the duty of trying to get up some organization that would in a measure reduce these accidents, and as my business all of my life has been with men and women and not with things, I believed that if I could put this proposition up right to the men on the North-Western railway—and I want to say right here that we have got the best bunch of railroad men that ever stood in shoe leather, just the same as we have got the best railroad in the world—I believed if I could ever make them see this thing the way I saw it, if I could impress upon them the sorrow and the suffering and the misery and the destitution that follows in the wake of these accidents, . . . that they would agree with me that they should do something to prevent their occurring in the future.[69]

At the heart of the Richards plan were the safety committees. These coordinated and localized units appeared on every operating division and in every roundhouse, shop, and terminal yard. Consisting of division officers, three of whom were permanent members, and one or more workers from "every class of labor employed in the shop, or from every class of labor employed in the roundhouse and in the yards," the committees gathered monthly to discuss "any defective condition or practice that is likely to cause an accident or that is likely to prevent accident or likely to increase efficiency of our organization." As Richards explained, "These men are paid by the company for the time they serve on these committees, the same as if they were working, and they are paid their expenses for attending these meetings." Employees cooperated and gladly wore a "neat button" with the safety-first slogan.[70]

Education was at the heart of the safety campaign. Richards and his associates frequently toured the system with their safety messages. One particular activity involved employment of a specially equipped coach that allowed safety personnel to provide the "latest signal information, advice and instructions among all operating employees." The lectures usually included a two-hour presentation, illustrated by stereopticon slides, which showed "every possible signal or interlocking device, position or difficulty, every piece of unusual track laying and all other conditions not immediately understood by average employees." Other formalized instruction followed, and then the employees faced oral and written tests. The company wisely based its educational philosophy on the notions that "absorption and intuition are beneficial, but without specific training and examination, that absorption and intuition unfortunately is [sic] liable to be of the wrong kind."[71]

Less intensive but still important was the effort to remind employees constantly of the need to perform their tasks safely. Throughout the workplace the Richards group plastered walls with "straight-from-the-shoulder" safety posters. The most common urged:

BETTER TO BE CAREFUL THAN CRIPPLED
BETTER TO BE SAFE THAN SORRY
BETTER CAUSE A DELAY THAN CAUSE AN ACCIDENT
IT TAKES LESS TIME TO PREVENT THAN REPORT
AN ACCIDENT [72]

The safety work on the North Western produced impressive, positive results. In January 1914 Richards told workers in Huron that "there have been during the past three years 265 fewer deaths and 8,461 less injuries." And the trend continued. Unquestionably Richards's efforts paid dividends for the company and ultimately for other careers as well.[73]

The efforts of the North Western to create a Best of Everything environment for its workers and for everyone associated with the property were bolstered by better, safer technology, including improvements mandated by the Safety Appliance Act and specific practices established by state and federal legislation. Although Congress passed the Hours of Service Act, or the "Sixteen Hour Law," in 1907, which limited the number of continuous hours an operating employee could be on duty without a rest period, the North Western had long realized that tired workers could become unsafe workers. Three years before the 1907 act, the company's general manager issued a circular to superintendents and yardmasters that stated in part:

> See that a minimum time is absolutely afforded train and engine crews for rest as follows:
> - Men ten hours or less on duty, eight hours' rest, minimum.
> - Men twelve hours on duty, ten hours' rest, minimum.
> - Men fourteen hours on duty or more, twelve hours' rest, minimum.
> - Keep before the train dispatcher such record of movement of crews as absolutely will prevent an engineman or trainman from going out on a run without the full allotted time for rest.
> - Check this matter up personally to see that the rule is being carried out, examining reports periodically as to rest actually allowed.[74]

The commitment to safety first had entered the North Western world before Ralph Richards started his much-heralded efforts.

Millions of older Americans by the 1950s fondly remembered the early part of the twentieth century as the "good ol' days." Before American involvement in World War I, the country was seemingly a happier, gentler place. Men were truthful, women were ladylike, and children obeyed their parents. People attended church, watched baseball games, and joined church, family, or fraternal gatherings; they took pleasure in the simple joys of community life. Most of this recollection was nostalgia—the longing of an aging generation for its lost youth. Yet often for the nation's railroads, including the North Western, these were their golden years. The companies enjoyed a virtual monopoly on profitable freight movements and had a similar hold on the passenger business. The only disturbing elements were increasing meddling by government, especially after political progressives reached Congress, and the developing electric interurban railways. The popular "trolleys" posed the first real threat to railroad domination of passenger traffic, but they never siphoned off long-distance travelers because of their short runs and their generally isolated or poorly integrated operations. Early in the interurban era the North Western felt the presence of the Aurora, Elgin & Chicago and Chicago & Milwaukee Electric railways. These interurbans took some riders away from commuter and local trains on the road's Galena and Wisconsin divisions. Management feared that other "juice" roads might appear in North Western territory.[75]

Before the outbreak of the Great War, the North Western experienced sound financial health. Annually it earned an average of 11.41 percent of the value of its common stock between 1898 and 1914. Only the "Road of Anthracite," the Delaware, Lackawanna & Western Railroad, claimed a better performance. Discerning investors, including large numbers of Europeans, eagerly acquired shares of the North Western and held on to them. Characteristic of the high regard that the financial community had toward the company are these statements that appeared in a 1918 report prepared by the Statistical Department of the New York investment house of Wood, Struthers & Co.: "[The] notable record of the careful expenditure of nearly a quarter of a billion dollars upon the up-building of a single railway system within the short space of fifteen years is, upon the whole, a striking illustration of the proverb that nothing succeeds like success." Continued Wood, Struthers, "If the result of it all has not been a manifest improvement of the position of the owners of the Company's securities, it has been at least the maintenance of the exalted position that they held at the outset. In view of the history of several other 'granger' roads among the Northwestern's neighbors this alone has been a memorable achievement."[76]

The North Western could afford to embrace the Best of Everything credo, and it lived out that commitment in multiple ways. Yet even a prosperous, well-developed carrier could encounter difficulties, and these came during World War I and the "Roaring Twenties," when government intervention, labor unrest, and rising motor competition caused serious financial problems for this stalwart granger road.

Toward the end of the Marvin Hughitt presidency, the company launched its first employee magazine, *The North Western Bulletin*. Several worker-oriented publications were to follow throughout the years. (Author's collection)

President Calvin Coolidge, who succeeded Warren G. Harding, and his wife, Grace, made several trips over the North Western during his tenure in the White House. On June 15, 1928, the Coolidges and, *right*, Cora McCoy Lenroot, wife of U.S. Senator Irvin L. Lenroot (R-Wisc.), greet the public from the platform of a North Western train in Superior, Wisc. The Coolidges were on their way to a summer vacation at Cedar Island Lodge, 35 miles from the end of their rail journey. (North Western/Union Pacific)

CHAPTER Seven

THE GREAT WAR AND THE ROARING TWENTIES

The presidency of the Chicago & North Western Railway changed three times during the 1910s and once during the 1920s. This was a decided break from the established pattern of leadership; the previous two chief executives, Albert Keep and Marvin Hughitt, had served a combined total of 37 years. The turnabout began when Hughitt, who had held the post since 1887, stepped aside on October 20, 1910, to make way for William A. Gardner. This seventh president performed his duties until his death on May 11, 1916. Richard H. Aishton took charge for two years, May 23, 1916, until June 11, 1918. His successor, William H. Finley, held the position until he retired on June 23, 1925, and was replaced by Fred W. Sargent. While disruptions seemed endemic, Hughitt provided continuity as chairman of the Board of Directors until 1925 and as head of the Finance Committee until his death in 1928. Several influential board members also remained active, including Chauncey M. Depew and William K. Vanderbilt of the powerful Executive Committee.[1]

At 73 Marvin Hughitt turned over the daily affairs of the North Western to his hand-picked successor, William Gardner. Like Hughitt, Gardner had moved steadily through the ranks to a major management position. Born in the central Illinois village of Gardner (not named for the family) on March 8, 1859, of old-stock English American parents, Hughitt's successor had little formal education. Even before his teenage years, Gardner worked informally at the local Chicago & Alton depot where he did odd jobs, mostly janitorial chores and telegram delivery. In exchange for his labor the agent taught him to send and receive Morse code. Once Gardner had gained telegraphic skills, the Alton hired him in 1872 to be an operator at Lemont, Illinois, a village near Joliet; he was only 13. Leaving the Alton in 1881, this young railroader joined the Atchison, Topeka & Santa Fe as a trainmaster in Emporia, Kansas, but soon returned to Illinois to accept an operating assignment with the North Western. Within a decade Gardner was superintendent of the busy Wisconsin Division and by 1906 was vice president in charge of system operations and maintenance.[2]

William Gardner's Horatio Alger-like career seems a natural outcome considering his overall abilities and personality. He was intelligent, diligent, and always eager to master his job. After he took charge of the Wisconsin Division in 1890, Gardner walked every mile of track. This hands-on railroader was apparently a driven man. A daughter remembered a workaholic father who tackled problems immediately. A modest, friendly person, Gardner was adored by his family and respected by his associates. "He had an unusually keen sense of humor, and a remarkable gift for witty repartee," notes an industry trade writer.[3]

As president, William Gardner embraced the basic policies of Marvin Hughitt. After all, he had been part of the Hughitt team, and the grand old man of the North Western was there to peer over his shoulder even though Hughitt told the *Chicago Tribune* that he would "give advice instead of orders." Neither Gardner nor his immediate successors wanted to alter the corporate structure. The concept of maintaining the time-tested centralized bureaucracy in Chicago remained firmly entrenched. Not unexpectedly, Gardner supported the "Best of Everything" philosophy, and he did much to advance it, particularly the "safety-first" campaign.[4]

Gardner's principal efforts focused on cutting expenses, which did not mean sacrificing capital improvements and general maintenance for savings but rather containing costs by eliminating waste. These efforts paid off handsomely in 1915. Even though the company earned $3,780,000 less that year than during 1914, largely because of continuing restrictive rate regulation and shorter average passenger trips, net operating revenues actually exceeded those of the previous year. The railroad saved nearly $4 million in expenses. More efficient locomotive fuel consumption constituted the principal economy. For one thing, engine crews took seriously the admonitions "SMOKE IS FUEL WASTED" and "SAVE COAL." Also reductions came from fewer payments for loss and damage of freight shipments and reduced injury claims because of a safer work place.[5]

Gardner and his successors had to confront the troublesome Valuation Act of 1913. As one of his final actions as president, William Howard Taft signed a bill that directed the Interstate Commerce Commission (ICC) to conduct a comprehensive evaluation of the nation's railroads. It was a predictable follow-up to the Hepburn Act of 1906 and the Mann-Elkins Act of 1910. Even though the ICC wielded great rate-making powers, it lacked an effective way to determine if charges were "just and reasonable." The ubiquitous progressives considered railroads to be greatly overcapitalized, and these reformers did not want the carriers receiving revenues based on inflated paper values. The Valuation Act caused the Division of Valuation (Bureau of Valuation after 1917) to balloon into a gigantic fact-gathering bureaucracy. The process consumed $48 million of public and $152 million of private funds in a vain quest to create guidelines by which to establish appropriate rates for each carrier. Unfortunately, and despite mighty efforts, the bureau never could ascertain "historic" original costs.[6]

Nevertheless the North Western had to endure this exacting and expensive probe. The company launched its own valuation department in 1915 to comply with the commission and also to protect its interests. "Mr. Gardner willingly cooperated with the law," an associate noted in 1916. "He worried that the government would produce the wrong figures even though he knew that the securities were hardly full of water." And, he added, "Mr. Gardner was troubled by the unwillingness of the Commission to allow rate increases that would produce a reasonable return on the enormous investments that had been made and were continuing to be made in this railroad. . . . A truthful evaluation would reveal that undeniable fact." North Western evaluators worked alongside those from the ICC, and eventually the government recognized the road's sterling qualities. This exercise cost the North Western more than $4.1 million, however, a sum comparable to the expenses of other large carriers.[7]

The death in 1916 of William Gardner, the victim of a chronic heart condition, came when extraordinary pressures were beginning to affect the North Western and the railroad industry. The outbreak of World War I in August 1914 shocked Americans, who had paid scant attention to matters in Europe. Soon, however, they closely followed the battlefront reports. This conflict ultimately had great consequences for the North Western, but initially the impact was largely unseen. Although the Woodrow Wilson administration proclaimed America's neutrality, which reflected the country's foreign policy heritage, the Allies, particularly France and Great Britain, made increasing demands on American agricultural and industrial output. This meant increased freight traffic for coastal destinations, and the North Western hauled its share of European-bound tonnage.

Succeeding William Gardner was Richard Henry Aishton. Resembling most railroad officers of the times, Aishton had learned the business from the bottom up. Born on June 2, 1860, in Evanston, Illinois, he entered service on the North Western as an axman for a survey crew in 1878 following the end of his formal schooling. After advancing in the engineering department, Aishton moved into general administration; he followed Gardner in 1906 as general manager and four years later as vice president in charge of operations and maintenance. Aishton was a loyal, hardworking lieutenant in the Hughitt regime and personally close to Gardner. Aishton too was "distinctly human" and highly respected, even idolized by co-workers. "I don't know whether or not I'm going to like this business," he told a friend after he had been picked to succeed Gardner. "I'm afraid that just because I happen to be president, I'm not going to see so much of the boys."[8]

Once Aishton assumed his presidential responsibilities, he probably saw less of the "boys" than he would have liked. He immediately confronted a troubling labor situation. The railroad brotherhoods announced their intention to win an eight-hour day and threatened a national strike if the industry refused. Discussions between the two sides were unproductive, and a union deadline of Labor Day, September 4, 1916, pointed to the start of a prolonged work stoppage.[9]

As the summer wore on, the impasse attracted the attention of the White House. Presi-

During the Great War a troop train departs from an unidentified station on the North Western. The "double-header," with white flags flying to designate an "extra" movement, pulls a heavy consist of cars. (Author's collection)

dent Wilson would not accept a shutdown of the rails; he had initiated a preparedness program because war seemed inevitable. The *Lusitania* tragedy of May 1915, German submarine activity in the North Atlantic, and skilled propaganda by the Allies had caused more Americans to question the country's neutrality. Wilson did not want a paralyzing strike in the midst of his bid for reelection in what was turning out to be a tight contest. The president asked Congress on August 29 to deal with the potential railroad labor crisis, and four days later it passed the Adamson Act. The measure, which bore the name of the Georgia progressive who chaired the House Interstate Commerce Commission, established the eight-hour day on American railroads and averted a paralyzing strike.[10]

Aishton and railroad management generally disliked the Wilson measure. The North Western and other carriers were forced to pay employees the same remuneration for eight hours of service they had previously paid out for 10. This amount was not insignificant for North Western; the company already had labor costs in 1916 of $38,624,721 or 59.31 percent of its operating expenses. Furthermore, the new law failed to provide any orderly mechanisms for handling future disputes between labor and management over hours, wages, and working conditions. The industry did more than fret; it tested the Adamson Act in the courts. But the strategy failed when the Supreme Court upheld the statute by a single vote in March 1917.[11]

The High Court gave the carriers a stinging defeat. Just as the federal government had increased its rate-making powers with the Hepburn and Mann-Elkins acts, it now entered into wage making. "[T]he government had taken over both sides of the ledger, income and expenses," observes historian Maury Klein, "and the mechanisms for regulating one were in no way coordinated with those for adjusting the other." It was more enterprise denied for the railroads.[12]

The Adamson Act became effective on January 1, 1917. But Richard Aishton and his colleagues surely were more upset when Washington "federalized" the North Western and most other railroads on December 28, 1917. The illusion of American neutrality ended on April 6, 1917, when Wilson signed a declaration of war against the German Empire. The United States immediately took up the challenge to subdue the "Huns," who were guilty of "throwing to the winds all scruples of humanity," and also to make the world "safe for democracy." A host of technical and logistical problems arose on the home front right away, most notably from shortcomings in the transport system. Wartime traffic had soared, and chaos reigned in Atlantic and Gulf terminals. Loaded cars clogged sidings at port side while shippers pleaded for empties. The Railroads' War Board, a voluntary organization of industry executives, attempted to untangle the congestion and alleviate equipment shortages, but its efforts to forge a "continental railway system" failed. Old rivalries, jealousies, and suspicions between trunk roads as well as the complexities of the task forced the Wilson administration to intervene. All the belligerent nations had nationalized their railroads; Great Britain, whose carriers were privately owned, took control the day war was declared.[13]

Railroaders soon learned to cope with the United States Railroad Administration (USRA), one of the most powerful federal agencies ever created. Authority granted to the federal government under a provision of the Army

Appropriation Act of August 29, 1916, made the USRA possible. Regulation by the Interstate Commerce Commission temporarily lapsed, and Washington leased the carriers. The Railroad Control Act, passed on March 21, 1918, then guaranteed companies compensation based on an average of incomes for the three years ending on June 30, 1917. The measure sensibly created a revolving fund of $500 million for the costs of federalization, and the government promised to return the rail properties to their owners no later than 21 months after the end of the war.[14]

The USRA evolved quickly. President Wilson selected William G. McAdoo, his secretary of the treasury and son-in-law, to be director general, a post that involved financial control as well as actual operation. (When McAdoo retired to private life in January 1919, his assistant director, Walker D. Hines, a Santa Fe official, took over.) To staff the eight main divisions at its headquarters in Washington, D.C., and seven regional offices, the USRA hired scores of railroad officials who assumed their tasks in haste. One of them was Richard Aishton.[15]

The North Western president thus became involved in the early work of the USRA. Director General McAdoo named him to take charge of the Western Region, a vast area west of Chicago and the Mississippi River. The other two regional directors, A. H. Smith of the Eastern Region (east of Chicago and the Mississippi and north of the Ohio and Potomac rivers), and Charles H. Markham of the Southern Region (east of the Mississippi and south of the Ohio and Potomac rivers), had also headed major railroads; Smith and Markham were president of the New York Central and Illinois Central respectively. As the complexities of federalization increased, McAdoo ordered additional subdivisions of the USRA bureaucracy in late spring of 1918. Aishton took charge of the Northwestern Region with jurisdiction over railroads from Chicago to the Pacific Northwest, including the North Western and the Milwaukee Road. At this time he officially resigned from the North Western presidency and devoted his efforts entirely to the USRA. He remained at this post until the government returned the carriers to their owners on March 1, 1920. Unlike most former USRA employees Aishton did not rejoin his company but instead assumed the presidency of the industry's principal trade group, the American Railway Association (later the Association of American Railroads).[16]

With an able body of patriotic railroaders the USRA fulfilled most of its mandates and provided badly needed unified railroad operation in various ways. First, it placed stringent controls on the movement of freight. The centralized management of car routings reduced congestion on the busiest lines by redirecting shipments over underutilized trackage. The USRA also governed freight at its source; personnel accepted shipments only when prompt delivery at their destinations was possible. To discourage unnecessary civilian travel, duplicate passenger runs were combined, sleeping-car service was curtailed, and some "limiteds" were required to make local stops. Trains that carried few passengers were annulled. Considerable consolidation took place as the USRA ordered the joint use of various equipment, repair shops, and terminals; scores of ticket offices, off-line freight and passenger agencies, and stations were either unified or closed. The USRA also purchased nearly 2,000 locomotives and 100,000 freight cars, all constructed to standard specifications. This rolling stock, which cost about $380 million and was ultimately charged to the railroads, depleted most of the revolving fund that Congress had appropriated.[17]

Federalization advanced efficiency, but it had other effects. Government control eliminated the profit motive and the need for repeated rate increases and other bureaucratic functions required by state and national regulation. The railroad brotherhoods welcomed the consequences: the eight-hour day was fully implemented; work rules were carefully delineated and favorable to labor; and wages rose. As for this last, the average hourly earnings of railroad employees, exclusive of managers, stood at an index number of 100 in 1915, climbed to 129 in December 1917, soared to 198 a year later, and reached 225 for the first quarter of 1920.[18]

The reaction of managers and workers at the North Western was similar to that of other roads. Like other carriers the railroad backed the war in many ways. Employees who entered the military, for example, won leaves of absences and seniority protection. When soldiers of Company E,

Thirteenth Engineers—a unit consisting largely of North Western men—reached France, they received money donated by the railroad for "buying kitchen equipment and to supplement the company mess."[19]

With railroaders rallying to the colors, the North Western changed its hiring practices. While the company made no concerted effort to recruit African Americans, Hispanics, or Native Americans, it did seek out women, and this was a decided break from the past. "[R]ailway life," noted the company in 1917, "more than commercial pursuits, has always been considered a man's field of work." Even before the war a woman might be hired if she possessed telegraphic skills, perhaps learned from a station agent father or husband. Most women who joined the company after 1917 received low-level assignments, such as coach cleaners, filing clerks, and depot custodians.[20]

One publicized hiring and exception to the pattern for women was the appointment of Julia A. Laughlin, widow of a North Western conductor, to be "Station Master" at Ames, Iowa. Although Laughlin did not know Morse code, she easily handled a multitude of responsibilities at this busy location. The job required much: "[to] announce the departures and arrivals of trains,

The spirit of patriotism expressed by employees of the North Western and other carriers is evident inside the depot at Agar, S.Dak. Agent Hugh Merritt and his wife, Nellie, are joined by their cat in this photograph of September 1917. (Author's collection)

The North Western readily acknowledged the presence of its first female stationmaster, Julia A. Laughlin. The photograph, dated October 22, 1917, was probably taken in Ames, Iowa, where Laughlin contributed to the war effort. (North Western/Union Pacific)

assist departing passengers to proper trains and direct arriving passengers about the city, help women and children on and off trains, see that mail and baggage is ready that trains may not be delayed, that no undesirable characters loiter around the station[,] and assist in selling tickets." Laughlin wore a smart dark blue uniform and donned a cap with STATION MASTER in gold braid. There is no record if she remained at the Ames depot after 1918. These "North Western Belles" were encouraged to "retire" following the armistice.[21]

The North Western needed more than another Julia Laughlin to accommodate the crush of soldiers and sailors at the Chicago passenger terminal. Management paid special attention to these patriots, who received "comfortable chairs, reading and writing materials, music in the shape of a victrola and piano, bathing facilities in the way of porcelain tubs and shower baths, and a modern lunch counter where lunches can be procured at the lowest prevailing prices." A social service bureau, staffed by volunteers, directly assisted men in uniform, many of whom were posted at nearby Camp Grant and the Great Lakes Naval Training Station. The feeling prevailed that harm lurked in Chicago, and military personnel, like immigrants, required protection. "Many of the soldiers and sailors are strangers in the city and exposed to the dangers growing out of chance acquaintances and unfortunate environments encountered in the quest for entertainment." Saloons and brothels dotted the neighborhood.[22]

While volunteers aided servicemen in the cavernous Chicago terminal, other public-spirited individuals, "wives, mothers, sisters and daughters of North Western employees residing in Chicago and suburbs," undertook projects sponsored by the American Red Cross in specially assigned rooms. Rose Whitbeck Aishton, wife of the president, was placed in charge of the workshop and oversaw preparation of surgical dressings, garments for hospital patients, and other needed items.[23]

For many within the North Western family, supporting the war effort meant making financial sacrifices. To pay for the fighting the federal government borrowed heavily from the public. Four Liberty Loan drives and the Victory Loan—sold after the armistice—brought into the national treasury more than $21 billion. Not only did committees in virtually every community organize Liberty Loan campaigns, but businesses, industries, and railroads also became involved. "A splendid record has been made by the employees of the Chicago & North Western Railway in subscribing for the Liberty Loan Bonds of the third issue," the *Passenger Department Monthly Bulletin* reported in May 1918. "Approximately 75% of the officers and employees, numbering 39,456 persons, have not only purchased bonds themselves, but they have been enthusiastic in their work of soliciting their fellow employees to do likewise and in making clear to them the liberal plan [of payments] offered by the Company which gives every officer and employee an excellent opportunity to purchase bonds in a manner that will not be burdensome." Added the *Bulletin,* "Much friendly rivalry has existed among the various groups of employees in striving to 'go over the top' and earn the 100% flag." No company publication mentioned zealous patriots who forced co-workers to buy bonds, but some German American, Irish American, and other employees questioned whether "Kaiser Bill" was the devil incarnate or this was a "just war."[24]

As an army travels on its stomach, food production became a high priority. A wartime Food Administration emerged to ensure availability of sufficient foodstuffs. This agency, headed by Herbert Hoover, effectively employed education and moral suasion to achieve its objectives. Although Americans were spared rationing, they were enjoined to substitute dark bread for white, use leftovers, and observe wheatless Mondays and Wednesdays, meatless Tuesdays, and porkless Thursdays and Saturdays. Citizens were urged to plant "victory gardens." Once more the North Western cooperated. Company personnel who operated dining services closely monitored food consumption, and soon after the war began Walter J. Towne, assistant general manager, sent a circular letter to division superintendents requesting them to have vacant railroad property cultivated. The road's Agricultural Department worked with agricultural colleges and experiment stations in promoting farm production. Projects focused on expanding potato production, especially in Minnesota and Wisconsin, and planting additional acres of wheat and barley in the range country of the Great Plains.[25]

The North Western did its part in the Great War. In Chicago, Huron, Marquette, Milwaukee, Norfolk, St. Paul, and Sioux City, wherever its rails extended, employees worked harder, cars carried heavier loads, and trains moved faster. The federalized rail network, of which the North Western was part, contributed to the Allied victory, proclaimed in a railway car in the French forest of Compiegne on November 11, 1918.

The war years had been a trying time. With respect to finances the North Western's experience mirrored what happened to other railroads and the nation generally. Inflation struck with a vengeance. Between December 1915 and December 1917 the cost of living rose a staggering 40 percent. Materials of all types became more expensive, and the company scaled down betterment plans. Still the North Western installed 41,443 tons of new steel rail in 1917; most of it replaced lighter rail along more than 300 miles of track. Not surprisingly, railroad workers became restive because of rising consumer prices; their wages failed to reflect the rate of inflation. In December 1917, for example, about half of all railroad employees earned $75 per month or less, and many struggled to make ends meet. Director General McAdoo granted them a major wage increase in May 1918, and additional raises followed. These actions pleased workers but worried managers. "Such obligations can eat us alive," proclaimed a North Western officer. "In a few years who knows what the consequences will be." The mounting labor costs, which were the largest part of the North Western's operating expenses, were graphically reflected in the financial data for 1917 and 1918:

	1917	1918
Operating revenues:	$108,264,983	$127,295,678
Operating expenses:	$ 78,758,988	$109,498,572

These figures also reflect McAdoo's willingness to boost freight and passenger rates in May 1918. Charges rose about 28 percent for freight and 18 percent for passengers.[26]

The statistics for 1918 are somewhat misleading, however. The North Western and the USRA in September established an annual rental of $23.2 million. This compensation and other income allowed payment of dividends and bond interest, war taxes, and additional expenses, and it led to a positive income for the year of approximately $2.4 million. The figures for 1919 remained largely unchanged, although income dropped to $2.03 million.[27]

When privatization occurred, the overall condition of the railroads differed greatly from what it had been at the time of federalization. Carriers commonly complained that the government had left them with a battered physical plant, disrupted traffic patterns, and damaged goodwill. Luckily for the North Western, the loss had not been as great as for some roads, particularly the Colorado Midland and Pennsylvania. Shareholders learned in early 1921 that the "property, when returned to the Company at the end of Federal control, was not in as good repair nor in as complete equipment as it was . . . when taken over by the Government." Nevertheless, most prewar traffic was quickly reclaimed and the Best of Everything standard largely retained.[28]

Another change also affected the North Western and the industry, the Esch-Cummins Act, which bore the names of its progressive Republican House and Senate sponsors, Representative John Jacob Esch of Wisconsin and Senator Albert Baird Cummins of Iowa. This measure, also called the Transportation Act of 1920, was much less radical than what some reformers, led by Senator Robert M. La Follette Sr. of Wisconsin, had wanted. These progressives embraced the "Plumb Plan," the handiwork of Glen E. Plumb, legal counsel for the several operating brotherhoods. The core of Plumb's scheme called for nationalization of the carriers, a process to be financed from the net earnings of the unified system. Even though government ownership of railways was gaining acceptance outside the United States, Americans generally rejected the idea. For the most part they wanted a return to "normalcy," and that meant less government intrusion in their lives.[29]

The future of the American railway industry would be shaped instead by the Esch-Cummins Act, the principal regulatory statute until the Transportation Act of 1940. Unlike previously enacted federal laws, Esch-Cummins sought to cartelize the railroad enterprise. The measure controlled entry, exit, and capital formation within the industry. Particularly significant were features to equalize the rate of return among carriers. The law directed the Interstate Commerce Commission to prepare a set of consolidation plans whereby strong and weak roads would be merged. The notion of enforced competition as a panacea for railroad abuses was rejected; instead the idea prevailed that the public interest would be served by encouraging the strong to take over the weak under strict government supervision. The act also contained an elaborate, albeit controversial plan for equalizing earnings between the mighty and the not-so-mighty. In what was termed the "recapture of excess earnings" clause, half of the earnings of railroads over 6 percent of their value were earmarked for a fund administered by the ICC, the proceeds of which were to be lent to impoverished roads for debt refunding and capital improvements. The other half was to be held as a reserve for interest, dividends, and rents when earnings fell below 6 percent. The act further granted the ICC the power to control *minimum* freight and passenger rates, and it could set aside rates fixed by state regulatory bodies if found to be "prejudicial" to interstate commerce. The measure permitted traffic pooling, if the ICC concurred.[30]

The 1920 law also considered labor-management relations. The fear of railroad strikes in the postwar era led to provisions that provided for both local boards of labor adjustment and a national labor board. The former, to be created by companies and their workers, would hear grievances over rules and working conditions. Wage disputes and matters left unsettled by adjustment boards would then come before the United States Railroad Labor Board. This national tribunal would be composed of nine members appointed by the president: three to be chosen from a list nominated by the industry, three to be suggested by labor, and three to be appointed to represent the public.[31]

Finally, the Esch-Cummins Act did not ignore the transition from federalization to private management. For the first six months after the return of the railroads the government guaranteed companies a net return equal to the rentals they had received from the USRA. Rates, fares, wages, and salaries were frozen at existing levels during the guarantee period, however, unless the government agreed to changes. Carriers could tap a revolving loan fund of $300 million during a two-year period following resumption of private control.[32]

It was William Henry Finley, president of the North Western from June 11, 1918, until June 23, 1925, who led the company through federalization, the return to privatization, and the effects of the Esch-Cummins Act. As did his predecessor Richard Aishton, Finley came to the executive office by way of the engineering department. Born on a farm in New Castle County, Delaware, on January 22, 1862, and educated in local schools and "by private instruction in engineering," Finley joined the Edge Moor Iron Company of

Wilmington in 1882 and remained there for five years. He entered railroading as a draftsman for the Chicago, Milwaukee & St. Paul Railway and soon became an assistant engineer in charge of bridge design. Finley moved to the North Western in 1892 as "engineer of bridge work" and in 1900 became the principal assistant engineer. He resigned in 1905 to serve as vice president and manager of the Widell-Finley Company, a Chicago-based engineering and contracting firm. But a year later he rejoined the North Western as its assistant chief engineer. Next, Finley was named chief engineer in 1913. The Board of Directors believed that the replacement for Aishton required the technical skills Finley possessed. He was a logical choice. Not only did Finley have that engineering background, he also was a thorough and precise individual in both his personal and professional life.[33]

The choice of William Finley proved fortuitous. This seasoned railroader quickly grasped most matters, even those associated with finance. He also aggressively presented the railroad's case before the public. An indefatigable speaker, Finley told a host of audiences that the North Western must generate sufficient revenues in order to make improvements. The strains of wartime exigencies had eroded the physical plant and rolling stock, and consequently heavy spending for betterments was essential. Operating costs, especially for labor, remained steep and necessitated higher income. "Only remember that Good Government, Sound Finance and Adequate Transportation are fundamental to your prosperity," he told attendees of the Western South Dakota Feeder Hog Show in Nisland, South Dakota, on September 5, 1923, "and may well be called your three best friends." No doubt these farmers agreed in the principle, but like other shippers they wanted the best possible rail service at the lowest possible price.[34]

The Finley administration encountered some rough track during the early postwar years, but no derailments. The Esch-Cummins Act did not materialize in the form that either its backers had intended or railroaders had feared. Most notably, the merger of the strong with the weak never happened. Under the tentative plan of consolidation released in August 1921, the proposed 19 groupings logically placed the Finley road in "System No. 13—Union Pacific-Chicago & North Western." The corporate elements of the existing North Western and Union Pacific units would be formally united and the new company would acquire the Lake Superior & Ishpeming, a 102-mile Michigan shortline, and the Wabash lines west of the Mississippi River. The finalized projection, published in 1929, and expanded to include 21 systems, dramatically relocated the North Western. Rather than being joined with the Union Pacific, the North Western became the principal component of "System No. 11—Chicago & North Western." The company would reach deep water under the plan, not the Pacific Ocean but the Gulf of Mexico. By absorbing the Chicago & Eastern Illinois and Mobile & Ohio and several Mid-South shortlines, the expanded North Western would resemble the Illinois Central, which wags dubbed as the "wrong-way" transcontinental. North Western rails in this scheme would stretch from Lander, Wyoming, and Duluth, Minnesota, to New Orleans, Louisiana, and Mobile, Alabama.[35]

North Western officials studied the maps and data, but they were really wasting their time. The commission guidelines came to naught. Stronger companies resisted assuming the burdens of weaker lines, although they coveted the best properties. In the case of System No. 11 of 1929, neither the Chicago & Eastern Illinois nor the Mobile & Ohio enjoyed especially good health. Moreover the ICC lacked jurisdiction over holding companies, and some major linkages occurred through that popular device. Two bachelor brothers from Cleveland, Ohio, Oris Paxton Van Sweringen and Mantis James Van Sweringen, "the Vans," were able by the mid-1920s through holding companies to assemble a 9,000-mile empire that included such trunk roads as the Chesapeake & Ohio, Erie, and Nickel Plate. The Vans continued to expand their rail holdings through a maze of holding companies until the early part of the Great Depression. When the Crash of October 1929 rattled the country, no railroad wished to take over an ailing property when its own financial life might be at stake. Federal authorities agreed.[36]

Life under Esch-Cummins offered the North Western and other major railroads more than meaningless sets of consolidation proposals.

The scheme to recapture excess earnings generated considerable paperwork and inflicted some financial damage. Even though the Supreme Court upheld the concept in the 1924 case of *Dayton-Goose Creek Railroad Company* v. *United States,* the "weak sisters" received little financial support. Stronger carriers such as the North Western effectively increased their betterment expenditures, thus curtailing profits that were subject to recapture. Companies reported excess earnings to the commission of about $24 million between 1920 and 1931, although the ICC estimated the amount to exceed $300 million. Then in 1933 the Emergency Railroad Transportation Act scrapped the recapture arrangement, and the ICC returned the retained funds to the contributing carriers on a pro rata basis.[37]

The Interstate Commerce Commission, with its enhanced rate-making powers, initially provided beneficial financial assistance. Recognizing the need to strengthen railroad income, the ICC granted a general increase in regional freight rates during the summer of 1920, ranging from 25 to 40 percent, and hiked passenger fares by 20 percent. Then the recession of 1921 and the decline in the cost of living prompted the commission to reverse itself; gains made by the North Western and the industry were partially lost. In the fall of 1921, for example, the ICC cut rates on farm products and livestock shipments from 10 to 22 percent. The commission reaffirmed that decision in May 1922 and ordered reductions of approximately 10 percent in all freight charges. In the aggregate these rollbacks cost the North Western more than $10 million in 1922 alone, and the company had to cope with these low rates for the remainder of the decade.[38]

Just as the commission initially adjusted freight and passenger rates upward, the Railroad Labor Board, also a creation of Esch-Cummins, granted railroad workers wage hikes in 1920 of approximately 22 percent. The following year, in keeping with the realities of the national recession, the board authorized a reduction of approximately 12 percent, except for operating employees, and in 1922 still another cut that nearly erased the gains of 1920.[39]

This last decision caused trouble. The Railroad Labor Board, which conducted hearings on the rates of pay of certain classes of employees, released its findings in May 1922. It called for reductions of from one cent to nine cents

While labor-management strife plagued the North Western after World War I, the company sought to promote a sense of esprit de corps among its workers. A railroad-sponsored band was one example. The musicians pose about 1925 in front of No. 2911, a 4-6-2 Pacific locomotive, at the Chicago Shops. (North Western/Union Pacific)

The mood of Americans was somber when they learned on August 2, 1923, of the sudden death of President Warren G. Harding. Mourning millions watched the funeral train moving from San Francisco, California, to Washington, D.C., and then to Marion, Ohio, Harding's hometown. The eastbound train crossed Iowa and Illinois on the North Western. Engineer J. Ertz readies the decorated locomotive at Omaha Union Station. (North Western/Union Pacific)

per hour in the wages of clerks, freight handlers and station employees, maintenance-of-way workers, and shopmen. In a subsequent order pay rates for maintenance-of-way workers were increased two cents per hour, however, and became effective on October 1, 1922. All of the workers who were covered by this decision, except the shopmen, grudgingly accepted the verdict. The shopmen struck on July 1, 1922, in what became a bitter work stoppage. "This shop strike was the most serious that had ever occurred on the transportation lines of the country," concluded W. H. Truesdale, president of the Delaware, Lackawanna & Western Railroad, in March 1923, "and had for its avowed purpose the crippling of the railroads to such an extent that, because of the loss and inconvenience resulting to the shipping and traveling public, the latter would force the railroads to make an immediate settlement with the strikers by granting all their demands."[40]

The effects of the first nationwide strike in American railroad history were immense. Approximately 400,000 members of the American Federation of Labor shopmen's unions, under the leadership of Bert Jewell, president of the Railway Employees' Division of the AFL, left their posts. Inevitably the walkout had a pronounced impact on the North Western. While more than 16,000 workers struck the company, the road in a sense was fortunate. The railroad was able to operate a majority of its freight and passenger trains and avoided most of the violence and vandalism associated with the strike. Some services had to be canceled; a national coal strike, rather than faulty equipment, largely explained these cutbacks. Perhaps the carrier's long-standing good labor relations, even maintained during the stormy Pullman Strike of 1894, led to "overtures from officials of the striking employees" in early September 1922 and to an end of the work stoppage on the 17th.[41]

Continuing management's triumphs over organized labor in nearly every national postwar dispute, railroad owners broke the strike. The enthusiastic backing of Harry M. Daugherty, the union-hating U.S. attorney general, who blamed "red borers" (Communists) for the stoppage, tilted the scales heavily against labor. A majority of the strikers reluctantly accepted a settlement and agreed to resume work in late September and early October. These men frequently lost their seniority rights and in some cases their previous positions. The Illinois Central, Pennsylvania, and

North Western President Fred W. Sargent and his daughter Fredrica wave good-bye to a locomotive engineer. (Regional History Center, Northern Illinois University)

Union Pacific, for example, had filled the shopmen's slots with strikebreakers, and they had no desire to employ ardent trade unionists. Workers on the North Western generally retained their prestrike seniority and job assignments.[42]

The North Western and several other railroads sought to prevent similar strikes in the future through implementation of the "B&O Plan." Shortly after the 1922 walkout the Baltimore & Ohio Railroad and its progressive president, Daniel Willard, created a scheme that vastly improved communications between managers and workers and made shop operations more efficient, economical, and generally better. The North Western copied this idea. Although conversations took place in autumn 1922 between the AFL's Bert Jewell and William Walliser, assistant general manager of the North Western, the two parties did not reach an understanding until March 6, 1925. Soon a pilot project began at the car shops in Clinton, Iowa, and later more than a score of car and locomotive repair facilities participated in the plan. The North Western mimicked the B&O by holding regular joint worker-manager meetings to raise and evaluate issues related to service quality. A meaningful dialogue resulted; rank-and-file operatives, whether they were blacksmiths, boilermakers, carmen, machinists, or sheet-metal workers, expressed their opinions about their jobs and the workplace. Apparently the cooperative plan met the expectations of the participants.[43]

Events during the remaining years of the Findley administration were comparatively calm. It was mostly business as usual, and the business was improving. The profitability of the North Western increased, especially during 1925, the first year of "Coolidge Prosperity." Operating expenses, which stood at $129,091,427 in 1921, dropped to $115,626,055 in 1925, and operating revenues rose from $144,775,475 to $148,538,269. The operating ratio (operating expenses divided by operating revenues) declined from 89.17 in 1921 to 77.84 in 1925, a truly positive sign.[44]

The North Western, however, fretted about the "serious burden" of property taxes. These assessments in 1924 consumed more than 6 percent of operating revenues. Tax obligations had greatly increased. The bill that was $3.76 million in 1913 exceeded $9 million a decade later. The company was not alone in coping with heavy tax strain; census reports revealed that with the exception of electric railways, steam carriers paid the largest percentage of their net income for taxes when compared to other businesses and industries.[45]

The business community was hardly thrown into a tizzy when William Finley resigned in June 1925. Although the North Western president was only 63, his health was failing, and he died a year later. The Board of Directors tapped not another civil engineer, but an experienced lawyer, Fred Wesley Sargent, making him at 49 the youngest president in company history. This able manager would guide the North Western through the remainder of the 1920s and into the Great Depression.[46]

Fred Sargent was born on May 26, 1876, in Akron, Iowa, a thriving agricultural community located about 30 miles north of Sioux City. Like so many lads of his generation, Sargent grew up on a farm and in a family where the patriarch ruled. His father, Wesley "Wes" Sargent, was fair, kind, and hardworking but a strict disciplinarian. The senior Sargent also possessed considerable business skills. He had been a successful cattle trader in Dakota and a pioneer flour miller in the region before becoming a prominent farm operator. "Indeed, Fred Sargent attributed much of his success to his dad's wise guidance," observes historian Frank P. Donovan Jr.[47]

Sargent received a better education than most of his peers. After graduating from his hometown high school in 1894, he entered the University of South Dakota in nearby Vermillion and later transferred to the State University of Iowa in Iowa City. Sargent received his bachelor of law degree in 1901. His decision to enter the legal world surprised no one; he had a passion for the law. "From the time I started to school," Sargent related to a magazine writer in 1928, "I planned my course with the thought of studying law. When I was in the high school at Akron, I sent for law books and read them evenings, and at that time I never had seen the inside of a court room."[48]

With sheepskin in hand and an early admission to the Iowa bar, Fred Sargent returned to northwest Iowa. He opened a law office in the area's largest metropolis, Sioux City, and soon developed a "large and extensive" general practice.

The newly arrived No. 3008, a mighty Class H 4-8-4 Northern locomotive, stands at Laramie Avenue in Chicago on October 27, 1929. The North Western took delivery of 35 of these general purpose engines from the Baldwin Locomotive Company in 1929 and 1930. Number 3008 remained on the roster until 1953. (Alfred W. Johnson photograph, George Krambles collection)

"I managed to get clients, good ones in Sioux City, among whom . . . were many of the principal banks and business houses." While in Sioux City Sargent made contact with the railroad industry. "[F]our years after I began to practice," he told *The American Magazine,* "I was appointed attorney for the Chicago, St. Paul, Minneapolis and Omaha Railway. . . . One year later I was asked to represent the North Western also, in Iowa. This was the beginning of my connection with railroads."[49]

Fred Sargent changed jobs in 1912. His considerable legal talent and his able work for the North Western was recognized by the Chicago, Rock Island & Pacific Railroad. That company, "considerably to his surprise," asked Sargent to serve as its general counsel, officially "State Attorney," for Iowa. Sargent agreed, and he and his family made their home in Des Moines for the next nine years. In 1920 the North Western asked Sargent to become its general solicitor in Chicago, and he accepted the offer. Three years later Sargent was named vice president and general counsel and also joined the Board of Directors.[50]

The many qualities of Fred Sargent caught the attention of the board. Obviously he was personable. A journalist described him as having "a most kindly manner and winning personality" while another wrote, "[He] is a quiet, soft-spoken man with thoughtful eyes, and a rare, charming smile." Sargent offered more, however. He not only developed a mastery of railroad law but also became increasingly knowledgeable about the business generally. Sargent showed an insatiable desire to learn, and he often learned by touring the property. "Those private-car trips were not pleasure trips," he observed in 1925. "They were study trips. Never a day passed but we discussed operations, finances, rates, roadbed condition, wages and conditions of employment, which might be done to improve our service in the communities through which the line passed, repairs, and so on. I talked repeatedly with officials and men. Every scrap of accurate information helped to complete my education. After a while, without intending it, I began to find that people were asking me about other matters than legal questions."[51]

The never-ending improvements for the North Western continued under the guidance of Fred Sargent for the rest of the 1920s, mostly well-conceived betterments that were financed by the good credit of the railroad. For one thing the company kept upgrading its rolling stock; steel freight and passenger cars steadily replaced those of the wood-car era. In 1925, for example, the firm purchased 3,200 steel underframe freight cars and rebuilt nearly as many. Part of these acquisitions included 1,000 40-ton automobile carriers, designed to accommodate a source of expanding and lucrative traffic.[52]

The equipment purchase that caught the public's eye was likely the 35 monster Class H (4-8-4) steam locomotives that the Baldwin Locomotive Company built for the North Western in 1929. The railroad was so pleased with this motive power that it issued an illustrated leaflet, "Zeppelins of the Rails: Giant Class 'H' Locomotives," in 1930. The first of the series, No. 3001, reached Chicago on October 10, 1929, the eighty-first anniversary of the arrival of the *Pioneer*, the Galena & Chicago Union's tiny 4-2-0. These Northern-type locomotives (so-called because the Northern Pacific first used them) weighed nearly 3,000 tons and could haul 26 passenger cars at 85 miles per hour or 150 freight cars at 50 miles per hour. The versatility of the Class "H" locomotives made them effective and popular on the road.[53]

The "Zeppelins of the Rails" were joined by some highly experimental locomotives. The North Western took delivery in April 1926 of 60-ton, 300-horsepower No. 1000, the product of a joint venture involving American Locomotive, General Electric, and Ingersoll-Rand. This "first oil-electric locomotive ever built for service in the West" was largely designed to reduce air pollution in downtown Chicago. No. 1000 and later two other identical oil (eventually converted to diesel) switchers shunted cars in the State Street and North Pier districts. The investment worked well; these locomotives functioned dependably and economically, and, of course, they were nearly smokeless. An experimental 110-ton battery-powered switcher, "the largest storage battery locomotive in the world," developed by General Electric and Exide Battery, failed to perform as expected after entering service in the fall of 1926, however. The North Western wisely decided to avoid this alternative to external and internal combustion locomotives.[54]

The physical plant, too, was not overlooked. The North Western installed additional main-line

The crew of oil-electric locomotive No. 1002, a product of the Ingersoll-Rand Company, performs switching chores at Chicago Junction in June 1927. (George Krambles collection)

tracks, cutoffs near Chicago and Milwaukee, longer passing tracks, especially after the arrival of the mighty Class H locomotives, and heavier rails, treated ties, and crushed-rock ballast. The company also built several mechanical coal handling plants and water-treatment facilities. And it constructed numerous viaducts and grade separations to remove trains from the constantly growing volume of highway traffic.[55]

A betterment that attracted considerable attention was a $3 million safety system, called Automatic Train Control (ATC), placed along the main line between Chicago and Council Bluffs. The North Western was the first railroad to install continuous ATC on such a massive scale. This improvement, however, was not self-initiated; the company complied with an order from the Interstate Commerce Commission in January 1922 that required 49 railroads to use such devices on their most heavily traveled lines. The North Western finished the ATC project in phases, and on May 1, 1928, the 485-mile Omaha line acquired this protection.[56]

The North Western likened Automatic Train Control, technically the General Railway Signal Automatic Two Speed Train Control, to "a giant hand or *invisible guardian*." The ATC system was a way to protect a train from ignoring a stop or caution signal by taking control away from the engineer and placing it with a device that automatically applied the brakes. This continuous-induction system, in which the track circuit itself was used to actuate induction coils mounted on the locomotive, responded to both signals and track conditions. The ATC system reacted to anything that interrupted the circuit, such as a broken rail or an open switch. In its extensive promotional literature, the railroad touted ATC as "Of Inestimable Value," and happily announced that "Automatic train control protects you in the worst kinds of weather, and materially aids in allowing your train to be brought through on schedule time. It also is of immense benefit to shippers in bad weather, especially shippers of perishable goods, as much delay is avoided because the engineer can run at the maximum speed allowable in spite of weather conditions."[57]

Freight cars speeding to Chicago destinations or Chicago connections reached a vastly improved Proviso Yard by the late 1920s. In 1923 the North Western began its long-term upgrade of this strategic facility, 13 miles west of downtown Chicago. Construction workers relocated the main tracks from the middle of the yard, "which had become a handicap in the operation of this large terminal facility," to a new location on the south side and installed a third track from Elmhurst at the west end of Proviso to West Chicago. This was "to handle expeditiously the greatly increased volume of traffic moving in and out of this yard in the most economical manner and for the avoidance of delays."[58]

After the preliminary work, the $16 million betterment became a priority project. The less-than-carload (LCL) freight transfer facility opened on October 1, 1927; its main "house," constructed of steel members, measured 1,420 feet in length and 626 feet in width and accommodated 690 cars. This LCL complex covered 21 acres under a single roof. Grading began in 1927 for the 59-track eastbound gravity classification yard and for a 21-track departure yard. This "largest individual freight terminal in the world" officially opened on July 1, 1929, and served as many as 26,000 freight cars daily. Such modern features as electronically operated car retarders, powerful electric floodlights, teletype machines, and pneumatic tubes for sending waybills contributed to making Proviso Yard the jewel in the North Western's freight crown.[59]

The investment at Proviso was worthwhile, though with the coming of hard times not long after its opening the capacity might have seemed excessive. But undeniably the North Western wasted money on its final major-line construction project before the 1980s, the 34-mile extension of the Norfolk-Winner branch, which opened between Winner and Wood, South Dakota, in 1929. Throughout the postwar years the company had built only minor appendages, the largest being 12 miles from Braden (Nisland) southeasterly to Vale, on the Belle Fourche River, in western South Dakota. This spur served a new sugar beet refinery owned by the Utah-Idaho Sugar Company, and the plant generated considerable carloadings.[60]

A rail-building craze swept sections of the Great Plains during the 1920s. Places that lacked access to the rails hoped then that their isolation would finally end. Railroads and not motor vehicles were still considered essential for economic growth. "From all corners of the state come the predictions that South Dakota, within

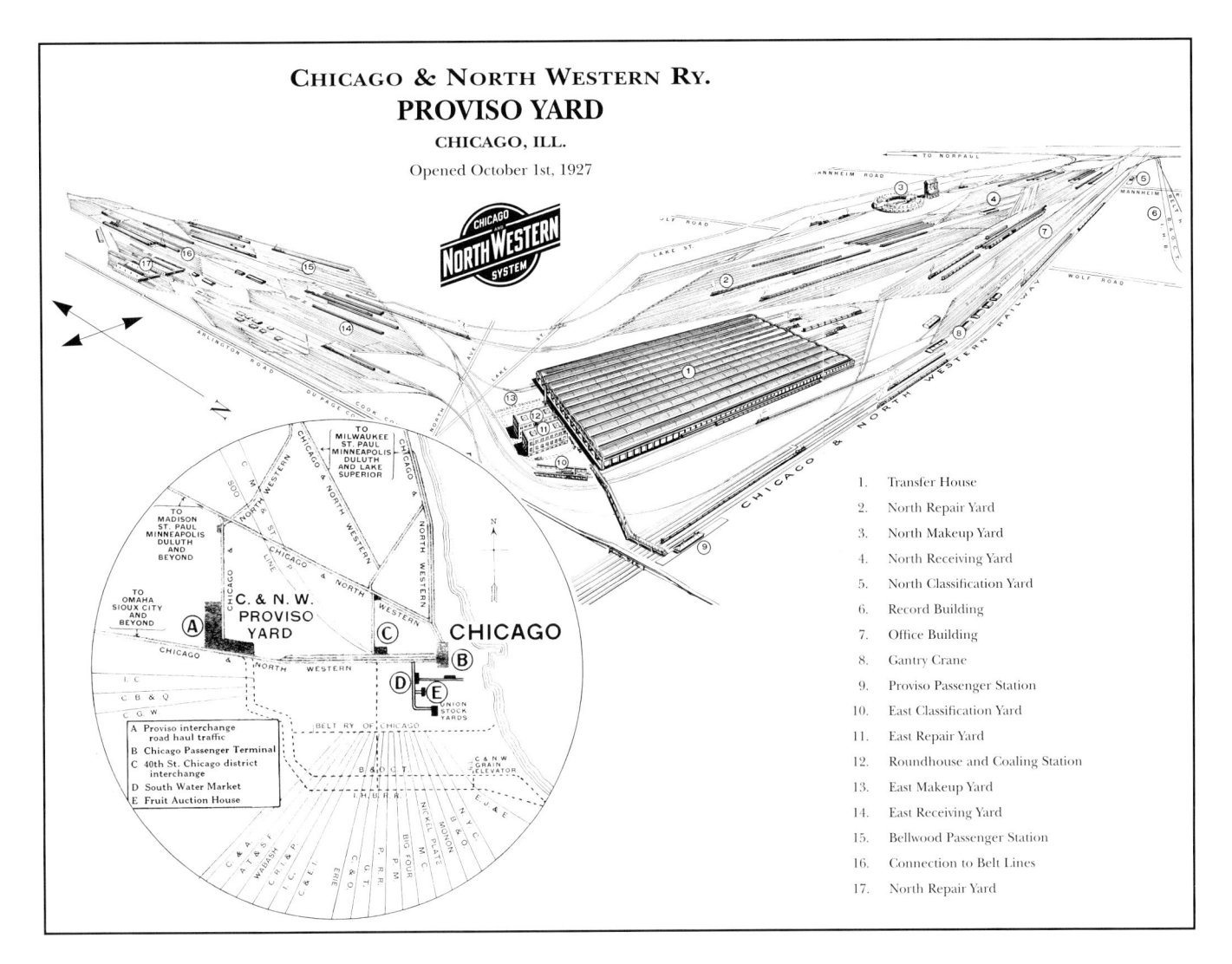

CHICAGO & NORTH WESTERN RY.
PROVISO YARD
CHICAGO, ILL.
Opened October 1st, 1927

1. Transfer House
2. North Repair Yard
3. North Makeup Yard
4. North Receiving Yard
5. North Classification Yard
6. Record Building
7. Office Building
8. Gantry Crane
9. Proviso Passenger Station
10. East Classification Yard
11. East Repair Yard
12. Roundhouse and Coaling Station
13. East Makeup Yard
14. East Receiving Yard
15. Bellwood Passenger Station
16. Connection to Belt Lines
17. North Repair Yard

A Proviso interchange road haul traffic
B Chicago Passenger Terminal
C 40th St. Chicago district interchange
D South Water Market
E Fruit Auction House

the next few years, will see another era of railroad building," editorialized the *Evening Huronite* in May 1929. "That era, from indications, is now upon us." The newspaper observed that several shortlines were either planned or under construction and that the North Western "is pushing its rails from Winner, in the Rosebud, to Wood." The *Huronite* and other South Dakota papers earlier had agitated for the extension to Wood and sought much more. "The [North Western should build] west from Winner and also help develop this great corn belt sections of the state, comprising the counties of Mellette, Todd, Bennett, Washabaugh, Washington and Shannon, an empire of 4,500,000 acres." This commentary concluded: "Order the ties and rails, Mr. Sargent, and this section will furnish the products to make it another great link in the C&NW system."[61]

While the North Western built the Wood extension to appropriate standards and established intermediate stations at Witten in Tripp County and Mosher in Mellette County, the line never produced much revenue. The stock market crash of October 1929, followed by depression and drought, the "Dirty Thirties," and highway competition made the construction seem unwise. But railroaders were hardly clairvoyant, and in this case Sargent and his company were unfortunate.[62]

The Sargent administration could have risked, and lost, vast sums of money if it had electrified suburban service in greater Chicago. In 1915 the Committee of Investigation on Smoke Abatement and Electrification of Railway Terminals, sponsored by the Chicago Association of Commerce, had recommended electrification of approximately 90 miles of North Western trackage, including lines from the passenger terminal to Des Plaines, Elmhurst, and Waukegan. But implementation of the proposal fizzled, in part because of unsettled conditions created by World War I. The company, however, seriously contemplated the possibility in the mid-1920s. At this time electrification of steam railways in Europe was becoming commonplace

The North Western took pride when it completed its new Proviso Yard and freight transfer station in Chicago. It distributed 30,000 copies of an elaborate publicity folder to celebrate the October 1, 1927, opening of this $16 million facility and to let freight patrons know that with this betterment it could handle "through traffic with the utmost efficiency." (Author's collection)

The North Western sent the refurbished, state-of-the-art *North Western Limited* on tour in 1923 before its entry into revenue service. The crack eight-car name train is seen at Lake Front Station in Milwaukee on December 17, 1923. (North Western/Union Pacific)

and when some New York and Philadelphia commuter routes were already under wire. And locally the Illinois Central electrified its suburban service between downtown Chicago and Matteson in August 1926. The "Illinois Central Electric Zone" immediately won praise and generated strong revenues. The estimated cost of installing the electrical system for the three Chicago suburban lines of the North Western exceeded $60 million, with additional expense for equipment and modifications to the physical plant. The plan was placed on hold. Another reason for inaction besides cost was that suburban service was a loser financially. In 1924 gross revenues were $3.7 million, but expenses stood at about $5 million. The feeling persisted that ultimately "heavy traction" would reduce operating expenses and "pay for itself." It was already known that electric locomotives could haul longer, heavier trains than their steam counterparts and at considerably greater speeds.[63]

The idea of electrification did not go away; another feasibility study appeared in 1929. "There has been no decision either for electrification or against," Sargent told reporters in October 1929 after examining the document. Although the study again called for millions of dollars of expenditures, the prevailing impression was that wiring the busiest line, trackage between Chicago and Waukegan, seemed viable. The Wall Street crash a few days after Sargent met the press sealed the fate of the project. Daily patrons, however, did encounter some betterments during the 1920s: several new suburban depots and scores of aluminum-alloy commuter cars.[64]

New passenger equipment for commuter trains was not the only benefit for North Western customers. The company continued the Best of Everything tradition in the 1920s, even though the dynamics of intercity travel were changing. North Western officials, including Finley and Sargent, believed that long-distance luxury trains remained viable and should be upgraded. The railroad, therefore, spent heavily on rolling stock for its name trains during the decade. The *North Western Limited*, the premier Chicago–Milwaukee–Twin Cities train, for example, greeted riders with replacement equipment on December 18, 1923. This "varnish" was magnificent. "The equipment consists of the latest type of standard Pullman sleeping cars, and includes observation-sleeping cars, free reclining chair cars, and dining cars," remarked an industry trade journal. "Special attention has been given to the electric lighting and also to ventilation throughout the entire train. A screened, adjustable ventilator in the outside window sash enables the occupant of the berth to control the temperature at night according to his liking. Obscured electric fixtures beneath the berths reflect a soft light in the aisles at night time."[65]

The North Western also added new or replacement equipment as the company desired to strengthen or at least maintain its passenger position. During the mid- and late 1920s numerous roads, including rivals Burlington, Milwaukee Road, and Rock Island, were also spending heavily on modern rolling stock, and the impact of these competitors' betterments could not be ignored. The North Western most notably introduced the *Corn King Limited* on August 20, 1928. This train, which appeared in a highly competitive market, was appropriately named; it raced through the corn-growing country from Chicago to Omaha and Sioux City. One section followed the main line directly to Omaha, while the other left it at Carroll, Iowa, for Sioux City, traveling over a heavy-duty branch to Onawa, via Wall Lake, and then on the rails of the old Sioux City & Pacific. The *Corn King*, immediately known for its "grand style and comfort," provided such luxuries as a glass-enclosed observation parlor and solarium car and highback, semiswivel seats in its coaches, "the first revolving type seat cars to be used in the West." It was a virtual copy of the most recent equipment assigned to the *North Western Limited*.[66]

Not everyone wanted to board the *Corn King* or any other train, however, during the "Roaring Twenties." At this time Americans were radically altering their travel habits: the automobile became for many the preferred choice. When President Warren G. Harding proclaimed in 1921 that "the motor car has become an indispensable instrument in our political, social, and industrial life," he stated the obvious. Already cars and improved roadways were transforming the nation. The statistics were impressive: 8,131,522 motor-vehicle registrations in 1920 and 23,034,753 ten years later; 390,000 miles of surfaced roads in 1920 and 694,000 in 1930. The comparative usage data between automobiles and trains were also dramatic: Americans in 1920 took their cars for intercity trips of 50 miles per year and trains for 450 miles; a decade later, however, they drove 1,691 miles and rode trains only 219 miles annually. For many the automobile had become indispensable. Sociologists Robert and Helen Lynd in their 1929 study of Muncie, Indiana, *Middletown,* noted that one working-class woman vowed to "go without food" before giving up her car, and another woman stated that her family would rather do without clothes than not have a car.[67]

Since the North Western had historically been a "heavy passenger line," management watched closely the trends in traffic. The company, more than most, kept investors informed about the changing passenger business. Both good and bad signs were evident by the early twenties. "The long distance travel has been steadily increasing but the benefits that come from these increases are more than offset by the shrinkage in volume of short-haul traffic, other than commutation," Finley told shareholders in May 1924. "In 1917, which is about the time the use of the automobile had reached a point where it was an important factor, your company carried 16,702,885 passengers in local intrastate traffic. In 1923 there were only 8,133,518 such passengers. This loss of over 50% in this class of business resulted in reducing the revenue in 1923 by over eight million dollars. For the most part this loss is attributable to the increase in the use of automobiles and motor busses for short distance travel."[68]

As with other railroads, the North Western did not ignore this threat. An obvious response was to remove trains that lost money. Regulatory constraints made some of these abandonments difficult, however, if not impossible. In mid-1924, for example, after struggling with the South Dakota Railroad Commission, the company won the right to discontinue two Sunday trains that operated between Huron and Pierre and obtained permission to curtail service between Redfield and Pierre. Subsequent efforts to abandon passenger operations on the Redfield-Pierre trackage came to naught.[69]

When government, either state or federal, refused to grant a discontinuance, the North

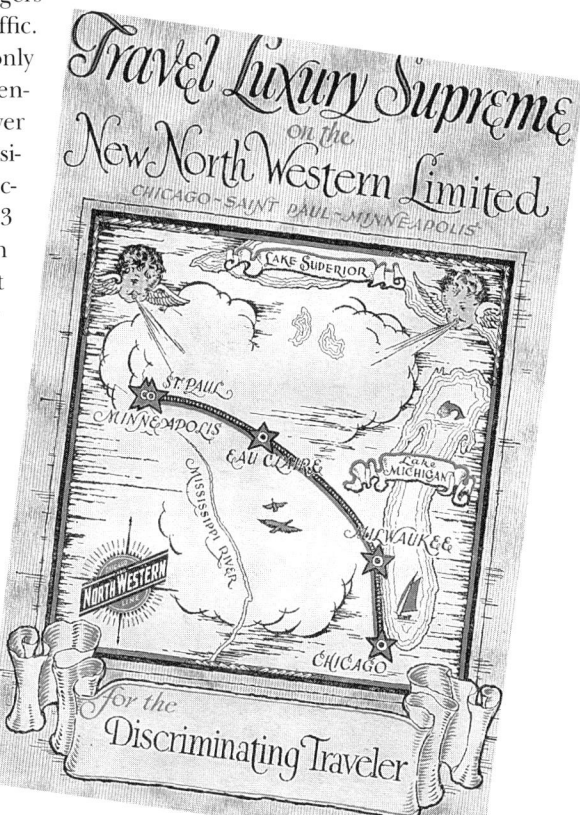

The North Western frequently distributed lavish publications to promote travel on its premier name trains. This brochure introduced the traveling public to the *New North Western Limited*. (Author's collection)

When the *Corn King Limited* made its debut in the 1920s, some promotional literature contained the specialized emblem with the altered corporate motto: "The Best of Everything in the Best of the West." (Author's collection)

Western tried to find ways to reduce the financial bleeding. An important counterresponse was the use of self-propelled gas-electric motor cars—popularly, even affectionately, called "doodlebugs" and "galloping geese." These units usually had ample space for passengers, mail, and express; some too could pull coaches, trailers, or even freight cars if needed. This rolling stock proved economical to operate because of reduced fuel and labor costs, yet it still accommodated riders and mail and express business that might exist in considerable quantity. Although the company had briefly placed a McKeen motor car in service on the 52-mile Fremont-Lincoln branch about 1912, repeated mechanical problems failed to prevent management from considering other self-contained vehicles. The road purchased more than a score of gas-electric motor units between 1926 and 1929, and a few years earlier had even successfully converted wooden passenger coaches into gasoline motor cars.[70]

Another option for cutting passenger expenses was operating "mixed" trains. These runs, where a few passengers joined the work crew and shipments of LCL freight and express in a caboose, "combine" (a combination coach and baggage car), or a wooden coach attached to freight cars, were hardly novel; they had existed since the earliest days of railroading. Some North Western branch lines, particularly those in the timber region of northern Wisconsin, never had received regular steam passenger trains.[71]

Mixed trains nonetheless appeared more commonly throughout the North Western system after World War I. Initially the company provided either steam or motor car trains on the Winner-Wood extension, for example, but it quickly won regulatory approval to substitute mixed service. At times the railroad continued to operate a conventional passenger train but allowed patrons to take a freight if they wished. In the late twenties the public could ride motor train No. 243 for the three-hour trip between Rice Lake and Park Falls, Wisconsin, a distance of 79 miles, or they could take freight No. 245 and endure a nearly eight-hour journey.[72]

As the 1920s wore on, the North Western joined numerous railroads, large and small, in concluding that railroad-owned or -controlled bus operations might bolster the local passenger business. The North Western entered the bus business in a modest way and by 1928 was involved in four small rural bus operations. In every case these motor coach lines fed passenger traffic to North Western trains: Deadwood to Lead, South Dakota, 5 miles; Eyota to Chatfield, Minnesota, 12 miles; Galesville to Trempealeau, Wisconsin, 7 miles; and Red Granite to Neshkoro, Wisconsin, 10 miles.[73]

This modest foray into highway passenger service revealed the positive benefits for both the traveler and the railroad. Mostly the service surpassed what had been available without a bus alternative. Take the case of a journey between the southeastern Minnesota communities of Eyota and Chatfield. In 1910 the North Western offered two daily steam trains each way. By the late 1920s it dispatched only a single daily train but operated three daily buses each way as well. Going to and from Chatfield was easier for the public and less expensive for the company.[74]

The North Western never lagged far behind the industry with its involvement with buses. As of January 1, 1925, only three major steam railroads operated motor buses. But more railroads came to realize that the bus was a potential competitor and a possible ally, and they responded accordingly. In the 20-month period that followed, railroads and their bus subsidiaries placed more than 1,200 vehicles on routes totaling 11,400 miles. These runs, however, were in competition with bus companies that operated nearly 20,000 buses and served 33,522 route miles. As was seen in the North Western's original bus affiliations,

In the 1920s the North Western acquired a fleet of gasoline-electric motor cars to reduce the cost of branch-line and local passenger operations. Near the end of World War II a motor train is seen in the station at Sioux City, Iowa. (Author's collection)

the idea was not solely to meet competition head-on but also to feed traffic from off-line or branch-line communities to trains on important passenger arteries. Similarly, buses were a way to solve problems that had existed since the railroad map had crystallized; a company's steel rails did not always reach the best places or go in the most logical fashion. Convenient, inexpensive, and flexible bus travel, moreover, would ideally attract riders who might want to leave their "tin lizzies" safely parked at home.[75]

The North Western made its big plunge into the bus business in 1929. Few barriers existed. State government, which regulated bus activities before 1935, usually accommodated the railroads' bus proposals. When Jesse Lee Haugh, the assistant to President Carl R. Gray of the Union Pacific and a former assistant chief engineer for the North Western, suggested to North Western management that the two railroads launch a joint bus operation, an agreement was quickly implemented. Regulatory approval came swiftly, and later the Interstate Commerce Commission endorsed the arrangement following a legal challenge from another bus carrier.[76]

Interstate Transit Lines became the joint venture. The North Western originally acquired 22,417 of the 69,000 outstanding shares, which represented an investment of approximately $1 million. Soon buses owned by Interstate and two related companies, Chicago & North Western Stages and Union Pacific Stages, provided largely companion service to communities along the main line of the North Western and Union Pacific. Other long-distance routes in the West and feeders were also part of this "Overland Route" bus network. By 1934 Interstate Transit offered "frequent daily schedules through 17 states," supported by a 7,260-mile route structure. A combination of extensive service and reasonable rates caused riders to flock to these North Western–Union Pacific buses: 1,417,032 in 1930 and 2,277,601 in 1934.[77]

The North Western vigorously promoted combined bus and rail travel. Since it wanted its highway subsidiary to tap territory for its main-line passenger trains, the railroad in its public timetables pointed to examples of improved connections. Illustrations described service from Rockford, Illinois, to Omaha and from Chicago to Lincoln, Nebraska. "The Interstate Transit Lines motor coach leaves Rockford, Ill. at 9:45

a.m., offering a connection with the 'Columbine' . . . leaving Dixon at 12:54 p.m. Passengers may also leave Rockford at 5:05 p.m., connecting with the 'Corn King Limited' at 8:06 p.m. [A] passenger can leave Chicago on the famous 'Corn King Limited' at 6:05 p.m., arrive Omaha 7:15 a.m. and leave there at 8:00 a.m. in a comfortable modern coach of the Interstate Transit Lines and arrive at Lincoln at 10:00 a.m." A rider wanting to do so could travel entirely by North Western trains, but the trip would have involved branch-line locals and substantially more time.[78]

The coordinated travel that captured greater press attention than the bus-train arrangements were plane-train operations sponsored by North Western. The concept enjoyed modest popularity during the formative years of commercial aviation. "The railroads have realized that they must do more than stick to the rail lines," voiced a Midwestern editor in 1928, "if they are to compete for passenger service." The successful flight made by Charles A. Lindbergh from New York to Paris in 1927 and development of the all-metal airplane, first by Fokker and then by Ford, positively affected air transport. The most acclaimed venture involved the arrangement between Transcontinental Air Transport, Inc. (TAT) and the Pennsylvania and Santa Fe railroads, which offered a 48-hour cross-country air-rail package. Starting in July 1929 westbound travelers could board the Pennsylvania's evening train, the *Airways Limited*, in New York City and detrain the next morning in Columbus. From "Port Columbus" in the Ohio capital they could fly during the daylight hours to Waynoka, Oklahoma, and board the Santa Fe's *Missionary* for

Promotional photographs of the exterior and interior of a bus belonging to the Chicago & North Western Stages date from the early 1930s. Responding to a changing travel market, the North Western used buses to be a profitable way to feed passengers to its trains. (North Western/Union Pacific)

the overnight trip to Clovis, New Mexico. Passengers made the final leg by air, again during the day, to Los Angeles and San Francisco. Better aircraft and guidance equipment soon eliminated the need for overnight rail trips; airplanes were able to bind the nation without a railroad partnership.[79]

While the TAT–Pennsylvania–Santa Fe operation captured national media attention, the North Western received mostly regional coverage for its air-rail service. In May 1928 the railroad announced that it would launch Chicago–Black Hills plane-train service with Rapid Air Lines via St. Paul, but the first travelers did not book passage until May 1, 1929. Despite this delay the railroad expected to attract affluent and adventurous passengers who vacationed in the Black Hills,
a recreational site popularized by visits of Calvin and Grace Coolidge. The schedule involved rail travel between Chicago and the Twin Cities and then air between the Twin Cities and Rapid City. The advantages were both the novelty and the savings of 12 to 15 hours over the all-rail route. Even though the North Western was the first railroad in the West after the Santa Fe to embark on this type of intermodal arrangement, the Chicago–Black Hills service was short-lived: it fell victim to the hard times caused by the subsequent stock market crash.[80]

A more enduring air-rail arrangement coincided with the Chicago–Black Hills coordinated service. This was the joint North Western–Kohler Aviation Corporation operation between Wisconsin and Michigan. A Kohler public timetable

The upgrading of train No. 1, the *San Francisco Overland Limited*, brought a crowd of well-wishers to the Chicago passenger terminal on November 13, 1926. (North Western/Union Pacific)

People who used the Chicago passenger terminal continued to have access to outstanding facilities. The barbershop was renovated in 1928 and Entel's Dining Room went "Parisian with outside service" during the summer of 1929. (North Western/Union Pacific)

for July 1, 1930, proclaimed it THE CONVENIENT ROUTE. "Passengers board the Kohler Planes at the Northwestern Railway Terminal in Milwaukee, and step from plane to Michigan Central Train in Grand Rapids." Air travelers rode in a six-passenger amphibian craft that had "equal facility on land or water." A changing technology and deepening depression, however, ended the railroad's participation by 1933.[81]

The North Western tried to bolster passenger revenues in yet another way: the Department of Tours lured individuals and groups to the rails. The company joined with the Union Pacific in 1900 to create the organization. The objective was to increase passenger business by promoting the scenic attractions of the American West through carefully arranged personal tours, an activity that several major Western carriers would follow. The department's initial efforts focused on Yellowstone National Park, the nation's first and largest recreational reserve. Results were modest, however, as the two roads carried only 38 vacationers in their inaugural year of escorted trips. The department's activities grew steadily, however, and for the 1925 season Manager C. J. Collins reported the transportation of 2,866 travelers on 35 escorted tours to Yellowstone together with "several large convention parties." Profits likewise rose, amounting to approximately $20,000 by the mid-1920s.[82]

The Department of Tours, after 1920 especially, revealed itself as an imaginative and sophisticated operation. In 1925 the department "loaned" a representative to assist H. M. Albright, superintendent of the Yellowstone National Park, in compiling statistics for his annual report to the secretary of the interior. The payoff was good. "In return for this man's services," noted Manager Collins, "we secured the list of names and addresses of all persons visiting Yellowstone Park this summer and also a copy of other valuable data, which in no other way can be procured." Department personnel carefully analyzed this information, and through its representatives, mostly associated with the company's off-line passenger agents, contacted hundreds of these individuals. The targeted group received information about forthcoming North Western–Union Pacific escorted parties to Yellowstone and to another popular attraction, Rocky Mountain National Park northwest of Denver. Literature describing trains on the Overland Route to California was mailed to them, and some even received telephone calls. When these statistics revealed sizable concentrations of previous park visitors in several Midwestern cities, including Chicago, Cleveland, Detroit, Indianapolis, and Milwaukee, the department either started new newspaper advertising campaigns or expanded existing ones.[83]

The Department of Tours showed a sensitivity to patrons' comments. Complaints were circulated among North Western and Union Pacific brass and appropriate actions taken. The surviving records contain few negative letters, and most contained only minor criticisms. A breakfast on the *Overland Limited,* for example, did not please a Chicago resident: "Several passengers had to stand in line while two or three colored waiters finished breakfast at the far table, as other tables were filled. Naturally, the service was poor without all waiters working. When one passenger complained to the Steward, he answered that the 'waiters had to eat.'"[84]

Compliments, on the other hand, were numerous. Typical was a glowing letter received in 1930 from Edward Snethen, a former officer of the Lions Clubs of America, to V. A. Hampton, general agent for the North Western in Indianapolis. Snethen, who had recently participated in a Lions Clubs of Indiana tour of Yellowstone, wrote in part:

> Your trains were all steel, finely equipped, with the best of service. The meals on your diners were most excellent, and the personally conducted tours through Yellowstone National Park . . . was [*sic*] handled in fine shape. All throughout Yellowstone, to and from the different points of interest, the transportation was taken care of in such manner that the passengers did not need to give any worry whatever with reference to their baggage, places of lodging, or looking after any details whatsoever in the trip. . . .[85]

The pampering of travelers took on various forms during the 1920s. While not a publicized part of this commitment, yet indicative of the North Western's continuing dedication to the Best of Everything credo, was the operation of the private car *Deerpath.* Starting in the spring of 1929 a group of wealthy and influential Chicago North Shore businessmen, which included Phillip Armour (meat packing), E. A. Cudahy (meat packing), Fred Preston (manufacturing), Edward Swift (meat packing), and Fred Wacker (machine tools), leased a club car that the North Western attached to regularly scheduled commuter runs between Waukegan and Chicago. The *Deerpath* allowed these men to travel in comfort, with an attendant looking to their needs. The car also remained in the Chicago passenger terminal for the use of the group, functioning as an exclusive club under the train shed. While this private use of rolling stock appeared on other railroads, the Erie and the New Haven for example, only the North Western provided the service in the Chicago area. Another club car leased from the company rolled for years between Barrington and Chicago.[86]

The calamitous break in the New York stock market in October 1929 heralded the slump that led to the greatest depression in world history. Economic dislocations not only befell the United States but also occurred elsewhere, particularly in Europe and Latin America. The feeling in America that an era of perpetual prosperity had been firmly established was so persistent that the stock market crash initially did not shatter confidence in the system. Fred Sargent and fellow officials, like most of their colleagues in the industry, did not seem immediately alarmed with the happenings in the financial sector. Freight and passenger traffic for the short term did not collapse. But by 1931 the national economy dramatically weakened, and rail usage declined. The North Western's net operating income, which stood at $26.2 million in 1929, slipped to $17.4 million for 1930 and plunged to $6.2 million a year later. Then in 1935 the North Western did what observers had once thought impossible; the company sought protection from creditors in bankruptcy court. After the North Western faltered and fell, it never again regained its exalted position as one of the bluest of the blue clips.[87]

It's dinner in the diner! This 1936 publicity photograph, showing passengers in the elegant "New Dining Car" of the *Portland Rose,* a daily Chicago-to-Portland train operated jointly by the North Western and Union Pacific, gives no indication that the nation is in the midst of the awful depression. (North Western/Union Pacific)

CHAPTER Eight

THE GREAT DEPRESSION AND BANKRUPTCY

Unlike the Panic of May 1893, which brought a sudden economic collapse, the stock market crash of October 1929 did not immediately throw the nation into depression. The New York market leveled off during the first several months in 1930 and so did various other indicators, including production, imports, and employment. President Herbert Hoover seemed hopeful, commenting in May that although he expected economic difficulties to continue, he believed that the most trying times had passed. While Hoover's first observation was correct, he erred badly with the second. Americans generally realized that the stock market tumble was the opening roll of thunder for an economic storm of epic proportions. Hard times had largely settled over the land by 1932, and the impact was immense. National income, a good barometer, plummeted from $82.8 billion in 1928 to only $42.5 billion four years later.[1]

America's railroads, dependent upon a high level of business activity for adequate revenues, faced mounting economic problems. The scope of these financial challenges was manifest in steeply declining annual operating revenues: $6.2 billion in 1929, $5.3 billion in 1930, $4.2 billion in 1931, and $3.1 billion in 1932. The net railway operating income for the North Western paralleled this dramatic fall of industry earnings: $26,220,149 in 1929, $17,432,850 in 1930, $6,272,136 in 1931, and a mere $1,422,835 in 1932.[2]

As the Great Depression deepened, the Fred W. Sargent administration understood that the North Western faced the economic fight of its life. As a way of explaining to shareholders why a prosperous property was encountering financial trouble, Sargent reviewed those forces that adversely affected income. Everyone comprehended the negative impact of the Wall Street debacle, but some perhaps were unaware of the way other factors reduced railroad revenues.

Sargent underscored the threat posed by highway carriers. He and his railroad colleagues were especially incensed that these competitors for freight traffic were largely uncontrolled. "During the depression truck competition has been enormously intensified," wrote the North Western president in April 1932. "One reason is that drivers of trucks can be secured at a very low cost and there are no regulations as to the length of time on duty." Sargent could have added that entry was easy; an unemployed factory worker could acquire a used truck, even on long-term credit, and immediately start hauling commercial goods.[3]

Then there was the matter of regulatory controls. Much governmental supervision of trucking was lacking before passage of the Motor Carriers Act of 1935, and even then regulation hardly touched "gypsy" operators. Railroads, on the other hand, operated in a highly controlled environment. "We're often in a regulatory straight-jacket," Sargent commented. The Interstate Commerce Commission, most of all, was not as supportive as the North Western executive would have liked. "In July, 1931, the carriers asked for emergency rates to help tide them over this unprecedented depression," Sargent observed. "The Commission finally decided that effective January 4, 1932, the carriers might make certain arbitrary increases on certain commodities, but it did not order such increases and left it to the railroads to secure favorable action in each of the states as to intrastate rates." Similarly, regulatory bodies were slow to approve applications to terminate passenger trains, which had a profound impact on the North Western, "a large passenger-carrying railroad." Sargent lamented that the company could not cut passenger train mileage as rapidly as business declined, so more financial losses resulted.[4]

The North Western president realized that the company possessed a physical plant with obsolete parts. He grasped the importance of closing scores of small-town stations and trimming the system's vast network of feeder lines. "In short, the railroad was built in the days of dirt roads and the horse and buggy. Stations are now more numerous than necessary, with concrete roads and the automobile. Unnecessary stations should be abandoned where the business can be handled at other stations on the same or

Porters attended to the needs of passengers, performing such tasks as the preparation of beds, and a few received assignments of a public relations nature. On March 8, 1930, a company photographer caught the "Pullman Porters' Quartet," men assigned to the *Victory*, a name train operating from Chicago to the Twin Cities with through equipment to Duluth, Minn., and Deadwood, S.Dak. (North Western/Union Pacific)

adjacent lines. Likewise, more branch lines were built in the horse and buggy age than would have been built in the age of the automobile and concrete highways." Sargent suggested that "railroads serving the same territory should enter into a co-operative arrangement to abandon branch lines and thus save large sums in maintenance and out-of-pocket costs of operation." Regulatory opposition was often keen; politicians listened to community leaders and shippers who demanded retention of both stations and rails. Still the company padlocked 45 depots during 1931, an impressive feat for the time; except for the Consol, Iowa, coal line, however, the North Western failed to abandon any significant trackage.[5]

Fred Sargent announced that the North Western would not play a passive role during the Great Depression. The company attempted a variety of measures, seeking to stop the flow of red ink as best it could, before filing for an unavoidable bankruptcy in mid-1935.

Self-help had been the standby remedy, and the North Western moved to initiate improvements. The company continued to make capital expenditures, mostly those approved prior to the crash, expecting that a more efficient physical plant would provide both immediate and long-term financial benefits. Sargent, who never expected such awful economic dislocations, told journalists in late November 1929, "We will go forward with our programs as though there had been no decline in the stock market. . . . I don't see that the market affects the general situation."[6]

The most costly of the early depression-era betterments took place in Chicago. The first, completed in 1930, was the rehabilitation of the Wood Street Yard to handle produce, especially potatoes. "A brick office building, platform scales in various locations, and other auxiliary facilities necessary to adapt the yard to the handling of [produce] . . . were installed as part of the facility." Then in the spring of 1931 the North Western opened its consolidated Wells Street freight station under the new Merchandise Mart; the railroad had earlier sold the air rights for this colossal structure. Located in the heart of the Windy City, this freight facility replaced four separate urban yards. "The Wells Street Freight Station is a mammoth affair," reported agent H. R. Terpning in 1932. "Its outbound platform stretches 1360 feet long and its in-bound platform 1000 feet long." He added, "The station is modern in every respect, both platforms being brick enclosed with wide steel doors opening to teamways and tracks. There are numerous approaches to the station and wide teamways serving the station giving shippers and receivers the best in freight service."[7]

As the national economy deteriorated, businesses large and small reduced wages. The North Western was no exception and joined other carriers in an agreement with the brotherhoods for a temporary 10 percent wage reduction effective February 1, 1932, which would end June 30, 1933. Paychecks, however, remained at the reduced levels when this arrangement was extended for another year. The industry restored the reduction as quickly as it could: 2 1/2 percent on July 1, 1934; 2 1/2 percent on January 1, 1935; and the remaining 5 percent on

On a June 1930 day, North Western personnel, who are turning No. 1559, a Pacific-type locomotive, at the West Chicago engine facility, probably had no idea that their employer was about to encounter its greatest economic challenges. (Alfred W. Johnson photograph, George Krambles collection)

April 1, 1935. These wage reductions saved millions of dollars for the North Western.[8]

Similarly, businesses furloughed employees, and the North Western again followed the national pattern. The size of the company workforce dropped during the hard times, a process mostly ongoing since before World War I. The railroad employed approximately 54,000 individuals in 1913 and fewer than 35,000 in 1932. Moreover, workers frequently became underemployed. At the close of 1930 the road had laid off about 7,000 employees, a majority of whom held assignments in the car and mechanical departments. Early the next year it recalled most of them on a three-day-week basis. Additional cuts occurred, and some workers remained off the job until 1934.[9]

Consolidation also appealed to North Western management. While the railroad had never favored decentralization, the exigencies of the times encouraged belt tightening through unification. In August 1931 the company announced that its Dakota, Madison, and Minnesota divisions would be fused into two districts, Dakota and Madison. Management also restructured the Black Hills, Eastern, and Wyoming divisions, which affected trackage west of the Missouri River. These changes occurred solely "for the sake of economy in administration."[10]

Two Chicago potato brokers gaze at a giant "Track List" blackboard in the clubroom of the Wood Street terminal. A boxcar's yard location and number are entered in chalk. (North Western/Union Pacific)

Even though a crippling depression gripped the greater Chicago area by 1933, commuters still traveled to and from the center city. The impressive lineup of suburban trains at West Chicago, Ill., on July 14, 1933, was photographed by Alfred W. Johnson, a commercial artist and railroad enthusiast. (George Krambles collection)

A self-help response that garnered a positive public reaction involved increasing shipments of less-than-carload (LCL) freight. With trucks siphoning off more of this lucrative traffic, North Western officials, like their counterparts at other progressive railroads, implemented a pragmatic solution. The company became a leader in door-to-door LCL service. Launched extensively in the early 1930s, the program allowed a shipper to contact the railroad for delivery to a customer without involving any trucking firms. "At the present time [1932], we have 277 stations where we offer this pick-up and delivery service," explained the company's vice president of traffic, Henry Beyers. "We do not absorb the trucking charge but add it to the regular shipping charge under this plan. However, no profit is made on the trucking by the road. The absolute cost of the service is all that is charged to the receiver or shipper." Later, the North Western assumed the costs for pickup and delivery.[11]

The North Western attempted other expedients to halt declining freight earnings. One experiment, the "magic box," did not work out as intended. For a few months in late 1930 and early 1931, the railroad used specially designed portable metal containers for shipping LCL goods between Chicago and Milwaukee. The idea was hardly new. Experiments during World War I, particularly the "Fitch Container," and additional efforts thereafter by the New York Central and several other roads caught the attention of North Western officials. The company was certainly familiar with United States mail traveling in this fashion. In May 1921 the New York Central contracted with the post office department for container shipments of mail, and some of these "moves" passed daily between La Salle Street Station and North Western Station in Chicago. It was obvious that LCL freight, which offered the potential for good profits, was also labor intensive, easily susceptible to damage and theft, and in need of a better method of hauling. Yet it was regulatory objections that ended the scheme on the North Western. The Interstate Commerce Commission in the spring of 1931 rejected a flat-rate schedule used by the North Western and several other carriers. The commissioners did not want customers to rent a box at a flat charge, which was cheap and simple, for they feared that modal competition would be damaged. "The ICC as a rate-making body," observes historian John H. White Jr., "could not abide containerization." And the conclusion reached by Vice President Beyers was valid: "We believe they [containers] would have been satisfactory if the rate situation could have been cleared up."[12]

The failure of containerization, however, led to a different approach that satisfied both shippers and regulators. The car and freight departments jointly developed the "compartment" car. "It is a freight car similar to the automobile freight car divided into four sections," observed Beyers. "The sections are sold on a space basis rather than a weight basis to shippers in Chicago and Milwaukee, the cars being in operation only between those two cities. These cars have worked out very well and we are inclined to believe are almost as satisfactory as the container idea." And he added, "When we did have the container cars in service, we found that the door to door idea, which is supposed to be the selling point of the container, was not as important as the fact that a shipper could buy what was virtually a sixth of a freight car at car load rates. The compartment car, you can see, has that same advantage."[13]

The public became much more aware of the self-help effort in the passenger rather than the freight sector. The North Western surprised the traveling public in January 1935 when it introduced a high-speed train, the *400*, between Chicago, Milwaukee, and the Twin Cities. Although this was a time when diesel-powered, lightweight aluminum and steel alloy "streamliners" represented a bold effort to lure Americans back to the rails, the North Western opted instead for conventional steam locomotives and standard, heavyweight equipment. The company's attempts to recapture and retain passenger business along this competitive corridor worked well; the trains made money and enhanced the corporate image.[14]

In 1934 North Western officials worried about the future of passenger revenues generated from the long-distance Chicago–Twin Cities market. The Burlington and Milwaukee Road seemed likely to upgrade significantly their services. Rumors spread by summer that the former planned to introduce stainless steel streamliners and the latter medium-weight equipment with streamlined steam locomotives. Whatever the nature of these trains, schedules might be slashed by three or four hours. The fastest trains covered the roughly 400 miles in about 10 hours. The threat of the Burlington *Zephyrs* surely unnerved North Western brass; the articulated, three-car diesel-powered *Zephyr* had caused a national sensation on May 26, 1934, when it made a record nonstop run from Denver to Chicago. The streamliner's subsequent national tour and successful assignment to revenue service augured well for high-speed internal combustion trains. Automobile competition also increased: more and more powerful and dependable vehicles rolling over better, all-weather highways allowed increased speeds and made trips more comfortable, predictable, and practical.[15]

Interrailroad passenger competition had already heated up for the North Western. The company found itself in a battle with the Milwaukee Road for business between Chicago and Milwaukee. While neither company selected *Zephyr* clones, both operated conventional steam-powered equipment on 90-minute schedules over this 85-mile route after mid-July 1934. Perhaps the success of the improved Chicago-Milwaukee trains convinced the North Western that it could do the same on a much grander scale. Traditional rolling stock appeared to be the plausible choice; replication of the Burlington's popular *Zephyr* would be too expensive and would take much time to acquire from the manufacturer.[16]

Once the North Western decided to introduce a premier Chicago–Twin Cities train, preparations began quickly and quietly. With the route selected—*400*s would travel through Milwaukee and along the Adams Cutoff rather than through Madison—crews laid new rail, improved curve elevations for high speed, and made other betterments to the track structure. Shopmen converted four 11-year-old Pacific-type locomotives (E-2 class 4-6-2s) from coal to oil to reduce engine changes and eliminate fuel and water stops at several intermediate points. Other workers renovated a group of coaches,

Locomotive No. 1154, a 4-6-0 Ten Wheeler, pulls a freight train across a mostly unprotected street crossing in St. Charles, Ill., in the mid-1930s. The era of automatic crossing-protection devices was mostly in the future. (Alfred W. Johnson photograph, George Krambles collection)

Train No. 401, the *400*, accelerates out of downtown Chicago for Milwaukee, the first leg of its "400 miles in 400 minutes." (North Western/Union Pacific)

The North Western aggressively promoted the *400*, its crack standard weight and steam-powered service between Chicago and the Twin Cities. Rand McNally printed 15,000 folders to announce the introduction of the train. (Author's collection)

diners, and parlor cars, some of which dated back to 1912. They installed air-conditioning equipment for the entire consist. With everything in readiness, press releases and paid publicity began to appear in late December 1934. One advertisement described the forthcoming service this way: "Again 'North Western' makes railroad history . . . clipping hours from the previous fastest morning time between Chicago, Milwaukee and the Twin Cities. 400 miles in 400 minutes. FASTEST TRAIN ON THE AMERICAN CONTINENT." The moniker also suggested sophistication and wealth: "the Four Hundred" in high society were the crème de la crème. "Besides being both unusual and easy to remember," observed one commentator, "[the name] . . . told the whole story. In a way, with the possible exception of the *Twentieth Century Limited*, it was the most effective train name ever devised."[17]

The *400*s made their maiden trips from Chicago and the Twin Cities on Wednesday, January 2, 1935. Everything went well: radio stations provided live broadcasts, crowds gathered at trackside, and the trains ran on time. The *400*s were a delight: they were comfortable and clean, and their speeds normally exceeding 80 miles per hour. Understandably these "new aristocrats of the rails" excited the public.[18]

The *400* project was a triumph for the beleaguered company. The North Western beat the Burlington and Milwaukee Road with popular, upgraded service and at the same time kept the cost remarkably low. Instead of spending a million dollars or more on trainsets, the railroad paid about $50,000 for refurbishing the locomotives and equipment.[19]

The popularity of the *400*s may have amazed North Western management. Nearly 10,000 passengers took the trains during the first month of operation, and ridership remained strong. The runs were frequently sold out for good reasons: the company did not charge an "extra fare," and scheduled the *400*s to allow patrons much of the working or shopping day in the terminal cities. Train No. 401 left Chicago at 3:30 P.M. and No. 400 departed from Minneapolis at 3:00 P.M. and St. Paul 30 minutes later. "The convenient late afternoon departure of the '400' permits the saving of practically an entire business day," explained a smartly designed *400* brochure, "and still gets you there before the evening is over." The northbound *400* arrived in St. Paul at 10:30 P.M. and Minneapolis 30 minutes later and the southbound train reached the Chicago terminal at 10:30 P.M.[20]

The North Western's *400*s on the Chicago–Twin Cities route caught the attention of the railway world, both competitors and connecting carriers. About a month after the service began, Albert J. Dickinson, passenger traffic manager for the Great Northern, wrote his former boss and president of the Burlington, Ralph Budd, the following observations:

> I thought you might . . . be interested in a little more information we have picked up concerning the C&NW #400 trains. . . . They seem to be securing a volume of commercial traffic that wants to spend one business day in Chicago with only one night away from home . . . , and it is also true of anyone who has to spend two days in Chicago but wants to get home late the same evening of the second day. This class of business usually moves on a ten day roundtrip rate of fare and one-third which necessitates the passenger using the same line in each direction between the Twin Cities and Chicago. . . .
>
> The Milwaukee [officials] are also complaining that the '400' train is making some inroads on their business . . . , there is no doubt that the C&NW are securing business from the Twin Cities destined to over-night points out of Chicago such as Detroit, Cleveland, Buffalo, Cincinnati, Indianapolis and St. Louis. On the Florida business the North Western seem to have been doing well with the '400' which makes convenient connections at Chicago with the Illinois Central Seminole leaving at 11:05 PM., C&EI Dixie Flyer at 11:25 PM., and the Pennsylvania Southland at 11:55 PM.

This Great Northern official concluded: "There is no question but what the North Western have [*sic*] capitalized and benefitted from the publicity and advertising of the Burlington and Union Pacific in connection with their streamlined high speed trains and a good many people perhaps out of curiosity are taking the '400.'" Curiosity alone did not adequately account for the North Western's triumph; speed, service, and price explained this success.[21]

While the *400*s were a solely North Western effort to bolster passenger revenues, the company shared a state-of-the-art streamliner with the more affluent Union Pacific. When the Union Pacific decided to place its experimental M-10001 in revenue service, it did so with a joint Union Pacific–North Western run between Chicago and Portland. This eye-catching seven-car articulated train, *City of Portland*, began racing along the 2,272 mile route on June 6, 1935, maintaining an approximately 40-hour schedule. The initial "City" streamliner, which averaged 57 miles per hour, shaved 18 hours from the fastest regularly scheduled run. Patrons gained more than impressive speed; the train was the first diesel streamliner to carry sleepers. Later, in mid-1936, the joint Union Pacific–North Western *City of Denver, City of Los Angeles,* and *City of San Francisco* (with the Southern Pacific) streamliners further enhanced service on the Overland Route.[22]

The management of the North Western could not reasonably expect self-help initiatives alone to solve its financial problems. Public policy decisions forced the North Western and other carriers to seek relief from regulatory bodies. In the passenger sector the Interstate Commerce Commission permitted the Western Lines, including the North Western, to make significant coach fare reductions after December 1, 1933. Rates dropped from 3.6 cents to two cents for coach travel. These low fares and the popularity of the World's Fair, "A Century of Progress Exposition," held in Chicago during the summers of 1933 and 1934, attracted more riders and stabilized passenger losses.[23]

Freight rates involved greater complexities. In June 1931 the nation's carriers asked the Interstate Commerce Commission for a 15 percent rate boost, but the ICC denied the request after prolonged hearings. Still the commission recognized that the railroad industry was rapidly failing, and in late 1931 it proposed an intriguing

Above, a passenger train, operating on the Galena Division in the mid-1930s, is powered by No. 2912, a 4-6-2 Pacific. People at trackside paid less attention to this typical consist than they did to the sleek streamliners. They flocked to see such trains as the *City of Portland*, the pioneer joint North Western-Union Pacific streamliner. Here it is pictured racing through Glen Ellyn, Ill., on January 27, 1939, bound for Chicago. (Author's collection; John F. Humiston photograph)

compromise: that rate hikes on designated commodities be granted, effective from the time of filing supplements to existing tariffs until March 31, 1933. Revenues generated would not go to the contributing roads, however, but would be pooled and awarded to those companies unable to meet their fixed charges. The industry preferred loans to gratuity payments, and in December the ICC agreed. Soon the Railroad Credit Corporation (RCC) was created to collect and administer the fund; the program made its debut on January 4, 1932, when the special rate increase took effect.[24]

The actions of the RCC had a positive impact upon the North Western. The railroad borrowed nearly $2.2 million from this short-lived body, which came to an end in 1933. The ICC extended emergency freight rates until September 30, 1933, but no longer endorsed the pooling plan. The RCC therefore liquidated its affairs after June 1, 1933, and distributed the remaining funds to the participating roads. The North Western used its share, which amounted to about $215,000, to reduce the principal on its RCC loans.[25]

The North Western tapped additional credit sources during these years of struggle. Since the company possessed an inadequate sinking fund and had depleted most of its revenues to pay interest on a series of convertible debentures that it sold to retire Omaha Road bonds in 1930, the Sargent administration needed cash to handle its maturing debt obligations. More than a dozen banks supplied $10 million in 1931, but the faltering economy prevented the railroad from receiving more financial support from these battered institutions. The major cash infusion came instead from the Reconstruction Finance Corporation (RFC). The dramatic contraction of credit forced the Hoover administration to back Congressional efforts in January 1932 to create a special federal agency to aid the weary business community. The RFC, which soon had access to several billion dollars, made loans to banks, industrial corporations, insurance companies, and railroads, hoping to prevent massive bankruptcies and escalating unemployment. By the end of 1932 the North Western had been the beneficiary of $17,039,933 in RFC loans. The company used this money and an additional $14,775,200 in 1933 to repay bank obligations and to refinance several maturing series of bonds. The RFC was "a God-send," said Fred Sargent, and this aid prevented the North Western from becoming an early casualty of the Great Depression.[26]

Once again the North Western turned to Washington for help. Just as management required approval from the ICC to adjust passenger and freight charges, it needed permission to pool ore traffic from the Gogebic Iron Ore Range in Michigan and Wisconsin with the Soo Line. While shipments of this commodity were badly depressed—iron ore movements in 1932 were but one-twentieth of normal amounts—this cargo remained important to revenues, and the North Western sought to reduce transport costs. Specifically, the North Western and Soo wanted to abandon about 25 miles of duplicate trackage and to share switching costs on the range and at the dock facilities in Ashland, Wisconsin. The ICC agreed, and the plan was implemented in 1934. "The results were entirely satisfactory," reported Sargent in April 1935, "although the contemplated savings were somewhat minimized by the small volume of ore moved."[27]

Iron ore was not the only commodity that traveled in limited quantities. The North Western and other granger roads felt the immediate sting of devastating drought in large sections of the Midwest and most of the Great Plains. Although dry periods had hurt railroad revenues before, particularly in the early 1890s, the effect of the "Dirty Thirties" was massive and disastrous for farmers, merchants, railroads, and every group associated with agribusiness activities. The overall scarcity of moisture after 1930 and the excessive middecade summer heat slashed animal and crop production and greatly reduced the buying power of the region's residents. The extensive agricultural relief-and-recovery schemes and related programs of the New Deal after March 1933 helped to mitigate the ruinous conditions, but intense suffering—economic, physical, and emotional—continued.[28]

Even running trains during the Dirty Thirties posed challenges. Dust storms disrupted operations and made them dangerous at times. "Dust drifts, gathered on the railroad tracks, were so thick that they derailed the [North Western's] Astoria branch train and landed the 75 ton engine in the ditch on its side recently," reported the *Winthrop* (Minnesota) *News* in the spring of 1934. "None of the trainmen were injured, except for being somewhat bruised and shaken up. The derailment occurred three miles west of Ivanhoe [Minnesota]. Striking the dust, the

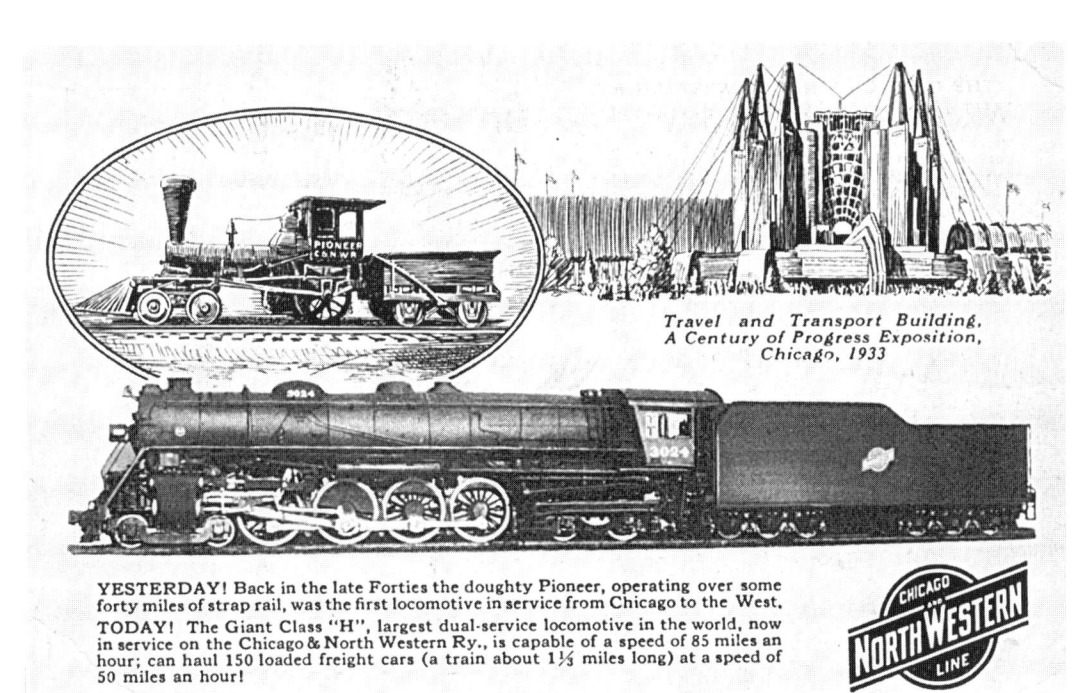

While battered by depression, the North Western distributed postcards that featured views of the *Pioneer* and the Class H locomotive. (Author's collection)

pilot wheels of the engine left the track and the rest of the engine followed, tearing up several rails of the track as it headed for the ditch and tipped over. Besides the engine and tender, there was only one freight car and the coach, which stayed on the track."[29]

Like other individuals and businesses the North Western was essentially powerless to cope with the agricultural crisis. The company did provide emergency rates, with regulatory approval, to farmers and ranchers beginning in 1931. In that year the railroad drastically reduced tariffs in South Dakota for carload lots of hay, straw, and feed grains and even transported some cattle free of charge to save their owners' investments. There was not much else to be done. The solution was better weather; no one could be blamed for the suffering caused by nature running through one of its more brutal cycles. Fred Sargent reported the obvious to shareholders in 1935: "Drought conditions which have prevailed in your Company's territory for the past three years reached disastrous proportions in 1934 in South Dakota, Minnesota, Nebraska and parts of Iowa. The loss in crop movement was immediately felt, but its effect on volume of live stock production and buying power of farmers and local industries will be felt for some time to come."[30]

Even worse weather came in 1935, 1936, and 1937. Summers were hot and dry and winters cold and snowy, greatly exacerbating the problems of 1934. If the territory of the North Western had experienced a normal climate during the depression, the company might have avoided bankruptcy in June 1935. Instead, the North Western became one of more than 20 major carriers, including archrival Milwaukee Road, that required court protection. The initials CNW, according to one wisecrack, had come to mean "*Can Not Worsen*."[31]

By early 1935 officials and board members knew that the North Western faced a financial crisis. The company had exhausted its lines of credit, including loans from the RFC, and operating income remained low. The railroad faced interest charges of more than $1.7 million on a series of convertible bonds due May 1, 1935. The Board of Directors, however, was not ready to admit financial defeat at its meeting of April 17. Instead the body decided to exercise a 60-day grace period on these obligations before formally deciding upon a course of action. But when conditions worsened, the board voted on June 27 to default on the convertible bonds. The company also faced nearly $30 million of obligations by the end of the year and no one was sanguine about prospects for payment.[32]

Directors of the North Western probably had fewer hesitations about bankruptcy than they might have had a few years earlier. The reason

While an agricultural depression had plagued the Great Plains since shortly after World War I, farm machinery manufacturers, like the J. I. Case Company of Racine, Wisc., continued to use the railroad for shipping and for advertising. (North Western/Union Pacific)

was that lawmakers had drastically altered the federal code in 1933. Worsening economic conditions had prompted the Hoover administration to accept an urgently needed business reform, the Federal Bankruptcy Act. This meant that a railroad with legal protection no longer needed a court-appointed receiver who would eventually sell the property, usually to a group of bondholders. Under Section 77 of the revised statute a protected carrier operated under the aegis of one or more trustees supervised by the court and the ICC. For the first time regulators played an active and positive role. "In the entire history of the ICC," comments transportation economist George W. Hilton, "probably nothing that the Commission undertook has met with such general approval as its behavior in reorganization of the bankrupt carriers of the 1930's." Argues Hilton: "The Commission helped bring about the reorganizations quickly and typically with conservatism concerning the railroad's future prospects." His conclusions, however, do not fully fit the bankruptcy case of the North Western.[33]

Early in the reorganization the revised law appeared to provide the benefits that George Hilton later observed. The process of bankruptcy originally moved along on the prescribed timetable. The plan, which the company filed with the Federal District Court for the Northern District of Illinois on June 27, 1936, and amended the next year, offered a blueprint for a financially viable property. Management wished to reduce fixed interest requirements from approximately $17 million to about $12.1 million. This reduction would benefit bondholders; the company could more easily meet future interest payments and debt retirements. Shareholders would not be neglected. Preferred stock would be exchanged one share of new 4 percent preferred and one share of new common for every two shares, and common stock would be exchanged at the rate of two shares of the old for one of the new.[34]

Neither the ICC nor the Federal Court rubber-stamped the North Western plan. Indeed, a serious rift erupted between the Board of Directors and the commission. The ICC ultimately concluded that the company could not generate significant revenues and said that all of its existing preferred and common stock should be eliminated. The leading creditors, namely institutional investors consisting of the Life Insurance Group Committee and the Mutual Savings Bank Group Committee, had taken that position during the public hearings conducted before the commission in late 1936 and 1937. These financiers wanted the railroad to be able to manage its debt obligations.[35]

The North Western opposed the reorganization philosophy of the commission and the principal creditors. Fred Sargent, who spoke for the board and management, strongly objected to wiping out the estimated $181 million of stockholder equity. He told the commission that it must consider the modern history of the company's earnings. In the five years from 1925 to 1929 inclusive, the railroad realized an average net operating income of about $23 million annually. But the ICC considered only the five years from 1931 to 1935 when annual average net income amounted to about $4.5 million. Sargent contended that the 1931–1935 period was an anomaly; these years represented the worst earnings ever and hardly reflected the firm's financial potential. "Your Board of Directors and management will continue to endeavor not only to keep faith with the Company's creditors," he told shareholders in 1938, "but also to preserve for the stockholders the ultimate equity which is believed to be inherent in this property, with its long, enviable record of solvency and prosperity and with its fine physical plant which has been adequately maintained

Although the North Western was bankrupt, trains still rolled. Freight extra No. 423, with its required white flags, chugs eastward on March 20, 1938, over the Galena Division at Marengo, Ill. (John F. Humiston photograph)

and is amply equipped to handle its reasonable share of the increased traffic which will surely ensure when the country returns to more normal economic conditions."[36]

The process of reorganization should have been completed by 1939 or 1940, four or five years being consistent with most contemporary rail bankruptcies. The Erie Railroad, for example, sought court protection in 1938 and regained its independence in 1941. But the commission and the railroad each dug in its heels over the issue of stockholder equity, and this extended the proceedings until June 1944.[37]

Participants in the reorganization surely did not anticipate a nearly nine-year-long bankruptcy. One positive sign seemed at hand in March 1938: a unit of the commission, the Bureau of Finance, recommended that sharcholders be included in the plan. These investors would receive a much less generous offer than the company wished: the bureau suggested one share of new common stock for every five shares of outstanding preferred stock and one share of new common for every ten shares of existing common. Still there was a rub. "If the earnings of the debtor during the depression period 1931–1936 are considered alone," concluded the bureau, "there is grave doubt that the existing stockholders have any equity remaining in the property."[38]

It was the equity issue that prompted considerable discussion in 1938 about a possible merger of the North Western and the Milwaukee Road. Since shareholders in both companies faced the loss of their investments, their representatives envisioned consolidation as a boon for everyone. Annual savings of "at least $10,000,000" were anticipated, money that would ensure solvency and would energize the combined system.[39]

Shareholders and their supporters argued that not only was the merger proposal a credible financial decision but the timing was excellent. The North Western and Milwaukee Road were believed to be in an "ideal situation" for testing the notion that consolidation could solve con-

On a wintry day in 1939 a company photographer visited Brookings, S.Dak., finding the ever-present Ten Wheeler, the workhorse of the North Western on its prairie lines. These locomotives performed so well that they remained in service until the end of steam. (North Western/Union Pacific)

temporary railroad ills, the same argument that would be heard frequently during the merger frenzy of the 1960s. While union was considered difficult under terms of the Esch-Cummins Act, it would be easier with both properties in bankruptcy. And with employment at record low levels fewer workers would be dislocated.[40]

The proposed marriage between the North Western and Milwaukee never progressed much beyond the idea stage. Kenneth Burgess, who represented insurance company holders of bonds of the two railroads, characterized the stockholders' consolidation plan as "fantastic and grotesque" and a "stalemate of reorganization." He wanted immediate restructuring, with the ensuing benefits for bondholders, before any efforts for merger took place.[41]

The commission agreed with the Burgess position. Regulators insisted that the data for 1931–1936 must be heeded. The reasoning centered on the perception that traffic would continue to erode: passengers lost to automobiles and buses and freight to barges, pipelines, and trucks. The ICC realized that labor costs and taxes constituted a sizable portion of the company's expenses, and both would undoubtedly increase. As in other bankruptcies the commission endorsed a cautious approach for reorganization. If fixed charges remained at modest levels, the North Western might become "depression-proof." *Railway Age* observed that "the commission is following a consistent policy which has become increasingly evident as each of the larger reorganization cases is decided."[42]

The specific details of the final reorganization package were intended to protect a new North Western. The plan of the commission, officially announced on December 15, 1939, reduced the company's capitalization from $547,567,847 (as of December 31, 1938) to $449,974,309. Fixed interest requirements would be cut from $16,549,740 in 1938 to $3,382,079. The proposal, however, allowed additional contingent interest charges of $5,988,529. As expected, preferred and common shareholders received nothing. They could keep their stock certificates as reminders of a good investment gone bad. Only a decade before a share of preferred stock sold in the range of $150 and common at about $100 a share.[43]

The next step toward financial renewal involved the federal court. District Judge John P. Barnes heard the appropriate testimony during the summer of 1940. The company and shareholders once more challenged the commission on the equity issue. On September 11, 1940, Judge Barnes announced his decision: he embraced the approach of the commission. In a 53-page opinion Barnes concluded that while the ICC's proposal "was not the best possible plan," nevertheless it "is fair and equitable and should be pursued in moving this property out of court as rapidly as possible."[44]

Howls of protest went up immediately. The reorganization was debated in the courts intermittently over the next three years. The North Western also attempted to reopen the case with the commission. But when on December 20, 1943, the nation's highest tribunal affirmed an appeals decision that had dismissed the "bill of complaint" by the railroad, the fight was over, and stockholders knew that they had forever lost their equity.[45]

While the legal battles raged, the Federal District Court moved ahead with the procedures prescribed by the bankruptcy code. In fall 1940 Judge Barnes ordered the commission to submit the plan to bondholders. The results of this balloting overwhelmingly favored the ICC-court reorganization proposal. This so displeased *Railway Age* that the influential trade publication editorialized: "We cite the case of the Chicago & North Western Railway Company as a classic example of the way this socialist economic philosophy works to ruin the middle class, especially when representatives of great investing institutions [seek] . . . to 'get theirs' regardless of consequences to anybody else."[46]

With creditors accepting the reorganization plan and the Supreme Court ending the disputatious protests, the North Western finally emerged from bankruptcy on June 1, 1944. The company reincorporated under the laws of Wisconsin (the former firm had held been incorporated in Illinois, Michigan, and Wisconsin), a new Board of Directors was elected, and the old bonds were exchanged for replacement securities.[47]

While dealing with the complications of reorganization, the North Western also experienced a change of leadership at its top level. When the railroad entered bankruptcy in June 1935, the Federal District Court named a trustee according to the 1933 law. The first appointee, Charles

Roland L. (Bud) Williams assumed the presidency of the North Western in 1939. Unfortunately, the many challenges the railroad encountered during the immediate post-World War II years proved overwhelming. (North Western/Union Pacific)

P. Megen, a leading Chicago attorney and president of the Illinois Bar Association, resigned in May 1939 to return to his law practice. Megen's replacement was Charles M. Thomson, a former United States congressman, Illinois jurist, and trustee of the insolvent Chicago & Eastern Illinois Railroad since 1933. Thomson, who possessed considerable talents, contributed significantly to the reorganization. He died on December 30, 1943, and Claude A. Roth, another Chicago lawyer, took over for the final several months of the bankruptcy.[48]

Not only did trustees come and go, the presidency changed. On June 1, 1939, Fred Sargent severed his ties with the North Western. At that time he was officially "Chief Executive Officer for the Trustee" and also a company director. Health problems, complications of an earlier kidney operation, and a chronic liver ailment, together with worry about the effects of depression and bankruptcy prompted Sargent's decision to retire. He moved to his farm near Mt. Vernon, Iowa, and died eight months later on February 3, 1940, at the age of 63.[49]

Sharing control of the North Western with the judge, trustee, and board following the departure of Fred Sargent was the company's eleventh president, Roland L. (Bud) Williams. Hardly a gifted executive, Williams with the worldview of an "auditor" was poorly educated, not particularly sophisticated, and intensely sensitive about his short stature. He won election primarily because of his perceived talents of corporate efficiency. Board members concluded that hard times mandated a leader who could control costs. "Bud Williams," they believed, "fits the ticket perfectly."[50]

A lifelong resident of Illinois, Williams was born in the downstate town of Salem on September 19, 1888. He entered railroading when he was 15 as a messenger for the Baltimore & Ohio Southwestern. As a teenager Williams mastered Morse code, which enabled him to gain employment with the Chicago & Eastern Illinois Railroad as a telegraph operator in 1907. Soon Williams became a timekeeper in the Danville office of the division superintendent and subsequently worked in a variety of clerical positions before being named chief statistician at the Chicago headquarters in 1918. Regular assignments focused on improving efficiency and affecting economies. By the 1930s Williams had caught the attention of industry executives in Chicago after recommending several money-saving changes on the C&EI, including purchase of more powerful freight locomotives and centralization of freight-car maintenance. Promotions followed: assistant to the president in 1932, senior executive assistant to the president three years later, and executive vice president in 1936.[51]

When Bud Williams assumed his duties as North Western president, he followed his inclination to create greater efficiency and savings. One of his first acts was to prepare a report for Trustee Thomson on the ways the railroad was already economizing under his direction. Williams proudly told of the consolidation of two operating divisions, the Southern Illinois and the Galena, the closing of divisional accounting offices, and the reduction of divisional maintenance-of-way and structures department stores from 12 to six. Williams also described his pet "Cleanup Campaign." As he wrote, "This campaign was conducted by individual divisional committee, and has resulted in a very substantial improvement in our housekeeping methods, and in return to the general stock of about $100,000 worth of materials and supplies, including stationery, which was found to be surplus at the individual locations." Williams went much further. His "good old-fashioned housecleaning" after three years resulted in the conversion of 700,000 tons of scrap metal into $7 million of much-needed cash.[52]

A gleaming *400*, with its sleek twin Electro-Motive E3A diesel-electric units and green and yellow Pullman-Standard consist, meant that the North Western had fully streamlined these popular Chicago–Twin Cities trains. On June 19, 1940, the *400* rounds the "Clinton-Kinzie curve" in Chicago. (Alfred W. Johnson photograph, George Krambles collection)

Although the nation reeled under the impact of the recession of 1937–1938, the worst economic decline since 1933, better growing conditions in the corn and wheat belts and the outbreak of World War II in Europe on September 1, 1939, strengthened the domestic economy. The North Western's operating ratios (the ratio of expenses to revenues) declined markedly during the latter part of the thirties: 90.6 in 1937, 87.7. in 1938, 82.8 in 1939, and 78.8 in 1940.[53]

Court protection from creditors and improved earnings after 1938 allowed the North Western to regain some of its Best of Everything sparkle. Most notably, the company could enter the streamliner era with its own trains. While the western *City* streamliners, operated jointly with the Union Pacific and Southern Pacific, had already thrust the North Western into the passenger revolution, the company was eager to upgrade its flagship varnish between Chicago and the Twin Cities. Admittedly the existing steam-powered, standard-equipped high-speed *400*s "set the pace for the world" in terms of speed and service, but they were hardly the ultimate form of intercity transport. Streamliners could offer

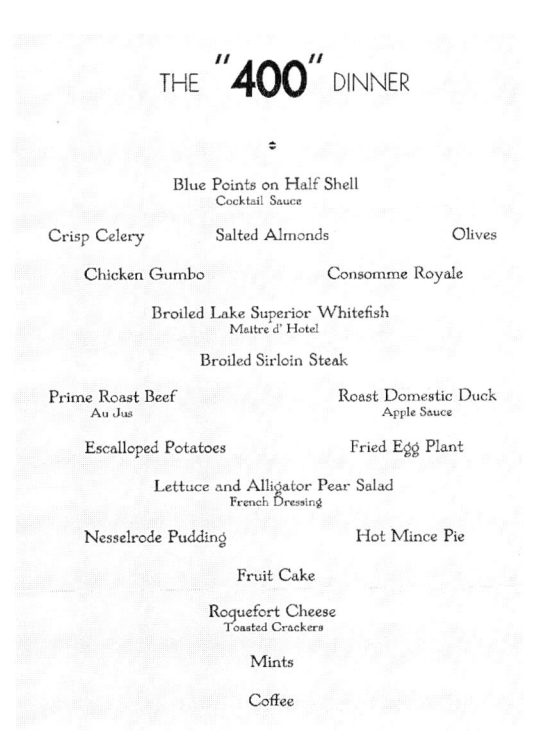

THE "400" DINNER

Blue Points on Half Shell
Cocktail Sauce

Crisp Celery   Salted Almonds   Olives

Chicken Gumbo   Consomme Royale

Broiled Lake Superior Whitefish
Maitre d' Hotel

Broiled Sirloin Steak

Prime Roast Beef   Roast Domestic Duck
Au Jus   Apple Sauce

Escalloped Potatoes   Fried Egg Plant

Lettuce and Alligator Pear Salad
French Dressing

Nesselrode Pudding   Hot Mince Pie

Fruit Cake

Roquefort Cheese
Toasted Crackers

Mints

Coffee

The *400* dinner menu offered a main course designed to appeal to everyone except die-hard vegetarians. Diners on the *400* had 14 tables seating four persons each and were staffed by seven waiters who each served two tables. (Author's collection)

In 1939 a Class E-4 streamlined locomotive, No. 4006, propels train No. 13 two miles east of DeKalb, Ill., toward the Milwaukee Road overpass. This type of engine regularly powered many Overland Route passenger trains from the late 1930s until the early 1950s. (Author's collection)

much more. For one thing economies provided by their diesel-electric locomotives and lightweight metal cars would be considerable. Moreover, an improved image was important. A state-of-the-art *400* would have great marquee value and would permit the North Western to battle successfully with the Burlington and Milwaukee Road in this competitive passenger market.[54]

The process of streamlining the *400*s moved along steadily. In December 1938 the North Western asked the federal court for authority to purchase 20 streamlined cars and four nonarticulated diesel-electric locomotives. Soon the judge approved the $2.3 million price tag, and Pullman-Standard and Electro-Motive Corporation then produced the smart green and yellow trains that revealed "exceptional imagination, research, care and study by the carbuilder, railway, and locomotive manufacturer." The new *400*s entered revenue service with much fanfare and public excitement on September 24, 1939. President Williams could tell shareholders in April 1940 that the two streamliners with "each train consisting of one double diesel power unit of 4,000 horse power, one tavern-lounge car, four coaches, one 56 seat diner, three parlor cars, and one parlor-observation-lounge car, a total of ten cars on each train" fully met expectations. "From October, to December 31, 1939, the number of revenue passengers handled on these trains between Chicago and Minneapolis and intermediate stations was 56,249, an increase of 17,340 over the same period of 1938, which provided a revenue increase of $84,835, or 45.6%."[55]

During the late 1930s and early 1940s the North Western further enhanced its long-distance passenger service. While a few of the older name trains remained, including the *North Western Limited*, a bevy of diesel-powered *400*s made their debut. These entries operated on lines other than the route of the original *400*s, which were renamed the *Twin Cities 400*s in January 1942 to avoid confusion. The *400* fleet featured the *Capitol 400* between Chicago and Madison; *Minnesota 400* between Chicago, Wyeville, Wisconsin, and Mankato, Minnesota; *Peninsula 400* between Chicago, Green Bay, and Ishpeming, Michigan; *Shoreland 400* between Chicago, Manitowoc, and Green Bay; and the *Valley 400* between Chicago, Appleton, and Green Bay. Several additional *400* trains appeared on the busy Chicago and Milwaukee corridor. "The beauty of appointments . . . the refinement of comfort . . . the smoothness of the original streamliner '400'—*all this is available in a fleet of new '400' Streamliners!*" proclaimed a company travel folder distributed in the autumn of 1942. "Flashing between Chicago, Wisconsin, Minnesota and Upper Michigan, these superb trains bring to important cities north and northwest of Chicago rail service that establishes a new era of speed and comfort in travel."[56]

On September 7, 1940, children watch the departure of train No. 153, *The Shoreland*, a Chicago to Green Bay train, at the Oostburg, Wisc., station. This name-train had yet to be modernized; it remained steam powered and used standard, heavyweight equipment. (John F. Humiston photograph)

Railroad enthusiasts found the North Western by the eve of World War II. On July 20, 1941, members of the Railroad Club of Chicago and friends traveled on the "Railfan Special" to Lancaster, Wisc. Car No. 7353 makes up the rear of "Extra No. 290 East." (John F. Humiston photograph)

The upgrading of the original *400* and the introduction of companion trains was timely. No one at the North Western or anywhere else really foresaw that an approaching war would create enormous demands for passenger service. Yet after America entered World War II on December 8, 1941, citizens who had abandoned flanged wheels for rubber tires rediscovered timetables and depots and patronized trains from the lowliest branch-line locals to the finest intercity runs. The expanded *400* fleet was a blessing for both the company and the traveling public.[57]

The North Western, still in receivership and led by a new president, soon encountered challenges as taxing as any caused by the Great Depression or bankruptcy. World War II strained the capabilities of the company as had no other conflict. The primary goal of the North Western and all railroads became the quick and safe transport of vast quantities of freight and hordes of passengers. The carriers responded splendidly and demonstrated immediately that they were essential to the national defense.

Women greatly contributed to the national wartime transportation effort. In October 1944 the North Western was already moving the heavy volume of Christmas mail for military destinations overseas. Princess Redfeather (right) and Adna McIntosh handle sacks of mail at the Chicago station. (North Western/Union Pacific)

CHAPTER

Nine

THE SECOND WORLD WAR AND POSTWAR RAILROADING

The Second World War had a dramatic impact upon the United States and its railroads. Even before the official act of war, the repeal of neutrality legislation, passage of the Lend-Lease Act to aid Great Britain, and the big defense appropriations of 1940–1941 had added six million workers to the payrolls, ending mass unemployment. These measures created an industrial boom reminiscent of the early stages of World War I. Once war came, Americans were united as never before to conquer enemies on three continents: millions rallied to the colors; even more civilians toiled on the home front; and the federal government marshaled resources to bring about an Allied victory over Germany, Italy, and Japan. The nation's railroads responded to the unprecedented demands to ensure victory. "Without transportation we could not fight at all," concluded Joseph B. Eastman, director of the Office of Defense Transportation (ODT), in 1943. "In these days there is nothing which enters into war, from troops to bullets, which is not dependent absolutely on transportation. Everyone must concede that they [railroads] have done an outstanding piece of work." Because gasoline, tires, and replacement parts were rationed, airline, bus, and truck companies could not maintain their prewar levels of service, let alone expand. The German U-boat offensive against American shipping during the early part of the war disrupted the flow of goods through the Panama Canal and between Texas and the eastern seaboard. As the only viable alternative to land and water transport, railroads managed to carry 83 percent of the increase of *all* traffic between 1941 and 1944, and they moved 91 percent of all military freight and 98 percent of all military personnel. Freight traffic, measured in ton miles, soared from 373 billion in 1940 to 737 billion in 1944 (the industry would not again equal the latter figure until 1966). Passenger volume, expressed in revenue passenger miles, soared from 23 billion in 1940 to 95 billion in 1944, a peak figure never again attained. The North Western and all railroads, which remained privately owned and managed during the conflict, accomplished far more than most politicians and others expected, a sharp and pleasant contrast to the experiences of the previous world war.[1]

The North Western carried an immense volume of goods and passengers during World War II. The company performed at levels that would have been difficult to imagine a few years earlier. The system (North Western and Omaha Road) moved more freight than it could comfortably handle: 43,542,619 revenue freight tons in 1940, a stupendous 62,181,898 tons in 1943, and an equally impressive 59,384,215 tons in 1945. The passenger figures were also awesome: 18,446,428 (commutation and all others) in 1940, 28,897,673 in 1943, and 30,586,195 in 1945. The organized movement of troops and furloughed military personnel often filled coaches and sleepers, and necessitated second or even third sections of the same train. Even before the Japanese attacked Pearl Harbor, the company demonstrated that it could cope with unusually heavy demands for its services. In August 1940, for example, the railroad dispatched 130 trains to transport 40,000 national guard troops to and from Second Army maneuvers at Camp McCoy, Wisconsin.[2]

The North Western found it easy to encourage its approximately 30,000 employees to support the war effort. An enemy victory was not inconceivable. The Axis powers speedily exploited their advantages, including opening their attacks unexpectedly. Their ruthless destruction of people and property swept aside most resistance and augured well for their military objectives. Still, these warmongers failed to anticipate the will to win of the Allied nations. That determination was seen graphically on the North Western. Employees joined the armed forces in great numbers: 3,623 were in uniform in 1943 and 4,415 two years later. Hundreds served in the company-sponsored 720th Railway Operating Battalion, which saw action in Europe. A smaller number of Omaha Road employees formed the core of the 714th Railway Operating Battalion, a unit that spent 25 months augmenting the civilian personnel of the

The North Western sponsored a wartime savings bond rally at the Chicago Shops. (North Western/Union Pacific)

The car foreman at the California Avenue facility in Chicago, C. P. Nelson, wearing a suit, speaks to Victory Club No. 3 about the need to back the war effort and buy war bonds. The crowd consists of both white and black workers, the latter having increased in number during the war. (North Western/Union Pacific)

Alaska Railroad. Those who remained at their posts accepted overtime assignments, donated blood, rebuilt broken equipment, and conserved scarce materials. Recalled a former official, "The spirit of patriotism was everywhere."[3]

A conspicuous expression of the patriotic spirit were the War Bond drives. The federal government concluded that one way to meet the enormous costs of war was to sell bonds to citizens. Though not essential, as bankers freely honored requests by Washington for money, bond purchases by individuals decreased the money supply and acted as a brake on inflation. The personnel of the North Western accepted the strategy. "Employes on the home front have continued their purchase of war bonds and 82% are regular subscribers under the Company's payroll deduction plan," noted Bud Williams in early 1945. "Total purchases during the year [1944] amounted to $5,689,000 maturity value." In employee publications the company regularly praised the financial loyalty of workers. Delbert Garwood, for example, a section foreman at Luverne, Iowa, in May 1945 sent a $506.25 check to the treasurer in Chicago for $675 worth of bonds during the Seventh War Loan Drive. While the amount was exceptional, Garwood was hardly alone in backing the war effort with his pocketbook.[4]

Another illustration of loyalty among North Western employees involved their "Victory Gardens." The company took pride in being the first railroad to open up its right-of-way to its workers for gardening. The North Western largely reinstated a scheme that had been used successfully during World War I. This time the road's agricultural department offered "advice and assistance whenever possible to promote the Victory garden program."[5]

While the North Western could take pride in its patriotic employees, the company encountered problems maintaining a workforce large and skilled enough to keep the trains running. As labor markets tightened, the railroad responded in a fashion similar to that of other carriers. The company encouraged employees, especially skilled workers, to postpone retirement, and it asked some retirees to return. It also sought out young males and used newspaper advertisements to lure them: "HIGH SCHOOL BOYS 16 OR OLDER RAILROADS NEED WORKERS Back up America's fighting forces. . . . Farm boys or farm trainees will not be considered." Similarly, the company hired Mexican nationals for seasonal maintenance-of-way jobs.[6]

The North Western also found additional female employees. Although most women took traditional assignments, usually as clerks, secretaries, and stenographers, others worked as station agents, mail handlers, and shop laborers. The company took special pride in claiming the services of a Native American woman, Princess Redfeather, a member of the Blackfoot tribe. Redfeather had not gone directly from her reservation in Montana to the North Western, however; instead she was a former model at the Chicago Art Institute and a graduate of Purdue University in home economics. Redfeather eschewed office work and joined both sexes as a mail loader in the Chicago passenger terminal. The North Western reported 1,569 women on the payroll in 1943, or about 6 percent of the workforce.[7]

Management not only strove to maintain adequate numbers of workers but also recognized the need to have them perform adequately. These men and women wished to contribute, and supervisors and foremen understood their responsibilities for "breaking in the new people." This desire to ensure a properly functioning railroad was illustrated by company participation in the Training Within Industry (TWI) program. Personnel management professionals, linked to the American Management Association and the War Manpower Commission, donated their skills to train workers in various businesses, including such railroads as the Erie, Lackawanna, New Haven, and North Western. The programs for assisting the recently hired apparently worked well. "In January 1944, TWI approached the accounting department of the Chicago & Northwestern Railway," reported TWI in 1945. "C.L. Dennis of the Brotherhood of Railway Clerks was present when the Job Instruction program was presented to management and added his endorsement, later saying that adoption of the TWI programs was the most constructive action taken by the company in twenty years. . . . By February, Institute training was provided, sessions were started, and on-the-job coaching under way."[8]

The war effort on the North Western included

ways to maximize efficiency with the fewest workers. By the early 1940s officials realized that dieselization would greatly enhance operations. The value of internal combustion had been demonstrated with the *City* and *400* streamliners and earlier with the gasoline-electric passenger units and oil-electric switch engines. Although the company was unable to acquire its first two 5,400-horsepower, four-unit diesel freight sets until near the end of the war, it steadily increased the number of diesel switch engines at various terminals and yards: 8 were acquired in 1941, 13 in 1942, 2 in 1943, 33 in 1944, and 23 in 1945. The diesel revolution was at hand and accelerated rapidly when the peacetime economy made it easier to procure this exceptional motive power.[9]

Another way to reduce personnel and also costs was to share or abandon trackage. In 1943 the North Western, with federal encouragement, retired 87 miles of its Wyoming line between Illco and Shoshoni, using adjoining Burlington trackage to reach the Lander terminus. The savings were estimated in 1944 at approximately $35,000 annually, and the sale or reuse of salvageable materials provided additional benefits. Moreover, the scrap metal was needed for the war effort. North Western officials took seriously the government-created slogan, "Salvage for Salvation!"[10]

A more complicated abandonment involved the former 103-mile Fremont, Elkhorn & Missouri Valley branch between Linwood (near Fremont) and Hastings, Nebraska. The freight business along this route through the South Platte agricultural region had dwindled since the 1920s, a casualty of truck competition and extended drought. The few passengers and the shipments of railway express traveled in the daily mixed-train between Fremont and Hastings. The latter community, an important trading center, was also served by the Burlington, Missouri Pacific, and Union Pacific, and the North Western received only a modest share of traffic. Understandably the company wanted to retire the line, and the ICC granted the request in late 1941. Then the Department of the Navy announced construction of a $45 million ordnance plant near Hastings, and the North Western recognized the possibility of increased business. Nebraska officials and organized labor also wanted to preserve the branch. But the federal government had its eyes on the rails and other metals, and that settled the matter. In 1943 the North Western sold three miles of line in the Hastings area to the Missouri Pacific, turned over the much-wanted scrap to Uncle Sam, and eliminated more than a score of employees, including section hands, station agents, and part-time custodians.[11]

During the war years the North Western noticeably trimmed its physical plant. The company abandoned nearly 400 miles of "unproductive" appendages and more than 650 miles of unnecessary side tracks. It also retired 137 coal and water facilities, 249 small-town depots, 659 shop buildings, and 1,344 "minor structures." "We wisely got rid of a lot of labor, maintenance and tax consuming properties at that time," remarked a former official. "But really they were the most obviously useless things that went. . . . It was really only the tip of the iceberg."[12]

A patriotic, more diverse workforce, which toiled on a somewhat pared-down physical plant, hardly guaranteed labor peace. The issue involved wages, and not the loss of some permanent jobs. The outbreak of the European war produced sharp increases in the cost of living, which jumped 27 percent between September 1939 and May 1943. The federal government finally responded by creating the Office of Price Administration (OPA) in 1942. Fortunately inflation moderated toward the end of the war, but before the OPA's efforts took hold, consumers felt the sting of rising costs. "Food is so high, although my wife is canning more from our garden," complained a shopman from Clinton, Iowa, in October 1942. "I can't seem to keep up with all the increases in prices at the stores."[13]

The wage-price squeeze caused workers nationwide to grow restive. In January 1943 nonoperating railroaders demanded an industry-wide wage boost; they sought a 20-cents-an-hour increase and a 70 cents-an-hour minimum wage. Simultaneously, operating personnel asked for a hike of 30 cents per hour in their basic daily rates and a minimum increase of $3 a day. Negotiations, at time rancorous, failed to produce a settlement, and a general strike loomed. Faced with a likely tie-up, President Franklin Roosevelt signed an executive order on December 27, 1943, seizing the nation's rail network and forcing workers to remain at their posts.[14]

Federal control, at least in name, ended when labor and management reached an agreement on January 18, 1944. Nonoperating employees won an increase of 10 cents an hour for the lowest hourly rated persons and 4 cents an hour for the highest hourly rated workers, retroactive to February 1, 1943. They received a graduated scale of hikes ranging from 9 to 11 cents an hour effective December 27, 1943. Operating personnel realized a gain of 32 cents per day, retroactive to April 1, 1943, and effective December 27, 1943, an additional 40 cents.[15]

The interventionist role by Washington took on various dimensions during the war, with seizure attracting the most attention. Although federalization was avoided, Congress created the Office of Defense Transportation soon after hostilities began. The ODT quickly produced a plethora of paperwork, including numerous "service orders" that required conservation of fuel and heavier loading of equipment. One directive, which inconvenienced overnight travelers toward the end of the war and affected railroad income, withdrew sleeping cars from trips of 450 miles or less and assigned them to troop transport. Patrons of the North Western no longer could take Pullmans between Chicago and Ashland, Green Bay, Ishpeming, Minneapolis, Rochester, and Watersmeet or between several other destinations, including Omaha and Chadron. This equipment did not return to commercial service until early 1946.[16]

The North Western like most railroads earned substantial though declining profits during the conflict. Net income for the system after fixed charges and contingent interest stood at $25,660,000 for 1942, $22,955,000 for 1943, $16,108,000 for 1944, and $15,084,000 for 1945. The last figure equaled approximately the income for 1929. Operating revenues, however, rose steadily: $162,125,000 for 1942, $188,288,000 for 1943, $193,938,000 for 1944, and $198,816,000 for 1945. The nationally mandated wage settlements cost carriers dearly, and special wartime excess profits taxes also damaged income.[17]

Nevertheless, with the end of bankruptcy in 1944, a new day seemed to have dawned for the North Western. "We will be our old railroad once the war is over," predicted Barret Conway, vice president and secretary, in June 1944. Free from court supervision, possessing a comfortable level of debt and solidly in the black, the company resumed payment of dividends in 1944 on its new issue of stock. Owners of preferred securities received $20 a share, although $15 represented funds accumulated from 1939 through 1943. (The date for the Plan of Reorganization was technically 1939.) Those who held common stock got $5 a share. The dividend rate was adjusted in 1945: $5 on preferred and $3 on common.[18]

The resumption of dividend payments portended well for the North Western. The company was not viewed by the investment community as a dying giant in 1945 but as a railroad that the Great Depression had brutally victimized. "The Chicago & North Western Railway is an attractive long-term investment," concluded a Chicago-based stock brokerage firm. "It will be a future leader of Midwestern rails."[19]

A careful examination of the property might have led to another conclusion. There were thunderstorms on the horizon, temporarily slowed by the impact of World War II. The conflict had solved the railroad's financial problems and had largely, albeit temporarily, reduced modal competition. A system map pointed to future trouble. The company possessed innumerable branches and twigs and few large sections of trunk. As Fred Sargent had noted already in the early 1930s, portions of the North Western had been designed to gather agricultural products and raw materials and to deliver consumer goods before the advent of motorized transport. With a preponderance of branch lines and secondary routes, the company could not benefit from long, through hauls. But there were also problems that were hardly visible. Most of all, the corporate culture, characterized by much ossification, produced an environment that hindered management from meeting the challenges created by a rapidly changing postwar America.

Optimism permeated the Chicago & North Western Railway during the immediate post–World War II period. While "reconversion" from a wartime to a peacetime economy was not without difficulty, the company appeared to be healthy. Operating revenues mostly rose between 1945 and 1948: $170 million in 1945,

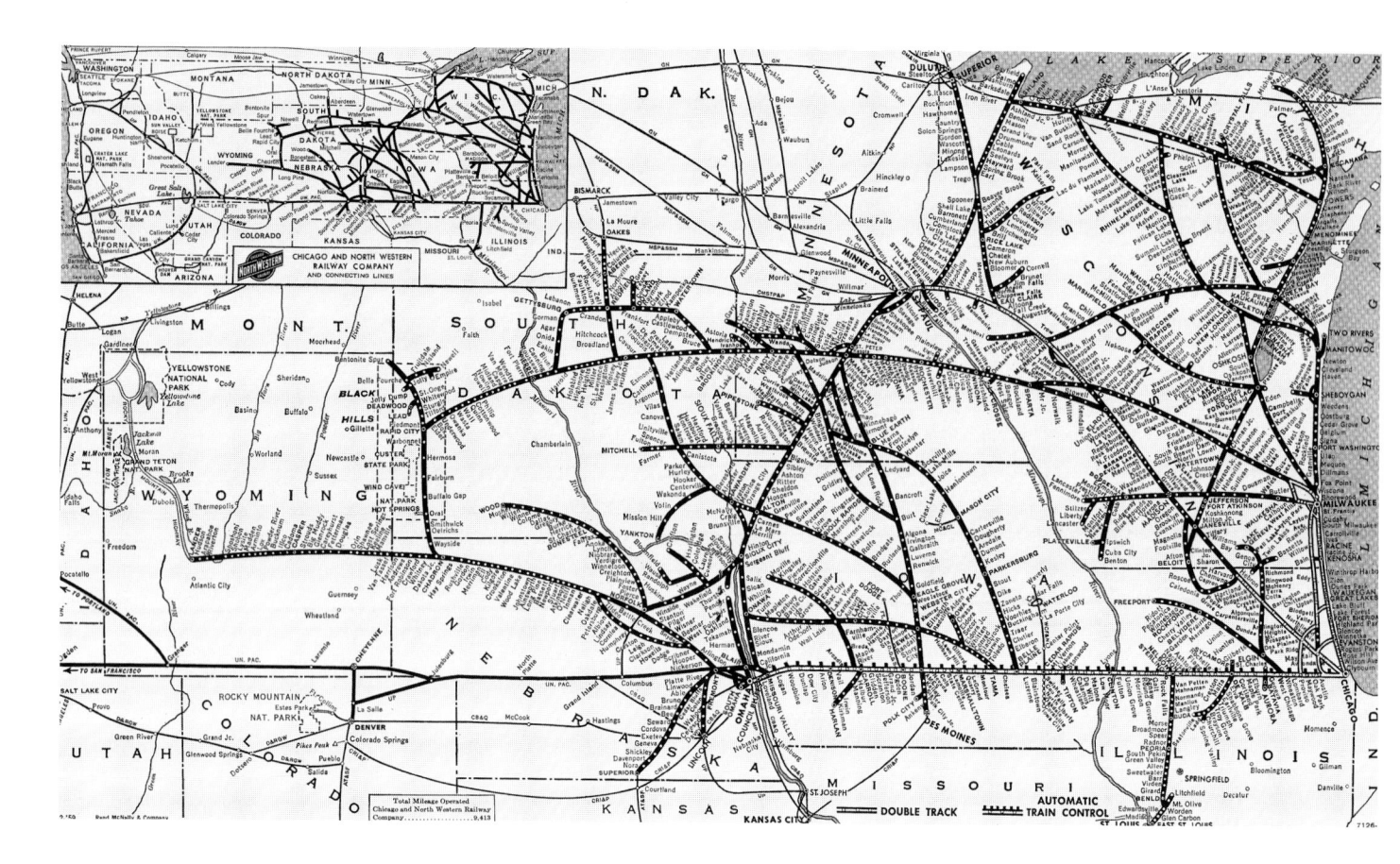

In the postwar era the North Western remained much branch and little stem. (Author's collection)

$160.5 million in 1946, $176.2 million in 1947, and $195 million in 1948. Net income likewise proved satisfactory. Although the railroad earned an impressive $18 million in 1945, the annual average from 1946 through 1948 was below $10 million.[20]

The problem was inflation. Following the midterm election of 1946, which gave laissez-faire-minded Republicans control of Congress for the first time since 1930, President Harry Truman issued an executive order ending federal controls on wages and prices. This action, coupled with brisk consumer spending, pushed the cost of living up dramatically. Wholesale prices soared 31 percent between July 1946 and May 1947. The spiral of inflation seemed inexorable; the rising costs of living prompted wage demands, and wage raises led to higher prices.[21]

Railroad labor understandably became restive. Demands for higher wages and more favorable work rules were ensured even before the war ended. Negotiations between the 20 railway labor organizations ultimately led to an agreement for a 16-cents-an-hour hike in early 1946. But two operating unions, Engineers and Trainmen, remained recalcitrant; in May 1946 the members struck, paralyzing the nation's rail-

roads. This work stoppage ended after two days when President Truman, a longtime friend of railway labor, assured the strikers that their position would be fully considered by the federal government.[22]

Still, troubles continued. In March 1947, members of nonoperating unions demanded another wage increase; this time these employees wanted 20 cents per hour. Arbitration resulted in a hike of 15 1/2 cents per hour, effective September 1, 1947. Operating brotherhoods in 1947 likewise sought more money, asking that their wages be increased 30 percent with a minimum of $3 per day. The railroads came to terms in November with conductors, switchmen, and trainmen, and these unionists received an additional $1.24 per basic day. This particular agreement called for several changes in work rules and further discussions of others. The engineers and firemen refused at first to accept the wage offer, but they finally relented in August 1948. The settlement was retroactive to November 1, 1947. Subsequently major work rule problems were solved.[23]

Wage demands had not yet run their immediate course. Persistent inflation set off a renewed round of negotiations. In June 1948 conductors and trainmen asked for a 25 percent hike, with a minimum of $2.50 a day. The firemen and engineers two months later demanded $1.76 per day, which represented the difference between their 1947 objective of $3 per day and the settlement of $1.24 per day. A national agreement came in the fall of 1948; operating brotherhoods received a boost of 80 cents per day, beginning October 16, 1948. Earlier, on April 10, 1948, nonoperating unions had filed for a pay increase of 25 cents per hour and major changes in wage agreements. Specifically, these brotherhoods sought 48 hours of pay for a 40-hour week, overtime in excess of eight hours per day, time and a half for work performed on Saturdays, and double time for Sundays and holidays. To prevent another strike a special presidential fact-finding board entered the process. After considerable study, the experts recommended a seven-cents-per-hour increase, starting October 1, 1948, and suggested a 40-hour week, with 48 hours pay, effective September 1, 1949. An agreement between the parties was reached in March 1949, and the position of the board prevailed.[24]

These various union compacts cost the North Western dearly. By 1949 annual labor obligations exceeded the 1945 level by more than $30 million. The average yearly compensation to individual workers reflected these hefty hikes: $2,796 in 1945, $3,186 in 1946, $3,294 in 1947, and $3,655 in 1948.[25]

Even though the ICC failed to offset fully the major income adjustments with freight-rate increases, North Western officials remained hopeful about the future. "I expect our shareholders will have steady or growing dividend checks for a long time to come," President Williams told security analysts in 1948. Indeed, the confidence of the Williams administration in postwar America was expressed in the extensive celebration in 1948 marking the centennial of the opening of the company's first unit, the Galena & Chicago Union Rail Road.[26]

Railroaders felt good about their industry. Corporate centennials and related celebrations reflected this optimism during the late 1940s and early 1950s. Chicago-based roads, in particular, conducted special observances, and most leading carriers had specific events to commemorate. These companies and others wished to bolster their public image, and they could do so because their coffers contained ample funds.[27]

Even if a company lacked an event to celebrate, it could join other carriers at the Chicago Railroad Fair of 1948 and 1949. This gala extravaganza, which the North Western spearheaded, was in itself a major part of the Williams administration's efforts to honor the historic Galena.

The idea for the Chicago Railroad Fair came from the creative mind of Francis V. (Frank) Koval, publicity manager for the North Western. A 1933 graduate in journalism from the University of Illinois, Koval worked in radio and public relations before he joined the railroad in 1943. At that time the company sought to upgrade its advertising and public relations program, which was then handled in an amateurish fashion by the chief traffic officer.[28]

Frank Koval viewed the centennial of the first train in Chicago as a wonderful opportunity for self-promotion of the North Western. President Williams agreed. Koval tapped company and industry money and resources in the city, including the *Chicago Tribune*, to hold the observance. On a mile-long strip along Lake Michigan south of the Loop, 35 railroads and the Pullman Company joined with the North Western to sponsor the Chicago Railroad Fair. Lenox R. Lohr, president of the Chicago Museum of Science and Industry, served as head of the board, with Williams as his vice president.[29]

The historic *Pioneer* and coach achieved star status at the popular, postwar Chicago Railroad Fair. On August 14, 1948, the train rests offstage at the Pageant of Transportation area near 23rd Street. Lake Michigan, seen behind the train, provided a backdrop for the show. (John F. Humiston photograph)

Since the late 1880s, company employees attended the trackside grave of the son of a construction worker. The "Little Fellow," whose name had been forgotten, had died in a bunk car near Elrod, S.Dak., on the Watertown-Redfield line, and was interred near that location. Frank Koval, the North Western's publicity coordinator during the 1940s, demonstrated the kind, dedicated North Western employees by promoting the "Little Fellow" story and having pictures taken as the crew of a motor train stopped on Memorial Day 1946 to decorate the grave. (North Western/Union Pacific)

The Chicago Railroad Fair exceeded all expectations. Between July 20 and October 2, 1948, more than 2.5 million visitors paid several million dollars to learn about the way railroads revolutionized Chicago and the nation. The colorful past and the bright future were part of the popular daily pageant, "Wheels a-Rolling," in which the venerable *Pioneer* locomotive, under steam, became a "star performer." The North Western did more: the company erected a replica of the Galena's first depot, a modest two-story wooden structure, and showed off its most recent rolling stock. The enthusiastic public response led to a repeat performance; more than 2.7 million people visited the exhibition grounds during the summer and early fall of 1949.[30]

The North Western, not limiting its celebratory activities to the Chicago Railroad Fair, sponsored special events in 58 on-line communities. A parade featuring motorized versions of the *Pioneer* and a *400* streamliner and the "Centennial Train" with an array of historic exhibits drew attention to these local festivities.[31]

The gala that took place in Huron, South Dakota, on May 24, 1948, was typical. The motorized replicas highlighted the parade, and the Centennial Train received hundreds of visitors. Window displays in downtown stores showed off vintage railroad artifacts and photographs. The Junior Chamber of Commerce, for one, joined the celebration; members did a brisk business selling wooden puzzles depicting the *Pioneer*. This was a fitting souvenir, for city officials proclaimed the occasion "Pioneer Day." A few days earlier a local editorial had suggested that the "Century of the C&NW's existence is one which calls for a proper celebration," which is just what this remote railroad town had.[32]

As midcentury neared, the North Western stood proud and confident. While the recession of 1949, two terrible blizzards that ravaged the Great Plains early the same year, and a national steel strike fouled the financial statements, the outbreak of the Korean War in June 1950 offset some of the financial losses by bolstering both freight and passenger revenues. Net railway operating income for 1949 stood at $2,783,000 and jumped to $9,113,000 the following year. Net income of $5,440,000 for 1950 was a dramatic change from the paltry $7,380 earned the previous year.[33]

Management did not plan radical changes. With air travel still a novelty and jet service years away, major carriers, including the North Western, remained committed to long-distance passenger travel. In 1950 the company introduced two modern streamliners, the *Dakota 400* and the *Flambeau 400*. The first of these name trains to enter revenue service, the *Dakota 400*, made its inaugural run between Chicago and Huron on April 30, replacing and extending the former *Minnesota 400*. The *Dakota 400* was an immediate sensation. Communities along the longest of the *400* routes praised the company and the streamliner in glowing terms. "It is surprising what the establishment of a first class train by a railway will do to public thinking about that railway," editorialized the Huron newspaper. "Before the Chicago and North Western Railway established the 'Dakota 400' the [South Dakota] public's opinion of the North Western line was nothing to brag about. It ranged from 'lousy,' 'antiquated,' to an absolute zero. But today the story is different. The establishment of the 'Dakota 400,' and the maintenance of that train at a high level of operating efficiency, passenger comfort and luxury travel has caused the public to revise completely its attitude toward the North Western." Concluded the writer, "Now the North Western is much more apt to be called 'progressive' than it is anything else."[34]

The *Flambeau 400* entered North Western timetables on May 26, 1950. This train provided service between Chicago and Ashland, Wisconsin, with connections during the summer months to Watersmeet, Michigan, and the adjoining resort territory. Already in 1935 the company had introduced the *Flambeau*, a mostly weekend-vacationer-oriented train that ran between Chicago and Ironwood, Michigan, and also to Watersmeet. Although steam-powered, the *Flambeau* featured air-conditioned coaches, a parlor car, and a diner to Ironwood. The North Western regularly adjusted the equipment, schedules, stops, and routing. In 1938, for example, the *Flambeau* added Green Bay to its somewhat circuitous path to the North Woods. After the Office of Defense Transportation in 1942 ordered seasonal trains to end "for the duration," the *Flambeau* did not reappear until August 1945.[35]

The debut of the *Flambeau 400* meant that the North Western supplanted and extended the previous *Flambeau*. In the process the new *400* replaced the *Shoreland 400* and the *Valley 400;* the train, operating northbound via Manitowoc and southbound via Appleton Junction, was no longer limited to a summer schedule. The *Flambeau 400* consisted of a mixture of older *400* equipment and some new Pullman-Standard cars, including an unusual cafe coach. The train, of course, was diesel-powered; two powerful E units pulled the green and yellow consist.[36]

Like the *Dakota 400* the *Flambeau 400* drew favorable comments. The editor of the *Ashland Daily Press* was hardly exceptional; he praised everything, including the "wonderfully accommodating steward, waiter and chef." The presence of the *Flambeau 400* enhanced the image of the North Western throughout the train's more than 450-mile territory.[37]

Even with the high quality of the *400* and *City* streamliners during the late 1940s and early

For the inaugural celebrations of the *Dakota 400* in April 1950, the North Western ordered special lettering for the E7 diesel-electric locomotive. The Chicago-to-Huron train, "America's Newest Luxury Streamliner," operated on the longest *400* route. (North Western/Union Pacific)

The North Western publicized acquisition of seven railway post office cars, which were assigned to the *City of San Francisco* streamliners. The first through RPO service began on October 1, 1949. The company wished to tell the public how it continued to modernize and to meet demands for better service, including mail delivery. (North Western/Union Pacific)

1950s not all travelers who chose the North Western encountered the once ballyhooed commitment to quality. Trains that plied branch lines and secondary main lines frequently were shabby. These runs usually lost money, and only "head-end" business of mail and express minimized the financial drain. The North Western found it easier to retain these trains than to battle with regulatory bodies for their abandonment. Not until the Transportation Act of 1958 would the removal process become somewhat easier.[38]

Complaints of passengers were often biting and probably justified. By the time the North Western removed trains No. 1 and No. 2, which linked Carroll, Iowa (and connections to Chicago), with Oakes, North Dakota, via Sioux City, Iowa, in the early 1950s, this service had deteriorated drastically and was a discredit to the company. A rider on No. 1 penned this revealing letter in January 1950: "A few days ago when returning to Huron from my Christmas in my home in Illinois, I took the unnameable and indescribable Chicago & North Western atrocity from Sioux City to Huron in the early morning hours," wrote Elizabeth Williamson, a Huron College professor. "It is the kind of thing one sees in nightmares from which one awakens, thankful that such a monster as one has dreamed about simply cannot exist. . . . It contains windows through which the light of day cannot penetrate because of decades of accumulated dirt. No one dares to touch the back of the seat, and the hand returns to its owner unrecognizable because of its sudden coating of black soot." Professor Williamson continued: "The monster comes to a stop and the alternative to having one's front teeth broken on the seat ahead is to have the neck bones cracked on the seat behind. One does not mention the penetration of cold, and the ceaseless clatter and grind of weary old wheels." She closed with these thoughts: "Let me suggest that on the coaches of this monstrous imposition be painted in yellow lettering: 'Abandon hope all ye who enter here.' The Hades of the ancients must have been a Paradise in comparison."[39]

Although inflation and the 1949 recession adversely affected the North Western, the company kept its financial house in reasonably good order until the early 1950s. The debt situation was encouraging. The company exploited falling interest rates to restructure its fixed obligations even as it reduced overall indebtedness. While the total debt (fixed interest bonds and notes, income bonds, and equipment obligations) stood at approximately $210 million in 1944, seven years later the total was only $184 million. Fixed charges dropped from $3.9 million to $2.9 million annually during this period. The company did not consistently make dividend payments to holders of preferred and common stock, however. It stopped payments in 1949, resumed them in 1950, suspended them for 1951, and made only modest payouts to owners of preferred stock in 1952, 1953, and 1954.[40]

The North Western might have paid dividends continually if management had shown greater creativity. Ossification had become the company hallmark; the "we've always done it this way" mentality seemed pervasive. President Williams belonged to the "cult of the operating man"; that is, he was a railroad official too tradition-bound to ever become a dynamic leader. "Williams's administration," recalled a onetime trade journalist, "epitomized a railroad that was over-built, old fashioned and lethargic."[41]

A marvelous illustration of the mind-set of Bud Williams toward innovation came after the war. A junior executive, Charles C. Shannon, learned that General Motors planned a truck "drive-away" scheme at its automobile assembly plant in Janesville, Wisconsin. Shannon thought that he had a way to save this traffic for the North Western. During his spare hours he tinkered with "O" gauge models of an auto flatcar. Soon he recognized the possibility of placing six vehicles on a standard-size flat rather than the four then being loaded into an Evans-type boxcar. When Shannon presented his idea to the president, Williams exploded. "God Damn it! You've been wasting company time!" Shannon retreated, and the North Western lost the GM business.[42]

Even the principal attribute of Bud Williams as a railroad executive was flawed. The North Western president rightfully received kudos for his efforts to economize and avoid waste, but at times penny-pinching backfired. The president's handling of maintenance expenditures characterized his shortcomings. "Williams with his pencil hooked maintenance to traffic," explained an associate. Namely, Williams adjusted the maintenance budget to business. When carloadings went up or down by 1 percent, he altered appropriations to match the fluctuation.

Little programmed maintenance resulted. "You would get organized and the traffic would go down. . . . Time and money would be wasted." Ralph Budd, who headed the Burlington at this time, took a different approach. When traffic declined, the railroad increased its outlays for maintenance; Budd correctly contended that the company received greater efficiency from its track personnel.[43]

No top officials challenged Williams. The president liked "yes men," and many questionable policies continued. Some appointments and promotions were good, most notably that of Lynne L. White. This "strong leader," who came to the North Western from the Erie in January 1940, served in major administrative capacities until he joined the Nickel Plate Road in 1948, becoming its president within a year. Despite a policy of economy Williams tolerated a bloated bureaucracy in

In the late 1940s, train No. 22, pulled by oilburning 4-4-2 Class D locomotive No. 1298, arrives at the Omaha Union Station with a baggage car, RPO car, and coach after its nearly 300-mile trip from Winner, S.Dak. (Don Christensen photograph, Author's collection)

The Ames-Hawarden-Huron train, No. 52-15-23, waits at the station in Alton, Iowa, on November 26, 1949. Only a brisk "head-end" business of mail and express prevented monumental annual losses for this 341-mile run. (Author's collection)

the Chicago headquarters. The law department in particular was huge and "full of lawyers who couldn't find jobs elsewhere." Furthermore, these attorneys "wouldn't fight for the company. . . . They were just plain lazy." Apparently the legal force arrived at the office late, took long lunches, and left early. If Williams disliked a white-collar employee, he might send the individual to the Omaha Road, "a dumping ground for the losers." Outright dismissals were rare.[44]

The corporate culture at the North Western continued to deteriorate even after Bud Williams left the presidential suite on December 31, 1952. This less-than-stellar executive remained active until April 1956; he continued a company tradition by serving as chairman of the Board of Directors. The new president, Paul Feucht, came from the operating side of the Pennsylvania Railroad. During his tenure of slightly more than three years the North Western endured its worst leadership of modern times, perhaps ever, and nearly failed financially. "We went from bad to worse under Feucht," opined a former official.[45]

Paul Eugene Feucht, nevertheless, possessed good credentials. Born in Indianapolis, Indiana, on January 4, 1900, he received a bachelor of science degree in civil engineering from Purdue University in 1923. Prior to joining the North Western as executive vice president on August 1, 1951, he had spent his entire career with the Pennsylvania system. Feucht steadily climbed the corporate ladder; for example, by 1939 he was general superintendent at Indianapolis where he supervised four operating divisions. Later promotions led him to the office of the vice president in Chicago with responsibility for the Western Region. In this assignment, which began in 1946, Feucht also served as president of several subsidiary firms and as vice president, director, or both of more than a dozen affiliated terminal, trucking, and warehouse companies.[46]

Why the North Western Board of Directors chose Paul Feucht as its twelfth president remains a mystery. His selection as the successor to Bud Williams may have been influenced by his involvement in the Chicago railroad fraternity. Area rail executives frequently belonged to the same clubs and social groups; both Feucht and Williams were active in the Traffic Club of Chicago. Another possibility is that the North Western leadership apparently wanted closer ties with the Pennsylvania, and Feucht presumably could help. Perhaps too there was the long-range objective of a corporate marriage.[47]

The longtime Vanderbilt–New York Central relationship ended with the bankruptcy of 1935. The subsequent reorganization conceivably sparked an interest in the Pennsylvania, the other principal route to the East. Even before Paul Feucht took charge, the North Western studied the feasibility of running the *City* streamliners into Union Station, the Chicago passenger terminal of the Pennsylvania. Moreover, the North Western and Pennsylvania successfully conducted a local joint-freight operation; North Western crews handled trains from Proviso to the 51st Street yard of the Pennsylvania and Pennsy personnel did the same from 51st Street to Proviso. At the time this was the only "cross-haul" arrangement with a company's own crews in the Windy City.[48]

Feucht's personality contributed little to the executive office because his "dull nature" hardly inspired anyone. One executive remembered Feucht as "not being a very stirring fellow." And phlegmatic Feucht had an ego problem. "He wanted people to come in every morning and say that he was the greatest president we have ever had." Indeed, this rodomontade railroader constantly sought praise. "You couldn't tell him anything was wrong with the property," recalled

The North Western and Omaha roads found that motor trains, like the *Namekagon* shown at Trego (Spooner), Wisc., usually cost less to operate than steam-powered consists and were more popular with patrons. (North Western/Union Pacific)

a colleague, adding, "I couldn't tell him that we didn't have enough grain cars."[49]

The personality of Paul Feucht helps explain a major public-relations setback. The Southern Pacific and Union Pacific railroads jointly terminated the five cross-country streamliners over the level tangents of the North Western after October 30, 1955, and rerouted them over the parallel, yet less-desirable Milwaukee Road trackage between Omaha and Chicago. Officials of the Southern Pacific and Union Pacific had good reason to end the agreements. The trains regularly ran late; they might arrive at their destinations an hour or more behind schedule. Rough track, which necessitated reduced speeds, led to annoying delays. "We had slow orders all over the place." An inspection party, which included Southern Pacific president Donald J. Russell, "not a bashful fellow," likely sealed the fate of the Overland Route varnish. "They really got shaken up on that 1955 trip." But Feucht ignored signs of possible cancellation; he was "quite willing to drift along with the status quo." Feucht's principal confidant, John E. (Jack) Goodwin, vice president of operations, "who made most of the day-to-day decisions," agreed with his boss that "they will never take the trains off." And Goodwin allegedly told Union Pacific officials: "We really don't want these trains. . . . Go to hell!"[50]

While most observers, particularly longtime employees and those associated with the passenger department and passenger-car maintenance, believed that the loss of the streamliners severely damaged the honor of the North Western, reality was somewhat different. The *City of Los Angeles* in particular was a financial drain. "Most of the time the *City of Los Angeles* ran with more crew members than passengers, except during the holidays," observed a North Western officer.

The North Western transported livestock until the early 1970s. In September 1950, cattle leave a string of well-used stock cars at the Chicago Union Stock Yards. For years the railroad annually operated a "Cattle Feeders Special" from Schleswig, Iowa, a town on the soon-to-be abandoned Wall Lake–Soldier branch, to the Windy City. (North Western/Union Pacific)

A three-unit diesel-powered freight creeps out of Proviso Yard. In the early 1950s, track maintenance had declined; weeds choked the "high-iron" rails. (North Western/Union Pacific)

Also the streamliners operated on schedules that were often inconvenient for local travelers, especially those with Chicago and Omaha destinations. Indeed, the Williams administration had seriously considered the introduction of a *400*-type train in the late 1940s to solve this problem. Winning the streamliner contract soon disappointed the Milwaukee Road. The company expected that its sizable investment in upgrading the Chicago to Council Bluffs line would pay off handsomely, but that never happened. The increasing popularity of air travel adversely affected the revenue picture. Most of all, the Milwaukee Road failed to receive the additional freight business that it anticipated from passenger-partner Union Pacific. "The deal [Overland Route contract] turned to dross," recalled former Milwaukee Road executive Burton Worley. The North Western, without the fast nametrains, could better handle the freight interchange needs of "Uncle Pete." The restructured passenger service on the North Western between Chicago and Omaha, which was hardly memorable except for the *Kate Shelley 400* between Chicago and Boone, Iowa, meant that these new trains were not given the special priority once accorded the streamliners. Dispatching time freights became easier.[51]

The North Western suffered more than a psychological blow with the loss of several of the nation's premier name trains. Annual statements showed increasing financial distress. Even though the Korean War bolstered freight and passenger revenues, the vicious winter of 1951–1952, severe flooding in the Midwest during 1952, major wage hikes in 1953, and another recession that started in the latter half of 1953 and continued through most of 1954 adversely affected net income. The promising figure of $5,440,000 for 1950 dropped dramatically to $2,035,000 in 1951, rose modestly to $2,839,000 for 1952, improved slightly to $2,935,000 in 1953, and then plummeted to a *negative* $4,592,000 for 1954.[52]

The response to a disappointing financial situation was mostly unremarkable. Management focused on reducing unproductive branch line mileage and trimming money-losing passenger operations. The system shrank by only 125 miles, however, between 1949 and 1955. Efforts to reduce passenger service worked out better. From mid-1949 to 1955 an average of 450,000 annual passenger-train miles were cut, but millions more were in need of elimination.[53]

The Feucht regime did demonstrate some imagination. While the merger craze was yet to come, the North Western and Milwaukee Road considered corporate marriage. In December 1954 these historic rivals hired William Wyer & Co., a respected railroad consulting firm, to study the "economics of consolidation and coordination." The final report, which William Wyer presented to Paul Feucht and Leo T. Crowley,

A publicity photograph from the late 1940s shows *City* streamliners at the servicing facility in Chicago. Although the North Western later permitted passenger service on its portion of the Overland Route to deteriorate, the company, especially employees, took enormous pride in this nationally acclaimed fleet of streamliners. After all, the North Western proclaimed itself the "Route of the Streamliners!" (North Western/Union Pacific)

In what was a major public-relations setback for the North Western, the company lost the *City* streamliners to rival Milwaukee Road. On Sunday, October 30, 1955, the operational changeover took place. The first of the Milwaukee Road streamliners to leave Chicago Union Station was the *Challenger–Midwest Hiawatha*, seen near Elgin, Ill., 37 miles west of Chicago. (Author's collection)

Milwaukee Road board chairman, on October 26, 1955, encouraged union. Although the Milwaukee Road reached southern Indiana, Kansas City, and the Pacific Northwest, the two roads largely paralleled each other elsewhere, except in Nebraska and Wyoming. Consolidation of administrations, facilities, and trackage could potentially produce impressive savings. "The studies indicate that the increased net income which might be realized from consolidation might run as high as $53,905,682," Wyer concluded. "We believe that this total should be reduced by 20% as an allowance for the contingencies . . . , so that our final estimate of increased net income is $43,124,546."[54]

As with earlier merger talks between the North Western and Milwaukee Road, this carefully crafted study went nowhere. Financial officers at the North Western expected the company to come out second in the arrangement and concluded that the merger might not be good for shareholders. Feucht himself, frightened by a possible hostile takeover, largely ignored what appeared to be a practical way to strengthen the company.[55]

Paul Feucht had good reason to worry about his fate at the North Western. In early 1956 it became evident that a changing of the guard was probable. Powerful investors, spearheaded by Eugene A. Schmidt Jr., a board member and the treasurer of Metropolitan Life Insurance Company, the largest stockholder in the railroad, concluded that the carrier was teetering on bankruptcy. A proxy fight loomed. Feucht decided to "leave the scene" when he learned that Schmidt was dealing with Chicago attorney Ben W. Heineman. Rather than resigning, Feucht took refuge in a Chicago hospital. Charles Shannon, a high-ranking officer, shielded his boss by announcing that Feucht had suffered a heart at-

North Western President Paul Feucht demonstrates a Pullman berth. He later autographed the publicity photograph. (North Western/Union Pacific)

tack. The end for Feucht came on February 10, 1956; the Heineman group reached an agreement with the board, taking five of the 17 director's seats and three places on the seven-person Executive Committee. Feucht left Chicago for Central America where he served as a consultant for the railroads of the United Fruit Company, his health by then much improved.[56]

By the mid-1950s the North Western was in serious trouble. If the Feucht administration had continued, the company likely would have experienced a second bankruptcy, an economic crisis that would have led to substantial changes. Reorganization would surely have meant a different management team and possibly even merger or partial liquidation. "I don't know how we could have continued as we were going under Feucht," Frank Koval remembered. "We were on a collision course and I don't know where the pieces might have landed."[57]

North Western Board Chairman Ben W. Heineman, with characteristic bow tie and pipe, stands near the Chicago passenger terminal in 1956 to tout dieselization of the road's commuter service. (North Western/Union Pacific)

CHAPTER

Ten

THE HEINEMAN ERA

A revolution swept the North Western after April 1, 1956, when the forces of Ben Heineman assumed power. With Heineman as chairman of the Board of Directors, what would be chief executive officer today, he could begin to work his magic. Those who knew Heineman realized that the beleaguered North Western had obtained an exceptional business leader. "He was sharp as a tack," remarked a veteran employee. Only a handful of contemporary railroad executives matched the balding, bow-tied Heineman for shrewdness and savvy. While not perfect, he unquestionably prevented financial disaster. "If you believe in reincarnation," chuckled an advisor, "then it was Marvin Hughitt who was there in the executive suite of the *Daily News* building." Some thought, and almost everyone hoped, that the North Western might return to its past days of glory. "Hughitt" and "Heineman" went together well.[1]

Ben Walter Heineman did not come from a railroad household. He was born in the central Wisconsin city of Wausau on February 10, 1914, where his paternal grandfather, a Jewish immigrant from Germany, had launched a lumber company in 1869 and later a bank. Ben's father, Walter, carried on the family businesses. In 1930 Walter Heineman went bankrupt and committed suicide, the year his only son graduated from high school.[2]

Although the Heineman family endured the trauma of indebtedness and death, Ben remained determined to get the best possible education. Since financial considerations prevented him from attending his first choice, Yale University, he entered the University of Michigan. After three years at Michigan, Heineman persuaded the law school at Northwestern University to admit him without a bachelor's degree. Northwestern administrators made no mistake; Heineman earned his bachelor of law degree in 1936, ranking third in his graduating class.[3]

With sheepskin in hand Heineman embarked on his legal and business career. Admission to the Illinois bar enabled him to join the Chicago law firm of Levinson, Becker, Peebles and Swiren and to learn more about the world of finance and law. Although deferred from military service during World War II because of blindness in one eye, Heineman still served his country, working as an assistant general counsel for the Office of Price Administration in Washington and later in a similar post with the Department of State. In 1944 Heineman returned to the Windy City where he formed a partnership with Max Swiren. Their firm, Swiren & Heineman, specialized in corporate law.[4]

That legal practice brought Heineman into railroading. In the early 1950s he represented a group of disgruntled stockholders of the Chicago Great Western Railway who demanded that the company pay out more than $6 million in accumulated preferred dividends; Heineman surprised many observers by bringing about a favorable out-of-court settlement. Three years later Heineman, who had acquired stock in the Minneapolis & St. Louis Railway (M&StL) on a suggestion made by Chicago businessman Frank Lyons, joined other shareholders to battle Lucian C. Sprague, the force behind this Minneapolis-based carrier for nearly 20 years. A nasty proxy fight prompted Sprague to retire in May 1954, and Heineman won election as chairman of the newly created Executive Committee.[5]

Heineman's activities at the M&StL revealed both his aggressiveness and overall common sense, a rehearsal of his career with the North Western. Heineman promoted modernization and improved marketing. He contributed more than good management; he sought to enhance the long-term health of this 1,400-mile road that tapped rich agricultural lands of Iowa, Minnesota, and South Dakota. While the railroad never reached St. Louis (Twin City–St. Louis traffic mostly moved through Albia, Iowa, and a connection with the Wabash), the M&StL did enter Peoria, Illinois. Heineman recognized the value of the "Peoria Gateway" and tried to acquire both the Toledo, Peoria & Western and the Monon to increase the central Illinois community's strategic importance. These properties, together with the M&StL, would allow freight to

While railroads encountered difficulties in acquiring diesel-electric locomotives during World War II, the North Western added this 1000 HP switcher built by the American Locomotive Company to its diesel fleet in August 1944. (Author's collection)

An early diesel switcher, No. 405, built by Whitcomb in 1943, works in the yards at Marshalltown, Iowa, on January 26, 1947. The North Western widely used the "Route of the Streamliners" slogan on motive power and freight cars. (Author's collection)

travel efficiently around congested Chicago terminals. Several major carriers, led by the Pennsylvania and Santa Fe, opposed Heineman's bold plan for an outer belt route, and they successfully thwarted the scheme.[6]

The North Western suffered from a long list of shortcomings when Ben Heineman took charge. The railroad was impaired by weak management, a cumbersome overcentralized organization, and too many employees. The company's wage-to-revenue ratio of 56.9 percent in 1955 was entirely out of line with the national average for major carriers of 47 percent. The reluctance to introduce labor-saving equipment and operating practices and the failure to consolidate, mechanize, and modernize yards and scattered shop facilities explained the dreadful wage-to-revenue ratio. With more than 700 diesel-electric locomotives, the North Western had enough units to dieselize fully "but didn't know it." Steam locomotives, which required special coaling and water facilities, were expensive remnants of the past. Furthermore, the railroad began to look like a transportation slum: "Track and roadbed were getting rough. Bridges and buildings had gone for years without maintenance or paint. Cars and locomotives were shabby in appearance and poor in performance."[7]

Contributing to the problems was the extensive network of lightly used branches. A traffic-density map for 1955 revealed that some trackage produced little business. The Wood to Winner branch in South Dakota, for example, based on a daily average compilation, generated a paltry 70 tons westbound and 50 tons eastbound. The North Western owned many lines that received only triweekly or even once-a-week service, except perhaps during the annual grain rush. The list of obvious candidates for abandonment was long. These largely useless appendages de-

By the late 1940s more diesel road locomotives powered North Western freight trains. A 4,500 HP A-B-A "F" unit, a product of the Electro-Motive Division of General Motors, works its way through Ames, Iowa, on Christmas Day in 1947. (Author's collection)

manded outlays for crews, car hires, and minimum maintenance and escalated taxes. On the other hand the North Western owned too few long-distance, high-density arteries. Collectively this 9,400-mile system created inadequate freight traffic and insufficient average hauls.[8]

Just as the system map was troubling, passenger operations also caused concern. The North Western operated far too many trains that lost money. Perhaps the most disquieting were the scores of commuter runs in the Chicago area that consumed precious funds, about $2.5 to $3 million annually. The red ink from the passenger sector threatened the solvency of the road. While the passenger deficit nationally absorbed an average of 40 percent of freight net operating revenues in 1956, the total for the North Western stood at more than 95 percent![9]

The Heineman regime had little time to turn around the rapidly declining property. "At the rate they were going I doubt they could have survived the year," was the assessment of Ben Heineman's highest-ranking operating officer, Clyde J. (Fitz) Fitzpatrick. Industry analysts agreed. "I know that the C&NW was on the verge of bankruptcy when Mr. Heineman took over," bond specialist Isabel H. Benham recalled years later. No wonder Heineman worked with dispatch and assembled the best possible management team.[10]

Heineman placed Clyde Fitzpatrick in the president's chair. "I picked Fitzpatrick because my opinion, now confirmed by our two-year association," observed Heineman in 1958, "was that he's the best railroadman in the business." Although a drinking problem that worsened as job pressures increased affected Fitz's ability to perform, he still was a knowledgeable and tough operating person. Fitzpatrick was born in Centralia, Illinois, on December 7, 1908, a third-generation railroader, and at 16 he took a part-time job as a telegrapher in his hometown with the Illinois Central. Following graduation from high school in 1925, Fitz "went railroadin" full time. Like so many others in the industry, he worked in various capacities, such as station agent, dispatcher, and trainmaster, before he became vice president in charge of the Operating Department in August 1953. At 44 he was the youngest operating vice president in the history of the Illinois Central.[11]

Since Heineman gladly delegated authority, he gave Fitzpatrick freedom to hire and fire. Fitz understood that the old Feucht policy of "doing things as they were always done" was wholly unacceptable. A major shake-up occurred in Chicago and elsewhere, and with the revamping of personnel several leading Illinois Central officials came to the North Western, "good railroaders but not exceptional ones."[12]

Three of the six new 2,000 HP E7-A passenger diesel-electric locomotives purchased from Electro-Motive arrive in Chicago in April of 1949. Number 5018-B remained on the roster until 1969. Its longevity attests to the quality of "first-generation" diesels. (North Western/Union Pacific)

The traffic density map of the North Western system for 1955 indicates that the company operated a vast array of lightly used branch lines. (Author's collection)

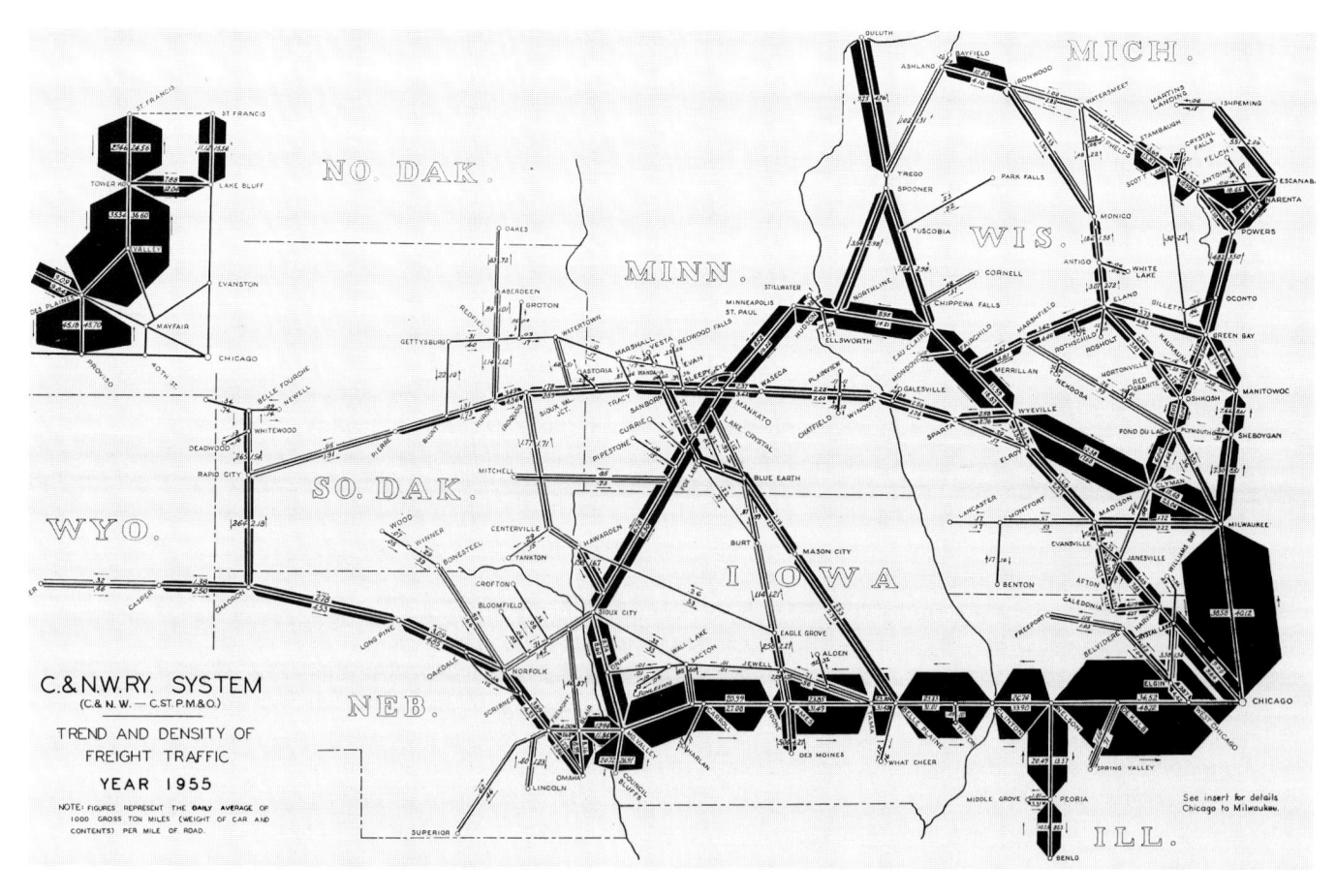

The arrival of the "IC mafia" troubled, even angered, some old-time employees. Sugar was put in the gas tanks of automobiles belonging to these former Illinois Central officers, and violence took place in the Proviso Yard, including shots taken at Carl Hussey, the assistant general manager. "People were scared to death."[13]

Not every new employee came because of Clyde Fitzpatrick. Undoubtedly the most important addition to the executive force was Larry S. Provo, who arrived at headquarters the day Heineman assumed power. This future president of the North Western was born in Minneapolis, Minnesota, on April 28, 1927, and graduated with distinction from the University of Minnesota with a degree in business administration in 1948. He soon became a certified public accountant and, after a stint with Arthur Andersen & Company, became comptroller of the Minneapolis & St. Louis in 1954. Heineman recognized Provo's business and intellectual prowess and wanted him in Chicago as comptroller and vice president. "Provo was a different type of CPA," remembered a colleague. "He wasn't dull. Provo was a hands-on guy."[14]

The Heineman team quickly let the public know that a new North Western was emerging. The railroad announced "D-Day" (for dieselization) on May 11, 1956, at least for thousands of commuters. In an appropriate ceremony Heineman, Fitzpatrick, Mayor Richard J. Daley of Chicago, reporters, and others gathered at the North Western station to watch the mayor give official city recognition to the exit of steam. Daley threw the "highball" sign to the engineer of a diesel locomotive whose unit then pulled the last steamer to enter the terminal away for permanent retirement. The festivities gave Fitzpatrick a forum to announce, "Equally important is the simultaneous dieselization of all road freight and passenger service. What little steam power remains is relegated to a few yard operations and switch runs on the northern divisions. Even these few steam engines are scheduled to be replaced by diesels in a matter of weeks." D-Day was possible because of better utilization of motive power; the company's 147 steam engines, of which 41 were concentrated in the Chicago area, were no longer needed. "In no case was a line or division shorted of diesel power," explained Fitzpatrick. "On each division advantage was taken of the high degree of utility inherent in diesel power for complete application in that area, the excess being relieved for duty in Chicago, the last major bulwark of steam on the railroad." Fortunately, the recently purchased diesels contained heavy-duty auxiliary generators and "so it was simple to use them in suburban service."[15]

Much less publicity surrounded numerous initiatives designed to modernize the North Western, "to make it a railway of the mid-20th century." In May 1956, for example, the company took the first step toward streamlining its operations when it eliminated the offices of four district superintendents. The restructuring of the Operating Department to function on a divisional rather than a departmental basis followed shortly. Management gave superintendents of each geographical division responsibility for their operations; personnel at headquarters focused primarily on formulating standards and overall matters of policy.[16]

Ben Heineman told shareholders in early 1957 that revamping the property would not be easy. "Just as it is necessary to dig before one can build, so it has been necessary laboriously to provide firm foundations for the sound structure we expect to erect. While this process has been slower than we might have wished . . . , we believe that with the passage of time progress toward the desired results will become increasingly apparent."[17]

An important step of that essential change entailed hiring Arthur Andersen & Co. in July 1956 to assist in the process of modernization. The accounting giant developed an integrated data-processing system that would provide faster and more accurate reporting of freight car and train movements. Thirteen months later Arthur Andersen informed Heineman that it had completed its task and estimated the cost of implementation at approximately $1.1 million annually. While expensive, the system would pay substantial dividends: "Any evaluation of the economics of the system must give consideration to the many potential and perhaps intangible benefits which cannot be estimated in terms of specific dollar savings through additions to revenues, better customer relations, reduction in car per diems, etc."[18]

It's "D-Day" for the North Western. Board Chairman Ben W. Heineman, *left*, Chicago Mayor Richard J. Daley, and President Clyde J. Fitzpatrick bid farewell to steam for commuter runs. Engineer Walter Herrli is in the cab. Locomotive No. 614 had emerged only weeks before from the Winona shops and was the last steam locomotive to be handled in that facility. The Class E Pacific attracted attention one more time, on a Chicago-to-Milwaukee fan trip, before being sold for scrap. (North Western/Union Pacific)

The work of Arthur Andersen & Co. enabled the North Western to reap the considerable benefits of state-of-the art accounting and support services. Integrated Data Processing (later called Car-Fax), installed at the Ravenswood accounting center in Chicago, did what was expected. The system, which utilized newly developed International Business Machine "Transceivers," permitted the accounting, operating, and traffic departments to control their operations better and allowed customers to learn the location and scheduled arrivals and departures of their shipments. "The Chicago & North Western is modernizing and mechanizing its accounting office to make accounting more of an adviser to management than a collector and belated analyzer of statistics," observed a trade journalist in April 1957. "The 56 stations for which Ravenswood does most of the paperwork account for nearly 70% of the North Western freight business. Twelve employees in the machine room do a job which formerly took 115 out on the line." Others too praised Car-Fax. E. L. DeVol, assistant superintendent at St. James, Minnesota, for example, told the local press in the spring of 1959 that the system "means a two-hour speedup for freight trains operating between Minneapolis and Sioux City. It means only about 40 minutes of switching operations in the St. James yards, instead of an hour and 20 minutes to an hour and a half. It means less hand-written record keeping for freight conductors. It means brakemen will know ahead of time exactly where to break trains for switching and it means the entire train consist will be forwarded to the next terminal at least an hour ahead of the train, expediting operations at every terminal."[19]

Other improvements in the corporate bureaucracy occurred during the formative years of Heineman's tenure. In July 1956 the company reorganized the Industrial Development Department and "added several able and experienced employees to its personnel." Two months later the railroad created a Foreign Freight Department, mostly in anticipation of the opening of the St. Lawrence Seaway. Then in November 1956 the purchasing and stores departments were consolidated, the initial step in modernizing inventory control and materials handling. The following year the railroad began to downgrade its less-than-carload (LCL) service by discontinuing free pickup and delivery. This action produced an annual savings of $1.5 million. The company soon razed its 21-acre LCL "shed" at Proviso. Also in 1957 the company hired the Real Estate Research Corporation of Washington, D.C., to survey the railroad's property and determine current values and possible alternative uses for this land. Heineman wanted to know how to convert land holdings from tax liabilities into producing assets. And in January 1958 the Traffic Department inaugurated a much-needed training program for its staff. "We wanted to make certain that our people know what to do and what others are doing and be familiar with the resources that are presently available."[20]

The Heineman management did not neglect much-needed betterments. Deferred maintenance plagued the system; understandably, expenditures increased for improving the basic infrastructure: track, roadbed, bridges, and signals. Since Heineman concluded that mechanization could solve many industry problems, the company acquired an array of modern maintenance-of-way equipment. The firm proudly depicted some of these devices in a two-page pictorial section, "Mechanization in Track and Rail Maintenance," in the 1957 annual report. This equipment generally performed well and ultimately saved money. One notable exception was an experiment to spray roadbeds with weed-killing chemicals by helicopters, which proved costly, ineffective, and at times dangerous to nearby flora and fauna.[21]

Continuing the emphasis on consolidation, mechanization, and modernization, North Western executives swiftly decided to overhaul the way in which rolling stock was maintained. Inefficiency reigned. The system for freight-car repairs was especially troubling. The company therefore announced plans on June 11, 1956, to construct a $6 million freight-car repair shop in

Not long after the start of the Heineman regime the North Western installed state-of-the-art office processing equipment at the Ravenswood (Chicago) Accounting Center. (North Western/Union Pacific)

While not a "piggyback" pioneer, the North Western entered the intermodal field in 1954 along with such carriers as the Baltimore & Ohio, Kansas City Southern, Lackawanna, Pennsylvania, and Wabash. (North Western/Union Pacific)

A track gang works in the early 1950s to install heavier rail on a busy section of the Omaha line in Illinois. (North Western/Union Pacific)

Clinton, Iowa, to replace 14 scattered and antiquated facilities, of which a dozen were outdoors, several in extremely cold climates.[22]

When the Clinton Car Shops officially opened on October 3, 1957, the railroad possessed a superb facility. The shops could provide major repairs on 7,000 freight cars annually and could construct a thousand cars a year. The focal point of the 32-acre complex of new and rehabilitated buildings was the erecting and fabricating shop. This was the largest structure and measured 1,000 x 160 feet, being divided into two bays. Overhead cranes operated the full length of each bay for transferring materials and for raising and lowering cars under repair or construction. The crane runways in the north bay extended outside for 700 feet over a material storage yard that covered 56,000 square feet. The paint shop, wheel shop, and air-brake and accessory shop complemented the core unit. The layout included an office building, powerhouse, employee center, fuel and oil supply house, and an acetylene generating plant. "It was really an impressive place," recalled a former official. "It was something that the North Western desperately needed and it was money very well spent."[23]

The North Western went beyond improving its freight and car repair and building capabilities. The company consolidated its diesel locomotive repair work in Chicago and closed three nonessential subyards at Proviso. Management also moved to eliminate various facilities that were once part of the Age of Steam. Coal chutes, water towers, and other obsolete structures and equipment were retired, saving both maintenance and tax money. In some cases these relics of the past generated cash income from their sale or scrap.[24]

While attentive observers read about or noticed the various physical changes on the North Western after 1955, they likely missed or paid little attention to another Heineman-inspired reform, the lease of the Omaha Road. The existence of this separate company, which the North Western controlled, was a wasteful operation that drained approximately $2 million annually by the mid-1950s. In Sioux City, for example, the Omaha controlled the switching, and the North Western was only a tenant, "a patch-work situation that was costly." Then there was the matter of personnel. "Omaha Road employees always felt superior to those on the C&NW," and the company had become a bastion of nepotism where "so many of the Omaha officers's children were junior officers." Also there were the "misfits" from Chicago headquarters.[25]

Previous administrations in Chicago had tolerated an independent Omaha. Bud Williams, in particular, was afraid to confront Carl R. Gray Jr., the longtime vice president and general manager. "Gray was a real king," remarked a North Western official. "He considered the Omaha to be his own and even had the shops in Hudson [Wisconsin] build him a pleasure boat." North Western brass knew that Gray's father was an influential railroader; the senior Gray served as president from 1920 to 1936 of the Union Pacific, a vital interchange partner for the North Western system. "Everybody thought Gray [Jr.] would use his connections with the Union Pacific if he ever got cornered." And perhaps he would.[26]

But by 1956 Gray had retired, and Ben Heineman was unwilling to tolerate a separate, cash-draining Omaha Road. The North Western legal department, energized and restructured, applied to the Interstate Commerce Commission on July 24, 1956, for authority to lease and operate the Omaha Road. Regulators worked with unusual dispatch; they gave their approval on December 28. In October shareholders of the two railroads had endorsed the arrangement, a simple task since the North Western owned 99.23 percent of the outstanding preferred and common stock of the Omaha. The lease took effect on January 1, 1957, with the North Western agreeing to maintain and operate the Omaha and assuming the revenues and expenses of the affiliate, except interest payable to the North Western on its first mortgage bonds and depreciation and retirement charges.[27]

While the legal details of the lease of the Omaha Road involved neither complexities nor opposition, the Heineman regime found itself embroiled in a lengthy and bitter battle with the Order of Railroad Telegraphers (ORT) over the staffing of small-town depots. On November 5, 1957, the North Western filed a petition with the South Dakota Public Utilities Commission to create a "central agency" system in that state,

Before the Heineman administration consolidated car work in Clinton, Iowa, small, inefficient shops dotted the system. A photograph taken in August of 1947 shows employees laboring under a blazing sun rebuilding hopper cars in Winona, Minn. (North Western/Union Pacific)

On October 10, 1955, two North Western Class E-S 4-6-2s, Nos. 650 and 647, take on coal at Clinton, Iowa, preparing to double-head train No. 16 to Chicago. The locomotives were formerly Nos. 1650 and 1647, but the company renumbered them to rationalize the numbering scheme for its growing diesel fleet. (Don Christensen photograph, author's collection)

thus eliminating unneeded stations. What the railroad proposed was sensible and straightforward: it wished to assign an agent to two or more stations. If that did not prove to be feasible, the company would close the lightly used depots. Unquestionably the telegrapher-agents were guilty of gross "featherbedding." There were 61 one-person stations in South Dakota in which duties of the agent did not require more than two hours per day. Some of these well-paid salaried employees worked on an average of only 15 minutes daily and received as much as $91 per hour for the time they actually performed their duties. The North Western claimed that these redundant agents cost hundreds of thousands of dollars yearly.[28]

The North Western did not blindly plunge into its confrontation with the telegraphers; it was acutely aware that such action carried risks. The railroad industry had virtually ignored matters of "make-work" or featherbedding, and heretofore the North Western had accepted this state of affairs. The company and the Order of Railroad Telegraphers had agreed, starting about 1954, that a station might be closed in some cases of worker attrition. The road averaged about two closings a year, which hardly solved the problem.[29]

Management wisely selected South Dakota for its initial effort, even though the railroad confronted idle agents elsewhere. "South Dakota law, as I read it, says that the state railroad commission is responsible for efficient operations of the carriers," recalled Charles Shannon, then assistant to the president for operations. "So why don't we confess that we are inefficient and see what they do about it." Thus the thrust of the argument was not wasted money but wasted time. The ploy worked. Within a short period the company won approval not only from South Dakota but also from four other state regulatory bodies to terminate these unnecessary employees.[30]

The aggressiveness of the North Western infuriated and frightened the ORT. In December 1957 the organization demanded that no ORT-filled job be abolished without union approval. The company ignored the ORT and eliminated approximately 500 positions during the next several years. The union fought back, attempting to block the actions by employing provisions of the Railway Labor Act. After exhausting all legal procedures of the law and ignoring the suggestions of two labor secretaries and a presidential emergency board that recommended generous allowances for telegraphers who would be displaced, the ORT struck the North Western on August 30, 1962. The walkout tied up the property until September 28 and cost the company approximately $600,000 a day. The strike disrupted the lives of many freight customers, long-distance passengers, and Chicago-area commuters.[31]

The North Western won broad support in its struggle with its disgruntled telegraphers. "Featherbedding, already a flagrant practice in the railroad industry, is no solution," editorialized the *Chicago Sun-Times*. "But that in effect is what the North Western telegraphers are demanding. Featherbedding, along with the competition of airlines and truck transportation, has already imperiled the financial structure of most railroads. In today's economy, characterized by the profit squeeze, neither the railroads nor any other industry can afford featherbedding." Even the liberal *Washington Post* concurred. "North Western Board Chairman Ben W. Heineman cannot be blamed for taking a resolute stand on an issue which involves the survival of the road. An efficient management does everything in its power to minimize costs."[32]

Widespread public displeasure, even anger at the striking telegraphers, pressured the ORT into agreeing to binding arbitration. Three individuals hammered out the settlement: head of the ORT George Leighty, Ben Heineman, and Pittsburgh attorney Sylvester Garett. Obviously the swing vote would come from Garett, the public arbitrator whom President John F. Kennedy selected to reach an accord. Garett was an excellent choice; he had already demonstrated his skills in mediating disputes in the steel industry.[33]

The North Western accomplished many of its goals in the arbitration process. *Time Magazine*, for one, called the final agreement a "stunning setback for the telegraphers." The railroad made its point that the number of telegraphers needed was a prerogative of management and not subject to a union veto. As a concession of sorts, the North Western agreed to provide the ORT with 90 days' notice of firings. The company also agreed to discuss changes and to pay discharged employees 60 percent of their annual earnings for as long as five years. Extra telegraphers would be guaranteed 40 hours of pay a week, but the company could determine the number of these employees. And, finally, an indication that toughness worked, telegraphers laid off prior to the strike would not be entitled to the benefits negotiated by this board.[34]

The settlement had both near-term and long-term effects. It ended considerable financial losses sustained by both sides: employees lost wages of $8.5 million, and the railroad lost revenues of $18 million. This was a landmark case, revealing to interested parties, most of all railroad management, that archaic work rules could be altered or eliminated. Make-work was costing the industry an estimated $500 million annually, and the North Western had dramatically altered the relationship between a carrier and the union. In an earlier dispute with the Southern

It's the twilight years for the Age of Steam on the North Western. The railroad corridor at Gilford, Iowa, where the Tama-Toledo line crosses the Minneapolis & St. Louis, retains a large, albeit weathered water tank to quench the thirst of the iron horse. (Author's collection)

Pacific Railroad the ORT had extracted major concessions. The company had guaranteed to retain its telegraphers until their death, retirement, resignation, or dismissal for cause.[35]

Soon the labor front saw much activity. In 1963 President John F. Kennedy asked Congress to demand that all matters of featherbedding be settled through arbitration. Lawmakers passed, and the president signed, legislation that required final and binding arbitration in only two areas, however: firemen on diesel locomotives and train-crew consists. This measure directed that other issues in dispute be negotiated between the parties within six months.[36]

Predictably, railroad brotherhoods opposed any binding decisions by arbitrators. They took the matter to court, challenging the constitutional right of Congress to dictate binding arbitration in a labor dispute. Eventually, a federal district court, the U.S. Court of Appeals, and the U.S. Supreme Court heard the pleas of labor; the courts consistently favored the companies.[37]

The Heineman administration remained steadfast in its efforts to reduce costs. Coinciding with the battle against the telegraphers was the company's determination to end money-losing passenger trains. The railroad moved on two fronts, long-distance trains and commuter runs, and focused on the heavy losses sustained in Wisconsin. On October 25, 1956, the North Western asked the Public Service Commission of Wisconsin (PSCW) for permission to eliminate 21 trains, but shrewdly offered state regulators something in return. The railroad would purchase two new trains and place them in areas where patronage warranted such service, and it would revamp schedules for the remaining trains. The PSCW surprised many by approving the plan. The annual savings from the train eliminations would offset the cost of the rolling stock, estimated at $2 million. In a calculated move the design of the new Pullman-Standard equipment allowed for possible use in Chicago commuter service. "We could easily tear out the parlor car seats and all of the other crap," noted one official, "and have these cars ready to carry commuters."[38]

Between 1956 and 1963 the North Western greatly scaled back its long-distance passenger service. Seventy-six trains were discontinued, representing a savings of 5,794,161 annual train miles and millions of dollars. The cuts occurred system wide and included such trains as Nos. 514 and 515 between Mankato and Huron on October 13, 1957; Nos. 203 and 204 between Minneapolis and Council Bluffs (Omaha) on October 25, 1959; Nos. 3 and 4 between Chicago and Clinton on July 15, 1961; and Nos. 518 and 519 between Chicago and Mankato on July 23, 1963.[39]

Toward the end of long distance passenger travel, the North Western operated a single train between Chicago and Clinton. Even though the company had officially dropped the *Kate Shelley 400* name in 1963, residents continued to call this train the "Kate Shelley," the "Katy," or simply the "Kate." (Author's collection)

The North Western did not always encounter friendly regulators. The removal of Nos. 13 and 14 between Omaha and Chadron is a case in point. Although the company initially considered termination of service along this 447-mile route in 1954, permission to eliminate the flagman was obtained from Nebraska authorities, and good "head-end" business minimized the red ink. "We had a special mail contract," explained an official. "The Chadron run was one of the most lucrative mail contracts that the North Western had. If we loaded the train with mail heavy westbound, we got the same rate for the eastbound." But financial conditions worsened. Out-of-pocket losses for 1956 amounted to $227,000, and they were expected to increase. The company was confronted by an unsympathetic Nebraska State Railway Commission. Regulators initially rejected a compromise offered by the railroad to maintain train service between Omaha and O'Neill (197 miles) and to provide bus service west to Chadron. The commission grudgingly granted the company its request for complete abandonment of the trains in February 1958, but this popularly elected body allowed protestors, mostly representatives from on-line communities, a rehearing. A month later the commission stayed its order, "citing improvement in C&NW's financial condition under the new management and a need to gather additional evidence." The railroad promptly appealed that decision to the state supreme court and received a favorable ruling in July. The company immediately annulled the trains, and service ended on July 6, 1958. But opponents continued their fight. The last appeal was finally dismissed in March 1959.[40]

The market for long-distance passenger trains steadily declined. Admittedly, residents along the "Cowboy Line" in Nebraska had limited access to alternative forms of public transportation. In time the state government subsidized a bus operation between Omaha and Chadron, but even that arrangement eventually ended because of financial problems. Americans, except in bad weather, increasingly wanted to use their automobiles and take advantage of an expanding network of divided, four-lane ribbons of concrete that the Interstate Highway Act of 1956 had made possible. Air service, too, grew in popularity especially after the debut of commercial jet aircraft in 1958. The best hope for the North Western as a passenger carrier came from its extensive Chicago commuter operations.[41]

For generations the North Western operated a large-scale commuter service; three suburban lines converged on downtown Chicago, linking the Loop district with more than 70 commuter stations. The northern route, known as the Milwaukee Division, served such lakeside suburbs as Evanston, Highland Park, and Lake Forest. Some commuters traveled as far as Kenosha, Wisconsin, 52 miles from the Windy City. The northwest line, called the Wisconsin Division, reached Arlington Heights, Mount Prospect, and Barrington. This was the longest artery, with riders coming from Harvard, 63 miles from Chicago, and Williams Bay, Wisconsin, 77 miles distant. The western route, the Galena Division, connected Chicago with such stations as Elmhurst, Glen Ellyn, and Wheaton. Geneva, 36 miles distant, was the western terminal.[42]

At one time the commitment to the "Best of Everything" meant comfortable and reliable daily trips for tens of thousands of patrons, but quality service had deteriorated during the Williams and Feucht years. One veteran rider recalled that crew members still lighted gas lamps in coaches on the Milwaukee Division. A writer compared the operation to "an alcoholic duchess expiring on Skid Row, still attired in silks and tiara," noting in particular that "the comfortable plush seats were stuffed with real horsehair, and through crazed, glass-thick varnish one could still see original walls, an exquisite mosaic of inlaid woods." Yet "car interiors had absorbed a hopeless quantity of soot and cinders. The windows were broken and the doors came off in your hand." A former executive put it bluntly: "We ran the world's worst commuter service." He vividly remembered the "umbrella cars," battered coaches inside of which passengers used their umbrellas during heavy rains.[43]

Commuting on the North Western got so bad at one time in 1954 that passengers on the Milwaukee Division held contests to compose the sharpest barbs and gleefully lampooned the company in song. A popular jibe was written to the tune of the Northwestern University fight song, "Go U Northwestern":

In 1950 the North Western purchased three rail diesel cars from the Budd Company for testing on its Chicago commuter lines. "We have wanted to try out the potentialities of this passenger car in suburban service ever since it was constructed," announced President R. L. Williams. But the experiment eventually dissatisfied the Williams administration, and after several years the cars were traded to the Chesapeake & Ohio for three nearly new streamlined passenger coaches. (Author's collection)

> O, O, my aching back
> Go, you North Western!
> Bounce right down that track,
> Broken springs and busted seats —
> O, O, my aching back!
> Choo, choo, choo

Another ditty, patterned on the same song, admonished:

> O, you North Western!
> Have some sympathy.
> Wipe off the shame
> From a once-proud name.
> Go, North Western! Show you're game![44]

A major revival for the harried and occasionally water-soaked commuter came with the new regime. Total dieselization in May 1956 made a positive impact and additional changes, designed to deal head-on with the "commuter problem," were fully in place by the early 1960s.

Railroaders knew that commuter trains were hopeless losers. "They bled cash like hell!" Ben Heineman recognized the dilemma and carefully reviewed the options: maintaining the status quo, abandoning the trains, upgrading the service. The first possibility would be economically unthinkable. "It was a money problem that had to be solved and quickly." The second would be politically difficult, if not impossible, as well as socially irresponsible. The "Stevensonian liberal" Heineman found that possibility wholly unacceptable. The third choice ideally would bring in profits or at least drastically reduce out-of-pocket losses. Understandably this alternative appealed to the board chairman, even though it would be dicey.[45]

The North Western proceeded to create what eventually was called "Chicago's Miracle." The company not only dieselized the trains but also hired Wyer, Dick & Co. to scrutinize the commuter business. As Heineman explained, "We were convinced that the suburban service problem couldn't be solved by piecemeal solutions." In December 1958, after successful hearings before the Illinois Commerce Commission, the railroad implemented the second major step of its renewal program—modernization of its ticketing and collection methods, revision of train schedules for better utilization of equipment, and major adjustments in rates. Here the company showed considerable imagination. To replace approximately 1,600 types of tickets and an irrational price structure, it decided to use a limited number of tickets and to encourage regular riders to buy monthly commutation cards by mail.[46]

The big change in the commuter service came with introduction of double-deck equipment and "push-pull" trains. The North Western was not the only line to acquire center-door, air-conditioned galley-type cars; the Burlington already used them in part to save on an expensive wheel tax at Chicago's Union Station. During the Feucht years the North Western had received 16 of these strikingly different pieces of rolling stock, another 32 in 1956, and 32 more in 1959. But as of January 1, 1960, these double-deckers represented only 20 percent of the total number of commuter cars. The company still operated 32 cars that had been built in 1910 and 84 dating from the period 1912 to 1917. The average age of the 335 conventional cars exceeded 37 years. On January 11, 1960, the railroad proudly announced that it would retire its historic car fleet and replace it with 116 high-capacity, double-deck coaches. This equipment would be in addition to 36 cars ordered the previous year.[47]

The great galley fleet ordered from Pullman-Standard and designed to create "the finest and the most modern suburban service in the world" operated in a push-pull fashion. This meant expansion of a revolutionary operating technique that the company had only recently pioneered: a diesel locomotive would always be at the same end of the train, pushing the coaches inbound to Chicago and pulling them on outbound trips. The last car of each train would have an engineer's control cab located at one end of the upper level. As such, push-pull trains resembled self-propelled cars—Rail Diesel Cars (RDCs), which the North Western had tried in commuter service beginning in 1950, for example—and multiple-unit electric trains.[48]

The push-pull operations offered considerable advantages. Most of all, the format permitted greater flexibility in employment of equipment and substantially reduced terminal switching. Complete modernization permitted the closing of the Erie Street coach yard and the release of nearly 40 acres of prime urban estate for development. Since double-deckers could handle more passengers, upgrading would also significantly reduce car miles. Similarly, the number of wheels and trucks and other parts to be maintained would be reduced. And fewer diesel units would be required, saving both motive power and fuel. The railroad also expected that the number of employees assigned to suburban duties could be cut by about 150.[49]

The Heineman administration shrewdly handled its power requirement for the push-pull service. In addition to the "cab cars" the railroad decided to rehabilitate 45 aging General Motors F-7 units, "which needed to be rebuilt if they remained in freight service." The company could then reassign from commuter runs its general purpose locomotives ("Geeps") to road freight and switching operations. This would save several millions of dollars in capital expenditures.[50]

The North Western publicized its major financial commitment to the commuter lines. The costs were high, involving $21 million for the new equipment and locomotive rehabilitation. An additional $6 million had already been spent for galley cars in 1959. The company was hardly a money machine; its net income for 1959 was a negative $2,890,000. Nevertheless Heineman obtained financing from the Metropolitan Life Insurance Company partly because Eugene Schmidt, Metropolitan's treasurer, served on the North Western board. The press and commuters applauded the announcement. Some commentators considered the investment a "daring gamble," but Heineman and his associates expected "bright spots" to benefit the undertaking.[51]

Greater Chicago changed rapidly during the late 1950s. Although the Recession of 1958 hurt the local economy, the region served by the North Western was growing. The populations of

When the North Western introduced push-pull commuter trains, it distributed a press release to describe the equipment. "Built above the lower level of seats, the cab provides a high, unobstructed view of the track ahead. The same controls and safety devices found on the locomotive are installed in the coach cabs." (North Western/Union Pacific)

Du Page, Kane, and Lake counties burgeoned during the Eisenhower era. "Some of the suburban towns and villages served by the North Western," noted the company, "have doubled and tripled their population in the last ten years." George Krambles, former head of the Chicago Transit Authority, recalled that "the very considerable white flight [from Chicago] to the northwestern suburbs certainly made the new commuter service on the North Western seem like a really smart move." The railroad closed more than 20 close-in stations, leaving those commuters to rely on public or alternative transport. The North Western could now concentrate on providing "true" suburban service. Said Heineman, "We don't want to run a street car type operation."[52]

Krambles also underscored the positive benefit to the North Western of the demise of two competing interurbans, the Chicago, Aurora & Elgin and the Chicago, North Shore & Milwaukee. "The Roarin' Elgin," severely hurt by the construction and then the opening of the "westside super highway" (Eisenhower Expressway), suspended its passenger operations in June 1957. This carrier had served such North Western communities as Geneva, Glen Ellyn, and Wheaton. The larger and more powerful rival, the North Shore, abandoned its "Shore Line" loop to Waukegan via Wilmette in 1955 and ran its last electric trains, largely parallel to the Milwaukee Division, on January 1, 1963. If electric riders continued to use flanged wheels, they usually took the North Western.[53]

The principal concern of the North Western was the private automobile and expansion of expressways and tollways in its suburban territory. The company did not panic, however. "There is a unanimous opinion on the North Western that a completely modernized suburban service can effectively compete with the highways," wrote Heineman. "If we do not modernize at this time [1959] in order to compete with the modern highways, we believe that as soon as the highways are completed our suburban service will start to show losses of several million dollars a year, and that we will be unable to eliminate the service."[54]

The Heineman administration deemed the multimillion dollar commitment to suburban service a success. The company reaped enormous goodwill from patrons, politicians, and the media that included city and suburban newspapers, popular national magazines, and a bevy of financial journals. The actual financial payoffs, however, came slowly. The operations posted a loss of $1,915,000 in 1961 and $2,090,000 in 1962, partly because of the month-long strike by telegraphers. Black ink appeared in 1963; net income reached $203,000. The results significantly improved for 1964 when the net stood at $706,000. In 1965 the railroad told shareholders that "suburban operations are now making an important contribution to net income." The service that year generated a net income of $1,387,000.⁵⁵

Some company officials questioned the "good" financial news about suburban service, however. Larry Provo for one thought that blue smoke and mirrors partly determined the results. Because Heineman had so closely identified himself with solving the commuter problem, Provo did not want to challenge his boss but privately told associates that Heineman sought to impress influential bankers from the North Shore communities.⁵⁶

The stratagem apparently worked. The impressions business leaders developed of "Ben Heineman's railroad" grew more positive. They judged the North Western by its commuter trains, which they consistently lauded. "Not one time has a train which I have been on been late," wrote a grateful executive about the upgraded service in 1966. "Not once have I received other than the most pleasant treatment from your employees. Not once have I had to stand. Never did the air-conditioning fail and always the cars were clean and comfortable." These influential individuals appreciated that this excellent service was profitable, a glowing testimonial to the genius of private enterprise and of course to Heineman himself. By the mid-1960s Heineman wanted the best possible image; he was then embarking on an ambitious program of nonrailroad acquisitions through a holding company, Northwest Industries.⁵⁷

Ben Heineman predicted difficulties in the financial rebuilding of the North Western. Deficits occurred in every year but one (1961) during the first seven years of his administration. The combined net income for this period was a minus $17,562,916, partly due to the 1958 recession and 1962 telegraphers' strike. The company finally broke out of the deficit mold; it reported a net income of $8,524,000 in 1963, $8,123,160 in 1964, and an impressive $16,063,760 in 1965, which was the highest in 20 years. With this much improved financial picture, the company reinstituted dividends. The board voted to pay preferred holders a quarterly dividend of $1.25 in late 1963, the first reward to these investors since 1954. And it paid the full $5 to preferred holders in 1964 and 1965. Although common shareholders received nothing in 1963, they earned $3 in 1964 and 1965; they had not seen a check since 1950.⁵⁸

No one could fault Ben Heineman for failing to respond to the challenges that confronted the North Western. He and his associates tackled the multitude of problems that plagued this old granger road and exploited its resources. The company battled to maintain the Oakes, North Dakota, gateway, for example. This avenue of interchange became an issue at the time of the proposed merger of the Hill roads, which led to the creation of Burlington Northern in 1970. The North Western wished to keep traffic flowing through Oakes because it provided a useful routing for lumber brokers. As Thomas Lamphier, an former Burlington Northern official, explained, "delivery could be delayed until the broker found a customer for a carload of lumber. The CNW hauled the cars to Huron, S.D. and stored them until the broker found a buyer. They [North Western] provided tri-weekly

A photographer for the St. Louis Car Company took an interior shot of the new North Western galley-type commuter car. The press release stated: "Features of the air-conditioned, streamlined cars include reversible seats upholstered in red vinyl plastic, green rubber tile floors, individual lighting, double pane safety windows." (North Western/Union Pacific)

The North Western received laudatory attention for its commitment to serving the Chicago area following the arrival of the new push-pull commuter trains. (North Western/Union Pacific)

service to Oakes from Huron, but we were handling train loads of this lumber from New Rockford and Jamestown, N.D. and we would just shove it down the CNW branch line." Added Lamphier, "This was all illegal—a violation of the Elkins Act, but it died a natural death, as the lumber companies started selling directly to lumber retailers, and in a few years [after the merger] the Oakes gateway dried up."[59]

While the Oakes lumber traffic boosted annual revenues during the Heineman years, probably the least successful task of management was paring down the number of unprofitable and marginal branch lines. "The company should have been more aggressive with line abandonments," reflected an industry consultant in 1988. The size of the historic North Western and Omaha Road properties did not shrink significantly during Heineman's tenure. The company simply concluded that it was better to retain many of these appendages, reasoning that abandonment procedures took time, caused political headaches, and might produce only limited savings. Management saw the possibility of accommodating shippers in an economical "cut-to-the-bone" fashion; trains would mostly handle the seasonal inbound and outbound cars of fertilizer and grain. If trimming took place, it would be in a manner designed to retain the maximize amount of business. The railroad, for example, retired the northern portion of the Superior branch in Nebraska between Seward and Platte River (near Fremont) and reached its major customers, which were largely located south of Seward, by trackage rights over the Burlington between Lincoln and Seward.[60]

The total mileage of the North Western actually increased substantially under Ben Heineman. The company entered the merger arena in the late 1950s and became a major player during the great wave of consolidations during the 1960s. Heineman joined others who concluded that the Midwest contained "excess capacity," and so he "worked very hard to spark merger madness." The North Western board chairman wanted to be certain that if the nation's railroad map were substantially redrawn, his company would not be irreparably damaged. "Ben Heineman did not take a head in the sand approach. He really sensed that big changes were about to take place in the industry."[61]

The first steps the North Western took into the turbulent world of mergers were modest. The company had officially leased the Omaha Road as of January 1, 1957, with the approval of the ICC. The next action brought the Litchfield & Madison Railway (L&M) into the fold. Lawyers filed the paperwork on August 1, 1957, and the ICC speedily granted the application. The effective date for this $8 million transaction was January 1, 1958. Ownership of this 44-mile bridge and coal-hauling line from Litchfield to East St. Louis, Illinois, gave the North Western its own entry into the busy St. Louis gateway. The company previously operated its trains over the L&M under a wheelage contract between Benld and East St. Louis.[62]

Acquisition of the L&M was a prelude for a major addition, the Minneapolis & St. Louis Railway (M&StL), on November 1, 1960. Earlier in the year the North Western had formally asked the ICC for permission to take over this 1,500-mile competitor. This was only the thirteenth petition since the Louisville & Nashville had fired the first salvo on the merger front in January 1955, when it filed an application to acquire the Nashville, Chattanooga & St. Louis.[63]

By 1960 the M&StL had considerable value, though that had not always been the case. Launched by Minneapolis boosters in 1870, the road expanded slowly, reaching Albert Lea, Minnesota, 107 miles south of the Mill City, in 1877. The 1880s saw much more growth as lines penetrated deeply into Iowa and eastern Dakota. The latter involved the Watertown extension and came during the "Rock Island Era," which began in 1882 and lasted for more than a decade. Rock Island's Ransome R. Cable aggressively expanded his railroad empire, and the M&StL became part of the story.[64]

Another dynamic railroader, Edwin Hawley, gained control of the M&StL, which became a much more important carrier under his tutelage. The first major addition involved the 135-mile Southwestern Extension, completed in 1900. Projected to Omaha, this branch reached only as far as Storm Lake, Iowa, although it offered connections to western and southwestern points. Soon Hawley invested heavily in the Iowa Central Railway. This 550-mile road, which linked Albert Lea with Peoria, Illinois, joined the M&StL on January 1, 1912. Hawley even had a Pacific dream, or at least the hope of pushing the Watertown line westward. If the M&StL could not reach the coast, the road might enter Canada and tie in with the transcontinentals. Between 1905 and 1907 the M&StL opened a 172-mile extension to LeBeau, South Dakota, on the Missouri River, and a 57-mile branch from Conde to Leola, South Dakota. Hawley also showed that he possessed true "Empire Builder" qualities. In 1910 he united the M&StL, Iowa Central, Chicago & Alton, and Toledo, St. Louis & Western railroads for a jointly coordinated operation. Though not a formal consolidation, this association involved centralization of authority in Chicago and unification of traffic solicitation. Hawley's system building efforts ended with his sudden death in February 1912.[65]

While the M&StL had expanded, it failed to sustain itself financially. The company entered receivership in 1923 and remained under court protection for the next 20 years. The M&StL seemed to deserve its nicknames: "Misery &

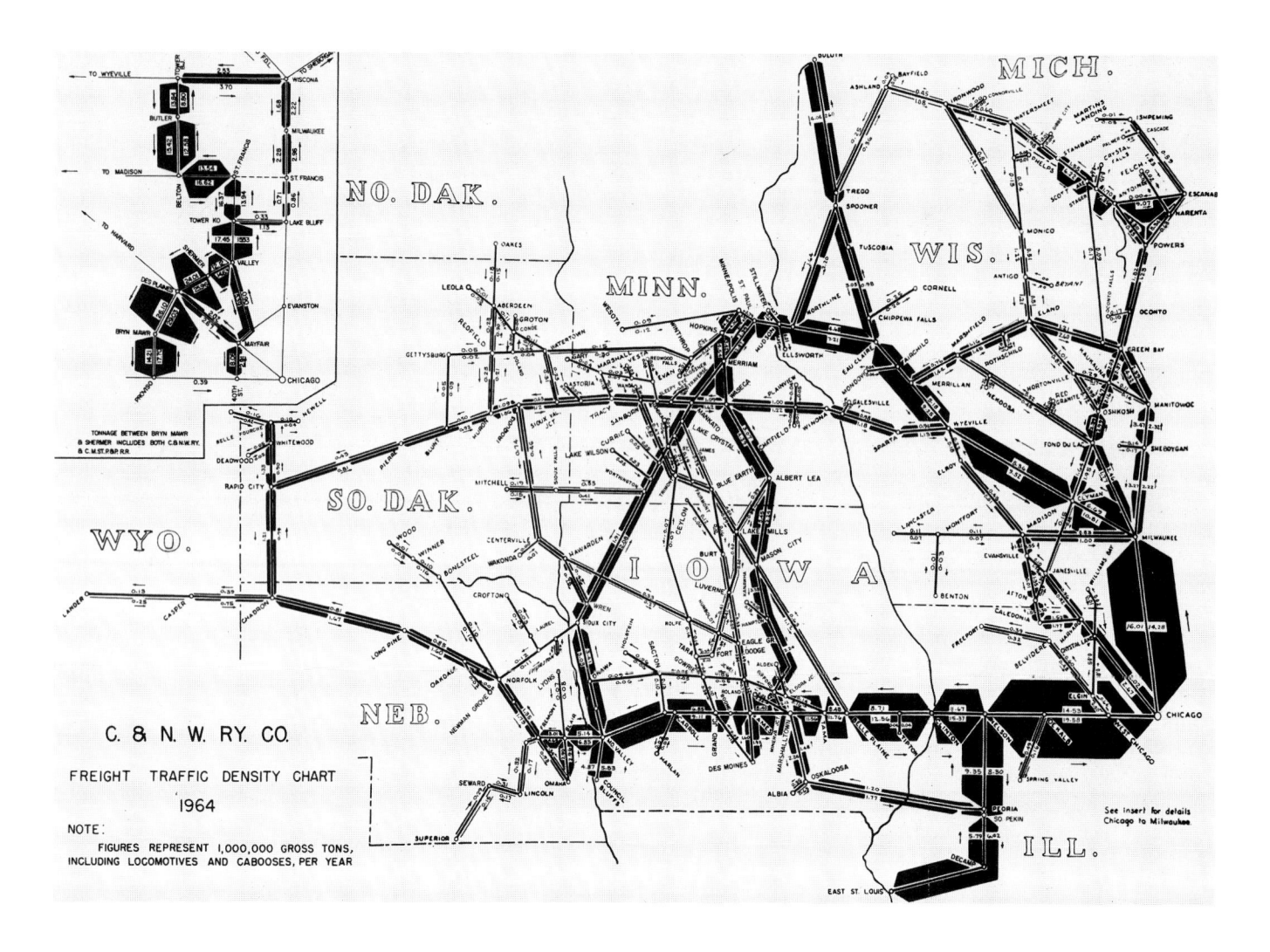

C. & N.W. RY. CO.
FREIGHT TRAFFIC DENSITY CHART
1964
NOTE:
FIGURES REPRESENT 1,000,000 GROSS TONS, INCLUDING LOCOMOTIVES AND CABOOSES, PER YEAR

Even though the Heineman regime abandoned some branch lines, it acquired even more as the result of its purchase of the Minneapolis & St. Louis in 1960. The freight traffic density map for 1964 reveals a railroad with few high-use lines. (Author's collection)

Short Life," "Maimed & Still Limping," and "Midnight & Still Later." The property appeared to be doomed; a proposal for liquidation emerged in 1935, but public opposition and improved management prevented dismemberment.[66]

The M&StL benefited from the traffic boom of World War II and became a renaissance road. Although some wags said that the M&StL went from somewhere (Twin Cites) to nowhere in particular (central South Dakota, Iowa, and west-central Illinois), the truth was that the M&StL served important agricultural shippers, switched major businesses in the Twin Cities, and reached the strategic Peoria gateway. The balance sheet looked good: net income before taxes averaged $3,149,000 annually during the 1950s. Its debt was modest: the only long-term obligations consisted of equipment trusts of nearly $9 million and a mortgage on the general office building of $1.45 million. The M&StL was a rare railroad in that it had no outstanding bonds, and, moreover, it owned a modern fleet of motive power and rolling stock.[67]

The company did have some problems. Officials worried especially about the impact of the St. Lawrence Seaway completed in 1959. "With the opening of the Seaway, grain from South Dakota and western Minnesota went only as far as the Twin Cities and then to Duluth," remembered Louis Gelfand, once executive assistant to the M&StL president, "but earlier it had gone via Peoria." The company had considered acquisition of the Gulf, Mobile & Ohio and a "connector road," the Chicago & Illinois Midland, to ensure the long haul of export grain. The M&StL fretted about increased truck competition. Better roads, including interstate highways, were being built in its territory. Management also agonized about the possibility of a merger of the Burlington, Great Northern, and Northern Pacific. The M&StL received considerable "bridge" traffic from the Great Northern and Northern Pacific, and these carriers would not "short-haul" themselves if the Burlington became part of a united system.[68]

Although the M&StL faced an uncertain future, the company remained a good prize, and the North Western easily handled the purchase. A first mortgage on the debt-free M&StL provided the acquisition money; the railroad fell into the lap of the North Western without cost. "The merger provided CNW with a cost-free expansion of territory, traffic, and revenues, plus a modern equipment fleet," observed a onetime M&StL official. "It was a fortuitous gift by a smaller line which could not have survived independently for very long against motor carriers on the Interstates and the massive traffic diversions that would come with the BN [Burlington Northern]." Gelfand echoed that conclusion: "In 1960 the world around the M&StL was changing and the company really had to find a merger partner."[69]

The process of melding the M&StL into the North Western outwardly went well. The latter turned the former into its "M&StL Division" and later its "Central Division." The North Western made the integration of the properties a priority. "We wanted to absorb the M&StL as soon as we could," Frank Koval remembered, "and we did it in a reasonably short time." With the M&StL in tow the North Western boasted that it owned 10,730 miles of trackage, making the company the nation's third longest railroad.[70]

The North Western paid a price for its claim. Employees of the M&StL almost universally despised the merger. When word of the deal first spread through the headquarters in Minneapolis, disgruntled workers responded variously: "We've been raped!" and "those Kike sons-of-bitches have stolen our railroad!" The latter expletive referred to Ben Heineman and Max Swiren, Heineman's former law partner who headed the M&StL's Executive Committee of the Board of Directors. Later that day many clerks got drunk. Reactions of M&StL personnel outside Minneapolis were similar. "I always felt Heineman was sort of a fifth columnist for the CNW who helped pave the way for the takeover," recalled a veteran station agent. "There were those who hated him so badly that if he had tried to become friendly with the M&StL employees, he might have been dragged out in the weeds and when he returned he'd be singing soprano. . . . It was a time of severe depression by all employees as it was akin to burying a dear old friend."[71]

Conditions appeared to worsen for the onetime employees of the M&StL. The words of a former Hedrick, Iowa, agent conveyed widely held sentiments:

> It was a million things, really. The CNW officials were arrogant and seemed to have it in for the M&STL people. They wanted to junk much of our railroad [M&StL], but they never told you anything. You could only judge by their actions or lack of them. In time 19 and 20 [time-freights between the Twin Cities and Peoria] were discontinued and were replaced by a local train operating west out of Monmouth [Illinois] as far as there was tonnage to move, and only once a week. Then the east switch at Oskaloosa [Iowa] was spiked, meaning that no train could pass through, or even enter town from the east. Nobody was ever told the reason why unless it was to dry up the business even further, and if such were the reason, they did splendidly because that, plus the once weekly service, soon reduced business between Wright, the first station east of Oskaloosa and Monmouth to near zero. . . . Then a crew was sent out to dismantle what interlocking plants there were west of Monmouth, including the one at Hedrick, then they took out the radios. Around 1965 sometime, my train order work was transferred from the dispatcher at Mason City, Iowa, to the CNW dispatcher at South Pekin, Illinois. After the inauguration of the weekly local service however, there was very little train order work. Then there was a storm that broke the wires somewhere between Morning Sun, Iowa and Monmouth, but the CNW would not allow the lineman to fix it, so for several years any train order work had to be handled via long distance phone. My company phone was disconnected purposely at Oskaloosa so I couldn't talk to him, so Morning Sun kept his telegraph wire grounded east of his depot and we would talk back and forth to each other nearly every day, otherwise I would have had nobody to talk to. . . . Working for the CNW was a different world, [and] you left if you could, especially if you had been a M&STL man.[72]

James R. Sullivan, a M&StL official who later worked for other major carriers and then became an industry consultant, expressed similar sentiments: "In sum, from a human relations standpoint, North Western's approach to the

M.St.L. acquisition could be characterized quite accurately as Neanderthal. It left behind a legacy of bitterness that over the years, in areas where I could influence the routing of railway freight traffic, my recommendation favored almost any alternative to the Chicago & North Western."[73]

The next takeover by the North Western happened on July 1, 1968. The company acquired another midwestern granger road, the Chicago Great Western Railway (CGW). About the size of the M&StL, the CGW linked the Twin Cities with Chicago, Kansas City, and Omaha. Unlike most of its neighbors, the CGW was shaped by a single individual, A. B. Stickney. This St. Paul lawyer-turned-railroader breathed life into the moribund Minnesota & Northwestern project by pushing it southward from St. Paul to a connection with an Illinois Central–controlled road in 1885. Unable to find a buyer, Stickney shrewdly extended the carrier to Chicago via Dubuque, Iowa, forging a through route in 1888. Stickney also eyed St. Joseph and Kansas City. By acquiring the Wisconsin, Iowa & Nebraska, an Iowa shortline, and constructing new trackage, he speedily reached these gateways. The banner was no longer the Minnesota & Northwestern, but the more appropriate Chicago, St. Paul & Kansas City. Stickney had the good sense to realize that the ultimate success of his hastily assembled property lay with trunk lines that connected thriving trade centers. Faced with numerous competitors, some of whom were vindictive, he needed every advantage.[74]

In the early 1890s Stickney reorganized the Chicago, St. Paul & Kansas City. The railroad took a new name, Chicago Great Western, and received an unusual financial structure, the English system of making the property mortgage-free but with a lien on income (an arrangement suggestive of the innovation that became a CGW hallmark). After the depression of the 1890s lifted, Stickney decided to enter the Omaha gateway. By using a former Hill road, the Mason City & Fort Dodge, as a springboard, the CGW spiked down the last rails on an extension that reached Council Bluffs in 1903.[75]

The Panic of 1907 proved that the Chicago Great Western had no immunity from economic dislocations, and in 1908 the company fell into receivership. Soon it was revived by J. P. Morgan & Company, and the new owners placed the "doctor of sick railroads," Samuel Felton, in charge. The next 20 years witnessed a revitalization, but the Felton era ended in the late 1920s when a group of speculators ousted the management. These plungers immediately cast a dark cloud over the road. Their holding company, the Bremo Corporation, headed by the flamboyant Patrick Joyce, proceeded to loot the CGW. This experience, coupled with an enormous decrease in traffic caused by the Great Depression, forced the CGW into receivership for a six-year period beginning in 1935. Reorganization and the boom created by World War II returned the railroad to a reasonable degree of financial health.[76]

The last major episode in the corporate life of the CGW began in 1948, when several Kansas City businessmen took control. The new owners placed lawyer-railroader William N. Deramus III into the president's chair in 1949, and by the early 1950s management had largely renovated the railroad. These improvements included dieselization and the abandonment of unprofitable passenger trains, branch lines, and obsolete facilities. Although Deramus left the presidency in 1957, his handpicked successor, E. T. Reidy, remained efficiency-minded.[77]

During the early 1960s merger frenzy, the CGW entered the fray. "The Great Western is a fine property," observed a company director, "but . . . it is being squeezed by increased competition, rate cuts and high labor costs and . . . merger with another railroad is the ultimate solution." After merger talks with the Soo Line broke off in November 1963, the North Western became an active suitor. Ben Heineman especially wanted the CGW's line from Marshalltown, Iowa, located on both the Omaha stem and the Twin Cities to Peoria line of the M&StL, to Kansas City, and he sought to rid himself of a spunky competitor. The CGW, for example, had pioneered "piggyback" traffic in the mid-1930s and aggressively promoted its intermodal services.[78]

The process of absorbing the Great Western moved forward. The North Western filed the merger petition on November 13, 1964. The ICC did not rubber-stamp the request, however. After four years of hearings and maneuvering, mostly with the Soo Line, the CGW officially joined the Heineman road. The former CGW became the "Missouri Division" between 1968 and 1974, although the North Western shortly began major line liquidation. The physical parts of this former competitor had largely disappeared by the late 1980s.[79]

Integration of the CGW into the North Western went more smoothly than had the merger with the M&StL, especially for workers. "I know we learned a lot about how to conduct a merger after the M&StL," reflected Frank Koval. Still, former CGW personnel complained about their new owners. "I'm not a North Western employee," snapped a former CGW locomotive engineer, "I'm a Great Western orphan."[80]

The financial arrangements benefited both companies. Negotiators for the CGW not only found a buyer but obtained a good price for their investors. Earlier, too, merger talks had driven up CGW stock from a 1963 low of $14.50 for a share of common to a 1967 high of $105. Unquestionably the CGW, like the M&StL, needed a new corporate home; both were vulnerable to industry consolidation. "If CGW was to be left alone with all surrounding railroads in the process of merger," observed a CGW director in 1967, "it could ultimately have only one result, . . . and that is, I believe, bankruptcy." The approximately $19.3-million deal gave the North Western an entry into Kansas City and the lucrative Roseport Industrial District near St. Paul as well as less competition.[81]

Twenty-nine days after the Chicago Great Western joined the North Western, two other midwestern roads entered the fold. The Heineman company acquired a pair of former Iowa interurbans, the 36-mile Des Moines & Central Iowa Railway (DM&CI) and the 110-mile Fort Dodge, Des Moines & Southern Railway (FtDDM&S). The former switched several important Des Moines–area businesses, including a large plant of the Firestone Tire & Rubber Company, and the latter connected Des Moines with Fort Dodge, once a center of M&StL and CGW activities. Gypsum mills were an attractive feature of the FtDDM&S: the company handled nearly 8,000 carloads of gypsum products in 1967. Murray M. Salzberg, a New York shortline magnate and junk dealer, headed a group that controlled both properties, and he apparently instigated merger discussions. Salzberg and his associates readily came to terms with Heineman. The North Western paid $5.1 million for 99.6 percent of the capital stock of the DM&CI, which possessed nearly all of the outstanding shares of the FtDDM&S. The ICC willingly endorsed the deal.[82]

Not long after the Salzberg agreement the North Western expanded again, but this time not through merger. The company invested approximately $8.25 million to acquire half-interest in the Alton & Southern Railroad, an important St. Louis–area terminal road. The North Western, which wished to strengthen its presence in the region, joined the Missouri Pacific to purchase this Aluminum Company of America (Aloca) property. The new owners reincorporated the railroad as the Alton & Southern Rail*way*, which the ICC authorized on April 19, 1968, and they completed the process three months later.[83]

Ben Heineman relished railroad mergers. What he accomplished during the 1960s did not fully disclose the extent of his ambitions. "It's no secret that I favor the construction of a vast railroad system centered broadly in the West, consisting of *at least* the North Western, the Milwaukee, the Rock Island and the Chicago Great Western, but including such other smaller roads as might care to join with us as well," he told *Forbes* magazine in 1964. "The object would be to create a useful economic organization corresponding to the increase in the size of the U.S. transportation market, to obtain greater efficiency of operation, and in the process to convert a number of marginal roads into a strong competitive medium." Heineman considered mergers as the salvation for the industry. Dieselization and other forms of replacement technology, while enhancing corporate earnings, could never become the total solution. The merger was an offensive weapon that could enable railroads to recapture traffic lost to barges, pipelines, and especially trucks.[84]

If Heineman had been successful, the final system would have exceeded 30,000 miles, stretching from Indiana and Chicago to the

Pacific Northwest and the Gulf Coast. The North Western chairman expected the megasystem to be profitable, perhaps generating annual pretax earnings of $100 million or more. Such a figure would be achieved in part through economies derived from the consolidation of administration, maintenance, and operations and abandonment of "burdensome excess capacity." Heineman consistently argued that the country, particularly its midsection, contained too much trackage, and corporate marriages could "rationalize" the railroad map.[85]

Ben Heineman did more than dream about forging a mammoth railroad. In addition to the several railroad acquisitions and purchase of a 13 percent interest in the Gulf, Mobile & Ohio in 1962 (which was soon sold), the North Western picked up on the Feucht regime's interest in the Milwaukee Road. While the Wyer report of 1955 had become badly dated, Heineman still anticipated substantial savings and solid profits following a North Western and Milwaukee Road merger. The Milwaukee, with its 10,500 mile network, including a line to the Pacific Northwest, complemented the North Western. The roads historically had competed in the heartland states of Illinois, Iowa, Minnesota, South Dakota, and Wisconsin.[86]

Action began in late 1960. Managements reopened negotiations, and these discussions soon led to formal merger talks. The prospects for union looked promising. "Differences over a plan . . . under consideration appeared to be so narrow," wrote Heineman, "that the managements felt justified in announcing jointly that they expected to present a plan of unification to their respective Boards of Directors at meetings to be held on March 16." But at this point a serious obstacle emerged. Leo Crowley, chairman of the Milwaukee Road board, presented Heineman with an alternative plan on March 13, which significantly differed from the earlier proposal. The formula for the exchange of securities alarmed Heineman. "It's a matter of price," he recalled three years later. "We came close in 1961 but not close enough." Still, Heineman publicly reiterated the value of this merger. "In our opinion there are no two railroads in the country that, in combination, could bring greater benefits to all interested groups."[87]

While Ben Heineman and his associates were disappointed and even angered over the outcome of the merger negotiations with the Milwaukee Road, they were not discouraged. If the North Western could continue to strengthen itself financially, the company would surely achieve a mutually acceptable agreement with the Milwaukee. The relationship between the two railroads improved, driven by the advantages offered by merger and the likelihood of support from the proposed Burlington Northern. The two boards agreed in September 1964 to resume consolidation talks, and on March 18, 1965, they approved a "definitive agreement" for merger. The unified property, the Chicago, Milwaukee and North Western Transportation Company, would issue one share of its preferred stock for each share of North Western and Milwaukee preferred stock, one share of its common stock for each share of North Western common, and seventh-tenths for each share of Milwaukee common. The North Western would name eight of the 15 directors. The next step involved approval by shareholders of the two roads, and they quickly agreed. On June 6, 1966, the companies filed their application with the ICC. The torturous process continued: public hearings were conducted between February 1967 and July 1968, and the ICC examiner endorsed the proposal in December 1968.[88]

But the Chicago, Milwaukee and North Western Transportation Company never absorbed the North Western and Milwaukee Road properties. The merger began to unravel when dissident Milwaukee stockholders accused their board of "selling out" to the North Western, and they filed a class action. A larger concern involved Northwest Industries, the holding company that by this time controlled the North Western. The bad news included a dramatic drop in earnings for Northwest Industries in 1969 and its failure to acquire several major nonrailroad corporations, including B. F. Goodrich. The ICC, concerned about the original stock-exchange ratio, ordered hearings to be reopened. Heineman refused to renegotiate the exchange ratio, and he may have shocked Milwaukee board members when he told them that his railroad was for sale. That beleaguered company, however, was in no position to propose an acceptable offer.[89]

The North Western soon encountered an even more trying merger experience. The company entered what ICC veterans considered "the most controversial rail merger case in memory," the battle for the Rock Island. As early as 1960 Ben Heineman had discussed the possibility of a Milwaukee Road, North Western, and Rock Island consolidation. These railroads, encouraged by several life insurance companies with major bond holdings, agreed that it was an attractive prospect. "[T]he concept was valid," said Heineman. "But we felt we should get two [North Western and Milwaukee Road] together first." The catalyst for the North Western moving aggressively on the Rock Island came in 1962. Giant Union Pacific revealed that it wanted "the Rock," wishing to break out of its historical position of remaining west of the Missouri River.[90]

In the early rounds of merger maneuvering the Union Pacific worried about future connections east of the Kansas City and Omaha gateways. After much study the transcontinental decided to acquire the Rock Island, a road that linked Kansas City with St. Louis and Omaha with Chicago, the nation's two greatest rail centers. But it was hardly a gem; the railroad badly needed a massive infusion of funds for modernization. By this time the carrier had become principally a hauler of agricultural products (corn and wheat); standard boxcars, rumbling over a deteriorating 7,500-mile, 14-state system, characterized the property.[91]

The Union Pacific pushed forward with its plan to acquire the Rock Island. Although the death in October 1961 of the venerable head of the Rock Island, John Dow Farrington, caused concern, the spokesperson for the railroad, Henry Crown, building materials czar of Chicago, agreed to talk. A major holder of Rock Island securities, Crown would back merger but for the right price. When the Union Pacific learned that the Southern Pacific was also eyeing the Rock Island, a deal between these two suitors was reached: the Southern Pacific would acquire what it coveted, most of the Rock Island south and west of Kansas City. The Union Pacific would take the remainder, including the strategic lines to Chicago and St. Louis. Negotiations between the interested parties started in early 1963, and a formal plan of consolidation followed. With agreement in hand the Union Pacific filed its merger papers with the ICC on September 10, 1964, and the Southern Pacific requested permission to buy a piece of the Rock on April 15, 1965.[92]

The hearings on the Union Pacific petition, which did not begin until 1966, faced a major complication as the commission had to consider more than the Union Pacific bid. Fourteen months before that paperwork arrived, the North Western had asked for permission to control the Rock Island. As the hearing process commenced, the ICC examiner reviewed the competing requests. While experts anticipated a dogfight between "David" North Western and "Goliath" Union Pacific, no one expected the longest merger battle in history.[93]

The presence of the North Western in the contest for Rock Island was understandable. The Rock fit into the Heineman strategy for a modern mid-American rail network; the doughty granger complemented both the North Western and Milwaukee Road and would make an "impressive inter-regional system that had some real hope for future profitability." More important, the prospect of a Union Pacific "invasion" of North Western territory rightly alarmed the historic eastern partner of the Overland Route. The North Western wanted to retain the extensive freight interchange, estimated at between 150,000 and 175,000 cars annually. The public announcement of the North Western's quest for the Rock, which came in May 1963, was rapidly followed by efforts to solicit Rock Island stockholders.[94]

The thought of the struggling North Western winning the Rock Island seemed ludicrous to many. "It looked like a wild thing to me," recalled Jervis Langdon Jr., who assumed the presidency of the Rock in May 1965. Yet Langdon and others realized that Ben Heineman was a talented corporate lawyer. "No one, and I mean no one," Langdon said with a smile, "should ever have doubted the brilliance and determination of Ben Heineman." Repeatedly the North Western chairman demonstrated his business acumen. While the Union Pacific thwarted North Western efforts in an early proxy fight, the public relations battle went in favor of the North Western. Journalists, especially those based in Chicago, liked the feisty Heineman; his actions provided them with good copy. In June

1964 the North Western surprised onlookers when it sold its holdings in the Rock Island, but Heineman had not surrendered. He shortly engineered a temporary legal roadblock and followed with a bid for Rock Island proxies. In January 1965 stockholders of the Rock Island, however, overwhelmingly approved the offer made by the Union Pacific.[95]

Even though the North Western encountered setbacks, the company astutely lined up anti–Union Pacific partners. The Heineman camp soon included the Frisco, Milwaukee Road, Missouri Pacific, Rio Grande, and Western Pacific. Undaunted, Union Pacific officials went ahead with their pursuit of the Rock. They foolishly avoided negotiations with Heineman or any other railroad executive.[96]

A formidable array of opponents hardly augured well for the Union Pacific. As the conflict continued, other events troubled the carrier. Langdon reversed the downswing of the Rock Island, and a healthier property caused some Rock Island investors to question the earlier stock-exchange agreement. The North Western also gained financial strength; Heineman's betterments were paying off. Although most Rock Island stock had been committed to the Union Pacific by September 1965, Heineman received commission permission to issue North Western certificates, and he offered them to Rock Island stockholders in exchange for comparable Union Pacific paper.[97]

Then came some good news for the North Western. In early fall of 1965 the Santa Fe made known its willingness to buy the southern lines of the Rock Island if the North Western gained control. Santa Fe intervention posed a real threat to the Union Pacific; this prosperous road added a psychological boost to the North Western cause and made the North Western bid appear more credible. Additional good news followed on March 31, 1966. The ICC ruled against the long-pending request of the Burlington, Great Northern, and Northern Pacific to unite. This decision weakened the Union Pacific case that a Burlington Northern would create unfair competition in the Midwest and West, and therefore the Union Pacific would have to expand.[98]

Public hearings on the future ownership of the Rock Island convened in Chicago on May 4, 1966, and droned on for months. The process lasted until October 1974, partly because of the profound strategic implications of the merger for other midwestern and western carriers. By the end of the 1960s the unification movement in the Midwest with few exceptions had become bogged down. The bright spot for consolidationists came when the ICC reconsidered the merger proposal for a Burlington Northern in January 1967 and endorsed the union 11 months later.[99]

The ICC finally determined that the Union Pacific should control the Rock Island, but the decision was a pyrrhic victory for the suitor. The ICC attached conditions that the Union Pacific found too onerous, and the deal collapsed. In the interim Rock Island management allowed the property to crumble. Unmistakably the Union Pacific had placed its eggs solely in the Rock Island basket, even rejecting a Heineman overture to sell the North Western. "When the Union Pacific finally 'won' the war," concludes historian Maury Klein, "there was nothing left to win."[100]

For all of the posturing between the North Western and Union Pacific for the Rock Island, Heineman had emerged victorious. He won on two counts: preventing the Union Pacific from entering Chicago and contributing to the dramatic decline and eventual collapse of the Rock.[101]

Ben Heineman recognized the difficulties of confronting railroad regulation. Nevertheless he understood how to cope with and even to manipulate the regulatory processes. He concluded by the mid-1960s that a better way to increase shareholder value would come not from modernization and mergers but from investments outside the transportation sector. Profits for the railroad were limited at best; the industry seemed unable to alter labor relations, pricing, and related regulatory matters. "To put it simply," Heineman told the business press, "I've been discontented with the railroad industry and its long-range outlook under present circumstances, because its rate of returns is disgustingly inadequate."[102]

The advantages to be derived from nonrailroad investments were considerable. If satellite enterprises generated profits, a stronger corporation would obviously result. The railroad could also benefit from the protection offered by contra-cyclical businesses. There would be attractive tax considerations as well, achieved by the nonrail concerns using the tax-credit carry-forwards of the parent railroad. If nationalization of the rail industry ever occurred, and some experts thought it possible, diversification would offer financial protection.[103]

The acquisition of nonrail firms began in 1965. The North Western acquired through a wholly owned subsidiary, Norwest Corporation (later Northwest Industries, Inc.), the entire capital stock of the Velsicol Chemical Corporation, which in turn controlled the Michigan Chemical Corporation. The North Western soon purchased additional shares of Michigan Chemical. By the end of 1965 the railroad's leveraged investment of $34 million meant that it either directly or indirectly owned more than 80 percent of Michigan Chemical. These "sound, stable and well-managed" manufacturing firms, which produced fungicides, herbicides, insecticides, paints, and industrial chemicals, contributed about $5 million of net income during the first six months of ownership.[104]

Encouraged by the acquisition of the chemical companies, Heineman and Northwest Industries (NWI) continued to expand. By 1968 NWI had become a full-fledged conglomerate. In that year a multimillion dollar securities transaction allowed NWI to take control of the Philadelphia & Reading Corporation, a holding and management company that had once produced anthracite coal (Philadelphia & Reading Coal & Iron). Philadelphia & Reading possessed numerous subsidiaries: Acme Boot, Fruit of the Loom (soft goods), Imperial Reading (clothing), Lone Star Steel (oil pipe), Union Underwear, and Universal Manufacturing (ballasts for fluorescent lights). Sales for 1966 approached $330 million, and NWI generated an after-tax profit of nearly $24 million. This diversification made an impression in business circles. It was mostly positive, although some bad publicity resulted from the failed takeover bid in 1969 of the poorly managed rubber product and chemical manufacturer, B. F. Goodrich.[105]

Many rail companies were busy acquiring un-related enterprises by the late 1960s. The Santa Fe, the Southern Pacific, and the Union Pacific had been pioneer diversifiers, and others, including the Illinois Central and Penn Central, joined the quest. Tax credits and the relative ease in obtaining government approval made nonrailroad acquisitions attractive. Perhaps the rail carriers should have turned to other transportation companies—airlines, barges, and motor carriers—but federal statutes severely restricted such modal expansion.[106]

What to do with the North Western was Ben Heineman's critical dilemma in the late 1960s. Net railway operating income for the mid-sixties had been good, averaging $25 million for 1964 through 1966. But that amount dropped in 1967 and declined steeply in 1968 and 1969. The railroad sustained a net operating loss of $5.7 million in 1969, a bad year for the entire industry. Heineman and his associates at Northwest Industries also worried about possible regulatory changes. "They feared . . . that the regulatory arm of the Interstate Commerce Commission might be extended to cover all of their manufacturing operations as well as the railroad." Heineman had sought buyers for the North Western, most notably the Milwaukee Road, but without success.[107]

By the late 1960s the North Western was becoming more decrepit. "During the late 1960s and early 1970s, C&NW was a pretty pathetic operation," recalled Don L. Hofsommer, a leading historian of midwest railroading. "I rode from Chicago to Clinton and return and I recall a very rough ride. There were many legitimate slow orders, the coach dropping frighteningly at bad spots where ties were pumping mud from a wretchedly maintained roadbed. Crewmen just shook their heads." The freight situation on the Omaha line was even more troubling. "The UPRR felt so wronged by C&NW service that a preferred routing was formed via Grand Island [Nebraska] and CB&Q, obviously shorthauling UPRR but saving its customers."[108]

The conundrum would have a solution. Larry Provo, who became vice president in May 1966 following the removal of Clyde Fitzpatrick for public drunkenness, had Heineman's trust and moved into the president's office in July

Small-town depots received little maintenance from the Heineman administration. By the mid-1960s many depots, including the one at Bancroft, Iowa, had grown shabby. (Author's collection)

1967. Although the new rail head was given considerable autonomy, Heineman kept a watchful eye. "Heineman drove me nuts!" Provo told an subordinate. The pressure of the job did not prevent the imaginative Provo from making an unusual offer to the board chairman, however, a leveraged buyout of the railroad by its employees. While Heineman wanted to spin off the property, he "didn't think that he [Provo] could pull it off." Yet Provo, backed by management and labor, did just that. On October 5, 1970, Northwest Industries entered into an agreement with the North Western Employees Transportation Company (NETCO) to sell substantially all of the assets of the Chicago & North Western Railway Company. For a modest sum, $19 million, to be paid over a 20-year period, and the assumption of the $340 million company debt, the railroad would become an employee-owned corporation. "The employees are getting what must be the cheapest railroad in history," concluded a financial writer. "They are paying little more than $100 a year per mile of railroad track." NWI would walk away from an unwanted operation with $200 million of tax credits that it could use to offset profits from its many subsidiaries. Once the sale was finalized, Heineman went his own way; he engineered the sale of NWI to Farley Industries in 1985 for $1.4 billion and retired from the business world.[109]

Larry Provo's scheme succeeded for several reasons. Ben Heineman provided encouragement, and Provo's top associates, particularly John Butler, Robert Russell, and James Wolfe, gave their endorsement. The buyout came about partly because of the good relations Provo established with organized labor. Leslie (Les) Dennis, who led the Brotherhood of Railway, Airline and Steamship Clerks, Freight Handlers, Express and Station Employees, or BRAC, which represented about a third of the North Western workforce, liked Provo. The North Western president projected the image of being "tough and fair." Dennis despised Heineman, particularly for "ending LCL and Railway Express on the North Western," but he did not consider Provo to be a clone of his old adversary. There was also a financial explanation. "I'm going to make you a rich man," Provo told the BRAC head. Under the ownership plan, workers (Dennis qualified because he remained on the company roster) could buy up to $100,000 of stock in the new company. While only about a thousand of the 14,000 employees took the opportunity to purchase the securities, Dennis invested the maximum amount of his eligibility, and "he made a killing." Provo also received support from the other powerful unions, the Brotherhood of Locomotive Engineers (BLE) and the United Transportation Union (UTU). "The key to making the LBO work was the backing received from BRAC and BLE," noted an official. "The UTU was not really enthusiastic, but it was not going to become a major roadblock."[110]

No obstacles of consequence stood in the way of the North Western Employees Transportation Company. None of the North Western adversaries in the recent merger contests objected. Without undue delays the hearings took place, and soon an ICC examiner recommended approval of the sale subject to certain conditions, mostly relating to bond obligations. But Larry Provo told the ICC that such restrictions, which Ben Heineman and Northwest Industries would not accept, were not desired by NETCO and he asked that they not be imposed. The ICC agreed, and on June 1, 1972, NETCO, renamed the Chicago and North Western Transportation Company, emerged. A new day had dawned for the elderly granger road, but the question remained whether this unusual employee venture could succeed.[111]

On March 21, 1984, workers west of Van Tassell, Wyo., install the first heavy steel rail on the coal line. The North Western soon took possession of one of America's most modern pieces of trackage. (North Western/Union Pacific)

CHAPTER
Eleven

EMPLOYEE OWNERSHIP AND AFTER
The Provo and Wolfe Administrations

When the Chicago & North Western Transportation Company made its corporate debut on June 1, 1972, the fate of this unique employee-owned firm was much in doubt. Some observers predicted a "rags to riches" scenario. Others expected the venture to disappear within several years, with the railroad entering the orbit of a competitor or a connecting carrier or even being largely abandoned. A combination of these expectations actually occurred. While employee ownership proved not to be a solution, a scrappy, innovative North Western sustained itself, prospering at times, until the Union Pacific, its principal interchange partner, purchased the property without opposition in 1995.[1]

In 1972 President Larry Provo and his associates were uncertain about employee response to the buyout opportunity. Although Provo told industry executives in November 1973 that "this past year and a half has been an incredible, fascinating, challenging and thoroughly delightful experience," concern developed over worker commitment. "We mailed out the offering circulars and sat back to wait," recalled Provo, "hoping, of course, that at least $1 million worth of stock was purchased since we had to have that much under terms of the I.C.C. order to enable us to consummate the deal."[2]

Even though employees purchased the entire equity offering of 72,905 shares at $50 each, the result was hardly a true worker-owned concern. Only about a thousand of the approximately 14,000-member North Western workforce initially acquired stock. About 600 nonunion personnel and 400 union members invested, "mostly engineers, conductors and clerks." An employee's earnings determined the number of shares that could be purchased. Most officers, including Provo, invested the maximum allowed ($100,000 of stock with an annual salary of $30,000 or more and $20,000 with income of $20,000 to $29,999), while others, usually blue-collar and office staff, invested only $500 for the minimum 10-share lot.[3]

The pattern of stock ownership in the recast North Western surprised few analysts. Federal regulations prevented management from actively soliciting sales. According to Provo, "we really did nothing to promote the offer." Other provisions probably impeded employee investment. The company could not pay dividends for the first five years, which were then limited at 8 percent of paid-in capital for the next five-year period. Furthermore, the firm could not diversify outside the transportation sector for a decade. Difficulties developed with the brotherhoods as well. "The unions told employees not to buy," Edward A. Burkhardt, an operating official, remembered. "They didn't like the idea of workers being close to the company." The rank and file, moreover, generally distrusted anything that smacked of "high finance." The offering circular itself was a forbidding document: boldface type announced that "these securities are offered as a speculation." In early 1973 a writer for *Forbes* concluded, "employees were told to go seek advice from a stockbroker or someone like that," which was not part of their culture. A veteran trainman recalled: "I didn't put money into the railroad because that Jew, Heineman, had already looted the railroad. He tore up part of the main line [in western Iowa] a few years before.... I didn't feel that I should buy that stock. I think I bought a refrigerator."[4]

Buying a refrigerator rather than North Western stock turned out to be a poor

Larry Provo, the talented protege of Ben W. Heineman, was the architect of employee ownership. (North Western/Union Pacific)

decision. Shortly after the company began operations some stockholders were privately selling shares for $300 or more apiece. Then in 1973 the three-member Board of Directors, eager to widen employee ownership, endorsed a 60-for-one stock split. The Interstate Commerce Commission readily went along. "We noted in the order approving the deal," observed an ICC official, "that they were making the big profit, but we couldn't say 'no' to people who wanted to buy the stock." The value of an initial $50 share had increased approximately 13-fold. If the largest shareholders had decided to liquidate, they could have recouped their $100,000 investments by selling only 150 of their original shares, leaving 1,850 shares, which were worth more than $1.2 million.[5]

Largely because of the deep mid-decade recession the common stock dropped in value. In early 1974 brokers in Chicago, Des Moines, and Milwaukee began to make a market at a price of approximately $5 a share for these after-the-split securities. Not long thereafter the stock traded over-the-counter on the NASDAQ exchange. During the first quarter of 1976 the price fluctuated between 4 1/8 and 5 3/4. By the second quarter of 1977 shares sold between 9 1/4 and 11 1/4 and continued in that range until they reached a high of 36 1/3 in 1981. An investment in North Western securities was a sound financial strategy.[6]

A substantial reduction in the size of the physical plant contributed to the generally positive financial picture of the North Western. Larry Provo, unlike Ben Heineman, energetically sought to eliminate unprofitable, low-density branch lines. "Approximately 40% of the North Western's mileage generates approximately 4% of the total revenues," he told reporters in June 1972.[7]

The railroad quickly compiled a "hit list" of unneeded trackage. "And believe me, these lines have long since passed any kind of economic justification for keeping them in service," Provo told grain dealers in May 1974. "They are an enormous drain on the railroad. Just to operate over these lines is a big cash drain. But the damage goes far beyond that. These lines waste freight cars and locomotives like nothing else can. And they waste precious and costly diesel fuel."[8]

The map of the North Western soon changed. During the Provo years the company retired nearly 1,800 miles of line. This "disinvestment" trend continued, even accelerated, under the subsequent James Wolfe administration. In 1981 the railroad junked a record 1,045 miles.[9]

A typical branch line abandonment initiated by the Provo regime was the Iroquois-Wren line. This 155.7-mile appendage linked Huron with Sioux City, a once busy route for agricultural traffic from Dakota to Iowa and Chicago. The North Western wished to retire nearly all this trackage, except for about a mile at Salem, South Dakota, where trains on the former Omaha Road between Mitchell and Sioux Falls could serve local customers.[10]

By the early 1970s the Iroquois-Wren branch had deteriorated badly. There had been seven derailments in 1972, for example, including a major mishap near Unityville, South Dakota, on May 13, 1972. More than 70 percent of the line was laid with 80-pound rail, with the remainder being 72-, 90-, and 100-pound steel. The dominant rail, manufactured between 1896 and 1910, had been installed shortly before World War I. Ties were often rotten and only about 175,000 of the 468,000 main line ties possessed any value. Ballast was also poor, "providing little, if any, bearing support for the track facility, nor does it provide drainage in the track zone area." Specifically, the ballast consisted of dirt, cinders, and gravel. Only the 48 steel bridges, 696 pile spans, and 298 culverts were judged to be in "fair" condition.[11]

A poor-quality branch line could be rehabilitated, but the North Western estimated that more than $1 million would be needed to permit speeds of 25 miles per hour. Traffic, both current and potential, hardly warranted such expenditures; the branch had lost about $400,000 in 1972 alone. "The potential for handling any significant amount of corn and other grains on the line does not exist," argued Maurice Reid, assistant chief engineer in administration and head of the Branch Line Committee. "Livestock feeding is prevalent in the area and there is a substantial amount of trucking [of grain] to river markets."[12]

The North Western began the abandonment process on January 2, 1973. The first hearings followed five months later in Sioux Falls. As in other cases company representatives were well prepared. They carefully reviewed physical conditions and financial matters and emphasized that through service between Huron and Sioux City would continue. The Tracy and Butterfield, Minnesota, route would permit greater speeds and equipment weight limits. Furthermore, the railroad encouraged the trucking of grain to stations on these arteries where it could be loaded into covered center-flow hoppers rather than random 40-foot boxcars and be moved efficiently in trains of 25 to 50 cars at multiple-car rates.[13]

The hearings did not lead to a speedy decision. Because of a ruling in a New York abandonment case that required an environmental impact statement, the administrative law judge abruptly halted the public process and "indefinitely" postponed the inquiry. The commission did not take up the matter until three years later in August and September 1976. Then after reviewing the environmental study, listening to the company's position, and considering the objections, the judge endorsed abandonment.[14]

Yet the battle to retire the money-losing Iroquois-Wren branch had not ended. The North Western encountered strong opposition from a grass-roots organization, Keep Our Railroad Running (KORR), an unincorporated association of on-line communities, merchants, and grain dealers. The Farmers Union, several state agencies, and various elected officials, including U.S. Senator George McGovern (D-SD), also backed KORR. In an appeal to the commission these opponents claimed that the trackage could become profitable "[because] the grain exports from the United States in the future years will result in a large number of carloads being shipped on the line." KORR and the state, moreover, charged the North Western with intentionally downgrading service so as to drive away customers. The railroad was viewed as wickedness incarnate. The ICC, however, rejected these arguments in a ruling on July 28, 1977, more than four and one-half years after the initial filing. Finally the company could annul its trains, remove salvageable materials, and sell real estate.[15]

The North Western continued to battle the regulatory maze as it pursued its abandonment program. Admittedly the process had become less burdensome following passage of the Transportation Act of 1958 and the Staggers Rail Act of 1980. While the latter partially deregulated the

An explanation for the poor condition of the Iroquis-Wren branch involves competition from truckers. A grain trunk crosses the railroad at Canistota, S.Dak. (M. S. Reid photograph, North Western/Union Pacific)

Most appendages needed upgrading by the early 1970s. The Carnarvon-Moville, Iowa, branch was no exception. The track east of Early, Iowa, necessitated slow speeds for the occasional way freights. (M. S. Reid photograph, North Western/Union Pacific)

industry, the bureaucracy still permitted protestors to air their opposition. Representatives from smaller communities, most of all, resisted abandonments, hoping to protect local businesses and attract new firms that wanted rail access.[16]

The Provo position on line retrenchment, however, received the backing of transportation specialists. "We know that we were right with our planning requests," noted Maurice Reid, "but experts told us what we already realized." Iowa State University and the Iowa Department of Transportation conducted a careful investigation in the mid-1970s and concluded: "If obsolete rail branch lines in Iowa were abandoned and the remaining viable lines were upgraded to permit heavier loads and multiple-car rates on grain, Iowa's economy and farmers would gain some $33,000,000 in annual income." The report argued that Hawkeye State communities located on dismantled trackage would be virtually unscathed. "There is comparatively little effect on communities when rail lines are abandoned. Population growth appears to be more influenced by town size, location and general economic conditions of the area than by availability of a railroad." The study added: "Essentially, there are only slight differences in population, retail sales, bank deposits and bank earnings of Iowa communities that have been abandoned in the past and those communities of similar size located on . . . [rail] lines."[17]

At the same time the North Western was diligently working to trim its unprofitable network of branch lines, it upgraded the major arteries, particularly the Omaha stem. This line assumed greater importance because of the expansion of freight interchanged with the Union Pacific. A harbinger of the future had taken place on May 20, 1960, when the Heineman regime expedited east-west traffic with a pair of trains between Chicago and Fremont, Nebraska, over the "Fremont Cut-off," via Blair, Nebraska. Interchange cars previously had been shunted between yards in Council Bluffs and Omaha. The revised operation saved time and distance (24 miles), making the North Western a more attractive connection for the Union Pacific.[18]

In 1974 officials of the North Western and Union Pacific pledged jointly to bolster the Chicago-Fremont line. A good relationship developed between Larry Provo and John Kenefick, the chief executive officer of the Union Pacific since 1970, in part because "Provo did not have Heineman's reputation in Omaha." And now the Union Pacific could avoid using less-desirable routes to Chicago, particularly those of the faltering Milwaukee Road and Rock Island. Their lines never equaled the North Western in quality of engineering, and by the mid-1970s "slow orders" had greatly reduced train speeds. Moreover, the Milwaukee Road and Rock Island "did not look like survivors." The Union Pacific earlier had found the Burlington to be its best connection for Chicago, but creation of Burlington Northern in 1970 altered the interchange picture. The UP liked having Fremont as the principal transfer rather than Council Bluffs because of labor costs and time considerations. The company also realized that the North Western possessed the best hump-yard facility in Chicago. Stronger ties between the North Western and Union Pacific at Fremont meant financial advantages for both roads, and the partnership pleased shippers. "It was not quite the same as single-line service," remarked Kenefick, "but it was the next best thing—what today is called elegantly, 'seamless service.'"[19]

The number of cars that moved along the Fremont Cutoff soared after employee ownership. Loads rose from nearly 170,000 in 1972 to about 500,000 within a decade. The North Western saw its share of interchange business from the Union Pacific Overland Route traffic climb from about 37 percent to nearly 90 percent.[20]

The North Western knew that it had much to do to upgrade the Chicago-Fremont line. Maintenance had been deferred, and approximately 50 miles between California Junction and West Denison, Iowa, had been reduced to a single track in 1964. Matters of economy prompted this regrettable action, namely, the desire to cut maintenance costs and generate funds from the sale of rail. On the positive side the Heineman administration had postponed single-tracking the Omaha line as far east as West Chicago, Illinois; financial and traffic improvements erased any cutback plans.[21]

Although the North Western reinvested earnings in its physical plant, the company lacked the wherewithal to renovate its principal arteries fully. In the early 1970s the firm acquired more than 40 miles of 136-pound steel rail for the busiest segments between Chicago and Nelson, Illinois, for example, but financial pressures forced the sale of this rail before it could be installed. "I nearly cried when we sold this rail to the Burlington Northern," recalled operating official James Zito. "We just couldn't afford to keep it." Fortunately federal funds and loan guarantees became available and the North Western effectively tapped them.[22]

During the early 1970s Congress grew concerned about the distressing state of the railroad industry, especially in the East. While the New York Central and Pennsylvania railroads became the 19,459-mile Penn Central Transportation Company on February 1, 1968, the highly touted consolidation failed within 28 months. A combination of limited premerger planning, poor management, truck competition, and other economic factors led to this largest business failure in American history. The Penn Central's fate was typical. The East was fast becoming a railroad graveyard: Central Railroad of New Jersey succumbed in 1967, Boston & Maine entered court protection in 1970, Lehigh Valley also fell in 1970, Reading entered bankruptcy in 1971, and Erie Lackawanna collapsed in 1972.[23]

A coalition of bankers, shippers, railroaders, and union members spent much of 1973 preparing rescue legislation. These activists told lawmakers that a national transport crisis would occur if Penn Central, most of all, shut down and liquidated. Their efforts succeeded; on December 20, 1973, Congress approved the Regional Rail Reorganization Act of 1973, shortened to the "3R Act." This multibillion dollar commitment largely ended the chaos in the East.[24]

Although the federal government laid the groundwork for creation of the quasi-public Consolidated Rail Corporation (Conrail) in April 1976 with the 3R measure, other carriers needed public assistance. The Rock Island and the Missouri-Kansas-Texas ("Katy"), two of the nation's most beleaguered roads, sought aid under Section 211 of the 3R Act, but only the Katy received financial support, mostly because it seemed to have a reasonable chance for survival. These requests led Congress to pass the Railroad Revitalization and Regulatory Reform Act ("4R Act"). This legislation, which became law in 1976, stabilized the industry, although the Rock Island failed and was later liquidated.[25]

Executives of the North Western watched the events in Washington. At first Provo distrusted government assistance; "he fretted about strings attached." But an associate in the law department convinced him that "4R money can't be passed up," and Provo directed the company to apply for funds under Title V. Specifically, the government offered financial aid through the purchase from "qualified" railroads by the secretary of transportation of $600 million of "redeemable preference shares," paper that held long terms of maturity and low rates of interest, and authorization of $1 billion in loan guarantees.[26]

In 1977 the Board of Directors of the North Western, a designated "qualified" carrier, issued more than $25 million of redeemable preference shares under terms of Section 505 of the 4R Act. This money underwrote installation of approximately 95 miles of heavy, continuous welded rail, new ties, and ballast on the Omaha line. The company also used these funds to rehabilitate part of the freight line between the Proviso Yard and Milwaukee. In the process of upgrading, the 136-pound welded rail replaced 112- and 115-pound jointed rail, much of which was welded into quarter-mile-long sections and installed on secondary and branch lines where it replaced mostly 90-pound rail. Reusable sections of this lighter rail, in turn, were spiked down in yards, replacing still lighter and older steel.[27]

Section 505 of the 4R Act generated even more money for capital improvements. In 1978 federal officials approved the issuance of $122.9 million in preference share financing. These funds permitted the completion of the 136-pound welded rail project and other betterments along the Omaha line. "By the early 1980s," James Zito reported, "we had the Chicago to Fremont line, especially the eastbound track, in excellent shape and that really pleased us, the UP and the shippers."[28]

The North Western also used loan guarantees that Section 511 of the 4R Act made possible. Initially about $16 million of these federally backed bank loans went for heavy repairs of 2,500 battered freight cars at the Clinton shops. A later guarantee of $20 million permitted refurbishing of an additional 2,600 bad-order cars. Not only did the railroad rehabilitate a large

By June 1969 the North Western had suspended service on the appendage between Tyler, Minn., and Astoria, S.Dak. Prairie grasses are reclaiming the right of way in the village of Arco, Minn. (M. S. Reid photograph, North Western/Union Pacific)

portion of its rolling stock, but it saved tens of millions of dollars on the cost of replacement equipment.[29]

The willingness of the federal government to assist the North Western delighted the company and annoyed competitors. Bureaucrats in Washington wished to honor the intent of Congress, and they did. The government was hardly taking a major risk with the North Western; the railroad possessed a decent record of earnings. Even though "Heineman left [the North Western] with no money to work with," the company posted a net income of $9,261,000 for its first partial year of operation. In 1973 and 1974 the net income stood at $18,095,000 and $14,400,000 respectively. After a setback in the recession year of 1975, which the company described as "the most severe economic downturn since the Great Depression of the 1930's," with the railroad losing $8,301,000, it came back strongly in 1976 with earnings of $8,248,000. And 1977 proved to be an even better year; net income reached $16,157,000.[30]

At the time the North Western was rationalizing and modernizing, the company experienced a change of leadership. Larry Provo, a heavy smoker, developed lung cancer and died on October 19, 1976, after an illness of only two months. "It is fair to say that in his relatively brief lifetime, Larry Provo accomplished more than most men could have given several multiples of those 49 years," said a resolution adopted by the Board of Directors. "It is certainly no exaggeration to state that without Larry Provo, there simply would not have been an employee-owned Chicago and North Western Transportation Company. He conceived the employee-owned company, played the major role in bringing about its reality and guided it through its first and most torturous years."[31]

The North Western did not have to face a managerial disruption. On September 1, 1976, six weeks before Provo died, the Board of Directors named James Wolfe president and chief operating officer. Provo became chairman and chief executive officer. The selection of Wolfe worked out well. Said an associate, "Jim Wolfe was an energizer and a modern thinker." Observed John Kenefick of the Union Pacific, "Fortunately, while many railroad presidents merely 'preside' over their railroads, Mr. Provo *ran* his—and so, later, did Mr. Wolfe." Others, while not questioning Wolfe's leadership abilities, considered him to be an outspoken, even an abrasive, chieftain.[32]

James Richard Wolfe, born in Hannibal, Missouri, on November 7, 1929, grew up in a railroad family. His paternal grandfather had worked as a fireman and engineer for the Wabash, and his father, James E. (Doc) Wolfe, had hired out with the Burlington in 1918, in time becoming a specialist in labor relations and later chairman of the National Railway Labor Conference.[33]

James Wolfe received a solid education and good preparation for a career at the North Western. He attended Georgetown University between 1947 and 1949 and graduated from Loyola University of Chicago in 1951. He entered the DePaul University School of Law in Chicago and received his degree in 1953. Wolfe then joined the Burlington and handled such matters as labor disputes, regulatory affairs, and personal injury claims. He interrupted his promising railroad career in 1955 to serve in the Judge Advocate General's Corps of the U.S. Army. Wolfe returned to the Burlington in 1958 but left a year later to be general counsel for the Southeastern Carriers' Conference. After four years he resigned to join the North Western as vice president for labor relations. Wolfe subsequently assumed responsibilities for corporate industrial engineering and in 1973 became vice president for operations, the post he held until his elevation to the presidency. Following Provo's death Wolfe received the title "President and Chief Executive Officer and Director."[34]

Considerable continuity existed between the Provo and Wolfe administrations. James Wolfe understood Larry Provo's objectives, and he had participated in the formulation of the principal goals. Moreover, the two executives shared a similar style of management.[35] Like Provo, Wolfe wanted to extricate the North Western from its money-losing Chicago-area commuter operations. While Heineman had touted the suburban trains, Provo and Wolfe had little enthusiasm for them. They believed that financing commuter transportation was a public responsibility; if the company continued the business, it should be through a purchase-of-service agreement with a governmental agency. After all, other railroads, most notably the Erie Lackawanna, had received such assistance for their commuter operations in the greater New York City area.[36]

The future looked promising for public intervention even before James Wolfe assumed his presidential responsibilities. On March 19, 1974, voters in the six-county Chicago region approved a referendum to create the Regional Transportation Authority (RTA). Wolfe, the consummate negotiator, helped to bring about a four-year, purchase-of-service agreement with the RTA. The arrangement, retroactive to July 1, 1975, called for RTA to pay the company $25,732,000 for the commuter service through June 30, 1979. Additionally, RTA agreed to purchase the company's fleet of suburban locomotives and coaches, which would be leased back to the road at a "nominal cost per year," and to spend $17 million for capital improvements and rehabilitation projects in the suburban territory. Not only did RTA's board chairman Milton Pikarsky present Wolfe with a check for $20,795,735.39 for the equipment on December 13, 1977, but the North Western also received an annual return of approximately 4 percent on its more than $50 million investment in suburban train service.[37]

With the favorable contract with the RTA the North Western no longer served as an independent operator of passenger trains. Earlier, the company had terminated its remaining noncommuter runs. By the time the quasi-public National Railroad Passenger Corporation (Amtrak) started up on May 1, 1971, the North Western provided only skeletal service. These few trains, with their distinctive bilevel equipment, connected Chicago and Green Bay (via Fond du Lac) and Chicago and Clinton. The seasonal service between Green Bay and Ashland had ended several months earlier. Amtrak decided not to run trains on any North Western routes, although it acquired some pieces of rolling stock.[38]

James Wolfe did more than contribute to a satisfactory solution of the nagging "passenger problem"; he effectively led the North Western to its greatest triumph during its twilight years, the Coal Line Project. "I can't think of a more significant improvement to the North Western than the Wyoming coal line," observed an industry consultant in 1988. "It probably turned around the railroad more than anything else."

A smiling James Wolfe poses in his Chicago office. He effectively led the North Western from shortly before the death of his predecessor, Larry Provo, in 1976, until his own passing twelve years later. (Cynthia Matthews photograph, North Western/Union Pacific)

In 1977 the North Western proudly called to the public's attention its financial comeback. Although financial troubles occurred in the mid-1980s, the company remained solvent. (Author's collection)

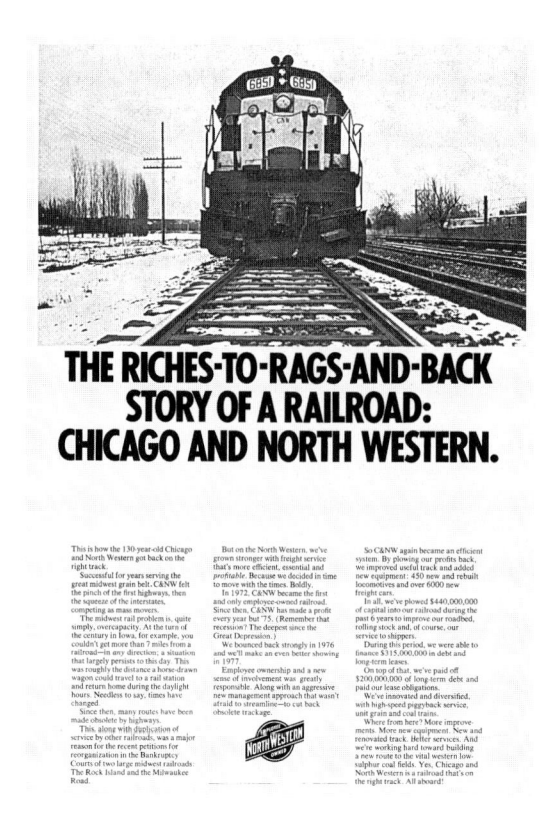

And he added: "Coal traffic freed the North Western from being so dependent on the grain business and bridge traffic." An analyst for Dean Witter Reynolds concluded a year later that the North Western realized a net profit of 35 cents for every $1 generated from this coal traffic. This income represented approximately two-thirds of the company's earnings.[39]

The Coal Line Project took more than a decade to develop. Even though the North Western recognized that the Powder River Basin in southeastern Wyoming contained billions of tons of subbituminous coal that were in thick seams close to the surface, these minerals seemed to have little value. The coal had relatively low heat content, and the fields were long distances from potential customers. But these handicaps were not important issues by the 1970s. In the previous decade a powerful political movement for environmental protection had begun. Science writer Rachel Carson had done much to set in motion this crusade with her warnings that pollution threatened all human and animal life. Congress responded with a series of landmark measures: the Clean Air Act (1970), the Clean Water Act (1971), and the Endangered Species Act (1973). Demand soon grew for Wyoming coal; its low ash and low sulphur content (about one-third to one-fifth of eastern deposits) would allow electric-power companies to comply with the clean-air legislation. Moreover, development of unit coal trains, which commonly consisted of scores of 100 or more 100-ton cars, made lengthy transport of coal more economical. These trains would also be more environmentally friendly than the transport alternative, a coal slurry pipeline.[40]

The North Western became interested in the Wyoming coal fields in 1973. The company sent Eugene Lewis, a civil engineer, to the Douglas area to develop traffic projections. The potential for coal-hauling revenues, Lewis told Provo, was "unbelievable." The railroad already had a presence in the area; the lightly used "Cowboy Line" between Norfolk, Nebraska, and Lander, Wyoming, was approximately 75 miles south of the principal deposits. But getting to them would be difficult. The company needed to enter the coal fields and to upgrade the Lander extension. At one early meeting about the Coal Line Project Provo asked an subordinate if a unit coal train could be operated between Douglas and Fremont. The answer came immediately: "Yes, sir—I think we might get one across. But I guarantee we'll never get two." The company faced rebuilding 519 miles of line that contained sharp curves, steep grades, flimsy trestles, few good ties, and "ancient" jointed rail.[41]

The North Western did more than simply discuss the coal project; in May 1973 the company sought ICC authority to construct 76 miles of track northward into the coal fields from the Lander line. In July the North Western suggested to the Burlington Northern (BN), which had asked the ICC seven months earlier for permission to build a 113-mile extension from near Gillette, Wyoming, on its Alliance-Billings route, to Orin, Wyoming, on its Casper line (Billings-Wendover route), that it consolidate their applications since each wished to penetrate what would be called "America's last railroad frontier." But in August the BN rejected the overture, arguing that the basin was "exclusively Burlington Northern territory." "[W]e took a dim view of the North Western effort to expand into an area already being served by BN," commented Robert W. Downing, a former BN executive, "and partly because we could not see how the North Western could finance even half of a line."[42]

The Burlington Northern failed to stop the North Western. In October the company petitioned the commission to consolidate its application with the BN's. The ICC, normally a proponent of rail competition, urged the carriers to create a *joint* project. At a December meeting held in Washington an agreement, at least in principle, was reached to build a 106-mile line together north from BN and North Western trackage near Douglas. The companies filed the necessary papers with the ICC in February 1974 and signed a formal document 15 months later. In the interim public hearings were held and engineering and environmental studies conducted.[43]

Although the commission approved the joint line in January 1976, snags developed. An appeal by environmental groups ensued. "[They] thought correctly that they could prevent mining if they could block [railroad] construction." Notwithstanding this roadblock, Burlington Northern wanted to proceed quickly with construction. "Delays were costing it money." The North Western also wished to build, but it could not obtain private financing for either its 50 percent share in the joint line or the Lander line upgrade. A recession was on, and banks snubbed the railroad. In June 1976 the companies signed a supplemental agreement whereby BN would push ahead with the joint project with the deadline for the North Western to pay its share set on November 30, 1977. When the North Western still lacked the money, the arrangement was extended until November 30, 1979. This happened not because the BN liked the North Western but because it liked the Union Pacific even less. That Omaha-based giant had told the ICC that if the North Western withdrew, it would gladly enter "as an alternative, competitive carrier for Power River Basin coal." Even though there was no love lost between rivals BN and Union Pacific, John Kenefick remembered that "this was really more of a bluff to help a friend than anything else."[44]

In need of a lender of last resort the North Western decided to take advantage of the provisions of the 4R Act. In 1977 the company discussed with federal officials the likelihood of loan guarantees. After receiving initial encouragement, the railroad began the paperwork. "As information was developed for the application,"

Though the massive headhouse of the Chicago passenger terminal became landfill in the late 1980s, the historic trainshed and track indicator boards remain in place. On August 16, 1989, the 2:40 P.M. train to Geneva waits on track No. 4. (John F. Humiston photograph)

To penetrate the Powder River Basin in the 1980s, the North Western opted for a connector and trackage rights arrangement with the Union Pacific rather than upgrading its trans-Nebraska "Cowboy Line." (Author's collection)

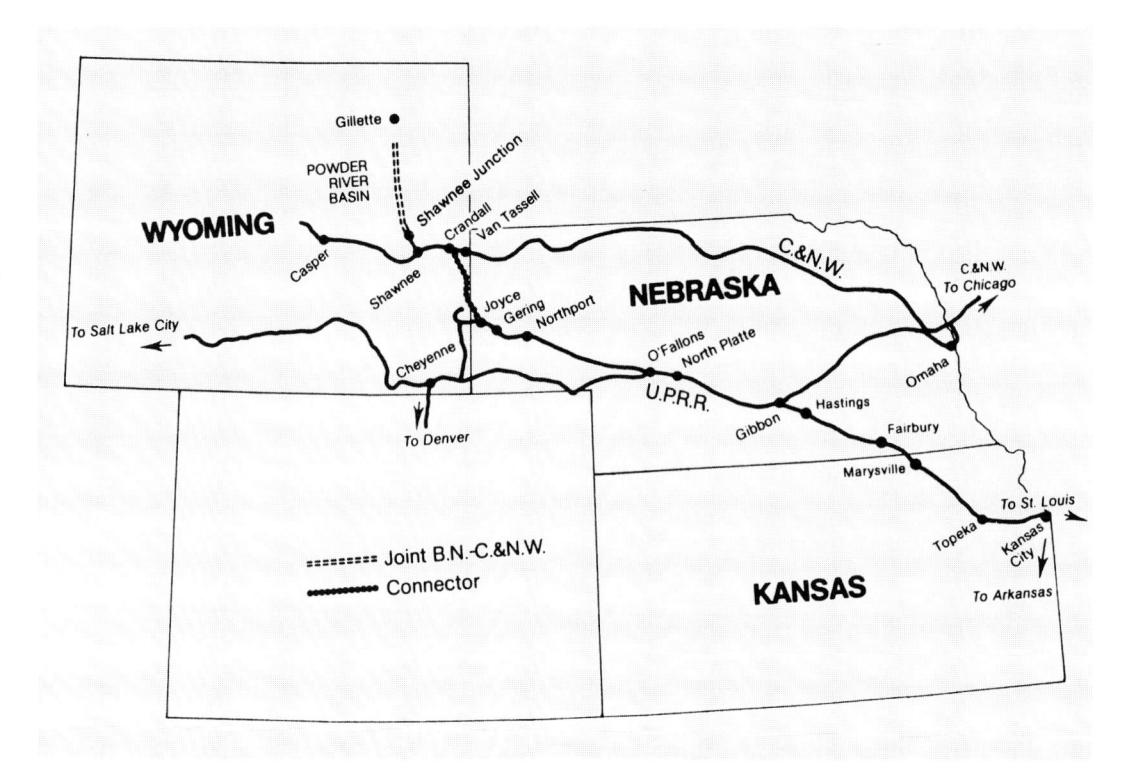

noted John M. Butler, senior vice president for finance and accounting, "it became increasingly evident that the cost of reconstructing over 500 miles of existing line to unit coal train standards would be prohibitive." The price tag exceeded $530 million. Apparently, the North Western sensed that Washington would not commit vast sums of money to a single project.[45]

While upgrading hundreds of miles of the Lander line across Nebraska might not be financially feasible, options existed. The Union Pacific, anxious for additional traffic destined to the south, southeast, and southwest, suggested to the North Western that it relinquish the Coal Line Project. Specifically, the Union Pacific offered the North Western a two-cent-a-ton royalty, or roughly $200 per loaded coal train, for a period of 20 years. In exchange the North Western would surrender both its rights to the joint line and its trackage in Wyoming.[46]

Although overall relations between the North Western and Union Pacific were cordial, the offer to exit the Powder River Basin displeased the Wolfe administration, but the overture did not discourage it. Some arrangement with the well-heeled Union Pacific offered the easiest way for the North Western to reap the coal bonanza. James Wolfe promoted discussions with the John Kenefick team about a mutually acceptable alternative. Fortunately for the North Western, "Wolfe developed a closer relationship with Kenefick than had Provo." A workable plan was reached, and the outlines were announced on December 4, 1978.[47]

The North Western–Union Pacific pact, which James Wolfe cheerfully told journalists would "permit the North Western to participate in significant movements of low sulphur Western coal at substantially less than half the estimated original costs," required a practical strategy. The joint North Western–Burlington Northern line would meet the Lander trackage at Shawnee, Wyoming, via a six-mile cutoff from the joint line at Shawnee Junction. Existing track of 45 miles would be completely rebuilt eastward to Crandall near the Nebraska border. The North Western would install a 56-mile connector southward to Joyce, Nebraska (South Morrill), a point on a grain-gathering branch of the Union Pacific that connected O'Fallons, 17 miles west of North Platte, with South Torrington, Wyoming. The UP had recently rebuilt 115 miles of this 200-mile appendage to handle coal trains from an interchange with the BN at Newport, Nebraska. Once unit trains reached the UP main line, they would travel to various connections, including the North Western at Council Bluffs and Fremont. "The Union Pacific's route from South Morrill is literally down hill all the way to Omaha," noted John

Kenefick, "a good route for unit trains."[48]

This new way to reach Wyoming coal, what the North Western called its "Yellow Plan," did not automatically mean that construction crews could start work. The Burlington Northern, "anxious to monopolize as long as it could the lucrative coal tonnage," continued to frustrate the North Western. Complaining to the ICC about the North Western's failure to pay its share of the completed project, the BN insisted that the North Western acted only as a surrogate for the Union Pacific. But the North Western received an important assist from the commission in late 1979. That body ruled that, although the North Western was unable to meet the contractual deadline of November 30, 1979, BN could not unilaterally deny the North Western the right to operate over the trackage. Earlier, after the North Western learned that the Federal Railroad Administration could not process the loan-guarantee application by November 30, largely because of environmental procedural requirements, it asked the ICC for a postponement. While the commission declined the request, it indicated that an extension was unnecessary because when it backed the application, it endorsed a *joint* line of railroad. The ICC stated that the terms of a private agreement between the North Western and the BN had no impact since it had never reviewed the matter. Thus the BN could not exclude the North Western. Later, on July 24, 1981, the ICC gave its final approval to the Coal Line Project.[49]

The Burlington Northern, living up to its "Big Nasty" epithet, remained a thorn in the side of the North Western. Wrangling continued over the price and other terms of the 93.2-mile joint line. The commission, which remained deeply involved, on October 22, 1982, set $76.2 million as the North Western's share; BN demanded $95.5 million. The ICC told the North Western that it had to demonstrate to BN by November 5 that it could tender the money, and it did so. But on November 8, BN rejected the offer and petitioned the Federal Court of Appeals in Washington to overturn the ICC decision. Several weeks later the North Western asked the court to expedite the proceedings. Both the ICC and Department of Justice joined in the motion, which coal producers, utilities, and the state of Texas also endorsed. These parties felt that rate competition, which the Staggers Rail Act allowed, would be an impossibility if the North Western were excluded from the basin. On November 14 the appeals court granted the North Western request, and oral arguments took place on March 2, 1983. The efforts by BN to receive more than $76.2 million failed when the court ruled in favor of the North Western on March 29. A wholly owned subsidiary of the North Western, Western Railroad Properties, Inc. (WRPI or "Werpy" for short), then formally purchased half interest in the coal line for the lesser amount.[50]

The financing for the Coal Line Project finally fell into place. John Kenefick explained that "the Union Pacific, which had nothing else if not money, arranged the financing for the whole thing." The North Western withdrew its application for federal loan guarantees and began to work with a group of banks, led by Manufacturers Hanover Trust Company, receiving in December 1981 a commitment that would supplement the funds it and the UP agreed to invest. "While there were a few strings tied to the bank's [*sic*] commitment," observed Keith Feurer, a Coal Line Project officer, "we basically had our money." By the end of 1983, $387.2 million was available; the company no longer faced a crisis as this was ample funding. The final cost was only about $300 million, partially due to "a lot of good contractors looking for work" because of the recession.[51]

Other problems were also solved. The North Western ultimately gained the necessary endorsements from various state and federal government units, including environmental agencies. And the company took title to the parcels of real estate, a triumph worth celebrating. Since early 1979 the railroad had sparred with the WyoBraska Landowners' Association (WLA), an irritating group of farmers and ranchers whose sole purpose was to block the new line construction. While Burlington Northern did not use the WLA as a stalking horse, the group helped the railroad by delaying regulatory approval.[52]

Construction work at last began. Following the official ground-breaking ceremony on June 27, 1983, crews tackled both the "Rehabilitated Line" and "Connector Line" projects. More than 150 workers, operating dozens of pieces of

Construction of the Connector Line between the reconstructed North Western track and the Union Pacific required the bridging of the North Platte River about five miles east of the Nebraska-Wyoming border. On a chilly January day in 1984 two Union Pacific engineers observe the progress. (North Western/Union Pacific)

heavy equipment, started their labors at four locations in Nebraska and Wyoming. The Neosho Construction Company, the prime contractor, launched various projects, from building highway overpasses to bulldozing the roadbed in advance of tracklaying gangs. The work was state of the art: 136-pound continuous welded rail and a geofabric that covered soft spots on the right-of-way. Centralized traffic control was later installed. After 14 months of frenzied building, the first unit coal train, 110 cars pulled by a North Western SD-40 and two Union Pacific C-30 locomotives, moved over the line on August 15–16, 1984. Its 11,000-ton cargo of black diamonds was headed from the North Antelope Mine to the Arkansas Power & Light Company plant at Newark, Arkansas.[53]

Not only did the coal business rapidly expand with long-term contracts with various electric utilities, but the North Western also, through WRPI, strengthened its position in the basin. Since the company lacked authority to serve the southern part of the Burlington Northern's own line, coal producers expressed their desire for competition. One firm, the Sun Company, built a 1.5-mile extension from its Cordero Mine to Coal Creek Junction, the northern most point of WRPI service. The lack of two-railroad access allowed the North Western to win approval from the ICC to construct track from Coal Creek Junction to East Caballo Junction, a distance of about 11 miles, to reach four mines on the line that BN served exclusively. WRPI surveyed its own route and was about to start construction when BN agreed to sell half-ownership to East Caballo Junction for $27 million. The formal sale took place on December 15, 1986."⁵⁴

Entry by the North Western into "exclusive" Burlington Northern territory rightly angered the St. Paul–based giant. "Provo assured us that the North Western would not ask for extension of the joint territory to the north in order to serve mines off the BN's line," Robert Downing of the BN remembered. "One of the things that provoked BN later was the disregard of that commitment by the North Western after Larry Provo's death."⁵⁵

The presence of the North Western in the Powder River Basin not only led to conflict with Burlington Northern, it resulted in a clash with a proposed coal slurry venture, Energy Transmission Systems, Inc. (ETSI). Before the North Western entered the coal picture, BN had become interested in moving coal by pipeline. Later ETSI, allied with electric power interests in Texas, asked BN to join as a partner, but BN refused. "We declined their offer because we knew enough about the economics of rail vs pipe line that the unit coal train was actually more economical," recalled Downing. "For financing very little equity was to be provided by ETSI and it was probable that the debt would have to be guaranteed by BN and the utility consumers since ETSI itself did not have much financial strength." ETSI got nowhere and in the mid-1980s sued several railroads for conspiring to block construction of the slurry for "anti-competitive" reasons. Both the North Western and BN were defendants, and later each railroad settled out of court for "substantial" amounts, although the North Western paid far less than BN. "In taking dispositions the ETSI lawyers seemed to imply that somehow the C&NW and BN were in cahoots by building the line jointly but this was not only not true," observed Downing, "but I do not believe that they ever tried to make the claim seriously. The settlement [was] . . . based on other factors perhaps not the least of which was that it would have been tried before a jury in Texas where unreasonable verdicts in damage cases were not uncommon."⁵⁶

Just as the Coal Line Project altered the system map, the North Western made a major acquisition in the early 1980s, the Twin Cities–Kansas City line and several grain-gathering branches of the bankrupt Chicago, Rock Island & Pacific Railroad (the Rock). The North Western purchased 718 miles of the Rock for $93 million. The principal addition, what the North Western called the "Spine Line," provided the best rail link between the Twin Cities and Kansas City. The existing North Western route, cobbled together from segments of the former Minneapolis & St. Louis and Chicago Great Western, was 36 miles longer and generally poorly engineered. "This was a hill and dale route and hardly competitive to the Rock Island's line."⁵⁷

Other railroads recognized the merits of the Spine Line. The Burlington Northern, in particular, coveted the property; it possessed an even circuitous route between Kansas City and the Twin Cities. The Soo Line also decided that the Spine Line could serve its needs.⁵⁸

Although the North Western gained strength during the 1970s and early 1980s, the condition of the rival Rock Island worsened to the point of collapse. The crisis at the Rock made headlines on March 17, 1975, when the Federal District Court in Chicago granted the company protection from its creditors. The railroad reportedly had just $200 in its cash drawer. The Rock Island Line was hardly the "Mighty Good Road" of musical verse.⁵⁹

As a new management team headed by John W. Ingram tried to keep the Rock Island alive, conditions deteriorated in August 1979. Two unions, the Brotherhood of Railway and Airline Clerks and the United Transportation Union,

Locomotive No. 6935 breaks through a banner on the Nebraska-Wyoming border marking the arrival of the first coal train on the North Western from the Powder River Basin. (North Western/ Union Pacific)

walked out over a wage dispute. A month later President Jimmy Carter declared an emergency and ordered the strikers to return to work for 60 days. Angry employees ignored the president and made it clear that unless they received their money, "those trains don't roll." At the insistence of the transportation secretary the ICC ordered the Kansas City Terminal Railway, a switching company based in Kansas City, Missouri, and owned by a dozen carriers, to operate the Rock and to pay the disputed wages with federal funds.[60]

The crisis deepened. Although the strikers returned to work, the accounting firm of Peat, Marwick, Mitchell & Company told bankruptcy judge Frank McGarr in January 1980, that the "road was beyond salvage." Later that month McGarr ordered the railroad liquidated. The process started in earnest after March 1980 when court-appointed trustee William Gibbons, with ICC approval, leased most of the lines to other railroads, including the North Western. Gibbons could then decide which parts of the Rock should be sold and which should be junked.[61]

Beginning on April 1, 1980, the North Western took over about 800 miles of the Rock, including the Spine Line and branches, mostly in Iowa. The North Western paid approximately $5 million annually ($407,500 per month) for usage rights. This was the first such agreement between the trustee and any of the railroads that would operate former Rock Island trackage.[62]

Absorbing pieces of the Rock caused problems. The North Western needed to build physical connections to establish efficient patterns of operation and to hire more personnel. The trackage itself was in generally poor condition with ever present slow orders. To heighten the challenges, 1980 turned out to be the biggest grain-hauling year on record for the railroads. In order to manage this burgeoning traffic, mostly corn and soybeans, the company set up a special command post in Mason City, Iowa, on the Spine Line, to control trains in its expanded grain territory.[63]

While the Rock Island trackage presented some drawbacks, the North Western decided that it should buy most of it. An upgraded Spine Line would provide the best avenue between the Twin Cities and Kansas City and a competitive

While the once ubiquitous caboose had mostly disappeared by the mid-1990s, these pieces of rolling stock could still be found systemwide in the early 1980s. "Waycar" No. 1095, painted in a bright, high visibility shade officially known as "Sunburst Yellow" or popularly as "Zito yellow," stands in Union, Ill., on November 8, 1981, clearly displaying the famed "safety first" slogan. (John F. Humiston photograph)

route from the upper Mississippi River valley and northern Great Plains to Louisiana and Texas ports. Since the export grain business was strong and there was the potential for more coal, chemical, and lumber traffic, the company wanted to improve its capacity to profit from it. As the North Western later demonstrated, the former Great Western main line between Marshalltown, Iowa, and St. Joseph, Missouri, was readily expendable; virtually no local traffic existed south of Des Moines.[64]

The grain-gathering branches were another attractive feature. Even though the North Western was pruning its own network of feeders, the Rock Island possessed some with major shippers on line. The Rock had pioneered the concept of unit grain trains, and this had spurred the development of large elevators on its lines, including those in the Iowa communities of Royal, Superior, and West Bend. The prospects of unit grain train business from these locations became more attractive with the Staggers Act. The company could negotiate rates with shippers and could offer rebates for guaranteed traffic volumes. Partial federal deregulation thus gave the North Western and other carriers more flexibility in their operations and greater confidence in their future.[65]

Although the North Western did not publicly admit this dimension during its quest for the Rock, the company wished to "lock-up" its "home territory." While praising competition in the Powder River Coal Basin, the North Western sought to protect the financial benefits that came from the demise of its old adversary in the granger country.[66]

Leasing Rock Island trackage turned out to be far easier than gaining ownership. Unfortunately for the North Western, a bidding war erupted with the Soo Line Railroad. In the fall of 1982 the Soo contacted William Gibbons about acquiring the Spine Line and several branches. This grain and lumber hauler wished to reach Kansas City and generally expand "into a size that could better balance the main competition in its service region." Recent acquisition of the Minneapolis, Northfield & Southern by the Soo allowed for convenient physical ties between it and the Spine Line. While some observers thought that the Canadian Pacific, which owned more than half of the Soo Line, was behind the expansion talk, the reality was quite the opposite. "Our problem," commented a Soo Line executive, "was getting CP interested in what we wanted to do."[67]

Although the North Western anticipated a struggle for a piece of the Rock, a few weeks after its contact with Gibbons the Soo Line apparently had second thoughts. The prospects for a sale to the North Western brightened. On February 24, 1983, Gibbons and the company signed a purchase agreement; the price was $76.35 million.[68]

The announcement of the sale alarmed the Iowa Department of Transportation (IDOT). This state agency, worried about the possible expansion of the largest local grain hauler, went on the offensive. The *Des Moines Register*, with its statewide circulation, agreed to cooperate. The paper published a series of news features and editorials that criticized the North Western–Rock Island deal. Such headlines as "DOT officials seek to block Iowa rail sale," "Rail purchase despicable act," "Public vs. private good," and "Saving rail competition" spread the anti–North Western message. IDOT lobbied for state aid to the Soo Line so that it could successfully bid against the North Western.[69]

The actions of the Iowa Department of Transportation incensed the North Western. A livid James Wolfe sent Iowa Governor Terry Branstad, members of the Iowa congressional delegation, and officials of state government a brisk letter, dated March 11, 1983:

> I have just been advised that the Iowa Railroad Finance Authority has agreed to accept for consideration a request by the Soo Line Railroad, a company controlled by Canadian interests, for public financing in the amount of $21 million to enable the Soo to bid competitively for the lines of railroad now owned by the Rock Island Railroad, lines which the Chicago and North Western has just signed a contract to buy. . . .
>
> The North Western is utterly appalled at the possibility of such discriminatory State governmental action. We have made an arms-length private agreement for the property after years of different negotiations and we will pay for it ourselves without any governmental financial assistance.
>
> Considering that we have operated these same railroad lines for almost three years on a lease basis at our expense under extremely difficult economic circumstances . . . and in the process served

the at times desperate shipping needs of the State and its people, it would be considered by us, Iowa's major railroad, as an extremely unfriendly act by State government if such an unfair request by foreign interests is favorably received. In this respect, two facts are extremely important. First, North Western has spent over $10 million on these Rock Island lines just to make them usable for Iowa commerce in the past three years. There were no other volunteers for this project at a time when Iowa desperately needed a railroad to pick up the Rock Island pieces. Secondly, North Western is Iowa's largest railroad, serving most of its major cities, some exclusively, and large sections of agricultural territory. If Chicago and North Western would lose, major portions of your state will also lose.[70]

Even though the Iowa Department of Transportation backed off, the Soo Line again had its eyes on the Rock Island prize. One week before the March 15 bankruptcy court hearing to consider the North Western bid, the Soo offered $81 million for most of the same trackage. The North Western countered with a $85.35 million bid. When the Soo Line learned of the response, it asked Judge McGarr for a 30-day delay. The judge granted only three days; he sided with attorneys for the major bond holders who fretted that postponement of a hearing on the liquidation, scheduled for March 28, might cost them dearly. Near the deadline, on March 11, the Soo gave Gibbons a bid of $88.5 million. Although delighted, the trustee gladly welcomed a counteroffer. The North Western responded with a $93 million bid. The Soo Line refused to raise the ante, arguing that its offer was superior. The company wanted only 673 miles of route, and its proposal amounted to more money per mile. Since representatives for the debtors and Gibbons liked the North Western proposal, the judge concurred. When the ICC endorsed the agreement on June 20, 1983, the drama ended. The ICC, however, noted that joint ownership and operation "might have been more in the public interest and benefit both carriers," but this statement was made only "in passing."[71]

While the bidding had raised the cost of the Rock Island properties, the North Western promptly took possession of valuable pieces of trackage through a wholly owned subsidiary, Midwestern Railroad Properties, Inc. "We're going to become a north-south as well as an east-west railroad," crowed James Wolfe. The road quickly moved to upgrade the additions, "to put the railroad up out of the mud," most of all the Spine Line. A combination of federal funds received under the 4R Act and proceeds from a $75 million bond offering permitted a major rehabilitation of the Spine Line in 1984. Following the betterments trains could move over the 430-mile artery at 40 miles per hour; later improvements allowed for faster speeds. The company installed a massive connection at Nevada, Iowa, where the Spine line crossed the Omaha stem, to facilitate the interchange of traffic to Chicago and the West.[72]

James Wolfe and his colleagues believed that the North Western was on the verge of making a "grand slam": the Coal Line Project, Spine Line, and then the purchase of the Milwaukee Road. While the North Western did not seek more of the Rock Island, the opportunity existed for the North Western to become the dominant carrier in the Upper Midwest, bringing Ben Heineman's dream to fruition.[73]

Like the Rock Island, the Milwaukee Road—officially the Chicago, Milwaukee, St. Paul & Pacific—floundered during the 1970s. The company filed for bankruptcy in December 1977 after suffering three years of heavy losses. Court protection was needed, according to parent Chicago Milwaukee Corporation (CMC), because the railroad operated "too many miles of unproductive track while saddled with regulatory burdens, outmoded labor requirements and heavy taxes." But unlike the Rock the Milwaukee Road avoided liquidation. Rather, the company scaled back its system from nearly 10,000 miles to slightly more than 3,000 miles. The most dramatic reduction was its Pacific Coast Extension, abandoned in 1980; the Milwaukee at first sent trains only as far west as Miles City, Montana, and then just to Ortonville, Minnesota.[74]

By the early 1980s the Milwaukee Road, nicknamed by some as "Milwaukee Lite," consisted of three principal routes: Chicago-Kansas City, Chicago-Louisville, and Chicago-Milwaukee-Twin Cities-Duluth. This core road, or "Milwaukee II," showed signs of economic viability.

Richard Ogilvie, the court-appointed trustee and former governor of Illinois, and Worthington (Worth) Smith, the company president, tried to revitalize the railroad; better rolling stock, track structure, and service characterized the slimmed-down carrier. The company seemingly possessed the potential to become a profitable regional operation and an attractive candidate for sale to another road.[75]

As Milwaukee II took shape, the Grand Trunk Corporation (GTC), the holding company for the American rail properties of the Canadian National (Central Vermont; Duluth, Winnipeg & Pacific; and Grand Trunk Western), expressed keen interest in this changing Chicago-based railroad. Passed over by the rail mergers of the previous decade, shut out from former gateways by the much larger systems around it, and heavily dependent on the cyclical automotive industry, the Grand Trunk Western, the core component of GTC, sorely needed to grow. It was "expand or die!" GTC officials and trustee Ogilvie announced on October 21, 1981, that they had initiated "discussion concerning the possible integration of the Milwaukee Road into the GTC system of railroads."[76]

Creation of a 5,000-mile carrier encircling much of the American side of the Great Lakes offered opportunities to the Grand Trunk Corporation. It would receive longer hauls, access to strategic gateways, most notably Kansas City, and a better mix of traffic. Furthermore, Milwaukee II would provide a direct connection between the Duluth, Winnipeg & Pacific and the Grand Trunk Western as it had trackage rights over the Burlington Northern (which came from the Northern Pacific) between Duluth and the Twin Cities.[77]

Grand Trunk Corporation and Milwaukee II appeared to be headed toward union. In late May 1982 the parties signed a letter of intent that provided for transfer of stock ownership to GTC. The deal involved GTC assuming approximately $250 million of Milwaukee debt and obligations, and allowed Chicago Milwaukee Corporation to retain tax credits and a valuable subsidiary, the Milwaukee Land Company. In June the two railroads backed a "Voluntary Coordination Agreement" (VCA) that invigorated interchange traffic. "We have established run-through trains, run-through locomotive power, expedited interchanges, pre-blocking arrangements and joint routes, rates and contracts, all stemming from the VCA," reported the GTC. "Through these activities we expect to attract in excess of 40,000 new carloads to the MILW during 1983."[78]

The North Western followed closely the demise of the Milwaukee Road. James Wolfe and his colleagues, however, shed few tears. The railroad map of the Midwest remained covered with rail lines, and Wolfe fervently believed that more restructuring and abandonments were necessary. "No single carrier has ever had the kind of density on its lines alone that would justify the enormous costs involved in a major upgrading of its roadbed as well as its fleet of grain-hauling cars and locomotives," Wolfe told a business group in January 1980. "It's the direct result of too many railroad corporations with too much track attempting to serve a market than cannot, indeed, never has or ever will in its present configuration, support such a proliferation of corporate entities and fixed plant."[79]

The North Western wanted to play a role in the future of the Milwaukee II. Even before Grand Trunk Corporation showed interest, the North Western approached the first trustee, Stanley Hillman (who preceded Richard Ogilvie), about some trackage that would not likely become part of the restructured property. Specifically, Wolfe wanted several hundred miles of agricultural feeders, most of all the 250-mile line across northern Iowa from Sheldon to Marquette "with the ability to reach the Mississippi River grain barge transloading facility." He also sought the automobile unloading dock in Council Bluffs and the joint Milwaukee Road–Kansas City Southern yard in Kansas City, Missouri. The North Western obtained little on its wish list, however. In 1981 the company acquired only two Milwaukee line segments of approximately 65 miles in northwestern and central Iowa.[80]

While Grand Trunk Corporation moved to acquire Milwaukee II, the North Western watched carefully and then became an official suitor on July 27, 1983. The explanation for the interest and a subsequent bidding battle involved several factors. The North Western fervently wanted to "save" granger railroading, "to end the era of railroad financial instability in the midwest." Since Milwaukee II contributed to the "badly overbuilt" trackage of the region, the North Western planned to unite the properties and in the process abandon approximately 1,000 miles of excess trackage. But other features of Milwaukee II appealed to the North Western. The company wanted the speedway between Milwaukee and the Twin Cities and access to the Louisville gateway. The truncated road also possessed several good grain-gathering branches. Indeed, Milwaukee II had even kept the trackage across northern Iowa that James Wolfe had eyed a few years earlier.[81]

Initially the quest for Milwaukee II involved comparatively low stakes. The Grand Trunk Corporation offered to assume the $250 million of Milwaukee debt and other obligations. But the North Western could provide something more: "We would assume all liabilities but leave the seller corporation in the hands of its shareholders, meaning that they would receive up to a $180 million tax shelter."[82]

The North Western did more than mimic the GTC position; it launched a vigorous public relations campaign to promote its case. It even invoked patriotism as an argument for acceptance. As with its successful pursuit of the Spine Line, the company repeatedly mentioned the "Canadian threat." This time it was the direct connection with Ottawa through Canada's nationalized railroad, the Canadian National; previously the target had been the privately held Canadian Pacific with its substantial position in the Soo Line.[83]

Until fall 1983 the North Western seemed to be in a good position, but on November 9 Richard Ogilvie jolted the company with an announcement that its proposal "does not currently satisfy reorganization requirements." The trustee preferred an end-to-end merger; he liked the performance of Grand Trunk Corporation–Milwaukee traffic arrangement and believed that labor would suffer under North Western control. Ogilvie labeled the offer as "more elimination than reorganization." Yet he later suggested that the North Western might participate. "The implication is put up some more dough," remarked a North Western official. Still, the ICC and the bankruptcy court needed to review the respective plans.[84]

Other events also worried the North Western. The Chicago Milwaukee Corporation, which owned 96 percent of the common stock of Milwaukee II, changed its thinking during the fall; rather than backing liquidation it promoted a stand-alone railroad. About the same time rumors spread that the Soo Line would seek the Milwaukee, too. "The Soo officials assure me," remarked Glenn Cameron, a railroad analyst with Lehman Brothers, "that they are not going to sit back and let their traffic be eroded by a Milwaukee Road merger with either the C&NW or Grand Trunk."[85]

The Soo Line formally revealed its intentions on January 19, 1984. The company entered the fray with an offer to the bankruptcy court of $40 million in cash and a commitment to assume "all or most" of the Milwaukee Road debt. The public pronouncement was unequivocal: "A Soo Line-Milwaukee Road combination would strengthen competition for rail traffic in the central United States." Like the Grand Trunk Corporation and other middle-sized carriers, the Soo felt threatened by recent mergers and acquisitions and concluded that it could not survive unless it grew larger. But unlike GTC, the company enjoyed excellent credit and strong cash reserves.[86]

The Soo Line apparently possessed the edge. Not only did it offer cash, but also it could rightly claim a "public-interest" position. Union of the 4,400-mile Soo and the 3,100-mile Milwaukee would be in many ways end to end with connecting points in Illinois, Minnesota, and Wisconsin. The proposal, much as the one made by Grand Trunk Corporation, garnered considerable grass-roots support. The potential involvement by the North Western, however, was commonly viewed as not ensuring long-term rail service to Milwaukee II customers.[87]

The bidding war intensified in late February 1984. The North Western proposed $60 million in cash and agreed to drop its plans to trim Milwaukee II. The North Western also listed four conditions that it could accept: the Soo Line could continue to operate over Milwaukee II through Milwaukee; the Soo could have access to Kansas City by way of Milwaukee II trackage; the Green Bay & Western, a Wisconsin shortline, could enter Milwaukee on Milwaukee II; and joint rates would be maintained with Burlington Northern for coal traffic to an electric power plant near Muscatine, Iowa.[88]

While GTC still wanted Milwaukee II, it refrained from making a cash offer. It did modify its stance to allow Milwaukee shareholders to keep the tax credits, which had an estimated value of $250 to $275 million. The GTC keyed its position to the argument of preservation of competition, contending that its offer was the only one that would maintain Milwaukee II as a vital force in the region.[89]

By the time the field of battle moved to the ICC in Washington in July, the North Western and Soo Line had sweetened the pot. In early April the North Western raised its bid from $60 million to more than $170 million in cash, cash equivalents, and guaranteed stock, and the Soo boosted the cash portion of its bid from $40 million to $168.5 million.[90]

The chances for a GTC victory diminished immediately. Its remaining hope was that the commission would dismiss the rival applications, but the body refused. Yet the ICC admitted that the voluntary coordination agreement between GTC and Milwaukee II "is probably the most important reason for the Commission having a number of suitors for the Milwaukee before it today." The statement, of course, provided small comfort to GTC.[91]

The fight between the North Western and the Soo Line continued. The North Western by this time showed considerable optimism, even preparing to unite physically with Milwaukee II. The company purchased 13 miles of the abandoned Rock Island "Golden State" line in southern Iowa (Allerton-Seymour) to forge a better Chicago to Kansas City route. Yet events at the commission suggested that the North Western had lost. On July 26 the ICC approved the Soo bid, but two of the four commissioners said that they would not grant final approval unless the railroad agreed to renegotiate the traffic interchange agreement between Milwaukee II and Grand Trunk Corporation. But that condition became moot in early September when GTC scrapped the arrangement in favor of a potentially more profitable alliance with Burlington Northern. Still the ICC left the door ajar for the North Western. The commission, which split on the North Western offer, returned the bid without action to the bankruptcy judge. Finally, on September 10 the ICC gave "unqualified" support to the Soo position.[92]

The North Western remained in the picture, however. On October 10, 1984, the deadline set by the court, the company improved its previous offer by $210,850,000. "The Soo Line did not increase its bid for acquisition of the assets of the Milwaukee Road," observed a more self-assured James Wolfe. "We are confident that despite challenges by the Soo and others, our modified proposal will be approved."[93]

The maneuvering persisted when the court reopened the bidding on October 29. Judge Thomas R. McMillen surprised trustee Richard Ogilvie by denying his recommendation that the North Western offer be sent to the commission with temporary approval. Instead, McMillen believed that the Soo should have an opportunity to raise its offer, while saying that he considered the bid made by the North Western to be final.[94]

Even though the Soo Line did not meet the North Western dollar for dollar, the Minneapolis-based company held its own during regulatory deliberations in December. The commissioners, by a four to three vote, backed the Soo proposal, worth an estimated $570 million. But the ICC also approved the North Western package, valued at $785,650,000, by a five to two tally. The ICC returned both proposals to the bankruptcy court.[95]

Openly optimistic, the North Western received the stunning news on February 4, 1985, that Judge Thomas McMillen preferred the Soo. "Sitting here today, if I would make a decision, I would rule in favor of the Soo Line." McMillen worried about the loss of competition and jobs; he thought that the Soo could better protect the public interest.[96]

James Wolfe and his colleagues were disappointed, but the decision infuriated others, including Richard Ogilvie and investors in the Milwaukee. They would receive about 30 percent less than what the North Western offered. Wolfe withdrew his bid shortly before the judge made his official pronouncement and decided against an appeal. "[A] protracted legal struggle would prevent the company from cultivating other growth opportunities by limiting financial flexibility," Wolfe

Branch lines, albeit fewer in number, continued to feed the North Western in the 1980s. On December 20, 1980, train No. 1026 East approaches Olson Road in Union, Ill., on the historic Galena & Chicago Union trackage. (John F. Humiston photograph)

told shareholders. "Also, lengthy periods of uncertainty simply aren't good for anyone." Perhaps the North Western president found some comfort in a note from John Riley, head of the Federal Railroad Administration: "We share your disappointment on the Milwaukee, but there are still a lot of worlds out there to conquer. I know we'll hear from you guys again!"[97]

The failure of the North Western to bring the Milwaukee Road into its orbit was a blessing of sorts. Although the North Western spent $3.8 million on acquisition expenses, the price it offered was excessive and could have damaged future earnings. "The wisdom of this fast exit from an overly high bid," concludes Michael Blaszek, a Chicago attorney and student of the North Western, "was demonstrated over the next four years as Soo struggled to make its Milwaukee acquisition pay." Still, a North Western official a few years after the Soo victory continued to believe that if the North Western controlled the Milwaukee, "We would have been in a wonderful position [in the Midwest]."[98]

James Wolfe and the North Western looked to the future. "The race will be won by those carriers who have a commitment to superior service, take a realistic look at their cost structure, and attempt to unleash the creative and entrepreneurial energy of their people," wrote Wolfe in 1985. This would be the course the North Western followed during its last decade.[99]

The North Western restructured itself in the aftermath of the Milwaukee defeat. Stockholders at the annual meeting on June 21, 1985, approved a board proposal for creation of a holding company, CNW Corporation (CNW Corp), which became the vehicle for diversification. "We need producing assets to balance our cylicality," Wolfe told shareholders. "We are a short-haul railroad and our densities are still among the lowest in the country. We need to look for ways to solve the structural deficiencies."[100]

After 1982 the North Western studied and even pursued several possible end-to-end rail mergers. The company showed particular interest in the Illinois Central Gulf, which would have provided direct access to the Gulf of Mexico and increased the average line-haul. But as James Wolfe said in 1988, "The other railroads either refused our proposal or demanded uneconomic terms."[101]

Even with access to credit as a result of the failed bid for the Milwaukee, CNW Corp made only a single acquisition. In May 1986 it purchased Douglas Dynamics, Inc., a manufacturer of snowplows and hydraulic log splitters, for $53.7 million. While the manufacturing subsidiary was profitable, CNW Corp sold it to Park-Kenilworth Industries in June 1988 for $100 million. CNW Corp seized the chance "to take the profit on it now" in order to retire high-interest bonds. At the time of the sale Wolfe still embraced diversification. "The factors which motivated our decision to diversity—the cyclical nature of the railroad business and C&NW's ability to shelter $510 million in taxable income—remain. We will continue to look for other diversification opportunities."[102]

With exception of Douglas Dynamics and a foray into the intermodal brokerage business with 400 Freight Services in 1985, the North Western followed the old Marvin Hughitt adage of "stick to our knitting." Ever since the transportation company emerged, various efforts had been made to improve freight operations. The "Falcon" intermodal service (trailer-on-flatcar or TOFC and container-on-flatcar or COFC) was introduced in spring 1973 between Chicago and Fremont, Nebraska. North Western sales people approached the Union Pacific with the idea of a high-speed, dedicated intermodal train; specifically a "run-through" 24 hours faster than existing service. A preblocked train would originate at the Wood Street Yard in Chicago and run express to the Union Pacific interchange where it would "highball" toward western destinations. The traffic grew, in part because of speed and dependability. "It's a simple philosophy C&NW people have," observed *Railway Age* in 1977. "You run as many trains as you need, you leave on time, you don't get in a Falcon's way out on the road, and you get in on time—or better."[103]

Even though conventional piggyback traffic eventually declined, the overall volume of intermodal business burgeoned. The North Western sensed the bright promise of container traffic. While the company had been handling COFC traffic and unit COFC trains since 1977, in March 1984 it joined with the Union Pacific to introduce double-stack container service between the West Coast and Chicago. Four months later the two carriers added a Conrail link to the East Coast, forging the first transcontinental double-stack container operation. These containers, loaded in Pacific rim nations, arrived at West Coast ports where cranes transloaded them from specially designed ships onto low-to-the rail, lightweight flatcars. This rolling stock permitted a train to carry twice as many containers with only a 30 percent increase in weight compared to conventional COFC trains.[104]

The North Western created the infrastructure to accommodate the double-stack business. In early 1985 the company purchased the Robey Street Yard in Chicago from a CSX affiliate, Baltimore & Ohio Chicago Terminal, for approximately $3.3 million. This property was adjacent to the Wood Street Yard, and the two facilities became "Global One," a $36 million state-of-the-art project designed solely to load and unload double-stack trains. The opening of Global One in late 1986 allowed the company to increase the number of double-stack round-trip trains handled from eight to 14 per week. By 1988 the volume had grown to 38 trains weekly.[105]

The North Western gladly let the intermodal genie out of the bottle. The company proudly announced in March 1988 that it had signed a long-term contract with American President Lines for transporting and handling its double-stack container cars. By 1992 the double-stack traffic accounted for 86 percent of the intermodal business, and this was a profitable activity. "Double-stack technology has enabled the C&NW to move 80 percent more loads per train at the same cost as traditional piggyback service," reported the company in its *1992 Annual Report*. "The average revenue per car earned for double-stack movements is lower than our other business groups, but profit margins are higher because of the inherent efficiencies of the operation."[106]

More stack trains necessitated additional facilities. The second container terminal, "Global Two," located on the site of "Piggyback Plaza" and Yard One at Proviso yard, officially opened on October 1, 1989, at a cost of approximately $16 million. Expansions followed. This facility was even more efficiently designed than Global One; the company used the knowledge that it had gained from five years of double-stack operations. The location of Global Two was superb: the central "Chicagoland" site was convenient to Interstate Highways 240 and 294 and an hour closer to the Union Pacific connection than Global One.[107]

The North Western did more than cultivate the double-stack business; the company applied the age-old Best of Everything credo to its customers. One innovation that worked well and

North Western power moves a unit grain train southbound through Crete, Ill., on the Union Pacific's Illinois Division, the former Chicago & Eastern Illinois Railroad. The date is May 7, 1987. (John F. Humiston photograph)

served as a model for the industry was the "Commoditrain." In 1971 management negotiated an agreement with the operating brotherhoods to permit a three-person crew to handle rock trains of 20 to 25 cars over five seniority districts without changing crews. Three round trips were made weekly between South Beloit, Illinois, and Chicago. What had previously been a marginal operation developed into a profit maker. The benefits were numerous: operating jobs increased, car utilization rose, and customers received better and faster service at attractive rates.[108]

The consumer-driven orientation of the North Western took other forms. With partial deregulation after 1980, the company negotiated with shippers for traffic at rates that would be mutually beneficial. Service to the iron ore and steel industries is an example. In December 1989 the railroad began to move unit ore trains for Granite City Steel from Partridge, Michigan (the Lake Superior & Ishpeming originated the ore at the Tilden Mine) via Escanaba, Green Bay, and Milwaukee to the East St. Louis area.[109]

The North Western also entered into more complicated traffic arrangements designed to assist customers and bolster revenues. Service to a new wet-corn milling plant, owned by Cargill, Inc. and located near Eddyville, Iowa, on the 81-mile former Minneapolis & St. Louis line between Albia and Marshalltown is a good example. By the early 1980s the North Western continued to handle business between Marshalltown and Oskaloosa, north of Eddyville, and to serve its small car shop at Oskaloosa before that facility closed in 1982. During the mid-1970s it had canceled trains on the 24-mile Oskaloosa-Eddyville-Albia segment. The trackage that remained in service deteriorated, and brush choked the rest. Understandably, the company pushed for abandonment of the entire subdivision. But prospects of obtaining 10,000 or more carloads annually of Cargill-generated business changed the picture. Financial assistance from the nonprofit Mid-Iowa Shippers Association, Cargill, government agencies, and others allowed the railroad to begin to upgrade the trackage during the summer of 1983. By the mid-1990s the line had been fully rehabilitated, except for the abandonment of the southern 1.5-mile portion between Maxon, a junction with the Burlington Northern, and the Albia yard. Shippers, including Cargill, who had backed these betterments with interest-free loans, received a rebate for each car that they originated or terminated until the debt was repaid.[110]

The Albia-Marshalltown project worked well. Traffic generated by the Cargill plant, which subsequently expanded, exceeded expectations. Additional agribusinesses, also eager for rail service, moved to the Eddyville area, and longtime patrons retained their rail outlet.[111]

Whether serving agricultural, industrial, intermodal, or mining customers, the North Western continued to upgrade its motive power and rolling stock. Predictably, the company used its newest diesel-electric locomotives to haul unit coal trains. In February 1989, for example, the company announced an order for 30 Dash 8-40C units from General Electric at a cost of approximately $40 million. At the time these six-axle, 4,000-horsepower locomotives were the most powerful units manufactured domestically. Older power was reassigned, traded in, sold, or scrapped.[112]

The same policy applied to the car fleet. Modernization meant such acquisitions as 500 jumbo covered hopper cars in 1980 and 574 open-top coal hoppers in 1991. Rolling stock was repaired, rebuilt, or retired. One innovative project conducted at the Clinton shops took place in 1988 when the company, under contract with the XTRA Corporation, converted 200 insulated boxcars into piggyback flatcars. Not only did obsolete rolling stock receive a second life, but these flats contributed to the intermodal business. "The current trend in shipping is toward 48-foot trailers," commented Robert Jahnke, vice president for equipment management. "The 89-foot piggyback cars worked well when the standard trailer length was 40 or 45 feet, but they pose a real problem with 48-foot trailers. The 50-foot XTRA conversions are more versatile and can handle any size trailer or container on chassis presently in use."[113]

While modern equipment contributed to the financial health of the North Western, the company struggled to cope with ever rising labor costs. The introduction of advanced technologies, such as computers, led to the elimination of hundreds of jobs. The major challenge involved reducing the number of employees who were protected by archaic work rules, and this battle raged for years.[114]

The North Western joined an industrywide effort to tackle employee "featherbedding." The national scene had seen some progress in the 1960s in altering outmoded work rules, but state-enacted restrictions proved difficult to change. Victories took place even so; the last important one came in Wisconsin in 1972. Badger State lawmakers, imbued with the anticorporate, proconsumer spirit of progressivism, had decided in 1907 that a "full crew" statute was essential to protect the public. The state mandated employment of an engineer, fireman, conductor, and several brakemen. Wisconsin was the first of 17 states to pass such a measure, although by 1972 only Arkansas and Wisconsin retained these costly laws. While the intent of full-crew legislation could be defended when slow-moving, steam-powered trains dominated the industry, such a statute had truly become an "excess crew" law by the diesel era. Workers represented by the United Transportation Union, a recent amalgamation of firemen and trainmen, and the carriers, served by the Wisconsin Railroad Association, reached an accord that permitted firemen to retire or transfer jobs without being replaced. A joint labor and management bill, subsequently enacted, provided that no railroad employee could be "discharged, laid off, furloughed, removed from train or engine service, cut in salary or transferred without his approval." Even though the companies argued that this agreement was "the most generous made to railroad employees by any state which ever repealed a full crew law," the North Western was still able to lower its labor costs.[115]

The North Western hardly rested with the

Wisconsin victory. Especially during the James Wolfe years, the road sought additional ways to end featherbedding. Its most significant effort centered on reducing the size of train crews from four to two (the issue of firemen having been settled), initially projected to produce an annual savings of $61 million. While no one questioned the need for a locomotive engineer, the company challenged the requirement to operate with a conductor and two brakemen. "We are required to utilize *three* ground service employees on most of our train crews," reported Wolfe. "Yet virtually all the jobs on our railroad can be safely and efficiently performed with only *one* ground service employee on each crew."[116]

The Wolfe administration forced the issue of crew size on May 15, 1987. The company served the United Transportation Union with a notice under Section 6 of the Railway Labor Act that it intended to alter the existing labor agreement. The railroad and the UTU began direct negotiations in June, but talks accomplished little. The union made known its determination to demand substantial protection for its members. The UTU frowned on the company offer to allow furloughed workers the choice of either resigning and taking a $25,000 separation allowance or remaining on furlough and receiving the pay of a yardman for one year. The UTU instead countered with a proposal that called for a lifetime earnings guarantee for ground service employees, elimination of some brakeman and yard helper positions on an attrition basis, and a salary boost ("lonesome pay") for trainmen who were part of reduced crews.[117]

The positions of the railroad and the United Transportation Union were too far apart to allow speedy settlement. "The union just dug in its heels . . . , fearful of what could likely happen to its membership." Management, on the other hand, was determined to realize an estimated annual savings of $61 million. The federal government entered the process in late July 1987 when the National Mediation Board, under terms of the Railway Labor Act, appointed a representative to resolve the dispute. Lengthy discussions followed, leading ultimately to a settlement.[118]

The process itself was difficult and at times tense. While the company increased financial incentives of its proposal in March 1988, the United Transportation Union rejected the offer and moreover refused a proposal for binding arbitration. The National Mediation Board then terminated its services on March 22, 1988. This action triggered a 30-day cooling-off period after which time the North Western could unilaterally implement its work rules and the UTU could strike.[119]

The National Mediation Board did not leave the scene and asked President Ronald Reagan to appoint a presidential Emergency Board to investigate the dispute. The president did so on April 20, 1988, and both labor and management were required to accept the status quo for 60 days. After this second cooling-off period had lapsed and frustrated by the lengthy negotiations, the UTU struck on September 9, 1988. The walkout lasted only eight hours. Congress passed a measure that day resolving the conflict, and President Reagan hurriedly signed it. This federal action, which embraced the recommendations of the Emergency Board, allowed the railroad, effective May 22, 1989, to operate its trains with three rather than four people; to permit the crew size on nonstop through trains to be reduced to two through additional arbitration, and to grant redundant employees a buyout of $50,000.[120]

Although the debate over crew size was largely settled, further wrangling ensued. Happily for the North Western, management and the United Transportation Union came to terms on December 13, 1991, about the third crew member. The train consist would now have only two persons, an engineer and either one conductor or a brakeman. The company would have sole discretion to add a third person, a "utility brakeman," to any assignment. In return, the North Western granted several concessions, foremost an offer to buy out unneeded brakemen who voluntarily resigned at $100,000 for individuals hired prior to the congressional legislation and $50,000 for persons hired after the September 1988 date. Employees who refused to resign were placed on "reserve boards" where they would remain until called to service. The agreement resulted in the elimination of approximately 580 brakemen positions and a projected savings of $21 million for 1992 alone.[121]

As the size of the workforce steadily declined (14,345 employees in 1981, 9,450 in 1986, 6,841 in 1991), largely through buyouts, attrition, technological changes, and line abandonments and sales, the morale of remaining workers was often low. "A lot of people were scared to death about their future with the railroad," commented a company official in 1986. "They really thought that management was cruel and rather heartless." Even though that perception was widespread, James Wolfe had tried to keep the most capable individuals and to recruit the best outside talent. Perhaps the most conspicuous effort to soothe workers and bolster productivity and profits was adoption of a Total Quality Improvement System (TQIS) in 1985. "Our goal," wrote Wolfe the next year, "is to produce a better quality transportation product through teamwork and open communication among all levels of employees."[122]

The force behind the Total Quality Improvement System was James Zito, senior vice president for operations. At the suggestion of an associate Zito attended several seminars on total quality management and soon became convinced of the soundness of the concept. "I wanted to get our people involved . . . [and] having a say in the decisions," reflected Zito. "People trained in TQIS became committed to the company. People talked to management more. It was a way to end a stodgy style [of management]."[123]

While some workers balked at Total Quality Improvement System seminars and characterized the concept as "happy horse shit," the program paid dividends. The number of company investigations of employee conduct significantly decreased, for example. The Robert Schmiege administration, which took over in 1988, showed less interest in TQIS, however, and the program languished.[124]

The Wolfe regime saw another opportunity to reduce expenses and advance efficiency: sale of redundant trackage. Ideally the company could "spin-off" marginally profitable lines to operators of shortlines. These carriers, which

A maintenance-of-way employee watches the welding of a rail joint in the continuous welded rail along the Belvidere subdivision. By the 1980s most important lines sported this kind of rail. The thermit charge in the crucible has been ignited, but the weld metal has not yet flowed into the mould. The weld in the near rail has already been made and the running surface ground smooth. (John F. Humiston photograph)

might be nonunion or at least minimally staffed, could profitably serve customers and direct interchange traffic to the North Western. The company would win on every front: cash from the sale, savings in overall operating costs, and future income from interline business.[125]

While the North Western eventually spawned several shortlines, large and small and with varying degrees of financial success, the company's principal legacies were the Dakota, Minnesota & Eastern Railroad (DM&E), and the Fox River Valley Railroad (FRVR). These properties, representing more than a thousand miles of former North Western trackage, developed somewhat differently.

The largest spin-off involved 965 miles of secondary and branch trackage in the Dakotas, Iowa, and Minnesota, including the 647-mile line between Rapid City, South Dakota, and Winona, Minnesota. What became the DM&E in 1986 began to take shape a year earlier when the North Western and L. B. Foster, Inc., a Pittsburgh-based railway equipment and shortline concern, agreed to a $26 million purchase price for the track and other assets. L. B. Foster later left the DM&E, but the management team headed by a former North Western operating official, J. C. (Pete) McIntyre, created a viable railroad. Assistance from state authorities for major betterments and supportive customers, mainly grain shippers, helped DM&E become a thriving "regional" carrier. In 1992 the company failed to acquire an additional 175 miles of North Western track in the Black Hills. The DM&E wished to haul more cars of Bentonite, cement, and wood chips, "but at the last minute the deal fell through."[126]

Although the North Western surrendered a substantial portion of its trackage to create the DM&E, the arrangement initially favored the Wolfe road. The North Western kept tight reins on trackage rights and interchange practices and even required that most traffic originating on the DM&E be loaded in North Western–owned cars. These pro–North Western provisions remained intact until 1994. To obtain DM&E support for the Union Pacific's application to the ICC for control of the company, the North Western agreed to modify its stringent requirements.[127]

The North Western concluded its second major route sale on December 9, 1988, when it sold 208 miles of line in eastern Wisconsin to FRVR Corporation, a noncarrier subsidiary of ITEL Rail Corporation. For approximately $60 million, ITEL received trackage that extended from Duck Creek (four miles north of Green Bay) through Appleton, Oshkosh, and Fond du Lac to Granville (13 miles north of Milwaukee), the "Valley Line," and from Green Bay through Manitowoc to Cleveland (10 miles north of Sheboygan), the "Shore Line." Branches between Appleton and Kaukauna, Appleton and New London, and Manitowoc and Two Rivers were also included. The FRVR Corporation acquired the North Western's depot, shops, and yard in Green Bay and received trackage rights between Granville and the Butler Yard near Milwaukee.[128]

As soon as the North Western–ITEL deal was announced in the fall of 1987, the railroad brotherhoods voiced their opposition. Union members worried about the loss of jobs and their relationship with ITEL. Following a series of legal maneuvers, the U.S. Supreme Court on November 28, 1988, decided not to hear an appeal from a ruling made by the Seventh Federal Court of Appeals that approved the sale and blocked labor from striking over the matter.[129]

What appeared to be another success for the North Western turned sour. In 1992, largely for financial reasons, ITEL decided to sell its three shortline railroads in Wisconsin, the Ahnapee & Western, the Fox River Valley, and the Green Bay & Western, to the Wisconsin Central Transportation Corporation. This regional, launched in October 1987 and headed by former North Western executive Edward Burkhardt, operated more than 2,000 miles of line in Wisconsin, upper Michigan, eastern Minnesota, and northern Illinois, trackage that had previously belonged to the Soo Line. The North Western protested the ITEL decision and did so for understandable reasons: the North Western competed with the Wisconsin Central and did not relish the loss of interchange traffic with the FRVR, estimated at $18 million annually. The North Western publicly emphasized that control of the FRVR by the Wisconsin Central would eliminate competition in certain markets, especially the movement of wood products. The ICC ultimately granted the Fox Valley & Western, Ltd., a Wisconsin Central subsidiary, permission to acquire the shortline.[130]

North Western management also anticipated the sale of the remaining 320 miles of trackage north of Green Bay (Duck Creek). In May 1987 it negotiated an agreement with a group of investors assembled by L. B. Foster that called itself the Escanaba & Northern Railroad Corporation. The buyers would pay $66 million and assume $8 million of North Western debt. But the deal unraveled. A combination of the stock market crash of October 1987 and labor protection concerns forced the North Western to retain these marginally profitable routes. Following the Fox River Valley sale trackage in northern Wisconsin and the Upper Peninsula was isolated from the rest of the system.[131]

The Wolfe administration moved as aggressively to sell unneeded real estate. In 1980 and 1981, for example, the company sold more than $15 million in surplus property. The most celebrated transaction came with the sale of the deteriorating Chicago passenger terminal to Tishman Midwest Management Corporation for $17 million in 1982. Negotiations had been under way since 1979. On January 31, 1984, the general contractor began work on a replacement station and office complex designed by architect Helmut Jahn. (Most of the old track sheds remained for commuter trains.) The 39-story glass and steel edifice, called the Northwestern Atrium Center, opened with much fanfare on April 14, 1987.[132]

The dazzling Northwestern Atrium Center in a way symbolized the North Western. The railroad might be labeled sleek like this bright addition to the Chicago skyline. "By the time Jim Wolfe passed from the scene, the CNW was in trim, fighting shape," reflected James Zito. "I would say that it would be grossly unfair to call the railroad old-fashioned; . . . it was lean and mean." North Western management had done a credible job in responding to the challenges that came immediately before and after the landmark Staggers legislation. Its leaders sought to make possible a profitable life in the constantly changing world of deregulation. This strategy continued until the consumation of a successful corporate sale in 1995.[133]

Until purchase by the Union Pacific, the North Western continually acquired replacement motive power. On July 1, 1994, newly purchased locomotives No. 8618 and 8671, General Electric C44-9Ws, stand on the Illinois Central's Markham Yard lead in Homewood, Ill. By 1995 the company owned more than 100 of these ultramodern locomotives. (John F. Humiston photograph)

CHAPTER Twelve

THE FINAL YEARS

In the midst of the North Western's effort to trim trackage and maximize returns on capital, the company underwent a change of leadership. James Wolfe, chairman and chief executive officer, died on August 8, 1988. Several years earlier Wolfe had developed colon cancer, and he managed to conceal the severity of his illness from colleagues and board members for some time. "Jim would have lost his job if his health condition would have been known," commented a close associate. Robert W. Schmiege, a ranking official whom Wolfe picked to be his successor, took charge.[1]

Robert Schmiege, the last president of the North Western, grew up in a financially secure midwestern family. His father worked as an engineer for Continental Can Corporation, and a great uncle served as chairman of the board of the Milwaukee Road. Born on May 24, 1941, in Madison, Wisconsin, Schmiege earned his bachelor's degree from the University of Notre Dame in 1963 and his juris doctor degree from the Notre Dame Law School three years later.[2]

Launching his professional career, Schmiege became an attorney with the National Labor Railway Conference. He resigned in 1968 to become a "bump and bruise type of trial lawyer" in the law department of the North Western. Schmiege remained in legal affairs until 1974, when he joined the legal staff of the Southern Pacific Transportation Company; he entered private law practice a year later. Then in 1976 Schmiege rejoined the North Western as assistant vice president for labor relations. In 1979 he became vice president for labor relations and five years later won promotion as senior vice president for administration, the position he held until becoming president and chief operating officer.[3]

The Schmiege regime largely reflected an already established corporate culture. "The Heineman tradition continued through Schmiege," observed an industry expert in 1994. "It remains a company with a no-nonsense attitude." Schmiege personally admired the "rigorous management thought of Heineman." As he put it, "Larry Provo was cut from the Ben Heineman mold and Jim Wolfe was cut from the Provo mold." Schmiege considered himself cut from the Wolfe mold.[4]

Yet Robert Schmiege was not James Wolfe, and there was a noticeable difference in style. Wolfe acted "imperially"; his was leadership of a "commanding nature." Conversely, Schmiege appeared less authoritarian and more democratic. "The top officials frequently have all-day meetings to arrive at a policy consensus," remarked an insider. "Schmiege likes the consensus approach." The new president was more open and candid with employees, shippers, and others than had been his predecessor, and his personal priorities were different. While Wolfe liked the trappings of his position, Schmiege cared much less about them. After Wolfe died, for example, Schmiege was asked if he wanted Wolfe's chauffeured automobile; he declined with the reply, "I can take a cab."[5]

Leading the North Western in the late 1980s was not an easy task. Although management had applauded the Staggers Act, this legislation led to intense competitive pressures. At first the company was at a disadvantage. The newly created regional railroads in its territory, most notably the Chicago Central & Pacific (former Illinois Central trackage), Iowa Interstate (a former Rock Island route), and Wisconsin Central (former Soo Line mileage) were either nonunion or benefited from concessions granted by the powerful United Transportation Union. Even though the issue of crew size was ultimately resolved to the advantage of the North Western, the company endured repeated rate battles with other carriers. The years 1982 to 1986 were characterized by a general rate war, instigated by the Burlington Northern and the Soo after its acquisition of the Milwaukee. These rate slashes meant roughly 8 to 10 percent decreases in annual revenues for the North Western in an era depressed by the recession of 1983–1984. The impact of market pressures was illustrated by the loss of income received for a carload of freight between Chicago and the Union Pacific connection: an average return of $625 in 1981 was reduced to $500 five years later although operating costs had risen.[6]

The rate war had a negative impact on the North Western, and the company was rapidly going downhill by 1987. "We were painfully close to bankruptcy," remarked one official. The response was varied. The railroad made deep cuts in the size of the workforce, especially white-collar employees, in 1985 and 1986; it restructured operating divisions; and, significantly, it moved toward a major liquidation.[7]

Massive downsizing never occurred, but it was considered. The proposed sell-off involved much of the 6,000-mile system; unwanted units would be sold to regional or shortline operators. Still the North Western would continue, but only as a "core" network of the most profitable pieces, including the Fremont-Omaha stem and the Wyoming coal lines. Company investors would join those of the successfully restructured Illinois Central Gulf Railroad in benefiting from the immediate sale of assets and from the profits a core carrier would provide. If the North Western were split up and auctioned off, the value of a share of common stock might triple. With management support the New York investment house of Gibbons, Green, van Amerongen entered the picture in November 1987. But concerns about the expense of labor protection flawed the breakup plan, and discussions ended in April 1988. This failed scheme cost the North Western about $4 million.[8]

Improving financial conditions followed the exit of Gibbons, Green as a marketer. The North Western's pretax income for 1988 increased to $43.4 million compared to a loss the previous year, and in February 1989 the company announced the first dividend for common shareholders since the stock was issued in 1972. Management became more sanguine, and the feeling was well founded. Freight rates finally "bottomed out" and began to rise, productivity increased, and the Wyoming coal operations generated even more income. "Western Railroad Properties really saved us," concluded Schmiege in early 1989.[9]

North Western management could not relax, however. Hostile takeover attempts and corporate restructuring soon caused much work and aggravation. The company was hardly immune from the "go-go" spirit of the "Roaring Eighties"; the Reagan years witnessed a corporate merger and takeover craze of unprecedented proportions.[10]

One takeover attempt hit the North Western in 1988. John E. Haley, a flamboyant railroader who had navigated the course of the Chicago Central & Pacific during its formative years, launched H. Comet Industries that bid for the North Western. Haley tried to elect four directors at the annual meeting, vaguely telling stockholders that he could make the North Western a "much better railroad." When asked about the activities of H. Comet Industries, James Wolfe said, "We believe that this represents the latest union attempt to stop the North Western from changing work rules to reduce the size of train crews." Indeed, one of the four candidates proposed by Haley was a union general chairman. Haley and his backers, who included Paul Kazarian of the corporate finance department of Goldman, Sachs & Company, got nowhere.[11]

The real threat came a year later from Paul Kazarian and the investor group that he headed, Japonica Partners, L.P. During the winter of 1988–1989, Kazarian and Michael Lederman, another former Goldman, Sachs officer, bought stock in CNW Corporation, the holding company for the Chicago & North Western Transportation Company (the railroad). By March 1989 Japonica owned an 8.8 percent stake in CNW Corp and duly acknowledged its position to the Securities and Exchange Commission.[12]

Paul Kazarian and Japonica Partners at first only annoyed North Western management. "Our Board of Directors and our management has [*sic*] made it very clear that the interests of all of its constituencies are best served by CNW remaining an independent company," curtly announced Robert Schmiege. "CNW's current business plan provides a base for improving earnings and for continued growth of the company to maximize value for shareholders." But Japonica demonstrated that it was not H. Comet. "Japonica really jarred the company that spring [1989]," and it did so for good reason. In late April the partnership offered to acquire the outstanding common stock of CNW Corp for $44 per share, $39.50 in cash and $4.50 in preferred stock. Kazarian indicated that his group had a commitment for financing from a "premier money center bank" and a "highly confident" letter from Drexel Burnham Lambert for subordinate financing.[13]

Wrangling soon intensified between the

North Western management and Japonica. The railroad maneuvered as best it could; it formed a special committee of the Board of Directors and sought assistance from Goldman, Sachs and Salomon Brothers. The decision was made to find a "friendly" buyer rather than to surrender to a "gang of corporate raiders" who would "destroy the company by selling off its assets."[14]

Organized labor quickly expressed interest in ownership. The proposal made in early June by the Association of General Chairmen, which represented 16 labor unions on the North Western, offered to give employees a one-third interest in the common stock of CNW Corp. The remainder of the shares would stay with the current owners.[15]

Entry of labor into the mix harkened back to the employee-ownership scheme guided by Larry Provo in 1972. Nine years later the company had recognized that it could no longer claim to be an employee concern; active workers owned less than 40 percent of the outstanding stock. Consequently, the railroad retired the phrase "Employee-Owned" from its ball and bar emblem and other advertising. Yet the idea of a leveraged employee buyout in 1989 might have had greater currency had James Wolfe been alive. "I bet he would have tried for a second employee LBO," argued James Zito, "and it could have worked."[16]

The North Western avoided the employee-ownership proposal because management had found an acceptable "white knight," one that it believed could derail Japonica. The railroad announced on June 6, 1989, that the board had approved a "definitive merger agreement" with Chicago and North Western Acquisition Corporation, a firm formed by Blackstone Capital Partners, L.P. and other investors including Donaldson, Lufkin & Jenrette Securities Corporation, Union Pacific Corporation, and senior North Western officers. The Blackstone Group significantly bettered the Japonica bid of $44.00 a share; it offered $45.50 a share in cash and $4.50 in preferred stock with a 17 percent dividend. This commitment amounted to approximately $1.6 billion.[17]

Who was this white knight? The Blackstone Group was created in 1985 by Peter Peterson, once president of Bell and Howell, onetime head of Lehman Brothers Kuhn Loeb, and former secretary of commerce in the Richard Nixon administration; and by Stephen Schwarzman, former chair of Lehman Brothers' merger and acquisition department. This "investment boutique" was involved in assisting leveraged buyouts, the rage of the 1980s, and providing bridge financing and other investment services. Blackstone knew railroading; it was the majority owner of Transtar, Inc., which operated more than 2,000 miles of lines formerly owned by USX Corporation (United States Steel).[18]

Joining the Blackstone Group were Donaldson, Lufkin & Jenrette and the Union Pacific. The former, an independently owned subsidiary of the Equitable Life Assurance Society of the United States, had been active in leveraged acquisitions. Clearly the latter wished to protect access to the Chicago gateway. Indeed, the Union Pacific became so anxious about the possibility of a Japonica takeover that it acquired a three-year option to buy the Iowa Interstate from Council Bluffs to Chicago in May 1989. The Union Pacific worried that if the North Western went to Japonica, the highly leveraged company would not be able to maintain the Omaha line as a modern speedway.[19]

The mechanics of the takeover of the North Western by the Blackstone Group went smoothly, and the plan was fully implemented. These efforts led to the nation's eighth largest railroad (in total operating revenues) being placed at the bottom of a paper superstructure. Chicago and North Western Holdings Corporation, incorporated in the state of Delaware in 1989, served as the parent of Chicago and North Western Acquisition Corporation, which in turn controlled CNW Corp, holding company for the railroad, Chicago and North Western Transportation Company.[20]

The North Western was held together for a price. The buyout saddled the Holdings corporation with more than $750 million in long-term debt, and interest payments during the first year amounted to $175 million. Although Japonica had lost, it benefited financially. Paul Kazarian and his associates reaped a windfall from the sale of their shares acquired only a few months earlier.[21]

The corporate machinations of the late 1980s prompted the North Western to conduct even more belt tightening. Additional buyouts

By 1994 the North Western was a shadow of its former self. The company's remaining lines in Michigan, South Dakota, and Wyoming had become isolated from the remainder of the system. Little too was left of either the former Minneapolis & St. Louis or Chicago Great Western railroads. (Author's collection)

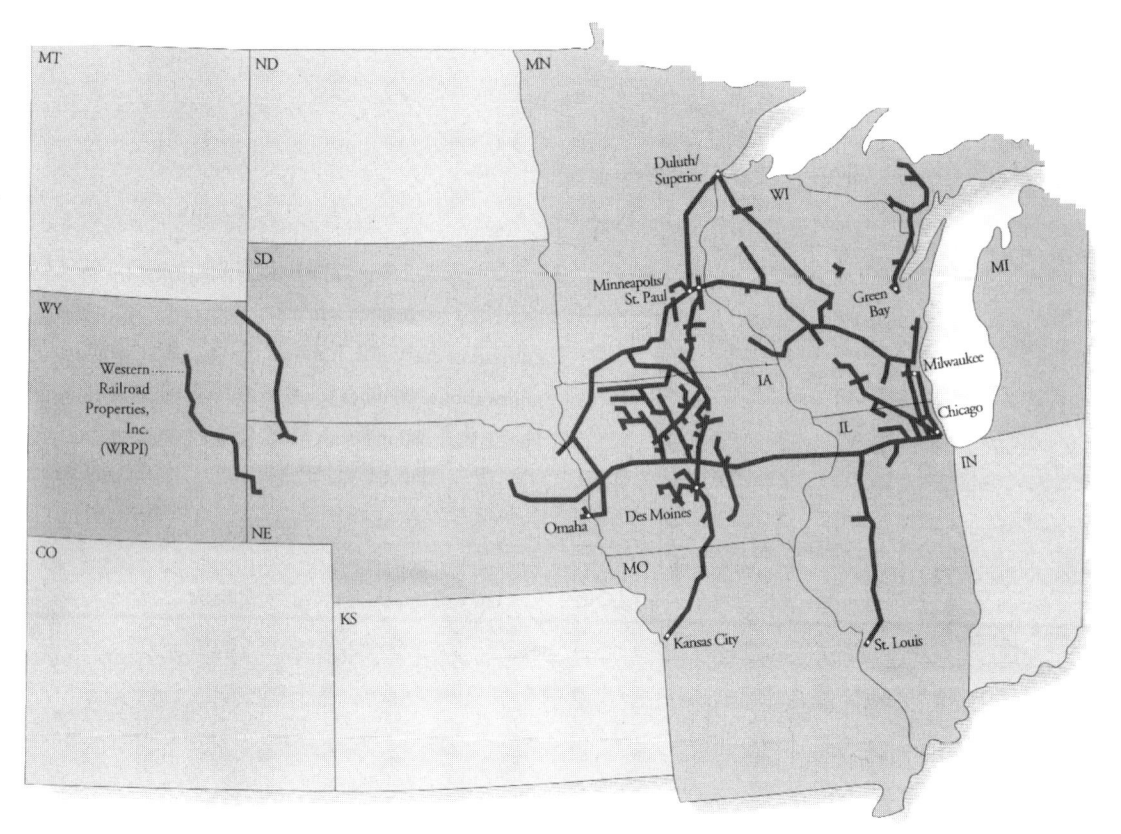

of employees took place, reducing the workforce to 6,269 in 1992. Other actions produced savings. The ongoing electronic and semiconductor revolution allowed the railroad to centralize its train dispatching in Chicago, and that epic change occurred in December 1989. Consumer service was also centered in the Windy City in 1992. That same year the company shut down yard control operations in Boone, Milwaukee, and St. Paul and closed the diesel shop in Council Bluffs. A similar fate subsequently befell the Oelwein, Iowa, locomotive repair and rebuilding facility. The Schmiege regime even sold rolling stock, including locomotives and part of the fleet of business cars assembled during the Wolfe years.[22]

The North Western remained interested in paring down its system. The ever aggressive Wisconsin Central purchased approximately 100 miles of the Itasca line (South Itasca–Cameron, Wisconsin) in 1992, although the North Western gained trackage rights between South Itasca (the company's Superior yard) and Wisconsin Rapids, via the Ladysmith line of the Wisconsin Central. Also in the Badger State the North Western abandoned its 90-mile Green Bay–Wausau branch in August 1993. The line, which generated mostly carloads of forest products and roofing granules, had deteriorated, and no buyer could be found. More significantly, several months earlier the company retired its 320-mile "Cowboy Line" between Chadron and Norfolk, Nebraska. A portion of that secondary trackage, the 77-mile Chadron-to-Merriman section, went to a shortline operator, the Nebkota Railway, and the remaining became a public "rails-to-trails" hike and bike project, the fate of hundreds of miles of former North Western mileage.[23]

By 1993 the 4,300-mile North Western, about 40 percent of its 1972 size, could report that "[1992] will be remembered as the year the railroad retired its 1988 LBO debt and emerged as a publicly traded company." A successful stock offering in April and $700 million in new borrowing enabled the Holdings firm to retire expensive "junk" bonds and other high-interest debt. This recapitalization benefited from both the lower cost of borrowing and the strong economy of the early 1990s. The company described it as "record volume of growth for the C&NW, [the firm] ended 1992 with it's [sic] 11th consecutive record quarter for total year-over-year loads." Although a severe winter followed and tremendous flooding struck much of the Midwest during the spring and summer months of 1993, the railroad, notwithstanding, experienced good financial health. Low-sulphur coal from Wyoming mines continued to be the principal revenue-producing commodity and was expected to promote future growth. This optimism was graphically reflected in the acquisition of several score of 4,500-horsepower Dash 9 locomotives from General Electric that were regularly assigned to unit coal trains.[24]

The life of the smaller, more efficient, and profitable North Western came to an abrupt end in April 1995. The Union Pacific, which had long watched its interchange partner, made its first move toward control in 1989; the giant carrier invested $100 million in the defensive leveraged buyout that kept the North Western from the clutches of Japonica. In March 1993 the Union Pacific formally asked the ICC to approve conversion of its nonvoting common stock, which it acquired when the North Western went public in 1992, into voting shares. The railroad also informed the commission that it wished to buy all of the North Western's common stock. Shortly before the Union Pacific request, Schmiege had announced that the "North Western's business plan does not contemplate our railroad becoming part of the Union Pacific. The managements of C&NW and UP have developed and continue to foster a strong business relationship, which recognizes and supports our many mutual goals and interests." The Schmiege pronouncement notwithstanding, the railroads did not remain separate.[25]

With a green light from the ICC the Union Pacific announced in March 1995 its intention to buy the 70 percent of North Western common that it did not own. The official press releases issued by both railroads on March 17 caught many by surprise and even shocked some, especially the rank and file on the North Western. "This acquisition will strengthen our capacity to compete in the key western freight corridors," said Union Pacific chairman and chief executive officer Drew Lewis. "It will increase Union Pacific's growing intermodal traffic from the major West Coast ports to the Midwest and enhance our low-sulfur coal shipments out of the Powder River Basin in Wyoming to the Mississippi Valley and the East. We are delighted to have this fine railroad joining the Union Pacific family." Robert Schmiege responded with these comments: "In addition to providing a substantial premium for our shareholders, this merger offers an opportunity for our customers and virtually all of our employees to participate in a larger railroad with

The failure to find a buyer for much of the "Cowboy Line" across Nebraska led to abandonment of this former Fremont, Elkhorn & Missouri Valley trackage. In August 1994 a section in the sand hills of western Cherry County was dismantled. (James F. Foote photograph)

broader horizons, greater resources and enhanced opportunities for the marketing of our customers' products and our employees' professional growth."[26]

The Union Pacific had acted for a variety of reasons. The management was badly disappointed that it had recently failed in its hard-fought battle with Burlington Northern for control of the Atchison, Topeka & Santa Fe Railway. The UP wanted to strengthen its position against the impending presence of the proposed Burlington Northern Santa Fe Corporation. Acquisition of the North Western would help. Moreover, Union Pacific had the financing to handle the approximately $1.1 billion offer to North Western shareholders; it enjoyed an extensive line of credit as a result of its hoped-for takeover of the Santa Fe. And UP managers had become unhappy with some of the operating practices of the North Western. "They [North Western] did a lot of annoying things," recalled John Rebensdorf, vice president of strategic planning for the UP. "They stopped coal trains, for example, at Council Bluffs and lashed on C&NW power and then there were lengthy checks for wheel defects on those trains." Rebensdorf added, "The trouble began when [James] Zito left the C&NW."[27]

News of the acquisition of the North Western by Union Pacific generally pleased customers. They planned to take advantage of the pricing that would result from the long-haul economies of having a single source for shipments between the Great Lakes and southern and western points. North Western patrons commonly felt that service would improve along principal lines; the UP, with its deeper pockets, could afford necessary expenditures. Those who worried about the likelihood of the UP discarding their trackage, especially the grain-gathering lines in Iowa, expected regional or shortline operators to keep the trains running.[28]

Not everyone applauded the purchase, however. Analysts estimated that Burlington Northern would lose about $10 million annually as a result of traffic diversions, and some other carriers would also be injured. Since the Union Pacific indicated that it would close some North Western facilities, most notably the freight car shop in Clinton and the diesel-repair operation in Marshalltown, the sale caused consternation among employees; no one wished a loss of employment or job transfers.[29]

Shortly before the North Western became a part of the Union Pacific, there was talk of North Western officers remaining in railroading apart from the UP. Discussions involved the possible purchase by Robert Schmiege and several associates of Transtar Inc, the Blackstone Group–controlled network of former United States Steel railroads, but no deal was consummated before the UP purchase. These senior North Western officials received attractive "golden parachutes" from the UP; 27 executives became eligible for $10.9 million in severance payments.[30]

The process of amalgamating the North Western into the Union Pacific seemed to start off in good fashion. Dick Davidson, the railroad head who would shortly assume duties as president and chief operating officer of the parent UP Corporation, told a group of union officials in mid-May 1995 that the merger "is really going well, much smoother that I had hoped." In October Davidson reiterated his optimism about the North Western purchase. He informed securities analysts that the UP had brought the North Western into its computerized train-control system "with only a few glitches" and bragged that 500 employees from the two carriers, one-tenth of them management, had accepted voluntary severance and "400 of the 500 have already left." Davidson anticipated the financial benefits from unification to be greater than initially projected. As he concluded, "Everyone at UP has been very pleased with the speed of implementation . . . we are right where we need to be."[31]

Less than a month after Davidson's positive pronouncements, the official UP tune had changed dramatically. Ronald J. Burns, Davidson's replacement at the railroad, publicly confessed that "many shippers are experiencing unprecedented problems with service provided by our railroad." And he added that "service has deteriorated to a level never before seen on UP." The director of grain transportation for Farmland Industries agreed, telling the *Wall Street Journal*, "It has been about the ugliest operational situation I have seen since I have been around railroads." The trouble, even crisis, explained *Traffic World*, stemmed from "the difficulties [UP] has experienced digesting the far smaller Chicago & North Western." An analyst for Merrill Lynch & Co. thought that he could pinpoint the cause: "Perhaps the significant employment cuts at CNW should have been delayed until the train operations of the two railroads were fully consolidated."[32]

Notwithstanding the later pain of corporate dyspepsia, the story of the North Western acquisition by the Union Pacific was overshadowed by a colossal merger proposal. In August 1995 the UP announced a deal with the Southern Pacific (SP) to acquire this western transportation giant, thus "rejoining" the former Harriman rail system. The UP decided "not to go transcontinental" but rather "to solidify our position in the West." The company wanted to prepare itself for the anticipated Burlington Northern–Santa Fe merger.[33]

The timing had been good for the North Western. A Union Pacific–Southern Pacific union would surely have damaged the North Western just as the Burlington Northern–Santa Fe merger would have drained business for an independent North Western.

The fate of the North Western itself contained a few ironic twists. The company had considered purchasing the Union Pacific in the 1890s. In those troubled economic times the "Best of Everything" powerhouse had the financial wherewithal to acquire this transcontinental. Government planners later realized that the North Western and UP would make a good fit. In the initial unification proposal, presented under the Esch-Cummins Act of 1920, "System Plan No. 13" consisted principally of these two carriers. Finally, it is arguable that the North Western left the corporate world in the Best of Everything tradition. The UP possessed stellar qualities; as one observer put it: "The North Western went with a winner."[34]

Just as the North Western was about to achieve "fallen flag" status, someone erected a SO LONG CNW sign along the right of way in DeKalb, Ill. While the North Western is no more, the activities of the Chicago & North Western Historical Society keep alive its memory. (John Morris photograph)

Notes

The following abbreviations have been used in the notes.

Blair papers	John I. Blair Papers, DeGolyer Library, Southern Methodist University, Dallas, Texas
CB&Q papers	Chicago, Burlington & Quincy Railroad Company papers, Newberry Library, Chicago, Illinois
C&NWHS	Chicago & North Western Railway Historical Society Collection, Regional History Center, Northern Illinois University, DeKalb, Illinois
C&NWTCo papers	Chicago & North Western Transportation Company papers, Chicago, Illinois
Chicago & North-Western	*Chicago & North-Western Railway Company and Proprietary Companies.* Chicago: Cameron, Amberg, 1892
Chicago and North Western 1910	*Chicago and North Western Railway Company and Components to April 30, 1910.* Chicago: Chicago & North Western Railway Company, 1910
Erie Lackawanna papers	Erie Lackawanna Railway papers, University of Akron Archives, Akron, Ohio
Harvey Fisk papers	Harvey Fisk & Sons papers, Princeton University Library, Princeton, New Jersey
Omaha Road papers	Chicago, St. Paul, Minneapolis & Omaha Railway Company papers, State Historical Society of Wisconsin, Madison, Wisconsin
Stennett	William H. Stennett, compiler. *Yesterday and To-day: A History of the Chicago & North Western Railway System.* Chicago: Rand McNally, 1910
Yesterday and Today	*Yesterday and Today: A History.* Chicago: Chicago & North Western Railway Co., 1899

Chapter 1: The Galena

1. John F. Stover, *Iron Road to the West: American Railroads in the 1850s* (New York: Columbia University Press, 1978), 7–8; William H. Brown, *The History of the First Locomotives in America* (New York: D. Appleton, 1874), 145.

2. Stover, *Iron Road to the West*, 11, 13, 24; George Rogers Taylor and Irene D. Neu, *The American Railroad Network, 1861–1890* (Cambridge: Harvard University Press, 1956), 2–5.

3. George W. Hilton, *American Narrow Gauge Railroads* (Stanford: Stanford University Press, 1990), 24–38; Slason Thompson, *A Short History of American Railways* (New York: D. Appleton, 1925), 76–78.

4. Edward Hungerford, *Men of Erie: A Story of Human Effort* (New York: Random House, 1946), 53–54.

5. Edward Harold Mott, *Between the Ocean and the Lakes: The Story of Erie* (New York: John S. Collins, 1899), 323–24.

6. See James A. Ward, *Railroads and the Character of America, 1820–1887* (Knoxville: University of Tennessee Press, 1986), 28–40.

7. Robert L. Frey, ed., *Railroads in the Nineteenth Century* (New York: Facts On File, 1988), xvii–xviii.

8. The *Weekly Chicago Democrat* of January 22, 1849, wonderfully captured the optimism associated with the coming railway age: "The great benefits to be derived to the world from improved modes of communications are as yet but dimly seen and appreciated. The United States is no doubt to be the field in which the greatest scope for a realization of the benefits of railroads in the widest view will be found, and the Mississippi valley the centre from which radii will diverge to the utmost limits of the nation."

9. *Historical Statistics of the United States: Colonial Times to 1957* (Washington: U.S. Department of Commerce, 1960), 13; Richard J. Jensen, *Illinois: A Bicentennial History* (New York: Norton, 1978), 3–31; Theodore Calvin Pease, *The Story of Illinois* (Chicago: University of Chicago Press, 1965), 82–131; William Cronon, *Nature's Metropolis: Chicago and the Great West* (New York: Norton, 1991), 103–4.

10. George Rogers Taylor, *The Transportation Revolution, 1815–1860* (New York: Rinehart, 1951), 32–73, 153–75; Stover, *Iron Road to the West*, 13.

11. Bessie Louise Pierce, *A History of Chicago*, vol. 1, *The Beginning of a City, 1673–1848* (New York: Knopf, 1937), 43–74.

12. Ibid., 75–76, 119; *Illinois Bounty Land Register* (Quincy, Ill.), October 16, 1835.

13. Ronald E. Shaw, *Canals for a Nation: The Canal Era in the United States, 1790–1860* (Lexington: University Press of Kentucky, 1990), 143–45; Ronald E. Shaw, "Canals in the Early Republic: A Review of Recent Literature," *Journal of the Early Republic* 4 (summer 1984): 132; Pierce, *History of Chicago*, 1:120.

14. Shaw, *Canals for a Nation*, 146; *Weekly Chicago Democrat*, May 16, 1848; Cronon, *Nature's Metropolis*, 70.

15. William K. Ackerman, *Early Illinois Railroads* (Chicago: Fergus, 1884), 17, 19.

16. Ibid., 22; John F. Stover, *History of the Illinois Central Railroad* (New York: Macmillan, 1975), 9–10.

17. Ackerman, *Early Illinois Railroads*, 23–25; Robert P. Howard, *Illinois: A History of the Prairie State* (Grand Rapids: William B. Eerdman, 1972), 200–202; Colleen A. Dunlavy, *Politics and Industrialization: Early Railroads in the United States and Prussia* (Princeton: Princeton University Press, 1994), 48–69.

18. Stover, *Illinois Central Railroad*, 38–57.

19. Pierce, *History of Chicago*, 1:114; Ralph William Marshall, "The Early History of the Galena and Chicago Union Railroad" (master's thesis, University of Chicago, 1937), 10–11; *Chicago Daily Tribune*, January 18, 1853.

20. Marshall, "Early History," 10–11.

21. Ibid., 12; Augustine W. Wright, "The First Chicago Railroad," *Railroad Gazette* 12 (February 20, 1880): 99.

22. Marshall, "Early History," 15–18.

23. John W. Wentworth, *Fort Dearborn* (Chicago: Fergus, 1881), 76–77.

24. Marshall, "Early History," 20–21.

25. Ibid., 21–27.

26. Pierce, *History of Chicago*, 1:109.

27. *Weekly Chicago Democrat*, April 13, 1849; September 29, 1848.

28. Pierce, *History of Chicago*, 1:110; Remley J. Glass, "Early Transportation and the Plank Road," *Annals of Iowa* 21 (January 1939): 502–34.

29. *Weekly Chicago Democrat*, February 22, 1848.

30. Pierce, *History of Chicago*, 1:113–14; Bessie Louise Pierce, *A History of Chicago*, vol. 2, *From Town to City, 1848–1871* (New York: Knopf, 1940), 36; Milo M. Quaife, *Chicago's Highways Old and New: From Indian Trail to Motor Road* (Chicago: D. F. Keller, 1923), 123–37.

31. Marshall, "Early History," 34.

32. Ibid., 34–49.

33. Ibid., 40–46.

34. *Dictionary of American Biography*, ed. Dumas Malone (New York: Charles Scribner's, 1934), 13: 644–45.

35. Ibid.; Isaac N. Arnold, *William B. Ogden and Early Days in Chicago* (Chicago: Fergus, 1881), 6.

36. Arnold, *William B. Ogden*, 7–8; Ogden's activities were hardly unusual. During times of migration and cheap land, aggressive individuals, whether urban or rural, often found real-estate bonanzas (A. T. Andreas, *History of Cook County, Illinois from the Earliest Period to the Present Time* [Chicago: Alfred T. Andreas, 1884], 128–31).

37. Andreas, *History of Cook County*, 9–15; *Biographical Sketches of the Leading Men of Chicago* (Chicago: Wilson, Pierce, 1876), 7; Marshall, "Early History," 48–49.

38. Arnold, *William B. Ogden*, 7–8; L. O. Leonard, "The Founders and Builders of The Rock Island: William B. Ogden," *Rock Island Magazine* 8 (August 1926): 7–8.

39. Marshall, "Early History," 46–47.

40. Ibid., 59–65; *Weekly Chicago Democrat*, October 5, 1847.

41. *American Railroad Journal* 6 (September 7, 1850): 566.

42. Richard P. Morgan, *Report of the Survey of the Galena and Chicago Union Rail Road* (Chicago, 1847), 10.

43. Ibid., 13, 15.

44. *Galena and Chicago Union Railroad Company, Report of William B. Ogden, Esq.* (Chicago, 1848), 6–7.

45. *Over Half a Century of Progress, 1848–1902* (Chicago: Chicago & North-Western Railway, 1902), 3–4 (Note: Because of the purchase of the Chicago & North Western by the Union Pacific in 1995, materials that are identified as belonging to the Chicago & North Western have been either transferred to the Union Pacific or donated to the Chicago & North Western Historical Society.); *Weekly Chicago Democrat*, August 21, 1848, November 28, 1848; "Report of John Van Nortwick, Chief Engineer," in *Third Annual Report of the Galena and Chicago Union Railroad Company* (Chicago, 1850), 3.

46. *Galena and Chicago Union Railroad* [1848] *Report*, 14.

47. *Weekly Chicago Democrat*, July 10, 1850; Frey, ed., *Railroads*

in the Nineteenth Century, 340–44; Dunlavy, *Politics and Industrialization*, 233; D.C. Prescott, *Early Railroading from Chicago: A Narrative with Some Observations* (Chicago, 1910), 72.

48. John H. White Jr., *The Pioneer: Chicago's First Locomotive* (Chicago: Chicago Historical Society, 1976), 5–15; *Chicago Sunday Tribune*, January 26, 1890; "'The Pioneer'— First Locomotive Out of Chicago," *Railway Journal* 27 (September 1921): 14; *Gem of the Prairie* (Chicago), October 28, 1848.

49. "First Rail Shipments," Box 2, C&NWHS.

While the Millican Hunt story is credible, there exists uncertainty about the exact time the "first" freight shipment moved over Galena rails. The *Chicago Journal* of November 21, 1848, reported the following: "While at the western end of the finished road, a farmer, driving a pair of oxen with a load of wheat and hides . . . on his way to the city, and his wheat purchased by Mr. C. Walker and the hides taken by Mr. J. Beecher, and bought to town, were the first receipts by the Galena and Chicago Railroad."

50. *Weekly Chicago Democrat*, December 5, 1848; *Chicago Journal*, December 9, 1848.

51. *Weekly Chicago Democrat*, May 4, 1849, June 19, 1849; *Chicago Journal*, July 3, 1849.

52. John H. White Jr., "A Few Words about This Picture," *Invention & Technology* 2 (fall 1987): 10.

53. [Caroline Kirkland], "Illinois in Spring-time: With a Look at Chicago," *Atlantic Monthly* 2 (September 1858): 484–85.

54. "Chicago's First Railroad," *Chicago History* (summer 1948): 356; *Weekly Chicago Democrat*, November 24, 1849; "Report of John Van Nortwick," 5; *Chicago Daily Tribune*, December 28, 1850; *American Railroad Journal* 6 (August 31, 1850): 551.

55. "Report of John Van Nortwick," 4.

56. Galena officials also worried about wolves. These wild creatures lived in abundance along the line and liked to scavenge through freight shipments.

57. Herbert H. Harwood Jr., "History Where You Don't Expect It: Some Surprising Survivors," *Railroad History* 166 (spring 1992): 103–14.

58. "Report of John Van Nortwick," 7.

59. *Fifth Annual Report of the Galena and Chicago Union Railroad Company* (Chicago, 1852), 6.

60. Ibid., 5–7; *Weekly Chicago Democrat*, October 5, 1850; Stennett, 21.

61. *Fifth Annual Report*, 7–8; *Sixth Annual Report of the Galena and Chicago Union Railroad* (Chicago, 1853), 5–6; *Seventh Annual Report of the Galena and Chicago Union Railroad Company* (Chicago, 1854), 5.

62. Stennett, 24–25; *American Railroad Journal* 11 (June 16, 1855): 374; *Sixth Annual Report*, 8; *Seventh Annual Report*, 5; *First Annual Report of the Beloit and Madison Rail Road Company* (Chicago, 1854), 5–7. 12; *Eighth Annual Report of the Galena and Chicago Union Railroad Company* (Chicago, 1855), 9.

63. Stover, *Illinois Central*, 54; *Eighth Annual Report*, 8.

64. *American Railway Times*, February 2, 1854; Maury Klein, *Union Pacific: Birth of a Railroad, 1862–1893* (Garden City, N.Y.: Doubleday, 1987), 8–9; William Edward Hayes, *Iron Road to Empire: The History of 100 Years of the Progress and Achievements of the Rock Island Lines* (New York: Simmons-Boardman, 1953), 15–18; *Chicago Daily Democrat*, February 20, May 22, May 27, 1852; *Chicago Daily Tribune*, April 11, 1853.

65. Hayes, *Iron Road to Empire*, 20, 27; *Sixth Annual Report*, 10–11; *Chicago and North Western 1910*, 27.

66. *Seventh Annual Report*, 5.

67. Richard C. Overton, *Burlington Route: A History of the Burlington Lines* (New York: Knopf, 1965), 8–9; *Seventh Annual Report*, 5–6; *Sixth Annual Report*, 11.

68. *Seventh Annual Report*, 5; *Chicago and North Western 1910*, 27; "The Mississippi and Rock River Junction Railroad Company," Valuation Records, Interstate Commerce Commission, The National Archives, Washington, D.C.; "The Life and Times of the Chicago and North Western," *North Western Newsliner* 3 (February 1948): 9.

69. Stennett, 25; *Tenth Annual Report of the Galena and Chicago Union Railroad Company* (Chicago, 1857), 7.

70. William W. Davis, *History of Whiteside County, Illinois* (Chicago: Pioneer Publishing, 1908), 194.

71. *Ninth Annual Report of the Galena and Chicago Union Railroad Company* (Chicago, 1856), 7–8; *Eleventh Annual Report of the Galena and Chicago Union Railroad Company* (Chicago, 1858), 15.

72. *Chicago Tribune*, ca. 1884, clipping in public relations files, C&NWTCo papers.

73. *American Railroad Journal* 7 (June 28, 1851): 407; Robert J. Casey and W. A. S. Douglas, *Pioneer Railroad: The Story of the Chicago and North Western System* (New York: Whittlesey House, 1948), 62; Arnold, *William B. Ogden*, 19–21.

74. Gerald Musich, "John B. Turner," in Frey, ed., *Railroads in the Nineteenth Century*, 390–91.

75. Ibid., 392.

76. Ibid.; *American Railroad Journal* 11 (July 28, 1855): 470.

77. H. Roger Grant, "Why Left-Handed?" *Trains* 49 (January 1989): 34–35.

78. Stennett, 25; *Tenth Annual Report*, 17–18.

79. *First Annual Report of the Directors of the Elgin & State Line R. R. Co.* (Chicago, 1860), 7–9; *Chicago and North Western 1910*, 28.

80. *First Annual Report of the President and Directors to the Stockholders of the Iowa Central Air Line Railroad Company* (Chicago, 1858), 2; *Tenth Annual Report*, 11; *American Railroad Journal* 12 (October 11, 1856): 645.

81. Frank P. Donovan Jr., "The North Western in Iowa," *The Palimpsest* 43 (December 1962): 546–48; *The History of Marshall County, Iowa* (Chicago: Western Historical, 1878), 411.

82. *American Railroad Journal* 12 (May 3, 1856): 276–77; P. B. Wolfe, *Wolfe's History of Clinton County, Iowa* (Indianapolis: B. F. Bowen, 1911), 122; *Twelfth Annual Report of the Directors of the Galena and Chicago Union Railroad Company* (Chicago, 1859), 11; *Thirteenth Annual Report of the Directors of the Galena and Chicago Union R.R. Company* (Chicago, 1860), 8.

83. *Statement of the Chicago, Iowa & Nebraska Railroad Company* (Chicago, 1857), 5–6; *The History of Clinton County, Iowa* (Chicago: Western Historical Company, 1879), 493–95; *Clinton* (Iowa) *Herald*, June 18, 1859.

84. *Clinton Herald*, November 2, 1861; *First Report of the President and Directors of the Cedar Rapids and Missouri River Rail Road* (Chicago, 1860), 3–5; Donovan, "North Western in Iowa," 549–51.

85. *A Communication of the Board of Directors of the Galena and Chicago Union Rail Road Company . . . Relative to the Cedar Rapids & Missouri River R.R.* (Chicago, 1860), 3–5.

86. Ibid., 8; "Act Granting the Lands to the Cedar Rapids & Missouri River Rail Road," March 26, 1860, C&NWTCo papers.

87. *First Report of the President and Directors of the Cedar Rapids and Missouri River Rail Road*, 3–4.

88. *History of Marshall County, Iowa*, 417; *Seventeenth Annual Report of the Directors of the Galena & Chicago Union Railroad Company* (Chicago, 1864), 9; Donovan, "North Western in Iowa," 551.

89. Anthony L. Cassen, "Surveying the First Railroad Across Iowa: The Journal of John I. Blair," *Annals of Iowa* 35 (summer 1960): 321–24; "Early Railroad Builders in Iowa," *The North Western* 7 (June-July 1911): 41.

Blair continued to promote expansion of railroads in Iowa and the Great Plains. His strategy largely repeated the one with the Cedar Rapids & Missouri River. The New Jerseyite bought into weak, locally promoted roads in promising areas. He expected profits from both the satellite construction companies and the sale of real estate, including townsite lots. Blair then sought to lease or sell the completed lines to the system into which they best fitted.

90. Donovan, "North Western in Iowa," 554–56.

91. Ibid., 552; *Fourteenth Annual Report of the Directors of the Galena & Chicago Union Railroad Company* (Chicago, 1861), 8; *Sixth Annual Report of the Chicago and North Western Railway Company* (New York, 1865), 7; *History of Clinton County, Iowa*, 497–99; Ronald D. Sims, Robert C. Guhr, and Paul Swanson, "The Mississippi River Bridge at Clinton, Iowa," *North Western Lines* 20 (spring 1993): 24–26.

92. *Clinton Herald*, June 29, 1861; *Sixteenth Annual Report of the Directors of the Galena & Chicago Union Railroad Company* (Chicago, 1863), 7; *Thirteenth Annual Report*, 9; *Clinton Herald*, August 9, 1862; *Chicago Tribune*, January 10, 1862; E. B. Talcott to John Blair, January 25, 1862, Blair papers.

93. Alfred D. Chandler Jr., *The Visible Hand: The Managerial Revolution in American Business* (Cambridge: Harvard University Press, 1977), 135.

94. *Chicago Tribune*, January 10, 1862.

95. *Eleventh Annual Report*, 11–12; see Galena & Chicago Union annual reports for 1856–1864; *Seventeenth Annual Report of the Directors of the Galena & Chicago Union Railroad Company* (Chicago, 1864), 5.

96. Stennett, 29–30, 45–46; *Over Half a Century of Progress*, 13; Peter Moshein and Robert R. Rothfus, "Rogers Locomotives: A Brief History and Construction List," *Railroad History* 167 (autumn 1992): 38.

97. *Seventeenth Annual Report*, 8; John H. White Jr., *The American Railroad Passenger Car* (Baltimore: Johns Hopkins University Press, 1978), 246–47, 417.

98. Stennett, 34–37; "Depots of the North Western," *North Western Newsliner* 3 (September 1948): 4.

99. *Fourteenth Annual Report*, 11. See also H. Roger Grant and Charles W. Bohi, *The Country Railroad Station in America* (Sioux Falls: Center for Western Studies, 1988), 17–24.

100. Galena & Chicago Union Railroad public timetable, Winter Arrangement, 1861.

101. *Weekly Chicago Democrat*, December 1, 1849. See also *American Railroad Journal* 8 (March 27, 1852): 199.

102. *Weekly Chicago Democrat*, March 21, 1850.

103. Prescott, *Early Railroading from Chicago*, 23, 25–32; James H. Ducker, *Men of the Steel Rails: Workers on the Atchison, Topeka & Santa Fe Railroad, 1869–1900* (Lincoln: University of Nebraska Press, 1983), 25.

104. Walter Licht, *Working for the Railroad: The Organization of Work in the Nineteenth Century* (Princeton: Princeton University Press, 1983), 145–47, 181–97, 240–44.

105. D. W. Yungmeyer, ed., "Selected Items from the Minute Book of the Galena and Chicago Union Railroad Company," *Bulletin of the Railway & Locomotive Historical Society* 65 (October 1944): 28.

106. George James Stevenson, "The Brotherhood of Locomotive Engineers and Its Leaders, 1863–1920" (Ph.D. diss., Vanderbilt University, 1954), 45–49; Licht, *Working for the Railroad*, 249.

107. Prescott, *Early Day Railroading from Chicago*, 75; William Stennett, "The Galena Road," n.d. C&NWTCo papers; *Annual Report of the Trade, Business and Growth of Chicago and the Northwest* (Chicago, 1865), 5.

Chapter 2: The North Western Emerges

1. Edward Hungerford, *Men of Erie: A Story of Human Effort* (New York: Random House, 1946), 106–22; John F. Stover, *History of the Illinois Central Railroad* (New York: Macmillan, 1975), 15–57.

2. *Yesterday and Today*, 6–7; William H. Taft to President Northwestern R. R. Company, n.d., C&NWHS.

3. Stennett, 50–53; Taft letter, C&NWHS; *Yesterday and Today*, 6–7.

4. Taft letter, C&NWHS.

5. Ibid.

6. *Chicago and North Western 1910*, 1.

7. *American Railroad Journal* 12 (December 6, 1856): 669–70; ibid. 11 (October 6, 1855): 626–27; ibid. 12 (December 6, 1856): 776–77; *Second Annual Report of the Directors of the Chicago, St. Paul & Fond du Lac Rail-Road Company, to the Stockholders* (New York, 1857), 3.

8. William F. Raney, "The Building of Wisconsin Railroads," *Wisconsin Magazine of History* 19 (June 1936): 389, 394–95.

9. DeWitt C. Prescott, *Early Day Railroading from Chicago: A Narrative with Some Observations* (Chicago: David B. Clarkson, 1910), 29–30.

10. Stennett, 55–56; *American Railroad Journal* 12 (November 29, 1856): 763.

11. Prescott, *Early Day Railroading from Chicago*, 31–32; *Yesterday and Today*, 23; Gustave William Buchen, *Historic Sheboygan County* (Privately printed, 1944), 183; "Early Railroading in Wisconsin," n.d., C&NWTCo papers.

12. *For Sale, Seven per. Cent. First Mortgage Bonds, . . ., Chicago, St. Paul, & Fond-du-Lac Railroad Company* (London, 1856), 6–7; F. H. Van Cleve, "Railroads of Delta County," *Michigan History* 5 (1922): 460–61.

13. August Derleth, *The Milwaukee Road: Its First Hundred Years* (New York: Creative Age Press, 1948), 14–36; "Early Railroading in Wisconsin," C&NWTCo papers.

14. *Yesterday and Today*, 23; Robert F. Fries, *Empire in Pine: The Story of Lumbering in Wisconsin, 1830–1900* (Madison: State Historical Society of Wisconsin, 1951), 86.

15. *Statement Showing Land Grants Made by Congress to Aid in the Construction of Railroads, Wagon Roads, Canals, and Internal Improvements* (Washington: Government Printing Office, 1888), 4–5; Stennett, 55.

16. *Sixth Annual Report of the Chicago and North Western Railway Company* (New York, 1865), 24, hereafter cited as *Sixth Annual Report*.

17. *Yesterday and Today*, 23; *Sixth Annual Report*, 27–29; Van Cleve, "Railroads of Delta County," 463; Fries, *Empire in Pine*, 86; Stennett, 60.

18. *The History of Rock County, Wisconsin* (Chicago: Western Historical, 1879), 77; Stennett, 59; *Sixth Annual Report*, 24–25.

19. Stennett, 46.

20. *Circular to the Stockholders of the Chicago & North-Western R'y Company, June 20th, 1864* (Chicago, 1864), 3–5; *Sixth Annual Report*, 3–4; *Yesterday and Today*, 12–13.

21. *Clinton* (Iowa) *Herald*, July 7, 1865; *Boston Journal*, February 23, 1865; *New York Commercial Advertiser*, July 20, 1865; H. H. Boody to Thomas J. Lee, February 27, 1865, C&NWHS.

22. *Circular to the Stockholders*, 4.

23. Ibid., 3.

24. *Sixth Annual Report*, 13–15; Stover, *Illinois Central Railroad*, 532; John F. Stover, *Iron Road to the West: American Railroads in the 1850s* (New York: Columbia University Press. 1978), 52, 122.

The mileage of the Illinois Central soared from 706 to 1,107 between 1865 and 1869. The Pennsylvania, as the result of mergers and leases, assembled a 5,814-mile system by 1873.

25. Alfred D. Chandler Jr., *The Visible Hand: The Managerial Revolution in American Business* (Cambridge: Harvard University Press, 1977), 145–87.

26. Stennett, 63–65.

27. *Report of the Chicago and North Western Railway Company, for the Seventh and Eighth Fiscal Years Ending May 31st, 1866, and May 31st, 1867* (New York, 1867), 15.

28. Stennett, 70.

29. Ibid., 70–71.

30. Ibid., 71; Maury Klein, *Union Pacific: Birth of a Railroad, 1862–1893* (Garden City, N.Y.: Doubleday, 1987), 217–27; *Report of the Chicago and North Western Railway Company, for the Tenth Fiscal Year, Ending May 31st, 1869* (New York, 1869), 10.

31. *A Compilation of the Acts of the Legislature of Minnesota and Provisions of Its Constitution, Acts of Congress, Deeds, Legal Papers, Documents and Records Affecting the Winona and St. Peter Railroad Company* (Chicago: Beach, Barnard, 1882); Franklyn Curtiss-Wedge, *The History of Winona County Minnesota* (Chicago: H. C. Cooper Jr., 1913), 461–62. 467; *History of Steele and Waseca Counties, Minnesota* (Chicago: Union Publishing, 1887), 114.

32. H. S. Larimer, "A Word about Land Grants," *North Western Newsliner* 3 (November 1947): 9–10; *Guide to an Unsurpassed Farming Region in Southern Minnesota and Eastern Dakota along the Winona & St. Peter Railroad* (Chicago: Chicago & North Western Railway, 1878), 3–5; C. F. Case, *History and Description of Lyon County, Minnesota* (Marshall: Messenger Printing House, 1884), n.p.

A railroad ultimately saved Lynd, Minnesota. The Willmar & Sioux Falls, part of the Great Northern system, reached the village by 1890.

33. *Guide to an Unsurpassed Farming Region*, i, 4.

34. *Agreement: Danford N. Barney and Others, with Winona and St. Peter Rail-Road Company* (October 31, 1867); *Report of the Chicago & North Western Railway Company for the Fiscal Year Ending May 31st, 1868* (Chicago, 1868), 9–10.

35. Curtiss-Wedge, *History of Winona County Minnesota*, 468–69; *Report of the Chicago & North Western, 1868*, 10–11; *Report of the Chicago and North Western Railway Company, for the Thirteenth Fiscal Year, Ending May 31st, 1872* (New York, 1872), 11–12.

36. *Report of the Chicago and North Western Railway Company for the Twelfth Fiscal Year, Ending May 31st, 1871* (New York, 1871), 19–20.

37. *Yesterday and Today*, 23; *Chicago & North-Western*, 14–15; *Annual Report of the Chicago and North Western Railway Company, for the Fifteenth Fiscal Year, Ending May 31st, 1874* (New York, 1874), 25.

38. *Report of the Chicago and North Western, 1871*, 26–27.

39. *Annual Report of the Chicago and North Western Railway Company, for the Fourteenth Fiscal Year, Ending May 31st, 1873* (New York, 1873), 17.

40. Ibid.

41. *Chicago and North Western 1910*, 38; *Sixth Annual Report*, 50; *Annual Report of the Chicago and North Western, 1873*, 40.

42. Ibid., 20.

43. Harold C. Livesay, *Andrew Carnegie and the Rise of Big Business* (Boston: Little, Brown, 1975), 79; *Annual Report of the Chicago and North Western, 1873*, 20.

44. Robert L. Frey, ed., *Railroads in the Nineteenth Century* (New York: Facts On File, 1988), 293.

45. *The National Cyclopedia of American Biography* (New York: James T. White, 1933), 23: 238–39; *Dictionary of American Biography*, ed. Dumas Malone (New York: Charles Scribner's, 1933), 10:286; ibid, 8:293–94; *New York Herald*, July 31, 1869.

46. *Milwaukee Sentinel*, April 20, 1887; *New York Times*, April 20, 1887; Derleth, *Milwaukee Road*, 68–71.

47. *Milwaukee Sentinel*, April 20, 1887; Derleth, *Milwaukee Road*, 87–94.

48. Frey, ed., *Railroads in the Nineteenth Century*, 261.

49. *Milwaukee Sentinel*, April 20, 1887; Julius Grodinsky, *The Iowa Pool: A Study in Railroad Competition, 1870–1884* (Chicago: University of Chicago Press, 1950), 15.

50. *Yesterday and Today*, 32.

51. William Edward Hayes, *Iron Road to Empire: The History of 100 Years of the Progress and Achievements of the Rock Island Lines* (New York: Simmons-Boardman, 1953), 44.

52. Grodinsky, *Iowa Pool*, 75.

53. Ibid., 15.

54. Richard C. Overton, *Burlington Route: A History of the Burlington Lines* (New York: Knopf, 1965), 117.

55. Grodinsky, *Iowa Pool*, 7.

56. Ibid., 15–18; Clyde H. Freed, *The Story of Railroad Passenger Fares* (Washington, D.C.: By the author, 1942), 181.

57. Grodinsky, *Iowa Pool*, 75–76.

58. *Yesterday and Today*, 32.

59. *Dictionary of Wisconsin Biography* (Madison: State Historical Society of Wisconsin, 1960), 200; *Who's Was Who in America, 1897–1942* (Chicago: A. N. Marquis Co., 1943), 659; *New York Times*, May 14, 1907.

60. Stennett, 172; Grodinsky, *Iowa Pool*, 76; Frey, ed., *Railroads in the Nineteenth Century*, 407–8; *Dictionary of Wisconsin Biography*, 200.

61. Records of Finance and Executive Committee, Number 1, March 14, 1867–April 29, 1891, Chicago & North Western Railway Company, 220–21, C&NWTCo papers; Augustus J. Veenendaal Jr., "The Kansas City Southern Railway and the Dutch Connection," *Business History Review* 61 (summer 1987): 294; *Railroad Gazette* 7 (July 10, 1875): 291; Augustus J. Veenendaal Jr., "An Example of 'Other People's Money': Dutch Capital in American Railroads," *Business and Economic History* 21 (1992): 150–51; Augustus J. Veenendaal Jr., *Slow Train to Paradise: How Dutch Investment Helped Build American Railroads* (Stanford: Stanford University Press, 1996), 18, 35, 55, 67, 100, 157–59, 162, 168–69, 181–85, 188, 208–9.

62. Maury Klein, *The Life and Legend of Jay Gould* (Baltimore: Johns Hopkins University Press, 1986), 3, 221; *American Railroad Journal* 34 (June 15, 1878): 669.

63. D. Sven Nordin, *Rich Harvest: A History of the Grange, 1867–1900* (Jackson: University Press of Mississippi, 1974), 214–37; Earl S. Beard, "The Background of State Regulation in Iowa," *Iowa Journal of History* 51 (January 1953): 32–36; Mildred Throne, "The Repeal of the Iowa Granger Law, 1878," *Iowa Journal of History* 51 (April 1953): 97–130.

64. Nordin, *Rich Harvest*, 214–37; Solon Justus Buck, *The Granger Movement: A Study of Agricultural Organization and Its Political, Economic, and Social Manifestations, 1870–1880* (Cambridge: Harvard University Press, 1913), 123–94; George H. Miller, *Railroads and the Granger Laws* (Madison: University of Wisconsin Press, 1971); Robert T. Daland, "Enactment of the Potter Law," *Wisconsin Magazine of History* 33 (September 1949): 45–54.

65. Charles Francis Adams Jr., "The Railroads and Granger Laws," *North American Review* 120 (April 1875): 406–8.

66. Mildred Throne, *Cyrus Clay Carpenter and Iowa Politics, 1854–1898* (Iowa City: State Historical Society of Iowa, 1974), 177–85.

67. Nordin, *Rich Harvest,* 217; *Proceedings of the Iowa State Grange of the Patrons of Husbandry, 1873–1875*; Ames (Iowa) *Intelligencer,* January 7, 1886.

68. *American Railroad Journal* 31 (February 20, 1875): 231; *Annual Report of the Chicago and North Western 1874,* 18–22.

69. *Memorial of the Chicago & North Western and Chicago, Milwaukee & St. Paul Railway Companies to the Senate and Assembly of the State of Wisconsin* (Chicago, 1875), 2.

70. Minutes of the Board of Directors, Chicago & North Western Railway Company, August 25, 1873, February 2, 1874, January 11, 1875, C&NWTCo papers; Stanley P. Caine, *The Myth of a Progressive Reform: Railroad Regulation in Wisconsin, 1903–1910* (Madison: State Historical Society of Wisconsin, 1970), 9.

71. Daland, "Enactment of the Potter Law," 54; Throne, "Repeal of the Iowa Granger Law," 97–130.

72. "The North Western Lines," C&NWTCo papers.

73. *Report of the Chicago and North Western, 1872,* 6.

74. David P. Morgan Jr., *Fast Mail: The First 75 Years* (Chicago: Chicago, Burlington & Quincy Railroad, 1959), 11–14.

75. Frey, ed., *Railroads in the Nineteenth Century,* 344–45.

76. Clark C. Carr, *The Railway Mail Service: Its Origin and Development* (Chicago: A. C. McClurg, 1909), 13–14.

77. Ibid., 15–16; Bryant Alden Long, *Mail by Rail: The Story of the Postal Transportation Service* (New York: Simmons-Boardman, 1951), 112–13.

78. Stennett, 44–45; "R.P.O.—Four Score and Four," *North Western Newsliner* 3 (July-August 1948).

79. Liston Edgington Leyendecker, *Palace Car Prince: A Biography of George Mortimer Pullman* (Niwot: University Press of Colorado, 1992), 145–62.

80. H. Roger Grant, ed., *We Took the Train* (DeKalb: Northern Illinois University Press, 1990), 33.

81. Chicago & North Western Railway broadside, ca. 1875.

82. Grant, ed., *We Took the Train,* 33.

83. *Williams' Pacific Tourist and Guide across the Continent* (New York: Henry T. Williams, 1876), 13.

84. Chicago & North Western Railway public timetables, 1865–1900.

85. Everett Chamberlin, *Chicago and Its Suburbs* (Chicago: T. A. Hungerford, 1874), 392, 427, 433, 458; Michael H. Ebner, *Creating Chicago's North Shore: A Suburban History* (Chicago: University of Chicago Press, 1988), 10, 23–27; Stennett, 72.

86. Chicago & North Western broadside, August 31, 1875, CB&Q papers.

87. Chicago & North Western Railway public timetable, October 1874.

Chapter 3: Years of Expansion

1. Marvin Hughitt to Charles E. Perkins, January 18, 1888, CB&Q papers.

2. Robert J. Casey and W. A. S. Douglas, *Pioneer Railroad: The Story of the Chicago and North Western System* (New York: Whittlesay House, 1948), 138; interview with Francis V. Koval, St. Charles, Illinois, September 6, 1986; Carlton J. Corliss, *Marvin Hughitt* (Chicago: Lakeside Press, 1927), 23.

3. "Marvin Hughitt," *North Western Railway Magazine* 1 (January 1923): 6; Thomas C. Cochran, *Railroad Leaders, 1845–1890: The Business Mind in Action* (Cambridge: Harvard University Press, 1953).

4. T. A. Busbey, comp., *The Biographical Dictionary of the Railway Officials of America* (New York: The Railway Age and Northwestern Railroader, 1893), 185–86; Stennett, 93.

5. "Marvin Hughitt," 4–5.

6. Stennett, 94; Harold Francis Lane, ed., *The Biographical Dictionary of the Railway Officials of America* (New York: Simmons-Boardman, 1913), 272.

7. Koval interview; *Chicago Evening American,* February 7, 1928.

8. *North Western Railway Magazine* 1 (January 1923): 71.

9. Maury Klein, *Unfinished Business: The Railroad in American Life* (Hanover, N.H.: University Press of New England, 1994), 39–40; Dolores Greenberg, *Financiers and Railroads, 1869–1889: A Study of Morton, Bliss & Company* (Newark: University of Delaware Press, 1980), 42, 90, 137; *Commercial and Financial Chronicle,* October 10, 1874; *Poor's Manual of the Railroads of the United States for 1877–1878* (New York: H. V. and H. W. Poor, 1878), x-xxix.

10. John Luther Ringwalt, *Development of Transportation Systems in the United States* (Philadelphia: Railway World, 1888), 228; *Chicago and North Western Railway Company Annual Report, for the Eighteenth Fiscal Year, Ending May 31st, 1877* (New York, 1877), 7, 47; *Annual Report of the Chicago and North Western Railway Company, for the Fourteenth Fiscal Year, Ending May 31st, 1873* (New York, 1873), 7; *Annual Report of the Chicago and North Western Railway Company, for the Nineteenth Fiscal Year, Ending May 31st, 1878* (n.p., 1878), 5.

11. *Annual Report of the Chicago and North Western Railway Company for the Twenty-Second Fiscal Year, Ending May 31st, 1881* (New York, 1881), 45; *Annual Report of the Chicago and North Western Railway Company for the Twenty-Sixth Fiscal Year Ending May 31st, 1885* (New York, 1885), 51; *Annual Report of the Chicago and North Western Railway Company for the Thirty-Fifth Fiscal Year* (n.p., 1894), 51.

12. *Chicago and North Western 1910,* 38; "Chicago & Northwestern Railway Co. Common Stock as an Investment," n.d., Harvey Fisk papers.

13. Stennett, 74–75, 88, 164–66; *Chicago and North Western Railway Company Annual Report for the Twenty-First Fiscal Year, Ending May 31st, 1880* (New York, 1880), 13.

14. *Chicago and North Western Railway Company, 1877,* 21.

15. Ibid., 21–22; *Chicago and North Western 1910,* 16.

16. Stennett, 95; *Chicago and North Western 1910,* 18.

17. *Chicago and North Western, 1880,* 23.

18. George W. Hilton, *American Narrow Gauge Railroads* (Stanford: Stanford University Press, 1990), 48–71, 295.

19. Ibid., 396–97; *Railway World* 5 (August 9, 1879): 753.

20. *Railroad Gazette* 12 (June 11, 1880): 325; ibid. 12 (August 27, 1880): 462.

21. Hilton, *American Narrow Gauge Railroads,* 557–58.

22. Ibid.; *Poor's Manual of the Railroads of the United States, 1879* (New York: Henry V. Poor, 1879), 769.

23. Hilton, *American Narrow Gauge Railroads,* 558; Stanley H. Mailer, "The Ridge Runner," *Trains* 30 (June 1971): 24–28.

24. *Chicago and North Western 1910,* 16; *Chicago and North Western, 1880,* 21; Hilton, *American Narrow Gauge Railroads,* 559; Gregg Condon et al., *The Dinky: C&NW Narrow Gauge in Wisconsin* (Marsh Lake, Wisc.: Marsh Lake Productions, 1993), 18.

25. *Historical Statistics of the United States: Colonial Times to 1957* (Washington: U.S. Department of Commerce, 1960), 428; *Statistics of the Chicago and North Western Railway Company . . . for the Fiscal Year*

Ending May 31st, 1890 (New York, 1890), 11.

26. *Iowa Official Register: Forty-Eighth Number, 1959–1960* (Des Moines, 1960), 290; Earle D. Ross, *Iowa Agriculture* (Iowa City: State Historical Society of Iowa, 1951), 71–91.

27. *Chicago and North Western 1910*, 30; *Annual Report of the Chicago and North Western, 1873*, 6; *Annual Report of the Chicago and North Western Railway for the Fiscal Year Ending May 31st, 1882* (New York, 1882), 19.

28. Stennett, 101, 186; *Chicago and North Western 1910*, 20; *Annual Report of the Chicago and North Western, 1885*, 8; *Railroad Gazette* 31 (July 28, 1899): 540.

29. *Railroad Gazette* 12 (August 27, 1880): 462; ibid. 14 (September 29, 1882): 605; ibid. 15 (April 3, 1883): 239; *Chicago and North Western 1910*, 17, 22; "The Toledo and Northwestern Railway," n.d., Valuation Records, Interstate Commerce Commission, The National Archives, Washington, D.C.

30. "Toledo and Northwestern Railway;" *Chicago and North Western, 1880*, 20; *Annual Report of the Chicago and North Western Railway Company for the Twenty-Fourth Fiscal Year Ending May 31st, 1883* (New York, 1883), 24.

31. *Annual Report of the Chicago and North Western, 1883*, 24; *Railway Gazette* 18 (June 25, 1886): 453.

32. *Annual Report of the Chicago and North Western, 1885*, 17; Stennett, 100–101.

33. *Annual Report of the Chicago and North Western, 1885*, 17; *Fremont* (Neb.) *Tribune*, April 23, 1884.

34. Marvin Hughitt to Charles E. Perkins, October [?], 1884, CB&Q papers.

35. *Chicago and North Western 1910*, 35; Tom W. Glaser, *A Guide to the Collection of John Isley Blair* (Dallas, Texas: DeGolyer Library, 1985), 1–2.

36. *Yesterday and Today*, 28; *Fremont Tribune*, March 5, 1869; Stennett, 41–42.

37. Maury Klein, *Union Pacific: Birth of a Railroad, 1862–1893* (Garden City, N.Y.: Doubleday, 1987), 14–15; Stennett, 41; "The Chicago and North Western," *North Western Newsletter* 3 (May-June 1948): 12; "To the Senate and House of Representatives of the United States," n.d., Blair papers.

38. William H. Buss and Thomas T. Osterman, eds., *History of Dodge and Washington Counties, Nebraska and Their People* (Chicago: American Historical Society, 1921), 332; David Seidel, *Fremont, Elkhorn & Missouri Valley R.R. Co.* (Columbus, Neb.: Harbor Mist Publications, 1988), 1–3; Jay Van Hoven, "The History of the Fremont, Elkhorn and Missouri Valley Railroad, 1868–1903" (master's thesis, University of Nebraska, 1940), 2–5.

39. *Manual of the Railroads of the United States* (New York: H. V. Poor, 1876), 592–93; John F. Stover, *History of the Illinois Central Railroad* (New York: Macmillan, 1975), 133–35; Stennett, 42.

40. *Fremont Tribune*, March 12, 1869; Seidel, *Fremont, Elkhorn & Missouri Valley R.R. Co.*, 6; *Railroad Gazette* 18 (July 9, 1886): 484; *Chicago and North Western 1910*, 20.

41. *Fremont Tribune*, September 23, 1869.

42. Ibid., April 9, 1869; *Chicago & North-Western*, 12; Harrison Johnson, *Johnson's History of Nebraska* (Omaha, Neb.: H. Gibson, 1880), 131.

43. Van Hoven, "History," 6–7.

44. *Fremont Tribune*, November 4, 11, 1869.

45. Van Hoven, "History," 81.

46. Ibid., 11; "List of Subscriptions to the Fremont, Elkhorn & Missouri Valley R.R.—1870," Blair papers.

47. Van Hoven, "History," 13–14.

48. *Chicago & North-Western*, 19; Van Hoven, "History," 16, 19; Johnson, *History of Nebraska*, 261.

49. James C. Olson, *History of Nebraska* (Lincoln: University of Nebraska Press, 1955), 181–84; "North Western Opens Contest for Employees," January 27, 1948, C&NWHS papers; Van Hoven, "History," 20.

50. Hilton, *American Narrow Gauge Railroads*, 438; Johnson, *History of Nebraska*, 131–32; Van Hoven, "History," 25.

51. Van Hoven, "History," 28, 30.

52. *Chicago & North-Western*, 19; Edward Albert Landgraf, *Early History of Norfolk, Nebraska and Madison County* (Norfolk, Neb.: The Norfolk Daily News, n.d.), n.p.; Van Hoven, "History," 32; Seidel, *Fremont, Elkhorn & Missouri Valley R.R. Co.*, 10.

53. *Chicago & North-Western*, 19; Johnson, *History of Nebraska*, 455; Richard C. Overton, *Burlington Route: A History of the Burlington Lines* (New York: Alfred A. Knopf, 1965), 279.

54. "The Fremont, Elkhorn and Missouri Valley Railroad Company," Valuation Records, Interstate Commerce Commission, The National Archives, Washington, D.C.; *Chicago & North-Western*, 19; A. J. Leach, *A History of Antelope County Nebraska* (Chicago: Lakeside Press, 1909), 154.

55. Van Hoven, "History," 34–36; Olson, *History of Nebraska*, 203–14.

56. *Poor's Manual of Railroads, 1884* (New York: H. V. Poor, 1884), 771–72; "A Report on the Fremont, Elkhorn & Mo. Valley R.R. Co., February 1, 1884," Blair papers.

57. Seidel, *Fremont, Elkhorn & Missouri Valley R.R. Co.*, 17; "A Report on the Fremont, Elkhorn & Mo. Valley R.R. Co., February 1, 1884," Blair papers; *Railroad Gazette* 16 (August 8, 1884): 595.

58. Julius Grodinsky, *The Iowa Pool: A Study in Railroad Competition, 1870–84* (Chicago: University of Chicago Press, 1950), 150–62.

59. Maury Klein, *The Life and Legend of Jay Gould* (Baltimore: Johns Hopkins University Press, 1986), 342; Overton, *Burlington Route*, 190–93.

60. *Chicago & North Western*, 19; *Railroad Gazette* 16 (August 22, 1884): 627.

61. *Chicago & North-Western*, 19; *Rapid City* (Dakota Territory) *Journal*, July 7, 1886.

62. August Derleth, *The Milwaukee Road: Its First Hundred Years* (New York: Creative Age Press, 1948), 295–96; Overton, *Burlington Route*, 227–28.

63. See Mildred Fiedler, *Railroads of the Black Hills* (Seattle, Wash.: Superior Publishing, 1964); Joseph H. Cash, *Working the Homestake* (Ames: Iowa State University Press, 1973), 14–28.

64. *Chicago & North-Western*, 19; Hilton, *American Narrow Gauge Railroads*, 513–16.

65. *Chicago & North-Western*, 19; Van Hoven, "History," 65.

66. *Chicago and North Western 1910*, 21; *Railroad Gazette* 20 (May 4, 1888): 295.

67. *Chicago & North-Western*, 19; Van Hoven, "History," 63–64; Seidel, *Fremont, Elkhorn & Missouri Valley R.R. Co.*, 38–39.

68. *Chicago & North-Western*, 19; Seidel, *Fremont, Elkhorn & Missouri Valley R.R. Co.*, 48–50.

69. Lawrence H. Larsen and Barbara J. Cottrell, *The Gate City: A History of Omaha* (Boulder, Colo.: Pruett, 1982), 74–77.

70. Seidel, *Fremont, Elkhorn & Missouri Valley R.R. Co.*, 40; Van Hoven, "History," 80; *Railroad Gazette* 14 (April 21, 1882): 244; ibid. 18 (December 31, 1886): 915; ibid. 33 (February 8, 1901): 103.

71. *Chicago & North-Western*, 19; Seidel, *Fremont, Elkhorn & Missouri Valley R.R. Co.*, 41–43; *Travelers' Official Railway Guide for the*

72. Seidel, *Fremont, Elkhorn & Missouri Valley R.R. Co.*, 42.

73. Van Hoven, "History," 67–70; Dorothy Weyer Creigh, *Nebraska: A Bicentennial History* (New York: Norton, 1977), 124–25; Ray H. Mattison, "The Burlington Tax Controversy in Nebraska over the Federal Land Grant," *Nebraska History* 28 (April-June 1947): 110–31.

74. Van Hoven, "History," 79–81.

75. Herbert S. Schell, *History of South Dakota*, 3d ed. (Lincoln: University of Nebraska Press, 1975), 158–74.

76. Ibid., 159; James F. Hamburg, "Railroads and the Settlement of South Dakota during the Great Dakota Boom, 1878–1887," *South Dakota History* 5 (spring 1975): 165–78; *Daily Huronite* (Huron, Dakota Territory), July 28, 1886; George W. Kingsbury, *History of Dakota Territory*; and George Martin Smith, ed., *South Dakota: Its History and Its People*, 5 vols. (Chicago: S. J. Clarke Publishing, 1915), 2: 1331; Hamlin Garland, *A Son of the Middle Border* (1917; reprint, New York: Macmillan, 1962), 312.

77. *Chicago and North Western, 1910*, 18; *Railway World* 9 (August 7, 1880): 756; Derleth, *Milwaukee Road*, 290; Doane Robinson, *Doane Robinson's Encyclopedia of South Dakota* (Pierre, S.Dak.: Privately printed, 1925), 601.

78. Casey and Douglas, *Pioneer Railroad*, 159–71; Kenneth M. Hammer, "Dakota Railroads" (Ph.D. diss., South Dakota State University, 1966), 105–6, 185; Minute Book, Western Townlot Company, 1881–1887, C&NWTCo papers.

79. See Roy M. Robbins, *Our Landed Heritage: The Public Domain, 1776–1936* (Princeton: Princeton University Press, 1942); and Thomas Le Duc, "The Disposal of the Public Domain on the Trans-Mississippi Plains," *Agricultural History* 24 (October 1950): 199–204.

80. *Railroad Gazette* 11 (April 4, 1879): 190; ibid. 11 (May 30, 1879): 302; ibid. 12 (August 27, 1880): 462.

81. *Chicago and North Western 1910*, 18; *Railroad Gazette* 13 (January 21, 1881): 42; *Railway World* 9 (October 23, 1880): 1015; Robinson, *Encyclopedia of South Dakota*, 601.

Another factor apparently plagued the extension to the Black Hills. The *Railroad Gazette* for December 30, 1887, explained it this way: "The company is having a survey made across the Sioux Reservation in Dakota. Eight years ago the survey for the same line was made, and the notes and profile were stolen."

82. *Chicago and North Western 1910*, 18; *Railroad Gazette* 16 (May 16, 1884): 385; ibid. 31 (August 18, 1899): 588.

83. *Chicago and North Western 1910*, 18.

84. Ibid.; *Railroad Gazette* 12 (July 23, 1880): 402; ibid. 17 (September 18, 1885): 606; Kurt John Stoebe, "The History of the Redfield-Gettysburg, South Dakota Branch Line of the Chicago and North Western Railway Company," unpublished M.A. thesis, University of South Dakota, 1977, 16–26; *Chicago and North Western Railway Company Annual Report for the Twenty-Ninth Fiscal Year, Ending May 31st, 1888* (New York, 1888), 7.

85. Derleth, *Milwaukee Road*, 290–93; Charles W. Bohi and H. Roger Grant, "Country Railroad Stations of the Milwaukee Road and Chicago & North Western in South Dakota," *South Dakota History* 9 (winter 1978): 1–23.

86. "Review of the Fiscal Year, 1901," C&NWTCo papers.

87. Charles Billing Hurst, "Spink County Reminiscences," *The Dakotan* 5 (May 1902): 43; Casey and Douglas, *Pioneer Railroad*, 172–74.

88. Marvin Hughitt to James J. Hill, April 2, 1886; James J. Hill to Marvin Hughitt, April 3, 1886; Marvin Hughitt to James J. Hill, July 29, 1886, all letters in James J. Hill papers, James Jerome Hill Reference Library, St. Paul, Minnesota, hereafter cited as Hill papers; Ralph W. Hidy et al., *The Great Northern Railway: A History* (Boston: Harvard Business School Press, 1988), 62, 110.

89. *Railroad Gazette* 14 (August 11, 1882): 490; Schell, *History of South Dakota*, 223; Gilbert C. Fite, *The Farmers' Frontier, 1865–1900* (New York: Holt, Rinehart and Winston, 1966), 106–9; Lemeuel E. Quigg, "New Empires in the Northwest: The Dakotas, Montana, and Washington," *Library of Tribune Extras* 1 (August 1889): 11.

90. *Chicago and North Western Railway Company Annual Report for the Thirty-Third Fiscal Year* (New York, 1892), 10–11.

91. Stennett, 107–8, 166; *The History of Rock County, Wisconsin* (Chicago: Western Historical Company, 1879), 180–81.

92. Ralph G. Plumb, *A History of Manitowoc County* (Manitowoc, Wisc.: Brandt Printing & Binding, 1904), 100–101, 105; D. I. Nelke, ed., *The Biographical Dictionary and Portrait Gallery of the Representative Men of the United States, Wisconsin Volume* (Chicago: Lewis, 1895), 233–34.

93. *Chicago and North Western 1910*, 19; Plumb, *History of Manitowoc County*, 102–3.

94. *Chicago and North Western 1910*, 19; *Railroad Gazette* 7 (September 25, 1875): 401; ibid. 7 (December 18, 1875): 525; *Poor's Manual of the Railroads of the United States, 1883* (New York: H. V. Poor, 1883), 755; *First Annual Statement of the Milwaukee, Lake Shore and Western Railway Company* (Milwaukee, 1876), 1; *New York Times*, January 10, 1942.

95. *Chicago and North Western 1910*, 19; Robert F. Fries, *Empire in Pine: The Story of Lumbering in Wisconsin, 1830–1900* (Madison: State Historical Society of Wisconsin, 1951); Robert C. Nesbit, *Wisconsin: A History* (Madison: University of Wisconsin Press, 1973), 296–310.

96. *Railroad Gazette* 11 (June 27, 1879): 361; ibid. 16 (September 5, 1884): 660.

97. *Chicago and North Western 1910*, 19; Alice E. Smith, *Millstone and Saw: The Origins of Neehah-Menasha* (Madison: State Historical Society of Wisconsin, 1966), 76; *Railroad Gazette* 17 (March 20, 1885): 191.

98. *Chicago and North Western 1910*, 19; *Rhinelander* (Wisc.) *News*, January 10, 1942; *Railroad Gazette* 20 (April 20, 1988): 263.

99. Charles H. Stats to author, April 26, 1994.

100. Stennett, 144, 168; *Poor's Manual of the Railroads, 1885*, 703, 984.

Railroad historian Charles Stats writes: "The backers of the StPEGT diverted [its line] . . . to Clintonville after the MLS&W beat them to Wausau (one of the intermediate cities the StPEGT planned to reach), and palmed it off on the MLS&W. The 200,000 acres of timberland were probably the icing on the cake that did it" (Charles H. Stats to author, April 26, 1994).

101. *Poor's Manual of Railroads, 1887* (New York: Henry V. Poor, 1887), 499; *Poor's Manual of Railroads, 1892* (New York: Henry V. Poor, 1892), 786.

102. *Railroad Gazette* 23 (December 18, 1891): 909; *Chicago and North Western Railway Company Annual Report for the Thirty-Third Fiscal Year*, 11; *Annual Report of the Chicago and North Western Railway Company for the Thirty-Fifth Fiscal Year* (n.p., 1894), 16.

103. *Chicago and North Western Railway Company Annual Report for the Thirty-Third Fiscal Year*, 10.

104. *Chicago and North Western 1910*, 16–18.

105. *Railroad Gazette* 17 (October 30, 1885): 702; ibid. 17 (December 18, 1885): 17; *Chicago and North Western 1910*, 17.

106. *Chicago and North Western 1910*, 16, 20; *Poor's Manual of the Railroads of the United States, 1879*, 778–79; *Poor's Manual of the*

Railroads of the United States, 1880 (New York: H. V. Poor, 1880), 811.

107. *Chicago and North Western 1910*, 16–18, 28.

108. Ibid., 16, 18.

109. *Railroad Gazette* 27 (August 9, 1895): 531; "A Review of 1895 . . . Comments by President M. Hughitt, January 1896, C&NWTCo papers.

110. *Chicago and North Western Railway Company Annual Report for the Thirty-Third Fiscal Year*, 5.

Chapter 4: The Omaha Road

1. *Annual Report 1956 Chicago and North Western Railway Company* (Chicago, 1957), 11; *Chicago, Saint Paul, Minneapolis & Omaha Railway Annual Report 1971* (Chicago, 1972), i; *Moody's Manual of Investments: Railroad Securities* (New York: Moody's Investors Service, 1930), 1134; New York News Bureau clipping, March 14, 1902, Harvey Fisk papers.

2. "Corporate History of the Chicago, Saint Paul, Minneapolis and Omaha Railway," April 1, 1940, 1, Chicago & North Western History Center, Northern Illinois University, DeKalb, Illinois, hereafter cited as "Omaha Corporate History."

3. Judson W. Bishop, "History of the St. Paul & Sioux City Railroad, 1864–1881," *Collections of the Minnesota Historical Society* 10 (1905): 399–401; "Omaha Corporate History," 2; S. M. Stockslager, *Statement Showing Land Grants Made by Congress to Aid in the Construction of Railroads, Wagon Roads, Canals, and Internal Improvements* (Washington: Government Printing Office, 1888), 8–9.

4. "Omaha Corporate History," 2–3.

5. Ibid., 4, Bishop, "History of the St. Paul & Sioux City Railroad," 402–3; Stockslager, *Land Grants Made by Congress*, 12–13; Roy V. Scott, "Early Agricultural Education in Minnesota," *Agricultural History* 37 (January 1963): 22; H. S. Jaynes to "My dear sir," February 15, 1896, Omaha Road papers.

6. "Omaha Corporate History," 4–5; Henry A. Castle, *History of St. Paul and Vicinity* (Chicago: Lewis, 1912), 223–24.

7. C. C. Andrews, ed., *History of St. Paul, Minn.* (Syracuse, N.Y.: D. Mason, 1890), 45–48; "Omaha Corporate History," 5.

Elias Franklin Drake was an experienced railroad executive. Before the Civil War he had helped to organize and manage several small carriers in his native Ohio. During the 1860s Drake entered railroading in Minnesota. See W. B. Hennessy, *Past and Present of St. Paul, Minnesota* (Chicago: S. J. Clarke, 1906), 225–28.

8. Ibid., 7–9. *Manual of the Railroads of the United States, 1881* (New York: Henry V. Poor, 1881), 684.

9. Ibid., 9.

10. Harrison Johnson, *Johnson's History of Nebraska* (Omaha, Neb.: Henry Gibson, 1880), 210, 213, 581; "Omaha Corporate History," 9.

11. George W. Hilton, *American Narrow Gauge Railroads* (Stanford: Stanford University Press, 1990), 438; "Omaha Corporate History," 9–10.

12. *Railroad Gazette* 12 (November 19, 1880): 621; Richard C. Overton, *Burlington Route: A History of the Burlington Lines* (New York, Knopf, 1965), 279.

13. "Omaha Corporate History," 17.

14. *The First Mortgage Land Grant Sinking Fund Seven Per Cent. Gold Bonds, . . . of the West Wisconsin Railway* (New York, 1871), 5; Stockslager, *Land Grants Made by Congress*, 6–7.

15. "The Life and Times of the Chicago and North Western," *North Western Newsliner* 3 (September 1948): 8; J. D. Condit, "Early History of the 'Omaha,'" *North Western Railway System Magazine* 2 (March 1924): 4; "Omaha Corporate History," 17–18.

16. "Omaha Corporate History," 18; H. H. Porter, "To the Bondholders of the West Wisconsin Railway Company," ca. 1875, 4, Omaha Road papers.

17. "Omaha Corporate History," 18; Porter, "Bondholders," 2–3.

18. *To St. Paul via the Chicago, Madison and St. Paul Line* (Chicago: Rand, McNally, January 22, 1876); "Abstract of Agreement between Chicago and North Western Railway Company and Chicago, Saint Paul, Minneapolis and Omaha Railway Company for Joint Through Line between Chicago and St. Paul Dated April 27, 1876," Omaha Road papers.

19. Franklyn Curtiss-Wedge, *History of Dunn County, Wisconsin* (Minneapolis: H. C. Cooper Jr., 1925), 92; A. E. Kidder, "The Railroads," in *History of Eau Claire County, Wisconsin*, ed. William F. Bailey (Chicago: C. F. Cooper, 1914) 2: 490–92.

20. Kidder, "Railroads," 489; Harold Weatherhead, *Westward to the St. Croix: The Story of St. Croix County, Wisconsin* (Hudson, Wisc.: St. Croix County Historical Society, 1978), 61, 68; Frank P. Donovan Jr., "The North Western in Iowa," *The Palimpsest* 43 (December 1962): 568; Arthur M. Wellington, *The Economic Theory of the Location of Railways* (New York: J. Wiley, 1893), 35.

21. *Manual of the Railroads of the United States, 1878* (New York: Henry V. Poor, 1878), 774–75; "Omaha Corporate History," 19–20.

22. "Omaha Corporate History," 20; *Poor's Manual of Railroads, 1878* (New York: H. V. Poor, 1878), 818.

23. *St. Paul Pioneer Press*, October 24, 1880.

24. Timetable No. 34, West Wisconsin Railway, April 5, 1874, Omaha Road papers; "Omaha Corporate History," 22.

25. "Omaha Corporate History," 22–23.

26. *Railroad Gazette* 12 (April 19, 1880): 200; *Eau Claire (Wisc.) Free Press*, February 5, 1880.

27. *Poor's Manual, 1878*, 770.

28. Stockslager, *Land Grants Made by Congress*, 6–7.

29. "Omaha Corporate History," 23.

30. Ibid., 23–24; Richard N. Current, *Pine Logs and Politics: A Life of Philetus Sawyer, 1816–1900* (Madison: State Historical Society of Wisconsin, 1950), 132–43.

31. *First Annual Report of the Chicago, St. Paul, Minneapolis and Omaha Railway Company, 1881* (Chicago, 1882), 8.

32. "Omaha Corporate History," 25–29; Stennett, 169.

33. "Omaha Corporate History," 27–28; *Railroad Gazette* 13 (October 7, 1881): 561.

34. Stennett, 170; *Twelfth Annual Report of the Chicago, St. Paul, Minneapolis & Omaha Railway Company* (St. Paul, 1893), 6.

35. *Report on Economics of Consolidation and Coordination, Chicago, Milwaukee, St. Paul and Pacific Railroad Company, Chicago and North Western Railway Company [,] Chicago, St. Paul, Minneapolis and Omaha Railway Company* (East Orange, N.J.: Wm. Wyer, 1955), Exhibit A.

36. *Annual Report of the Chicago and North Western Railway Company for the Twenty-Fourth Fiscal Year Ending May 31st, 1883* (New York, 1883), 22; *Chicago, St. Paul, Minneapolis & Omaha Railway Co.: A Review of the Financial Development of the Chicago & North Western System* (New York: Wood, Struthers, 1920), 1; New York News Bureau clipping, March 14, 1902, Harvey Fisk papers.

37. William Edward Hayes, *Iron Road to Empire: The History of 100 Years of the Progress and Achievement of the Rock Island Lines* (New York: Simmons-Boardman, 1953), 98–105; Maury Klein, *The Life and Legend of Jay Gould* (Baltimore: Johns Hopkins University Press, 1986), 438; Frank P. Donovan Jr. *Mileposts on the Prairie: The Story of*

the Minneapolis & St. Louis Railway (New York: Simmons-Boardman, 1950), 63.

38. *Chicago, St. Paul, Minneapolis & Omaha Railway Co.*, 1; Overton, *Burlington Route*, 165.

39. *First Annual Report of the Chicago, St. Paul, Minneapolis and Omaha Railway Company*, 3; *Official Time Tables* (Philadelphia: National Railway Publications, April 1877), 158.

40. New York News Bureau clipping, March 14, 1902, Harvey Fisk papers, *Chicago, St. Paul, Minneapolis & Omaha Railway Co.*, 4.

41. *Railroad Gazette* 41 (September 28, 1906): 259; *Second Annual Report of the Chicago, St. Paul, Minneapolis & Omaha Railway Company* (St. Paul, 1883), 3; Robert M. Frame III, "William Drew Washburn," in Robert L. Frey, ed., *Encyclopedia of American Business History and Biography: Railroads in the Nineteenth Century* (New York: Facts On File, 1988), 426–27.

42. May [?] 1887 clipping, Harvey Fisk papers; Stennett, 117, 166; Robert J. Casey and W. A. S. Douglas, *Pioneer Railroad: The Story of the Chicago and North Western System* (New York: Whittlesey House, 1948), 316; *Railroad Gazette* 16 (February 8, 1884): 119.

43. *Railroad Gazette* 41 (September 18, 1906): 259; *Chicago, St. Paul, Minneapolis & Omaha Railway Co.*, i.

44. A. L. McClurg, "Chicago, St. Paul, Minneapolis & Omaha Ry. Co.," April 14, 1936, 14, Omaha Road papers.

45. Ibid.; Robert F. Fries, *Empire in Pine: The Story of Lumbering in Wisconsin, 1830–1900* (Madison: State Historical Society of Wisconsin Press, 1951), 87; Weatherhead, *Westward to the St. Croix*, 60.

46. W. A. Gardner to J. T. Clark, November 16, 1907, Omaha Road papers.

47. *Annual Report of the Chicago and North Western, 1883*, 23.

48. W. A. Gardner to J. T. Clark, November 16, 1907, Omaha Road papers; *The Daily Huronite* (Huron, S.Dak.), February 12, 1914; *Railroad Gazette* 13 (July 8, 1881): 379.

49. *Railroad Gazette* 24 (August 5, 1892): 588; unidentified newspaper clipping, May 2, 1889, Omaha Road papers.

50. *Butterfield* (Minn.) *Times*, December 6, 1901.

51. Unidentified newspaper clipping [?1891], Omaha Road papers.

52. John S. Kennedy to James J. Hill, December 20, 1882, Hill papers; *The Official Guide of the Railways* (New York: National Railway Publications, January 1909), xxvii; Wayne Andrews, *The Vanderbilt Legend: The Story of the Vanderbilt Family, 1794–1940* (New York: Harcourt, Brace, 1941).

53. See Overton, *Burlington Route*, 219–25.

54. *Eighth Annual Report of the Chicago, St. Paul, Minneapolis & Omaha Railway Company* (St. Paul, 1889), 10.

55. C. R. Fitch to W. F. Merrill, February 3, 1896, Erie Lackawanna papers. See also Albro Martin, *Enterprise Denied: Origins of the Decline of American Railroads, 1897–1917* (New York: Columbia University Press, 1971).

56. James E. Moore to J. N. Rivers, November 22, 1892, letterpress book of Northwestern Town Lot Co., 386, Omaha Road papers.

57. Interview with Charles Shannon, Arlington Heights, Illinois, October 1, 1988; Overton, *Burlington Route*, 165; Hayes, *Iron Road to Empire*, 164.

58. Marvin Hughitt to Cornelius Vanderbilt [II], February 28, 1890, C&NWTCo papers.

Chapter 5: The Hughitt Era

1. *Annual Report of the Chicago & North Western Railway Company for the Forty-Second Fiscal Year Ending May 31, 1901* (Chicago, 1901), 7; *The Daily Huronite* (Huron, S.Dak.), December 2, 1899.

2. *Annual Report of the Chicago & North Western Railway Company for the Forty-Second Fiscal Year Ending May 31, 1901*, 5; *New York Times*, May 30, 1898.

3. *Chicago and North Western 1910*, 38; New York News Bureau clipping, June 10, 1903, Harvey Fisk papers.

4. *Historical Statistics of the United States: Colonial Times to 1957* (Washington: U.S. Department of Commerce, 1960), 427, 429; Robert J. Casey and W. A. S. Douglas, *Pioneer Railroad: The Story of the Chicago and North Western System* (New York: Whittlesey House, 1948), 314–16, 319–320.

5. Interview with Charles Shannon, Arlington Heights, Illinois, October 1, 1988.

6. George S. May, "Getting Iowa Out of the Mud," *The Palimpsest* 46 (February 1965): 66–67.

7. William H. Thompson, *Transportation in Iowa: A Historical Summary* (Ames: Iowa Department of Transportation, 1989), 93.

8. *Chicago and North Western Railway Company Annual Report for the Fortieth Fiscal Year Ending May 31st, 1899* (Chicago, 1899), 22–23; John F. Stover, *History of the Illinois Central Railroad* (New York: Macmillan, 1975), 142–43.

9. *Chicago and North Western 1910*, 17; Don L. Hofsommer, "A Chronology of Iowa Railroads," *Railroad History* 132 (spring 1975): 76; H. Roger Grant, *The Corn Belt Route: A History of the Chicago Great Western Railroad Company* (DeKalb: Northern Illinois University Press, 1984), 63–65.

10. *Annual Report of the Chicago & North Western Railway Company for the Forty-First Fiscal Year* (Chicago, 1900), 26.

11. *Annual Report of the Chicago & North Western Railway Company for the Forty-Third Fiscal Year Ending May 31, 1902* (Chicago, 1902), 20.

12. Paula M. Nelson, *After the West Was Won: Homesteaders and Town-Builders in Western South Dakota, 1900–1917* (Iowa City: University of Iowa Press, 1986), 7–8, 14–23.

13. Casey and Douglas, *Pioneer Railroad*, 315–16; Herbert S. Schell, *History of South Dakota*, 3d ed. (Lincoln: University of Nebraska Press, 1975), 252–55.

14. *Chicago and North Western 1910*, 18; August Derleth, *The Milwaukee Road: Its First Hundred Years* (New York: Creative Age Press, 1948), 293.

15. *Fifty-First Annual Report of the Chicago and North Western Railway Company, Fiscal Year Ending June 30, 1910* (Chicago, 1910), 22; *Fifty-Second Annual Report of the Chicago and North Western Railway Company, Fiscal Year Ending June 30, 1911* (Chicago, 1911), 22; *Railway Age Gazette* 49 (September 9, 1910): 482; Derleth, *Milwaukee Road*, 187, 198.

16. Shannon interview.

17. *Fifty-First Annual Report of the Chicago and North Western*, 21–22; Marvin P. Riley, W. F. Kumlien, and Duane Tucker, *50 Years Experience on the Belle Fourche Irrigation Project* (Brookings: South Dakota State College, 1955), 8–10.

18. Shannon interview; *Railroad Gazette* 40 (June 22, 1906): 181; *Railroad Age Gazette* 45 (June 5, 1908): 47; Frank P. Donnovan Jr., *Mileposts on the Prairie: The Story of the Minneapolis & St. Louis Railway* (New York: Simmons-Boardman, 1950), 123–31.

19. *Chicago and North Western Railway Company Annual Report for the Thirty-Seventh Fiscal Year Ending May 31st, 1896* (New York, 1896), 16–17.

20. *Chicago and North Western Railway Company Annual Report for the Thirty-Ninth Fiscal Year Ending May 31st, 1898* (Chicago, 1898), 19; *Annual Report of the Chicago and North Western, Forty-First Fiscal Year*, 24.

21. *Chicago and North Western 1910*, 20.

22. *Poor's Manual of the Railroads of the United States, 1909* (New York: Poor's Railroad Manual, 1909), 499; *Poor's Manual of Railroads, 1922* (New York: Poor's Publishing, 1922), 221.

23. *Annual Report of the Chicago & North Western, 1901,* 19.

24. *Railroad Gazette* 32 (December 7, 1900): 817; *Annual Report of the Chicago & North Western, 1901,* 21; Dorothy Schwieder, Joseph Hraba, and Elmer Schwieder, *Buxton: Work and Racial Equality in a Coal Mining Community* (Ames: Iowa State University Press, 1987), 88–112.

The North Western likely considered the southern Iowa coal line to be an avenue to Kansas City, Missouri. "The company's engineers are surveying from Weller [Monroe County, Iowa] to Corydon, on the Keokuk & Western [Burlington Railroad], about 32 miles," reported the *Railroad Gazette* in 1900. "It is understood that a further extension is to be made from Corydon to Spring Valley in Decatur County [Iowa], near the southern boundary of the State, and from thence into Missouri. The ultimate terminus is understood to be Kansas City." *Railroad Gazette* 32 (November 30, 1900): 784.

25. Albro Martin, *Enterprise Denied: Origins of the Decline of American Railroads, 1897–1917* (New York: Columbia University Press, 1971), 55–61.

26. *Annual Report of the Chicago & North Western, Forty-First Year,* 26.

27. Ibid., 25.

28. Ibid., 25–26; Shannon interview.

29. *Chicago and North Western 1910,* 20; Casey and Douglas, *Pioneer Railroad,* 319.

30. *Annual Report of the Chicago & North Western, Forty-First Year,* 26; George Miller to Frank Koval, n.d., C&NWTCo papers.

31. *Annual Report of the Chicago & North Western, 1901,* 21; *Annual Report of the Chicago & North Western, 1902,* 20.

32. David P. Thelen, *Robert M. La Follette and the Insurgent Spirit* (Boston: Little, Brown, 1976), 32–51; Robert S. Maxwell, *Emanuel L. Philipp: Wisconsin Stalwart* (Madison: State Historical Society of Wisconsin, 1959), 90–110; New York News Bureau clipping, May 28, 1904, Harvey Fisk papers; Stanley P. Caine, *The Myth of a Progressive Reform: Railroad Regulation in Wisconsin, 1903–1910* (Madison: State Historical Society of Wisconsin, 1970), 202.

Governor Emanuel L. Philipp, a loyal supporter of the North Western, had once worked as a station agent and dispatcher on the Madison Division and later served as a freight solicitor. According to Philipp's biographer, "officials of the C&NW remained his warm friends throughout [his] life" (Maxwell, *Emanuel L. Philipp,* 12).

33. *Forty-Sixth Annual Report of the Chicago & North Western Railway Company for the Fiscal Year Ending June 30, 1905* (Chicago, 1905), 19–20.

34. *Fifty-First Annual Report of the Chicago and North Western, 1910,* 23.

35. Ibid.; Shannon interview.

36. *Fifty-First Annual Report of the Chicago and North Western, 1910,* 22.

37. *Annual Report of the Chicago & North Western, 1901,* 22; *Fifty-Second Annual Report of the Chicago and North Western, 1911,* 22–23.

38. *Annual Report of the Chicago & North Western, 1902,* 19, 39; *Fifty-Third Annual Report of the Chicago and North Western, 1912,* 19; *Fifty-Fourth Annual Report of the Chicago and North Western Railway Company, Fiscal Year Ending June 30, 1913* (Chicago, 1913), 20; *Fifty-Fifth Annual Report of the Chicago and North Western Railway Company, Fiscal Year Ending June 30, 1914* (Chicago, 1914), 19.

39. John E. Blunt to M. Hughitt, January 25, 1902, C&NWHS; *Fifty-Second Annual Report of the Chicago and North Western, 1911,* 23; Stenographers' Minutes, Interstate Commerce Commission, Washington, D.C., April 28–30, 1927, C&NWTCo papers; Richard C. Overton, *Burlington Route: A History of the Burlington Lines* (New York: Knopf, 1965), 278.

40. John Sherman Porter, ed., *Moody's Manual of Investments: Railroad Securities* (New York: Moody's Investors Service, 1930), 81–82; George H. Drury, compiler, *The Historical Guide to North American Railroads* (Milwaukee: Kalmbach, 1985), 175–76.

41. *Forty-Seventh Annual Report of the Chicago & North Western Railway Company, Fiscal Year Ending June 30, 1906* (Chicago, 1906), 20–21.

42. Memorandum by Samuel A. Lynde, August 21, 1918, C&NWTCo papers; *The Daily Huronite,* October 29, 1903.

43. Casey and Douglas, *Pioneer Railroad,* 315; Shannon interview; *Eastern Pennington County Memories* (Wall, S.Dak.: American Legion Auxiliary, 1964), 9; *Railroad Gazette* 41 (August 3, 1906): 32; ibid. 42 (June 14, 1907): 878; B. A. Botkin and Alvin F. Harlow, *A Treasury of Railroad Folklore* (New York: Crown, 1953), 505.

44. *Wind River Mountaineer* (Lander, Wyo.), November 17, 1905; Alfred James Mokler, *History of Natrona County Wyoming, 1888–1923* (Chicago: Lakeside Press, 1923), 47–49.

45. E. M. Lewis, "Chicago and North Western Ry. and the Projected West Coast Extension, 1904–1906," C&NWHS; New York News Bureau clipping, August 4, 1907, Harvey Fisk papers. See also H. Roger Grant, "Seeking the Pacific: The Chicago & North Western's Plans to Reach the West Coast," *Pacific Northwest Quarterly* 81 (April 1990): 67–73.

46. Derleth, *Milwaukee Road,* 170–71; New York News Bureau clipping, December 1, 1905, Harvey Fisk papers.

47. "A Pacific Advance," C&NWTCo papers; Casey and Douglas, *Pioneer Railroad,* 139; *Railroad Age Gazette* 47 (September 17, 1909): 487.

48. New York News Bureau clipping, n.d., Harvey Fisk papers; *Chicago Tribune,* January 8, 1928.

49. Derleth, *Milwaukee Road,* 187, 198–225.

50. Don DeNevi, *The Western Pacific: Railroading Yesterday, Today and Tomorrow* (Seattle: Superior, 1978), 51–58.

51. Albro Martin, *James J. Hill and the Opening of the Northwest* (New York: Oxford University Press, 1976), 309–10, 552–55; *One Square Mile of Nebraska Grazing Land Free to the Settler under the Terms of the Kincaid Bill* (Chicago: Chicago & North Western Railway, 1908).

52. *Alfalfa: The Money Crop of the West and Northwest* (Chicago: Chicago & North Western Railway, 1910); Roy V. Scott, *Railroad Development Programs in the Twentieth Century* (Ames: Iowa State University Press, 1985), 48; *The Daily Huronite,* July 8, 1909.

53. *One Square Mile of Nebraska Grazing Land.*

54. Scott, *Railroad Development Programs,* 41; "Potato Growing and Industrial Development," *[C&NW] Traffic Department Monthly Bulletin* 2 (April 1914): 14–15.

55. *The Daily Huronite,* July 26, 1886; June 20, 1910.

56. Ibid., May 26, 1887; December 9, 1890; March 14, 1891.

57. *Statistics of the Chicago and North Western Railway Company for the Fiscal Year Ending May 31st, 1900* (Chicago: Chicago & North Western Railway, 1900), 57; "Agriculture in Review," (1900), C&NWTCo papers.

58. *Railroad Gazette* 9 (August 3, 1877): 354; ibid. 30 (January 7, 1898): 2; G. W. Tilton to H. B. Stone, March 27, 1880, CB&Q papers; *The Daily Huronite,* January 23, 1886, December 23, 1902; Almont Lindsey, *The Pullman Strike: The Story of a Unique Experiment and of a Great Labor Upheaval* (Chicago: University of Chicago Press, 1942), 287–88.

59. *The Daily Huronite,* June 1, 1893.

60. Overton, *Burlington Route,* 158–60; Donald L. McMurry, *The Great Burlington Strike of 1888: A Case History in Labor Relations* (Cambridge: Harvard University Press, 1956), 13–14; C. H. Salmons, *The Burlington Strike: Its Motives and Methods* (Aurora, Ill.: Press of Bunnell & Ward, 1889), 159–60.

Income for workers tended to vary more by region than by carrier. The supply of labor and the cost of living affected payment scales. Generally railroaders in the West made the best wages; those in the South the lowest. See James H. Ducker, *Men of the Steel Rails: Workers on the Atchison, Topeka & Santa Fe Railroad, 1869–1900* (Lincoln: University of Nebraska Press, 1983), 12.

61. *The Daily Huronite,* August 1, 1908.

62. Fred C. Henson, "Apprentice to Greatness," *The Conductor & Brakeman* 72 (November 15, 1955): 310–13; Edward H. Meyers, "The Kate Shelley Incident," manuscript in author's possession; *Boone County* (Iowa) *Republican,* July 13, 1881; *Ogden* (Iowa) *Reporter,* July 14, 1881; H. Roger Grant, "Kate Shelley and the Chicago & North Western Railway," *The Palimpsest* 76 (Fall 1995): 138–44.

63. Meyers, "Kate Shelley Incident."

64. Walter Licht, *Working for the Railroad: The Organization of Work in the Nineteenth Century* (Princeton: Princeton University Press, 1983), 212–13.

65. Ducker, *Men of the Steel Rails,* 25; Marvin Hughitt to Frederick D. Underwood, March 27, 1908, Erie Lackawanna papers.

66. T. Addison Busbey, ed., *The Biographical Directory of the Railway Officials of America* (Chicago: Railway Age, 1906), 298.

67. Shannon interview; interview with James A. Zito, St. Charles, Illinois, May 4, 1994.

68. *The Daily Huronite,* July 21, 1892; "Sioux City Man Traces His Unique Railroad Roots: Largest Railroad Family to Work for C&NW," news release, n.d., C&NWTCo papers; "Pensioners' Letters to the Family," *The North Western* 7 (October 1911): 4–18.

69. *The Daily Huronite,* January 9, 1901; *Railroad Gazette* 33 (January 11, 1901): 17–18.

70. George H. Burgess and Miles C. Kennedy, *Centennial History of the Pennsylvania Railroad Company, 1846–1946* (Philadelphia: Pennsylvania Railroad, 1949), 665; *Railroad Gazette* 32 (December 28, 1900): 866.

71. "What a North Western Pension May Mean," *The North Western* 7 (November 1911): 10; "Pensioners' Letters to the Family," 10.

72. "The Surgical Department of the Chicago & North-Western," *Railroad Gazette* 39 (December 1, 1905): 518.

73. Licht, *Working for the Railroad,* 239–43.

74. Ducker, *Men of the Steel Rails,* 126–39.

75. Ibid.; Lewis Atherton, *Main Street on the Middle Border* (Bloomington: Indiana University Press, 1954), 173–74, 189–90.

76. *The Daily Huronite,* February 4, 1887.

77. "The Worker and the Rail-road," 1899, C&NWTCo papers.

78. John F. Moore, *The Story of the Railroad "Y"* (New York: Association Press, 1930); *Rules and Regulations for the Government of Employes of the Operating Department* (Chicago: Chicago & North-Western Railway, 1893), 6.

A revised rule book, which was issued in 1902, extended supervision over addictive substances when it forbade "trainmen to use tobacco in any form, at or near stations." The reason likely involved a concern for public health and cleanliness (*The Daily Huronite,* April 11, 1902).

79. "The C.& N.W. Ry. Co. Employees' Mutual Aid Association," *The North Western Bulletin* 4 (February 1909): 32; ibid. 4 (July 1909): 35.

80. *The Daily Huronite,* July 20, 1914.

81. H. Roger Grant, "Midwestern Railroad Leader: Marvin Hughitt of the Chicago & North Western," *Hayes Historical Journal* 8 (fall 1988): 5–16.

82. Edward E. Loomis to Marvin Hughitt, May 15, 1910, Erie Lackawanna papers.

Chapter 6: "The Best of Everything"

1. Newspaper clipping, May 3, 1911, in author's possession.

2. "'The Ball with the Bar across It:' The North Western's Trademark Is the Offspring of Eight Illustrious Ancestors," *North Western Newsliner* 8 (May–June 1953): 10–11.

3. Ibid.

4. Ibid.; James A. Ward, "On the Mark: The History and Symbolism of Railroad Emblems," *Railroad History* 153 (autumn 1985): 46.

5. *The Daily Huronite* (Huron, S.Dak.), November 8, 1888, clipping, C&NWTCo papers.

By the late 1920s the North Western modified the phrase to read "The Best of Everything in the Best of the West," and then the motto disappeared. In the early 1990s the company selected another promotional slogan, "On Track for Excellence!" and renewed an advertising tradition.

6. H. Roger Grant, *Living in the Depot: The Two-Story Railroad Station* (Iowa City: University of Iowa Press, 1993), 13; Freeman H. Hubbard, *Railroad Avenue: Great Stories and Legends of American Railroading* (New York: McGraw-Hill, 1945), 34–35; *The Official Guide of the Railways* (New York: National Railway Publications, July 1900), 427, 529, 656.

7. *Railroad Gazette* 9 (May 11, 1877): 216.

8. "In the Days of the 'Hotel Car,'" *The North Western* (January 1911): 14; Chicago & North Western Railway public timetable, April 1, 1884.

9. H. Roger Grant, "The Chicago & North Western and the 'Overland Route,'" *National Railway Bulletin* 52 (1987): 4; *Chicago Journal,* December 17, 1887; "Chicago and North-Western Line Through Train Service," December 30, 1897 (Chicago: Chicago & North Western Railway).

10. Arthur D. Dubin, *Some Classic Trains* (Milwaukee: Kalmbach, 1964), 173–74.

11. Ibid., 174; Chicago & North Western Railway public timetable, November 14, 1909.

12. "Contracts, Agreements, Leases, Etc., Union Pacific System, 1880–1893," 1.

13. Maury Klein, *Union Pacific: The Rebirth, 1894–1969* (New York: Doubleday, 1989), 84–100.

14. "From Prairie Schooner to the Overland Limited," *The American Monthly Review of Reviews* 26 (July 1902): 33, 40.

15. Lucius M. Beebe, *The Overland Limited* (Berkeley, Calif.: Howell-North, 1957), 9–10, 26–29; James Edward Kranefeld, "What This Train Needs Is a Good 5c Cigar!" *National Railway Bulletin* 52 (1987): 36–37; Dubin, *Some Classic Trains,* 172; *The Daily Huronite,* May 26, 1926.

The S. S. Pierce Company continued the "Overland" brand long after the *Overland Limited* disappeared. In the early 1950s, for example, the cigar label contrasted a modern diesel-electric locomotive with a mid-nineteenth-century passenger train.

16. *The Official Guide of the Railways* (New York: National Railway Publications, June 1903), 577–78, 589–93, 659–662, 683–84, 689; Chicago and North-Western Line public timetables, December 14, 1903.

17. Dubin, *Some Classic Trains,* 157–58; Chicago & North

Western Railway public timetable, June 9, 1879.

18. Dubin, *Some Classic Trains,* 158.

19. *The Railroad Gazette* 39 (November 24, 1905); Dubin, *Some Classic Trains,* 10; *The New North Western Limited* (Chicago: Chicago & North Western Railway, 1913), 3–5, 8–9.

20. H. Roger Grant, "Experiencing the 'Best of Everything:' Passenger Service on the Chicago & North Western Railway," *Railroad History* 169 (autumn 1993): 38; Chicago and North Western Line public timetable, December 14, 1903.

21. *The Railroad Gazette* 36 (May 20, 1904): 388; *The Duluth-Superior Limited* (Chicago: Chicago & North Western Railway, 1906).

22. Chicago & North Western Railway public timetable, September 6, 1908.

23. *The Daily Huronite,* December 7, 1898, December 20, 1907.

24. *Annual Report of the Chicago & North Western Railway Company for the Forty-First Fiscal Year* (Chicago, 1900), 5; Edwin A. Pratt, *American Railway* (London: Macmillan, 1903), 70–71.

25. *The Daily Huronite,* November 14, 1888.

26. H. Roger Grant, "The Chicago & North Western and Freight: An Historical Overview," *North Western Lines* 17 (spring 1990): 18.

27. Emory R. Johnson and Grover G. Huebner, *Railroad Traffic & Rates* (New York: D. Appleton, 1911), 1:270; *Chicago Daily Inter-Ocean,* n.d., clipping in Harvey Fisk papers.

28. John H. White Jr., *The American Railroad Freight Car: From the Wood-Car Era to the Coming of Steel* (Baltimore: Johns Hopkins University Press, 1993), 122; *Chicago and North Western Railway Company Annual Report for the Thirty-Third Fiscal Year* (Chicago, 1892), 14.

29. White, *American Railroad Freight Car,* 602.

30. *The Railroad Gazette* 39 (November 10, 1905): 431; *The Daily Huronite,* July 22, 1896.

31. "Car for Transportation of Horses, C.& N.W. Railway," *American Engineer, Car Builder and Railroad Journal* 72 (June 1898): 193.

32. H. Roger Grant, ed., *Brownie the Boomer: The Life of Charles P. Brown, an American Railroader* (DeKalb: Northern Illinois University Press, 1991), 86–87.

33. *Chicago and North Western Railway Company Annual Report for the Thirty-Seventh Fiscal Year* (New York, 1896), 13; *Annual Report of the Chicago & North Western, Forty-First Fiscal Year,* 16; Charles T. Knudsen, *Chicago & North Western Railway Steam Power, 1848–1956* (Chicago: Knudsen Publications, 1965), 46–77; *The Railroad Gazette* 29 (October 29, 1897): 762, 43 (July 5, 1907): 6; "New Class 'D' Passenger Locomotives," *The Railroad Gazette* 32 (August 3, 1900): 520–21.

34. "Powerful 8-Wheel Passenger Locomotives," *The American Engineering and Railroad Journal* 78 (June 1899): 79.

35. "Hughitt and Finley Retire," *Railway Age* 78 (June 27, 1925): 1641; Gregory Lee Thompson, *The Passenger Train in the Motor Age: California's Rail and Bus Industries, 1910–1941* (Columbus: Ohio State University Press, 1993), 138; Knudsen, *Chicago & North Western Steam Power,* 164–73.

36. *The Railroad Gazette* 27 (November 15, 1895): 754, and 28 (April 10, 1896): 251; Knudsen, *Chicago & North Western Steam Power,* 78–84; *Railway Age Gazette* 48 (April 22, 1910): 1052.

37. *Over Half a Century of Progress, 1848–1902: The Only Double Track Railway between Chicago and the Missouri River* (Chicago: Chicago & North Western Railway, 1902), 17.

38. Ibid.

39. *Chicago and North Western Railway Company Annual Report for the Thirty-Second Fiscal Year* (New York, 1891), 17; *Chicago and North Western Railway Company Annual Report, Third-Third Fiscal Year,* 15; *Omaha World,* July 12, 1896.

40. *Annual Report of the Chicago & North Western Railway Company for the Forty-Second Fiscal Year Ending May 31, 1901* (Chicago, 1901), 17.

41. Ibid., 18–19.

42. *Over Half a Century of Progress,* 17.

43. *Annual Report of the Chicago & North Western Railway Company for the Forty-Third Fiscal Year Ending May 31, 1902* (Chicago, 1902), 17.

44. John Anson Ford, "Twenty Millions for a Station," *Technical World Magazine* 14 (February 1911): 676; *Fifty-Second Annual Report of the Chicago and North Western Railway Company, Fiscal Year Ending June 30, 1911* (Chicago, 1911), 17; John A. Droege, *Passenger Terminals and Trains* (New York: McGraw-Hill, 1916), 131.

45. *The Railroad Gazette* 13 (June 3, 1881): 306; Carroll L. V. Meeks, *The Railroad Station: An Architectural History* (New Haven: Yale University Press, 1956), 23; Ira J. Bach and Susan Wolfson, *A Guide to Chicago's Train Stations: Present and Past* (Athens: Ohio University Press, 1986), 10; Stennett, 35; Knudsen, *Chicago & North Western Steam Power,* 101; Walter G. Berg, *Buildings and Structures of American Railroads* (New York: John Wiley, 1900), 400.

46. W. C. Armstrong, "The New Passenger Terminal of the Chicago and North Western Railway," *Journal of the Western Society of Engineers* 16 (December 1911): 933.

47. *The Railroad Gazette* 41 (October 12, 1906): 314; Armstrong, "New Passenger Terminal," 934–37.

48. Armstrong, "New Passenger Terminal," 993; *Chicago Record-Herald,* August 8, 1908; Meeks, *Railroad Station,* 122; *Railroad Age Gazette* 45 (August 14, 1908): 711; *The Daily Huronite,* August 19, 1908.

49. *Railroad Age Gazette* 45 (August 14, 1908): 711.

50. Interstate Commerce Commission, Bureau of Valuation, Engineering Report upon Chicago & North Western Railway Company, Valuation 898, vol. 3, box 685, The National Archives, Washington, D.C.

51. H. Roger Grant, "Midwestern Railroad Leader: Marvin Hughitt of the Chicago & North Western," *Hayes Historical Journal* 8 (fall 1988): 10; Armstrong, "New Passenger Terminal," 949, 963, 990–92.

52. "The Chicago and North Western Passenger Terminal, Chicago," *The Official Guide of the Railways* (New York: National Railway Publications, August 1911), xxxvi–xxxviii.

53. Ibid., xxxvi; H. Roger Grant, Don L. Hofsommer, and Osmund Overby, *St. Louis Union Station: A Place for People, A Place for Trains* (St. Louis: St. Louis Mercantile Library, 1994), 95–96.

54. *Chicago and North Western Traffic Department Monthly Bulletin* 2 (November 1913): 31–33; *The Care and Protection Afforded the Immigrant in the New Passenger Terminal* (Chicago: Chicago and North Western Railway, 1913), 3, 5.

55. J. R. Sandy, "Emigrants at Wells St. Station, Chicago," *The North Western Bulletin* 4 (June 1909): 13–18; *Care and Protection Afforded the Immigrant,* 7, 9, 15–25; "Where Immigrants Are Happy," *The North Western* (August 1911): 10–12.

56. *The North Western* 7 (February 1921): 11.

57. "Chicago & North Western $23,000,000 Passenger Terminal," *Live Stock Journal* 51 (July 6, 1911): 4; Bach and Wolfson, *A Guide to Chicago's Train Stations,* 26; Droege, *Passenger Terminals and Trains,* 132; *The Official Guide of the Railways* (New York: National Railway Publications, July 1911), xxix.

58. Ford, "Twenty Millions for a Station," 674; *Railroad Age Gazette* 47 (July 9, 1909): 41.

59. Grant, *Living in the Depot,* 8; *Annual Report of the Chicago &*

North Western, Forty-First Fiscal Year, 22; E. B. Stillman, *Past and Present of Greene County, Iowa* (Chicago: S. J. Clarke, 1907), 86.

60. "The Pace That Kills," *The World's World* 13 (March 1907): 8595–96.

61. H. I. Cleveland, *A Thrilling Night's Ride on the North-Western Fast Mail* (Chicago: Chicago & North Western Railway, 1899).

62. *Chicago Herald*, April 22, 1891.

63. "A Great Time Record," *The North Western Bulletin* 5 (September 1909): 37.

64. *Sioux City Journal*, February 11, 1914.

65. Mark Aldrich, "Safety First Comes to the Railroads, 1910–1939," *Railroad History* 166 (spring 1992): 7; Charles H. Clark, "The Railroad Safety Movement in the United States: Origins and Development," unpublished Ph.D. diss., University of Illinois, 1966; Christopher Clark, "The Railroad Safety Programs in the United States," *Transport History* 7 (summer 1974): 97–123.

66. *The Daily Huronite*, January 8, 1894.

67. Ralph C. Richards, *Conservation of Men* (Chicago, 1910), 8–9.

68. *The North Western* 7 (October 1921): 3; Edward L. Tinker, "Ralph C. Richards," *American Magazine* 76 (December 1913): 44–45; *The Daily Huronite*, January 19, 1914.

69. "The Industrial Toll of Death and Chicago & North-Western Railway's Exemplary 'Safety First' System," *Chicago Commerce* 8 (April 11, 1913): 12.

70. Ibid., 13, W. T. Gale, "Safety on the Chicago & North Western," *American Engineer* 87 (March 1913): 137–41; *The Daily Huronite*, January 26, 1911.

71. "Chicago and North Western Railway's Campaign on Signal Instruction," *Chicago & North Western Traffic Department Monthly Bulletin* 2 (January 1914): 10–11; "Some Good Ideas on Discipline," *Railroad Age Gazette* 45 (September 25, 1908): 998.

72. *The North Western*, October 1921, 3.

73. *The Daily Huronite*, January 24, 1914.

74. *The Railroad Gazette* 37 (December 16, 1904): 636.

75. Albro Martin, *Enterprise Denied: Origins of the Decline of American Railroads, 1897–1917* (New York: Columbia University Press, 1971), 173–93; George W. Hilton and John F. Due, *The Electric Interurban Railways in America* (Stanford: Stanford University Press, 1960), 118, 335–36; "Competition with Suburban Steam Service," *Street Railway Journal* 25 (March 25, 1905): 1.

76. *Chicago & Northwestern Railway Company: Some Account of Its Resources of the Past Fifteen Years and of the Use That It Has Made of Them* (New York: Wood, Struthers, 1918).

Chapter 7: The Great War and the Roaring Twenties

1. Robert J. Casey and W. A. S. Douglas, *Pioneer Railroad: The Story of the Chicago and North Western System* (New York: Whittlesey House, 1948), 289, 294.

2. *The Biographical Dictionary of the Railway Officials of America* (New York: Simmons-Boardman, 1913), 203; Willamine A. Gardner Cook, *The W. A. Gardner Story* (Evanston, Ill.: Privately printed, 1956), 3–4, 8–10, 16.

3. Cook, *W. A. Gardner Story*, 85–89; *Railway Age Gazette* 60 (May 19, 1916): 1078.

4. "Changes in the North Western Family," *The North Western* 6 (November 1910):4; *Railway Age Gazette* 60 (May 19, 1916): 1078.

5. *Fifty-sixth Annual Report of the Chicago and North Western Railway Company* (Chicago, 1915), 13, 22.

6. Bowman Hilt Moore, *The Federal Valuation of the Railroads in the United States* (Chicago: American Railway Engineering Association, 1952), 8–10, 26; Albro Martin, *Enterprise Denied: Origins of the Decline of American Railroads, 1897–1917* (New York: Columbia University Press, 1971), 177.

The North Western had already confronted valuation requirements before the 1913 federal legislation. It had launched such efforts for Wisconsin in 1903, Michigan in 1904, and Minnesota in 1905 (Stenographers' Minutes before ICC, Interstate Commerce Commission Valuation Reports, Valuation No. 898, The National Archives, Washington, D.C.).

7. New York News Bureau clipping, December 3, 1916, Harvey Fisk papers; *Sixty-First Annual Report of the Chicago and North Western Railway* (Chicago, 1921), 18–19; *Seventy-Second Annual Report of the Chicago and North Western Railway* (Chicago, 1932), 27; interview with Lynn D. Farrar, Overland Park, Kansas, September 23, 1994.

8. *The Biographical Directory of the Railway Officials of America* (Chicago: Railway Age, 1906), 5; *New York Times*, April 4, 1946; *The Daily Huronite* (Huron, S.Dak.), June 3, 1916.

9. Richard C. Overton, *Burlington Route: A History of the Burlington Lines* (New York: Knopf, 1965), 294.

10. Winthrop M. Daniels, *American Railroads: Four Phases of Their History* (Princeton: Princeton University Press, 1932), 84–86; *New York Times*, September 1, 1916.

11. A. B. Garretson, "The Attitude of the Railroad Brotherhoods toward Hours and Wages," *Annals of the American Academy of Political and Social Science* 69 (March 1918): 265–67; *Supplement to Fifty-Seventh Annual Report of the Chicago and North Western Railway Company* (Chicago, 1917), 6; K. Austin Kerr, *American Railroad Politics, 1914–1920: Rates, Wages, and Efficiency* (Pittsburgh: University of Pittsburgh Press, 1986), 13–16.

12. Maury Klein, *Union Pacific: The Rebirth, 1894–1969* (New York: Doubleday, 1989), 218.

13. Kerr, *American Railroad Politics*, 39–100; John F. Stover, *The Life and Decline of the American Railroad* (New York: Oxford University Press, 1970), 161; Richard Saunders, *The Railroad Mergers and the Coming of Conrail* (Westport, Conn.: Greenwood Press, 1978), 36–37; T. R. Gourvish, *British Railways, 1948–73* (Cambridge: Cambridge University Press, 1986), 13–16.

14. Walker D. Hines, *War History of American Railroads* (New Haven: Yale University Press, 1928), 1–21, 27–29, 93–95.

15. I. Leo Sharfman, *The American Railroad Problem: A Study in War and Reconstruction* (New York: Century, 1921), 105–14.

16. *Railway Age* 64 (January 25, 1918): 201; ibid. 64 (June 14, 1918): 1439, 1451.

17. *New York Times*, January 10, 1918; Keith L. Bryant Jr., ed., *Railroads in the Age of Regulation, 1900–1980* (New York: Facts On File, 1988), 447.

18. Kerr, *American Railroad Politics*, 91–102; Overton, *Burlington Route*, 308; Ralph W. Hidy et al., *The Great Northern Railway: A History* (Boston: Harvard Business School Press, 1988), 152.

19. *North Western Passenger Department Monthly Bulletin* 6 (January 1918): 4–5; *Railway Age* 64 (April 12, 1918): 996.

20. *North Western Passenger Department Monthly Bulletin* 6 (December 1917): 4; *Daily Huronite*, December 11, 1917, June 5, 1918, September 4, 1918.

21. *North Western Passenger Department Monthly Bulletin* 6 (December 1917): 4.

22. *Railway Age Gazette* 63 (December 28, 1917): 1183–84.

23. *Railway Age* 64 (February 8, 1918): 329.

24. *North Western Passenger Department Monthly Bulletin* 6 (May 1918): 3.

25. *Daily Huronite,* May 3, 1917.

26. *Fifty-Eighth Annual Report of the Chicago and North Western Railway Company* (Chicago, 1918), 10; Kerr, *American Railroad Politics,* 91–100; *Daily Huronite,* May 24, 1918; *Fifty-Ninth Annual Report of the Chicago and North Western Railway Company* (Chicago, 1919), 7.

27. *Fifty-Ninth Annual Report of the Chicago and North Western,* 6–7; *Sixtieth Annual Report of the Chicago and North Western Railway Company* (Chicago, 1920), 6.

28. *Sixty-First Annual Report of the Chicago and North Western,* 9.

29. William Norris Leonard, *Railroad Consolidation under the Transportation Act of 1920* (New York: Columbia University Press, 1946), 53–54; Saunders, *Railroad Mergers,* 38–42.

30. Sharfman, *Railroad Problem,* 397–431; Ari and Olive Hoogenboom, *A History of the ICC: From Panacea to Palliative* (New York: Norton, 1976), 94–97.

31. Interview with D. Keith Lawson, Rogers, Arkansas, October 18, 1980; *New York Times,* February 25, 26, 1920.

32. *New York Times,* February 24, 1920.

33. *The Biographical Dictionary of the Railway Officials of America* (New York: Simmons-Boardman, 1922), 211–12; *The National Cyclopedia of American Biography* (New York: James T. White, 1929), 20:141.

34. *Sixty-Second Annual Report of the Chicago and North Western Railway Company* (Chicago, 1922), 6–10; *The North Western* 8 (October 1921): 10–11; *Brookings* (S.Dak.) *Register,* October 4, 1923.

35. Leonard, *Railroad Consolidation,* 306, 326.

36. Saunders, *Railroad Mergers,* 48–49; "Memorandum on the Van Sweringen Railroads," (n.d.), 1–6, John W. Barriger Collection, The Mercantile Library, St. Louis, Missouri.

37. *Dayton-Goose Creek Railroad Company* v. *United States,* 263 U.S. 456; Leonard, *Railroad Consolidation,* 193–225.

38. Julius Kruttschnitt, "Railroad Efficiency: Past and Present," *Atlantic Monthly* 129 (January 1922): 106–9; *Sixty-Third Annual Report of the Chicago and North Western Railway,* (Chicago, 1923), 9.

39. John F. Stover, *History of the Baltimore and Ohio Railroad* (West Lafayette: Purdue University Press, 1987), 248–49; *Sixty-First Annual Report of the Chicago and North Western,* 9.

40. Bert M. Jewell, "The Railroad Strike: Striker's Viewpoint," *Current History* 17 (November 1922): 207; *Annual Report of the Delaware, Lackawanna and Western Railroad Company* (New York, 1923), 6.

41. *Evening Huronite,* July 26, 1922; *Sixty-Third Annual Report of the Chicago and North Western,* 10.

42. James N. Giglio, *H. M. Daugherty and the Politics of Expediency* (Kent, Ohio: Kent State University Press, 1978), 147; *Railway Age* 73 (September 23, 1922): 549; Robert H. Zieger, *Republicans and Labor, 1919–1929* (Lexington: University of Kentucky Press, 1969), 138–39.

43. David M. Vrooman, *David Willard and Progressive Management on the Baltimore & Ohio Railroad* (Columbus: Ohio State University Press, 1991), 66–67; *Evening Huronite,* October 15, 1925.

44. *Sixty-Second Annual Report of the Chicago and North Western,* 5; *Sixty-Sixth Annual Report of the Chicago and North Western Railway Company* (Chicago, 1926), 5.

45. *Sixty-Fifth Annual Report of the Chicago and North Western Railway Company* (Chicago, 1925), 7–8.

46. *Railway Age* 78 (June 27, 1925): 1641–42; *Minneapolis Morning Tribune,* June 24, 1925.

47. Frank P. Donovan Jr., "The North Western in Iowa," *The Palimpsest* 43 (December 1962): 591–92.

48. Neil M. Clark, "'Wes' Sargent's Boy," *The American Magazine* (December 1925): 202–3.

49. Ibid., 202.

50. Ibid.; "Little Stories about Big Men," *Transportation* 6 (January 1930): 80.

51. *North Shore News* (Evanston, Ill.), July 27, 1928; "Little Histories of Our Big Men: Fred W. Sargent," *Townsfolk* 1 (October 1928): 60; Clark, "'Wes' Sargent's Boy," 203.

52. *Sixty-Sixth Annual Report of the Chicago and North Western,* 6–7.

53. "Zepplins of the Rails: Giant Class 'H' Locomotives," (Chicago: Chicago & North Western Railway, 1930); Charles T. Knudsen, *Chicago & North Western Steam Power, 1848–1956* (Chicago: Knudsen Publications, 1965), 164–73.

54. *Railway Review* 78 (May 8, 1926): 834; *Evening Huronite,* October 12, 1926; *Railroad Herald* 31 (August 1927): 22–23; *Brotherhood of Locomotive Firemen and Enginemen's Magazine* 81 (November 1926): 423–25.

55. "Recent betterments," n.d. [ca. 1930], C&NWHS.

56. *Railway Review* 71 (October 28, 1922): 601; *Sixty-Seventh Annual Report of the Chicago and North Western Railway Company* (Chicago, 1926), 8; *Sixty-Ninth Annual Report of the Chicago and North Western Railway Company* (Chicago, 1929), 7.

57. "Automatic Train-Control—How It Operates on Main Line between Chicago and Omaha, Chicago and North Western Railway," C&NWHS; "A Superhuman Engineer Protects This Train," (Chicago: Chicago & North Western Railway, 1930).

The obvious glitch with the ATC system was that it could not guarantee the prevention of an accident. If a switch engine, for example, pulled out in front of a crack passenger train, the cab signals would warn of impending danger but probably not in time to avoid a mishap (interview with Wallace Abbey, Chicago, Illinois, September 20, 1994).

58. *Sixty-Fourth Annual Report of the Chicago and North Western Railway Company,* (Chicago, 1924), 15–16.

59. *Sixty-Eighth Annual Report of the Chicago and North Western Railway Company* (Chicago, 1928), 7; *Seventieth Annual Report of the Chicago & North Western Railway Company* (Chicago, 1930), 7; "The General Freight Classification and Hump Yards, Proviso, Ill.: A $16,000,000 Project," (Chicago: Chicago & North Western Railway, 1930).

60. Casey and Douglas, *Pioneer Railroad,* 316; *Sixty-Eighth Annual Report of the Chicago and North Western,* 9.

61. Donovan L. Hofsommer, *Katy Northwest: The Story of a Branch Line Railroad* (Boulder, Colo.: Pruett, 1976), 79–86; *Evening Huronite,* February 25, 1925, July 19, 1927, August 25, 1927, November 17, 1928, May 27, 1929.

62. *Seventieth Annual Report of the Chicago and North Western,* 12–13; Chicago & North Western public timetable, September 25, 1932, 41; interview with Charles C. Shannon, Arlington Heights, Illinois, October 1, 1988.

63. *Smoke Abatement and Electrification of Railway Terminals in Chicago* (Chicago: Rand McNally, 1915), 774, 778–79; Michael Bezilla, *Electric Traction on the Pennsylvania Railroad, 1895–1968* (University Park: Pennsylvania State University Press, 1980), 27–31, 91; John F. Stover, *History of the Illinois Central Railroad* (New York: Macmillan, 1975), 301–3; *New York Times,* October 7, 1926.

64. *Chicago Tribune,* October 22, 1929; *Sixty-Eighth Annual Report of the Chicago & North Western,* 8; *Seventieth Annual Report of the Chicago and North Western,* 13; "Aluminum Used Extensively in New C. & N. W. Suburban Cars," *Railway Mechanical Engineer* 101 (October 1927): 665–67.

65. *Railway Review* 73 (December 22, 1923): 914.

66. Interview with Arthur D. Dubin, Chicago, Illinois, September 21, 1994; "A New Steel Train: Northwestern Limited," *Railway Journal* 30 (January 1924): 19; *Railway Age* 85 (September 1, 1928): 419–20.

67. James J. Flink, *The Car Culture* (Cambridge: MIT Press, 1975), p. 140; Robert Lynd and Helen Lynd, *Middletown: A Study in American Culture* (New York: Harcourt, Brace, 1929), 255–56; *Historical Statistics of the United States. Colonial Times to 1957* (Washington: U.S. Department of Commerce, 1960), 458, 462; *Passenger Traffic Report* (Washington: U.S. Office of the Federal Coordinator of Transportation, 1935), 14, 20–21, 111–12.

68. *Sixty-Fourth Annual Report of the Chicago and North Western*, 7–8.

69. Robert E. Bader, "The Curtailment of Railroad Service in Nebraska, 1920–1941," *Nebraska History* 36 (March 1955): 33–40; *Evening Huronite*, June 7, 1924; December 7, 1928.

70. *McKeen Motor Car Co. 124 Cars in Service* (Omaha: McKeen Motor Car, 1912), 52; "C. & N. W. Ry. Converts Passenger Coach into Gas Motor Car," *Railway Review* 76 (April 2, 1925): 771–75; *Sixty-Seventh Annual Report of the Chicago & North Western*, 7; *Sixty-Eighth Annual Report of the Chicago and North Western*, 10; *Sixty-Ninth Annual Report of the Chicago and North Western*, 11; *Seventieth Annual Report of the Chicago and North Western*, 13.

71. Interview with Charles H. Stats, Chicago, Illinois, September 25, 1994.

72. Shannon interview; Chicago & North Western public timetable, February 17, 1929, 21.

73. *Railway Age* 84 (June 23, 1928): 1490.

74. *The Official Guide of the Railways* (New York: National Railway Publications, January 1911), 749; Chicago & North Western public timetable, February 17, 1929, 38.

75. Burton B. Crandall, *The Growth of the Intercity Bus Industry* (Syracuse: Syracuse University, 1954), 33–34; Douglas V. Shaw, "Ralph Budd, the Great Northern Railway, and the Advent of the Motor Bus," *Railroad History* 166 (Spring 1992): 57–64.

76. Klein, *Union Pacific: The Rebirth*, 265.

77. Ibid., 266; Crandall, *Intercity Bus Industry*, 132; *Bus Transportation* 9 (January 1930): 45; Interstate Transit Lines . . . , "Improved Bus Service from Coast to Coast," [folder, ca. 1935].

An example of the desire to expand Interstate Transit Lines came in 1931 when the North Western spent $275,000 for the bus operations of the largest Iowa electric interurban, the Fort Dodge, Des Moines & Southern. The deal gave Interstate 38 additional buses and 550 more highway route miles. See *Chicago Journal of Commerce*, February 20, 1931.

78. Chicago & North Western public timetable, September 25, 1932, 51.

79. *Evening Huronite*, May 25, 1928; George H. Burges and Miles C. Kennedy, *Centennial History of the Pennsylvania Railroad Company, 1846–1946* (Philadelphia: Pennsylvania Railroad, 1949), 603–4.

80. *New York Tribune*, June 23, 1929; *Evening Huronite*, April 20, 1929, April 30, 1929.

81. Kohler Aviation Corporation public timetable, July 1, 1930.

82. *Report from Bureau of Service National Parks and Resorts . . . To Chicago & North Western Railway, and Union Pacific System* (n.p., 1922); ? to R. Thomson, December 4, 1933, Union Pacific papers, Nebraska State Historical Society, Lincoln, Nebraska, hereafter cited as Union Pacific papers; *Report from the Department of Tours . . . to Chicago & North Western Railway and Union Pacific System* (n.p., 1925).

83. [1925] *Report*.

84. John C. Pollock to F. E. Lewis, August 20, 1934, Union Pacific papers.

85. Edward O. Snethen to V. A. Hampton, December 27, 1930, Union Pacific papers.

86. *Highland Park* (Ill.) *Press*, April 4, 1929; Dubin interview.

87. *Seventieth Annual Report of the Chicago and North Western*, 6; *Seventy-First Annual Report of the Chicago and North Western Railway Company* (Chicago, 1931), 6; *Seventy-Second Annual Report of the Chicago and North Western*, 6.

Chapter 8: The Great Depression and Bankruptcy

1. Charles P. Kindleberger, *The World in Depression, 1929–1939* (Berkeley: University of California Press, 1973), 83–170; *Historical Statistics of the United States: Colonial Times to 1957* (Washington: U.S. Department of Commerce, 1960), 139.

2. *Yearbook of Railroad Information* (New York: Committee on Public Relations of the Eastern Railroads, 1936), 40; *Seventieth Annual Report of the Chicago and North Western Railway Company* (Chicago, 1930), 6; *Seventy-First Annual Report of the Chicago and North Western Railway Company* (Chicago, 1931), 6; *Seventy-Second Annual Report of the Chicago and North Western Railway Company* (Chicago, 1932), 6; *Seventy-Third Annual Report of the Chicago and North Western Railway Company* (Chicago, 1933), 5.

3. *Seventy-Second Annual Report of the Chicago and North Western*, 7; Merrill J. Roberts, "The Motor Transportation Revolution," *Business History Review* 30 (1956): 57–79.

4. Address by Fred W. Sargent [ca. 1932], C&NWHS; *Seventy-Second Annual Report of the Chicago and North Western*, 16–17.

5. *Seventy-Second Annual Report of the Chicago and North Western*, 17–18.

6. *Seventieth Annual Report of the Chicago and North Western*, 7–8; *Wall Street Journal*, February 10, 1931; *The Evening Huronite* (Huron, S.Dak.), November 26, 1929.

7. *Chicago Journal of Commerce*, April 21, 1930; *Seventieth Annual Report of the Chicago and North Western*, 7; H. R. Terpning, "The New Wells Street Freight Station (Merchandise Mart)," 1932, C&NWHS.

8. *Annual Report of the Delaware, Lackawanna and Western Railroad Company, 1932* (New York, 1933), 10; *Seventy-Fifth Annual Report of the Chicago and North Western Railway Company* (Chicago, 1935), 6.

9. *The Evening Huronite*, January 6, 1931, April 18, 1934; *Minneapolis Journal*, June 9, 1932; *Seventy-Third Annual Report of the Chicago and North Western*, 7.

10. *The Evening Huronite*, April 13, 1931; *St. Paul Dispatch*, August 13, 1931.

11. "Motor-Rail Shipping—Door to Door" [ca. 1932], C&NWHS; "C.& N. W. Pick-Up and Delivery," *Traffic World* 55 (January 19, 1935): 114.

12. John H. White Jr., "The Magic Box: Genesis of the Container," *Railroad History* 158 (spring 1988): 73–93; "Container Car Service," *Traffic World* 46 (December 6, 1930): 1425–26; "Motor-Rail Shipping."

13. "Motor-Rail Shipping."

14. Jim Scribbins, *The 400 Story* (Park Forest, Ill.: PTJ Publishing, 1982), 9–10, 17.

15. Richard C. Overton, *Burlington Route: A History of the Burlington Lines* (New York: Knopf, 1965), 396–98; *Traffic World*, Jan-

uary 19, 1935, p. 114; Scribbins, *400 Story*, 9.

16. Scribbins, *400 Story*, 9; interview with James Larson, St. Louis, Missouri, September 29, 1989.

17. "North Western '400' High-Speed Train," *Railway Mechanical Engineer* 109 (February 1935): 52–54; *Chicago Daily News*, December 25, 1935; Scribbins, *400 Story*, 10; "Trains That Are Making Good, No. 8*—The 400," 62, clipping C&NWHS.

18. Scribbins, *400 Story*, 17–24; *Chicago Daily Tribune*, January 3, 1935, quoting Fred Sargent.

19. *Seventy-Fifth Annual Report of the Chicago and North Western*, 6; *St. Paul Pioneer Press*, January 3, 1935.

20. Scribbins, *400 Story*, 24–25; "The '400' 400 Miles 400 Minutes," n.d., C&NWHS.

21. Albert J. Dickinson to Ralph Budd, February 6, 1935, Great Northern Railway Collection, Minnesota Historical Society, St. Paul, Minnesota.

22. Maury Klein, *Union Pacific: The Rebirth, 1894–1969* (New York: Doubleday, 1989), 306; *Railway Age* 98 (June 8, 1935): 875–76; Roy G. Clark, "Denver Streamliner," *Trains* 6 (July 1946): 30; "Streamliners to West Coast," *Railway Mechanical Engineer* 115 (September 1941): 337–40.

23. *Seventy-Fourth Annual Report of the Chicago and North Western Railway Company* (Chicago, 1934), 6; *Seventy-Fifth Annual Report of the Chicago and North Western*, 6.

24. *The Evening Huronite*, September 3, 1931, December 5, 1932; *Seventy-Third Annual Report of the Chicago and North Western*, 6.

25. *Seventy-Fourth Annual Report of the Chicago and North Western*, 6.

26. *The Commercial and Financial Chronicle*, August 19, 1933; *Seventy-Third Annual Report of the Chicago and North Western*, 6–7; *Seventy-Fourth Annual Report of the Chicago and North Western*, 7.

27. *Seventy-Third Annual Report of the Chicago and North Western*, 6; *Seventy-Fourth Annual Report of the Chicago and North Western*, 7; *Seventy-Fifth Annual Report of the Chicago and North Western*, 7.

The Interstate Commerce Commission in 1936 granted the request of the North Western and Milwaukee Road to pool interstate iron ore traffic from the Menominee Range in Michigan and Wisconsin to Escanaba, Michigan. Once again savings resulted, especially after ore movement increased on the eve of World War II.

28. *Fifty-Third Annual Report of the Chicago, Saint Paul, Minneapolis and Omaha Railway Company* (St. Paul, 1935), 4; *Seventy-Seventh Annual Report of the Chicago and North Western Railway Company* (Chicago, 1937), 6–7.

29. *Winthrop* (Minn.) *News*, May 10, 1934.

30. *The Evening Huronite*, September 3, 1931; *Seventy-Fifth Annual Report of the Chicago and North Western*, 6.

31. See H. Roger Grant and L. Edward Purcell, eds., *Years of Struggle: The Farm Diary of Elmer G. Powers, 1931–1936* (Ames: Iowa State University Press, 1976); August Derleth, *The Milwaukee Road: Its First Hundred Years* (New York: Creative Age Press, 1948), 244–45; interview with Charles C. Shannon, Arlington Heights, Illinois, October 1, 1988.

32. *Seventy-Sixth Annual Report of the Chicago and North Western Railway Company* (Chicago, 1936), 5; *Commercial and Financial Chronicle*, October 6, 1934, June 6, 1935; "Two Roads Petition Federal Court to Reorganize," *Railway Age* 99 (July 6, 1935): 11.

The Omaha Road, because of its debt structure, avoided bankruptcy.

33. William James Cunningham, *The Present Railroad Crisis* (Philadelphia: University of Pennsylvania Press, 1939), 16–22; George W. Hilton, *Monon Route* (San Diego: Howell-North, 1978), 153.

34. *Seventy-Sixth Annual Report of the Chicago and North Western*, 5; "North Western Files Reorganization Plan," *Railway Age* 101 (July 4, 1936): 35; *Amended Plan of Reorganization of Chicago and North Western Railway Company* (December 15, 1937), 1943, 1961.

35. "C.& N.W. Reorganization," *Railway Age* 103 (December 18, 1937): 890; *Railway Age* 104 (February 26, 1938): 400.

36. *Seventy-Eighth Annual Report of the Chicago and North Western Railway Company* (Chicago, 1938), 5–6.

37. H. Roger Grant, *Erie Lackawanna: Death of an American Railroad, 1938–1992* (Stanford: Stanford University Press, 1994), 24–33; *Eighty-Fifth Annual Report of the Chicago and North Western Railway Company* (Chicago, 1945), 3.

38. "Bureau of Finance Proposes Tentative Plan for C.& N.W.," *Railway Age* 104 (March 19, 1938): 544–45.

39. "Views Vary on Merger in N.W.," *Railway Age* 105 (December 24, 1938): 923, 931.

40. Ibid.; "C.& N.W.—Milwaukee Merger?" *Traffic World* 60 (October 16, 1937): 825; *The Evening Huronite*, October 27, 1938; *Chicago Daily News*, August 11, 1938.

41. "Views Vary on Merger in N.W.," 931.

42. "I.C.C. Wipes Out C.& N.W. Equities," *Railway Age* 107 (December 23, 1939): 967.

43. Ibid., 967–68; *Chicago Journal of Commerce*, June 26, 1940.

44. "C.& N.W. Reorganization Plan Approved by Federal Court," *Railway Age* (September 14, 1940): 377.

45. "C.& N.W. Reorganization," *Traffic World* 66 (August 17, 1940): 389–40; "C.& N.W. Reorganized," *Railway Age* 116 (June 10, 1944) 1120; *Chicago Daily News*, April 8, 1941.

46. "C.& N.W. Reorganization," *Traffic World* 67 (June 28, 1941): 1638–39; *Eighty-First Annual Report of the Chicago and North Western Railway Company* (Chicago, 1941), 6; "Wars to Grab Property—Abroad and at Home," *Railway Age* 111 (July 5, 1941): 1–2.

47. *Eighty-Fifth Annual Report of the Chicago and North Western*, 3.

48. *Seventy-Sixth Annual Report of the Chicago and North Western*, 5; *Railway Age* 99 (October 5, 1935): 449; *Timely Topics* 4 (June 1939): 3, and 4 (July 1939): 4; *Eighty-Fourth Annual Report of the Chicago and North Western Railway Company* (Chicago, 1944), 9; *Who's Who in America* (Chicago: A. N. Marquis, 1948), 2126.

49. "Fred W. Sargent Resigns," *Railway Age* 106 (June 3, 1939): 945; *Eightieth Annual Report of the Chicago and North Western Railway Company* (Chicago, 1940), 2.

50. Shannon interview.

51. "R. L. Williams Appointed Chief Executive Officer of C.& N.W.," *Railway Age* 107 (July 29, 1939): 180–81; *Timely Topics* 4 (August 1939): 1–2.

52. "[To] Mr. Charles M. Thomson, Trustee," C&NWHS; "Feucht to Succeed Williams As North Western's Head," *Railway Age* 133 (December 29, 1952): 42.

53. *Seventy-Ninth Annual Report of the Chicago and North Western Railway Company* (Chicago, 1939), 19; *Eightieth Annual Report of the Chicago and North Western*, 13; *Eighty-First Annual Report of the Chicago and North Western*, 13.

54. Scribbins, *400 Story*, 39.

55. Ibid.; "Saga of the '400,'" *Trains* 2 (November 1941): 4–5; *Eightieth Annual Report of the Chicago and North Western*, 6; *Railway Mechanical Engineer* 113 (January 1989): 37.

56. "Now! Not One '400'—But a Fleet of Them," (Chicago: Chicago & North Western Railway, December 1942).

57. Shannon interview.

Chapter 9: The Second World War and Postwar Railroading

1. "Right-of-Way," 16–mm. film produced by the Office of War Information, 1943, National Archives, Washington, D.C.; *Historical Statistics of the United States: Colonial Times to 1957* (Washington: U.S. Department of Commerce, 1960), 427, 430–31.

2. *Eighty-Second Annual Report of the Chicago and North Western Railway Company* (Chicago, 1942), 37; *Eighty-Fourth Annual Report of the Chicago and North Western Railway Company* (Chicago, 1944), 35; *Eighty-Sixth Annual Report of the Chicago and North Western Railway Company* (Chicago, 1946), 35; press release, June 17, 1940, C&NWHS.

3. *Eighty-Fourth Annual Report of the Chicago and North Western*, 9; *Eighty-Sixth Annual Report of the Chicago and North Western*, 11; *Timely Topics* 9 (March 1944): 3, and 10 (July 1945): 1; *North Western Newsliner* 1 (December 1945): 25; Carl R. Gray, Jr., *Railroading in Eighteen Countries: The Story of American Railroad Men Serving in the Military Railway Service, 1862 to 1953* (New York: Charles Scribner's Sons, 1955), 53–54; interview with Frank Koval, Wheaton, Illinois, September 9, 1988.

4. *Timely Topics*, 7 (July 1942): 1; *Eighty-Fifth Annual Report of the Chicago and North Western Railway Company* (Chicago: Chicago & North Western Railway, 1945), 11; *Timely Topics* 10 (June 1945): 1.

5. Press release, March 15, 1944, C&NWHS; "Victory Garden Special," *North Western Newsliner* 2 (June 1946): 4–5.

6. Interview with Charles C. Shannon, Arlington Heights, Illinois, October 1, 1988; *The Evening Huronite,* June 3, 1944.

7. *Timely Topics* 9 (October 1944): 1; *Eighty-Fourth Annual Report of the Chicago and North Western*, 11.

8. *The Training within Industry Report, 1940–1945* (Washington: War Manpower Commission, 1945), 140–41.

9. *Eighty-Second Annual Report of the Chicago and North Western*, 7; *Eighty-Third Annual Report of the Chicago and North Western* (Chicago, 1943); *Eighty-Fourth Annual Report of the Chicago and North Western*, 7; *Eighty-Fifth Annual Report of the Chicago and North Western*, 8; *Eighty-Sixth Annual Report of the Chicago and North Western*, 9.

10. *Eighty-Fourth Annual Report of the Chicago and North Western*, 8.

11. "U.S. Takes C.& N.W. Rails," *Traffic World* 70 (July 18, 1942); "M.P Buys C&NW's Hastings Terminal," *Missouri Pacific Lines Magazine* 17 (February 1943): 7; *The Railway Gazette* 79 (August 13, 1943): 159–60.

12. *Eighty-Sixth Annual Report of the Chicago and North Western*, 10; Shannon interview.

13. Richard Polenberg, *War and Society: The United States, 1941–1945* (Philadelphia: J. B. Lippincott, 1972), 30–31, 95–96; Richard R. Lingeman, *Don't You Know There's a War On? The American Home Front, 1941–1945* (New York: G. P. Putnam's, 1970), 80–81; newspaper clipping, October 14, 1942, C&NWHS.

14. *Erie Railroad Company Annual Report, 1943* (New York, 1945), 22–24.

15. Ibid.

16. Claude Moore Fuess, *Joseph B. Eastman: Servant of The People* (New York: Columbia University Press, 1952), 270–96; *Timely Topics* 10 (July 1945): 10.

17. *Eighty-Sixth Annual Report of the Chicago and North Western*, 3.

18. Newspaper clipping, June 29, 1944, C&NWHS; *Eighty-Fifth Annual Report of the Chicago and North Western*, 11; *Eighty-Sixth Annual Report of the Chicago and North Western*, 11.

19. Newspaper clipping, ca. 1945, C&NWHS.

20. *Eighty-Ninth Annual Report of the Chicago and North Western Railway Company* (Chicago, 1949), 3.

21. Herbert Stein, *The Social Revolution in America* (Chicago: University of Chicago Press, 1969), 197–240.

22. *Eighty-Seventh Annual Report of the Chicago and North Western Railway Company* (Chicago, 1947), 8.

23. *Eighty-Eighth Annual Report of the Chicago and North Western Railway Company* (Chicago, 1948), 9; *Eighty-Ninth Annual Report of the Chicago and North Western Railway*, 8.

24. *Eighty-Ninth Annual Report of the Chicago and North Western Railway Company*, 8; *Ninetieth Annual Report of the Chicago and North Western Railway Company* (Chicago, 1950), 7–8.

25. *Ninetieth Annual Report of the Chicago and North Western*, 8.

26. Clipping from *Chicago Tribune* [ca. 1948], C&NWTCo papers.

27. H. Roger Grant, *Erie Lackawanna: Death of an American Railroad, 1938–1992* (Stanford: Stanford University Press, 1994), 63; Richard D. Overton, *Burlington Route: A History of the Burlington Lines* (New York: Alfred A. Knopf, 1965), 548.

28. Koval interview; C. B. Tavenner, *Who's Who in Railroading in North America* (New York: Simmons-Boardman, 1954), 404.

29. Koval interview; *Chicago Railroad Fair: Official Guide Book* (Chicago, 1948), 1.

30. Koval interview; *Chicago Guide Book and Program for the Pageant 'Wheels a-Rolling'* (Chicago, 1949); *Eighty-Ninth Annual Report of the Chicago and North Western*, 14–15; *100 Years of Railroad Progress: Railroad Poster Stamp Album* (Chicago, 1948).

31. *Eighty-Ninth Annual Report of the Chicago and North Western*, 15.

32. *Daily Plainsman* (Huron, S.Dak.), May 9, 14, 24, 25, 1948.

33. *Ninetieth Annual Report of the Chicago and North Western*, 3–4; *Ninety-First Annual Report of the Chicago and North Western Railway Company* (Chicago, 1951), 3–4.

34. *Daily Plainsman,* August 24, 1950; Jim Scribbins, *The 400 Story* (Park Forest, Ill.: PTJ Publishing, 1982), 96, 98–99, 102–03, 105.

35. Scribbins, *400 Story,* 121–25.

Flambeau is French for "flaming torch." French fur trappers and traders were struck by the Native Americans of northern Wisconsin who fished at night with the aid of burning torches. The route of the *Flambeau 400* served Lac du Flambeau, Flambeau flowage, and the Flambeau River.

36. Scribbins, *400 Story,* 125–26, 128–29.

37. Ibid., 132.

38. Shannon interview; George W. Hilton, *The Transportation Act of 1958: A Decade of Experience* (Bloomington: Indiana University Press, 1969), 97–154.

39. *Daily Plainsman,* January 8, 1950.

40. *Ninety-Third Annual Report of the Chicago and North Western Railway Company* (Chicago, 1953), 11; Review of income and dividends [1955], C&NWTCo papers.

41. Interview with John P. Fiskwick, Roanoke, Virginia, June 6, 1989; interview with Wallace Abbey, Memphis, Tennessee, September 26, 1985.

42. Shannon interview.

43. Ibid.; interview with Charles J. Myers, Livingston, New Jersey, May 25, 1988.

44. Interview with Jervis Langdon Jr., Akron, Ohio, April 26, 1990; Shannon interview; Tavenner, *Who's Who in Railroading,* 769.

45. Shannon interview.

46. Tavenner, *Who's Who in Railroading,* 220; "Feucht to Suc-

ceed Williams As North Western Head," *Railway Age* 133 (December 29, 1952): 42–43.

47. Koval interview; Shannon interview.

48. Shannon interview.

49. Interview with William N. Deramus III, Kansas City, Missouri, October 15, 1980; Koval interview; Shannon interview.

Charlotte Fritz Feucht may have affected her husband's career at the North Western. She was extremely protective, demanding that a special cubicle be built in Feucht's business car so that food preparation could be watched. Apparently she believed that her husband might be poisoned by a jealous underling or rival.

50. Shannon interview.

51. Koval interview; interview with Arthur D. Dubin, Highland Park, Illinois, October 3, 1986; Shannon interview; Scribbins, *400 Story*, 167–68, 170–71.

52. *Ninety-Third Annual Report of the Chicago and North Western*, 4–5; *Ninety-Fourth Annual Report of the Chicago and North Western Railway Company* (Chicago, 1954), 4–5. 8; *Ninety-Fifth Annual Report of the Chicago and North Western Railway Company* (Chicago, 1955), 3–5.

53. "The State of the North Western Railway" [ca. 1955], C&NWTCo papers.

54. Grant, *Erie Lackawanna*, 84–85; *Report on Economics of Consolidation and Coordination: Chicago, Milwaukee, St. Paul and Pacific Railroad Company*[,] *Chicago and North Western Railway Company* [and] *Chicago, St. Paul, Minneapolis and Omaha Railway Company* (East Orange, N.J.: Wm. Wyer, October 26, 1955), 1–6; "Chicago & North Western and Milwaukee Road Talk about 'Coordination' Savings," *Trains* 15 (January 1955): 6–7.

55. Shannon interview.

56. Ibid.; Koval interview, *Chicago Daily Tribune*, January 18, 1956; Minutes of the Board of Directors, Chicago & North Western Railway Company, February 10, 1956, C&NWTCo papers; *New York Times*, June 6, 1965.

57. Koval interview.

Chapter 10: The Heineman Era

1. Interview with Frank Koval, Wheaton, Illinois, September 9, 1988; interview with Jervis Langdon Jr., Akron, Ohio, April 26, 1990.

2. Richard W. Barsness, "Ben W. Heineman," in *Railroads in the Age of Regulation, 1900–1980*, ed. Keith L. Bryant Jr. (New York: Facts On File, 1988), 194; *Chicago Tribune*, January 9, 1965.

3. Barsness, "Ben W. Heineman," 154; Joseph Poindexter, "The Return of Ben W. Heineman," *Dun's Review* 99 (March 1972): 36; *Chicago Tribune*, January 9, 1965.

4. Barsness, "Ben W. Heineman," 194.

5. Poindexter, "Return of Ben W. Heineman," 36; David Karr, *Fight for Control* (New York: Ballantine, 1956), 109–17; interview with D. Keith Lawson, Rogers, Arkansas, October 18, 1980.

6. Barsness, "Ben W. Heineman," 194; interview with Louis I. Gelfand, Minneapolis, Minnesota, January 13, 1986.

7. Interview with Wallace Abbey, Memphis, Tennessee, September 26, 1985; William D. Middleton, "What Are They Doing to North Western?" *Trains* 18 (July 1958): 18–19; interview with Charles C. Shannon, Arlington Heights, Illinois, October 1, 1988.

8. Traffic density map (1955), C&NWTCo papers; Shannon interview.

9. Middleton, "What Are They Doing to North Western?" 18; Shannon interview.

10. Middleton, "What Are They Doing to North Western?" 16; interview with Isabel H. Benham, New York, New York, June 6, 1989.

11. Middleton, "What Are They Doing to North Western?" 20; interview with James Zito, St. Charles, Illinois, May 4, 1994; C. B. Tavenner, *Who's Who in Railroading* (New York: Simmons-Boardman, 1954), 225.

12. Shannon interview; Zito interview.

13. Zito interview.

14. Russell F. Moore, ed., *Who's Who in Railroading in North America* (New York: Simmons-Boardman, 1959), 517; Zito interview.

15. *Ninety-Seventh Annual Report of the Chicago and North Western Railway Company* (Chicago, 1957), 14–15; Shannon interview; news release, May 14, 1956, C&NWTCo papers.

16. Koval interview; Middleton, "What Are They Doing to North Western?" 20.

17. *Ninety-Seventh Annual Report of the Chicago and North Western*, 3.

18. Arthur Andersen & Co. report to B. W. Heineman, August 30, 1957, C&NWTCo papers.

19. *Chicago and North Western Railway Company Annual Report 1957* (Chicago, 1958), 7; Frank Richter, "C&NW Converts to Responsibility Accounting," *Modern Railroads* 12 (May 1957): 75–77; "Are We Making Any Money Today?" *Railway Age* 142 (April 29, 1957): 34–35; "C&NW Steps Up Data Processing," *Modern Railroads* 14 (June 1959): 96–98, 100, 103–4; unidentified clipping, May 7, 1959, C&NWTCo papers.

20. *Ninety-Seventh Annual Report of the Chicago and North Western*, 6–7; Shannon interview; *Chicago and North Western Railway Company Annual Report 1957*, 18; Middleton, "What Are They Doing to North Western?" 29.

21. *Chicago and North Western Railway Company Annual Report 1957*, 13–16; *Daily Plainsman*, August 24, 1959; Shannon interview.

22. *Ninety-Seventh Annual Report of the Chicago and North Western*, 15; "Facts about CLINTON CAR SHOPS," October 3, 1957, C&NWTCo papers.

23. "Facts about CLINTON CAR SHOPS"; Koval interview.

24. *Ninety-Seventh Annual Report of the Chicago and North Western*, 13–14.

25. Interstate Commerce Commission, Finance Docket No. 19432, Chicago, Saint Paul, Minneapolis & Omaha Railway Company Lease, Decided December 28, 1956; *St. Paul Dispatch*, July 23, 1956; *Chicago, Saint Paul, Minneapolis and Omaha Railway Company Annual Report 1956* (Chicago, 1957), 2–3; Shannon interview.

26. Shannon interview.

27. *Chicago, Saint Paul, Minneapolis and Omaha Railway Company Annual Report 1957* (Chicago, 1958), 3.

28. Shannon interview; *Daily Plainsman*, November 6, 1957; *Chicago and North Western Railway Annual Report 1958* (Chicago, 1959), 14; W. J. Stender to W. L. Smith, July 29, 1966, Great Northern Railway papers, Minnesota Historical Society, St. Paul, Minnesota.

29. Shannon interview; Lawson interview.

30. Shannon interview.

31. *Huronite and Daily Plainsman*, November 9, 1958; *Daily Plainsman*, August 27, 1962; "Kennedy Defaults on C&NW," *Trains* 23 (November 1962): 3, 6; *Report to the U.S. President by the Emergency Board* (Washington, D.C., June 14, 1962).

32. *Chicago American*, August 31, 1962; *Chicago Sun-Times*, August 31, 1962; *Washington Post*, September 3, 1962.

33. "An End to Featherbedding," *Time* 80 (October 19, 1962): 81.

34. Ibid.; *Rapid City* (S.Dak.) *Journal,* October 1, 1962.

35. "An End to Featherbedding," 81; "End of Strike," *Trains* 23 (December 1962): 12; *Chicago and North Western Railway Company Annual Report 1962* (Chicago, 1963), 3, 6; Shannon interview.

36. Interview with Joseph D. Allen, Cleveland, Ohio, May 10, 1989; Shannon interview.

37. Ibid.

38. *Ninety-Seventh Annual Report of the Chicago and North Western,* 7–8; *Chicago and North Western Annual Report 1957,* 8; Shannon interview.

39. "Chicago and North Western Railway Company Through Passenger Train Eliminations since January 1, 1955," December 11, 1963, C&NWTCo papers.

40. Shannon interview; James J. Reisdorff and Michael M. Bartels, *Railroad Stations in Nebraska* (David City, Neb.: South Platte Press, 1982), 34–35.

41. The problems the North Western encountered with its passenger service during the 1950s were well remembered by Boris Blick, a retired professor of history at the University of Akron, in February 1995:

> In the winter of 1956 I was relatively new at driving and completely inexperienced on snow-covered roads. At the time I was shuttling between the small Wisconsin cities of Sheboygan and Manitowoc teaching in the University of Wisconsin Extension System.
>
> One wintry Tuesday afternoon a blizzard hit Manitowoc. My car stalled; I could go no further. Walking downtown, I was delighted to learn that I could get back to Sheboygan by rail and so I caught a C&NW train.... It was such a pleasure, I thought, to ride in a dry, warm, pleasant train with none of the anxieties of driving on icy highways.
>
> There was only one other passenger in the car. From what I could hear of the conversation with the conductor, he was a railroad employee, with a free pass. When the conductor came over to check my ticket, I naively told him that it was wonderful to have the trains around when the roads were covered with snow. He gave me an unfriendly look and sarcastically demanded, "And how often do you use the trains in good weather?" I understood instantly and did not reply. I never forgot that exchange.

42. *Chicago Daily News,* December 20, 1957.

43. Abbey interview; Andrew Schiller, "Chicago Miracle," *Harper's Magazine* 230 (January 1966): 66; remarks of James Larson, Lexington Group in Transportation History, Milwaukee, Wisconsin, September 25, 1992.

44. *Chicago Tribune,* February 7, 1960.

45. Shannon interview; interview with James Larson, Los Angeles, California, May 6, 1989; Zito interview.

46. Shannon interview; *Chicago Sun-Times,* December 20, 1957; *Chicago and North Western Annual Report 1957,* 9; *Chicago and North Western Annual Report 1958,* 11–12.

47. Shannon interview; "Facts in Brief on C&NW Suburban Service," C&NWTCo papers; *Chicago Tribune,* January 9, 1960; *Chicago Sun-Times,* January 10, 1960.

48. "Good News for North Western Commuters," *The Carbuilder* (January-February 1960); Donald Duke and Edmund Keilty, *RDC: The Budd Rail Car* (San Marino, Calif.: Golden West Books, 1990), 158–59.

49. *Du Page Press* (Elmhurst, Ill.), December 31, 1959; Memorandum and Related Schedules for Board of Directors in Connection with Proposed Suburban Modernization Program, December 28, 1959, C&NWTCo papers.

50. Shannon interview.

51. Ibid.; *Chicago Daily News,* January 16, 1960; *Chicago Tribune,* January 16, 1960.

Others associated with the North Western were not convinced that upgrading Chicago commuter operations was a good idea. "Shippers and the broad public in Iowa, and likely Nebraska, Minnesota, South Dakota, etc. looked with wonder at C&NW in these days, spending endlessly for Chicago commuters while offering rotten freight service" (Don L. Hofsommer to author, September 8, 1995).

52. Press release, Chicago and North Western Railway Company, January 11, 1960, C&NWTCo papers; interview with George Krambles, Oak Park, Illinois, June 25, 1985; Schiller, "Chicago Miracle," 68; *Chicago Daily News,* December 3, 1960.

53. Krambles interview; George W. Hilton and John F. Due, *The Electric Interurban Railways in America* (Stanford: Stanford University Press, 1960), 335–37; *Chicago and North Western Railway Company Annual Report 1961* (Chicago, 1962), 12–13.

54. Memorandum and Related Schedules for Board of Directors.

55. Koval interview; *Chicago and North Western Railway Company Annual Report 1965* (Chicago, 1966), 9–10.

56. Zito interview.

57. Koval interview; *Chicago Tribune,* February 8, 1963; Louis W. Menk to Ben W. Heineman, August 25, 1966, C&NWTCo papers.

58. *Chicago and North Western Railway Company Annual Report 1963* (Chicago, 1964), 2–3; *Chicago and North Western Railway Company Annual Report 1964* (Chicago, 1965), 2–3; *Chicago and North Western Annual Report 1965,* 3.

59. Thomas J. Lamphier to author, July 31, 1995.

60. Shannon interview; interview with D. B. (Del) Carlisle, Chadron, Nebraska, November 12, 1986.

61. Ben W. Heineman, "America's Railroads—and Their Future," *Progressive Railroading* (January-February 1965): 41; interview with John Harper, Omaha, Nebraska, September 25, 1987; Koval interview.

62. *Chicago and North Western Annual Report 1957,* 12; Gus Welty, ed., *Era of the Giants: The New Railroad Merger Movement* (Omaha: Simmons-Boardman, 1982), 86; *Moody's Transportation Manual* (New York: Moody's Investors Service, 1958), 387; minutes of the Board of Directors, Chicago & North Western Railway Company, May 21, 1957, June 6, 1957, C&NWTCo papers.

63. Welty, *Era of the Giants,* 86–87.

64. Frank D. Donovan Jr., *Mileposts on the Prairie: The Story of the Minneapolis & St. Louis Railway* (New York: Simmons-Boardman, 1950), 9–76.

65. Ibid., 91–135; Don L. Hofsommer, "Edwin Hawley," in *Railroads in the Age of Regulation,* 190–91.

66. Donovan, *Mileposts on the Prairie,* 173–244.

67. "The Minneapolis and St. Louis Railway Company" (1955), Northwestern University School of Business; *The Minneapolis & St. Louis Railway Company Annual Report 1959* (Minneapolis, 1960), 14–15; *Chicago and North Western Railway Company Annual Report 1960* (Chicago, 1961) 15.

68. *Minneapolis Star,* August 29, 1960; Gelfand interview; James R. Sullivan to author, August 19, 1985.

69. Minutes of the Board of Directors, Chicago & North Western Railway Company, April 7, 1960, C&NWTCo papers; Sullivan to author; Gelfand interview.

70. Koval interview; Memorandum and Related Exhibits for Board of Directors in Connection with Proposed Acquisition of the Minneapolis & St. Louis Railway Company, C&NWTCo papers.

71. Dan Knight to author, March 23, 1983; Gelfand interview.

72. Knight to author.

73. Sullivan to author, August 6, 1985.

74. H. Roger Grant, *The Corn Belt Route: A History of the Chicago Great Western Railroad Company* (DeKalb: Northern Illinois University Press, 1984), 1–34.

75. Ibid., 35, 48, 60–67; Gerald Berk, *Alternative Tracks: The Constitution of American Industrial Order, 1865–1917* (Baltimore: Johns Hopkins University Press, 1994), 116–49.

76. Grant, *Corn Belt Route*, 73–87, 110–17, 125–30.

77. Ibid., 135–46, 152–58.

78. Ibid., 158–64, 166–69.

79. Ibid., 169–70, 172–74; Shannon interview.

80. Koval interview; Grant, *Corn Belt Route*, 176.

81. Grant, *Corn Belt Route*, 176, 181–82; Lawson interview.

82. *Chicago and North Western Railway Company Annual Report 1968* (Chicago, 1969), 4; *Chicago Sun-Times*, November 17, 1966; *Fort Dodge, Des Moines & Southern Railway Company Annual Report for the Year Ended December 31, 1967* (Boone, Iowa, 1968), 5–6; minutes of the Board of Directors, Chicago & North Western Railway, January 5, 1967, C&NWTCo papers; *Wall Street Journal*, November 17, 1966.

83. Welty, *Era of the Giants*, 92; *Chicago and North Western Railway Company Annual Report 1968*, 4; Koval interview.

84. "Ben Heineman's Shrewd Poker Game," *Forbes* 94 (September 1, 1964): 20; Benham interview.

85. "Ben Heineman's Shrewd Poker Game," p. 20.

86. Chicago and North Western Railway Company: Selected Gulf, Mobile and Ohio Railroad Data, March 27, 1962, C&NWTCo papers; Shannon interview.

87. *Chicago and North Western Annual Report 1960*, 3; Chicago, Milwaukee, St. Paul and Pacific Railroad Company Proposal for Unification of the Milwaukee Road and Chicago and North Western Railway Company, March 7, 1961; "Ben Heineman's Shrewd Poker Game," 22; Ben W. Heineman to Leo T. Crowley, March 15, 1961, C&NWTCo papers.

88. *Chicago and North Western Annual Report 1964*, 20; *Chicago Sun-Times*, May 19, 1965; Richard Saunders, *The Railroad Mergers and the Coming of Conrail* (Westport, Conn.: Greenwood, 1978), 232–33; Welty, *Era of the Giants*, 92.

89. Saunders, *Railroad Mergers*, 234–35; John Brooks, *The Go-Go Years* (New York: Weybright and Talley, 1973), 176–77; Shannon interview.

90. Dan Cordtz, "The Fight for the Rock Island," *Fortune* 73 (June 1966): 141; Maury Klein, *Union Pacific: The Rebirth, 1894–1969* (New York: Doubleday, 1989), 517–20.

91. Klein, *Union Pacific*, 519; Langdon interview.

92. Cordtz, "Fight for the Rock," 141; Don L. Hofsommer, *The Southern Pacific, 1901–1985* (College Station: Texas A&M University Press, 1986), 266–68; Welty, *Era of the Giants*, 90–91.

93. Shannon interview; Welty, *Era of the Giants*, 90; *Railway Age* 164 (June 10, 1964): 46–47; *Wall Street Journal*, December 18, 1964.

94. Shannon interview; Langdon interview; Koval interview; *Chicago and North Western Annual Report 1963*, 19–20.

95. Langdon interview; Klein, *Union Pacific*, 524–28.

96. Klein, *Union Pacific*, 527; *Chicago Daily News*, January 11, 1965; *Wall Street Journal*, January 17, 1966; Meyer interview.

97. Cordtz, "Fight for the Rock," 209; Klein, *Union Pacific*, 528; *Chicago and North Western Annual Report 1965*, 4.

98. *Chicago Tribune*, October 27, 1965; *New York Times*, October 27, 1965; Klein, *Union Pacific*, 528–29.

99. *Chicago Tribune*, May 5, 1966; Saunders, *Railroad Mergers*, 225–45; Welty, *Era of the Giants*, 88.

100. Klein, *Union Pacific*, 530–31.

101. Meyer interview.

102. Poindexter, "Return of Ben W. Heineman," 33–34, 36–37, 39.

103. Shannon interview.

104. *Chicago and North Western Annual Report 1965*, 3, 14–15.

105. Arthur D. Little, Inc., "Evaluation of Philadelphia & Reading Subsidiaries; Report to Chicago and Northwestern Railway Company," November 1967, C&NWTCo papers; *Philadelphia and Reading Corporation Annual Report 1967* (New York, 1968), 2–3; Barsness, "Ben W. Heineman," 196.

106. Hofsommer, *Southern Pacific*, 276–78; Klein, *Union Pacific*, 539–41; John F. Stover, *History of the Illinois Central Railroad* (New York: Macmillan, 1975), 465–82; Keith L. Bryant Jr., *History of the Atchison, Topeka and Santa Fe Railway* (New York: Macmillan, 1974), 360–76; "Is It Endsville for the Railroads?" *Forbes* 104 (October 15, 1969): 39.

107. *Chicago and North Western Annual Report 1965*, 2; *Chicago and North Western Railway Company Annual Report 1966* (Chicago, 1967), 2; *Chicago and North Western Railway Company Annual Report 1968*, 1; *Chicago and North Western Railway Company Annual Report 1969* (Chicago, 1970), 1; speech by Larry S. Provo, Western Railway Club, Chicago, Illinois, November 19, 1973, C&NWTCo papers.

108. Don L. Hofsommer to author, September 8, 1995.

109. Frederick C. Osthoff, ed., *Who's Who in Railroading in North America* (New York: Simmons-Boardman, 1968), 405; Zito interview; *Chicago and North Western Railway Company Annual Report 1970* (Chicago, 1971), i; Poindexter, "Return of Ben W. Heineman," 36; Barsness, "Ben W. Heineman," 197.

110. Zito interview; Osthoff, *Who's Who in Railroading*, 130; interview with Edward A. Burkhardt, Fremont, Nebraska, November 11, 1986.

111. Poindexter, "Return of Ben W. Heineman," 34, 36; *Chicago and North Western Transportation Company Annual Report 1972* (Chicago, 1973), 3.

Chapter 11: Employee Ownership and After

1. Interview with Frank Koval, Wheaton, Illinois, September 9, 1988; interview with James A. Zito, St. Charles, Illinois, May 4, 1994.

2. Speech by Larry S. Provo, president, Chicago and North Western Transportation Company, Western Railway Club, November 19, 1973, C&NWTCo papers.

3. Zito interview; "Employee Ownership Refuels a Railroad," *Business Week* (December 9, 1972): 48–49.

4. Speech by Larry S. Provo, November 19, 1973, C&NWTCo papers; Proposal of NETCO, C&NWTCo papers; interview with Edward A. Burkhardt, Fremont, Nebraska, November 9, 1986; "Fable for Our Times," *Forbes* (March 1, 1973): 22; confidential interview, Clinton, Iowa, July 23, 1986.

5. "Making Railroaders Rich," *Newsweek* (November 17, 1980); *Chicago and North Western Transportation Company Annual Report 1973* (Chicago, 1974), 1–2; *Chicago Daily News*, June 9, 1976.

6. Unidentified newspaper clippings in C&NWTCo papers;

Des Moines Register, April 27, 1976; *Chicago and North Western Transportation Company Annual Report 1976* (Chicago, 1977), 14; *Chicago and North Western Transportation Company Annual Report 1981* (Chicago, 1982), 23.

7. Interview with Charles Shannon, Arlington Heights, Illinois, October 1, 1988; press release, June 15, 1972, C&NWTCo papers.

8. "The Branch Line Problem: 'Is Anyone Listening?'" address by Larry S. Provo, president, Chicago and North Western Transportation Company, before the Grain Transportation Workshop, Iowa State University, Ames, Iowa, May 14, 1974, C&NWTCo papers.

9. Status of Branch Line Abandonments as of July 1, 1984, C&NWTCo papers.

10. Iroquois-Wren, AB-1 (Sub. No. 9) file, C&NWTCo papers.

11. Ibid.

12. Ibid.

13. *Decisions of the Interstate Commerce Commission of the United States* (Finance Reports) (Washington: U.S. Government Printing Office, 1979), 354:114–15.

14. Ibid., 114–20.

15. Ibid.; *Argus-Leader* (Sioux Falls, S.Dak.), May 11, May 23, 1973; *Daily Plainsman* (Huron, S.Dak.), May 20, 1973; *The Republic* (Mitchell, S.Dak.), May 29, 1973; statement by Senator George McGovern, May 22, 1973, C&NWTCo papers.

16. Shannon interview; interview with D. B. (Del) Carlisle, Chadron, Nebraska, November 11, 1986.

17. The Railroad Branch Line Study by Iowa State University of Science and Technology and the Iowa Department of Transportation: A Summary, C&NWTCo papers.

18. *Chicago and North Western Railway Company Annual Report 1960* (Chicago, 1961), 8–9.

19. Zito interview; John C. Kenefick to author, August 11, 1995, hereafter cited as Kenefick letter.

John Kenefick recalled that the Union Pacific worried about changing patterns of transcontinental traffic. "When I became chief executive officer of the Union Pacific in 1970 one of my problems was establishing an efficient route to Chicago that would compete with the single-line route of the Santa Fe from California and the soon-to-be single-line route of the Burlington Northern from the Pacific Northwest.... I made two overtures to the Rock Island—with whom we were supposed to be merging—to establish a kind of 'most favored nation' relationship through Council Bluffs, but they were not interested in giving up their long hauls via Tucumcari and Denver and turned us down flat." Added Kenefick, "I have often wondered ... what might have happened if the Rock Island had responded positively to our overtures in 1970" (Kenefick letter).

20. Crew Consist Dispute: Chicago and North Western Transportation Company and United Transportation Union: The North Western's Recent History, Statement of James R. Wolfe ..., 1988, 10, hereafter cited as Wolfe statement, C&NWTCo papers.

21. Zito interview.

22. Ibid.

23. H. Roger Grant, *Erie Lackawanna: Death of an American Railroad, 1938–1992* (Stanford: Stanford University Press, 1994), 188–89.

24. Joseph Albright, "The Penn Central: A Hell of a Way to Run a Government," *The New York Times Magazine,* November 3, 1974, 16–17 ff.

25. *The Great Railway Crisis: An Administrative History of the United States Railway Administration* (Washington: National Academy of Public Administration, 1978), 391; *Wall Street Journal,* February 5, 1975.

26. Zito interview; Railroad Revitalization and Regulatory Act of 1976, C&NWTCo papers.

27. *Chicago and North Western Transportation Company Annual Report 1977* (Chicago, 1978), 2.

28. *Chicago and North Western Transportation Company Annual Report 1978* (Chicago, 1979), 2–3.

29. Ibid., 3; *Chicago and North Western Transportation Company Annual Report 1980* (Chicago, 1981), 5.

30. Zito interview; Burkhardt interview; Financial Review Statement, 1972–1977, C&NWTCo papers; *Chicago and North Western Transportation Company Annual Report 1975* (Chicago, 1976), 2.

31. *Chicago Sun-Times,* October 20, 1976; *Chicago Tribune,* October 20, 1976; *Chicago & North Western Transportation Company Annual Report 1976,* inside front cover.

Larry Provo's funeral graphically revealed the high regard that he enjoyed. "[A]t the funeral, there were two conspicuous pews filled with Union Pacific senior officers as well as Mrs. Kenefick to demonstrate our respect for him and for our partner railroad" (Kenefick letter).

32. *North Western News,* October 15, 1976, 1; Zito interview; Burkhardt interview; Kenefick letter; "A Hero for the North Western," *Trains* 43 (October 1983): 3.

33. Frederick C. Osthoff, ed., *Who's Who in Rail Transit* (New York: Simmons-Boardman, 1971), 448; interview with D. Keith Lawson, Rogers, Arkansas, October 18, 1980; *Journal of Commerce,* March 6, 1985.

34. *North Western News,* September 1, 1976, 1; Biography of James R. Wolfe, C&NWTCo papers; "James R. Wolfe Is Elected Vice-President of C&NW," *Traffic World* 134 (April 13, 1968): 39.

35. Zito interview.

36. Ibid.; "The RTA: An Enormously Important Beginning," remarks by Larry S. Provo before the Financial Executives Institute, April 18, 1974, C&NWTCo papers; Grant, *Erie Lackawanna,* 143–46.

37. *Chicago and North Western Transportation Company Annual Report 1976,* 2; *RTA Transfer,* February 1977, 1; *North Western News,* January 1, 1978, 1.

38. Jim Scribbins, *The 400 Story* (Park Forest, Ill.: PTJ Publishing, 1982), 129, 150, 170, 201.

As the North Western cut back its intercity passenger service, the Burlington, Great Northern and Northern Pacific railroads formed a "blind pool" to purchase the modern North Western cars. As Thomas J. Lamphier, former Great Northern officer, explained, "[This occurred] so that no road would get all the good cars, nor would they get all the bad order cars. This purchase allowed the three roads to get rid of virtually all their old heavy weight passenger cars" (Lamphier to author, October 24, 1995, hereafter cited as Lamphier letter).

39. Shannon interview; Fred W. Frailey, "Powder River Country, *Trains* 50 (November 1989): 43.

40. Frailey, "Powder River Country," 44–45; Burkhardt interview; Lamphier letter.

41. Frailey, "Powder River Country," 46; Keith E. Feurer, "Railroad Land Acquisition in the '80's—It Takes More Than Money," American Railway Development Association, Dearborn, Michigan, May 16–18, 1984, C&NWTCo papers.

42. Frailey, "Powder River Country," 45–46; *Chicago and North Western Transportation Company Annual Report 1974* (Chicago, 1975), 1–2; Robert W. Downing to author, August 31, 1995, hereafter cited as Downing letter.

43. *Chicago and North Western Transportation Company Annual Report 1975,* 3; Frailey, "Powder River Country," 46; Feurer, "Railroad Land Acquisition."

Robert Downing described that December 1973 meeting in Washington, D.C., between the Burlington Northern and North Western:

> [T]he two companies were requested to meet under the Commissions [*sic*] auspices to resolve the matter. I represented the Burlington Northern at the meeting with Commissioner Rupert Murphy. Larry Provo attended for the North Western, each of us with a lawyer present. Commissioner Murphy made it clear that the Commission would not approve either application as long as there were two competing applications before them, told us that he had arranged for an adjoining room for the four of us and not to come out until we had reached agreement. It was clear that we would have to do so and Larry and I were willing to try. We agreed in principle to the jointly owned line but also agreed on several other important points. First although the southern terminus had by then been fixed at Orin the C&NW application was vague on where the northern end of the joint line would be. We reached agreement on the exact location. Secondly since this was to be a main BN line over which trains would operate to and from other points of the system we needed to have operational control but would give C&NW trains equal handling. This was agreeable to Provo. Third it was agreed that each road would build half of the new line. The C&NW was concerned that the BN might not build its half expeditiously so they asked to build the south half which would give them access to mines if the BN did not complete the north half. This was agreeable to BN. Finally it was agreed that it would require assistance from staff people to work out the details of an agreement but that Provo and I would personally see that our people cooperated. At that point we reported to Commissioner Murphy that we had reached agreement in principle to proceed with the line jointly and he responded that the Commission would give prompt consideration to a joint application. (Downing letter)

44. *Chicago and North Western Transportation Company Annual Report 1976,* 3; Feurer, "Railroad Land Acquisition"; Joseph P. Marren, "The North Western's New Coal Line: Good for Energy and Good for the Country!" C&NWTCo papers; Kenefick letter.

The details of Union Pacific involvement in the Wyoming coal country are elaborated in these remarks by former UP head John C. Kenefick:

> Mr. [Louis] Menk [head of Burlington Northern] to this day . . . is convinced that I, while his guest [on an inspection trip of the Powder River Basin], was inspired to put the "Yellow Peril," as we [Union Pacific] were called, into the basin and that I put the North Western up to the whole deal. He is still not too pleasant about it. Also, fairly early in the game, Richard Bressler, the executive vice president of Arco in charge of their coal operations, met with me and urged strongly that we build into the basin to provide competitive service to his mine. Not too much later he left Arco to succeed Mr. Menk as chairman of the Burlington Northern and spent the next few years trying his best to keep us out. (Kenefick letter)

45. Statement by John M. Butler, attached to undated memorandum, C&NWTCo papers; interview with Jim Farrell, Fremont, Nebraska, November 9, 1986.

46. Frailey, "Powder River Country," 53.

47. Farrell interview; Zito interview; *Chicago and North Western Transportation Company Annual Report 1979,* 3; *Chicago Tribune,* December 5, 1978.

48. Press release, December 4, 1978, C&NWTCo papers; Frailey, "Powder River Country," 53–54; Kenefick letter.

49. *North Western News,* February 15, 1979; Interstate Commerce, Finance Docket No. 29066F, decided November 30, 1979; *Wall Street Journal,* November 5, 1979; *Chicago Tribune,* July 25, 1981.

50. *Traffic World,* July 4, 1983, 10, 98; Frailey, "Powder River Country," 54; James H. Brownlee, "CNW Competes for Western Coal," *Modern Railroads* 39 (August 1984): 30; *Burlington Northern Railroad Co.* v. *United States of America and Interstate Commerce Commission,* No. 82–2341; *Chicago and North Western News,* January–March 1983, 4–5.

51. Kenefick letter; Feurer, "Railroad Land Acquisition"; *Chicago and North Western News,* June 1981, 3; *Chicago and North Western Transportation Company Annual Report 1983* (Chicago, 1984), 9–10; Brownlee, "CNW Competes for Western Coal," 31.

The actual ownership of the Coal Line was complex. Western Railroad Properties, Inc. (WRPI) possessed the right-of-way title to the rehabilitated and connector lines and leased them to WRPI Trust, an affiliate of the Union Pacific. WRPI Trust owned the actual facilities such as bridges and track. WRPI Trust then leased these facilities to WRPI, which arranged with the North Western to perform WRPI's obligations as a common carrier.

52. *Wyoming State Tribune* (Cheyenne), May 14, 1980; *Casper* (Wyo.) *Star-Tribune,* August 22, 1980; *Torrington* (Wyo.) *Telegram,* April 24, 1982; J. S. Eberhardt to J. P. Marren, August 15, 1979, C&NWTCo papers; telephone interview with Carl Franklin, Yerington, Nevada, July 24, 1995.

53. *Chicago and North Western News,* September 15, 1983, 4–5; *Omaha World-Herald,* August 15, 1984; *Lusk* (Wyo.) *Herald,* August 23, 1984; *Arkansas Democrat* (Little Rock), October 28, 1984.

54. Press releases, March 27, 1984, March 26, 1985, C&NWTCo papers; "C&NW News Highlights #27," September 4, 1985; *Chicago Tribune,* January 16, 1985; Bob Baker, "The Powder River Coal Line: Construction, Operation, Photography," *North Western Lines* 14 (spring 1987): 37–39.

55. Downing letter.

56. Robert Downing to author, November 9, 1995.

57. Telephone interview with Don L. Hofsommer, St. Cloud, Minnesota, April 10, 1995.

58. Lamphier letter; Zito interview.

59. Dan Rottenberg, "The Last Run of the Rock Island Line," *Chicago Magazine* (September 1984): 200.

60. Ibid., 201, 234–35; *Wall Street Journal,* September 27, 1979; *New York Times,* September 27, 1979.

61. Rottenberg, "Last Run," 235–37.

62. *Chicago and North Western Transportation Company Annual Report 1980,* 4; press release, May 6, 1980, C&NWTCo papers.

63. Burkhardt interview; Carlisle interview.

64. *Crain's Chicago Business,* June 16, 1980.

65. Hofsommer interview; Burkhardt interview.

66. Interview with Joseph P. Marren, Chicago, Illinois, July 17, 1985.

67. *Des Moines Register,* September 21, 1982; Bryan D. Olsen to

Don L. Hofsommer, October 11, 1991, courtesy of Don L. Hofsommer, St. Cloud, Minnesota.

The Soo Line was not alone in its interest in the Spine Line. Representatives of Burlington Northern also met with William Gibbons, but they later broke off discussions (Lamphier letter).

68. *Chicago Tribune*, March 16, 1983; *Chicago and North Western Transportation Company Annual Report 1982* (Chicago, 1983), 8.

69. Newspaper clippings, C&NWTCo papers.

70. James R. Wolfe to Governor Terry Branstad et al., March 11, 1983, C&NWTCo papers.

71. *Crain's Chicago Business*, June 27, 1983; *Des Moines Register*, June 30, 1983; *Traffic World*, June 27, 1983, 54, and July 4, 1983, 8.

72. *Chicago Sun-Times*, July 1, 1983; undated press release, C&NWTCo papers; *Chicago and North Western News*, September 15, 1983, 3; *Chicago and North Western News*, October-December 1983, 4, 6–7; *Nevada* (Iowa) *Evening Journal*, July 25, 1983.

73. Zito interview; James Cook, "The Turning Point," *Forbes* (September 24, 1984): 51.

74. *Trains* 51 (November 1990): 39–41; Manalytics, Inc., "Analysis of Impacts of Grand Trunk Corporation's Proposed Acquisition of the Milwaukee Road," June 7, 1983, C&NWTCo papers.

75. Report and Recommendations for the Future of the Milwaukee Road, May 15, 1980, C&NWTCo papers; Why the Milwaukee Core Railroad Should Be Joined to the North Western, August 1983, 2, C&NWTCo papers.

76. *Chicago Tribune*, October 28, 1981; *Chicago Sun-Times*, October 29, 1981; *Wall Street Journal*, October 28, 1981.

77. *Chicago Sun-Times*, October 15, 1983.

78. *Milwaukee Sentinel*, December 28, 1983; *lst Monday 3rd Monday* (publication of the Milwaukee Road), February 22, 1983; "The Grand Trunk/Milwaukee Combination Begins to Look Like a Winner" [ca. October 1983], Grand Trunk Western Railroad Co., C&NWTCo papers.

79. "Rationalizing the Midwest's Rail Plant: Our Last Chance," James R. Wolfe, annual luncheon of the Midwest Advisory Board, Dundee, Illinois, January 16, 1980, C&NWTCo papers.

80. James R. Wolfe to Stanley Hillman, May 2, 1979, C&NWTCo papers; press release, September 22, 1980, C&NWTCo papers; *Chicago and North Western Transportation Company Annual Report 1981*, 5.

81. *Chicago Tribune*, June 26, 1983, July 22, 1983; *Modern Railroads* 38 (August 1983: 9; *Des Moines Register*, July 22, 1983.

82. *Chicago Sun-Times*, July 29, 1983.

83. *Chicago Tribune*, January 26, 1983; *Chicago Sun-Times*, July 31, 1983.

84. *Chicago Tribune*, November 13, 1983; *Chicago Sun-Times*, November 9, 1983.

85. *Chicago Sun-Times*, December 14, 1983; *Wall Street Journal*, November 9, 1983.

86. *Wall Street Journal*, January 20, 1984; *Chicago Sun-Times*, January 20, 1984.

87. *Des Moines Register*, January 20, 1984; *Chicago Sun-Times*, February 7, 1984; *Mason City* (Iowa) *Globe Gazette*, February 18, 1984.

88. *Chicago Tribune*, February 29, 1984; *Wall Street Journal*, March 1, 1984.

89. *Des Moines Register*, March 2, 1984; *Chicago Tribune*, March 6, 1984; *Traffic World*, March 12, 1984, 64–65.

90. *Wall Street Journal*, April 9, 1984; *Chicago Sun-Times*, April 10, 1984; press release, Milwaukee Road, April 14, 1984, C&NWTCo papers.

91. Interstate Commerce Commission, Finance Docket 28640, Washington, D.C., July 27, 1984.

92. *Chicago and North Western News*, January-April 1984, 4–5; *Chicago Tribune*, July 27, 1984, September 5, 1984, September 6, 1984; *Wall Street Journal*, July 27, 1984, September 11, 1984; *Chicago Sun-Times*, August 18, 1984; *Journal of Commerce*, August 29, 1984; Milwaukee Acquisition: Treatment of VCA Traffic in Soo and CNW Applications, September 4, 1984, C&NWTCo papers.

93. *Wall Street Journal*, October 10, 1984; *Chicago Tribune*, October 10, 1984; press release, Milwaukee Road, October 16, 1984, C&NWTCo papers.

94. *Chicago Sun-Times*, October 17, 1984, October 30, 1984; press release, October 10, 1984, C&NWTCo papers; *Wall Street Journal*, October 30, 1984.

95. Press release, December 20, 1984; *Chicago Tribune*, December 21, 1984; *Wall Street Journal*, December 21, 1984.

96. *Chicago Tribune*, February 5, 1985; *Wall Street Journal*, February 11, 1985.

97. *Journal of Commerce*, March 6, 1985; press release, undated, C&NWTCo papers; *Chicago and North Western Transportation Company Annual Report 1984*, 3; John Riley to Jim [James Wolfe], March 13, 1985, C&NWTCo papers.

98. *Chicago and North Western Transportation Company Annual Report 1984*, 3; Michael W. Blaszak, "Chicago & North Western: Evolution of a Survivor," *Trains* 54 (April 1994): 37; interview with Robert W. Schmiege, Chicago, Illinois, March 7, 1989.

99. *Chicago and North Western Transportation Company Annual Report 1984*, 3.

100. *Journal of Commerce*, June 20, 1985.

101. Zito interview; *Chicago Tribune*, March 21, 1985; Wolfe statement, 20.

102. *Chicago and North Western News*, spring 1986, inside cover; *CNW Corporation 1986 Annual Report* (Chicago, 1987), 2; press release, June 24, 1988, C&NWTCo papers; Zito interview.

103. *Chicago and North Western News*, May 1, 1978, 2, and spring 1986, 8–9; "With Service Improved, C&NW's Falcons Are Bagging Bigger Game," *Railway Age* 178 (May 30, 1977): 16–20.

104. Wolfe statement, 10–11; David J. De Boer, *Piggyback and Containers: A History of Rail Intermodal on America's Steel Highways* (San Marino, Calif.: Golden West Books, 1992), 83–97.

105. The Chicago and North Western's Global One, C&NWTCo papers; *CNW Corporation 1986 Annual Report*, 2, 9–10; *CNW Corporation 1987 First Quarter Financial and Operating Data* (Chicago, 1987), 32; *CNW Corporation 1988 Annual Report* (Chicago, 1989), 12–13; *Chicago & North Western News*, July-August 1985, 7–8; "Global One Lifts C&NW's Hopes," *Railway Age* 198 (February 1987): 36–37.

106. Press release, March 23, 1988, C&NWTCo papers; "Great Intermodal Service Reward with Volume Increase," *The North Western Dispatch* 7 (March 1993): 1; *Chicago and North Western Holdings Corp. 1992 Annual Report* (Chicago, 1993), 9–10.

107. "Global Two Terminal To Begin Operations," *The North Western Dispatch* 3 (October 1989): 1; interview with Chris Burger, Chicago, Illinois, May 20, l989.

108. *Chicago and North Western Railway News*, May 1972, 4; Daniel L. Overbey, *Railroads: The Free Enterprise Alternative* (Westport, Conn.: Quorum Books, 1982), p. 79.

109. *North Western Lines* 16 (winter 1989): 13.

110. *Monroe County News* (Albia, Iowa), June 21, 1983, July 26, 1983; *Albia* (Iowa) *Union-Republican*, September 29, 1983, July 11, 1985; *Chicago and North Western News*, October-December 1983, 5; *Des Moines Register*, February 3, 1985.

111. Zito interview; *The North Western Dispatch* 7 (April 1993): 1, 4.

112. Press release, February 21, 1989, C&NWTCo papers.

113. Press release, September 8, 1980, C&NWTCo papers; "Coal-Hauling Capacity To Increase," *The North Western Dispatch* 5 (August 1991): 1; "New Life for Old Boxcars at Clinton Car Shop," *The North Western Dispatch* 2 (July 1988): 4.

114. Shannon interview.

115. *Capital Times* (Madison, Wisc.), March 22, 1972; *Wisconsin State Journal* (Madison, Wisc.), March 23, 1972; *Milwaukee Sentinel*, March 23, 1972.

116. Telephone interview with J. D. Allen, Cleveland, Ohio, February 4, 1992; Wolfe statement, 1.

117. *CNW Corporation 1987 Annual Report* (Chicago, 1988), 4; "C&NW Requests Mediation in Crew Consist Negotiations," *The North Western Dispatch* 1 (July 1987): 1.

118. "Mediator Appointed in Crew Consist Impasse," *The North Western Dispatch* 1 (August 1987): 1; Schmiege interview; "Mediation Moves to Washington," *The North Western Dispatch* 2 (January 1988): 1.

119. Press release, March 16, 1988, March 22, 1988, C&NWTCo papers; "Crew Consist Mediation Ends," *The North Western Dispatch* 2 (April 1988): 1.

120. "No Progress Made at Latest Mediation Session," *The North Western Dispatch* 2 (March 1988): 1; "President Reagan Appoints Emergency Board in Crew Consist Dispute," ibid. [Special Edition] (May 1988): 1; "Crew Consist Dispute Resolved," ibid. 2 (September 1988): 1; R. J. Cuchna to D. F. Markgraf and P. H. Bauch, August 1, 1988, C&NWTCo papers; press release, August 3, 1988, January 25, 1989, C&NWTCo papers.

121. "North Western to Reduce Train Crew Size," *The North Western Dispatch* 5 (December 1991): 1; press release, December 16, 1991, C&NWTCo papers; Chicago and North Western Corp. Form 10–K [Annual Report to Securities and Exchange Commission] for the Fiscal Year Ended December 31, 1991, 1.

122. Wolfe statement, 14; Chicago and North Western Corp. Form 10–K, for the Fiscal Year Ended December 31, 1993, 4; Burkhardt interview; Zito interview; *CNW Corporation 1986 Annual Report*, 4.

123. Zito interview; *C&NW Quality Update: Company Highlights* (December 1986): 1–6.

124. Confidential interview; Zito interview.

125. Schmiege interview.

126. *Sioux Falls Argus-Leader,* November 15, 1987; Peter A. Briggs, "The 'People-Oriented, Customer-Driven' DM&E," *Modern Railroads* 42 (September 1987): 28–30, 32; *Railway Age* 193 (March 1992): 22; *North Western Lines* 19 (winter 1992): 14–15; *Rapid City Journal*, September 23, 1995.

127. *North Western Lines* 21 (spring 1994): 19.

128. *CNW Corporation 1988 Annual Report*, 28; *North Western Lines* 15 (spring 1988): 9–10.

129. "C&NW Announces Agreement to Sell Trackage," *The North Western Dispatch* 1 (October 1987): 1; *Railway Age* 188 (November 1987): 23; press release, December 7, 1987, March 16, 1988, C&NWTCo papers; "Supreme Court Clears Way for Line Sale," *The North Western Dispatch* 2 (December 1988): 1.

130. *Railway Age* 194 (February 1993): 16; "Competitor Announces Plan to Buy Wisconsin Lines," *The North Western Dispatch* 6 (January-February 1992): 1; *North Western Lines* 19 (summer 1992): 16–17; *Chicago and North Western Holdings Corp. 1992 Annual Report*, p. 3; *Chicago and North Western Holdings Corp. 1993 Annual Report* (Chicago, 1994), 12.

131. *North Western Lines* 14 (summer 1987): 5; telephone interview with Henry Posner III, Pittsburgh, Pennsylvania, June 20, 1995.

132. *Chicago and North Western Transportation Company Annual Report 1980,* 7; *Chicago and North Western Transportation Company Annual Report 1981,* 9; "C&NW to Sell Chicago Passenger Terminal," *Chicago and North Western News* 1 (December 1979): 4; ibid. 2 (June 1981): 2; ibid. 5 (January-April 1984): inside cover; *Chicago Tribune*, March 13, 1981; *Chicago and North Western Transportation Company Annual Report 1982*, 19; "Northwestern Atrium Center Opens to Public," *Chicago and North Western News* 8 (spring 1987): 23.

133. Zito interview.

Chapter 12: The Final Years

1. Press release, August 9, 1988, C&NWTCo papers; interview with James A. Zito, St. Charles, Illinois, May 4, 1994.

2. Interview with Robert W. Schmiege, Chicago, Illinois, March 7, 1989; *Who's Who in America, 1990–1991* (Wilmette, Ill.: Marquis Who's Who, 1991), 2: 2908; "Administration Department Changes," *Chicago & North Western News* 5 (November-December 1984): 12.

3. Schmiege interview; press release, August 9, 1988, C&NWTCo papers.

4. Interview with Tom Shedd, Overland Park, Kansas, September 22, 1994; Schmiege interview.

5. Zito interview; interview with Michael W. Payette, Chicago, Illinois, March 7, 1989.

6. Schmiege interview; "Crew Consist Dispute: Chicago and North Western Transportation Company and United Transportation Union: The North Western's Recent History, Statement of James R. Wolfe . . ., 1988," 16–17, hereafter cited as Wolfe statement; *Modern Railroads* 42 (August 1987): 19.

7. Payette interview; Zito interview; "North Western Consolidates Operating Divisions," *The North Western Dispatch* 1 (July 1987): 1.

8. Zito interview; *North Western Lines* 15 (winter 1988): 8; ibid. 15 (summer 1988): 13; *CNW Corporation 1988 Annual Report* (Chicago: CNW Corporation, 1989), 28.

9. *CNW Corporation 1988 Annual Report*, 2; press release, February 28, 1989, C&NWTCo papers; Schmiege interview.

10. Leigh B. Trevor, "Hostile Takeovers in Perspective," *Vital Speeches of the Day* 54 (June 15, 1988): 528–29; "Running the Biggest LBO," *Business Week* (October 2, 1989): 72–75, 78–79.

11. Schmiege interview; *Wall Street Journal*, April 18, 1988; *Railway Age* 189 (May 1988): 16.

12. Press release, March 13, 1989, C&NWTCo papers.

13. Press releases, April 6, 26, 27, 1989, C&NWTCo papers; Zito interview.

14. Press releases, May 2, 4, 9, 1989; *Wall Street Journal*, April 7, 1989; Zito interview.

15. *Wall Street Journal*, June 5, 1989.

16. *Chicago and North Western News* 2 (October-November 1981): 5; Zito interview.

17. Press release, June 6, 1989, C&NWTCo papers.

18. Ibid.; *Washington Post*, July 30, 1989.

19. Press release, June 6, 1989; *Wall Street Journal*, May 15, 1989.

20. Chicago and North Western Holdings Corp. Form 10–K, for the Fiscal Year Ended December 31, 1990, 1–2.

21. Michael W. Blaszak, "Chicago & North Western: Evolution of a Survivor," *Trains* 54 (April 1994): 40–41; Zito interview.

22. Chicago and North Western Holdings Corp. Form 10-K, for the Fiscal Year Ended December 31, 1991, 4; "Centralized Dispatching Facility Begins Operation," *The North Western Dispatch* (December 1989): 1; *Chicago and North Western Holdings Corp. 1992 Annual Report*, 11, 14; *Omaha World-Herald*, July 3, 1992.

23. "North Western Sells Itasca Line to Wisconsin Central," *The North Western Dispatch* 6 (August 1992): 1; *Chicago and North Western Holdings Corp. 1993 Annual Report*, 13; "Fate of the Nebraska Line Finalized," *The North Western Dispatch* 8 (September 1994): 1; *Lincoln* (Neb.) *Star*, April 1, 1992; *Norfolk* (Neb.) *Daily News*, December 2, 1992; Rick W. Mills, "Happy Trails, Cowboy Line," *Trains* 53 (April 1993): 26–27.

24. Press release, January 24, 1992, March 8, 1993, C&NWTCo papers; Blaszak, "Chicago & North Western," 42–43; *Chicago and North Western Holdings Corp. 1993 Annual Report*, 1–2; "1992 North Western in Review," *The North Western Dispatch* 7 (January 1993): 1; "C&NW Boosts Horsepower of Locomotive Fleet with Acquisition of New Engines," ibid. 7 (November 1993): 1.

25. *Omaha World-Herald*, August 23, 1992; David M. Cawthorne, "Western Rails Unveil Rights Request as Condition to UP-C&NW Control Plan," *Traffic World* (April 26, 1993): 16–17; "North Western Affirms Intent To Remain Independent," *The North Western Dispatch* 6 (September 1992): 1.

26. Union Pacific press release, March 17, 1995; Chicago & North Western press release, March 17, 1995.

27. *Wall Street Journal*, March 8, 23, 1995; *Corporate Growth Report*, No. 836, March 20, 1995, 7748; interview with John Rebensdorf, Omaha, Nebraska, September 1, 1995.

28. *Wall Street Journal*, December 14, 1994, March 13, 1995.

29. "Union Pacific Seeks C&NW Control," *Distribution* 92 (March 1993): 20; *Chicago Tribune*, May 28, 1995.

30. *Traffic World*, April 24, 1995: n.p.

31. Rebensdorf interview; Gus Welty, "From UP, A Lesson in Management-Labor Relations," *Railway Age* 196 (July 1995): 9; *Traffic World*, November 13, 1995, 13.

32. *Traffic World*, November 13, 1995, 13; *Wall Street Journal*, November 30, 1995.

33. *Trains* 55 (October 1995): 18; Rebensdorf interview.

34. Telephone interview with Don Snoddy, Omaha, Nebraska, June 12, 1995.

Additional Works on the North Western

Arlington Heights Railroad History: Chicago and North Western and Other Railroads. Arlington Heights, Ill.: Arlington Heights Historical Society, 1983.

Baker, Bob. *Wisconsin Rails II: A Passage of Time.* Racine, Wis.: National Railway Historical Society, 1994.

Caine, Stanley P. *The Myth of a Progressive Reform: Railroad Regulation in Wisconsin, 1903–1910.* Madison: State Historical Society of Wisconsin, 1970.

Casey, Robert, and W. A. S. Douglas. *Pioneer Railroad: The Story of the Chicago and North Western System.* New York: Whittlesey House, 1948.

Chicago & North Western Railway. *Chicago & North-Western Railway Company and Proprietary Companies.* Chicago: Cameron, Amberg, 1892.

———. *Corporate History of the C&NW Railway Company and of Auxiliary Railway and Bridge Companies.* Chicago: Chicago & North Western, 1923.

———. *Over Half a Century of Progress, 1848–1902.* Chicago: Chicago & North Western Railway, 1902.

Cleveland, H. I. *A Thrilling Night's Ride on the North Western Fast Mail.* Chicago: Chicago & North Western Railway, 1899.

Cole, Francis. *Locomotives of the Chicago and North Western Ry.* Boston: Railway & Locomotive Historical Society, 1938.

Condon, Gregg, Robert Felten, and James Nickoll. *The Dinky: C&NW Narrow Gauge in Wisconsin.* Marsh Lake, Wis.: Marsh Lake Production, 1993.

Cook, Preston. *Chicago and North Western Memories, 1970–1980.* Chicago: Old Line Graphics, 1989.

Cook, Willamine A. Gardner. *The W. A. Gardner Story.* Evanston, Ill.: Privately printed, 1956.

Dorin, Patrick. *Chicago and North Western Power: Modern Steam and Diesel, 1900 to 1971.* Seattle: Superior Publishing Co., 1972.

Fiedler, Mildred. *Railroads of the Black Hills.* Seattle: Superior Publishing Company, 1964.

Grant, H. Roger. *The Corn Belt Route: A History of the Chicago Great Western Railroad Company.* DeKalb: Northern Illinois University Press, 1984.

Grodinsky, Julius. *The Iowa Pool: A Study in Railroad Competition, 1870–1884.* Chicago: University of Chicago Press, 1950.

Hilton, George W. *American Narrow Gauge Railroads.* Stanford, Calif.: Stanford University Press, 1990.

Knudsen, Charles. *Chicago and North Western Railway Steam Power.* Chicago: Knudson Publications, 1965.

Koval, Francis. *A Pioneering Railroad: Its First Century.* Chicago: C&NW Railway, 1948.

Luecke, John. *The Chicago and Northwestern in Minnesota.* Eagan, Minn.: Grenadier Publications, 1990.

Miller, George H. *Railroads and the Granger Laws.* Madison: University of Wisconsin Press, 1971.

Mills, Rick. *The High, Dry, and Dusty: Memories of the Cowboy Line.* David City, Neb.: South Platte Press, 1992.

———. *Making the Grade: A Century of Black Hills Railroading.* Hermosa, S.Dak.: Privately printed, 1985.

Olmsted, Robert. *Prairie Rails.* Woodridge, Ill.: McMillan, 1979.

Porter, Russ. *Chicago and North Western—Milwaukee Road Pictorial.* Forest Park, Ill.: Heimburger House, 1994.

Prescott, DeWitt C. *Early Day Railroading from Chicago: A Narrative with Some Observations.* Chicago: David B. Clarkson Co., 1910.

Randall, W. David. *Chicago and North Western.* Godfrey, Ill.: Railway Production Classics, 1990.

Rapp, William. *The Chicago and North Western: The Nebraska Division.* Crete, Neb.: J-B Publishing Co., 1989.

Richardson, Helen, ed. *Chicago and North Western Railway Company, a Centennial Bibliography.* Washington, D.C.: Bureau of Railway Economics, Association of American Railroads, 1948.

Scribbins, Jim. *The 400 Story.* Park Forest, Ill.: PTJ Press, 1982.

Seidel, David. *Fremont, Elkhorn & Missouri Valley R.R. Co.* Columbus, Neb.: Harbor Mist Publications, 1988.

Simon, Marvin, *Chicago & North Western Railroad from Stockton to Lewiston.* M. J. Simon, 1980.

Stennett, William H. *A History of the Origin of the Place Names Connected with the Chicago and North Western.* Chicago: Chicago & North Western, 1908.

———, compiler. *Yesterday and To-day: A History of the Chicago & North Western Railway System.* Chicago: Chicago & North Western Railway, 1910.

Thompson, John. *The Chatfield Branch Line and Planks Crossing, C&NW Railway System, 1878–1969.* Eyota, Minn.: T. R. Thompson, 1974.

White, John H., Jr. *The Pioneer: Chicago's First Locomotive.* Chicago: Chicago Historical Society, 1976.

Williams, Rowland. *The Chicago and North Western Railway: A Centenary Address.* New York: Newcomen Society, 1948.

Index

Aberdeen, South Dakota, 61
Acme Boot Company, 215
Adams, Charles Francis, Jr., 37
Adamson Act (1916), 129
Afton, Wisconsin, 65
Ahnapee & Western Railroad, 244
Airways Limited (passenger train), 148
Aishton, Richard H., 127–28, 130
Aishton, Rose Whitbeck, 132
Akron, Iowa, 139
Alaska Railroad, 173
Albert Lea, Minnesota, 76, 207
Albia, Iowa, 240–41
Albion, Nebraska, 55
Albright, H. M., 150
Alden, Iowa, 49
Alfalfa, 93–94
Allerton, Iowa, 237
Alliance, Nebraska, 55
Alton, Iowa, 78
Alton & Southern Railroad, 211
Alton Railroad. *See* Chicago & Alton Railroad
Aluminum Company of America (Alcoa), 211
American Land Company, 9
American Locomotive Company, 141
American Management Association, 173
American President Lines, 239
American Red Cross, 132
Ames, Iowa, 46, 131
Ames, Oakes, 52
Amtrak. *See* National Railroad Passenger Corporation
Anamosa, Iowa, 17, 32, 48
Aniwa, Wisconsin, 63
Appleton, Wisconsin, 62, 168, 244
Appleton & New London Railroad, 62, 64
Appleton Junction, Wisconsin, 179
Arkansas Power & Light Company, 230
Arlington, Nebraska, 57
Arlington Heights, Illinois, 201
Armour, Phillip, 151
Armstrong, George, 39–40
Army Appropriation Act (1916), 129, 193
Arnold, Isaac, 16
Arthur Andersen & Company, 193–94
Ashland, Nebraska, 71
Ashland, Wisconsin, 63–64, 69, 75, 161, 178, 225
Ashland Junction, Wisconsin, 75
Ashland Limited (passenger train), 105

Association of American Railroads, 130
Association of General Chairmen, 249
Astoria, South Dakota, 85
Atchison, Topeka & Santa Fe Railway, 57, 127, 148–49, 190, 214–15, 252–53
Atlantic Express (passenger train), 102
Audubon, Iowa, 48
Aurora, Elgin & Chicago Railway, 124
Aurora, Illinois, 66
Aurora Branch Railroad, 15
Austin, Illinois, 20
Automobiles, 145, 157
Avoca, Harlan & Northern Rail Road, 85
Avoca, Iowa, 85
Avoca, Minnesota, 81
Avoca, Wisconsin, 25

Babcock's Grove, Illinois. *See* Lombard, Illinois
Baldwin, D. A., 73
Baldwin Locomotive Company, 141
Baltimore & Ohio Chicago Terminal Railroad, 239
Baltimore & Ohio Railroad, 96, 109, 139
Baltimore & Ohio Southwestern Railroad, 166
Bannerman, Wisconsin, 89
Baraboo, Wisconsin, 33
Barnes, John P., 165
Barney, Danford, 31
Barrington, Illinois, 151, 201
Batavia, Illinois, 66
Bayfield, Wisconsin, 69, 74–75
Beebe, Lucius, 104
Belle Fourche, South Dakota, 55, 86
Belle Fourche Irrigation Project, 86
Belle Fourche Valley Railway, 86
Belle Plaine, Iowa, 48, 88, 105
Belle Plaine, Minnesota, 69
Beloit, Wisconsin, 14, 65, 113
Beloit & Madison Railroad, 14
Belvidere, Illinois, 13–14, 65
Bement, Illinois, 20
Benham, Isabel H., 191
Benld, Illinois, 90, 207
Benson, Minnesota, 61
Best Friend of Charleston (locomotive), 3
Beyers, Henry, 256
B. F. Goodrich Company, 212, 215
Big Suamico, Wisconsin, 87
Bismarck, North Dakota, 60
Black Hawk War, 4

Black Hills, South Dakota, 55
Black Hills & Fort Pierre Railroad, 55
Black River Falls, Wisconsin, 72
Blackstone Capital Partners, 249, 252
Blacktail Junction, South Dakota, 55
Blair, John Insley, 18, 50, 52, 54
Blair, Montgomery, 39
Blair, Nebraska, 49, 71, 222
Blaszek, Michael, 238
Bloomfield, Nebraska, 75
Blue Earth, Minnesota, 88
Blunt, John E., 91
Blunt, South Dakota, 86
Bonesteel, South Dakota, 55, 85–86, 107
Boone, Iowa, 18, 40, 97, 112, 184, 250
Boone County Railroad, 112
Boston & Maine Railroad, 223
Boyer, Iowa, 84
Boyer Valley Railroad, 84–85
Boyington, William W., 113
Bradgate, Iowa, 48
Bradley, Page & Company, 25
Breckenridge, Minnesota, 61
Breese, Sidney, 5
Bremo Corporation, 210
Brotherhood of Locomotive Engineers, 22–23, 97–98, 217
Brotherhood of Railway, Airline and Steamship Clerks, 217, 231
Brotherhood of Railway Carmen, 99
Brown, Charles P., 109
Budd, Ralph, 181
Buffalo, New York, 159
Buffalo Gap, South Dakota, 54–55
Burgess, Kenneth, 165
Burkhardt, Edward A., 219, 244
Burlington, Cedar Rapids & Northern Railway, 76, 81
Burlington, Iowa, 76
Burlington & Missouri River Railroad in Nebraska, 41
Burlington Northern Railroad, 205, 209, 212, 214, 222–23, 226–31, 235, 237, 241, 247, 252–53
Burlington Northern Santa Fe Corporation, 252
Burlington Railroad. *See* Chicago, Burlington & Quincy Railroad
Burns, Ronald J., 252
Burt, Iowa, 79, 88
Butler, Charles, 9
Butler, John, 216, 228

Butler, Wisconsin, 90
Butterfield, Minnesota, 79–80, 221
Buxton, Iowa, 87–88

Cable, Ransom R., 76, 85, 207
California Junction, Iowa, 50, 222
California Limited (passenger train), 104
Callanan, Iowa, 46
Cameron, Glenn, 236
Cameron, Wisconsin, 250
Camp Douglas, Wisconsin, 73
Camp McCoy, Wisconsin, 171
Canadian National Railways, 235–36
Canadian Pacific Railway, 81, 233, 236
Canals, 4–5. *See also* Illinois & Michigan Canal
Canova, South Dakota, 122
Canton, South Dakota, 60
Capitol 400 (passenger train), 168
Carey, Illinois, 25
Cargill, Inc., 240–41
Cario, Illinois, 5–6
Carnegie, Andrew, 33
Carpenter, Cyrus Clay, 37
Carroll, Iowa, 48, 85, 112, 145, 180
Carson, Rachel, 226
Carter, Jimmy, 232
Casper, Wyoming, 54, 91–92
Cassat, Alexander J., 97
Castlewood Junction, South Dakota, 60
Cedar Falls, Iowa, 88
Cedar Rapids, Iowa, 17, 76, 111
Cedar Rapids & Missouri River Rail Road, 17–19, 30, 45, 49–51
Centerville, South Dakota, 60
Central Pacific Railroad, 30, 51
Central Railroad. *See* Illinois Central Railroad
Central Railroad of New Jersey, 223
Central Vermont Railway, 235
Century of Progress Exposition (Chicago), 159
Chadron, Nebraska, 54, 201, 250
Chamberlain, South Dakota, 60
Chamberlin, Everett, 41
Chandler, Wisconsin, 74
Chatfield, Minnesota, 46, 146
Chatfield Rail-Road, 46
Chelsea, Iowa, 18
Cherry Valley, Illinois, 13
Chesapeake & Ohio Railway, 135
Chicago, Aurora & Elgin Railroad, 204
Chicago, Burlington & Northern Railroad, 54
Chicago, Burlington & Quincy Railroad, 15–16, 30, 35–36, 49, 53–55, 57, 71, 76, 81, 91, 94, 104, 119, 145, 157–59, 168, 174, 181, 203, 207–9, 214–15, 222, 225
Chicago, Illinois, 4–7, 9–14, 16, 19, 23, 26–27, 29, 38, 40–41, 66, 75, 88, 97, 102, 104–5, 107–9, 111, 113–15, 118–19, 122, 132, 141–44, 148–49, 151, 156–59, 167–68, 177–79, 182–84, 193, 197, 200–1, 203–4, 210, 213–15, 220, 222–23, 225, 239–40, 245, 250
Chicago, Indianapolis & Louisville Railway, 189
Chicago, Iowa & Dakota Railway, 48
Chicago, Iowa & Nebraska Railroad, 17–19, 49, 51
Chicago, Milwaukee & North Western Transportation Company, 212
Chicago, Milwaukee & St. Paul Railroad (Chicago, Milwaukee, St. Paul & Pacific Railroad), 38, 44, 49, 55, 59–62, 73–74, 76, 85–86, 92–93, 104–5, 119, 135, 145, 157–59, 162, 168, 183–84, 186, 211–15, 222, 234–35, 236
Chicago, North Shore & Milwaukee Railroad, 204
Chicago, Rock Island & Pacific Railroad, 14, 30, 35–37, 54, 76, 81, 85, 104, 140, 145, 207, 211, 213–14, 222–23, 231, 232, 247
Chicago, St. Charles & Mississippi Airline Railroad, 14, 16
Chicago, St. Paul & Fond du Lac Railroad, 25–26
Chicago, St. Paul & Kansas City Railway, 210
Chicago, St. Paul & Minneapolis Railway, 74–75, 78
Chicago, St. Paul, Minneapolis & Omaha Railway (Omaha Road), 48–49, 57, 67, 69–70, 74–81, 83, 88–90, 112, 140, 160, 171, 182, 197, 207
Chicago & Alton Railroad, 102, 119, 127, 207
Chicago & Dakota Railway, 59
Chicago & Eastern Illinois Railroad, 135, 159, 166
Chicago & Illinois Midland Railway, 208
Chicago & Milwaukee Electric Railway, 124
Chicago & Milwaukee Railway, 29–30
Chicago & North Western Railway:
—Adams cut-off, 77–78, 89, 157
—acquisitions: Blair Roads, 49–50; Chicago & Milwaukee, 29–30; Chicago Great Western, 210–11; Chicago, St. Paul & Fond du Lac, 26–27; Des Moines & Central Iowa, 211; Fort Dodge, Des Moines & Southern, 211; Fremont, Elkhorn & Missouri Valley, 54; Galena & Chicago Union, 28–29; Iowa Midland, 31–32; Kenosha, Rockford & Rock Island, 28; Milwaukee, Lake Shore & Western, 64–65; Minneapolis & St. Louis, 207, 209–10; North Western Union, 31, Spine Line (Rock Island), 231–34; Winona & St. Peter, 31
—agricultural development and promotion, 93–94, 133
—air-mail service, 148–49
—bankruptcy (1935–1944) and reorganization, 162–67, 175, 184, 225
—betterments, 33, 88, 111–15, 118–20, 133, 140–43, 195–97, 222–23, 234, 239
—branch line problems and retrenchment, 190–91, 206–7, 220–22
—bridges: Des Moines River, 112; Mississippi River, 18, 31; Missouri River, 50
—bus operations, 146–48
—Car-Fax, 194
—centennial celebrations (1948), 177–78
—Chicago & North Western Acquisition Corporation, 249
—Chicago & North Western Holdings Corporation, 249
—Chicago & North Western Transportation Company, 217, 219, 249
—CNW Corporation, 238–39, 248–49
—Chicago fire (1871), 38, 113, 118–20, 132, 245
—Chicago Passenger Terminal, 113–15
—Chicago Railroad Fair (1948–1949), 177–78
—Clinton (Iowa) car shops, 195–97, 223, 241
—Coal Line Project, 225–231
—commuter service, 41, 191, 201–5, 225
—container and intermodal freight, 156, 239
—co-ordination, modernization, and retrenchment, 153–55, 161, 166, 174, 190, 193–97, 200–1, 204, 220–21, 243–45, 248–50
—*Deerpath*, 151
—depots, 119–20 (*see also* Chicago Passenger Terminal)
—dieselization, 174, 190, 193, 203
—diversification, 214–15
—double-tracking, 111–13
—Dutch investment, 36–37
—electrification proposal, 143–44
—Elroy Route, 73, 79, 104–5
—Employee Mutual Aid Association, 98–99
—Employees, labor relations, and unions, 94–99, 128–29, 131–32, 137, 139, 155, 173–77, 197–200, 219, 241–42, 244, 249
—employee ownership, 216–17, 219–20, 249
—Esch-Cummins Act, 135–36
—expansion, 27–31, 33, 45–51, 54–55, 57, 61, 65–67, 83–92, 142–43
—financial condition, 33, 44–45, 67, 83, 124–25, 127, 133–34, 136, 139, 151, 153, 160–62, 167, 175–76, 178, 180, 184, 187, 205, 215, 224, 248, 250
—Four-R Act, 223–24, 227, 234
—freight service, 107–9, 194, 205–6,

239–40 (*see also* LCL freight and rolling stock)
—Great Depression (1930s), 153–55, 161–62
—interurbans, 124
—Iowa Pool, 36
—land promotion, 41
—LCL freight, 156–57, 195
—left-hand operations, 16
—logo and public image, 101–2
—mail service (RPO), 39–40
—merger proposals: Milwaukee Road, 164–65, 184–86, 212; Rock Island, 213–14
—Midwestern Railroad Properties, 234
—Milwaukee II bid, 234–38
—motive power, 109–110, 141, 146, 157, 174, 190, 241
—North Western Employee Transportation Company, 216
—Omaha Road lease, 197
—Overland Route, 30, 104, 151, 159, 183, 213, 222
—Pacific Extension plans, 92–93
—passenger service, 40–41, 102–5, 107, 144–46, 157–59, 167–69, 175, 178–80, 183–84, 191, 200–1, 225
—pension, 96–97
—Railroad Credit Corporation, 160
—rates and regulation, 37–38, 159–60, 247–48
—Reconstruction Finance Corporation, 160–62
—rolling stock, 107–9, 195–96, 200, 203, 239, 241, 251
—Safety-First campaign, 122–24, 127
—speed of trains, 120–22
—stock purchase in Alton & Southern, 211
—stock purchase in Gulf, Mobile & Ohio, 212
—Surgical Department, 97
—take-over attempts of C&NW, 248–49
—telegraphers' (ORT) strike, 197–99
—Total Quality Improvement System (TQIS), 243
—Tours Department, 150–51
—Training Within Industry (TWI) program, 173
—Union Pacific purchase, 251–53
—valuation work, 128
—Western Railroad Properties, 229, 248
—World War I, 128–33
—World War II, 169, 171, 173–75
—wrecks, 111–12
See also Aishton, Richard; Feucht, Paul; Finley, William H.; Fitzpatrick, Clyde J.; Gardner, William A.; Heineman, Ben W.; Hughitt, Marvin; Keep, Albert; Keep, Henry; Mitchell, Alexander; Ogden, William Butler; Schmiege, Robert W.; Williams, Roland; Wolfe, James

Chicago & North Western Stages, 147
Chicago & Rock Island Railroad. *See* Chicago, Rock Island & Pacific Railroad
Chicago & Tomah Railroad, 47
Chicago & Vincennes Railroad, 6
Chicago Great Western Railway, 81, 85, 189, 210–11, 231, 232
Chicago Milwaukee Corporation, 234–36
Chicago Special (passenger train), 104
Chicago Tribune Company, 97, 177
Chippewa Falls, Wisconsin, 75
Chippewa Falls & Northern Railway, 75
Cincinnati, Ohio, 159
City of Denver (passenger train), 159
City of Los Angeles (passenger train), 159, 183
City of Portland (passenger train), 159
City of San Francisco (passenger train), 159
Clayman Junction, Wisconsin, 90
Clayton, Wisconsin, 74
Clean Air Act (1970), 226
Clean Water Act (1971), 226
Cleveland, Ohio, 151, 159
Cleveland, Wisconsin, 244
Clinton, Iowa, 17, 109, 111, 121, 139, 196, 200, 215, 223, 225, 241, 252
Clintonville, Wisconsin, 63–64
Clovis, New Mexico, 149
Clowry, Michigan, 65
Clybourn Junction, Illinois, 120
Coal Creek Junction, Wyoming, 230
Colburn Junction, Nebraska, 71
Collins, C. J., 150
Colome, South Dakota, 86
Colorado Midland Railway, 133
Colorado Special (passenger train), 104
Columbia, South Dakota, 60
Columbine (passenger train), 148
Columbus, Nebraska, 52, 55
Columbus, Ohio, 148
Committee of Investigation on Smoke Abatement and Electrification of Railway Terminals (Chicago), 143
Como, Illinois, 20
Conde, South Dakota, 207
Consol, Iowa, 88, 154
Consolidated Coal Company, 87–88
Consolidated Rail Corporation (Conrail), 223, 239
Conway, Barret, 175
Coolidge, Calvin, 149
Coolidge, Grace, 149
Coos Bay, Oregon, 92
Cordero Mine, Wyoming, 230
Corn King Limited (passenger train), 145, 148
Cottage Hill, Illinois, 12
Council Bluffs, Iowa, 30, 40, 109, 121, 200, 210, 222, 228, 235, 250, 252
Covington, Columbus & Black Hills Railroad, 52, 71

Covington, Nebraska, 52–53, 71
Crandall, Wyoming, 228
Crandon, Wisconsin, 87
Creighton, Nebraska, 53, 55
Crocker, Lucius B., 18
Crowley, Leo T., 184, 186, 212
Crown, Henry, 213
Crystal Falls, Michigan, 65
Cudahay, E. A., 151
Cudahay Packing Company, 57
Cumberland, Wisconsin, 74
Cummins, Albert B., 134

Daley, Richard J., 193
Dallas, South Dakota, 86
Dakota, Minnesota & Eastern Railroad, 58
Dakota Central Railway, 49, 58–61, 78
Dakota 400 (passenger train), 178
Dakota Junction, Nebraska, 54
Dakota Southern Railroad, 58
Daugherty, Harry M., 137
David City, Nebraska, 57
Davidson, Dick, 252
Deadwood, South Dakota, 55, 59, 146
Deadwood Central Railroad, 55
Dean Witter Reynolds, 226
Deerpath (private car), 151
DeKalb, Illinois, 65, 121
Delaware, Lackawanna & Western Railway, 124, 137, 173
Denison, Iowa, 84, 120
Dennis, C. L., 173, 217
Denver, Colorado, 49, 57, 157
Denver & Rio Grande Railway, 102
Denver & Rio Grande Western Railroad, 214
Denver Express (passenger train), 102
Department of Justice, 229
Depew, Chauncey M., 127
Deramus, William N., III, 210
Des Moines, Iowa, 46, 211, 220
Des Moines & Central Iowa Railway, 211
Des Moines & Minnesota Railroad, 46
Des Moines Register, 233
DeSoto, Nebraska, 50
Des Plaines, Illinois, 13, 143
Detroit, Michigan, 151, 159
DeVol, E. L., 194
Dickinson, Albert J., 159
Dixie Flyer (passenger train), 159
Dixon, Illinois, 15, 148
Dodgeville, Wisconsin, 47
Doland, South Dakota, 60
Donaldson, Lufkin & Jenrette Securities Corporation, 249
Donovan, Frank P., Jr., 139
Doon, Iowa, 70
Douglas, Stephen A., 6, 15
Douglas, Wyoming, 54, 226–27
Douglas Dynamics, 238–39
Downing, Robert W., 226, 231

Dows, David, 76
Drake, Elias F., 71
Drexel Burnham Lambert, 248
Drifting Goose (Sioux chief), 61
Droege, John A., 113, 118
Drought of 1930s, 161–62
Dubin, Arthur D., 102–3, 105
Dubuque, Iowa, 18–19, 210
Dubuque & Pacific Railroad, 18, 50
Duck Creek, Wisconsin, 89, 244–45
Duluth, Huron & Denver Railway, 61
Duluth, Minnesota, 69, 75, 208, 235
Duluth, Winnipeg & Pacific Railway, 235
Duluth-Superior Limited (passenger train), 105
Dunleith, Illinois, 6, 19
Dyer, Thomas, 9

Eagle Grove, Iowa, 48
Earling, Albert J., 93
East Caballo Junction, Wyoming, 230
East Elgin, Illinois, 16
East St. Louis, Illinois, 91, 207, 240
Eastern Express (passenger train), 104–5
Eastman, Joseph B., 171
Eau Claire, Wisconsin, 72–73, 75, 89, 105
Eau Claire & Chippewa Falls Railway, 75
Eddyville, Iowa, 240–41
Eland Junction, Wisconsin 63, 89
Elburn, Illinois, 121–22
Electro-Motive Corporation, 168
Elgin, Illinois, 10–11, 13, 66
Elgin & State Line Railroad, 17, 66
Elkhorn Land & Town Lot Company, 52
Ellensburg, Washington, 93
Ellsworth, Wisconsin, 75
Elm Grove, Wisconsin, 27
Elmhurst, Illinois, 12–13, 142–43, 201
Elmore, Minnesota, 48–49, 70–71
Elroy, Wisconsin, 69, 72–73, 76, 112–13, 122
Emergency Railroad Transportation Act (1933), 136
Emerson Junction, Nebraska, 75
Emporia, Kansas, 127
Endangered Species Act (1973), 226
Energy Transmission Systems, 231
Equitable Life Assurance Society of the United States, 249
Erie Lackawanna Railway, 223, 225
Erie Railroad, 3, 9, 25, 81, 109, 135, 151, 164, 173, 181
Escanaba, Michigan, 28, 45, 65, 240
Escanaba & Lake Superior Railroad, 65
Escanaba & Northern Railroad, 245
Esch, John J., 134
Esch-Cummins Act (1920), 134–36, 165, 253
Eureka, California, 92
Eureka, South Dakota, 86
Evan, Minnesota, 85

Evanston, Illinois, 111, 201
Evansville, Wisconsin, 112–13
Exide Battery Company, 141
Eyota, Minnesota, 46, 146

Fairmont, Minnesota, 88
Fargo, William, 31
Farley Industries, 216
Farmers Union, 221
Farmland Industries, 252
Farrington, John D., 213
Faulkton, South Dakota, 60, 86
"Featherbedding" (make-work), 198–200, 241
Federal Bankruptcy Act (1933), 163
Federal Bureau of Reclamation, 86
Federal Railroad Administration, 229
Felton, Samuel, 210
Fennimore, Wisconsin, 47
Feucht, Paul, 182–84, 186–87
Feurer, Keith, 229
Finley, William H., 127, 134–35, 139, 144–45
Finnegan, Arthur, 97
Fitch Container, 156
Fitzpatrick, Clyde J., 191, 193, 215
Flambeau (passenger train), 179
Flambeau 400 (passenger train), 178–79
Fond du Lac, Wisconsin, 25, 32, 65, 89, 225, 244
Food Administration, 133
Ford, John Anson, 119
Fort Dodge, Des Moines & Southern Railway, 211
Fort Dodge, Iowa, 85, 211
Fort Pierre, South Dakota, 91
400 (passenger train), 157–59, 167–68. *See also Twin Cities 400*
Fox Lake, Minnesota, 88
Fox River Valley Railroad, 17, 66
Fox River Valley Railroad (new company), 244
Fox Valley & Western, Ltd., 245
Freemasons, 96
Freeport, Illinois, 14, 47
Fremont, Elkhorn & Missouri Valley Railroad, 49–55, 57–59, 71, 85
Fremont, Nebraska, 49–51, 57, 146, 174, 207, 222, 228, 239
Frisco Railway. *See* St. Louis–San Francisco Railway
Frost, Charles S., 113
Frost & Granger, 113
Fruit of the Loom Company, 215
FRVR Corporation, 244
Fulton, Illinois, 15, 19

Galena, Illinois, 5–6, 10, 14, 47
Galena & Chicago Union Railroad, 2, 6–7, 28; betterments, 13, 15, 19–20; Cedar Rapids & Missouri River Railroad, 18–19; Chicago Group, 9–10; Chicago & North Western merger, 28–29; Chicago, Iowa & Minnesota Railroad, 18–19; construction, 11–16; Dixon Air Line, 14–15; Elgin & State Line Railroad, 17; employees, 22–23; financial condition, 15, 19; formation, 7–11; operations, 12–13, 16, 22; social impact, 20–21
Galena & Southern Wisconsin Railroad, 47
Galena & Wisconsin Railroad, 47
Galesville, Wisconsin, 66, 146
Galesville & Mississippi River Railroad, 66
Garden City, Kansas, 57
Gardner, Illinois, 127
Gardner, William A., 90, 127–28
Garland, Hamlin, 58
Garrett, Sylvester, 199
Garrison, Montana, 93
Garwood, Delbert, 173
Gary, Charles, 22
Gary, South Dakota, 58
Gelfand, Louis, 208–9
General Electric Company, 141, 241
General Motors Corporation, 181
General Railway Signal Automatic Two Speed Train Control, 142
Geneva, Illinois, 66, 121–22, 201, 204
Geneva, Nebraska, 57
Genoa, Wisconsin, 66
George H. Hammond & Company, 57
Gettysburg, South Dakota, 60, 86
Gibbons, Green, van Amerongen, 248
Gibbons, William, 232–34
Gifford, Iowa, 48
Gillett, Wisconsin, 87
Gillette, Wyoming, 226
Girard, Illinois, 90–91
Gladbrook, Iowa, 48
Glenbeulah, Wisconsin, 65
Glen Ellyn, Illinois, 201, 204
Glen Rock, Wyoming, 54
Glidden, William, 52
Goldman, Sachs & Company, 248–49
Goodwin, John E., 183
Gould, George, 93
Gould, Jay, 37, 121
Grand Island, Nebraska, 215
Grand Rapids, Michigan, 150
Grand Rapids, Wisconsin, 89
Grand Trunk Corporation, 235–37
Grand Trunk Western Railway, 235
Granger, Alfred Hoyt, 113
Grangers. *See* Patrons of Husbandry
Granite City Steel Company, 240
Granville, Wisconsin, 244
Grasshoppers, 52
Gray, Carl R., 197
Gray, Carl R., Jr., 197
Gray, Hugh, 108
Great Dakota Boom, 58–59, 86

Great Depression (1930s), 151, 153
Great Northern Railway, 53, 159, 208, 214. *See also* St. Paul, Minneapolis & Manitoba Railway
Great Sioux Indian Reservation, South Dakota, 59
Green Bay, Milwaukee & Chicago Railroad, 29
Green Bay, Wisconsin, 27, 40, 45, 62, 65, 89, 168, 179, 225, 240, 244, 250
Green Bay & Western Railroad, 236
Green Bay Transit Company, 28
Gregory, South Dakota, 86
Groton, South Dakota, 60
Gulf, Mobile & Ohio Railroad, 208, 212

H. Commit Industries, 248
Haley, John E., 248
Hamlin, John, 7
Hampton, V. A., 151
Hannibal & St. Joseph Railroad, 39
Harding, Warren G., 145
Harlan, Iowa, 85
Harlan & Kirkman Railway, 85
Harriman, E. H., 92–93, 103–4
Harrison, Wisconsin, 64
Harvard, Illinois, 112–13, 201
Harvard, Nebraska, 57
Hastings, Nebraska, 57–58, 174
Hatch, Rufus, 34
Haugh, Jesse Lee, 147
Hawarden, Iowa, 48–49, 60, 88, 90
Hawley, Edwin, 207
Hedrick, Iowa, 209
Heineman, Ben W., 186–87, 189, 191, 195, 199, 202–5, 207, 209–16, 219, 222, 247
Heineman, Walter, 189
Hepburn Act (1906), 128–29
Heron Lake, Minnesota, 70
Highland Park, Illinois, 120, 201
Hill, James J., 61, 92–93
Hillman, Stanley, 235
Hilton, George W., 46, 163
Hines, Walker D., 130
Hitchcock, South Dakota, 86
Hofsommer, Don L., 215
Homestead Act (1862), 59
Hoops, David, 101
Hoover, Herbert, 133, 153
Hortonville, Wisconsin, 63
Hosicon, Wisconsin, 25
Hot Springs, South Dakota, 55
Hours of Service Act (1907)
Hubbard, Elijah Kent, 7–8
Hudson, Wisconsin, 72
Hudson & River Falls Railway, 75
Huebner, Grover, 107
Hughitt, Marvin, 43–44, 49, 54–55, 58–59, 61, 65, 67, 77, 80–81, 83, 85, 89–90, 92–94, 96–99, 101, 108–10, 112–14, 127

Hughitt, Marvin, Jr., 96
Humbird, Jacob, 73
Hunt, Millican, 11
Hurley, Wisconsin, 64
Huron, South Dakota, 60–61, 98–99, 107, 145, 178, 180, 200, 205–6, 220–21
Huron Furniture Company, 107
Hussey, Carl, 193

Illco, Wyoming, 174
Illinois & Michigan Canal, 5–6, 9
Illinois & Missouri Telegraph Company, 43
Illinois & Wisconsin Railroad, 25–26
Illinois Central Gulf Railroad, 238, 248
Illinois Central Railroad, 5–6, 14–15, 19, 29, 36, 43–44, 47, 50, 85, 90, 130, 137, 144, 159, 191, 210, 215, 247
Illinois Commerce Commission, 203
Illinois Parallel Railroad, 29
Immigrants' Protective League, 115, 118
Imperial Reading Corporation, 215
Indianapolis, Indiana, 151, 159
Ingersoll-Rand Company, 141
Ingram, John W., 231
International Association of Machinists, 99
International Brotherhood of Blacksmiths, 99
Interstate Commerce Act (1887), 81
Interstate Commerce Commission, 81, 128, 130, 134–35, 142, 147, 153, 156, 159–61, 163–64, 174, 177, 197, 207, 210–16, 219–21, 226–27, 229–30, 232, 234, 236–37, 245, 251
Interstate Highway Act (1956), 201
Interstate Transit Lines, 147–48
Iowa Central Air Line Railroad, 17, 31
Iowa Central Railway, 207
Iowa Department of Transportation, 222, 233–34
Iowa Falls, Iowa, 49
Iowa Falls & Sioux City Railroad, 50, 70
Iowa Interstate Railroad, 247, 249
Iowa Leased Lines. *See* Cedar Rapids & Missouri River Railroad; Chicago, Iowa & Nebraska Railroad
Iowa, Minnesota & North Western Railway, 88–89
Iowa Midland Railway, 31–32, 45, 48–49
Iowa Pool, 36, 54
Iowa Railroad Construction Company, 18
Iowa Railroad Finance Authority, 233
Iowa Railroad Land Company, 18
Iowa South-Western Railway, 48–49, 85
Iowa State University, 222
Iron Range Express (passenger train), 105
Iron Range Railway, 65
Ironwood, Michigan, 179
Iroquois, South Dakota, 49, 60, 88, 220
Irvington, Nebraska, 57
Ishpeming, Michigan, 65, 168
ITEL Rail Corporation, 244

Jahn, Helmut, 245
Jahnke, Robert, 241
James River Valley & North Western Railway, 86
Jamestown, North Dakota, 60, 206
Janesville, Wisconsin, 25–26, 65, 181
Janesville & Evansville Railway, 65–66
Japonica Partners, 248–49, 251
Jefferson, Iowa, 120
Jewell, Bert, 137, 139
Jewell Junction, Iowa, 46, 48
Johnson, Emory, 107
Johnson, John, 44
Johnson, Peter, 95
Joliet, Illinois, 14
Joy, James F., 35–36
Joyce, Nebraska, 228
Joyce, Patrick, 210
J. P. Morgan & Company, 210
Junction Railway Company, 66

Kansas City, Missouri, 48, 210–11, 213, 231–32, 235–36
Kansas City Southern Railway, 235
Kansas City Terminal Railway, 232
Kate Shelley 400 (passenger train), 184
Kaukauna, Wisconsin, 244
Kazarian, Paul, 248–49
Keep, Albert, 36–38, 43, 45, 49, 73, 76, 79, 127
Keep, Henry, 34
Keep Our Railroad Running (KORR), 221
Kenefick, John, 222, 224, 227–29
Kennedy, John F., 199–200
Kenosha, Rockford & Rock Island RailRoad, 28
Kenosha, Wisconsin, 28, 201
Kettle, Robert, 51–52
Kirkland, Caroline, 12
Kirkman, Iowa, 48, 85
Klein, Maury, 129, 214
Kohler Aviation Corporation, 149–50
Koval, Francis (Frank) V., 177, 187, 209, 211
Krambles, George, 204

Labor. *See* Brotherhood of Locomotive Engineers; Brotherhood of Railway, Airline and Steamship Clerks; Brotherhood of Railway Carmen; Farmers Union; International Brotherhood of Blacksmiths; National Brotherhood of Boilermakers; United Transportation Union
Lac Du Flambeau, Wisconsin, 64
Lackawanna Railroad. *See* Delaware, Lackawanna & Western Railroad
Lacona, Wisconsin, 87
La Crosse, Wisconsin, 31
La Crosse, Trempealeau & Prescott Railroad, 31

INDEX

La Follette, Robert M., Sr., 89, 134
La Fox, Illinois, 121–22
Lake, Alice, 104
Lake Benton, Minnesota, 95
Lake City, Iowa, 48
Lake Crystal, Minnesota, 70
Lake Forest, Illinois, 201
Lake Forwarding Company, 28
Lake Geneva, Wisconsin, 66
Lake Geneva & State Line Railway, 66
Lake Gogebic, Michigan, 63
Lake Kampeska, South Dakota, 58, 61
Lake Shore & Michigan Southern Railroad, 36
Lake Shore Junction, Wisconsin, 112
Lake Superior & Ishpeming Railroad, 135
Lake View, Iowa, 49
Laketon, Nebraska, 71
Lamphier, Thomas, 205
Lancaster, Wisconsin, 47
Lander, Wyoming, 91–92, 174, 226
Langdon, Jervis, Jr., 213–14
La Salle, Illinois, 5
Laughlin, Julia A., 131–32
L. B. Foster, Inc., 244–45
Lead, South Dakota, 55, 146
Lederman, Michael, 248
Lee, George P., 26
Le Mars, Iowa, 70, 90
Lemont, Illinois, 127
La Salle Street Station (Chicago), 113
Le Beau, South Dakota, 207
Lehigh Valley Railroad, 223
Leola, South Dakota, 207
Leslie, Florence, 40
Le Sueur, Minnesota, 70
Levinson, Becker, Peebles & Swiren, 189
Lewis, Drew, 251
Lewis, Eugene, 226
Liberty Loans, 132–33
Life Insurance Group Committee, 163
Lincoln, Nebraska, 55, 57, 146, 148, 207
Lindbergh, Charles A., 148
Lindsay, Nebraska, 55
Lindwerm, Wisconsin, 77, 89
Lindwood, Nebraska, 57, 174
Litchfield, Illinois, 207
Litchfield & Madison Railway, 91, 207
Little Bay de Noquet, Michigan, 27
Lodi, Illinois, 20, 33
Logan, Iowa, 111
Lohr, Lenox R., 177
Lombard, Illinois, 13
Lone Pine, Nebraska, 53
Lone Star Steel Company, 215
Los Angeles, California, 103, 149
Los Angeles Limited (passenger train), 103
Louisville & Nashville Railroad, 207
Luverne, Minnesota, 70
Lynd, Helen, 145
Lynd, Minnesota, 30–31

Lynd, Robert, 145
Lyons, Frank, 189
Lyons, Iowa, 17, 32

McAdoo, William G., 130, 133
McCagg, Reed & Company, 16
McCormick, Alexander, 115, 118
McGarr, Frank, 232, 234
McGovern, George S., 221
McGregor, Malcolm, 104
McIntyre, J. C., 244
McKeen Motor car, 146
McMillen, Thomas R., 237
Macoupin County Railway, 90
Madison, South Dakota, 60
Madison, Wisconsin, 14, 45, 47, 65–66, 105, 122, 168
Manitowoc, Green Bay & North Western Railway, 89
Manitowoc, Wisconsin, 62, 89, 107, 168, 179, 244
Mankato, Minnesota, 70, 88, 168, 200
Mankato & New Ulm Railroad, 88
Mann-Elkins Act (1910), 128–29
Manufacturers Hanover Trust Company, 229
Maple River Junction, Iowa, 45, 112
Maple River Rail-Road, 45, 48–49
Mapleton, Iowa, 45, 49
Marinette, Michigan, 64
Markham, Charles H., 130
Marshall, Minnesota, 85
Marshalltown, Iowa, 18, 109, 210, 233, 240, 252
Marquette, Iowa, 235
Marshfield, Wisconsin, 63, 65, 77, 89
Mason City, Iowa, 88, 105, 209, 232
Mason City & Fort Dodge Railroad, 210
Matteson, Illinois, 144
Maxon, Iowa, 241
Mayo Brothers' Clinic, 95
Mayville, Wisconsin, 25
Medill, James, 39
Megen, Charles P., 166
Mendota, Minnesota, 69–70
Memominee River Railroad, 45, 65
Merchandise Mart (Chicago), 154
Mergers, 207, 211–12, 214
Merrill Lynch & Company, 253
Merrillan, Wisconsin, 72, 76, 89
Merriman, Nebraska, 250
Metropolitan, Michigan, 65
Metropolitan Life Insurance Company, 186, 203
Michigan Central Railroad, 150
Michigan Chemical Corporation, 215
Michigan Southern & Northern Indiana Railroad, 14, 34
Michigamme, Michigan, 65
Mid-Iowa Shippers Association, 241
Midwestern Railroad Properties, Inc., 234

Miles City, Montana, 234
Millett, Stephen C., 45
Milwaukee, Lake Shore & Western Railway, 62–65, 78
Milwaukee, Manitowoc & Green Bay Railroad, 62
Milwaukee, Sparta & North Western Railway, 89–90
Milwaukee, Wisconsin, 27, 32–34, 38, 62–63, 65, 75, 90, 107, 111–13, 142, 149–51, 156–59, 168, 220, 236, 240, 250
Milwaukee & Madison Railway, 47, 65
Milwaukee & Mississippi Rail Road, 26–27
Milwaukee & Northern Railroad, 62, 64
Milwaukee & Prairie du Chien Railroad, 34
Milwaukee & St. Paul Railroad, 31, 34–35, 72–73
Milwaukee Land Company, 235
Milwaukee Road. *See* Chicago, Milwaukee & St. Paul Railway
Minneapolis, Minnesota, 46, 74, 104, 157–59, 168, 194, 200, 207, 209
Minneapolis, Northfield & Southern Railway, 233
Minneapolis, St. Paul & Sault Ste. Marie Railroad, 81, 87, 161, 210–11, 231, 233–34, 236–38, 244, 247
Minneapolis & Cedar Valley Railroad, 17
Minneapolis & St. Louis Railway, 81, 86, 189, 193, 207–11, 231, 240
Minneapolis Eastern Railway, 74
Minnesota & Iowa Railway, 79, 88
Minnesota & Northwestern Railroad, 210
Minnesota & South Dakota Railway, 85
Minnesota 400 (passenger train), 168, 178
Minnesota Railway and Warehouse Commission, 79
Minnesota Valley Railroad, 69–70
Minnesota Valley Railway, 46
Minnesota Western Railway, 85
Missionary (passenger train), 148–49
Mississippi & Missouri Railroad, 18
Mississippi & Rock River Junction Railroad, 15
Missouri-Kansas-Texas Railway, 223
Missouri Pacific Railroad, 57, 174, 211, 214
Missouri River Junction, Iowa, 49
Missouri River Transfer Company, 71
Missouri Valley, Iowa, 50, 112
Missouri Valley & Blair Railway & Bridge Company, 49–50
Mitchell, Alexander, 34–35, 38
Mitchell, South Dakota, 60–61, 76
Mobile & Ohio Railroad, 135
Moingona, Iowa, 95–96
Mondamin, Iowa, 84
Monico, Wisconsin, 64
Monmouth, Illinois, 209
Monon Railroad. *See* Chicago, Indianapolis & Louisville Railway

Montfort, Wisconsin, 47
Montrose, Illinois, 66
Moore, James E., 81
Morgan, Richard Price, 10
Morning Sun, Iowa, 209
Morrison, Illinois, 15
Mosher, South Dakota, 143
Motor Carriers Act (1935), 153
Mount Prospect, Illinois, 201
Muchakinock, Iowa, 48
Muncie, Indiana, 145
Muscatine, Iowa, 237
Mutual Savings Bank Group Committee, 163

Nachusa, Illinois, 20
Narenta, Michigan, 65
Nashville, Chattanooga & St. Louis Railway, 207
National Brotherhood of Boilermakers, 99
National Mediation Board, 242
National Railroad Passenger Corporation, 225
National Road, 4
Nebkota Railway, 250
Nebraska & Western Railroad, 53
Nebraska Land Grant Act (1869), 51
Nebraska State Railway Commission, 201
Necedah, Wisconsin, 77
Negaunee, Michigan, 28
Neillville, Wisconsin, 77
Nekoosa, Wisconsin, 89
Neligh, Nebraska, 53, 94
Nelson, Illinois, 90, 223
Neosho Construction Company, 230
Neshkoro, Wisconsin, 146
Nevada, Iowa, 18, 234
Newark, Arkansas, 230
Newberry, Walter, 8–9
Newcastle, Nebraska, 76
Newell, South Dakota, 86
New Haven Railroad. *See* New York, New Haven & Hartford Railroad
Newlands Act (1902)
New London, Wisconsin, 62–63, 244
Newport, Nebraska, 228
New Richmond, Wisconsin, 74
New Rockford, North Dakota, 206
New Ulm, Minnesota, 58, 88
New York, Albany and Buffalo Telegraph Company, 43
New York, Chicago & St. Louis Railroad, 135, 181
New York, New Haven & Hartford Railroad, 151, 173
New York, New York, 148
New-York & Erie Rail Road. *See* Erie Railroad
New York Central Railroad, 101–2, 130, 156, 182, 223
Nickel Plate Road. *See* New York, Chicago & St. Louis Railroad
Nickerson, Nebraska, 52
Nishland, South Dakota, 135, 142
Norfolk, Nebraska, 53, 75, 107, 226, 250
North Antelope Mine, Wyoming, 230
North Evanston, Illinois, 66
Northwest (horse car), 109
North Western Employees Transportation Company, 216
North Western Limited (passenger train), 104–5, 144
North Western Union Railway, 31–33, 45
North Wisconsin Junction, Wisconsin, 74
North Wisconsin Railway, 69, 74–75
Northern Cross Rail Road, 6
Northern Illinois Railway, 65
Northern Nebraska Air Line Rail Road, 50
Northern Pacific Railroad, 44, 54, 60, 75, 104, 208, 214
Northwestern Atrium Center (Chicago), 245
Northwestern Express and Transportation Company, 60
Northwest Industries, 205, 212, 215–16
Norwest Corporation, 215

Oakdale, Nebraska, 53, 55
Oakes, North Dakota, 60, 107, 180, 205–6
Oakland, Nebraska, 71
Oak Park, Illinois, 11, 16
Oconto, Wisconsin, 64, 120
Oelwein, Iowa, 250
O'Fallons, Nebraska, 228
Office of Defense Transportation, 175, 179
Office of Price Administration, 174
Ogden, Iowa, 112
Ogden, Utah, 30, 51, 54, 107
Ogden, William Butler, 8–9, 15–16, 26–29, 33–34
Ogilvie, Richard, 235–37
Ogle, Illinois, 20
Omaha, Nebraska, 57, 69, 71, 85, 145, 148, 183–84, 200, 210, 222
Omaha, Niobrara & Black Hills Railroad, 53
Omaha & Northern Nebraska Railway, 71
Omaha & North Western Railroad, 71
Omaha Packing Company, 57
Omaha Road. *See* Chicago, St. Paul, Minneapolis & Omaha Railway
Onawa, Iowa, 49, 145
Oneida, South Dakota, 86
O'Neill, Nebraska, 53, 201
Order of Railroad Telegraphers, 197–200
Ordway, South Dakota, 60
Oregon Express (passenger train), 104
Orient, South Dakota, 86
Orin, Wyoming, 226
Ortonville, Minnesota, 234
Oshkosh, Wisconsin, 27, 63, 75, 244
Oskaloosa, Iowa, 209, 240

Ottumwa, Cedar Falls & St. Paul Railway, 48
Overland Flyer (passenger train), 102
Overland Limited (motion picture), 104
Overland Limited (passenger train), 102–4
Overland Route, 30, 104, 151, 159, 183, 213, 222

Pacific Express (passenger train), 102
Pacific Railway Act (1862), 50
Palatine, Illinois, 41
Park Falls, Wisconsin, 146
Park-Kenilworth Industries, 239
Parrish, Wisconsin, 64
Partridge, Michigan, 240
Patrons of Husbandry, 37–38
Peat, Marwick, Mitchell & Company, 232
Peck, Ebenezer, 7
Peck, Keep & Company, 36
Pekin, Illinois, 90
Pelican, Wisconsin, 87
Peninsula Express (passenger train), 105
Peninsula 400 (passenger train), 168
Peninsula Rail-Road of Michigan, 27
Penn Central Transportation Company, 215, 223
Pennsylvania Railroad, 19, 29, 33, 35, 83, 97, 102, 119, 133, 137, 148–49, 159, 182, 190, 223
Peoria, Illinois, 90–91, 189, 207–8
Peoria & North Western Railway, 90
Peoria & Pekin Union Railway, 90
Perkins, Charles, 54, 94
Perkins, Michigan, 87
Peru, Illinois, 14
Peterson, Peter, 249
Philadelphia & Reading Corporation, 215
Philip, South Dakota, 91
Philipp, Emanuel L., 89
Pierre, Rapid City & North Western Railway, 91–92
Pierre, South Dakota, 59, 61, 145
Pigney, William, 122
Pikarsky, Milton, 225
Pioneer (locomotive), 11–12, 141, 178
Pipestone, Minnesota, 70
Pittsburgh, Fort Wayne & Chicago Railroad, 29
Plainview, Minnesota, 46
Plainview, Nebraska, 53
Plainview Rail-Road, 46
Platteville, Wisconsin, 47
Plumb, Glen E., 134
Plymouth, Wisconsin, 65
Ponca, Nebraska, 52, 71
Pony Express, 39
Portage, Wisconsin, 14
Port Washington, Wisconsin, 62
Porter, Henry H., 74–77
Portland, Oregon, 159
Postville, Iowa, 76

Potter Railroad Law (1874), 37–38
Powder River Basin, Wyoming, 226, 231
Powers, Michigan, 45, 65
Prairie du Chien, Wisconsin, 26–27
Pratt, Edwin, 107
Pratt, George, 64
Pratt Junction, Wisconsin, 64
Prescott, Wisconsin, 31
Preston, Fred, 151
Princeton, Wisconsin, 65, 89
Princeton & North Western Railway, 89
Princeton & Western Railway, 77
Provo, Larry S., 193, 205, 215–17, 219–26, 231, 247, 249
Public Service Commission of Wisconsin, 200
Pulaska, Wisconsin, 89
Pullman Palace Car Company, 40, 102
Pullman-Standard Company, 168, 200, 203

Quinnesec, Michigan, 45, 65

Rail diesel cars, 203
Railroad Control Act (1918), 130
Railroad Credit Corporation, 160
Railroad Labor Board, 134, 136–37
Railroad Revitalization and Regulatory Reform Act (1974), 223
Railroads, betterments, 88; gauges, 3; Great Depression, 153; growth, 3–6, 13–14, 47–48, 83; World War I, 129–30; World War II, 171
Railroads' War Board, 129
Railway Age, 165
Railway Labor Act, 199, 242
Randolph, Nebraska, 75
Rapid Air Lines, 149
Rapid City, South Dakota, 54–55, 91, 93, 149, 244
Reading Railroad, 223
Reagan, Ronald, 242
Real Estate Research Corporation, 195
Rebensdorf, John, 252
Reconstruction Finance Corporation, 160–61
Redfeather, Princess, 173
Redfield, South Dakota, 60–61, 145
Red Granite, Wisconsin, 89, 146
Redwood Falls, Minnesota, 46
Regional Rail Reorganization Act (1973), 223
Regional Transportation Authority (Chicago), 225
Reid, Maurice, 220–21
Reidy, E. T., 210
Republic, Michigan, 65
Rhinelander, Frederick W., 62
Rhinelander, Wisconsin, 64
Rice Lake, Wisconsin, 146
Richards, Ralph C., 122–24
Richmond, Illinois, 16

Riley, John, 238
River Falls, Wisconsin, 75
River Forest, Illinois, 41
Rochester, Minnesota, 46, 95
Rochester & Northern Minnesota Railway, 46
Rockefeller, William, 93
Rockford, Illinois, 8, 13–14, 28, 147–48
Rock Island, Illinois, 14
Rock Island Junction, Illinois, 121
Rock Island Railroad. *See* Chicago, Rock Island & Pacific Railroad
Rock River Railway, 65
Rock River Valley Union Railroad, 25–26
Rocky Mountain National Park, 151
Roosevelt, Franklin D., 174
Root River Valley & Southern Minnesota Rail Road, 69
Rosebud Indian Reservation, South Dakota, 86
Roseport Industrial District, 211
Roth, Claude A., 166
Round Grove, Illinois, 20
Royal, Iowa, 233
Russell, Donald J., 183
Russell, Robert, 216

Sac City, Iowa, 45
Sacramento, California, 30
Safety Appliance Act (1893), 122, 124
St. Charles, Illinois, 66
St. Charles Railroad, 66
St. Croix & Lake Superior Railroad, 75
St. James, Minnesota, 70, 194
St. Joseph, Missouri, 39, 48, 210, 233
St. Lawrence Seaway, 208
St. Louis, Alton & Chicago Railway, 43
St. Louis, Missouri, 90–91, 159, 213
St. Louis, Peoria & North Western Railway, 90
St. Louis-San Francisco Railway, 214
St. Paul, Minneapolis & Manitoba Railway, 61
St. Paul, Minnesota, 27, 69, 70, 72, 77, 104, 122, 157–59, 210, 250
St. Paul, Stillwater & Taylor Falls Rail Road, 72, 75
St. Paul & Duluth Railroad, 104
St. Paul and Minneapolis Express (passenger train), 104
St. Paul & Pacific Railroad, 104
St. Paul & Sioux City Railroad, 69–72, 74–75, 78
St. Paul Eastern Grand Trunk Railway, 64, 87
St. Peter, Minnesota, 88
Salem, South Dakota, 70, 122, 220
Salomon Brothers, 249
Salzberg, Murray M., 211
Sanborn, Minnesota, 79, 88
San Francisco, California, 30, 102, 149
San Pedro, Los Angeles & Salt Lake Railroad, 103

Santa Fe Railway. *See* Atchison, Topeka & Santa Fe Railway
Sargent, Fred W., 127, 139–40, 143–44, 151, 153–54, 161–64, 166
Sargent, Wesley, 139
Sauk Center, Minnesota, 61
Saunders, Michigan, 87
Savanna, Illinois, 14
Sawyer, Philetus, 75
Schenectady Locomotive Works, 110
Schmidt, Eugene A., Jr., 186, 203
Schmiege, Robert W., 247–48, 251–52
Schwarzman, Stephen, 249
Scribner, Nebraska, 55
Seattle, Washington, 93
Seminole (passenger train), 159
714th Railway Operating Battalion, 171
Seward, Nebraska, 207
Seymour, Iowa, 237
Seymour, James, 7
Shakopee, Minnesota, 69
Shannon, Charles C., 181, 186, 198
Shawnee, Wyoming, 228
Shawnee Junction, Wyoming, 228
Sheboygan, Wisconsin, 62, 65, 89
Sheboygan & Fond du Lac Railroad, 65, 89
Sheboygan & Mississippi River Railroad, 65
Sheldon, Iowa, 235
Shelley, Kate, 95–96
Shirk, Harry, 122
Shopmen's strike of 1922, 137, 139
Shoreland 400 (passenger train), 168, 179
Shoshoni, Wyoming, 91–92, 174
Shoshoni Indian Reservation, Wyoming, 91–92
Sioux City, Dakota & North Western Railway, 90
Sioux City, Iowa, 49–50, 58, 60, 69–71, 90, 139–40, 145, 180, 194, 197, 220–21
Sioux City & Nebraska Railroad, 71
Sioux City & Pacific Railroad, 49–52, 54, 71, 78
Sioux City & St. Paul Railroad, 70
Sioux Falls, South Dakota, 61, 70, 221
Sioux Falls Junction, Minnesota, 70
Sleepy Eye, Minnesota, 46
Smith, A. H., 130
Smith, Angus, 31
Smith, Theophilus, 7
Smith, Worthington, 235
Snethen, Edward, 151
Soo Line Railroad. *See* Minneapolis, St. Paul & Ste. Marie Railroad
South Beloit, Illinois, 240
South Carolina Canal & Rail Road Company, 3
South Dakota Public Utilities Commission, 197, 199
South Dakota Railroad Commission, 145
Southern Iowa Railway, 87
Southern Minnesota Rail Road, 69

Southern Pacific Railroad, 102–4, 159, 167, 183, 199–200, 213, 215, 247, 253
South Itasca, Wisconsin, 250
Southland (passenger train), 159
South Norfolk, Nebraska, 53
South Omaha, Nebraska, 57
South Omaha Land Company, 57
South Pekin, Illinois, 209
South Torrington, Wyoming, 228
Sparta, Wisconsin, 89
Spooner, Wisconsin, 75
Sprague, Lucian C., 189
Spring Valley, Illinois, 65
S. S. Pierce Grocery Company, 104
Staggers Rail Act (1980), 221–22, 229, 233, 245, 247
Stambaugh, Michigan, 65
Stanton, Nebraska, 53
Stanwood & Tipton Railway, 48–49
Stark, Iowa, 87
State Center, Iowa, 18
State Line, Illinois, 29
State Line & Union Railway, 66
Sterling, Illinois, 15
Stickney, A. B., 85, 210
Stiles Junction, Wisconsin, 64
Storm Lake, Iowa, 207
Stratford, Iowa, 48
Stroude, James, 7
Sullivan, James R., 209–10
Summit Lake, Wisconsin, 63
Sun Company, 230
Superior, Iowa, 233
Superior, Nebraska, 57
Superior, Wisconsin, 75
Swift, Edward, 151
Swift & Company, 57
Swiren, Max, 209
Swiren & Heineman, 189
Sycamore, Illinois, 65
Sycamore & Cortland Railroad, 65

Tacoma, Washington, 93
Taft, William Howard, 128
Talcott, Edward, 19
Tama, Iowa, 48–49
Tarrant, Robert, 26
Tekamah, Nebraska, 71
ten Have, J. L., 36
Terpning, H. R., 154
Thatcher, Nebraska, 53
Thomson, Charles M., 166
Thomson, J. Edgar, 33
Tigerton, Wisconsin, 63
Tilden Mine, Michigan, 240
Timber Culture Act (1873), 59
Tishman Midwest Management Corporation, 245
Toledo, Iowa, 48
Toledo, Peoria & Western Railroad, 189
Toledo, St. Louis & Western Railroad, 207

Toledo & North Western Railway, 46, 48–49, 71, 88
Tomah, Wisconsin, 47, 72–73
Tomah & Lake St. Croix Railroad, 72
Tonawanda Railroad, 11
Towne, Walter J., 133
Tracy, John F., 35–36
Tracy, Minnesota, 59, 95, 221
Traffic Club of Chicago, 182
Training Within Industry (TWI) program, 173
Transcontinental Air Transport, Inc., 148–49
Transit Railroad, 30
Transportation Act (1920). *See* Esch-Cummins Act
Transportation Act (1958), 180, 221
Transtar, 249, 252
Trego, Wisconsin, 75
Trempealeau, Wisconsin, 66, 146
Truesdale, W. H., 137
Truman, Harry, 176
Turner, John Bice, 16, 20
Turner Junction, Illinois. *See* West Chicago, Illinois
Twentieth Century Limited (passenger train), 104, 158
Twin Cities 400 (passenger train), 168
Two Rivers, Wisconsin, 62, 244
Tyler, Minnesota, 85

Union Pacific Railroad, 30, 37, 49–53, 55, 57, 67, 75, 92, 102–4, 135, 139, 147, 150–51, 167, 174, 183–84, 197, 213–15, 219, 222–23, 227–29, 239, 244, 249, 251
Union Pacific Stages, 147
Union Station (Chicago), 119, 182, 203
Union Underwear Company, 215
United Fruit Company, 187
United States Railroad Administration, 129–30, 133–34
United States Railroad Labor Board, 134
United Transportation Union, 217, 231, 241–42, 247
Unityville, South Dakota, 220
Universal Manufacturing Company, 215
University of Wisconsin Extension Service, 94
Utah-Idaho Sugar Company, 142

Vale, South Dakota, 142
Valentine, Nebraska, 49, 53–54
Valley 400 (passenger train), 168, 179
Valuation Act (1913), 128
Vanderbilt, Cornelius, 36, 80
Vanderbilt, Cornelius, II, 80
Vanderbilt, William H., 36, 80
Vanderbilt, William K., 80, 93, 127
Van Nortwick, John, 11, 13
Van Sweringen brothers (O. P. and M. J.), 135

Velsicol Chemical Corporation, 215
Verdigre, Nebraska, 55, 85
Verdon, South Dakota, 60
Vesta, Minnesota, 88
Vestibuled Limited (passenger train), 104
Vilas, Joseph, 62
Villard, Henry, 75
Volga, South Dakota, 59
Voluntary co-ordination agreements, 235, 237

Wadsworth, Julius, 28
Wabash Railroad, 135
Wabeno, Wisconsin, 87
Wacker, Fred, 151
Wahoo, Nebraska, 57
Wall, South Dakota, 92
Wallace, John, 113
Walliser, William, 139
Wall Lake, Iowa, 45, 48, 84, 145
Walter, Charles, 9
Ward, James A., 101
War Manpower Commission, 173
Warren, Wisconsin, 72–73
Waseca, Minnesota, 32
Washburn, William Drew, 77
Wasta, South Dakota, 91
Waterloo, Iowa, 88
Watersmeet, Michigan, 65, 179
Watertown, South Dakota, 25, 30, 58, 60–61
Waukegan, Illinois, 143–44, 151, 204
Wausau, Wisconsin, 63, 250
Wayne, Nebraska, 75, 80
Waynoka, Oklahoma, 148
Webster City, Iowa, 48
Wells Street Freight Station (Chicago), 154
Wells Street Passenger Station (Chicago), 20, 113, 115
Wentworth, John, 7
West Allis, Wisconsin, 90
West Bend, Iowa, 233
West Chicago, Illinois, 13, 15–16, 122, 142, 222
West Denison, Iowa, 222
Western Pacific Railroad, 93, 214
Western Railroad Properties, 229–30
Western Townlot Company, 59
West Point, Nebraska, 52
West River Country, South Dakota, 85–86, 91
West St. Paul, Minnesota, 70
West Wisconsin Railway, 69, 72–74, 76
Wheaton, Illinois, 13, 201, 204
White, John H., Jr., 156
White, Lynne L., 181
White, Morris & Company, 72
Whitewood, South Dakota, 55
Wichita, Kansas, 57
Widell-Finley Company, 135
Willard, Daniel, 139

William Wyer & Company, 184
Williams, Henry T., 41
Williams, Roland (Bud), 166–68, 173, 177, 180–82, 197
Williams Bay, Wisconsin, 66, 201
Williamson, Elizabeth, 180
Willmar, Minnesota, 61
Wilmette, Illinois, 204
Wilson, Woodrow, 128–30
Winner, South Dakota, 86, 142–43, 146, 190
Winnetka, Illinois, 41
Winona, Mankato & New Ulm Railroad, 31
Winona, Minnesota, 30–31, 244
Winona, St. Peter & Missouri River Railroad, 30
Winona & St. Peter Railroad, 30–32, 45–46, 58, 61, 78, 88
Winona Junction, Wisconsin, 31, 45
Wisconsin, Iowa & Nebraska Railroad, 210
Wisconsin & Northern Railroad, 87
Wisconsin & Superior Rail Road, 27
Wisconsin Central Transportation Company, 244–45, 247, 250
Wisconsin "Full Crew" Law (1907), 241
Wisconsin Marine & Fire Insurance Company, 34
Wisconsin Northern Railway, 87
Wisconsin Potato Growers' Association, 94
Wisconsin Railroad Association, 241
Wisconsin Railroad Commission, 89
Wisconsin Rapids, Wisconsin, 250. *See also* Grand Rapids, Wisconsin
Wisner, Nebraska, 51–53
Wisner, S. P., 52
Witten, South Dakota, 143
Wolfe, James, 216, 220, 224–25, 228, 233–38, 242–45, 247–49
Wolfe James, E., 224
Wolfe & Wisconsin Rivers Railroad, 64
Wood, South Dakota, 142–43, 146, 190
Wood, Struthers & Company, 77, 124–25
Woodman, Wisconsin, 47
Woodstock, Minnesota, 70
Wood Street Yard (Chicago), 154
Woodville, South Dakota, 55
Woonsocket, South Dakota, 60
Worley, Burton, 184
Wren, Iowa, 90, 220
Wright, Iowa, 209
Wyer, Dick & Company, 202. *See also* William Wyer & Company
Wyer, William, 184, 186
Wyeville, Wisconsin, 77, 89, 168
WyoBraska Landowners' Association, 229
Wyoming & North Western Railway, 91–92
Wyoming Central Railway, 54

XTRA Corporation, 241

Yankton, South Dakota, 58, 60
Yellowstone National Park, Wyoming, 54, 92, 150–51
York, Nebraska, 57
Young Men's Christian Association, 98

Zephyr (passenger train), 157
Zito, James, 223, 243, 249, 252
Zumbrota, Minnesota, 46

BOOKS BY H. ROGER GRANT

THE COUNTRY RAILROAD STATION IN AMERICA
(with Charles W. Bohi)

INSURANCE REFORM:
Consumer Action in the Progressive Era

SELF-HELP IN THE 1890s DEPRESSION

THE CORN BELT ROUTE:
A History of the Chicago Great Western Railroad Company

SPIRIT FRUIT:
A Gentle Utopia

KANSAS DEPOTS

LIVING IN THE DEPOT:
The Two-Story Railroad Station

ST. LOUIS UNION STATION:
A Place for People, A Place for Trains
(with Don L. Hofsommer and Osmund Overby)

RAILROAD POSTCARDS IN THE AGE OF STEAM

ERIE LACKAWANNA:
Death of an American Railroad, 1938–1992

OHIO'S RAILWAY AGE IN POSTCARDS

BOOKS EDITED BY H. ROGER GRANT

YEARS OF STRUGGLE:
The Farm Diary of Elmer G. Powers, 1931-1936
(with L. Edward Purcell)

WE GOT THERE ON THE TRAIN:
Railroads in the Lives of the American People

WE TOOK THE TRAIN

BROWNIE THE BOOMER:
The Life of Charles P. Brown, an American Railroader

MONTANA
Helena
NORTH DAKOTA
Bismarck
SOUTH DAKOTA
Pierre
WYOMING
YELLOWSTONE NATIONAL PARK
IDAHO
UTAH
COLORADO
Denver
NEBRASKA
Lincoln
KANSA
GREAT NORTHERN
NOR. PAC.
GT. NOR.
OREGON SHORT LINE
UNION PACIFIC
UN. PAC.
M. ST. P. & S. S. M.
CHICAGO & NORTH WESTERN
W. & N. W.
P.R.C. & NW.
C. ST. P. M. & O.
Missouri River
Yellowstone River
Musselshell R.
Big Horn River
Powder River
Green River
OAKES
REDFIELD
WATERTOWN
GETTYSBURG
HURON
BROOKINGS
DEADWOOD
Newell
RAPID CITY
MITCHELL
SALEM
SIOUX FALLS
BONESTEEL
YANKTON
HAWARDEN
LANDER
CASPER
CHADRON
NORFOLK
Fremont
OMAHA
HASTINGS
SUPERIOR